Springer Series in Language and Communication 6

Editor: W. J. M. Levelt

Springer Series in Language and Communication
Editor: W. J. M. Levelt

Semantics from Different Points of View

Editors
R. Bäuerle   U. Egli   A. von Stechow

With 15 Figures

Springer-Verlag Berlin Heidelberg New York 1979

Dr. Rainer Bäuerle
Professor Dr. Urs Egli
Professor Dr. Arnim von Stechow

Universität Konstanz
Sonderforschungsbereich 99, Linguistik, Postfach 5560
D-7750 Konstanz, Fed. Rep. of Germany

Series Editor:

Professor Dr. Willem J. M. Levelt
Max-Planck-Projektgruppe für Psycholinguistik
Berg en Dalseweg 79, Nijmegen, The Netherlands

ISBN 3-540-09676-0 Springer-Verlag Berlin Heidelberg New York
ISBN 0-387-09676-0 Springer-Verlag New York Heidelberg Berlin

Offset printing and bookbinding: Brühlsche Universitätsdruckerei, Giessen
2153/3130-543210

Preface

This volume contains the papers read at the conference on 'Semantics from different points of view' that took place at Konstanz University in September 1978. This interdisciplinary conference was organized by the 'Sonderforschungsbereich 99 - Linguistik' and sponsored by the Deutsche Forschungsgemeinschaft. Linguists, philosophers, logicians, and psychologists met to discuss recent developments in the study of the semantics of natural language from the point of view of their disciplines.

But this is not to say that there was one particular topic shared by all the participants. The conference was organized because the seven research groups that constitute the Sonderforschungsbereich wanted to discuss their results in an international context and to get advice and guidance for the work still to be done. Therefore, quite a number of topics were covered, though at different levels of precision, under the general label 'semantics'. And the selection of topics, as well as the relative importance given to them, is due to the research interests currently represented in the Sonderforschungsbereich.

Given such a situation, it is all the more important to note that the relative diversity of topics is not paralleled by a diversity of methods. The core of the papers in this volume is based on possible-worlds semantics, which at the moment seems to be the most productive and influential paradigm for semantic research in linguistics and philosophy. And it is with respect to this central issue that the present volume may claim to give a representative survey of 'the state of the art'.

The arrangement of the papers in this volume represents an attempt at a loose thematic grouping (with the exception of Hans Kamp's paper, which for technical reasons had to be ordered last), which is by no means more than tentative.

The first paper, Barbara Partee's plea to make semantic theories more psychologically realistic, provides the link between the logical and the psychological (Cohen/Kelter/Woll; C. Heeschen) approaches contained in this volume. Here we regret that the paper read by Huber/Poeck/Vogels ('Semantic confusion in aphasia') is not included, because it had already been promised to another publisher.

The majority of papers belong to the realm of philosophical semantics. These range from more fundamental considerations concerning the logical properties of temporal operators and events (Gabbay/Rohrer; H. Kamp) to detailed analyses of individual problems such as conditionals (A. Kratzer), particles (E. König; D. Wunderlich), and event expressions (M. Cresswell), to mention only a few.

Pragmatic aspects of meaning are discussed in the papers of D. Lewis, A. Kasher, F. Kambartel, and H. Schneider. And the fact that syntax is also to be taken seriously is obvious from the papers by U. Egli and A. von Stechow, where the authors try to motivate semantic representations that are not too far from the syntactic structure. More basically concerned with syntactic theory itself is the paper by K.J. Engelberg, who introduces recursive tree functions as a model for syntax.

How our present-day concepts can be used to shed light on aspects of ancient theories of language is shown by U. Egli and K. Hülser, who discuss Stoic linguistic theory.

And last, the papers of Hauenschild/Huckert/Maier and Ch. Schwarze investigate problems of semantics that arise from the point of view of translation and interlingua.

It was hard work to discuss all these topics in just one week, but this effort was all the more rewarding in that working together soon created an atmosphere of understanding.

We would like to take the opportunity to thank all those that read a paper or participated in the discussions for their contribution to the success of the conference. Indeed they all encouraged us to mention yet another problem: the problem of referring expressions. The problem of referring by names has quite a tradition in philosophy and linguistics (just think of names used in fiction). And in order to make the reader think about the reference of authors' names, we insert a photograph of the conference participants at the page opposite to the Index of Contributors.

As everybody knows, the success of a conference depends heavily on what is going on backstage. Here we owe a great debt of gratitude to our secretary Helga Baeckmann, who joined our team only a couple of weeks before the conference, but was at the heart of everything in almost no time. We would also like to thank the "Deutsche Forschungsgemeinschaft" - especially Dr. Fleischmann - for providing the funds with a minimum of administrative expense, and the publishers for their patience with the inevitable delays in the completion of the manuscript for this volume.

Konstanz, June, 1979

R. Bäuerle
U. Egli
A. von Stechow

Contents

Semantics – Mathematics or Psychology?

Barbara Hall-Partee

The Commonwealth of Massachusetts, University of Massachusetts,
Department of Linguistics, Amherst, MA 01003, USA

1. Introduction

My goal in this paper is to argue that the question in the title is one that
urgently needs attention from both linguists and philosophers, although I do
not have an answer for it. I believe that we will not be able to find an
adequate account of the semantics of propositional attitudes without a
theory which reconciles the conflicting demands of the two kinds of views
of what semantics is.

Where do these two views come from? The view that semantics is a branch
of psychology is a part of the Chomskyan view that linguistics as a whole is
a branch of psychology. This view, which is shared by many linguists, derives
from taking the central goal of linguistic theory to be an account of what
the native speaker of a language knows when he or she knows a language, and
of how such knowledge is acquired. Most linguists take it for granted that
people know their language; within the Chomskyan view, it is the knowledge
of the individual language user that is criterial for determining what his
or her language _is_.

The contrasting view is ascribed to MONTAGUE (and endorsed) by THOMASON
in his introduction to [22]: "Many linguists may not realize at first glance
how fundamentally MONTAGUE's approach differs from current linguistic conceptions. ...According to MONTAGUE the syntax, semantics, and pragmatics
of natural languages are branches of mathematics, not of psychology." (p. 2.)
(THOMASON holds that lexicography is an empirical science that demands considerable knowledge of the world, but is not part of semantics proper. I
will return to that issue below.) The view that semantics is not psychology
can also be reasonably ascribed to FREGE [10], and seems to be either implicit or explicit in the work of many logicians and philosophers.

It might seem from the recent growth of cooperation among linguists, philosophers, and logicians that the question really doesn't matter. And for
many purposes I believe it doesn't. To put some perspective on what I take
to be the real problem, let me list some respects in which the question is
not a problem.

1.   There is no reason why a psychological theory can't be expressed in
mathematical terms. In fact on a Chomskyan view it should be, since we
are trying to discover something about the structure of a certain mental
faculty, and mathematics is the best available tool for describing structure.
So I am not suggesting that there is any incompatibility between mathematics
in general and psychology in general.

2. The fact that some logician is not interested in psychology does not preclude the possibility that he or she may develop a theory which can be taken as a serious candidate for a psychological theory. This was an argument that can be used in urging linguists to take MONTAGUE's theory seriously [26]; it may be hoped that one might turn MONTAGUE's general theory of language [21] into a theory of possible human languages simply by adding additional constraints, constraints designed to reflect human linguistic capacities. I still have hopes that such a program can be carried out for a theory bearing some resemblance to MONTAGUE's, since the progress that has been made in syntax and semantics working in constrained versions of that theory and similar ones seems too great to be an artifactual illusion. But I now believe that MONTAGUE's theory (and relevantly similar ones) cannot be the basis of a linguistic theory without some radical revisions in the foundations of the semantics.

3. As far as I can see, there are no problems with logicians' treatment of syntax analogous to the problems in the semantics. But I can't say any more about the difference until I have described the semantic problems. I will return to this later.

Having said what I think the problems are not, let me turn to the discussion of what they are.

2. Idealizations

Idealizations are of course indispensable for making headway in any science. Linguists are accustomed to making a distinction between competence and performance, and CRESSWELL [5] shows that the same distinction can be used to argue for the reasonableness of truth-conditional semantics as an account of semantic competence. But the arguments of PUTNAM [30] [31], CHOMSKY [3], and LINSKY [18] can be used to show that some of MONTAGUE's idealizations are incompatible with the view of semantics as psychology. In [27], I discussed the PUTNAM arguments and concluded that speakers of a language do not in fact know their language; but LINSKY's arguments and further reflection on the semantics of propositional attitudes have convinced me that even if this is so, some of MONTAGUE's idealizations must be given up.

The crucial idealizations that MONTAGUE makes are the following:

   (i)   The objects of propositional attitudes are propositions.

  (ii)   The intensions of sentences are propositions.

 (iii)   The intensions of sentences are compositionally determined, i.e. recursively built up from the intensions of their parts.

  (iv)   Intensions are functions from possible worlds to extensions.

   (v)   Words have intensions.

The crucial linguistic assumptions which I believe are incompatible with those are the following:

  (vi)   People know their language.

 (vii)   The brain is finite.

A typical PUTNAM example is the intension of natural kind terms such as
gold, water, or tiger. PUTNAM has shown that a speaker can, by all reasonable standards, be in command of a word like water without being able to
command the intension that would represent the word in possible worlds semantics.

We might attribute this difficulty to the more general impossibility of
fitting a MONTAGUE model into a speaker's head, since by any reasonable assumptions there must be non-denumerably many possibly worlds, and hence the possible worlds could not all be represented distinctly within a finite brain.
I don't think this is the source of the problem, however. For one thing,
you don't need to represent all of the possible worlds distinctly in order
to know a function which has them as domain. We know the function for adding arbitrary real numbers without being able to represent all the real
numbers distinctly.[2] For another thing, it makes sense independently to
assume that our knowledge of meanings of lexical items should be represented
by partial functions rather than total functions from possible worlds to
extensions. The finite brain could be just a special sort of "performance"
limitation, just as finite memory span is often assumed to be in syntax.

KASHER [14] focusses on similar problems with a similar goal in mind,
which he characterizes as the goal of achieving a "logical rationalism" in
semantics. Accepting the linguists' assumptions, (vi) and (vii) above, he
makes finite representability a condition of elementary adequacy on a semantic theory, and explores the kinds of restrictions and modifications that
would be required to make Montague grammar finitely representable. He suggests as one major modification that the possible worlds not be viewed as
atomic but as constructs from a finitely and uniformly representable (conceptual) "logical space". He also proposes the quite reasonable restriction
that the interpretation of all operators (functions from functions to functions) be required to be computable.

If we didn't worry about propositional attitudes, I think we might be
able to achieve a reconciliation of psychological semantics with the possible
worlds approach in another way, along the following lines. Take the Fregean
or Montague semantics as representing a kind of super-competence: what we
would be like if not limited by finite brains and finite experience (e.g.
if we were God.) Finiteness restricts us to constructing partial models,
and in place of complete intensions of words we construct imperfect algorithms
which yield partial functions on these partial models. Different individuals
will have different partial models and different algorithms, since our brains
and our real-world experience are not identical. Communication will be possible as long as there is sufficient similarity in our partial models and
our imperfect semantics. Viewed in this way, there may be no problem in
principle in regarding a theory like MONTAGUE's as a kind of competence model.
It could be telling correctly how we can determine the meaning of a sentence
from the meanings of its parts, with "performance" factors like finite brains
explaining why we don't have complete meanings of lexical items to begin with
and why we sometimes make logical mistakes along the way.

But such a story remains plausible only so long as we ignore the propositional attitudes.

3. Propositional Attitudes

The trouble is that we know that we have these limitations, and this knowledge is reflected in propositional attitude sentences. The difficulty of formulating an appropriate semantics for belief-sentences and other sentences about propositional attitudes is well-known, and I would certainly not want to suggest abandoning any semantic theory out of hand simply because that theory did not so far seem to allow any adequate treatment of the propositional attitudes. But I believe that some of the idealizations that we take as fundamental in possible worlds semantics are the source of some of the problems we have in dealing with the propositional attitudes, and that an attempt to make our theories more psychologically realistic may be essential for solving those problems.

Among the problems associated with propositional attitude sentences, I believe that possible worlds semantics works relatively well for the problem of "quantifying in" and the problems associated with demonstratives and other indexical words inside propositional attitude contexts. More "quotational" or "linguistic" approaches have serious difficulties with those problems. A quotational analysis of a sentence such as (1)

Smith believes that the earth is flat   (1)

on its natural opaque reading, will treat believes as a relation between Smith and something like the sentence "the earth is flat", with perhaps the suggestion that (1) is true if Smith is in a certain mental state that involves something like a semantic representation of the sentence "the earth is flat". The sorts of difficulties I am referring to can be illustrated by the following sentence:

Smith believes that that door is locked, but she doesn't believe   (2)
that that door is locked.

Sentence (2) can be used to make a non-contradictory statement, so long as the two occurrences of the demonstrative expression "that door" are used to refer to different doors. So the relation of believing here cannot be a relation simply between Smith and the sentence type "that door is locked". So one may try something like saying that Smith stands in the opaque believing relation to some sentence of the form $\ulcorner \alpha$ is locked $\urcorner$ where α represents or denotes that (first) door for Smith, and doesn't stand in that relation to some other sentence $\ulcorner \beta$ is locked $\urcorner$, where β represents that other door for Smith. The problem here, as BURGE [1] clearly points out, is that in many typical cases of de re beliefs, it is implausible to assume that the believer's internal name or description (the α or β above) is one which will individuate the object in question in a context-independent manner. And if it does not, it is not reducible to a purely de dicto belief or to a relation between a person and a sentence-type.

This kind of problem arises for any sentence containing indexical elements: demonstratives, deictic pronouns, tenses, here, now, etc. It is a problem for any theory that identifies propositions with sentence types or with meanings of sentence types, taking these to be characterizable purely in terms of internal mental states of language users independently of the real-world environment or context in which the sentence-tokens occur. FODOR [9] provides a clear example of such a theory with what he calls "the computational theory of the mind". He requires that "two thoughts can be distinct in content only if they can be identified with relations to formally distinct representations" (p. 4). "If mental processes are formal, then they have access only to the formal properties of such representations of the environment as the senses provide. Hence they have no access to the seman-tic properties of such representations, including the property of being true, of having referents, ..." (p. 9). (I should say that FODOR does acknowledge that demonstratives are so far an unsolved problem for his approach.)

But there are two major problems that are not dealt with at all in MONTA-GUE's sort of theory.

3.1. The Logical Equivalence Problem

The first is the well-known non-substitutivity of logical equivalents in propositional attitudes. If P and Q are logically equivalent, we cannot validly make an inference from (3) to (4).

Irene believes that P.   (3)

Irene believes that Q.   (4)

This problem is widely admitted, but seldom confronted within MONTAGUE sem-antics, since it results directly from the assumption that propositions are the intensions of sentences and are functions from possible worlds to truth values.[4] MONTAGUE's semantics requires that logical equivalents be inter-substitutable everywhere, and it will take a major modification to remove that requirement. To describe what I see as the source of the problem, let me refer informally to a language with no propositional attitude expressions as a level 0 language, one with a single layer of propositional attitudes as a level 1 language, and so on. (This is an informal borrowing from RUSSELL's theory of ramified types.) And suppose we were to accept something like the view of MONTAGUE's theory as a theory of competence for speakers of a level 0 language, as I sketched in the previous section. Then we could express the argument of LINSKY [18] by saying that the performance limitations of speakers of a level 0 language must be acknowledged at the competence level of speakers of a level 1 language, and in general the level i performance limitations must be acknowledged at the level $i+1$ competence level. That is, as LINSKY argues, even if an idealized speaker will always recognize the logical equivalence of P and Q, he or she should not make the inference from (3) to (4), since part of his or her competence would be the knowledge that holders of propositional attitudes can make logical mistakes. I see this as one deep-rooted connec-tion between the demands of a psychological theory of semantics and the demands of an adequate account of the semantics of propositional attitudes.

Another way of putting the point is this. Suppose we view MONTAGUE's semantics as a super-competence model: a semantics for English as spoken by God. Then the semantics works perfectly well for the level 0 parts of the language, but it still fails for the propositional attitudes, since God would not make the inference from (3) to (4).

Note that we cannot get around this problem by assigning the objects of propositional attitudes to some other semantic type within a Montague-like system that retains his intensional logic, since substitution of logical equivalents is valid in such a system for every semantic type. Nor can we solve it by allowing non-standard interpretations for the logical connectives if, as I believe, the typical case of the failure of the inference from (3) to (4) arises simply because holders of propositional attitudes don't always recognize logical equivalence, independently of what logic they are using. [5]

3.2. The Rigid Designator Problem

The second major inadequacy of MONTAGUE's treatment of propositional attitudes has to do with the nature of lexical meaning. Let me add some background before stating it. Within the non-psychological semantic tradition, there are excellent arguments for why certain words such as proper names and perhaps natural kind terms should be viewed as rigid designators, that is, intensions which pick out the same extension in every possible world. As PUTNAM and others have persuasively argued, such intensions cannot be identified with psychological states narrowly defined. The mystery of how people can use such words at all can be solved by the causal chain story (see KRIPKE [16], DONNELLAN [6], EVANS [8]). On such a story, a person who knows nothing about Frege can use the name Frege to refer to Frege, for instance in asking the question "Who is Frege?", simply by intending to use the name in the way that others before him have used it, so long as there is an appropriate causal chain tracing back to a situation that makes an appropriate connection to the individual Frege himself. Similar remarks apply to certain words that designate natural kind terms such as names of species, chemical elements, etc.

In these cases the gap between the "mathematical" view and the psychological view seems much wider, perhaps unbridgeable. What is in a speaker's head in association with a proper name bears almost no resemblance to the intension.[6] The intension is a rigid designator, while the psychological representation is probably more like an incomplete and possibly incorrect definite description, or a partial algorithm for picking out the referent across times and worlds by qualitative characteristics. One complicating factor is that if the rigid designator theory is correct, then people in effect intend to use proper names as rigid designators, and therefore do not regard their associated descriptions and identifying procedures as constituting the meaning or intension of the name. Thus on a kind of meta-level (all this is unconscious, of course), our psychological states may be quite compatible with the rigid designator analysis, but on the ground level the individual speaker's psychological state will not in general determine a rigid designator.

As MONDADORI [19] says, the intension in the modal semantics sense is a function from really possible worlds to extensions therein, whereas the kind of concept that can be "grasped" (by us) is a function from epistemically possible worlds to extensions therein, and these are likely to diverge in the case of proper names and other rigid designators.[7]

With this background, we can state the second problem, which is that rigid designators do not remain rigid designators in propositional attitude contexts. Almost everyone agrees that sentence (5) does not entail sentence (6) and that (7) does not entail (8).[8]

The ancients did not know that Hesperus was Phosphorus.   (5)

The ancients did not know that Hesperus was Hesperus.   (6)

John wonders whether woodchucks are groundhogs.   (7)

John wonders whether woodchucks are woodchucks.   (8)

The standard treatment in intensional logic works well enough where either or both of the terms are non-rigid descriptions, but it seems to fail in cases like these where the two terms are rigid designators which rigidly designate the same entity or species. The failure seems to me to be directly attributable to the fact that the rigid designators are not "in our heads". The identity statement (9)

Herperus is Phosphorus. (9)

is necessarily true but not known a priori; the ancients may have used 'Herperus' and 'Phosphorus' as rigid designators for the same planet, but they didn't know it. The two names were not psychologically equivalent for them (nor are they for us.) Sentence (5) can have a different truth value from sentence (6) because it involves a psychological modality, and not a metaphysical modality, applied to a sentence which is (psychologically) informative although metaphysically necessary. Therefore I believe that this is another case where even a super-competence model (the 'God's language' model) cannot ignore the psychological view of semantics.

There are at least two other approaches to diagnosing the problem. One is to say that these cases are peculiarly metalinguistic, and should perhaps not be treated quite literally, since they are really statements about their subjects' lack of knowledge of the language. In favor of this view[9] is the fact that these sentences are not as readily translatable into other languages as are most propositional attitude sentences. And such sentences seem to make no sense at all when their subjects are dogs, pre-linguistic children, etc., to whom many propositional attitudes can reasonably be attributed.

Yet I think one would be hard pressed to find criteria for dividing propositional attitude sentences into two classes, one metalinguistic in this sense and the other not. When we judge the truth of a propositional attitude sentence we often take into consideration both the subject's dispositions to assent and his or her dispositions to act. When we attribute beliefs to dogs we are generally judging by their actions, and when we utter (5) we are generally judging by the ancients' assertions, or by actions which essentially include linguistic acts. But this is not enough to show that there is an ambiguity, either lexical (in the attitude verbs) or structural (e.g. true that-clause vs. quotation.) Perhaps there is, but it remains to be shown.

Another approach which has been suggested recently involves ideas of STALNAKER's and KAPLAN's about the role of context in determining the content of an utterance.[10] STALNAKER [34] includes the possible world in which an utterance occurs as part of the context, which lets us bring into play the fact that it is contingent that the expressions in the utterance mean what they do and refer to what they refer to. It is contingent that "Hesperus" and "Phosphorus" are names of the same planet. What STALNAKER calls the propositional concept associated with the linguistic form "Hesperus is Phosphorus" is a function from contexts of use, including a possible world, to propositions (functions from possible worlds to truth values.) (I believe this is very close to what DAVID KAPLAN [13] calls character.) In the context of the actual world, that propositional concept picks out the necessary proposition, but in a world compatible with the beliefs of someone who thinks the names are names of distinct planets, it picks out the necessarily false proposition.

This sounds like it has the ingredients we need, but I am still quite uncertain about how to incorporate it into a compositional semantics of belief-sentences. The appeal to the context can explain why an assertion of "Hesperus is Phosphorus" in isolation is informative; but when a sentence like (5) or (7) is uttered, the world of the context of the utterance is (loosely speaking) the speaker's world, not the subject's world. To somehow invoke the context of the ancients (for (5)) or of John (for (7)), contexts must be recursively manipulated. And it seems to be still an open question within this approach [11] whether it is character or content that is the object of the attitudes. At any rate, this seems to me potentially a very promising approach to this problem (although I do not so far see that it would bear on the first problem, the problem of logical equivalence.)

There is an additional example that I will mention here because I think it is closely related to the rigid designator problem, although I am not certain. PIAGET [28] observes that many children go through a stage of believing that clouds are alive. On first encounter, we may be quite unsure what that means, since it may seem to us analytic that clouds are not alive. We can be sure that the children have some belief that differs from some belief of ours, but without further investigation we don't know whether it's a belief about what "clouds" means, or about the nature of clouds, or about what "alive" means, or about the nature of life, or something else. (The explanations the children give when queried further tend to rest on the auxiliary beliefs that clouds move by themselves, cause wind, manage not to "sink", etc.)

Perhaps such examples should be dismissed. We might justify dismissing them on the grounds that if someone's whole belief structure, including beliefs about what many words mean, differs very radically from mine, I cannot hope to describe his or her belief in my language. A compositional semantics may be impossible without the assumption of a homogeneous interpretation system (both the model theory and the interpretation into it.)

Yet I am uneasy about dismissing them, because it seems to me that the difference between the children's language and ours is greater in degree but not in kind from the differences between any two of us, and that we often use belief sentences to report beliefs that differ from our own in cases where we really don't know how much of the difference is "linguistic" and how much is "factual". Assuming homogenous interpretation may be a necessary idealization for getting started, but it carries the danger of making us all seem egocentrically dogmatic when we attribute beliefs to others.

Let me summarize the two problems that I have been discussing. The first is the non-substitutability of logical equivalents in propositional attitude contexts. My claim is that this problem arises in formal semantics because of the idealization away from psychological limitations on our capacity to do logic; but propositional attitudes are psychological, and it is just these psychological limitations that make substitutions of logical equivalents fail in such contexts. The second problem is that rigid designators are not always rigid in propositional attitude contexts and more generally, that words do not appear always to have their usual intensions in propositional attitude contexts. I believe this problem to have a similar source: the psychological semantic representation of a word is often very different from its intension, and properties of the psychological representation are often the crucial factor in propositional attitude contexts.

4. Is Semantics Possible?

My general theme so far has been that the view of natural language semantics as psychology is not just a reflection of a Chomskyan approach to what linguistics is all about. We can start from the logician's goal of giving a correct account of the entailment relations among sentences of a natural language, even with the idealization to a super-ideal speaker who is omniscient about all possible worlds and who never makes logical mistakes. Montague's semantics, and any other semantics that has a similar treatment of intensions, will make false predictions about entailment relations among the propositional attitude sentences for such a speaker.

So I don't see how we can get a correct account of propositional attitudes without bringing psychology into the picture, but I also don't see how we can get along <u>with</u> it. The relevant psychological factors are ones which vary from speaker to speaker and moment to moment. No one can infallibly recognize logical equivalence, but there is no general way of determining who will recognize which equivalence when. The psychological correlates of word intensions are similarly variable across speakers and times. These were the very reasons why FREGE suggested that if we want propositions to stand in a close relation both to language and to truth, we must not equate them with ideas.

At this point, I think it can be made clear why I think syntax does not face the same difficulty that semantics does. In syntax, we can safely use the notion of an idiolect of a single speaker, determined completely by what's in his or her head. At no point do the syntactic rules of one speaker have to be sensitive to the syntactic rules of any other speaker, or to non-linguistic context. There are no syntactic analogs to the propositional attitude problems. (It might be thought that direct quotation could present a similar problem, but [25] argues that quotations should not be regarded as linguistic parts of the sentences that contain them.)

The problem we are faced with in trying to give a semantics for propositional attitudes is twofold: first, to determine what kind of semantic entities the objects of the propositional attitudes are, and second, to determine the compositional rules that will assign the appropriate such entities to the syntactic objects of the propositional attitude verbs. For the first problem, I have no solution; my arguments have been mainly negative, to the effect that there is no semantic type of the right sort available within MONTAGUE's intensional logic.

The second problem cannot be solved before the first has been, but we can make some tentative claims about some of the factors that need to be involved:

(i) The structure of the embedded sentence matters. We lose too much information if we just compute out intensions as we proceed up the analysis tree of the embedded sentence. This factor is related to the notion of intensional isomorphism in [2] and to what LEWIS calls "meanings" in [17].[12]

(ii) Context clearly matters, not only for indexicals, but also in the broader senses discussed above in connection with STALNAKER's and KAPLAN's suggestions.

(iii) The believer's interpretation of lexical items matters for the rigid designator problems, and the believer's "logical performance factors" matter for the logical equivalence problems. Neither of these can be determined compositionally, since the speaker of the sentence may not know what they are. But perhaps there is a way of introducing variables for such factors, and introducing existential quantifiers connect those variables to the subject of the propositional attitude predicate.

One conclusion we may be forced to is that there are virtually no valid inferences from the propositional part of propositional attitude sentences except via additional premises. Within an approach like MONTAGUE's, this would make it much harder to see what the adequacy criteria for a correct account of propositional attitudes would be.[13]

5. Conclusion

I certainly have not answered the question whether semantics is mathematics or psychology. There are undoubtedly too many different kinds of mathematics and psychology for a general answer to be possible. What I have tried to suggest is that the linguist's concern for psychological representation may be relevant to every semanticist's concern for an account of the semantics of propositional attitudes. So far I don't see how to achieve either goal; my only positive suggestion is that a good theory might be expected to achieve both at once.

Acknowledgements

I received many helpful criticisms and suggestions from the participants in the Konstanz colloquium for which this paper was prepared, and also from the audiences at the 1978 Chapel Hill Philosophy Colloquium and at M.I.T., where slightly revised versions of the first draft were read. Many people read the first draft and gave me useful suggestions; I would particularly like to thank Emmon Bach, Tyler Burge, Greg Carlson, David Dowty, Elisabet Engdahl, Janet Fodor, Jerry Fodor, Frank Heny, Stephen Isard, Hans Kamp, David Kaplan, Asa Kasher, David Lewis, John McCarthy, Julius Moravcsik, Robert Stalnaker, Richmond Thomason, and Bas van Fraassen. I am also grateful to Noam Chomsky for his comments on an earlier paper which led to some changes in my thinking that are reflected in this one.

Notes

[1]DOWTY [7], citing recent arguments of PUTNAM's, suggests that "possible worlds semantics on the one hand and most linguistic theories of semantics on the other should not be taken as competing explanations of the same phenomenon but rather as complementary theories of distinct though related phenomena." On this view, Montague's theory is a theory of truth and reference, or correspondence, and what linguists are aiming for is a theory of language understanding, and both kinds of theories will be needed to explain all of what is usually called "meaning".

I believe that even if this view is correct, Montague's semantics still needs radical revision just to do its own job adequately, and that its inadequacies reflect certain properties of human understanding.

[2]STEPHEN ISARD (personal communication) has suggested that we can't really be said to know the function for adding arbitrary real numbers. We don't know it extensionally; that is, we don't have any representation of the entire set of ordered triples (a,b,c) such that a and b are real numbers and c = a + b. And any finitely specifiable algorithm for addition must operate on representations of numbers; e.g. the algorithm for adding fractions is different from the algorithm for adding decimals. Then since we can't have finite representations of all the real numbers which the algorithm is to operate on, we can't have a finite specification of the algorithm itself. (You certainly can't build a Turing machine that will add arbitrary real numbers, even if you let it run forever, since you can't get the inputs onto the tape to begin with.) I'm not sure whether I believe this argument; but I will postpone considering it further to a later occasion. Finite representability of infinite structures seems to me to be a question deserving much more attention in semantics than it has had, and one where we could probably learn a good deal from computer scientists. The work of FRIEDMAN et al. [11] is certainly relevant here.

[3]I am thinking here of something along the lines of CRESSWELL's communication class in [4].

[4]KATZ and KATZ [15] make this point forcefully. It should be noted that MONTAGUE addressed this problem in at least two places. In [20], he defends the substitution of logical equivalents in belief contexts as correct, with the remark that "its counterintuitive character can perhaps be traced to the existence of another notion of belief, of which the objects are sentences or, in some cases, complexes consisting in part of open formulas" (p. 139 in [27]). In [21], he provides a framework which he says permits "a natural treatment of belief contexts that lacks the controversial property of always permitting interchange on the basis of logical equivalence" (p. 231 in [22]). However, he does not spell that treatment out, since he still prefers to allow substitution of logical equivalents. I believe he had in mind a treatment in which logical words receive non-standard interpretations at certain "unactualizable" points of reference; as I mention below, I don't believe that solution is on the right track.

[5]JOHN McCARTHY (personal communication) pointed out that this problem arises as much for machines as for people. His observation suggests that the real tension is not between a mathematical and a psychological view of semantics but between a purely Platonistic semantics (which Montague's is) and an operational (his term) semantics.

HINTIKKA solves this problem by analyzing belief sentences in terms of epistemically possible worlds which are not all logically possible worlds. His notions of surface and depth information are directly related to the problem of logical non-omniscience, and RANTALA [32] and HINTIKKA [12] offer an interesting non-standard model theory ("urn models") to provide a semantic backing to the notion of "impossible possible worlds". I do not understand the system well enough to know how difficult it would be to incorporate into a system like MONTAGUE's.

For examples of some very interesting psychological work on people's performance on various kinds of inference tasks, see [36].

[6]MORAVCSIK [23] argues in this connection that FREGE's and KRIPKE's differing theories of proper names are really theories of very different things,

built from different conceptions of "mastery of a language." FREGE was concerned with the _informativeness_ of identity statements involving proper names, KRIPKE with their necessary truth. In the terms of footnote 1, FREGE was after a theory of understanding and KRIPKE a theory of correspondence. MORAVCSIK doubts that a single theory can or should achieve both.

[7]This is clearly a central and pervasive problem, not just for proper names. MONDADORI [19] and MORAVCSIK [23] use it to argue against the likely fruitfulness of an attempt to construct a unitary theory of meaning; KASHER [14], like me, sees it as a place where the foundations of MONTAGUE's semantics need to be changed, the open question being whether they can be changed without sacrificing the logicians' goals.

[8]We are concerned here with the readings on which the terms in subordinate clause are entirely within the scope of _know_ or _wonder_, i.e. the "opaque" readings. The trouble is that (at least in MONTAGUE's system) the rigid designator treatment of proper names makes all the readings of (5) come out equivalent, and likewise for (6); the same would be true of (7) and (8) if either (a) _woodchuck_ and _groundhog_ are given the same intension, or (b) _woodchucks_ and _groundhogs_ are treated as rigid designator names of species.

[9]GREG CARLSON kindly brought this point (back) to my attention.

[10]This approach was not mentioned in the first draft of this paper, and I am grateful to DAVID LEWIS, DAVID KAPLAN, and BAS VAN FRAASSEN for suggesting it and to ROBERT STALNAKER for a helpful and stimulating conversation about it. Their suggestions did not all agree, and none of them thinks the problems have all been solved. None of them is responsible for my description of this approach.

[11]This is a point on which there was not agreement among those mentioned in note 10. I won't say who thinks what because some of them were expressly tentative.

[12]THOMASON [35] proposes a method for achieving this effect in a system which takes propositions as a primitive semantic type. PARSONS suggests something similar in [24].

[13]TYLER BURGE (personal communication) suggests that this conclusion is not grounds for the pessimism of my earlier draft. Compositional semantics can provide an important part of the basis on which we make practical or probabilistic inferences, even if there are no valid entailments to be gotten. It may be that the seeming impossibility of giving a semantics for propositional attitudes is partly the result of MONTAGUE's narrow focus on capturing valid entailments as virtually the sole criterion for the adequacy of semantics -- indeed, as _the_ job of a semantic theory.

References

1. Tyler Burge: "_Belief_ De Re", _Journal of Philosophy_ 74, 338-362 (1977)

2. Rudolf Carnap: _Meaning and Necessity_: A study in Semantics and Modal Logic, University of Chicago Press, enlarged edition (1956)

3. Noam Chomsky: _Reflections on Language_, Pantheon Books, New York (1975)

4. M.J. Cresswell: Logics and Languages, Methuen, London (1973)

5. M. J. Cresswell: "Semantic competence", in M. Guenthner-Reutter and F. Guenthner, eds., Meaning and Translation: Philosophical and Linguistic Approaches, Duckworth, London (1978)

6. Keith Donnellan: "Speaking of nothing", Philosophical Review 83, 3-32, reprinted in [33]

7. David Dowty: Word Meaning and Montague Grammar, Synthese Language Library, D. Reidel Publishing Co., Dordrecht (forthcoming)

8. Gareth Evans: "The causal theory of names", Aristotelian Society Supplementary Volume 47, 187-208, reprinted in [33]

9. J.A. Fodor: "Methodological solipsism considered as a research strategy in cognitive psychology", M.I.T., Cambridge (unpublished)

10. G. Frege: "Der Gedanke", Beiträge zur Philosophie des deutschen Idealisms, Vol. 1 (1919); trans. by A. Quinton and M. Quinton as "The thought: a logical inquiry", Mind 65, 289-311 (1956)

11. Joyce Friedman, Douglas Moran, and David Warren: "Dynamic Interpretation", N-16, Dept. of Computer and Communication Sciences, University of Michigan, Ann Arbor (unpublished)

12. Jaakko Hintikka: "Impossible possible worlds vindicated", Journal of Philosophical Logic 4, 475-484 (1975)

13. David Kaplan: "Demonstratives: an essay on the semantics, logic, metaphysics and epistemology of demonstratives and other indexicals", read in part at the March 1977 meeting of the Pacific Division of the American Philosophical Association, "Draft #2", manuscript, UCLA (1977)

14. Asa Kasher: "Logical Rationalism: on degrees of adequacy for semantics of natural languages", Philosophica 18, 139-157 (1976)

15. Fred M. Katz and Jerrold J. Katz: "Is necessity the mother of intension?", The Philosophical Review 86, 70-96 (1977)

16. Saul Kripke: "Naming and necessity", in D. Davidson and G. Harman, eds., Semantics of Natural Language, D. Reidel, Dordrecht (1972)

17. David Lewis: "General Semantics", Synthese v. 21 (1970)

18. L. Linsky: "Believing and necessity", Proceedings and Addresses of the American Philosophical Association 50, 526-530 (1977)

19. F. Mondadori: "Interpreting modal semantics" in F. Guenthner and C. Rohrer, eds., Studies in Formal Semantics, North-Holland, Amsterdam (1978)

20. Richard Montague: "Pragmatics and intensional logic", Synthese 22, 68-94, reprinted in [22]

21. Richard Montague: "Universal grammar", Theoria 36, 373-398, reprinted in [22]

22. Richard Montague: Formal Philosophy: Selected Papers of Richard Montague, edited and with an introduction by Richmond Thomason, Yale University Press, New Haven (1974)

23. J.M.E. Moravcsik: "Singular terms, belief, and reality", Dialectica 31, 259-272 (1977)

24. Terence Parsons: Nonexistent Objects, forthcoming, Yale University Press

25. B. H. Partee: "The syntax and semantics of quotation", in S.R. Anderson and P. Kiparsky, eds., A Festschrift for Morris Halle, Holt, Rinehart, and Winston, New York (1973)

26. B. H. Partee: "Montague grammar and transformational grammar", Linguistic Inquiry 6, 203-300 (1975)

27. B.H. Partee: "Montague grammar, mental representations, and reality", to be published in proceedings of the symposium "Philosophy and Grammar", Uppsala University, June 1977, Stig Kanger and Sven Ohman, eds. (forthcoming)

28. Jean Piaget: The Child's Conception of the World, trans. J. and A. Tomlinson, 1972 edition, Littlefield, Adams, & Co., Totowa, N.J. (1929)

29. Hilary Putnam: Mind, Language and Reality: Philosophical Papers, Vol. 2, Cambridge University Press, Cambridge (1975)

30. Hilary Putnam: "The meaning of 'meaning'", in K. Gunderson (ed.), Language, Mind and Knowledge, Minnesota Studies in the Philosophy of Science VII, University of Minnesota Press, Minneapolis, reprinted in [29]

31. Hilary Putnam: "Language and reality", in [29]

32. Veikko Rantala: "Urn models: a new kind of nonstandard model for first order logic", Journal of Philosophical Logic 4, 455-474 (1975)

33. Stephen R. Schwartz: Naming, Necessity, and Natural Kinds, (ed), Cornell University Press, Ithaca (1977)

34. Robert Stalnaker: "Assertion", in Peter Cole, ed., Syntax and Semantics, Vol. 9: Pragmatics, Academic Press, N.Y., 315-332 (1978)

35. Richmond Thomason: "A model theory for propositional attitudes", ms. 1977, University of Pittsburgh (unpublished)

36. P.C. Wason and P. N. Johnson-Laird: Psychology of Reasoning: Structure and Content, Harvard University Press, Cambridge, Mass. (1972)

Do We Really Need Tenses Other Than Future and Past? *

Dov Gabbay

Bar-Ilan University, Department of Mathematics, Ramat-Gan, Israel

Christian Rohrer
Universität Stuttgart, Institut für Linguistik, Schloßstraße 26
D-7000 Stuttgart 1, Fed. Rep. of Germany

Section 1

Some languages have more tense forms than others. They seem to have more expressive power. Compare English with Hebrew. Hebrew has practically only two tenses, future and past; while English has others, such as perfect. This gives the impression that in English one can express more. This impression is reinforced by the fact that often translation from English into Hebrew is awkward, from the point of view of tense expressions.

How does Hebrew compensate for the lack of the perfect? This is a serious and interesting question. We know that we can use time adverbs and time reference points in Hebrew, (as in any other language) but then, how does it exactly compensate? Is there a more extensive use of reference events (points) in Hebrew than in English?

We shall try to pose and answer these questions within the framework of tense logic. Another dialect we use is the Swabian German dialect, where the only tenses used are present and past (so perhaps we can say future (= present) and past), with possibility to iterate past to achieve an equivalent of the pluperfect.

Our general conclusion shall be that all natural languages have the same temporal expressive power no matter what their grammatical tense system is.

Section 2

Consider a flow of time $(T,<)$, assumed to be linear. Consider a propositional tense logic with atomic propositions, q, q', v, v' ... the classical connectives $\sim$, $\wedge$, V, $\rightarrow$ and the two priorian unary operators Fq, Pq. We imagine our propositions vary in truth value along the time axis. We write $||A||_t = 1$ to mean A is true at t. Atomic propositions get arbitrary truth value distribution, i.e. there is a function h, such that for all atoms q, $h(q) \subseteq T$ and $||q||_t = 1$ iff $t \epsilon h(q)$.

We understand Fq as saying q will be true and Pq as saying q was true.

So $\quad ||FA||_t = 1 \quad <=> \quad \exists s>t \quad ||A||_s = 1$

$\quad\quad ||PA||_t = 1 \quad <=> \quad \exists s<t \quad ||A||_s = 1$

So for example if q is: <u>John visits Mary.</u>
Fq = <u>John will visit Mary.</u>
Pq = <u>John visited Mary.</u>

If   G = $\sim F\sim$, H = $\sim P\sim$
Then   q∧Hq = <u>John has always visited Mary.</u>
GFq = <u>John will never stop visiting Mary.</u>

Thus we see that some tense statements are definable using future F and past P.

Not all tensed expressions are definable.
Take   U(p,q)   = <u>q will be true until p</u>
$$||U(p,q)||_t = 1 \iff \exists s > t(||p||_s = 1 \land \forall u(t<u<s \to ||q||_u=1)).$$
Similarly define since S(p,q).
$$||S(p,q)||_t = 1 \iff \exists s < t(||p||_s = 1 \land \forall u(s<u<t \to ||q||_u=1)).$$

<u>Theorem 1</u> (H. KAMP)

U, S are not definable using P, F, over linear time.
Of course if the flow of time has some special properties, then U may be definable using F, P. For example we can take the pessimistic view that the future has only one point s. Then U(p,q) = Fp. So for such a flow of time U is definable.

<u>Section 3</u>

Consider the perfect tenses, for example, future perfect. For the future perfect you need a reference point s in the future, and if t is the present then <u>future perfect</u> (A) is true at s iff for some u t<u<s; A is true at u.
If we take a proposition p that is true exactly at s, we can say <u>when p will be (becomes) true, q will have been true.</u> That is a connective
$$\pi(p,q) \text{ with } ||\pi(p,q)||_t = 1 \iff$$
$$\exists s > t(||p||_s = 1 \land \forall u(t<u<s \to ||p||_u = 0) \land \exists u'(t<u'<s \; ||q||_{u'} = 1)).$$

Since the point s is the first where p becomes true it is unique, so we can also write
$$||\pi(p,q)||_t = 1 \iff \forall s(t<s \land \forall u(t<u<s \to ||p||_u = 0) \land ||p||_s = 1 \to$$
$$\exists u'(t<u'<s \land ||q||_{u'} = 1)).$$

<u>Theorem 2</u> (DOV GABBAY)

The perfect tenses and their mirror images (i.e. π and its mirror image) are equivalent in power of expression to <u>Since</u> and <u>Until</u>. (i.e. <u>Since</u> and <u>Until</u> on the one hand and π and its mirror image on the other hand are interdefinable).

<u>Corollary</u> From this we conclude that F and P alone cannot express the perfect future and its mirror image.

Some argument may be put forward whether π really represents the future perfect or some other operator. In principle we know that a future reference point is needed for the future perfect and so in principle we can still get for any reasonable presentation of the future perfect that it is interdefinable in some way with <u>Since</u> and <u>Until</u>, and so the corollary to Theorem 2 can be seen as valid.

So how do we manage to express a distribution of events in languages with future and past tense only? In Hebrew we use the word "already" like this:

<u>When he will come the bill will already be paid.</u>
i.e. <u>When (p will) already (q will).</u>

In Hebrew: .כאשר הוא יגיע החשבון כבר ישולם

This is bad English but correct Hebrew. The word "already" forces q to be in past of p but the tense form <u>will</u> in q forces q to remain in the future. So this is future perfect. For example, if we were to use this "trick" in French we could say:

(1) Quand Jean arrivera - Marie
    (a) aura deja gagne
 *(b) gagnera deja

(2) Quand Jean arrivera
    (a) le soleil se sera (déjà) couché
 * (b) le soleil se couchera déjà.

(a)b is the form used in Hebrew. In Swabian form (1)b is used but instead of future form in (b) past is used. So the perfect is expressed:

(3) (a) In Hebrew: When future form of p - already future form of q.

      <u>When John will arrive Mary will already win.</u>

    (b) In Swabian: When present form of p (with possibly a time adverb) already past form of q.

      <u>When John arrives (tomorrow) Mary already won.</u>

    (c) In English: When present form of p, (already) future perfect form of q.

      <u>When John arrives Mary will have (already) won.</u>

    (d) In French: When future form of p, (already) future perfect form of q.

      <u>When John will arrive Mary will have already won.</u>

Sentence (2)b above in French may be acceptable for durative verbs. In that case English uses future progressive for q: <u>When John arrives Mary will already be eating.</u>

(Hebrew cannot express directly the sentence (2)b for durative verbs). We cannot use such a trick in the tense logic itself because when we write Fq, <u>q does not take any surface change.</u> Only in natural language can we use this device. So, any language with the word "already" can do that. Linguists have noticed the close connection (semantic similarity) between perfect and already cf. <u>not yet</u> etc.

<u>Section 4</u>

Another device that language with future and past can use are time adverbs or time reference points. Let ν be a variable for reference point. Suppose we are at time t. We can fix ν to be t. We can regard ν to be a proposition true exactly at t. E.g. you can say "The time is t." Then we can define e.g. π (p,q) using ν as a parameter.

$$\nu \wedge H\nu \vee \wedge G \sim \nu \rightarrow [\pi\ (p,q) \longleftrightarrow \pi'(p,q,\nu)= F(p\wedge H(\sim p\ V\nu\ V\ F\nu)\wedge P(a\wedge P\nu))]$$

This says if ν denotes the time t then π (p,q) is $\pi'(p,q,\nu)$.

Theorem 3 (DOV GABBAY)

If we allow as many reference parameters $\nu_1,\ldots\nu_n$ as needed any tensed expression is definable using P,F.

Since this theorem is important, saying that anything can be expressed using P,F and time adverbs, we must make it more precise.

Let $(T,<,Q_1,\ldots,Q_n)$ be the flow of time with $Q_i \subseteq T$. Q_i corresponds to a proposition q_i, with $h(q_i) = Q_i$. Any wff ψ (t) in the first order language of $(T,<,Q_i)$ with t free is a time expression because it says how Q_i are distributed around t. For example:

$$\psi_\pi(t,P,Q) = \exists s>t\ (P(s) \wedge \forall u(t<u<s \rightarrow \sim P(u)) \wedge \exists u'(t<u'<s \wedge Q(u'))$$

says exactly that π (p,q) is true at t.

Given any wff A built up from $q_1,\ldots q_n$, we can ask is A true at t? Since the value of A depends on when $q_1,\ldots q_n$ are true and nothing else, there corresponds to A a wff $\psi_A(t,Q_1,\ldots,Q_n)$. The expressive power of a tense language is how many ψ_A can be obtained. Theorem 2 says that ψ_π cannot be obtained using any A built up from F,P alone.

Theorem 3 (reformulation)

For any $\psi(t,Q_1,\ldots,Q_n)$ there exists an m (dependent on ψ) and an A and reference parameters $\nu_1\ldots\nu_m$ such that given t, the values of $\nu_1,\ldots,\nu_m$ can be fixed in such a way that for all h

$$||A(q_1,\ldots,q_n,\nu_1,\ldots,\nu_m)||_t^h = 1 <=> \psi(t,h(q_1),\ldots,h(q_n)).$$

This theorem does not solve the problem of the expressive power of languages with P,F only. We must consider the following objections.

(1) The number m of reference points increases with different ψ's. It is not fixed. Thus there should be a proliferation of time adverbs in the language (which is not true).

(2) The dependence of ν_i on ψ is awkward. A small change in ψ calls for a complete change in the choice of the ν_i. (e.g. change a negation sign inside ψ and a completely new set of ν_i may be needed). One gets the feeling that we don't think in these terms.

H. KAMP has shown the following:

Theorem 4

For time dedekind complete (e.g. real or integer numbers time) U and S are sufficient to define all other tensed expressions (without parameters).

Theorem 5 (DOV GABBAY)

The same holds for a system with P,F and future perfect and future in the past (would), for dedekind complete time.

The above gives a satisfactory answer for the case of e.g. real numbers time, because we have (a) perfect tenses (b) since + until (c) the use of reference parameters. Each of (a) - (c) is sufficient to express all tensed statements and so in practice we choose a comfortable combination. The above is true for dedekind complete flow of time only.

Theorem 6 (H. KAMP)

U. S is not sufficient for arbitrary linear time. A similar theorem holds for the perfect tenses.

So our problem is not yet solved. We don't feel in our everyday life that time is e.g. the real numbers. We may feel that time is linear but not necessarily real.

Section 5

There is another use, however, that all languages practice with P and F. We can say FA and mean that the "entire story" of A happens in the future. For example:

(1) Mary waited until Bill came.

(2) When we arrived John was reading.

The entie story takes place in the past. Denote this use of future by F^0. Similarly P^0.

Consider:

(3) I knew him before he had been to prison.

(4) I knew him after he had been to prison.

(4) is o.k. but how about (3)? This is a puzzle unless we read it like P^0 (I knew him before he has been to prison).

Theorem 7 (DOV GABBAY)

F^0, P^0 are sufficient to express all tensed expressions over linear time.

The above theorem requires further explanation. We saw that with each sentence $A(q_1,...q_n)$ we can associate a formula $\psi_A(t,Q_1,...Q_n)$ which says exactly what is required for A to be true at moment t. We assume, of course, that Q_i is the truth set of q_i. $Q_i = \{x \mid q_i$ true at $x\}$. For example, $U(p,q)$ has the formula $\psi_U(t,P,Q)$; where $\psi_U(t,P,Q) = \exists y > t(P(y) \wedge \forall x(t<x<y \rightarrow Q(x)))$. This formula reads q until p. So if p = Bill comes, q = Mary waits, then $U(p,q)$ = Mary waits until Bill comes.

Now given A, we can form the sentence PA, reading A was true. So PA is true at t iff for some s<t, A is true at s. But A is true at s iff $\psi_A(s)$ holds. Thus PA is true at t iff $\exists s<t$ $\psi_A(s)$. But PA is true at t iff $\psi_{PA}(t)$ holds.
Thus we get: $\psi_{PA}(t) = \exists s<t$ $\psi_A(s)$.

So let us compute now ψ of $PU(p,q)$.

$$\psi_{PU}(t) = \exists y{<}t \; \psi_U(y) = (\exists y{<}t)\,(\exists s{>}y)(P(s) \land \forall x(y{<}x{<}s \to Q(x)))).$$

$PU(p,q)$ does not read Mary waited until Bill came for the q,p chosen above. This is so because the time chosen (for Bill came) is not restricted to be in the past of t, in the formula $\psi_{PU}(t)$. What we are really saying when we use the English sentence is P^0U, i.e. the "entire story" of A is in the past of t. Thus $P^0U(p,q)$ will have the table:

$$\psi_{PO_U}(t) = (\exists y{<}t) \; \exists s(y{<}s{<}t) \; (P(s) \land \forall x(y{<}x{<}s \to Q(x))).$$

The s must also be chosen in the past of t. Thus from the above example we see that $\psi_{PO_A}(t) = \exists y{<}t \; \psi_A^{<t}(y)$, where $\psi_A^{<t}$ means that all quantifiers $\exists x, \forall x$ in ψ_A are relativised to $\exists x{<}t, \forall x{<}t$. This really reads that all points involved in the computation of the truth value of A at y are chosen smaller (in the past of t).

When we use natural language we sometimes use P^0, F^0, sometimes P,F and sometimes reference points, etc. The theorem says that for linear time, for any condition $\psi(t)$ there is always an A such that $\psi_A(t) = \psi(t)$, provided we are allowed the use of P^0, F^0.

We can thus conclude that the temporal expressive powers of practically all languages are equivalent and are the strongest possible. This is plausible because practically all languages allow for P^0 and F^0. One can always restrict the "entire story" to a specified time interval.

Footnote

*Research carried out under DFG contract Ro 245/10 at the Universitat Stuttgart, Institut fur Linguistik Romanistik.

References

1 Gabbay, D.M.   A tense logic with split truth table, Logique et Analyse, 1978, pp. 1-38.

2 Gabbay, D.M.   Functional completeness in tense logic, Journal of Symbolic Logic, To appear.

3 Kamp, H.   Tense Logic and the Theory of Linear Order, Thesis UCLA 1968.

4 Needham, P.   From the speaker's point of view, Synthese, 1976, pp.309-327.

5 Rohrer, C.   How to define temporal conjunctions, Linguistische Berichte, 1977, pp. 1-12.

Context Change, Truth and Competence

Thomas T. Ballmer

Sprachwissenschaftliches Institut Ruhr-Universität Bochum

Universitätsstraße 150, D-4630 Bochum, Fed. Rep. of Germany

> Et vous, vous dites toujours
> ce que vous avez à dire pour
> vous faire comprendre?
>
> Zazie, dans le mêtro

1. Introduction

In this short paper I would like to display some of the basic ideas which justify an investigation of the notion of *context change* as *one* basic notion of linguistics. It is by far not the only important notion, but it is of special interest, because it connects with a series of other notions relevant for linguistics which tend to conflict with some traditional conceptions in linguistics and even in the philosophy of language. One of these notions context change connects with is the *instrumental character of natural language*. For, to conceive of language as an instrument, or more precisely as a set of instruments, is to disagree implicitly with (at least) two basic assumptions on which part of the linguists rely today, namely first with the possibility of a clean separation of competence and performance (or "langue" and "parole") and, secondly with taking a theory of truth as fundamental for semantics and pragmatics. To deny a clean separation of competence and performance opposes a deeply rooted structuralist hypothesis which has been accepted also by most transformationalists. To deny that the notion of truth is fundamental for the semantics and pragmatics of natural language stands in opposition to the view of most logical grammarians. However, the work of certain transformationalists (cf. LAKOFF [8]) casts doubt on the competence performance distinction. Likewise, certain students of artificial intelligence (cf. WINOGRAD [17]) objected to the declarative approach to semantics and advocated a procedural approach. This amounts in their view to rendering the truthfunctional approaches inadequate.

One may question whether these objections by linguists and students of artificial intelligence are put forward and argued for in a sound way. What I would like to demonstrate - with reference to my work on the notion of *context change* and related notions - is that there is some truth in their *challenge*.

2. The Instrumental Character of Natural Language and Context Change

In order to demonstrate my point, we ought to be clear about what the instrumental character of natural language and the notion of context change are and how they connect to more familiar notions such as meaning, truth and inference. In doing this, we have to strictly keep in mind that it is our primary objective to look out for a *best possible analysis of language* and of the way it functions. Having taken this into consideration, we of course should be willing to establish the relation to the more traditional views. In this respect let us be as conservative as possible (sometimes, of course, there may be no such possibility).

Because my point of view deviates in some respect from what is usually accepted today, we shall start at the basis of linguistic analysis and give a fresh explication of what language is. One important aspect of it is, as is well accepted, that it can be *used* by its user. It can be used for certain purposes. Sometimes these purposes are public, sometimes they are private, sometimes they are not even consciously known to the user: there may be purposes which pertain to the social system to which the user belongs. Whether there are uses of language in the proper sense without any purpose in this general sense I leave open at this point, but we assume for the moment that there are none. Nothing hinges on that assumption.

The fact that in various languages we may say that language is *used*, demonstrates linguistically that language is taken to be an *organ* or an *instrument*. For what we *use* typically are our hands, feet, eyes or hammer, scissors, cups etc. Many aspects of language can be, but need not be controlled consciously. This is so with the production of words and sentences. Certain other aspects of language, however, are not consciously controllable normally, as is the case with certain parts of intonation e.g. timbre. Organs unlike instruments belong inalienably to the body of the user. Only a few organs, like the limbs, eyes, tongue, lips and lungs, are consciously controllable, many are not. Instruments normally are consciously controlled, unless the user is extremely used to them. These few considerations show that language is in certain respects rather an *organ* than an instrument, but in many important respects, especially in those which we are interested in, it can safely be taken to have *instrumental character*.

In order to understand more explicitly what it means to say that language is a (set of) instrument(s), we should clarify to some extent what an instrument (or organ) is.

Thus we should know under what circumstances instruments (and organs) are used, and what their usage amounts to.

Organs and instruments are aids for those who use them to achieve an aim or purpose. They are normally necessary aids in that they facilitate the attainment of a goal in a radical manner: it is possible but normally very hard to drive in a nail with your bare hands. Using linguistic expressions facilitates the achieving of certain purposes in a similar fashion. Thus the circumstances in which organs and instruments are used are normally such that one could not dispense with them in a case where one aims at fulfilling a certain purpose.

What is involved, then, in using an organ or instrument? An organism uses his organs and instruments to maintain certain states which are in danger of vanishing but are of some value for him, and likewise he uses his organs and instruments to reach a certain valuable state which does not obtain at present. These two cases we comprise by saying that the organism uses his organs and instruments to reach a certain (conscious or nonconscious) purpose. In these terms to reach a purpose is to *change the normal course* of the world (or certain aspects of the world) in some valuable respects, i.e. valuable for the organism. Because we want to leave it open at this point what the exact nature of what is changed is, we call that entity which is changed by organisms using their organs and instruments *context*. For an organism to use an organ or an instrument is then to *change the context* in a specific manner.

In this framework language is the *ability* to make use of a set of (organs and) instruments (say linguistic expressions) which are used by the user in a certain manner, namely as a necessary means to *change* (or maintain) *the context* (consciously or unconsciously) in order to fulfil some individual or collective purpose.

In a succinct way we may hence say that a *language* is a set of instruments. It is understood then that the user knows how to use them.

Using language - which is roughly synonymous with speaking, writing, signing or more generally with communicating linguistically - is *to behave* (or *to act*) in a certain manner, namely to use linguistic instruments appropriately.

3. Context Change and Truth

On this basis it is already possible to show the differences of the approach presented here and of some more standard positions. Let us then, first, show that our approach is in an important sense more general than *truthvalue semantics* and moreover that it is methodologically more prospective than *truthvalue semantics*.

In order to show that the instrumental approach to semantics (and pragmatics) is *more general* than the truthvalue approach we show first in what way the second is a special case of the first. This is a simple matter. To say that a sentence is true (or false) in a situation is the same as applying (abstractly) this sentence to a given situation and (abstractly) assigning to it a truthvalue. This is a reformulation of the truthvalue approach. But it is also a reformulation of the following instrumental characterization: apply the linguistic instrument (the sentence) to a context which is a pair of a situation and an (undetermined) truthvalue. The effect of this application (in the intended case) changes the context such that the truthvalue fits the satisfaction relation between the sentence and the situation. In short a truthvalue assignment is a specific context change.

Right from the beginning it should be made clear that in one sense the truthvaluational approach is as powerful as the context change approach: Every context change can in principle be described in a scientific (meta-)language: the context *before* and *after* the application of an instrument is described and a causal relation between them is stated. This is not what is questioned here. What is questioned is rather that a notion of truth is presupposed for the *user of the instruments* causing the context changes. In other words, the individuals described by our scientific (meta-)language need not themselves have a notion of truth at their disposal from the outset. What is philosophically and linguistically interesting is that it is possible to understand that (and how) individuals without a notion of truth at hand may develop one in certain specific circumstances starting from their more elementary abilities to change contexts. The notion of truth, to put it more radically, can be considered to be a product of a bio-sociological evolution in very much the same way as are, say, the human beings themselves.

Now we should look out for cases for which the truthvalue approach is no longer applicable adequately from the point of view of the user of an instrument. Let us therefore start with the cases for which the truthvalue approach works in the typical sense, and then proceed to cases where it gets less and less adequate. We will finally reach a point where everybody is forced to agree that it no longer works in the required way.

In typical, but relatively rare cases of natural language use, the form of the linguistic expression used depicts in a transparent manner the proposition and illocutionary force which determine the way in which the notion of truth is involved in controlling the context change. This is true for the ideal cases for which "nothing goes wrong". An example may be a policeman in the appropriate situation saying to a person: 'I arrest you'. By the utterance of this sentence in that situation the context is changed in such a way as to make the sentence 'The addressee is arrested.' true. If Danny asks Patricia: 'Do you love me?', then the context is changed so as to make the sentence 'Danny asked Patricia whether she loves him' true, which implies normally the truth of the sentence 'Patricia knows that Danny wants to know whether she loves him or not'. The following considerations show that these cases of explicitness are pretty rare. There are a lot of cases for which the form of the linguistic expression is not telling. The notion of truth is involved, if at all, only indirectly for the determination of the context change.

Examples for which the form of linguistic expressions is not telling are refrains like 'oh la lâ, oh la lâ', 'trâla trâla trâlala', or nonsense sequences like 'kriketikraketi', 'flktschr', 'flaflafla', expressions which may be uttered by young children in certain stages of their linguistic development. Poetic products may be another point in question, especially some modern forms of poetry. Another source of such phenomena are expressions used ritually and purely conventionally (STRAWSON [13]). They are used in certain places as a part of a fixed pattern of actions. Greetings ('Hello') and certain prayers may be of that kind.

Of course we may as linguists describe the situation by saying that, say, the context has changed in such a manner as to make the sentence 'somebody said 'flaflafla'' true. This is an extrinsic view which does not conflict with our claim about the relation of the two approaches.

The interesting point is that for all these expressions there are no sentences related perspicuously to the form of the expressions which are made true in the situation in which the linguistic expressions above are uttered. Nevertheless there are definite context changes every time such expressions are uttered (or not uttered when expected), depending on the context in question of course. I do not go into details here.

Comparable cases are indirect speech acts, cases where maxims of quality, quantity, relation, and manner are violated, and also fictional speech. In all these cases there is a clash between the linguistic form and its content or the intention of the speaker. It is possible to remedy these cases for the truthvaluational approach by taking into account content, (speaker-) intention, and even the context to determine the context change. Approaches giving an account of these phenomena in other frameworks than ours have been proposed for some of the examples mentioned (cf. SEARLE [11], GRICE [5], SEARLE [12]). An idea how these cases could be remedied in our framework is the following. If form and content (intention) clash one could choose the possibility of making the content (or intention) - and even the current context - determine the context change by rendering the content (or intention) true. This would in fact render some of the above-mentioned cases reducible to truth (i.e. context change which is controlled by truth). But indirect speech acts and violations of maxims require in practice so much contextual determination of the effected context changes that one may question seriously whether a truth functional approach alone would suffice.

Cases of deviant intentions like lies, double-dealings, concealed examination questions, deceptions are of a similar kind. The form of the linguistic expression is not telling - it only appears to be telling. In these cases the (speaker-)intentions do not determine overtly the context changes, only the content of the expressions do. Contextual factors play a role especially if the deceitful character of the utterance is unmasked.

If it is allowed to take into account (user-)intentions the truthvaluational approach can be stretched even further; it can then be extended to uses of non-linguistic instruments. The use of an instrument may depend in the following way on a notion of truth. Consider a case in which somebody uses a hammer. Normally he has an intention to use it. He may have the intention to hit some spot, say. In this case performing the action of hitting that spot is trying to make his intended purpose *true*. He may fail to reach his aim, a case in which his "success" is false with respect to his intention. Again, a notion of *truth* is involved. But the effect of the context change is no longer determined truthvaluationally, however, in general! Cases in which somebody uses linguistic instruments are often of the same type: user intention is involved. If an officer commands, he tries to make it true that the soldier addressed is under a certain commitment. If a professor defines a "notion", he tries to make it true that for the time being a certain word is used in a certain manner, or denotes some (abstract) object and the like.

This much should be sufficient as a preparation for the following examples which demonstrate a decisive weakness of the truthfunctional approach.

These cases do not rely on a notion of truth determining the effect of the context change even in the unusual, but most favorable conception concerning truthvalued control of the effect. Take the situation as follows. Egon intends to hit a certain nail with a certain hammer (which his children have broken recently), but because it is dark in the cellar when looking for the hammer he gets caught in a trap (another instrument) for foxes which he set up the other day. The example demonstrates that it is possible to have necessarily failing intentions and to be involved with another instrument than the one required - and still have a welldefined effect. In short, the intentions may be wrong (or even impossible to fulfil) and the instrument may be inappropriate, still there may be a definite effect. Such cases, I think, demonstrate a definite superiority of a context change approach over the truth valuational approach. A function determining the effect of a context change need not rely on propositions and the like, still the effect can be calculated.

No systematic relation between intention, instrument and effect need be present in such cases. This is true even for certain linguistic examples. An important one is this. There is a salient event happening, say calm meditation among a group of people. All of a sudden somebody says loudly 'damn it'. He remembers that he forgot to turn off the stove at home. The effect was, as it happened, that this meeting got the name 'dammit'. Again the relation of the intention (to utter 'damn it') and the linguistic instrument ('damn it') to the effect (that the meeting is called 'dammit') is not truthvaluational. Every other intention or instrument *might* have had this effect.

What is shown by the preceding discussion is the following. For many cases the meaning (or the effect) of (linguistic or non-linguistic) instruments is more or less determined by making something true, namely rendering the intention of the user of the instrument or, in case the instrument is a linguistic sentence, rendering this sentence or a formally related sentence true. In some odd but linguistically basic cases, however, the meaning (or effect) of such instruments is not connected with some proposition being relevant for the user or the language in the situation.

In these cases, *though we may describe the effect in a scientific metalanguage* (which is not our concern here) changing the context is different from making something true for the participants.

We shall conclude this section with some remarks on the value of the method of the context change approach. Because it is more general than the competing truth value approach - in the sense we have specified -, the context change approach lends itself much better to explaining certain phenomena of historical and ontogenetic language development. Not presupposing a full-blown notion of meaning (and truth), it is more naturally relatable to these developmental facts.

Most important is that the context change approach, based on the instrumental interaction of a user with his environment, is kinematic (and even dynamic) from the outset. It leads in many cases directly to the appropriate restrictions of instrumental (linguistic) phenomena. Being kinematic (dynamic) in this way, the context change approach is a candidate to bridge the gap to the various studies of dynamical systems as they are under investigation in many branches of science (like physics and biology).

4. Context Change and Competence

The following remarks are designed to show that the context change approach stands, in some respect, in conflict with at least some interpretations of the transformational (and structuralistic) claim that there is a distinct notional difference between competence and performance ("langue" and "parole"). There are various ways to conceive of such a difference, and some of them seem to be acceptable. Thus for instance if the competence performance distinction amounts to separating what a speaker *knows* of a language from what he *does* when he speaks, there is nothing wrong with this. We should also, with CHOMSKY, reject "langue" as merely a systematic inventory of items and rather conceive underlying competence as a system of generative processes (CHOMSKY [4], p. 4). Whether competence is *exclusively* mentalistic and does not include physicalistic aspects, I would prefer to leave open at the moment. Likewise I would like to leave open how much of (linguistic) competence is inborn or learned. It seems obvious that both factors play their role. The question whether competence is the exclusive object of linguistic study is not easily answered either. An answer depends very much on how competence is defined in detail. According to our explication of what language is, namely the ability to use certain instruments, namely linguistic instruments, the study of language is the study of a certain ability (or competence, if taken in its prescientific sense of ability). But this leads to certain problematic consequences for structuralism and generativism.

The linguistic ability to perform context changes is only one, though important, among many human abilities. It cannot be separated completely from certain other abilities, like perceptual, cognitive and especially effectory abilities. It is one of the effectory abilities. What seems crucial for the abilities of linguistic context change is that they include mechanisms to overcome memory limitations, distractions of various kinds, shifts of attention and interest and all kinds of errors.

If the linguistic abilities were not to include a rich set of correction and control procedures the effectiveness of context change would be seriously damaged. Thus a linguistic theory in our sense is explicitly concerned with more than CHOMSKY's ideal speaker-listener (CHOMSKY [4], p. 3). With respect to ideality the notion of linguistic abilities to change the context is essentially *different* from CHOMSKY's notion of competence, it comprises more. In CHOMSKY's terminology we would be concerned with performance. In our terminology we should, however, rather say that we are (to say the least) concerned with linguistic competence (abilities!) to perform, i.e. with a competence of performance. In our view it is impossible to separate competence and performance as is done in generative grammar: competence controls performance, performance influences and sometimes changes quite definitely competence (for an example see below).

Moreover the abilities to use linguistic expressions as instruments in the intended way have to include mechanisms to select and optimally assemble those instruments. The interpreter of linguistic instruments has to parse and analyse these instruments and to judge and modify (consciously or not) their effect or meaning. Therefore there is here another gap to CHOMSKY's competence. Our conception of a grammar includes the possibility that it is a model for a speaker and/or listener. It is *no* continuing misunderstanding to do so (cf. CHOMSKY [4], p. 9).

The CHOMSKYan competence/performance distinction relying on his conception of an ideal speaker, and his failure to include that part of competence which could be called the performance competence in a model of a speaker/listener stands in opposition to our conception of linguistics based on the instrumental character of language.

The instrumental character of natural language also contradicts in some respects the structuralist view of language as a *system*. Especially the distinction between synchronic and diachronic linguistics is to be modified. According to DE SAUSSURE "langue" forms a system (DE SAUSSURE [10], pp. 30 ff.). Because the instrumental force of language can be applied to language itself the system of language may be affected, also voluntarily (we are acquainted for instance with speech regulation by propaganda from a certain despotic regime some decades ago) and even be disrupted. But already the artistic and the natural development of languages provide enough evidence to cast doubt on the idea of language as a global monolithic system. Linguistic instruments are just the means to overcome possible difficulties in understanding in case the system, i.e. the regularities, break(s) down.

There are certain context changes which are (localized) operations on the language itself. E.g. definitions, explanations, clarifications affect the *meaning* of the expressions, i.e. the *conventionalized future effect* of these expressions; rehearsing sentence patterns, reciting modern poems or simply speaking long enough may influence somebody's grammar and pronunciation; listening to somebody else, say a foreigner, may have the same effect. Thus the historical development of language including its phonetic (phonologic), morpho-syntactic and semantico-pragmatic aspects, may be influenced to a considerable degree by single context changes operating upon the language as it is used. Because some of these context changes follow certain rules there must be some (localized) regularities recoverable in historical language change. Thus diachronic language states form at least to the same degree as synchronic ones a "system" in DE SAUSSURE's terms. This contradicts his distinction of synchronic and diachronic linguistics (cf. DE SAUSSURE [10], p. 140). In our view one synchronic language state is at the same time diachronic, because a synchronic state provides the devices (cf. the above mentioned examples) to change language in one detailed aspect (diachrony), while leaving it in globo the same (synchrony).

The conception of context change, being a dynamic conception from the onset, endowed even with devices to alter the language which is used to induce the context changes renders synchronic language "states" diachronic on a small scale. Nevertheless we should conceptually keep apart the two kinds of dynamics, this *microdynamics* and on the other hand the large scale developments as they happen in *secular* historical language changes. The difference of the two kinds of dynamics is comparable to the difference, in physics, between mechanics and thermodynamics. The historical language changes can and *should* be taken as arising from individual context (esp. language) changes. It should be conceived as a collective effect of the "synchronic" microdynamics of language.

5. Some Further Consequences of the Context Change Approach

Before coming to the end of this paper let us evaluate briefly some other important consequences of a context change approach to natural language. We should point out in this respect that both syntax *and* semantics of natural language are affected in the same way, adopting the context change approach. We shall concentrate here, however, on the *semantics* (and/or *pragmatics*). A basic semantic notion, beside truth, is *meaning*. Without a (fundamental) notion of truth at hand the notion of meaning should not, reasonably, be reduced to truth. Propositions(taken e.g. as sets of possible worlds), intensions, intensional isomorphisms, hyperintensions and similar constructions cannot therefore serve as explincanda for meaning. The notion of meaning should be tied more narrowly to context change. A reasonable candidate - in due generalization to the notion of proposition - would be the *function* assigning to the linguistic expression and contexts in which this expression is used the *effect* of such uses of the linguistic expression.

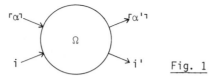

Fig. 1

If Ω is the effect function of the entire language (i.e. of all expressions $\ulcorner\alpha\urcorner$ in all contexts i) assigning a [possibly altered] expression $\ulcorner\alpha'\urcorner$ in a new context i', then $\lambda i\Omega$ ($\ulcorner\alpha\urcorner,i$) is the meaning of $\ulcorner\alpha\urcorner$. Loosely speaking the meaning of an expression could be said to be the (systematic) effect of the expression. It should be borne in mind however that the meaning of an expres-

sion is the transition function $\lambda i\Omega(\ulcorner\alpha\urcorner,i)$ and *not* the outcome of its application to a context. Thus the meaning *is not*, simply, the effect. The value of
two applications of the function $\lambda i\Omega(\ulcorner\alpha\urcorner,i)$ may be the same, though the meaning may differ. This is in analogy to the extension-intension distinction of
truth based semantics, of course. This gives us the reason of not briefly
identifying *meaning* and *effect*.

A complication arises in this picture, if one faces the fact that meaning may be changed itself by the use of linguistic expressions. As such the
effect function Ω of the entire language is no invariant. It, or at least
part of it, belongs to the context itself. It could be that there is a hard
core of such effect functions which can never be affected by language "use".
This core would then represent the semantics/pragmatics of the language in
its most basic form.

This variant of a context change approach to meaning allows for a fairly flexible conception of meaning. The interpretation of a sentence may
start from a primary assignment of meanings to the words occurring in the
sentence. These primary meanings are taken from the lexicon providing word
meanings which are approximately valid for typically occurring contexts.
These primary meanings are then normally modified by the context being built
up in a conversation or text, the meanings of the other words in the sentence
and the syntactic construction of the sentence. The resulting meaning of
the words in a sentence may differ considerably with respect to their primary
lexical meanings, and likewise the resulting meaning of the sentence with
respect to its "literal" meaning assignment. Along these lines the context
change approach allows us to model what is sometimes called a *hermeneutic*
interpretation of texts. All three basic operations of context change logics,
the *introduction* of new contexts, the *transport* of contexts to other places
in a sentence or text, and the *use* of contexts at certain places of interpretation thereby play an indispensible role.

Primary meanings are *conventional* in the sense that they express the
common knowledge about how certain linguistic expressions (e.g. words, simple
phrases) are systematically used in certain contexts commonly accepted as
typical. This *common knowledge* arising from various sources (such as innate
concepts, averaging over experiences) can be *suspended* for every single case,
if appropriate context changes by already understood expressions lead the
interpreter to the intended *nonstandard* interpretation. This context change
is probably a basic mechanism to give nature language its unlimited expressive power. Expressive power, a semantic notion, cannot be expressed in syntactical terms as CHOMSKY [4] did. An infinity of sentences does not necessarily imply an infinity of thoughts expressed by these sentences (cf. $\ulcorner p\urcorner$,
$\ulcorner p \wedge p\urcorner$, $\ulcorner p \wedge p \wedge p\urcorner$, ...). Two sources of expressive power, however, should
be warranted at least. Firstly, how can the conventional meanings be over-
come and individual meanings be assigned, if there is a need to do so, and
secondly, how are basic new meanings created in certain designated contexts
(cf. end of section 3). As we are aware from this paper, the context change
approach is able to account for both cases.

Apart from the consequences of the context change approach to meaning
there are some furthergoing considerations concerning the notion of *truth*
we should briefly deal with. It seems that on quite acceptable grounds we
may argue for a *relative* rather than an *absolute* notion of truth. It can be
made plausible that the context change approach allows for inferences where
classical and intuitionistic logic does no longer apply.

For that, let us leave the linguistic paradigm we usually work in and
let us adopt a scientific paradigm more specifically a biophysical paradigm
in which it is believed that human beings and their abilities have evolved

from inanimate materia by, say, a mechanism of mutation and selction. It is known that evolution in this biophysical sense takes place only in energetically and informationally *open systems* (cf. v. WEIZSÄCKER [16]). In the paradigm we are adopting right now it is *not* questioned that the biosocial and psychomental evolution obeys the same laws as the biophysical evolution. In the very same way it is tacitly assumed that the development of linguistic behavior (in a more comprehensive sense than a narrowed-down behavioristic sense, namely in one including mental behavior) can occur only in energetically and informationally open systems (*with restricted means*) too. This being so, it is suggestive that an intrinsic notion of truth used by organisms participating in the biochemical evolution (read: human beings) cannot be generalized or extended uniquely to an objective notion of truth. An *objective* (extrinsic) notion of truth certainly makes sense for *closed* systems. It is questionable, however, whether it generally makes sense to accept the fiction of absolute truth (cf. v. WEIZSÄCKER [15], p. 339, "Wahrheit ist die Art von Irrtum, ohne den eine bestimmte Art von lebendigen Wesen nicht leben könnten") for *open* systems for which neither the memory for past events nor the determination of future events is safe enough to warrant an invariant conceptual and linguistic basis. Only then would it be possible to assess what the notions of truth, proposition etc. amount to, and which statements express which "proposition" and are in same to be specific sense "true". In science by way of using models (in the *scientific* and *not* the *logical* sense) the *path* for a *relative notion of truth* is paved. Truth is relativized to such models or frames. In science there is a well established historical consciousness of the *relativity* of scientific notions, even very basic ones. Thus the relativity of truth may be taken as one case among many others. The context change approach, being radically intertwined with the context, is more likely to provide a framework in which these complexities can be treated adequately. The metalogic of context change logics *should* accordingly differ in important respects from a classical as well as an intuitionistic approach. Not only is there a place for yet *undecided statements* in context change logics (as is in intuitionistic logic) but there is also a possibility of *revising* the truth of statements. These revisions obey certain restrictions, however, and are *not* totally arbitrary. This still allows then for certain weakened forms of contextually limited inferences. One central contextual limitation of our inferences stems from the fact that we are bound to express ourselves in a specific language, which in other contexts may have a radically different interpretation. This fact again stresses relativity.

These logical and even philosophical considerations are in harmony with the biophysical paradigm where it is accepted that various notions of truth are considered to be biological achievements, where human beings are in the midst of an evolution far from arriving at a physical or intellectual finish (and it would therefore be extremely fortuitous to have found the ultimate [notion of] truth) and also with NEURATH's saying that we are like "Schiffer, die ihr Schiff auf offener See umbauen müssen, ohne es jemals in einem Dock zerlegen und aus besten Bestandteilen neu errichten zu können".

6. Closing Remarks

In this short paper I have tried to exhibit some consequences of an approach to linguistics based on the instrumental character of natural language. After an explication of the notion of language based on its instrumental character and the concept of context change, the notion of truth and the notion of competence have been investigated. Because of the lack of space I was not able to enter upon the technical details of a context change logic, especially upon the introduction of special constants, operators, connectives and their interpretation, and upon an illustration of these ideas by examples from the domain of pronominal reference. The reader who is interested in learning about that and a grammar based on the idea of context change is referred to the literature (BALLMER [1], [2], [3]). He will find there various applications also concerning syntax, speechacts, textlinguistics, presuppositions, and the like. Some historical remarks (BALLMER [3]) will also be found.

Because there was no space to enter in sufficient detail into these issues I had to change the original title "Context Change and Reference" of my talk to the one chosen for this paper.

7. References

1   BALLMER, Th., "Einführung und Kontrolle von Diskurswelten", in: WUNDER-LICH, D., *Linguistische Pragmatik*, Athenäum, Frankfurt a.M., 1972

2   BALLMER, Th., "Logical Language Reconstruction and Reference", in: MUF-WENE, S. et al. (eds.), *CLS* 12 (Papers from the Twelfth Regional Meeting of the Chicago Linguistic Society), Chicago, 1976

3   BALLMER, Th., *Logical Grammar*, North-Holland, Amsterdam, 1978

4   CHOMSKY, N., *Aspects of the Theory of Syntax*, M.I.T. Press, Cambridge, Mass., 1965

5   GRICE, P., "Logic and Conversation", in: COLE, P. and MORGAN, J.L. (eds.), *Syntax and Semantics*, vol. 3, Academic Press, New York, 1975

6   ISARD, St., "Changing the Context", in: KEENAN, E. (ed.), Cambridge University Press, Cambridge 1973/75

7   KUHN, Th., *The Structure of Scientific Revolution*, Chicago Univ., Chicago

8   LAKOFF, G./THOMPSON, H., "Introducing Cognitive Grammar", in: COGEN, C. et al. (eds.), *BLS* I (Proceedings of the First Annual Meeting of the Berkeley Linguistic Society), Berkeley, 1975

9   LEWIS, D.K., "General Semantics", in: DAVIDSON, D.; HARMAN, G. (eds.), *Semantic for Natural Language*, Reidel, Dordrecht, 1972

10 DE SAUSSURE, F., *Cours de Linguistique Générale*, Payot, Paris, 1971

11 SEARLE, J., "The Logical Status of Fictional Discourse", in: *New Literary History*, vol. VI, 1974-75, pp. 319-332

12 SEARLE, J., "Indirect Speech Acts", in: COLE, P. and MORGAN, J.L. (eds.), *Syntax and Semantics*, vol. 3, Academic Press, New York, 1975

13 STRAWSON, P., "Intention and Convention in Speech Acts", in: SEARLE, J. (ed.), *The Philosophy of Language*, Oxford University Press, Oxford, 1971

14 TARSKI, A., "Der Wahrheitsbegriff in den formalisierten Sprachen", in: BERKA, K.; KREISER, L. (eds.), *Logik-Texte*, Akademie, Berlin, 1971, pp. 447-559

15 WEIZSÄCKER, C.F. v., *Einheit der Natur*, Hanser, München, 1971

16 WEIZSÄCKER, E. v., *Offene Systeme* 1, Klett, Stuttgart, 1974

17 WINOGRAD, T., "On some Contested Suppositions of Generative Linguistics about the Scientific Study of Language", in: *Cognition*, 5, 1977, pp. 151 -179

How to Refer with Vague Descriptions

Manfred Pinkal

Universität Düsseldorf, Seminar für allgem. Sprachwissenschaft
Universitätsstr. 1, D-4000 Düsseldorf 1, Fed. Rep. of Germany

This paper deals with the question how reference with vague descriptions should be analysed formally, and gives a proposal for a solution. More precisely, it suggests a formal treatment for the reference identifying function of a special type of vague expressions, as they are used in a special type of definite descriptions. The results of the analysis, however, seem to be of more general importance. The paper consists of:

(i)   some remarks on vagueness and the formal treatment of one type of vagueness;

(ii)   some remarks on definite descriptions and the formal treatment of one kind of descriptions;

(iii)   a short outline of the formal frame which is used to describe both phenomena;

(iv)   an exemplary interpretation of one sentence containing a definite description with a vague predicate within this frame;

(v)   some remarks on the results of the formal analysis concerning reference, vagueness and their mutual relations[1].

1. Vagueness and Truth Values

Nearly all natural language expressions seem to be vague to some extent. There is a subgroup of expressions which are vague in a quite obvious way. And there is a subgroup of this subgroup which is usually discussed as the paradigmatic case of vagueness, since it contains expressions with relatively simple meaning intuitions. It is the scalar adjectives or adjectives of degree which can be related to a one-dimensional physical scale, like *tall, small, hot, cold, heavy, light, quick, slow*, the latter subgroup consists of. The former, more comprehensive group contains all kinds of one- and multi-dimensional adjectives, adverbs of space and time, modal verbs and adverbs etc. On the following pages, the discussion is restricted to the second group for reasons of intuitive simplicity; the central results, however, can be extended to a large part of the first group, too.

Scalar adjectives are vague, and they are context-dependent; they stay vague and context-dependent also in case they are used attributively or in connection with modifiers of different types. Thus, neither to treat them as sharp predicates nor as sharp common noun modifiers, like MONTAGUE does [12], yields intuitively adequate results[2]. As far as vagueness is concerned, two-valued context-dependent interpretations employing a 'comparison value' coordinate are inadequate as well as approaches which let the context provide for a comparison set. An advantage of the latter is that it is capable of semantically treating ad-adjectival constructions which specify sets of individuals rather than values. Nevertheless, being a two-valued approach, it has to specify an algorithm for the computation of a sharp numerical comparison value (something like the average) on the basis of the comparison set, and thus cannot do justice to the fact that a lot of accidental historical and psychological data may influence a native speaker's opinion of what is 'normal' with respect to a set of individuals. Obviously, there is no well-defined function connecting sets and values but just a loose probabilistic correlation between, say, the set of men and what is tall for a man[3]. The fact is taken into account informally by CRESSWELL's formulation that, roughly speaking, for a sentence *A is a tall man* to be true the degree of A's tallness has to be "towards the top of the scale" which is inherent to the semantics of *tall man* [3]. But which formal framework allows for a precise reconstruction of vagueness and inexactness?

Classical two-valued logic won't do the job. In three-valued logics, the inadequacy of a sharp boundary between truth and falsehood is replaced by the more subtle inadequacy of two sharp boundaries between boundary cases and truth and falsehood, resp., at the cost of abandoning the Law of Excluded Middle. No problems concerning boundaries arise with infinitely-valued logics, and yet the values assigned to vague expressions are completely precise entities. In fuzzy logic, sentences denote truth-values in the closed interval [0,1] , predicates denote functions from the set of individuals into [0,1] (cf. [8],[18]). For predicates like *red* or *tall*, the continuity of the set of possible denotations thus reflects the continuity of the colour spectrum and the scale of spatial distances, resp.

There is, however, an objection to fuzzy logic which is as old as multi-valued logics are: It is not possible to give an interpretation to logical connectives which renders fuzzy logic a conservative extension of two-valued logic. Classical tautologies and contradictions like (a) and (b) take truth-values different from 0 and 1, in case partial truth-values are assigned to their constituents, and, moreover, (a) and (b) may take the same truth-value in certain cases.

(a) *John's hair is red or it isn't*
(b) *John's hair is red and it isn't*

An interpretation of vague concepts which avoids these undesired results is offered by the theory of **super-valuations**[4]. Roughly speaking, expressions are differently evaluated at different 'indices' [9] or 'specification points' [4]. These valuations are classical, but additionally a higher level valuation takes place which assigns to the expressions higher-level values with respect to <u>sets</u> of standard interpretations. Truth in the super-valuation sense is defined as classical truth at each single valuation, super-falsehood correspondingly as falsehood at each single valuation; sentences containing vague expressions may be assigned a third super-truth value, indeterminateness, in case the respective sentence is true for some, false for some other precisifications. The crucial point in the super-valuation semantics is that the values of complex expressions are calculated from the values of their constituents not on the super-truth level, but on the elementary level, at each specification. Since the elementary level valuations are standard, the values of (a) and (b) will at each index, in each possible precisification be true and false, resp. - and therefore true and false, resp., at the super-valuation level, too.

Supervaluation semantics has three (super-) truth values at its disposal, so far. It can be provided with an infinite and numerical truth value inventory, too, in a formally quite simple way: by the definition of a probability measure on the set of all classical valuations [6]. Thus, the super-valuation approach

(i)   provides for precise and, if desired, numerical value assigments for vague expressions in terms of

(ii)   a conservative extension of standard predicate logic, but

(iii) it is no more truth functional in a direct sense.

In this paper, vague expressions will be analysed in a super-valuation framework, but before doing so, two substantial problems have to be considered[5].

First: The property (i) holds of the multi-valued approach, too. From a logical point of view, the second item may be regarded as the fundamental advantage of super-valuations - at the price of the abandonment of truth-functionality (iii). From an empirical linguistic position the argumentation is somewhat doubtful. Native speaker's intuitions about the possible truth values of sentences (a) and (b) are not very clear, and, moreover, supposed the colour of John's hair is a real border-line case native speakers tend to consider the contradiction (b) as true - a result which gives reason for the question if (ii) actually is an advantage of super-valuation semantics. Now, the reason for unsure and seemingly counter-logical intuitions with (a) and (b) can be found in the conversational extremity of these sentences[6]. There are slightly modified versions of (a) and (b) which may be used in ordinary communication in their standard sense.

(a') *John's hair is red or Bill's isn't (either)*
(b') *John's hair is red and Bill's isn't*

Provided that Bill's and John's hair are identical with respect to their colour which again be a borderline case of *red*,
at least (b') is clearly false since the predicates in both
atomic constituent sentences correlate. This nicely corresponds
to the super-valuation result, as well as the fact that (c)
and (d) may be regarded as partially true to a different extent,
resp., also in case the super-valuations of their constituents
are identical.

(c) *John's hair is red, and so is Bill's*
(d) *John's hair is red, and Bill's is brown*

Thus, the statement concerning the advantage of super-valuation
semantics remains true, but the argument has to be reversed:
It is the lack of plain truth-functionality which makes super-
valuations a proper means for the description of vague natural
language expressions; that analytic expressions of standard logic
save their truth-values is a special by-product.

The second question to be taken into consideration is still
more basic than the problem of compositionality with partial
truth: It concerns the concept of partial truth itself. What is
the intuitive correlate of degrees of truth in natural language
analysis? Natural language use of *true, false,* and, maybe,
indefinite is quite clear and unproblematic. Natural language
expressions referring to degrees of truth do not occur very often,
and when they are used, this usually happens in an ambiguous and
metaphorical manner. *true by half* e. g. can be used to designate
complex statements parts of which are true and parts of which
are false, or sentences which are definitely true, but leave relevant information unmentioned. It therefore seems impossible
to explain degrees of truth by referring to ordinary language
intuitions. Now, whereas in fuzzy logic numerical truth-values
are undefined basic terms, in super-valuation semantics they can
be defined as probabilities. But probabilities of what? Surely
no epistemic probabilities: That (e) is true to degree 0.5 cannot
mean that it is likely to 50% that (e) is (definitely) true.

(e) *John's hair is red*

Could it mean the probability that a native speaker will accept
(e) as true? Probably not, for whether a hearer of an utterance of
(e) will accept it as true depends mainly on the special conversational function of that utterance. In case (e) is used to describe
an unknown person, the hearer will accept it anyway (if there are
no reasons to doubt the sincerity of the speaker); he might or
might not accept it in case he faces John, and the same, but with
different criteria, holds in case he faces several persons, and
(e) is used to identify John. There is, however, one precise
task vague expressions observe: they contribute to reference
identification in definite noun phrases. If it can be shown in an
intuitively satisfying way how partial truth and partial membership are employed in the context-dependent evaluation of complex
NPs, this will give at least some intuitive support to semantics
with numerical values. As will be seen later on, the analysis

can actually be carried out in a super-valuation framework: as far
as definite NPs are concerned, it will follow the way informally
indicated in the next section.

2. Definite Descriptions

Definite descriptions are used to refer to single individuals[7].
There are at least two types of definite descriptions to be
distinguished with respect to the way they refer to individuals.
One type is represented by expressions like *the king of France*
and *the father of John*, or, shortly, *the king* and *the father*.
These noun phrases presuppose that there be one and only one
thing which possesses the property specified by the respective
common noun phrase: The CN phrase is a function expression,
either with or without an explicitly given argument. In the latter
case, the context of utterance has to answer the question whose
king or whose father is talked about, rather than which king
or which father is the individual under consideration: Context has
to specify the argument of the function rather than its value.
Once the argument is identified, existence and uniqueness presupposition hold for the elliptical version, too.

The second class of definite NPs,which is of special interest
in connection with the vagueness phenomenon, behaves completely
different. *the girl, the dog, the pig, the girl over there, the
small dog, the small pig over there with the floppy ears* do not
contain function expressions, neither explicit nor hidden ones.
The denotations of the respective CN constituents are more or
less comprehensive sets of individuals – there usually is no
opportunity for them to satisfy a uniqueness presupposition in
the sense first type descriptions do. Nevertheless, second type
descriptions are used to refer to single individuals, and, moreover,
once they denote an individual in an utterance at all, they denote
the same individual (during that utterance) independently of
world and time talked about. Similarly to proper nouns, they
are exclusively used as rigid designators, whereas first type descriptions have a de dictu reading as well as a de re reading[8].

RUSSELL's classical analysis of definite descriptions or at
least its reformulation in terms of the presupposition concept
[7] may be applicable to first type NPs. It should be clear from
what has been said so far that second type descriptions require
a completely different treatment. M. CRESSWELL suggests to employ "e-specifying context properties" where e is a set of
candidates for definite NP reference ([2], p. 180 f.). A description is evaluated in those and only in those contexts which
specify a set e containing exactly one individual of the kind
indicated by the CN phrase. As D. LEWIS pointed out, the inadequacy of this approach is shown by (f).

(f) *The pig is grunting, but the pig with the floppy ears
isn't*

If just one pig is given by the context - which is necessary
for the evaluation of the first part of (f) - the whole sentence
gets either an odd reading (in cases this pig has floppy
ears), or no one at all (in case the pig has not). This problem,
among others, caused LEWIS to replace the set by a salience
ranking [10]. The definite NP refers to the individual of
highest salience which is member of the extension of the
CN-expression. Thus a second type NP the α does not request
the hearer of an utterance in which it occurs to assume that
there is just one α among the things under consideration. It
rather asks him to look up the most salient α - which may of
course be an individual different from the most salient α'.

The intuitions underlying the analysis of definite descriptions suggested in this paper run along these lines, except for
one item: The approach allows for more sensitive modifications
of the salience ranking than the LEWIS approach does, and thus
does justice to the fact that vague expressions like *small* in
the small dog influence the relative position of individuals
in the preference scale rather than separating the individuals
into two distinct classes. For, which of two dogs is to be selected as the object referred to, if one of them is slightly
more salient in advance, whereas the other one is slightly
smaller? Formally, the analysis avoids the introduction of an
isolated preference scale, and treats the phenomenon of preference modification within a general semantic framework. In
advance, some informal remarks may indicate the way the analysis
will proceed. The formal framework will be described in the
next section.

Although which individual is referred to by a definite
NP depends on the situation of utterance, natural situations
of communication usually do not determine one single individual
completely. Except for the speaker, it is only more or less
likely for the discourse participants that a special individual
is the one thought of, where "likeliness" correlates to LEWIS'
salience. In other words the possible precisifications of
the under-determined context may differ with respect to the
referred-object coordinate, and different precisifications may
be more or less plausible, which can be modelled in a probabil-
istically extended super-valuation frame without problems. CN
phrases contribute to reference identification by increasing
the hearer's knowledge about context. More technically speaking: the CN phrase in the α excludes precisifications from the
super-assignment which yield as the referred object an individual which is no α.

3. The Formal Framework

Before the analysis of vague expressions in definite descriptions
can take place, it is necessary to give a survey of the employed
technical devices. There is no need to go too much into details,

since the notations and central parts of the theory are related to well-known systems in formal semantics. In short terms, the framework presented is a combination of the LEWIS [9] coordinate approach and the theory of super-valuations, written down in the λ-categorial notation of CRESSWELL [2][9].

According to the previous informal considerations, the formalism is defined in two steps. The central concept to be defined in the first step is that of <u>context</u>. A context t is a function from a - possibly <u>infinite</u> and non-empty - arbitrarily chosen set I. The values for each $i \epsilon I$ have to be taken from some predefined inventory Γ_i, which is a possibly infinite, non-empty set, too. The definition of the set of contexts is given by (1)[10].

$$\mathcal{L} = \{ t \mid t \text{ is function from I and } t(i) \epsilon \Gamma_i \text{ for each } i \epsilon I \} \quad (1)$$

The difference of the function writing to the usual notation is not a substantial one. Like a context n-tuple, a function t singles out an appropriate value for each context coordinate: an individual for the 'speaker' and 'referred-object' coordinate, resp., a triple of real numbers for the 'place-of-utterance' coordinate, a set of individuals for the 'comparison set' coordinate, etc. Intuitively, a context may be understood as a 'world relative to a single utterance event' including the most remote and unimportant information, but without taking into account focus of attention and knowledge of the discourse participants. According to the informal remarks in the preceding sections, contexts may be conceived of as complete precisifications of the shared knowledge of the discourse participants.

Given the definition of context set, an interpretation of a λ-categorial language can be defined as an ordered sextuple $\mathcal{V}$, in accordance with standard second-order semantics.

$$\mathcal{V} := < W, U, D, \mathcal{L}, \Gamma_{i<i\epsilon I>}, V > \quad (2)$$

W (the set of possible words) and U (the set of individuals) are non-empty; the system of possible denotations consists of indexed sets of possible values for each category, with $D_0 = \mathcal{P}(W)$ and $D_1 = U$ and the respective sets of complex functions for derived categories: $\mathcal{P}(W)^U$ for one-place predicates, the set of functions from predicate denotations into predicate denotations for predicate modifiers, etc. The meaning of each basic expression α is given by the assignment function V as a function from contexts into the set of possible denotations of α.

There is a substantial restriction placed upon the context-dependent value-assignment. For every basic expression α, $V(\alpha)$ must be definable in terms of a function of at most finitely many context coordinates. Informally speaking, the denotation of an elementary expression depends on a limited set of context features. - One more restriction, which is not less important, can be seen from (3), the definition of the value assignment function for complex expressions.

$$V^+(<\beta,\alpha_1,\ldots,\alpha_n>)(\mathcal{T}) := \tag{3}$$
$$V^+(\beta)(\mathcal{T})(V^+(\alpha_1)(\mathcal{T}), \ldots , V^+(\alpha_n)(\mathcal{T}))$$

The denotation of a complex expression at one context depends only on the denotations of its constituents at the same context, not on their meanings as a whole. To use CRESSWELL's term, meanings are regarded as distributive ([2], p. 119). An argument for this treatment of context-dependence which differs from the way most semanticists proceed is given by THOMASON [16]. One more reason which strictly demands the distributive treatment is the way contexts and context-dependent interpretations are employed on the second level of the system the presentation of which will follow after a final remark concerning definition (2). The first level assignment is two-valued, except at one point: the denotations of expressions of a derived category, at some contexts, may be undefined for certain arguments. Thus, each context $\mathcal{T}$ induces a classical interpretation for each expression - in case it induces an interpretation at all.

The central notion of the second level is that of a <u>situation</u>. Intuitively, a situation $\mathcal{R}$ is a cluster of information taken from the physical surroundings, previous talk and common-sense knowledge; it comprises anything which is available to the discourse participants for the evaluation of an utterance, and approximately may be thought of as a fragment of a context (in the sense of 'context' described above). Formally, a situation is definable as a subset of the context set, i. e. the set of those contexts which are compatible with the accessible knowledge.

$$\mathcal{R} \subseteq \mathcal{L} \tag{4}$$

As each context $\mathcal{T}$ induces a standard valuation, each situation $\mathcal{R}$ induces a super-valuation. Expressions are indetermined at a situation $\mathcal{R}$ in case context coordinates relevant for their evaluation are not uniquely specified in $\mathcal{R}$. Expressions are genuinely vague, if in ordinary discourse it is not possible to specify their relevant coordinates completely. Expressions can be made more precise in a situation by partially undefined modifiers. By preventing the valuation of the expression at certain members of $\mathcal{R}$, they specify the situation: imcompatible subsets of $\mathcal{R}$ are filtered out.

For the following, a couple of subsidiary definitions are required.

$$\mathcal{R}_i^\delta := \{\mathcal{T} \mid \mathcal{T}(i) \varepsilon \delta\} \quad (i \varepsilon I, \ \delta \subseteq \Gamma_i) \tag{5}$$

$$\mathcal{R}_\alpha^d := \{\mathcal{T} \mid V^+(\alpha)(\mathcal{T}) \ \varepsilon \ d\} \quad (\alpha \varepsilon E_\sigma, \ d \varepsilon D_\sigma) \tag{6}$$

$$\mathcal{R}_\alpha^\phi := \{\mathcal{T} \mid V^+(\alpha)(\mathcal{T}) \text{ is undefined}\} \tag{7}$$

$\mathcal{R}_i^\delta$ is the situation the only information of which consists in the fact that coordinate i takes one of the values of δ. By (6) the set of those contexts is defined at which α is assigned one of the values of d. $\mathcal{R}_\alpha^\emptyset$ is the set of alternatives excluded by context-modifying phrases contained in α. Now, let P be a probability measure on the context set $\mathcal{L}$[11]. Given P and an interpretation $\mathcal{U}$, a super-assignment function V^* is definable which at each situation $\mathcal{R}$ assigns to each expression α a probability distribution on the set of possible denotations of α.

$$V(\alpha)(\mathcal{R})(d) := \frac{P(\mathcal{R} \cap \mathcal{R}_\alpha^d)}{P(\mathcal{R} - \mathcal{R}_\alpha^\emptyset)} \tag{8}$$

Loosely formulating, V^* gives an estimate of the denotation of each expression. In advance, however, the situation can be precisified by constituents of the expression, as the denominator in the definiens of (8) shows.

So far, V^* and P are a means to describe context-dependence, vagueness and verbal context modification in a formally correct, but very general and abstract way. But P as a probability measure on the set of contexts not only assigns probabilities to possible denotations, but moreover completely determines (intuitively: reflects) the probabilistic correlations between context coordinates. Therefore, it is possible to proceed the opposite way and to define P in terms of correlations among coordinates, and, furthermore, to replace V^* by a set of elementary estimate functions γ_i^*, for each coordinate i, which, loosely speaking, represent the inductive procedures a discourse participant employs to find out the unknown value of context features which are relevant for the evaluation of an utterance, starting off from information given by the situation. Technically, the domain of each γ_i^* is the set of situations[12], the ranges contain probability distributions on the respective sets of coordinate values Γ_i. The mutual relation of the γ^* and P is described by (9), which formally is a definition of γ^*-functions on the basis of P.

$$\gamma_i^*(\mathcal{R})(\delta) := \frac{P(\mathcal{R} \cap \mathcal{R}_i^\delta)}{P(\mathcal{R})} \qquad \text{for} \quad \delta \subseteq \Gamma_i \tag{9}$$

Given (8) and (9), it is possible to prove a theorem concerning the way V^* can be expressed in terms of the γ^*-functions, using a couple of quite elementary theorems of the theory of probabilities. The theorem - which is presented in a footnote here because its formulation is rather complicated and not necessary for the comprehension of the applications in the next section[13] - allows to reduce the estimate for a complex expression to the estimates of the values for its finitely many coordinates, which again base on the available context information represented by the situation $\mathcal{R}$

4. The Small Dog

Underlying intuitions and facilities of the system which has been described in a quite abstract way so far will become more apparent by the exemplary interpretation of a couple of expressions of English, given in this section.

(g) *The small dog barks.*
(h) *It barks.*

Sentences (g) and (h) will be analysed; the lexical entries for basic expressions employed in the sample sentences are given at a time, in advance. As with the definitions of the last section, the formal correctness of the following interpretations sometimes is neglected in favour of greater lucidity. For the same reason, syntactic surface phenomena are not taken into account. In opposition to the general framework defined above, the whole interpretation will be an extensional one. There are certain additional problems connected with the intensional version[14], but they do not directly affect the aims of this paper, and thus will not be discussed further.

At a context t, in the following, sentences denote truth-values, predicate expressions denote characteristic functions from U, which correspond to sets of individuals, etc. Relevant context coordinates employed in the interpretation are qu (comparison value), ref (referred object), and mqu (comparison set), with

$$\Gamma_{qu} = \mathbb{R}^+ \quad ; \quad \Gamma_{ref} = U \quad ; \quad \Gamma_{mqu} = \mathcal{P}(U) \tag{10}$$

'gr' denotes a function which, intuitively, settles individuals on a tallness scale, by assigning positive real numbers to them[15].

dog: $<0,1>$ $\hspace{3cm}$ (11)

$V(dog)(t) = V(dog)(t')$ $\hspace{1cm}$ for each $t, t' \varepsilon \mathcal{L}$

$barks$: $<0,1>$ $\hspace{3cm}$ (12)

$V(barks)(t) = V(barks)(t')$ $\hspace{1cm}$ for each $t, t' \varepsilon \mathcal{L}$

$small$: $<0,1>$ $\hspace{3cm}$ (13)

$V(small)(t)(a) = 1$ $\hspace{0.5cm}$ iff $\hspace{0.5cm}$ $gr(a) < t(qu)$

$\hspace{5cm}$ for each $t \varepsilon \mathcal{L}$, $a \varepsilon U$

it : $<0,<0,1>>$ $\hspace{3cm}$ (14)

$V(it)(t)(\omega) = \omega(t(ref))$ $\hspace{1cm}$ for each $\omega \varepsilon D_{<0,1>}$

the: $<0,<0,1>,<0,1>>$ $\hspace{2cm}$ (15)

$V(the)(t)(\omega,\omega') = \begin{cases} \omega'(t(ref)) & \text{, if } \omega(t(ref)) = 1 \\ \text{undefined else} \end{cases}$

$\hspace{3cm}$ for each $\omega,\omega' \varepsilon D_{<0,1>}$

$$att: \quad <<0,1>,<0,1>,<0,1>> \tag{16}$$

$$V(att)(\mathcal{T})(\omega,\omega')(a) = \begin{cases} \min(\omega(a),\omega'(a)) & , \text{ if } \mathcal{T}(mqu) \subseteq \omega' \\ \text{undefined else} \end{cases}$$

$$\text{for each } \omega,\omega' \in D_{<0,1>}$$

dog and *barks* are analysed as sharp and constant one-place predicates, although both are - like most natural language predicates - vague to a certain extent. *small* is classified as a predicate, too. Alternatively, it could be analysed as a predicate modifier (of category $<<0,1>,<0,1>>$) in which case instead of the deep-structure operator *att* a different one would be required for the conversion of adjectives into predicates (cf. [2], p. 185). The semantics of *small* is defined as simply as possible. Of course, *small* is more correctly paraphrased by *significantly smaller than standard* than by *smaller than standard*. *small* does not exclusively refer to the aspect 'maximal distance in vertical direction', but to other aspects of shape, too (and therefore smallness will not induce a strict ordering); after all, which individual is to be considered as small does not only depend on a standard or average, but also on various norms and requirements (which are context-specific, too; cf. [13], pp. 104 ff.). The crucial point of (13), however, consists in the fact that *small* is interpreted by means of a comparison value coordinate rather than a comparison set coordinate - seemingly in contradiction to our former considerations. As usual, *it* is defined as a basic term phrase dependent on the referred-object coordinate; the reference-specifying function of gender is neglected. According to (12) and (14), (h) is interpreted in the following way:

$$V^+(<it, barks>)(\mathcal{T}) = V(barks)(\mathcal{T}(ref)) \tag{17}$$

As opposed to the lexical items considered so far, the interpretation of *the* and *att* yields incomplete functions for certain contexts. *the* is analysed as a quantifier, i.e., according to [2], as a phrase which takes two predicate expressions and makes a sentence thereof. According to (15), *the dog barks*, which is $<the, dog, barks>$ in λ-categorial representation, is assigned truth at $\mathcal{T}$ if the object referred to at $\mathcal{T}$ barks, falsehood otherwise. But an assignment of either truth or falsehood takes place just in case the referred object is a dog; otherwise, the interpretation is blocked up. - *att* combines two predicates to a complex one, and for this complex predicate introduces a new relevant context coordinate. According to (16), the denotation of $<att, small, dog>$ is the set of those individuals which are dogs and are smaller than the comparison value given by the context; a denotation, however, is assigned only in case the comparison set consists of dogs only. Otherwise, the interpretation is blocked up.

The λ-categorial representation of sentence (g) is given by (18), its interpretation by (19)-(21), where (20) specifies the conditions placed upon context by the context-specifying elements of (g), and (21) comprises the result of the interpretation in a more lucid manner.

<the, <att, small, dog>, barks>   (18)

$$V^+((18))(\mathcal{C})\qquad\qquad (19)$$

$$= V(the)(\mathcal{C})(V(att)(\mathcal{C})(V(small)(\mathcal{C}),V(dog)(\mathcal{C})),V(barks)(\mathcal{C}))$$

$$= \begin{cases} V(barks)(\mathcal{C}(ref)), & \text{if (20)} \\ \text{undefined else} \end{cases}$$

$$V(att)(\mathcal{C})(V(small)(\mathcal{C}),V(dog)(\mathcal{C}))(\mathcal{C}(ref)) = 1 \qquad (20)$$

if $V(small)(\mathcal{C})(\mathcal{C}(ref))=V(dog)(\mathcal{C}(ref))=1$, if $\mathcal{C}(mqu) \subseteq V(dog)$

undefined else

$$V^+((18))(\mathcal{C}) = V(barks)(\mathcal{C}(ref)) , \qquad (21)$$

        if: (i) $\mathcal{C}(ref)\ \varepsilon\ V(dog)$

           (ii) $gr(\mathcal{C}(ref))<\mathcal{C}(qu)$

           (iii) $\mathcal{C}(mqu) \subseteq V(dog)$

In natural language terms: If (g) is evaluated at all, it is assigned truth exactly in case the referred individual given by the
context barks; i.e., once there is assigned a denotation to (g),
this denotation is identical with the denotation of (h), given in
(17). But differently from (h), (g) is assigned a denotation only
if the individual referred to is a dog (i), and is smaller than
the context-given comparison value (ii), and the context-given
comparison set consists only of dogs (iii).

What has been done up to this point concerns the first level
of completely specified contexts. The super-valuation which will
follow now does not require any new information or decisions:
V^* of sentence (g) is completely determined by (21). In connection
with the super-valuation, however, a difficulty arises which in
part is due to the fact that the analysis is purely extensional.
In an intensional interpretation, different individuals as values
of the referred-object coordinate cause different valuations for
sentences containing personal pronouns or definite descriptions.
If the analysis is restricted to extensions, all valuation alternatives for definite NPs on the sentence level collapse to truth
and falsehood, resp., and the truth estimate does not reflect
the - more interesting - probability distribution on possible
noun phrase denotations. Therefore it is more illucidating to compute the V^*-value of the definite NP *the small dog* separately[16],
which is in λ-categorial notation

$$<\lambda x_{<0,1>}<the,<att,small,dog>,x_{<0,1>}> \qquad (22)$$

A straight-forward V^*-assignment for (22) is possible without
serious difficulties; it will, however, be easier and more instructive to give a second-level interpretation of (22) in terms
of V (*it*).

Be $\mathcal{R}^*$ the set of those contexts which are compatible with
the noun phrase (22). *barks* in (18) does not contribute to context restriction; therefore the value of $\mathcal{R}^*$ may directly be taken

from the restrictions listed in (21), the first-level interpretation of (18):

$$\mathcal{R}^* = \mathcal{R}_{ref}^{V(dog)} \cap \mathcal{R}_{mqu}^{\mathcal{R}(V(dog))} \cap \{\tau \mid gr(\tau(ref)) < \tau(qu)\} \quad (23)$$

Since (24) holds[17], and for all contexts admitted by (22) the denotations of *the small dog* and *it* are identical, the estimate of the NP may be reduced to the estimate of the personal pronoun as shown in (25).

$$V^*((22))(\mathcal{R}) = V^*((22))(\mathcal{R} \cap \mathcal{R}^*) \quad (24)$$

$$V^*((22))(\mathcal{R}) = V^*(it)(\mathcal{R} \cap \mathcal{R}^*) \quad (25)$$

The V*-valuation of *the small dog* is the same as for the personal pronoun, but it is based on a situation which has been enriched with the information that the individual referred to is a dog, that it is smaller than standard, and that the comparison set the standard relates to consists of dogs only.

Furthermore, using (26), the estimate of the definite description can be reduced to the estimate function of the referred-object coordinate; ζ_a in (26) and (27) be the term denotation which referentially corresponds to the individual a.

$$V^*(it)(\mathcal{R} \cap \mathcal{R}^*)(\zeta_a) = \gamma_{ref}^*(\mathcal{R} \cap \mathcal{R}^*)(a) \quad (26)$$

$$V^*((22))(\mathcal{R})(\zeta_a) = \gamma_{ref}^*(\mathcal{R} \cap \mathcal{R}^*)(a) \quad (27)$$

According to (27), the probability that an individual a is referred to by (22) in a situation $\mathcal{R}$ is given by the respective γ^*-value of the referred-object coordinate on the basis of a properly specified situation.

5. Results

Result 1 (concerning vagueness): Common nouns accompanied by adjectival attributes have a function they share with several types of adjective-modifying phrases: they specify features of the situation of utterance which are relevant for the valuation of the adjective. Like certain prepositional phrases (e. g. *for a dog*) they specify a comparison set rather than a comparison value. In the given interpretation, the set is related to a numerical standard by a probabilistic correlation rather than a sharp algorithm, which fits to natural language intuitions.

Result 2 (concerning vagueness): Context dependence and vagueness are preserved in case of explicit modification. They are, however, reduced in a proper way by the interaction of situation and explicit specification. Lexical items of different categories may be treated in the same way[18].

Result 3 (concerning definite descriptions): Definite descriptions, as they are used in ordinary discourse, often neither take one individual as their definite value, nor are they left without any value. They are assigned an estimate of the individual referred to, which is modelled by the given interpretation. Whether the utterance is accepted by its addressee, depends on the current standards of exactness (cf. [10]). The speaker of an utterance may (and has to try to) satisfy the standards by using more or less specific common noun phrases.

Result 4 (concerning definite descriptions): Definite descriptions and personal pronouns are reduced to the same type of context dependence, the former being treated as specified pronouns. Analogously, proper nouns could be treated as an extreme case of specification. The 'salience ranking' of LEWIS [10] may be defined in terms of the probability distribution which is assigned to the personal pronoun by the γ^*-function of the referred-object coordinate, with respect to a given situation.

Result 5 (concerning both): The way definite descriptions are related to pronouns is very similar to the way complex common noun phrases containing adjectives are related to adjectives in predicative use: in both cases, the more complex phrases are interpreted as context-specifying versions of the simpler ones.

Result 6 (concerning both): The referred-object coordinate in definite descriptions may be specified by vague expressions, e. g. scalar adjectives and adverbs of space, as well as by exact predicates. Accordingly, the way specifications take place, is neither described by set-theoretical intersection nor by deletions in a preference ordering of the LEWIS type, but in terms of a more sensitive procedure, by which the comparative salience of two individuals may be reversed.

Result 7 (concerning both): The analysis is not restricted to constructions of type *the* + adjective + CN; without great effort, it can be extended to noun phrase constructions of considerable variance and complexity. E. g., it treats descriptions containing sharp and context-invariant attributives like *married* and *rectangular* and recursive attributive constructions without any modification; combinations of vague modifiers of different type, like in *the small dog over there*; common nouns which are vague themselves (which indeed seems to be the case for nearly all natural language common nouns to some extent); modifying phrases containing vague CN-phrases (*the small dog with the large ears barking at the red-haired guy*) - provided, of course, suitable value assignments for adverbs and vague common nouns in the given framework.

Result 8 (concerning both): On the other hand, a quite fundamental result may be obtained by considering the most elementary cases of definite NPs. In a sentence like (k), the connection between the V^*-valuation of the definite NP and the super-valuation of the vague predicate *red* is rather plain, since for colour adjectives the influence of the comparison set coordinate on the denotation may be neglected.

(k) *Give me the red box*

Now, take an utterance of (k) in an elementary situation which
e.g. consists of the information that there are exactly two
candidates for the referred-object coordinate, and that neither
of them is favoured. Provided that the felicity of the utterance
only depends on the condition that the standard of precision in
is satisfied by the description *the red box*, and further provided the standard of precision is explicitly available, it is
possible to draw a direct line from the behaviour of discourse
participants to partial truth-values: usually, the reaction of
the addressee of (k) can be taken as an evidence for the felicity of the utterance; (k) is uttered successfully, if and only
if the standard is satisfied; the comparative degree of redness
of the two individuals under consideration may be computed on thé
basis of the standard[19]; finally, there is a direct correspondence
between partial membership relations contained in the second-
level valuations of adjectives and partial truth. - Of course,
these considerations are rather hypothetical in different respects.
Independently of the question to which degree standards of precision for standard situations can be made available, however, they
show that in the system described in this paper straight-forward
connections can be established between ordinary communication
and partial truth-values, in an intuitively acceptable way.

There are a lot of problems concerning vagueness and definite
descriptions which are not taken into account in this paper. Two
of these problems are so closely connected with the topics discussed that they at least should be mentioned. First, context
coordinates relevant for an adjective may be specified not only
by direct modifiers, but also by independent constituents of the
sentence.

(l) *This dog is small*
(l')*This is a small dog*
(m) *Ascot is small*

An interpretation which generally treats (l) and (l') as paraphrases does not provide for a satisfactory solution of the
problem. As well as *this dog* in (l), *Ascot* in (m) modifies the
value of *small*, provided Ascot is known to be a dog. Both (l)
and (m), however, may have different readings, due to different
underlying comparison predicates (e.g. *animal* or *beagle*). In the
version of the system presented in this paper, context-specifying expressions prevent first-level valuations for the whole
sentence, anyway - at the price of undesirable interferences
between different definite NPs occurring in the same sentence.
Thus, (l) and, possibly, (m) are assigned the (l') reading anyway - the latter in case proper nouns are treated as modifiers.
The system may be adjusted to the second (non-specifying) reading,
in which case however the first one is lost. The ambivalence of
weak specification cannot be modelled.

Secondly, the estimate of the referred individual is not only based upon the situation of utterance and modifiers of different type, but additionally influenced by the attempt of the addressee to evaluate the utterance in such a way that it comes out to be true. In case (g) is uttered in a situation which specifies a set of exactly two possible referents a and b, which both are dogs and of equal stature and the salience of which is identical, a will be preferred if a barks and b does not, and vice versa - to render (g) true. Unlike the first problem mentioned, interactions between sentence denotations and estimates of context features cannot be treated in the system without far-reaching modifications.

Notes

1 The topics referred to in (i) and (ii) are discussed in greater detail in [15] and [14], resp. A full-length description of the formal framework is given in [13]. The analysis of vagueness presented in this paper is strongly related to KAMP's view, as described in [6]. The intuitions underlying the analysis of definite descriptions correspond to ideas pointed out by LEWIS in his talk given at the Constance Colloquium, too [10].

2 KAMP [6] gives a detailed argument for the inadequacy of MONTAGUE's analysis.

3 BARTSCH and VENNEMANN who give a detailed account of the comparison set approach in [1] mention this problem (p.63) as well as WHEELER does in [17], but in both cases the problem is abandoned from linguistics and attached to psychology and other disciplines. Indeed, which correlation holds between set and value may be a matter of psychology; the fact however that only a correlation holds has to be taken into account for a semantic theory of adjectives.

4 For a detailed discussion of formal variants of supervaluation semantics, cf. [4]

5 To a great deal, the following arguments are due to extensive discussions of the the intuitive implications of the system presented, at the "Arbeitsgemeinschaft Sprache und Logik", Bielefeld.

6 Since (a) and (b), in their direct reading, violate general conversational postulates (cf.[5]) in being trivial and false, resp., they are to be interpreted differently in ordinary discourse; e.g. (b) could be understood as a meta-language hypothesis that *red* is a sharp predicate (with respect to hair colour), or as a request to attach one colour predicate definitely, based on that hypothesis.

7 The generic use of the definite article is not taken into account here, as well as descriptions containing collective, abstract and mass terms, to keep the analysis free from additional problems.

8   Correspondingly, there exist characteristic restrictions on
    common noun modifiers: *the former pig* sounds as strange as
    the king over there. Both phrases, however, are acceptable
    in special contexts, which seems to indicate that the semantics
    of the CN phrase suggests one interpretation of the NP rather
    than determines it.

9   A full-length account of the semantic system can be found in
    [13]. - The syntax is exactly that of [2]. Basic categories
    are 0 (sentence) and 1 (proper noun); derived categories are
    combined of less complex ones in the usual way ($<0,1>$ for one-
    place predicate, $<<0,1>,<0,1>>$ for predicate modifier etc.).
    Complex expressions are built up from simpler expressions of
    proper category by concatenation ($<John,runs> \epsilon E_0$ from
    John ϵF_1 and *runs* $\epsilon F_{<0,1>}$) and λ-abstraction ($\lambda x_1 <x_1,runs>$
    $\epsilon E_{<0,1>}$ with $<x_1, runs> \epsilon E_0$).

10 It might be convenient to exclude combinations of incompat-
    ible context features by defining $\mathcal{L}$ as a subset of the τ-funct-
    ions which are formally possible:

$$\mathcal{L} \subseteq \underset{i \epsilon I}{\times} \Gamma_i$$

    The problem, however, can be solved in the second step, too,
    by means of a suitable definition of the probability measure.

11 Roughly speaking, a probability measure on an occurrence set
    M assigns to each subset of M a value from the closed interval
    $[0,1]$, with $P(M)=1$, $P(\emptyset)=0$, and, for $N_1, N_2 \subseteq M$, if $N_1 \cap N_2 = \emptyset$,
    then $P(N_1 \cup N_2) = P(N_1) + P(N_2)$. The definition only holds good
    for enumerable M; for non-enumerable sets of contexts P would
    have to be defined in a far more complicated way; cf. [13]
    p.54ff.

12 For non-enumerable $\mathcal{L}$, the set of situations would have to be
    restricted to something like standard situations, two of
    which e.g. would have to differ at least at one coordinate
    relevant for the interpretation of a basic expression.

13 Be $\alpha \epsilon E_\sigma$, dϵD_σ, $\mathcal{R} \subseteq \mathcal{L}$, $P(\mathcal{R}) \neq 0$, $I' = \{i_1, \ldots, i_n\}$ the set of
    coordinates relevant for at least one constituent of α, and

$$K = \{\phi | \text{ex.} \tau \epsilon \mathcal{R}_\alpha^d \text{ and } \phi = \tau \upharpoonright I'\}$$

    Then the following holds:

$$V^*(\alpha)(\mathcal{R})(d) = \sum_{\phi \epsilon K} \prod_{j=1}^{n} \gamma_{ij}^* (\mathcal{R} \cap \bigcap_{k=1}^{j-1} \mathcal{R}_{i_k}^{\phi(i_k)})(\phi(i_j))$$

    A proof is given in [13], p.51. The theorem requires the set of
    contexts to be enumerable, cf. n.11,12. - By the way, the
    theorem reflects the fact that V^* is not compositional in a
    straight-forward manner.

14 E.g. the question which extension of a CN phrase should be
    employed for the specification of the referred-object coordin-
    ate in tensed or modalized constructions. - In an intensional

version of the interpretation, the comparison coordinates for adjectives might be treated in a way that non-intensional comparison values are maintained, whereas the comparison set coordinate is replaced by a comparison predicate coordinate.

15 There are general formal problems concerning adjectives and scales, which however will not be taken into account here. A detailed discussion as well as a proposal for a solution is given in [3].

16 There seems to exist a more general reason, too, for proceeding this way. The standards of precision required for an utterance primarily seem to concern the definite NPs of the sentence uttered rather than the utterance as a whole: a pragmatic rating takes places in the course of the supervaluation, at an intermediate level. Cf. the following sample sentence, an utterance of which may be rejected also in case its V^*-valuation unequivocally yields one proposition, because it is unclear which of the two noun phrases designates which of the two possible referred objects:

The small dog is as snappish as the other one

17 which can be seen from the following:

$$V^*((22))(\mathcal{R} \cap \mathcal{R}^*) = \frac{P(\mathcal{R} \cap \mathcal{R}^* \cap \mathcal{R}^d_{(22)})}{P((\mathcal{R} \cap \mathcal{R}^*) - \mathcal{R}^\phi_{(22)})}$$

$$= \frac{P(\mathcal{R} \cap \mathcal{R}^d_{(22)})}{P(\mathcal{R})} = V((22))(\mathcal{R})$$

since $\mathcal{R}^d_{(22)} \subseteq \mathcal{R}^*$, and $\mathcal{R}^* \cap \mathcal{R}^\phi_{(22)} = \phi$

The NP specifications are redundant with respect to a previously given situation which is a subset of $\mathcal{R}^*$.

18 In the framework, e.g. adverbs of space, local prepositions and their modifiers (*immediately, straight* etc.) can be given an interpretation analogously to the interpretation of adjectives and adjective modifiers. Cf.[13], pp. 94ff.,114f.

19 In the framework presented, an algorithm can be derived which does the job, under the above-mentioned assumptions. Since the whole argument is quite tentative, this algorithm will not be presented in this paper. It should, however, be clear that it does not consist in the plain identification of the maximal amount of partial membership with the standard of precision. The latter seems approximately to be the case with conditioned orders like:

If there is a red box on the table, give it please to me

If there is only one table among the things under consideration, and only one box on the table (which is definitely a box), the order will be carried out in case the box is red at least to the degree which is required by the standard of precision.

References

1 Bartsch, R./ Th. Vennemann: Semantic structures. A study in the relation between semantics and syntax. Frankfurt (M): Athenäum 1972

2 Cresswell, M.J.: Logics and languages. London: Methuen 1973

3 - : "The semantics of degree". B. Hall Partee (ed.): Montague grammar. New York: Academic Press 1976: 261-292

4 Fine, K.: "Vagueness, truth and logic". Synthese 30, 1975: 265-300

5 Grice, H.P.: Logic and conversation. Published in part in: P.Cole/ J.Morgan (eds.): Speech acts. New York 1975:41-58

6 Kamp, J.A.W.: "Two theories about adjectives". E.Keenan (ed.): Formal semantics of natural language. Cambridge 1975

7 Karttunen, L.: "Presuppositions and linguistic context". Theoretical Linguistics 1, 1974: 181-194

8 Lakoff, G.: "Hedges: A study in meaning criteria and the logic of fuzzy concepts". Journal of Philosophical Logic 2, 1973: 458-508

9 Lewis, D.: "General semantics". G.Harman/D.Davidson: Semantics of natural languages, Dordrecht: Reidel 1972: 169-218

10 - : "Score-keeping in a language game". In this volume.

11 Montague, R.: Formal philosophy. Selected papers. New Haven: Yale Univ. Press 1974

12 - : "English as a formal language". [11] :188-221

13 Pinkal, M.: Kontext und Bedeutung. Ein probabilistisch erweiterter pragmatischer Beschreibungsansatz. Tübingen:Narr 1977

14 - :"Kontext und Kennzeichnung". M.Conte/A.G.Ramat/P.Ramat (eds.): Wortstellung und Bedeutung. Akten des 12. Linguistischen Kolloquiums. Tübingen: Niemeyer 1978

15 - : "Semantische Vagheit". Forthcoming

16 Thomason, R.H.: Introduction to [11]: 1-69

17 Wheeler, S.C.: "Attributives and their modifiers". Noûs 6, 1972: 310-334

18 Zadeh, L.A.: "Fuzzy logic and approximate reasoning". Synthese 30, 1975: 407-428

Concealed Questions

Irene Heim

Universität of Massachusetts, Department of Linguistics,
Amherst, MA 1003, USA

The use of noun phrases as so-called concealed questions may be a rather
marginal phenomenon in natural languages, but it touches quite fundamentally
on considerations about the notion of noun phrase scope and its proper role
in a formal semantic description of natural language. My main point in
this paper is that a theory that handles ordinary noun phrases fails to
carry over to concealed questions in a simple straightforward manner. To
illustrate this, I will list some inadequacies of an unsophisticated extension of MONTAGUE's PTQ fragment [8]. I will then offer a choice of two
different remedies, neither of which seems to be the ultimate solution, however. Throughout my argumentation, I will completely ignore the fact that
there are paraphrase relations between concealed and overt questions which
may suggest interpreting the former via the latter. This doesn't mean that
I have any evidence which would rule out that sort of approach, but I do
have some practical justification for my neglect. Unless otherwise indicated, I presuppose everything in PTQ, but that is just a matter of convenient presentation.

1. What are Concealed Questions?

Roughly speaking, a noun phrase is used as a concealed question if it has
the meaning of an embedded wh-question. Take e.g. the underlined NP in (1):

John knows Bill's telephone number. (1)

As we naturally understand the sentence we could paraphrase it as "John
knows what Bill's telephone number is.", where the overt embedded question
"what Bill's telephone number is" replaces the NP "Bill's telephone number".
Here are some more examples:

John's favorite drink is obvious. (2)
They revealed the winner of the contest. (3)
Everything that John did surprised Mary. (4)
The temperature of the lake depends on the season. (5)

Paraphrases we could use instead of these are e.g. "It is obvious what John's
favorite drink is", "What the temperature of the lake is depends on which
season it is.", etc. As far as German is concerned, mostly the literal
translations of those verbs behave just the same, except for "know", which
splits into two German verbs "wissen" and "kennen". Some German dialects
syntactically restrict "wissen" to sentential and infinitival complements,
but where an NP object is permitted with "wissen", it clearly gets a concealed question reading:

Hans weiß Willis Telefonnummer. (6)

Most of our examples are ambiguous and admit of an alternative "straight-forward" reading under which the NP is not a concealed question. E.g. (3) need not always mean that they revealed who had won the contest, but could sometimes say about the winner of the contest that they removed what he had been wrapped in. Similarly, we have "He depends on his rich parents." along with (5), "The Pythagorean theorem is very obvious." along with (2), and so forth. Maybe the only reason why sometimes, e.g. in (1), the concealed question reading is the only one available, is that the alternative non-question reading happens to violate certain selectional restrictions: John just can't know the number 665-4839 in the sense in which one can know a person.

2. Concealed Questions Paraphrased Away?

I have offered paraphrasability by a wh-clause as a heuristic aid for identifying concealed questions, and it seems promising to exploit this relationship between concealed and overt questions in working out a formal semantic description of the former, especially since the latter have been studied quite successfully by semanticists already. This would also be in line with a tradition in transformational syntax which conceives of concealed questions as derived from wh-questions via a special deletion transformation, such as the one proposed by BAKER [1]. Obviously, a Montague grammar fragment that already handles wh-questions could easily be augmented by a syntactic rule modelled after BAKER's transformation and a trivial rule of translation to go with it, and this would give us a complete syntactic and semantic description of concealed questions. I am not going to proceed that way, however, because GRIMSHAW [4] has shown that there are significant generalizations about the distribution of concealed questions which cannot be captured as adequately in a theory which relates them transformationally to wh-clauses as they could in a theory which generates them as genuine noun phrases.

Instead, I am going to comment on the following closely related approach, which meets GRIMSHAW's objections while still utilizing the same putative paraphrase relations as a basis for interpreting concealed questions in terms of previously established interpretations for wh-questions. Suppose we start from some fragment designed for wh-questions, e.g. KARTTUNEN [6], and add a new rule S-CQ to its syntax. S-CQ performs a trivial syntactic operation, i.e. takes a noun phrase and returns it unchanged, but the associated translation rule T-CQ yurns the translation of the input noun phrase α into what would normally be the translation for the wh-clause "who (what) α is". The reader familiar with [6] may verify that this amounts to a translation such as (7).

$$\hat{p} \; \lor x \; [^{\lor}p \; \& \; p = \; ^{\land}[\alpha' \; (\hat{y} \; [^{\lor}x=^{\lor}y])]] \tag{7}$$

Having made this addition, we now possess a full-grown fragment for concealed questions, ready to be tested against the data.

Some potentially crucial examples have been pointed out by GREENBERG [3], although in a less formal context, and possibly aimed at a different point. He observes that in the following pair of alleged paraphrases, the overt variant (9) exhibits an ambiguity that is absent from its concealed counterpart (8):

John found out the murderer of Smith. (8)

John found out who the murderer of Smith was. (9)

(9) cannot only be used to express that John solved the question who murdered Smith, but has a further reading which is perfectly compatible with John's being entirely ignorant about Smith's murder, and which only amounts to the claim that John found out some essential fact or other (e.g. that he was his brother) about the person referred to as "the murderer of Smith". But this is not an available reading for (8), which can only be used in the first-mentioned way.

At first sight, GREENBERG's observations look like a straightforward challenge to the theory sketched above: if it is to survive it should either already predict the extra reading in (9) and its absence from (8), or at least lend itself to refinements which would bring about these predictions. As set out so far, it generates (8) as well as (9) with two significantly different scope constellations. If the noun phrase "the murderer of Smith" is generated in place, i.e. with narrowest scope, both (8) and (9) translate into equivalents of (10).

found-out'$_*$(j, $\hat{p}$ $\vee$x $[$p & p = $\wedge$$\wedge$v[murderer-of-Smith'$_*$(v) $\longleftrightarrow$ $^\vee$x=v]]) (10)

If widest scope is chosen for "the murderer of Smith", i.e. it is quantified in after either wh-clause formation or application of S-CQ, then either sentence receives a translation equivalent to (11).

$\vee$u[$\wedge$v[murderer-of-S.'$_*$ (v) $\longleftrightarrow$u=v] & found-out'$_*$(j, $\hat{p}$ $\vee$x [$^\vee$p & p = (11)
$\wedge$[$^\vee$x=u]])]

Presumably, (10) represents the first reading of (9) and the appropriate reading of (8) and is hence a welcome prediction of the fragment. But (11),contrary to what we may have expected, does not express the second reading observed by GREENBERG in (9), because the set of propositions denoted by "$\hat{p}$ $\vee$x [$^\vee$p & p = $\wedge$[$^\vee$x=u]]" turns out to be the unit set of the necessarily true proposition at any point of reference. Maybe (11) corresponds to what we would express by the English sentence: "John found out about the murderer of Smith that he was himself." In any case, it doesn't seem to capture GREENBERG's intuition about the second reading of (9).

This is not the only case where a sentence containing an overt embedded question has more readings intuitively than the grammar under consideration provides for. E.g. (12) can be used to say that John found out about every member of the conspiracy that that person was indeed a member of the conspiracy. But neither of the translations (13) and (14) fits that meaning.

John found out who every member of the conspiracy was. (12)

found-out'$_*$(j,$\hat{p}$ $\vee$x [$^\vee$p & p = $\wedge$$\wedge$u[member-of-the-conspiracy'$_*$(u) (13)
$\longrightarrow$ $^\vee$x = u]])

$\wedge$ u[member-of-the-conspiracy'$_*$(u) $\longrightarrow$ found-out'$_*$ (j, $\hat{p}$ $\vee$x[$^\vee$p & p (14)
= $\wedge$[$^\vee$x=u]])]

Note that (12) has a concealed counterpart, i.e. (15), which therefore ends up with the same two logical representations (13) and (14), despite its intuitively sensible meaning, which it has in common with (12).

John found out every member of the conspiracy. (15)

But now it is time to remember that this paper is not supposed to be about puzzles in the semantics of wh-, i.e. overt, questions, and that we are primarily trying to determine whether an adequate interpretation of concealed questions is likely to result from attaching something like S-CQ/ T-CQ to an interpretation of wh-questions. Unfortunately, the question has to remain unanswered: we can't tell how easy or ad hoc it would be to block the extra reading of (9) from appearing with (8), because we can't even predict it for (9) in the first place. And there is no point treating a case like (15) by relating it to one like (12), as long as the latter one itself can't be handled. That is my "practical" justification for temporarily disregarding the paraphrase approach without having disconfirmed it. All three of the tentative treatments to be discussed below approach concealed questions directly rather than via their overt paraphrases.

3. A First Attempt: The Scope Ambiguity Approach

Let's go right ahead, add "know" as a transitive verb to the PTQ lexicon, and see what happens if we generate and interpret sentence (16):

John knows the capital of Italy. (16)

There are at least two possible derivations, according to whether or not we quantify in "the capital of Italy", and their translations are equivalent to (17) and (18) respectively:

$$j*(^\wedge know' (\check{P} \; \bigvee v[\bigwedge u[capital\text{-}of\text{-}Italy'_*(u) \leftrightarrow u=v] \; \& \; P\{^\wedge v\}]))$$ (17)

$$\bigvee v[\bigwedge u[capital\text{-}of\text{-}Italy'_*(u) \leftrightarrow u=v] \; \& \; know'_*(j,v)]$$ (18)

Are they also equivalent to each other? That depends on whether we subject "know" to the extensionality postulate (19) (=(4) on p. 263 in [8]):

$$\bigvee_S \bigwedge x \bigwedge \mathcal{P} \; \square \, [\, \delta(x, \mathcal{P}) \leftrightarrow \mathcal{P}\{\hat{y}_S\{^\vee x, ^\vee y\}\}]$$ (19)

It looks like a good idea not to do so, because (16) intuitively does have two distinct readings: for one thing, it can mean that John is acquainted with a certain town, i.e. the capital of Italy, and on that reading, entailment (20) is valid:

John knows the capital of Italy. (20)
The capital of Italy is the largest town in Italy.
∴ John knows the largest town in Italy.

This is exactly what results from choosing the quantifying-in derivation with its translation (18). On the other hand, there is of course the concealed question reading of (16), with respect to which (20) is a fallacy. And that's just what we get from the derivation that goes with translation (17).

So everything has gone fine for "know" so far, and we are tempted to move right on to a minor problem with verbs like "surprise", or "depend on", which take concealed-question-subjects. Suppose we modify PTQ by lifting IVs up from category t/e to category t/T. Then there will be two non-equivalent scope possibilities in (21) as well, and the concealed question reading is thereby separable from the straightforward non-question reading, just as it was in (16).

The winner of the elections surprised Mary. (21)

4. Some Inadequacies of The First Attempt

(A) My first criticism is more of an intuitive suspicion than a counter-
argument: the ambiguities between concealed question readings and their
non-question alternatives seem to involve true lexical ambiguities in
verbs like "know", "depend on", "reveal", etc., rather than a structural,
i.e. scope, ambiguity. This suspicion is supported by two considerations:
(i) there is at least one verb, i.e. (South) German "wissen", whose arguments can never be interpreted as anything other than concealed questions.
This would be hard to explain on a scope ambiguity account. (ii) The question embedding and the straightforward senses of some of those verbs are
not related in a completely predictable way, but more like in cases of
metaphoric extension. This is especially plausible with e.g. "reveal".

(B) Our current attempt to interpret concealed questions fails to capture
certain valid entailments between utterances involving quantified concealed
questions:

John knows every phone number. (22)
∴John knows Bill's phone number.
John's last girlfriend surprised Bill. (23)
∴One of John's girlfriends surprised Bill.

I take it that (22) and (23) are valid not only on a non-question interpretation of the relevant NPs, but also under their concealed question readings.
But this conflicts with the idea that concealed question readings arise by
narrow scope.

(C) A related observation applies to pronominalized concealed questions, as
in (24) and (25):

If anything that John did escaped Mary, it also escaped Bill. (24)
John guessed everybody's favorite movie before it became obvious. (25)

In these cases, a concealed question NP serves as the antecedent to a bound
variable pronoun. Therefore, it should have wide scope, contrary to our
present treatment.

(D) An even stronger objection against viewing the ambiguities between concealed question and non-question readings of NPs as resulting from ambiguous
scope configurations comes from the behavior of concealed-question-embedding
verbs in restrictive relative clauses:

The only birthday I forget is my grandmother's. (26)
Every price that was not influenced by the oil crisis remained (27)
    stable.

(26) is just as ambiguous as (28):

I forget my grandmother's birthday. (28)

(28) can mean either that I don't have any memories of a certain day, i.e.
my grandmother's birthday, or (as a concealed question) that I forget when
.my grandmother's birthday is. According to our current theory, these two

readings correspond to wide and narrow scope of "my grandmother's birthday" respectively. But the same kind of ambiguity is present in (26), which can be understood either as "The only birthday I don't have any memories of is my grandmother's.", or as "Only in the case of my grandmother, I don't remember when her birthday is." The point is that there is no NP in the structure of (26) at all whose scope could be held responsible for this ambiguity, because restrictive relatives modify common noun phrases, not noun phrases.

5. A Second Attempt: The Individual Concepts Approach

It seems that all four of the objections (A) - (D) can be met by the following theory: there are two homonyms of each of our verbs, e.g. "$know_1$" for the plain sense of being familiar with something or somebody, and "$know_2$" for the sense that goes with a concealed question reading of the object. "$Know_1$" is presumably extensional, i.e. obeys (19), and won't be talked about any further. "$Know_2$" is not extensional, but it still obeys a meaning postulate that would be wrong to impose on certain other intensional verbs, e.g. "seek". This meaning postulate is formulated in (29):

$$\forall T \land x \land \mathcal{P} \Box [\, \delta \,(x, \mathcal{P}) \leftrightarrow \mathcal{P}\{\hat{y}T\{^{\vee}x,y\}\}] \tag{29}$$

T is short for $v_{0, <s,<<s,e>, <e,t>>>}$. The point is that "$know_2$" does not reduce to a relation between two individuals, but it does reduce to a relation between an individual and an individual concept. Intuitively, this represents the relation of knowing, as referred to in "John knows Bill's phone number.", as a relation between a person on one side and a certain function from points of reference into numbers on the other side. It is the case that John knows Bill's phone number, if and only if this relation holds between the person John and the individual concept denoted by "Bill's phone number", i.e. the function that assigns to every point of reference i the number which is Bill's phone number at i. Roughly characterized, this relation of knowing holds between X and Y at i iff X is at i able to identify the value Y(i) that Y yields when applied to i.

One more assumption is needed to make this view into a solution of our problems: the common noun "phone number" is like "price" and "temperature" and unlike "fish", "pen", and "man", in that it is not subject to meaning postulate (30) (=(2) on p. 263 in [8]).

$$\Box[\, \delta \,(x) \rightarrow \forall u[x=^{\wedge}u]] \tag{30}$$

This goes also for the CN-phrases "capital", "favorite drink", "thing that John did", etc., i.e. they all must be exempt from (30) and allowed to denote properties of possibly non-constant individual concepts. Incidentally, there seems to be a first problem coming up: are we going to have any "ordinary" common nouns left? But let me point out what we have gained by the new proposal before asking what we might have lost.

The explanation for why (20) under the concealed question interpretation is still a fallacy now parallels MONTAGUE's solution of the "ninety-rises"-paradox [8]. The logical representation for (20) is roughly (31):

$$\forall y[\land x[\text{capital-of-Italy}'(x) \leftrightarrow x=y] \& K(j,y)]$$
$$\forall y_1[\land x_1[\text{capital-of-Italy}'(x_1) \leftrightarrow x_1=y_1] \& \tag{31}$$

$$\bigvee y_2 [\bigwedge x_2 [\text{largest-town-in-Italy}'(x_2) \leftrightarrow x_2 = y_2] \ \& \ {}^{\vee}y_1 = {}^{\vee}y_2]]$$
$$\therefore \bigvee y [\bigwedge x [\text{largest-town-in-Italy}'(x) \leftrightarrow x = y] \ \& \ K(j,y)]$$

K abbreviates $\lambda y \, \lambda u [\text{know}_2'(\hat{} u, \hat{P}P\{y\})]$. For the argument to be valid, the second premise would have to contain "$y_1 = y_2$," whereas in fact it contains only "${}^{\vee}y_1 = {}^{\vee}y_2$".

Instead of going through objections (B), (C), and (D) individually, I pick out only (B) to show how the new proposal does better than the previous one. The essentials carry over to (C) and (D). I use a simpler version of example (22):

> John knows every phone number. (32)
> ∴ John knows a phone number.

We want (32) to come out valid, even under the concealed question interpretation. Here are the formulas our current translations of (32) reduce to:

> $\bigwedge x [\text{phone-number}'(x) \rightarrow K(j,x)]$ (33)
> $\therefore \bigvee x [\text{phone-number}'(x) \ \& \ K(j,x)]$

That is obviously good enough to warrant the inference.

I move right on to the objectionable features of the individual concepts approach. I have already mentioned that, as we multiply examples of concealed questions, not many "ordinary" ("extensional") CNs will be left over. Maybe we could live with that; but there is a more serious objection to be derived from a careful look at examples like (34):

> John knows the price that Fred knows. (34)

Imagine a situation where people talk about e.g. the price of milk, the price of bread, and the price of meat, and it is already known that Fred knows the price of one of these, e.g. he knows that milk costs 1.42 per gallon. In this context, an utterance of (34) could be used two different ways: either to say that John also knows, like Fred, that milk is 1.42, or to say that John knows that the price of milk is the price that Fred knows. But despite this intuitive ambiguity, we get only one logical representation, the one in (35):

> $\bigvee y [\bigwedge x [[\text{price}'(x) \ \& \ K(f,x)] \leftrightarrow x = y] \ \& \ K(j,x)]$ (35)

This formula expresses the first reading, i.e. the one where both John and Fred know the same thing, e.g. that milk is 1.42. There is no room for the second reading, unless we modify the current theory. I think we would have to introduce a homonym of "price" that denotes properties not just of individual concepts, but of "individual concept concepts", i.e. functions from points of reference to functions from points of reference to numbers. But then how about (36)?

> John knows the price known to Fred that Bill knows. (36)

If we disregard limitations of performance, examples like this can be constructed to prove that any finite number of homonyms is insufficient.

6. A Third Attempt: The Context Dependence Approach

Keeping the assumption that there are two homonyms of "know", and leaving "know$_1$" unchanged, we now take a different view about "know$_2$": "know$_2$" depends for its interpretation on the context in which it is uttered, more specifically: on a property that is somehow salient in the context. The intuitive idea is to analyze "John knows Bill's phone number" as something like "John knows Bill's phone number as Bill's phone number", or "John knows Bill's phone number with respect to its being Bill's phone number". Neither of these are of course good English paraphrases, but maybe they still serve to convey the intuition.

A theory of context dependence can be implemented in Montague Grammar in several different ways, and since it doesn't matter for my purposes, I choose at random a generalized version of MONTAGUE's procedure in [7]. It amounts to expanding points of reference by a further index, which is a variable assignment, and translating certain sentences of English into IL-expressions which contain free variables. (Variants of this method have been used by several authors, among them COOPER [2].)

For the cases at hand, the homonym "know$_2$" of the English verb "know" has to receive a translation of the form "KNOW(P)", where "KNOW" is an IL-constant of type $\ll s, \ll s, e\rangle, t\gg, f(TV)\rangle$, and P is as usual an IL-variable of type $\langle s, \ll s, e\rangle, t\gg\rangle$. To make the whole thing work, we require that meaning postulate (19) applies to "know$_2$", i.e. that "KNOW(P)" is reducible to an extensional relation, denoted by "[KNOW(P)]$_*$". We will see shortly that this does not force us to consider (20) a valid argument under the concealed question reading, because its fallacious character can now be explained in terms of the newly acknowledged context dependence of "know$_2$". Let's reconsider (20), which is paired up with formulas (37) this time:

$$\forall v[\wedge u[\text{capital-of-Italy}_*'(u) \leftrightarrow u=v] \ \& \ [\text{KNOW}(P)]_*(j,v)] \qquad (37)$$
$$\forall v[\wedge u[\text{capital-of-Italy}_*'(u) \leftrightarrow u=v] \ \& \wedge w[\text{largest-town-in-I.}_*'(w)$$
$$\leftrightarrow w=v]]$$
$$\therefore \forall v[\wedge u[\text{largest-town-in-I.}_*'(u) \leftrightarrow u=v] \ \& \ [\text{KNOW}(P)]_*(j,v)]$$

(37) is a valid entailment in one sense: for any fixed pair of a point of reference i and a variable assignment g, if the two premises are true, then so is the conclusion. But if we change the variable assignment from g to some g' as we proceed from the premises to the conclusion, then g(P) might differ from g'(P), and the premises might be true with respect to g, whereas the conclusion is false with respect to g'. What intuitive sense would there be behind changing g to g'? Remember that we think of a variable assignment as a component of the context, depending on such factors as the relative salience of various entities, among them properties of the kind required for the interpretation of "know$_2$". Now suppose there is a very strong pragmatic principle to the effect that whatever property is mentioned in the object term occurring after "know$_2$" tends to be so salient that it is assigned to the free variable in the translation of "know$_2$". If this principle operates, then an utterance of the first premise of (20) creates a context whose variable assignment component assigns to "P" the property of being-a-capital-of-Italy, whereas an utterance of the conclusion of (20) creates a context such that its variable assignment component assigns to "P" the property of being-a-largest-town-in-Italy. Under this assumption,

there is no mystery about "$[KNOW(P)]_*$" denoting different relations in its occurrences in the premise and in the conclusion.

This appeal to pragmatic principles, which solely carry the burden of cutting down on a vast overgeneration of semantically admissible readings, is probably the weakest point in the approach, and it becomes all the more problematic, as we realize that the examples cited in my objections (B), (C), and (D) above call for generating an even wider choice of translations than we have been imagining. Again, I pick out just (B) to illustrate the point: a crucial example was the argument (22), which we want to come out valid:

John knows every phone number   (22)
∴ John knows Bill's phone number.

Our current theory pairs this up with IL-formulas (38):

$$\bigwedge x[\text{phone-number}'(x) \to [KNOW(P)]_*(j, {}^{\vee}x)] \tag{38}$$
$$\therefore \bigvee y[\bigwedge x[\text{of}'({}^{\wedge}b\star) ({}^{\wedge}\text{phone-number}')(x) \leftrightarrow x=y] \& [KNOW(P)]_*(j, {}^{\vee}y)]$$

I take it for granted that a suitable meaning postulate for "of" tells us that a phone number of someone is always a phone number. Still, things don't work out: why should the same property be assigned to the occurrences of "P" in the premise and in the conclusion? According to the pragmatic principle I have invoked so far, it should be two different properties: the property of being-a-phone-number in the premise, and the property of being-Bill's-phone-number in the conclusion. The problem is that the premise intuitively doesn't mean that John can identify everybody's phone number as just being a phone number, but as being that person's phone number. So whatever value "P" assumes, it won't do, unless it somehow depends on the quantifier "every".

Here is a generalization of the theory that might help: instead of translating "know$_2$" into "KNOW(P)" uniformly, we allow for a whole bunch of alternative translations, including "KNOW(P)", "KNOW($\hat{x}R(x,y)$)", etc. Perhaps everything should be allowed in the place of "P", as long as it is of category $\langle s, \langle\langle s,e\rangle, t\rangle\rangle$ and made up of variables only. If we use this trick (which I have copied from [2], by the way) the premise and conclusion of (22) will translate -- among numerous other possible translations -- into formulas equivalent to (39) and (40):

$$\bigwedge x[\text{phone-number}'(x) \to [KNOW(\hat{y}R(y,x))]_*(j, {}^{\vee}x)] \tag{39}$$
$$\bigvee y[\bigwedge x[\text{of}'({}^{\wedge}b\star)({}^{\wedge}\text{phone-number}')(x) \leftrightarrow x=y] \& \tag{40}$$
$$[KNOW(\hat{z}R(z,y))]_*(j, {}^{\vee}y)]$$

Note that in order to achieve (39), not only the appropriate translation for "know$_2$" must be chosen, but moreover, "every phone number" must be quantified in. The advantage of (39) and (40) over our former translations (38) is that only R occurs free, i.e. a variable for a relation-in-intension (type $\langle s, \langle\langle s,e\rangle, \langle\langle s,e\rangle,t\rangle\rangle\rangle$). An utterance of each sentence therefore requires a context which specifies some relation of this type. It seems reasonable that the most salient such relation will be the one of being-the-phone-number-of in either case.

I have expressed uneasiness about the extent to which this theory relies on pragmatic explanations wherever its semantic machinery fails to pick out the intuitively good readings of an example among a host of intuitively bad ones. But on an open-minded reconsideration of the facts, this might turn out to be a virtue rather than a flaw. Let's take one more look at the premise of (22), "John knows every phone number." All along, we took it to mean that for every person, John knows what that person's phone number is, and we asked from a satisfactory theory to predict this reading as straightforwardly as possible. But there are indeed other readings conceivable for that sentence. Suppose, John's task is to assign to a new phone a number which is not yet taken by any other phone. Then he needs to "know every phone number", not in the sense of knowing which number is whose, however, but merely in the sense of knowing which numbers are somebody's at all. Among the theories I have sketched, the last one seems suited best to account for the possibility of this reading: it is due to the special contextual background, in which the property of being-somebody's-phone-number is most relevant, and therefore the most salient candidate for an assignment to the free property-variable in the translation of the utterance.

Acknowledgments

I was originally motivated by Bill Greenberg's paper [3]. Further suggestions and clarifying insights have come from reading Anil Gupta's dissertation [5], and from talking to Rick Saenz, Paul Hirschbuhler, Elisabet Engdahl, Barbara Partee, Terry Parsons, and especially Emmon Bach. I am grateful for the time these people have spent, and for the encouragement many of them have given me. I also want to thank Arnim von Stechow, who made my participation in the Konstanz colloquium possible and most rewarding.

References

1   Baker, C.L. Indirect Questions in English, Doctoral Dissertation, University of Illinois, Urbana, 1968.

2   Cooper, R. The Interpretation of Pronouns, in F. Heny and H. Schnelle (eds.) Selections from the Third Groningen Round Table, Syntax and Semantics, Vol. 10, Academic Press, New York, forthcoming.

3   Greenberg, B. A Semantic Account of Relative Clauses with Embedded Question Interpretations, ms., U.C.L.A., 1977.

4   Grimshaw, J. English Wh-Constructions and the Theory of Grammar, Doctoral Dissertation, University of Massachusetts, Amherst, 1977.

5   Gupta, A. The Logic of Common Nouns, Doctoral Dissertation, University of Pittsburgh, 1978.

6   Karttunen, L. Syntax and Semantics of Questions, Linguistics and Philosophy I, 1:3-44, 1977.

7   Montague, R. Universal Grammar, in R. Thomason (ed.) Formal Philosophy, Yale University Press, New Haven, 1974.

8   Montague, R. The Proper Treatment of Quantification in Ordinary English, in R. Thomason (ed.) Formal Philosophy, Yale University Press, New Haven, 1974.

Questions and Answers

Rainer Bäuerle

Universität Konstanz, Sonderforschungsbereich 99, 'Linguistik',
Postfach 5560, D-7750 Konstanz, Fed. Rep. of Germany

I shall be concerned in this paper with a tripartite classification of interrogative sentences which is all too familiar to us. There are questions that
contain an interrogative pronoun or adverb and that have the inflected form
of the verb in 'normal' second position, such as

> Where did you buy this?,

and there are questions with the inflected verb-form in first position, which
do not contain an interrogative word. Such questions can again be divided into
two sorts, differentiated by the presence or absence of a disjunction, and,
where this is not sufficient, by different intonation patterns. Examples are

> Did you catch the train?

and

> Did he take the bus or did he come by train?

This is the syntactic basis for differentiating between so-called *wh-questions*,
on the one hand, and *alternative* and *yes/no-questions* on the other.

Corresponding to this syntactic dichotomy, KARTTUNEN ([13], p. 6) remarks,
there undoubtedly is some semantic difference as well, but so far there has
been no consensus on what exactly it amounts to. It seems to be interesting,
therefore, to discuss the fate of this distinction in the various approaches
to a semantic description of interrogatives, to compare the results with
some intuitive ideas about this partition, and to come up in the end with
some suggestions of my own. That the paper is entitled 'Questions and Answers'
reflects the fact that a semantic characterization of our syntactically obvious distinction hinges crucially on the type of answer required.

As an aside, let me mention that in what follows the term *question* is used
indiscriminately to refer to interrogative sentences and to their propositional content. No confusion should arise from this. There is of course more to
a question than just a propositional content, but I do not aim at a full description of questions at the moment and shall therefore entirely disregard
the problem of illocutionary types. No harm can be done by restricting our
attention to the propositional content, because the classification we are
dealing with is quite uninfluenced by considerations whether the question
under discussion is meant to be an information-question, an exam question,
or what not.

In traditional grammars as well as in more recent writings on the semantics
of interrogatives it is normally assumed that there are two subclasses of
questions. But whereas for the traditional grammarian these two classes were

represented by wh-questions and yes/no-questions, recent writers rather adopt
the view that the basic categories are wh-questions and alternative questions.
The more syntactically-minded traditional grammarian tends to think of alternative questions as being 'of lesser importance' (QUIRK [16], p. 387); he
either does not mention them at all (DUDEN [3], p. 466), or else counts them
off in passing as a mere disjunction of yes/no-questions (JESPERSEN [11],
p. 480). For more semantic reasons, because of the equivalence between

Will he be there?

and

Will he be there or not?,

which both ask you to make a choice between p and non-p, one is inclined today
to assume that yes/no-questions can always be expanded to or reduced to alternative questions as the basic category.

Thus we have to do with a well-established and obvious dichotomy between wh-
questions and the rest, and a less obvious relation between alternative and
yes/no-questions, which seem to belong together more closely. This distinction
is heavily supported by syntactic phenomena such as the presence or absence
of a question-word and the position of the inflected verb-form. On the semantic level, however, these distinctions are not that obvious. If we have a look
at the answers required by the three types of questions, as e.g. in

Whom did you meet? - Your sister

Did you meet my brother or my sister? - Your sister

Did you meet my sister? - No,

the great gulf seems to open between yes/no-questions and the others. For
whereas wh-questions and alternative questions ask for the same type of categorial answer, the answer to a yes/no-question seems to be of a rather different type.
And even if we keep within the realm of syntax, it is astonishing that there
are interrogative sentences that are never quoted in the literature and to
which the aforementioned criteria do not apply:

When did you see him, yesterday or the day before?

Where did you see him, in London?

Questions that are yes/no-questions and alternative questions and yet do contain a question-word. We will later come back to questions of this type. Here
they are only mentioned to underline our problem: the problem of how to account
for the differences between the three types of questions semantically, and
whether two of them are more closely related to each other than to the third
type.

Let us for this purpose first have a look at the treatment of our classification of questions within the various approaches towards the semantics of
interrogatives. The different reconstructions of the propositional content
of questions can best be characterized on the basis of the type of answer
they are biased towards.

A question can either be answered by a whole sentence - we disregard the
possibility of non-verbal answers and also questions that are typically ans-

wered by a longer text-sequence - or by simply supplying the item missing in the question sentence, such as, for instance, the noun phrase 'your sister' when asked 'Whom did you meet at the cinema?'. We shall therefore speak of sentence answers and categorial answers.

As it is to be expected, there is a theory based on sentence answers, which has been developed by HAMBLIN [6] and later been adopted by EGLI [5] and KARTTUNEN [[12], [13] , and there is a theory based on categorial answers. Such a theory is advocated by, e.g., EGLI [4], KEENAN/HULL [14], and HAUSSER [[7], [8], [9]]. But curiously enough the most widespread and influential approach is a mixture of these two types of description. Thus it is maintained by BELNAP [1], HINTIKKA [10], and WUNDERLICH [17], among others, that wh-questions are categorial questions, whereas alternative and yes/no-questions are described as propositional questions. It is obvious that this is meant to mirror the old dichotomy, but let us nevertheless give a short account of the merits and shortcomings of all these approaches with respect to our classification problem.

But first of all, what are, intuitively speaking, the differences between the three types of questions that we should like any theory of questions and answers to reflect? I think that all the authors mentioned would agree that an interrogative act somehow involves a choice situation: the question presents a couple of alternatives, out of which the respondent has to make his choice. This idea leads BELNAP [1] to make the following distinction:

Either the alternatives are explicitly listed in the question or else they are described by reference to some condition or matrix, where a condition or matrix is a statement with variables holding the place of names.

BELNAP calls them whether- and which-questions, respectively, which is the old dichotomy between alternative and yes/no-questions vs. wh-questions. Much the same distinction is made by HAUSSER [9], where restricted and unrestricted questions are distinguished. Alternative and yes/no-questions are called restriced

because the possible values of the variables in their translation is restricted via explicit enumeration.

There is a subtle difference in that for BELNAP there is either a matrix or an explicit enumeration (of statements, that is), whereas for HAUSSER, if I understand him correctly, there always is a matrix plus eventually an explicit enumeration. We shall come back to this, suffice it for the moment to observe that there is agreement that the classificatory basis is whether the question just characterizes the type of answer required or else explicitly mentions the alternatives in question.

1. The Propositional Approach

HAMBLIN's propositional approach copes quite nicely with these intuitive remarks, if only because some of the problems of a categorial approach just do not arise. For HAMBLIN, a question represents a set of propositions with at least two members, one-membered sets are declarative sentences. Thus all questions are of the same logical category, and so are of course all answers (remember that only sentences are admitted as answers). Therefore the only means of differentiating between different sorts of questions can in fact be the manner of presentation of the alternatives.

A wh-question such as 'Who walks?' denotes, according to HAMBLIN, the set whose members are the propositions denoted by 'Mary walks', 'John walks', ... and so on for all individuals. The denotation set of a yes/no-question like 'Does Peter come?' must have as members just the denotation of 'Peter comes' and the denotation of the negation of 'Peter comes'. HAMBLIN himself does not mention alternative questions, but is can be imagined that their denotation set contains precisely as many propositions as there are alternatives. Such a treatment can be found in KARTTUNEN, who slightly modifies the approach in that questions denote sets of true propositions.

Thus we seem to have arrived at what we wanted: wh-questions can be so re-constructed as to specify their denotation set by means of properties of pro-positions, whereas alternative questions specify their denotation set by enumeration, yes/no-questions being just a special type of alternative questions Nevertheless the approach has a serious drawback in that yes/no-questions, where the alternatives have to be reconstructed, are treated in the same way as alternative questions, where the alternatives are given. That this is a mistake shall be pointed out in the section on the "mixed" approach, because HAMBLIN himself does not deal with alternative questions. Another flaw of this approach is that it cannot account for the more natural categorial answer, except perhaps by a battery of deletion transformations, which I should like to avoid if possible. It can be shown, on the other hand, that the categorial approach can be so extended as to incorporate sentence answers as well. There-fore it seems preferable if it can be made to work as smoothly as HAMBLIN's approach.

2. The Categorial Approach

It is quite an old observation, which also found its way into the grammar books, that wh-questions have some resemblance to mathematical equations or to functions, because the value of a variable has to be specified. Thus JESPERSEN [[11], p. 480], speaks of *x-questions* and COHEN [2] of *propositional functions*. The basic idea of the categorial approach, as developed in EGLI [4], then is that the propositional content of the whole question-answer-sequence is equivalent to a proposition, or, to put it differently, that questions are functions from categorial answers into propositions. Different categorial answers, such as noun phrases or adverbs, belong to different logical types, and consequently, so do different questions.

As is to be expected, this works quite well for wh-questions, where we always have a gap, so to say, in the assertive structure for the categorial answer to be put in:

Who comes: $\lambda x_{NP}(x_{NP} \text{ comes})$

When does he come: $\lambda x_{ADV_t}(x_{ADV_t}(\text{he comes}))$

The treatment of yes/no-questions, however, is less convincing. A question like 'Will he come?' does not have any obvious gap in the assertive structure. It seems to be clear, on the other hand, that the only candidates for a cate-gorial answer have to be 'yes' and 'no'. EGLI therefore supposes that any assertion can be split up logically into two parts called *Modus* and *Dictum*, the 'Modi' being 'yes' (which is equivalent to 'it is the case, that') and 'no' (equivalent to 'it is not the case, that').

The assertive structure of our question 'Will he come' then becomes something like

$$\lambda x_M(x_M(\text{he will come})).$$

Accepting such an analysis would imply that the difference between wh-questions and yes/no-questions is not a matter of the presentation of the alternatives, it is now a difference in logical type: it is the questioned variable that is different. Yes/no-questions thus become a special type of wh-questions, as far as the semantics is concerned. In contrast to the other categories, that usually have a large number of members, the category of 'Modus' is a very small one with only two members: 'it is the case' and 'it is not the case'. This is perhaps the reason why HAUSSER, whose approach is quite similar to EGLI's in other respects, nevertheless subsumes yes/no-questions under the heading of restricted questions and analyses them as disjunctive questions.

HAUSSER's [9] analysis is carried out within the framework of MONTAGUE grammar. His analysis of

Did John leave?

as

$$^\wedge\lambda V_n(V_n(^\wedge\text{leave}'(^\wedge j))\wedge((V_n\overset{\cap}{=}p(^\vee p))\vee(V_n\overset{\cap}{=}p(^\vee\negthickspace\sim p))))$$

clearly shows a question-matrix with a 'Modus'-variable plus an explicit enumeration of these 'Modi', namely 'it is the case that' and 'it is not the case that'. But note that such an enumeration is only explicit in disjunctive questions like

Did she kiss John or Bill?,

whereas it is, contrary to HAUSSER's assertion in [9], p. 37, not explicitly given in yes/no-questions. That HAUSSER is able to enumerate the possibilities is only due to the fact that the category of 'Modus' is a finite as well as a very small one. The cardinality of the set of possible answers and the number of alternatives explicitly mentioned should not be confused, and therefore I do not see any real reason for treating yes/no-questions as disjunctive questions within the categorial framework. Anyway, we would still be left with a categorial difference as the main feature of discrimination between wh-questions and yes/no-questions.

EGLI's attempt to reduce disjunctive questions to yes/no-questions may serve as an example of some intuitively unattractive peculiarities inherent to any such approach. These peculiarities have already been pointed out by WUNDERLICH. First, remember that the propositional content of the question-answer-sequence is equivalent to a proposition. Thus in the case of 'Will Bill come or John?', the answer 'Both' or 'John and Bill' yields the proposition

Bill will come and John will come.

Therefore the disjunction in the question has to be rendered as a conjunction as in EGLI's analysis

$$\lambda x_{M1} \lambda x_{M2} (((x1(Bill\ comes)) \wedge (x2(John\ comes))))).$$

And second, the answer to such a construct being e.g. 'Yes, Yes' or 'Yes, No', there seems to be no intuitively convincing way to get from 'Yes, Yes' to 'both', or to 'Bill and John', or from 'Yes, No' to the simple 'Bill'.

Therefore HAUSSER's analysis seems to be preferable in this respect and also more in keeping with our intuitive account of the differences between the three types of questions. As we have already seen, HAUSSER bases his account of disjunctive questions on a question matrix plus an added question scope which explicitly mentions the answering possibilities.

Thus his analysis of 'Did John kiss Mary or Suzy?' amounts to

$$\hat{P}_n(kiss'(^{\wedge}j,P_n) \wedge ((P_n=\hat{P}P\{^{\wedge}m\}) \vee (P_n=\hat{P}P\{^{\wedge}s\}))))$$

Now HAUSSER's terminology becomes obvious: unrestricted questions are categorial questions without any scope restrictions, and parallel to every type of unrestricted questions there are restricted questions of the same type to which a scope restriction in the form of a disjunction of elements of the appropriate type is added. This seems to account very neatly for the difference between so-called wh-questions and alternative or disjunctive questions.

But yes/no-questions do not seem to fit into this picture. We have already rejected the idea of analysing them as disjunctive questions within this framework, and we now get additional support for this: if yes/no-questions as analysed by HAUSSER would belong to the class of restricted questions, where is the appropriate type of unrestricted question to go with it? If we cancel HAUSSER's scope-indicator, we are just left with what is EGLI's account of yes/no-questions. And it doesn't work the other way round either. If yes/no-questions are but a special type of wh-questions, different only in logical type, there should be a corresponding alternative question with an answer category of the same type. You may answer the question

Will John come or Mary?

as well as the question

Who will come?

with either 'John' or 'Mary'. Now the only obvious disjunctive counterpart for

Will Peter come?

is

Will Peter come or not?

The former question can be answered by 'yes' or 'no', this however, is impossible for the latter question. Although both these questions may be

answered by 'He will' or 'He won't', this does not count as a categorial
answer to a yes/no-question within the approaches presented here, and it
would also pose the further problem of how to account for 'yes' and 'no'.

To sum up: the categorial approach in its present stage of development
distinguishes quite nicely between wh- and alternative questions in that
both are categorial questions differentiated by the presence or absence of
a scope-marker. Yes/no-questions can be set apart from wh-questions only by
their logical type, by a special type of possible answers. But their relation
to alternative questions is far from being clear, and this in turn disturbs
and blurs the neat generality of the restricted/unrestricted, that is alter-
native/wh-distinction.

3. The Mixed Approach

After presenting the two basic theories, nothing much has to be said about
the mixed approach. Wh-questions are analysed the categorial way, alternative
and yes/no-questions the propositional way. Thus there is a sharp distinction
between wh-questions, which are said to represent a *predicate term* by
WUNDERLICH, and the rest, which is assumed to represent a *propositional term*
(Prädikatsbegriff vs. Propositionsbegriff). This seems to avoid all the trouble
with yes/no-questions, on the other hand however, we just get a mixture of
different types of answers. I therefore subscribe to EGLI's judgement that
this is somewhat inconsequent and would only require some paperwork to be
reduced to either the propositional or the categorial approach.

Let me add, however, that the categorial treatment of alternative vs. wh-
questions looks much more appealing than the sharp distinction drawn by the
mixed approach if we compare such pairs as

Who will come?

Will John come or Mary?

with the intermediate

Who will come, John or Mary?

And furthermore, the seeming ease and uniformity with which yes/no-questions
are treated along with alternative questions is a fake, really, in HAMBLIN's
approach as well as in the mixed one. The alternatives presented are explicitly
mentioned in alternative questions, they have to be recovered in yes/no-
questions. This is a pitfall we have already discussed in connection with
HAUSSER's analysis. BELNAP explicitly says that it is the manner of the presentation of the alternatives that is the criterion of differentiation. And
the manner of presentation certainly is different here. Again it is only the
smallness of the class of possible answers that tempts us to lump together
yes/no-questions and alternative questions. But the fact remains that the
alternatives are not given, but have to be reconstructed, and such a reconstruction is theoretically always possible, even for wh-questions. And given
the right kind of category, it is also practicable, let us say for a question
like

What is the colour of your car?,

because the set of colour terms certainly is not too large a set. Therefore the possibility of reconstruction cannot serve as a criterion, and we are indeed left with the manner of the presentation of the alternatives.

It therefore seems to me that this approach suffers from two shortcomings, as far as the topic of types of questions is concerned: the sharp distinction between wh-questions and the rest is overstated, and the lumping together of alternative and yes/no-questions is an oversimplification.

Now that we have presented the three major approaches towards the semantics of questions (remember that attention has only been given to the treatment of the propositional content), it has become obvious that my sympathies lie with the categorial approach. In what follows, I shall therefore try to have a closer look at the weak point of this approach, a closer look at yes/no-questions and how they fit into the general pattern.

It is not only that - given the usual interpretation of yes/no-questions - a clear picture of the relation between different types of questions does not emerge. The analysis of yes/no-questions in itself has some doubtful aspects. It has, e.g., often been observed that the term *yes/no-question* is a misnomer. And indeed, such questions do not have to be answered by 'yes' or 'no'. In German we may easily answer a question like

Wird Peter kommen? (Will Peter come?)

with one of the following adverbials

vielleicht   (perhaps)
gewiss   (certainly)
wahrscheinlich   (most likely) (and so on).

EGLI [5], p. 40, seems to assume that they belong to the category of 'Modus' along with 'yes' and 'no'. But it seems to me that the behaviour of these adverbs is so entirely different from that of 'yes' or 'no', that such a classification would be rather awkward. 'Peter will perhaps marry Sheila' is perfectly normal, 'Peter will yes marry Sheila' is not English, and 'Yes, Peter will marry Sheila' is unthinkable except embedded in the content of at least one other sentence. What is more, 'yes' and 'no' can easily be added to these adverbs to form an answer. We are therefore left with the rather puzzling situation that answers to one and the same question would belong to two different categories, which we cannot allow.

Furthermore, yes/no-questions show another quite unusual feature, if we take them to be 'Modus'-questions. Whereas wh-questions are answered either by giving the missing item or else by a whole sentence, categorial answer and sentence answer co-occur quite naturally in the context of yes/no-questions, as in

Will he come? - Yes, he will come.

I take the fact, that 'yes' and 'no' co-occur with both sentence answers and categorial adverbial answers, together with the observation, that 'yes' and 'no' only occur in discourse situations (not in isolated sentences) to express agreement or disagreement with what has been said before, to indicate that they are not to be taken as answers, but as discourse elements that relate the answer to the question in some way or other, but similar to their function in a discourse like the following:

A (to C): But you have always been in favour of this proposal.

B (co C): Yes, I heard you say so.

C: No, what I was trying to say was quite another thing.

But this is not to mean that we should just take 'perhaps, surely' and other adverbs to be the categorial answers to yes/no-questions, because this would not account for question-answer-pairs like the following, which are taken from Old Greek and Latin:

Old Greek: δοκεῖ τί cοι εἶναι ἵππου ἔργον; ἔμοιγε

Scheint dir das Pferd eine Aufgabe zu haben; mir

Latin: Num venditor iniuste fecit? ille vero

Hat der Verkäufer ungerecht gehandelt? Er fürwahr.

Here we seem to have to do with straightforward categorial questions that do not differ from wh-questions in type, but only in scope - as it is the case with alternative questions.

This observation is backed up by a number of other phenomena, the most obvious of which is the existence of a mixed wh-//yes/no-type, which can be divided into question matrix and scope indicator as it has been the case with disjunctive questions:

Who has eaten the pudding, Mary?

What has Mary eaten, the pudding?

If we take writing as the basis of observation, both these questions translate into one and the same 'normal form' of yes/no-questions:

Has Mary eaten the pudding?

But in spoken language we have a difference in intonation:

Has Máry eaten the pudding?

Has Mary eaten the púdding?.

Thus the simple surface form

Have you eaten the pudding?

may be about *who* has eaten the pudding, it may be about *what* you have eaten, and it may be about *what has happened* to the pudding. Quite similar to wh-questions and scope-restricted alternative questions, what is asked for is the specification of an element of a certain category.

If there were no such gap in the underlying propositional structure, to be filled with a specific item, how would we know what else to say except an impolite 'no' when asked

Are you Dr. Livingstone?

Surely I would give my own name and not just the bare 'no', or else I would point out Dr. Livingstone among those present - depending on whether I interpret the question to be an inquiry for Dr. Livingstone - 'Who is Dr. Livingstone?', that is - or an inquiry for my name: 'Who are you?'.

My thesis therefore is that the difference between wh-questions, alternative and yes/no-questions is solely a matter of scope. As far as types are concerned, every type of question is represented in all three categories, e.g.

When does he arrive?

Does he arrive tomorrow or the day after tomorrow?
(= When does he arrive, tomorrow or the day after tomorrow?)

Does he arrive tomorrow?
(= When does he arrive, tomorrow?)

Thus wh-questions are unrestricted questions, as HAUSSER terms them, in that they do not have a scope-indicator, whereas alternative and yes/no-questions are restricted questions in that an explicit list of alternatives is given, which is maximally reduced in the case of yes/no-questions. Given such an explanation for yes/no-questions, there is no need to try to reduce them to another sort of question, no need to 'recover' the alternatives presented, and there is no need to lump positive questions like

Will you go to the dentist?

together with negative questions like

Won't you go to the dentist?

In the propositional as well as in the mixed approach, they cannot be kept apart, because they are said to represent the same set of propositions, namely: 'You will go to the dentist' and 'You will not go to the dentist'. In our approach, they will have the same scope, but a different question-matrix, which accounts for their different surface form.

A few things have to be explained now: if the scope-indicator of a yes/no-question does only contain one element, in what sense may we say that there is an alternative, which is the basic requirement of a question situation; and how do we account for answers like 'yes', 'no', or adverbs such as 'perhaps', 'maybe' and so on, and what about our categorial answers that hardly ever show on the surface.

Questions like

Will Peter come or Mary?

are said to be alternative questions, because we may choose from a list of alternatives: Peter, or Mary, or both of them. This cannot hold for yes/no-questions like

Will Peter come?

because our list does only comprise one item: Peter. So we do not seem to have a real choice. But we must not forget that in order to specify the true alternative out of a given list we first of all have to accept that at least one of these alternatives is true, which may not be the case. And this is where the only choice can be made in the case of yes/no-questions; we do not choose between different items given, but we decide whether the only item given is correct or not. More generally speaking, the first decision is whether the given list does or does not contain an appropriate item (which is all we have to do in the case of yes/no-questions), and it is only then that we may go on to specify the appropriate item, as it is in the case of alternative questions.

A wh-question like

Wer kommt?   (Who will come?)

may be answered by either

Niemand   (Nobody at all)

or else by noun phrases such as

John, Mary, the constable, and so on.

The same is true for alternative questions, which we may answer by

Keiner von beiden   (None of the two)

or else by

Hans, Fritz, beide   (Both of them),

if the question is 'Kommt Hans oder Fritz' (Will Hans come or Fritz?). And in the case of yes/no-questions like

Wird Hans kommen?   (Will John come?)

we may either reject the list whose only member is 'John' and say

(Nein), *der* nicht   - or simply: Nein

or accept it, the categorial answer being

(Ja), *Hans*   - or simply: Ja

But the categorial answers will only rarely turn up in the surface structure of German or English, although we have seen that there are examples in Greek and Latin. So we shall now have to explain how to get to the surface answers, which are 'yes' or 'no' or an adverb such as 'perhaps', 'most likely', or a combination of the two.

It does not seem to be difficult to think of examples where the categorial answer does show on the surface, e.g. in the German

Hast Du das im Radio gehört?   Ja, im Radio.
Did you hear that on the radio? Yes, on the radio.

But it is interesting that even where a categorial answer turns up, it is bound up with 'yes' or 'no'. And here seems to lie the explanation for the bulk of answers to yes/no-questions, where the categorial answer is suppressed. 'Yes' and 'No' signal agreement or disagreement with what has been said before. Thus they already tell us whether the list of alternatives, which in this case has only one member, is accepted or not, and there is no need to repeat an item already given - it is the only item on the list.

With regard to 'yes' and 'no', different languages show a variety of forms, a very detailed discussion of which can be found in POPE [15], on whose information I rely heavily in what follows. Whereas modern English has only 'yes, no (plus eventually a tag)', medieval English has 'yes, no, nay, yea', and German has 'ja, nein, doch', French 'oui, non, si' etc. This again is, I think, a point in favour of my approach, because the difference between these forms can easily be explained. Most analyses of yes/no-questions lump together 'Will John come' and 'Won't John come', because both are said to represent the two propositions 'John will come' and 'John won't come'. In such an approach, 'yes' is taken to mean 'it is the case that', and 'no' to mean 'it is not the case that'. This would be sufficient for e.g. Old Icelandic, where we only encounter the two forms 'ja' and 'nei'. 'Ja' being the answer to both 'will he come?' and 'won't he come?' with the meaning 'it is the case that he will come' vs. 'it is the case that he won't come'.

But it doesn't work for other languages, where we either have more than two forms or two forms that also take into account whether the preceding question is negated or not. Consider 16th century English:

		or German:
question not negated + I agree: yea		ja
question negated + I agree: no		nein
question not negated + I disagree: nay		nein
question negated + I disagree: yes		doch

In my approach to yes/no-questions, this can easily be accounted for, because positive and negative questions are distinguished by a positive or negative question matrix:

Whom did you invite for the party, the president?

Whom didn't you invite for the party, the president?

The occurrence of adverbs like 'perhaps', 'certainly' and so on without a categorial answer can be explained in much the same way.

Vielleicht Hans (John perhaps)

and Wahrscheinlich Hans (Most likely John)

make perfect answers to wh-questions and alternative questions. The adverb functions as a modifier of the categorial answer asked for. And it should now be obvious that the same holds true for yes/no-questions, where the only possible categorial answer is given in the scope-list and therefore need not be repeated.

It has been my aim in this paper to show that BELNAP was right in his book to say that the only difference between the types of questions discussed here is in the manner of the presentation of the alternatives, although he did not draw the necessary consequences himself. The result was a completely new analysis of yes/no-questions (I hesitate to still use the term). The necessity of such a new analysis has already been pointed out by RYSZARD ZUBER in [18]. Let me therefore, to conclude with, quote the abstract of his paper:

> The general (yes-no) question Q: "Is it true that ..." is presuppositionally ambiguous: Q(S is P) can have either S or P as 'argument'. In the former case one presupposes "Something has the property P" and one asks if this given property P is a property of S. In the latter case one presupposes "S has some property" and one asks if the given object S has also a property P.
> It is not possible to ask both in the same question.

References

1 Belnap, Nuel D. Jr. and T. B. Steel (1976)
  The logic of questions and answers;
  Yale University Press, New Haven and London

2 Cohen, Felix S. (1929)
  What is a question?;
  The Monist 39, p. 350-364

3 Duden
  Grammatik der deutschen Gegenwartssprache;
  2. Auflage 1966, Bibliographisches Institut, Mannheim

4 Egli, Urs (1974)
  Ansätze zur Integration der Semantik in die Grammatik;
  Skriptor, Kronberg

5 Egli, Urs (1976)
  Zur Semantik des Dialogs;
  Papiere des SFB 99, Konstanz

6 Hamblin, C.L. (1973)
  Questions in Montague English;
  Foundations of language 10, p. 41-53

7 Hausser, Roland and Dietmar Zaefferer (1976)
  Questions and answers in a context-dependent Montague grammar,
  to appear in: Guenthner/Schmidt (eds.), Semantics and
  pragmatics of natural language;
  Reidel, Dordrecht

8 Hausser, Roland (1977)
  The logic of questions and answers;
  photocopied

9 Hausser, Roland (1978)
  Surface compositionality and the semantics of mood,
  to appear in: Kiefer/Searle (eds.), Speech act theory
  and pragmatics;
  Reidel, Dordrecht

10 Hintikka, Jaakko (1976)
    The semantics of questions and the questions of semantics;
    Acta Philosophica Fennica, Vol. 28, No. 4, North Holland,
    Amsterdam

11 Jespersen, Otto (1940)
    A modern English grammar on historical principles, part V;
    Munksgaard, Copenhagen

12 Karttunen, Lauri (1977a)
    Syntax and semantics of questions;
    Linguistics and Philosophy 1, p. 3-44

13 Karttunen, Lauri (1977b)
    Questions revisited;
    photocopied

14 Keenan, Edward L. and Robert D. Hull (1973)
    The logical presuppositions of questions and answers;
    in: Petöfi/Franck (eds.), Präsuppositionen in Philosophie
    und Linguistik, p. 441-446;
    Athenäum, Frankfurt

15 Pope, Emily Norwood (1976)
    Questions and answers in English;
    Mouton, The Hague (= Janua Linguarum, Ser. practica 226)

16 Quirk, R./Greenbaum, S./Leech, G./Svartvik, J. (1972)
    A grammar of contemporary English;
    Longman, London

17 Wunderlich, Dieter (1976)
    Fragesätze und Fragen;
    in: D. Wunderlich, Studien zur Sprechakttheorie, p. 181-250;
    Suhrkamp, Frankfurt

18 Zuber, Ryszard (1972)
    A propos de la question dite générale;
    Dialectica 26, p. 131-137

Comparison and Gradual Change

Joachim Ballweg and Helmut Frosch

Institut für Deutsche Sprache, Friedrich-Karl-Str. 12
D-6800 Mannheim, Fed. Rep. of Germany

1.1 In our paper, we would like to develop a semantic analysis of verbs of change, i.e. verbs like *to wake up, to fall asleep, to grow* etc.

1.2 To our intuition, a simple declarative sentence containing such an item as a main verb designates a change from one state of affairs to another - whence the name.

To test our intuition, let us look more closely at sentence (1):

(1) *John falls asleep.*

This sentence is true not at a single time-point t, but at an interval $\bar{t}$ which fulfills the condition that

(2) *John does not sleep* and (3) *John sleeps*

are true at the beginning and the end of $\bar{t}$, respectively.[1]

The truth conditions of (1), then, can be constructed on the basis of the truth-conditions of (3), i.e. for (1) to be true at an interval, (2), the negation of (3), must be true at the beginning of this same interval, and (3) must be true at its end.[2]

There is one proposal for the analysis of these verbs in the literature which we want to look at more closely, namely David DOWTY's. We hope that our discussion of its shortcomings will shed some light on the problems we will have to face when trying to find a more satisfactory solution.

DOWTY has an operator BECOME, which takes sentences into sentences; our sentence (1), then, would be rendered in this framework as, roughly

(1)' [BECOME[*John sleeps*]].

The truth-conditions of the BECOME-operator are given as follows:

[BECOME $\emptyset$] is true at a time-point t iff $\emptyset$ is true at t, and [$\neg \emptyset$] is true at a t' before t, and at all t'' between t' and t.[3]

In this analysis, (1) would come out true at a time-point t if (3) is true at t, and (2) is true for a stretch of time-points before t.

But, in our opinion, this is rather an analysis of

(4) *John has just fallen asleep.*
or   (5) *John has just nodded off.*

than of (1).

This analysis could be improved if it were based on intervals rather than time points; [BECOME ∅] would then come out true at an interval t̄ if ∅ is true at the last time-point t of t̄, and if [¬ ∅] is true at all t'ε t̄, where t ≠ t'.

But even this emended version of the DOWTY analysis will not do, because it reconstructs the process of falling asleep as a change between two states taking place all of a sudden. This would make a sentence like

(6) *It took John half an hour to fall asleep.*

self-contradictory. That is empirically inadequate. Falling asleep should rather be analyzed as a gradual change (not necessarily a steady one). On the other hand, it is not clear how the progressive could be handled in such a framework, since for

(7) *John was walking to the station.*

to be true at an interval t̄, it suffices that John is, at the end of t̄, nearer to the station than at the beginning of t̄.

(8) *John is falling asleep.*

then, would be true at an interval t̄ iff John, at the end of this interval t̄, is 'nearer' to the state of sleeping than he was at the beginning of t̄.

We do not intend to give an account of the progressive, but the analysis of verbs of change given below will render possible such an account, as Max CRESSWELL pointed out to us at the conference.

From these preliminary considerations, it seems clear that some notion of comparison of states relative to predicates is vitally involved in an analysis of gradual change. Attempts to analyse this in formal systems are to be found in BRENNEN-STUHL's "Semantics for a door's closing" and in HOEPELMANNS "Activity verbs in Montague Grammar." Both authors adopt the framework of fuzzy logic, where, obviously, (1) can be analysed as 'It becomes more and more true and finally is true that John sleeps'.

We will not discuss these proposals in more detail, as we have strong reservations and qualms about the possibility of giving an intuitively and logically satisfactory definition of the sentential connectives in these frameworks with infinitely many truth values, let alone the possibility of justifying the numerical values between 0 and 1 attributed to the sentences.[4]

Another solution has recently been proposed by ÅQVIST/GUENTHNER. Their analysis of the 'fascinating notion' of 'gradual becoming' has greatly influenced our own views on the subject, as will become obvious below.

The main idea of their approach is to introduce an ordering $\geq_\emptyset$ over that subset of the power-set of time-points where a sentence $\emptyset$ is true; $t \geq_\emptyset t'$ is fulfilled iff "t exhibits $\emptyset$ at least as much as t'."[5]

Letting SLEEP (JOHN) be the state of affairs corresponding to

John sleeps.

(1) can be explained straightforwardly, its truth conditions being rendered (1) is true at an interval $\bar{t}$ iff first, there is a proper subinterval $\bar{t}'$, at the beginning of $\bar{t}$, such that (2) *John does not sleep.* is true at each element of $\bar{t}'$, and for all time points t, t' in $\bar{t}'$, if t is before $\bar{t}'$, then $t \geq_{not\ (sleep(John))} t'$, and second, there is a proper subinterval $\bar{t}''$ with $\bar{t}' = \bar{t} \setminus \bar{t}'$, such that (3) *John sleeps* is true at each element of $\bar{t}''$, and for all t'', t''' in $\bar{t}''$ if t'' is before t''', then $t'' \leq_{sleep\ (John)} t'''$.

We fully agree with ÅQVIST and GUENTHNER, that the <u>degree of realization of a state of affairs</u> is the key notion in the analysis of gradual change, and that it should not be confused with a concept like "being more true", said of a <u>sentence</u> describing this state of affairs.[6]

Our own aim in this paper is to give a more general account of comparison which goes further than just temporal comparison, and to sketch some possible fields of application it could have. Finally, we will use it as a base for an analysis of verbs of change.

1.3 Looking at sentence (1) once again, we see that an analysis of this sentence involves a comparison of 'the degree of John's sleeping' at different time points; this could be rendered in the ÅQVIST/GUENTHNER-system. However, it should also be possible to compare, at <u>one</u> time-point, the degree of two different individuals, with regard to a predicate α, as in examples like

(9) *John is taller than Hugo.*

(10) *Hugo is more of a detective than Humphrey.*

In these cases, we do not compare different time-points with respect to their different realizations of states of affairs, but rather different individuals with respect to their degree of α-ness (letting α vary over predicates).

Furthermore, none of these sentences intuitively implies the positive case, i.e. (9) does not imply

(9') *John or Hugo is tall,*
(10) does not imply
(10') *Hugo or Humphrey is a detective.*

Therefore, the analyses of (9) and (10) cannot be based simply on the classificatory one-place predicates *tall*, or *detective*. We rather need comparative two-place predicates such as 'sleep at least as much as' or 'sleep more than' as conceptually basic, the one-place concept being derived.

The noun *detective* would be interpreted by means of a two-place relation between individuals, this relation being a reflexive, antisymmetrical and transitive ordering $\geq_{detective}$. In this analysis, (10) would be true if $\langle Hugo, Humphrey \rangle \in \geq_{detective}$. The noun *detective* is then analysed as' at least as much of a detective as d', where d is the 'threshold-detective', or the 'minimal definite detective'.

This analysis is, in many respects, similar to some proposed analyses for adjectives.[7] This proposal might look awkward at first sight, as verbs do not occur in comparative constructions as often as adjectives do. It even seems difficult to find good examples, since in most cases the comparison with respect to a verb is expressed by means of an 'intensifying adverb' such as *closely*. These adverbs have, in addition to the comparative morpheme of the adjectives, specific meanings that have to be "added" to the pure comparison.

Before we show how to accommodate our analysis to the syntax of English, we want to give some further justifications for it. Above all, we feel that the problems of vagueness and context-dependency can be tackled in a quite natural way in such a framework.

Let us take as an example the predicate 'stool' and imagine, with Max BLACK a 'museum for applied logics', where visitors are confronted with a long row of objects, starting with a log of wood and ending at the right with a beautiful old hand-crafted stool. The poor visitor, now, will probably be unable to draw a sharp borderline between two objects, saying 'The left one is no stool, and the right one is'. But, despite this fact, which indicates the vagueness of the predicate 'stool', he will be able to give judgements like 'This object here is more of a stool than the object to its left', or: 'If we take this object to be a stool, then all the other objects to its right are stools too'. That means, for our discussion, that the vagueness of a classificatory predicate 'stool' vanishes, if we go to a comparative notion 'stooler than'. The classificatory predicate, then, can be construed from the comparative one by the introduction of a designated member of the ordering as the 'minimal definite stool'.[8]

The vagueness of the classificatory predicate can then be explained by the fact that in the context of the museum it is impossible to designate a unique object as the 'minimal definite stool'. On the other hand, any of the doubtful stools, or even some of the negative ones may play this role in an appropriate context, e.g. on a long trip through the woods searching for a nice place for a picnic, one might very well accept a sentence like

(1) *Sit on that stool.*

coupled with a gesture pointing towards a trunk of a tree. But if an assistant in a furniture shop should utter (1), pointing to a trunk-like object, one would not accept it, but would be inclined at least to doubt whether the assistant was serious, if not to worry about his mental health.[9]

Along these lines, it seems, all classificatory predicates of everyday language can be taken as based on comparative ones, the 'minimal definite individual' being furnished more or less precisely by the context.

1.4 Following this strategy we consider verbs of natural language as being based on comparative notions. But to treat them syntactically this way in English seems odd. We might construct a formal language which contains for each English n-place verb a 2n-place predicate constant and interpret English indirectly via translation into this formal language.

A closer examination of the *stool*-example shows, however, that neither in English nor in the syntax of the formal languages are such 2n-place predicates needed, because the range of the 'at least as stool as'-relation serves primarily to determine the stock of possible threshold stools. In other words: we must not take these ordering relations as direct interpretations of predicates, they serve rather to determine the interpretation (or the extension) of predicates with respect to a given context. Only comparative expressions (provided they enter into the language) are interpreted directly by the orderings. So, we treat n-place verbs of e.g. English as n-place predicates of the respective formal language that is semantically interpreted, and we take care that they are based on comparative notions by the construction of their semantic evaluation, that is, we do not, as usual, identify the extension of an n-place-predicate α with a set of individuals, but with the set of n-tuples standing in the 2n-place-relation $\geq \alpha$ at least as high as the 'minimal definite' member of that relation in a context. As the analysis of verbs of change, e.g. *to fall asleep* involves a comparison of one individual at one time-point with the same individual at another time-point, we extend the orderings to pairs of n-tuples of individuals and time-points.[10]

In intensional semantics, the relation should, of course, at least cover triples of n-tuples of individuals, time-points and possible worlds.

We are now in a position to construct a formal language based on the concepts discussed so far. In doing so, we introduce some new concepts, especially the concept of a scale. We do this, we would like to stress, only for reasons of technical convenience, so these notions can be eliminated, as they are defined in terms of the concepts discussed and analytically well-founded up to now.[11]

First, every relation $\geq_\alpha$ involved in the interpretation of a predicate α defines, in an obvious way, an equivalence relation $=_\alpha$ on the domain of individuals D. By $=_\alpha$, D is split into equivalence classes of (n-tuples of) individuals, where all elements of one such class 'realize the predicate α to the same degree'. Using our original relation $\geq_\alpha$ and the set Σ_α of these equivalence classes, we define a strict ordering $>_\alpha$ on Σ_α, such that for all δ_α, $\delta'_\alpha \epsilon \Sigma_\alpha$, and all $y \epsilon \delta_\alpha$, $y' \epsilon \delta_\alpha$, it holds:

$$y \geq_\alpha y' \wedge y \neq_\alpha y' \longleftrightarrow \delta_\alpha > \delta'_\alpha.$$

So, in the further construction of a semantic apparatus for describing predicates, we can concentrate on the pair $\langle \Sigma_\alpha, >_\alpha \rangle$, as it can be looked at as a scale, at least as an ordinal scale, where the elements δ_α of Σ_α represent the degrees of realization of α. Henceforth, we will call these δ_α 'values' provided the rest is clear from the context. The element of our scale which is the equivalence class of the 'minimal definite individuals' will be called τ_α, the threshold value.

Finally, we introduce a function μ_α from D^n into Σ_α, which maps individuals into the scale $\langle \Sigma_\alpha, >_\alpha \rangle$. Given $\langle \mu_\alpha, \Sigma_\alpha, >_\alpha, \tau_\alpha \rangle$, the extension of a predicate α can now be given as:

$$\{ y: y \epsilon D^n \wedge (\mu_\alpha(y) >_\alpha \tau_\alpha \vee \mu_\alpha (y) = \tau_\alpha)\}$$

2. In the following section, we introduce a language L of PL[1] with both context dependent and classical interpretations, based upon the concepts introduced in section 1. We define its syntax in the usual way, that is, we specify the symbols of the language and than give a recursive definition of the set of well-formed formulae.

2.1. The Language L of PL[1]

Symbols:

Individual constants: { *PORKY, JOHN, ARABELLA* } = IC
Individual variables: { x_1, x_2, ..., x_n, ...} = IV
Individual expressions: IV $\cup$ IC = IE
Predicate constants: { *GRUNT, SLEEP, ALIVE* }= $_1$PC
{ *SEE, LOVE* } = $_2$PC

The Quantifier: $\forall$
The one-place connective: $\neg$
The two-place-connective: $\wedge$
Auxiliary symbols: [ ], ( )

Syntax: WFF, the set of well-formed formulae of L, is the smallest set X such that:

If $\alpha \epsilon nPC$, and $\beta_1 \epsilon IE$, and ... $\beta_n \epsilon IE$, then $\alpha(\beta_1, ..., \beta_n) \epsilon X$.

If $\alpha \epsilon X$, and $\gamma \epsilon IV$, then $\forall \gamma [\alpha] \epsilon X$

If $\alpha \epsilon X$, then $[\neg \ \alpha] \epsilon X$

If $\alpha \epsilon X$, and $\beta \epsilon X$, then $[\alpha \wedge \beta] \epsilon X$

The other connectives and the existential quantifier are now defined as usual:

$$[\beta \vee \gamma] =_{df} [\neg [[\neg \ \beta] \wedge [\neg \gamma]]]$$
$$[\beta \rightarrow \gamma] =_{df} [\neg [\beta \wedge [\neg \gamma]]]$$
$$[\beta \leftrightarrow \gamma] =_{df} [[\beta \rightarrow \gamma] \wedge [\gamma \rightarrow \beta]]$$
$$\exists \gamma [\alpha] =_{df} [\neg [\forall \gamma [\neg \alpha]]]$$

We do not think we have to discuss this broadly here, nor should we discuss too much the classical semantics for this language L of predicate logic, which we present here:

Semantics for L

A model M for L is a quintuple

$\langle D, \{p, j, a\}, v, \langle Ext_\alpha \rangle_{\alpha \epsilon nPC} \rangle$, where D is a non empty set, the individual domain

$\{p, j, a\} \subseteq D$ is a set of designated elements of D

v is a function from IV into D

$\langle Ext_\alpha \rangle_{\alpha \epsilon_n PC}$ is a family of sets, indexed by the set of n-place predicates, whereby $Ext_\alpha \subseteq D^n$ is the extension of the predicate α for each $\alpha \epsilon_n PC$.

V is the evaluation function, such that for any $\alpha, \beta, \gamma \epsilon WFF$:

```
If α =     PORKY,     V(α) = p
If α =     JOHN,      V(α) = j
If α =     ARABELLA,  V(α) = a
If α ε IV         ,   V(α) = v(α)
If α ε nPC        ,   V(α) = Ext_α
If α ε WFF        ,   V(α) ε { 0, 1}
If α =[¬ β]       ,   V(α) = 1 iff  V (β) = 0
If α =[β ∧ γ]     ,   V(α) = 1 iff  V (β) = 1 and
                                   V (γ) = 1
```

If $\alpha = \forall \gamma [\beta]$, $V(\alpha) = 1$ iff for all $y \epsilon D$, $V^*(\beta) = 1$, and V^* is like V, with the possible difference that $V^*(\gamma) = y$.

If $\alpha = \beta (\gamma_1, \ldots, \gamma_n)$, where $\beta \epsilon_n PC$, $\gamma_1 \epsilon IE, \ldots, \gamma_n \epsilon IE$, $V(\alpha) = 1$ iff $\langle V(\gamma_1), \ldots, V(\gamma_n) \rangle \epsilon V(\beta)$

<u>If $\alpha \epsilon WFF$, then α is true relative to M</u> iff $V(\alpha) = 1$, for all models M', which differ from M at most in having v' instead of v.

The purpose of this presentation is to give you the possibility to compare the classical semantics for our language L with our context dependent semantics which we introduce in 2.2.

2.2. Context Dependent Semantics for L

Now what we do here is replace in the classical model for first order predicate logic the interpretation of n-place predicate constants by the technical apparatus introduced above. Thus a context dependent model CM for L is a quintuple

$$\langle\ D, \{p,j,a\}\ , v\ \langle\ \Sigma_\alpha,\ >_\alpha,\ \mu_\alpha,\ \tau_\alpha\ \rangle_{\alpha\ \epsilon\ _n PC}\ ,\ V'\ \rangle,$$

where D, $\{p,j,a\}$, v are as in M.

$$\langle\ \Sigma_\alpha,\ >_\alpha,\ \mu_\alpha,\ \tau_\alpha\ \rangle_{\alpha\ \epsilon\ _n PC}$$

replaces

$\langle\ Ext_\alpha\ \rangle_{\alpha\ \epsilon\ _n PC}$ in CM, and for all $\alpha\ \epsilon\ _n$ PC:

- Σ_α is a set which contains at least two elements.

- $>_\alpha$ is a transitive, irreflexive, and connected ordering in Σ_α. So $\langle\ \Sigma_\alpha\ ,\ >_\alpha\ \rangle$ is a scale for α. If the cardinality of Σ_α is exactly 2, it is a so-called nominal scale; if it is more than 2, it is an ordinal scale.

- μ_α is a function from D^n into Σ_α that specifies, so to speak, the degree of α-ness of each n-tuple of individuals. So $\langle\ \Sigma_\alpha,\ >_\alpha,\ \mu_\alpha\ \rangle$ is a scalar measurment for α.

- τ_α is a designated element of Σ_α, the threshold value, determined by the actual context.

The evaluation function V' of CM is like V with the exception that for any predicate constant α,V'(α) is the clause determined by:

If $\alpha\ \epsilon\ _n$PC, then V'(α) = $\{y\ :\ y\epsilon D^n\ \wedge\ \mu_\alpha\ (y)\ \geq\ \tau_\alpha\}$

If $\alpha\ \epsilon$ WFF, then α is true relative to CM iff

V'(α) = 1, for all models CM', which differ from

CM at most in having v' instead of v.

As we have seen, the τ_α may vary from one context to another. Consequently, the truth relative to CM is to be regarded as truth in a context, which we identify for our present purpose with the family $\langle\ \tau_\alpha\ \rangle_{\alpha\ \epsilon\ _n PC}$ of threshold values. Truth in all (or some) contexts can be defined in an obvious

way as truth in all models differing from CM at most in
$\langle \tau_\alpha \rangle_{\alpha \epsilon_n}$ PC .

2.2.2. Now, the mere substitution of CM for M does not affect
the expressive power of the language L itself. In an obvious
way, however, L can be extended to a language that expresses
comparison and the concept of degree.

Even without formulating such an extension, the model CM
allows for an adequate metalinguistic definition of <u>antonymy</u>
of predicates. It has been noted   in the literature[12]
that the notion of antonymy is highly related to comparison,
to give LYONs' example: *big* is regarded as antonymous of *small*,
since the bigger an object a is, the less small it is. Within
our framework the following definition formally reflects these
intuitions:

> If α and β are n-place predicate-constants, then
> <u>α is antonymous of β</u> iff for all y, y' ϵ D^n:
> $\overline{(\mu_\alpha(y) \leq \mu_\alpha(y')\ iff\ \mu_\beta}$ (y) $\geq \mu_\beta$ (y')) and
> if μ_α (y) $\geq \tau_\alpha$, then not μ_β (y) $\geq \tau_\beta$

Now what this amounts to, if we paraphrase it loosely,is
simply that two predicates α and β are antonymous of each
other if the scale for α is the reverse scale of the scale
for β, and there are two threshold values within this scale,
one τ_α, and one τ_β, which are different; this guarantees that
the extensions of these two predicates are in turn disjoint.

As a second result, a definition of <u>synonymy</u> (of predicates)
can be given that allows for the non - synonymy of predicates
with identical extensions:

> <u>α is synonymous of b</u> iff for all y, y' ϵ D^n:
> $\overline{(\mu_\alpha(y) \leq \mu_\alpha(y')\ iff\ \mu_\beta}$ (y)$\leq \mu_\beta$(y')) and
> $\mu_\alpha(y) = \tau_\alpha$iff $\mu_\beta(y)$ = τ_β

2.3. Extension of L to T L

Add to the symbols of L the following constants: $\boxed{P}$, $\boxed{F}$,
$\langle\!\!\langle P \rangle\!\!\rangle$, $\langle\!\!\langle F \rangle\!\!\rangle$

Add to the recursive definition of WFF the following clauses:

> If $\alpha \epsilon$ WFF, then $\boxed{P}$ (α) ϵ WFF
>
> $\boxed{F}$ (α) ϵ WFF
>
> $\langle\!\!\langle P \rangle\!\!\rangle$ (α) ϵ WFF
>
> $\langle\!\!\langle F \rangle\!\!\rangle$ (α) ϵ WFF

Now to give the semantics we will have to extend our context
model introduced above to a temporal context model, and we do
this by adding a temporal frame and than revising our notion
of an interpretation function:

Extension of CM to TCM:

$$TCM = \langle\ D,\ \{p,j,a\},v,\langle\ \Sigma_\alpha,\ <_\alpha,\ \mu_{t,\alpha},^\tau{t,\alpha}\rangle\ {}_{t\epsilon T},\ \alpha\epsilon_n PC,$$

$$\langle\langle T,\ <\ \rangle,\ T,\ t_0\rangle,\ V\ \rangle$$

where D, p,j,a ,v are as in CM,

$$\langle\ \Sigma_\alpha,\ <_\alpha,\ \mu_{t,\alpha},\ ^\tau{t,\alpha}\rangle t\epsilon T,\ \alpha\epsilon_n PC$$

is again as in CM with the exception that μ_α, τ_α are indexed with the set of time-points, or, loosely speaking, μ_α, τ_α are dependent on time.

$\langle\langle\ T,\ <\ \rangle,\ t_0\rangle$ is a temporal frame, where T is a set of time-points and t_0 is a designated element of T.

< is an irreflexive, transitive, dense and connected ordering on T, and for all t in T, there is a t' such that t < t', and there is a t", such that t"<t

Now again we have to specify the evaluation function for our new model TCM:

V^- is the evaluation function, such that for any expression α, for all $t\ \epsilon\ T$,

(1) If α = *PORKY*, $V^-(\alpha, t) = p$
(2) If α = *JOHN*, $V^-(\alpha, t) = j$
(3) If α = *ARABELLA*, $V^-(\alpha, t) = a$
(4) If $\alpha\ \epsilon$ IV, $V^-(\alpha, t) = v(\alpha)$
(5) If $\alpha\ \epsilon_n$PC, $V^-(\alpha, t) = \{y : y\epsilon D^n \wedge\ \mu_{t,\alpha}(y)\geq^\tau{t,\alpha}\}$
(6) If $\alpha\ \epsilon$ WFF, $V^-(\alpha,t)\epsilon\{0,1\}$
(7) If α = $[\underline{\quad}\ \beta],V^-(\alpha,t) = 1$ iff $V^-(\beta,t) = 0$
(8) If α = $[\beta \wedge \gamma]$, $V^-(\alpha,t) = 1$ iff $V^-(\beta,t) = 1$, and $V^-(\gamma,t) = 1$
(9) If α = $\forall\gamma\ [\beta]$, $V^-(\alpha,t) = 1$ iff, for all $y\epsilon D$, $V^*(\beta,t) = 1$, where V^* is like V^- with the possible exception that $V^*(\gamma,t) = y$
(10) If α = $\beta(\gamma_1,\ldots,\ \gamma_n)$, where $\beta\ \epsilon_n PC$, and $\gamma_1\epsilon PE,\ldots,$ $\gamma_n\ \epsilon I\ E$, $V^-(\alpha,t) = 1$ iff $\langle V(\gamma_1,t)$ $,\ldots,\ V^-(\gamma_n,\ t)\rangle\ \epsilon\ V^-(\beta,t)$

Thus, the evaluation function V^- is like V' with the exception that V is two place, i.e. the expressions are evaluated at a time-point.

For the new constants of TL, we put

(11a) If α = $\boxed{P}$ (β), $V^-(\alpha,t) = 1$ iff $V^-(\beta,t') = 1$, for all $t':t'< t$
(11b) If α = $\langle\!P\!\rangle$ (β), $V^-(\alpha,t) = 1$ iff $V^-(\beta,t') = 1$, for at least one $t':t'< t$
(12a) If α = $\boxed{F}$ (β), $V^-(\alpha,t) = 1$ iff $V^-(\beta,t)) = 1$, for all $t':t< t'$

(12b) If $\alpha = \langle\!\!\langle c \rangle\!\!\rangle$ (ß), V^- $(\alpha, t) = 1$ iff V^- (ß,t') = 1,
for at least one t':t< t'

A truth definition then, for this model, is: a well-formed formula α of tense logic is said to be true with respect to a model TCM, as above, if and only if V^- $(\alpha, t_0) = 1$ for all models TCM' which differ from TCM at most in having v' instead of v.

2.4. Gradual Change

We finally extend our language TL to TChL by the following stipulations:

If ß ϵ_n PC, and $\delta_1 \epsilon$ IE,..., $\delta_n \epsilon$ IE
then COME ABOUT (ß, δ_1,...,δ_n) ϵ WFF,
and CEASE (ß, δ_1,..., δ_n) ϵ WFF

For the evaluation of our extended language TChL, we have to extend the model TCM to a model TChM; this is done by adding $\bar{T}$, the set of time-intervals, to the temporal frame, and by changing t_0 to an interval $\bar{t}_0$:

$\bar{T}$ is the set of time intervals, which is the set of all non-empty subsets of T, in which < is irreflexive, transitive, dense and connected

$\bar{t}_0$ is a designated element of $\bar{T}$.

In addition, the evaluation V^+ for TChM is defined for intervals:

(13) If $\alpha \epsilon$ WFF, other than COME ABOUT (ß,δ_1,...,δ_n) or
CEASE (ß,δ_1,...,δ_n), and $\bar{t} \epsilon$ $\bar{T}$, then
V^+ $(\alpha,\bar{t}) = 1$ iff, for all $t \epsilon \bar{t}$:$V(\alpha,t)=1$ in TCM.

For the interpretation of our new constants, we set:

(14a) If α = COME ABOUT (ß, δ_1,...,δ_n), where ß ϵ_n PC,
and $\delta_1 \epsilon$ IE, ..., $\delta_n \epsilon$ IE then
V^+ $(\alpha,\bar{t}) = 1$, iff for all t, t', t" in $\bar{t}$,
there is a proper subinterval $\bar{t}^*$ of $\bar{t}$,
such that for all t* in $\bar{t}^*$:

(1) if t* < t, then t ϵ $\bar{t}^*$, and

(3) V^+ (ß(δ_1,...,δ_n), $\bar{t}^*$) = 1, and

(2) $\mu_{t,ß}$ (< V^- (δ_1,t),..., V^- (δ_n,t)>)<$\tau_{t,ß}$,if $t \notin \bar{t}^*$, and

(4) $\tau_{t',ß} = \tau_{t",ß}$.

This definition looks a little awkward at the outset so
a comment is in order: the first part of the definition just
specifies that $\bar{t}^*$ is at the end of $\bar{t}$, and the second part
says that for the time-points before that interval $\bar{t}^*$, the μ-
function for the predicate ß and the time-point t gives for
the n-tuple of extensions of the individual expressions δ_1,
..., δ_n at t a value which is smaller than the threshold value
of the predicate ß at t, and the third part of the definition
says that the extensions of a sentence, built up of ß and δ_1,...,
δ_n must be   1 at this interval $\bar{t}^*$, and finally the fourth
part of the definition guarantees that the threshold value for
the particular predicate ß is the same throughout the interval
of evaluation. This last clause seems in order in view of
examples like Hans KAMPs' "clever" namely: Let's say there is
one ordering of cleverness according to being quickwitted,
and one ordering of individuals clever as according to
being quick in solving mathematical problems, and you cannot,
at the outset, say which one is the everlasting ordering for
cleverness. But it depends on time, as in our model.

Now suppose the situation where one person, Jones, is clever
according to the quickwittedness - scale and another person,
say Smith, is clever according to the quickness-in-mathemati-
cal-problems-scale, and think of a situation where they both
meet at a party, and at its beginning Jones is very clever because it's just smalltalk and quickwittedness that count
and then somehow the conversation changes to problems of
arithmetic, and then of course Smith is very clever because
he is very quick at solving such problems.[13]

Now it would be very awkward indeed to give a comment on
this situation by saying *Jones turned dull and Smith turned clever
during the party* or *Jones became dull and Smith became clever during the
party*, and so to avoid this, we need a clause like the above
one, which guarantees that for all time-points in the interval of evaluation of a sentence built up with this COME ABOUT
operator, the threshold value $\tau\alpha$ for the predicate employed
must be the same.

Turning to CEASE, we see that V^+ for CEASE simply is the
mirror image of V^+ for COME ABOUT.

(14b) If α = CEASE$(ß, \delta_1, \ldots, \delta_n)$, where $ß \epsilon_n PC$, and

$\delta_1 \epsilon IE, \ldots, \delta_n \epsilon IE$, then $V^+ (a, \bar{t})$ = 1,

iff for all t, t', t" in $\bar{t}$, there is

a proper subinterval $\bar{t}^*$ of $\bar{t}$, such

that for all t^* in $\bar{t}^*$:

(1) if $t < t^*$, then $t \epsilon \bar{t}^*$, and

(2) $\mu_{t,ß}(< V^+(\delta_1,t), \ldots, V^-(\delta_n,t)>) < \tau_{t,ß}$, if $t \notin \bar{t}^*$, and

(3) $V^+ (ß(\delta_1, \ldots, \delta_n), \bar{t}^*)$ = 1, and

(4) $\tau_{t',ß} = \tau_{t",ß}$

Finally, we can remark that the definition given for COME
ABOUT is indeed liberal enough, as it does not suppose any restrictions about the way of *falling asleep*, for example,
that is, we can have all sorts of crazy curves in our time-
interval $\bar{t}$, as you see on the little picture below, and the
only requirement is that before the time-interval where V^+
$(ß(\delta_1,...,\delta_n)) = 1$, the μ-value of the individuals denoted
by the expressions in this sentence is smaller than the
threshold value.

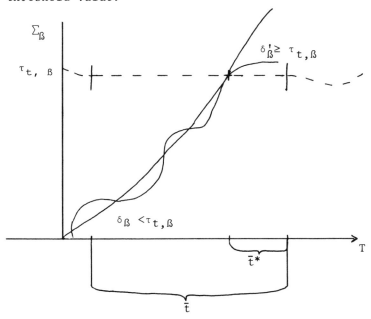

(1) *John falls asleep* can now be translated into the
TChL-formula COME ABOUT(SLEEP,JOHN), and likewise for other verbs of change.

3. If we look again at the solution we have given for a semantic treatment of gradual change we see that the trick of the
proposal put forward here is that it is so to speak 'fuzzy under the rug'. That is we have one evaluation as according to
degrees, that is the μ_α-function, and, as we do not have restrictions as to the cardinality of Σ_α, except that it be
$\geq$ two, we can of course handle what fuzzy logic claims it
can deal with. On the other hand, we have a second evaluation, V^+, according to truth of sentences in the model,
which is connected with the first, but which is perfectly classical, and so, unlike fuzzy logic, leaves the standard connectives unchanged. And we think that just this is a great

advantage of our proposal. A further advantage, in our view,
is that it treats the problem of giving semantics
for degree expressions and semantics for gradual change expressions by means of the same technical apparatus.[14]

Notes

1 The idea to evaluate English sentences in the simple
present tense at intervals is due to CRESSWELL 77.

2 At this point, it is not recessary to specify whether
'the begin' and 'the end' of $\bar{t}$ should be taken as an
interval or as a single time-point.

3 Cf. DOWTY 76, p. 208.

4 Cf. KAMP 75, pp. 130, 131.

5 Cf. ÅQVIST/GUENTHNER 78.

6 Indeed, we feel that the popularity of fuzzy logics is
due to this very confusion.

7 Cf. BARTSCH/VENNEMANN 72 and CRESSWELL 76.

8 At least if we ignore for the time being the problem of
multi-dimensionality mentioned in BLAU 77, p. 29.

9 In Lewisian terms, it defines the 'score' of the predicate
in that context. Cf. LEWIS 79.

10 With regard to adjectives, an analysis along these lines
would nicely explain the fact that positive constructions
with adjectives are context-dependent, while comparatives
are not.

11 See CRESSWELL 76 for similar views.

12 E.g. LYONS 68, p. 463 f.

13 This very example is discussed in KAMP 75, p. 146.

14 A very preliminary version of this paper was discussed
in Stuttgart, summer 78, and we owe much help
and encouragement to J. HOEPELMANN, D. GABBAY, and
especially H. KAMP. We wish to thank too all the people at
the conference who made valuable criticisms and suggestions. A. KIRKNESS patiently emended our English.

References

Åqvist, L. and Guenthner, F., Fundamentals of a Theory of
Verb Aspects and Events within the Setting of an Improved
Tense Logic, in: Guenthner/Rohrer.

Black, M., Language and Philosophy, Ithaca 1949.

Bartsch, R. and Vennemann, Th., Semantic structures,
Frankfurt 1972.

Blau, U., Die dreiwertige Logik der Sprache, Berlin 1978.

Brennenstuhl, W., Time-logic for a door's closing, mimeo.,
   TU Berlin 1974.

Cresswell, M., The Semantics of degree, in: Partee.

--, Interval Semantics and Logical Words, in: Rohrer (ed.),
   On the Logical Analysis of Tense and Aspect. Tübingen
   1977.

Dowty, D., Montague Grammar and Decomposition of Causative
   Verbs, in Partee.

Fine, K., Vagueness, truth and logic, in: Synthese 30, 1975.

Hoepelman, J.Ph., The Analysis of Activity Verbs in a Montague-
   type Grammar, in: Guenthner/Rohrer.

Kamp, J.A.W., Two theories about adjectives, in: Keenan (ed.),
   Formal Semantiçs of Natural Language, Cambridge 1975.

Lewis, D., General Semantics, in Partee.

--, Scorekeeping in a Language Game, in this volume.

Lyons, J., Introduction to Theoretical Linguistics, Cambridge
   1968.

Partee, B. (ed), Montague Grammar, N.Y. 1976.

Interval Semantics for Some Event Expressions

Max J. Cresswell

Victoria University of Wellington, Department of Philosophy, Private Bag, Wellington, New Zealand

This paper is the third in a series which investigates the properties of spatio-temporal modifiers in a categorial language with an interval-based semantics. Although intended to complement its predecessors ([13] and [15]) it is intended to be self-contained and a summary of the syntax and semantics presupposed is given in section 10. I shall also be making reference to [11] where categorial languages are set out and discussed more fully. (Though, as in [13] and [15], I shall not always be sticking to all the details of [11]). I shall also be making reference to [12].

In [13] a spatio-temporal adverb *quickly* was treated as a predicate modifier (in category ((0,1), (0,1)), *vide* section 10) while in [15] a number of pre-positional phrases were also so treated. In both cases it was shewn how to give an interval-based semantics for some simple senses of these phrases. The analyses presented there are certainly very crude but I still believe that they at least make a beginning.

My aim in this paper is to investigate what happens when we try to apply these modifiers to nouns which designate events.

1. Problem

Because of its restriction to a few spatio-temporal modifiers the paper is somewhat limited in scope. It has, however, a wider interest in that the predicate modifier view of adverbials is not the only view. DONALD DAVIDSON (in [16] and elsewhere) has argued that prepositional phrases should be ex-pressed by predicates holding of events; and his approach has been taken up by some linguists.[1]) Indeed in [12] I shewed how an event approach to adver-bials could be integrated into a categorial language of the kind set out in [11]. Part of the point of [13] and [15] was to shew that the reasons adduced in [12] for the event approach need not be compelling when we restrict our-selves to spatio-temporal modifiers. In other words the approach to adverbials I adopted in [12] is at odds with the view I favoured in [11] and returned to in [13], [15] and in the present paper. The approach of [12] is semantically akin to DAVIDSON's although syntactically it treats adverbs as predicate modifiers, but modifiers of predicates of events. When I refer to the 'predi-cate-modifier' view of adverbs I mean to exclude the approach taken in [12].

I will, in a moment, explain why I think it desirable to see how far one can go with the predicate modifier view of adverbs, but granted that one does there is an obvious question which must be faced. It is this. Whether or not we want to treat adverbs as predicate modifiers or as event predicates

there are certainly event words in our language and event phrases which receive adjectival modification in a way which has an intimate connection with
the predicates which receive adverbial modification. Thus we have

> (1) John walks quickly to the station.

related to

> (2) John takes a quick walk to the station.

(1) and (2) may not be quite synonymous but the adverb *quickly* seems closely
related to the adjective *quick* and the prepositional phrase *to the station*
does not seem equivocal. Between (1) and (2) there is

> (3) John's quickly walking to the station demonstrated his willingness
>   to aid the travellers.

In this case it is the complex verb-phrase *walk quickly to the station* which
has been nominalized.

But it is in (2) that we have the strongest claim for an analysis in terms
of events. For if the phrase *a quick walk to the station* does not denote an
event it is unclear what does. Further the adjectival form *quick* suggests
that it and the prepositional phrase are adjectival modifiers of the common
noun *walk*. If we were to adopt an event analysis of (1) on the model say of
[12] then the semantic relationship is quite clear. So in order to defend the
predicate modifier analysis of adverbials we will have to show how to give
an analysis of (2) which makes clear its links with (1). One way is to say
that (2) is simply a transformationally obtained variant of (1).[2] But the
way I prefer to go is to give a semantic analysis of both sentences which
makes clear the relationship between them. But first perhaps I should say a
little about why I prefer not to follow DAVIDSON at this point.

2. Should Events be Basic Entities?

The title of this section is intended to convey the suggestion that although
I don't really have any strong argument against the taking of events as basic
in the analysis of adverbials, yet I do have one or two qualms. These may
reflect no more than my prejudices, and it may well turn out that my mistrust
of the use of events as primitives in formal semantics is quite unjustified,
but I feel bound to say why I prefer to see how far we can get without them.[3]

The possible-worlds framework I am using is quite an elaborate one. As well
as the possible worlds we have a domain of individuals in each world (possibly
over-lapping but not necessarily) and further a system of temporal co-ordinates
in the form of time intervals (Spatial co-ordinates are probably needed too
but we have been able to get a surprising way without them.). All these entities may seem far more suspicious than events. Nevertheless despite this there
are, it seems to me, problems about the nature of events which do not arise
with worlds or times. The basic problem is the question of whether events stand
in certain logical relations. If we consider an event, say the arrival of the
train, then there are certain phrases which seem to denote things which are
logically incompatible with the arrival of the train e.g. the non-arrival of
the train. Now it may be that the non-arrival of the train is not an event;
indeed those who, like DAVIDSON, want to maintain that events are exactly on
a par with individuals would almost certainly say that the non-arrival of the
train is not an event. But even so there seems nothing at all comparable in

the case of individuals. And even if the phrase *the non-arrival of the train* does not denote an event, it must still denote something as in

(1) The non-arrival of the train surprised us.

Some linguists and philosophers[4] have divided the things referred to by phrases of the above kind into events processes and states. It may be that the non-arrival of the train is something like a state but these two phrases

(2) The arrival of the train

and

(3) The non-arrival of the train,

whatever they may denote exactly, seem to denote two incompatible things. Now on the possible-worlds framework that I am assuming we can explain this, at least to some extent; for we can say that (2) is, in some way, associated with the proposition that the train arrived, and this is understood as the set of worlds in which the train arrived, while (3) is associated with the proposition that the train did not arrive, and this is understood as the set of worlds in which the train did not arrive. The incompatibility is explained because there is no overlap between these two sets of worlds.

The moral of this is simply to point out that if we have adopted a possible-worlds framework we should look for an analysis within the framework.

In fact the semantics used in [13] and [15] treats the meaning of a sentence as a set of pairs (w,t) in which w is a possible world and t a time interval. The importance of the fact that t is an interval rather than a single moment will hopefully become clear as we proceed, but it is worth noting that the most valuable semantic analysis of the distinction between activities processes and states is one which has treated verbs as predicates true of things with respect to intervals of time. This analysis is given by BARRY TAYLOR in [34] and in my option his analysis not only appears to achieve the intuitively correct classification but also seems to explain *why* the members of each class have the properties they do.

3. Nominalizations

In the last section it was noted that nominalizations cover a much wider range than events. One very crucial problem is the problem of negation. For it seemed that if events are to be thought of as like individuals then it ought not to be possible to negate them the way one can negate predicates or propositions. Yet of course, we can say things like

(1) The non-arrival of the train caused consternation.

The point about a sentence like (1) is that although we *can* specify a time for the non-arrival we need not do so. Indeed it is not clear that there is *any* event which counts as the train's non-arrival. Other cases are like this too. A phrase like

(2) The alleged murder

may well be used when there is no event at all we can point to and say, that is the alleged murder. (I owe this point to a discussion with EMMON BACH and BARBARA PARTEE. I don't know which of us was responsible for it.) Actually, as ISMAY BARWELL has pointed out to me, and contrary to what I had thought, this sort of situation is possible even when the phrase refers to an individual.

(3) The alleged murderer

seems able to be used even though there is no particular person who is being alleged to be a murderer.

In an initial attempt to get to grips with (1) I will suggest (4) as a paraphrase.

(4) The fact that the train did not arrive caused consternation.

I think it is uncontroversial that at least some uses of (1) are the same as (4). There is a halfway house between (1) and (4).

(5) The train's not arriving caused consternation.[5]

(4) seems clearly to be a case of apposition, one nominal being *the fact* and the other nominal being a *that* clause. I shall assume as in [11], p. 166 that a *that* clause is the name of the proposition expressed by the sentence which follows the *that*. In (5) also we have a nominalization which seems to be made up from an embedded sentence. Not only does the presence of *not*, as opposed to the *non* in (1), indicates this but also the fact that as in (6) the phrase can be modified by the adverb *quickly* rather than the adjective *quick*.

(6) The train's not arriving quickly caused consternation.[6]

(6) seems pretty clearly to be dealt with as in some way analogous to (4). There seems no way in which *quick* can modify *non-arrival* in (1).

(7) The quick non-arrival of the train.
does not seem to make much sense at all.

(8) The non quick arrival of the train caused consternation.

perhaps seems a little better, and I suppose that if it does have a meaning it is the same as (6).

I shall not attempt in this paper to give a formal analysis of the kind of nominalization involved in (1). It is perhaps not as straight-forward as the impression given in [11], pp. 205-208, would suggest but I think that cases like this where a nominalizing symbol operates on a complex verb phrase or sentence can all be treated as similar if not semantically identical with *that* clauses.

Those nominalizations which work like *that* clauses have a close connection with what MONTAGUE calls generic events [29], p. 150. MONTAGUE defines a generic event as a property of moments of time. In his semantics this means that it is a function from times to sets of possible worlds. It is not difficult to see that this is set-theoretically equivalent to sets of world-time pairs.[7] As we mentioned at the end of section 2 these are precisely the kind of entities we wanted to be the value of sentences, so that *that* clauses have a semantics which makes them equivalent to MONTAGUE's generic events. MONTAGUE even allows the time to be an interval, at least in the case of what he calls protracted generic events, though he says that he will not consider intervals in his discussion, [29], p. 150. Since moments are a limiting case of intervals I will speak as if MONTAGUE had himself used intervals instead of moments. For myself I prefer not to think of generic events as events at all. For generic events are involved in sentences like (1) and (6) and in both cases we can it seems give the nominalization a semantics equivalent to a *that* clause.[8] It is of course a perfectly good set of world time pairs.

But of course we often want to talk about particular events. This is because events are countable and subject to criteria of sameness and difference.

We can say things like

    (9) Scott took two walks yesterday.

or

    (10) The bird was seen on the same walk as the elephant.

It may be that these sentences have paraphrases in which the noun *walk* does not occur but it is at least clear that *walk* is a predicate true of particular walks and not a predicate of the generic event of walking. The key ontological question here involves the criteria for when one walk counts as the same walk as another.[9] It is worth noting that if the DAVIDSON analysis of adverbials is used it must be particular events which are involved since one event of walking might be to the station and another one might not be.

MONTAGUE's analysis of generic events treated them as properties of times. We have seen that this makes them equivalent to the values of sentences in a semantics based on world-time pairs. But events have often had a spatial location and there may well be two events whose occurrence at any given time is logically equivalent but whose spatial location is different. KIM[10] instances the death of Socrates and the widowing of Xanthippe. Now since it is presumably not true in all worlds that Socrates is the husband of Xanthippe it is not certain that these are logically equivalent, but what is certain is that in all such worlds the one event happens at exactly the same time as the other. But as KIM observes the place where the one occurs is quite different from the place where the other occurs.

One way of dealing with spatial reference is to add a spatial index, but the other way is to use not sentences but predicates, for then the argument of the predicate can supply the spatial position. And this view of course dovetails well with the analysis of adverbs and prepositions offered in [13] and [15].

But we are still not quite at the analysis of particular events. MONTAGUE's discussion of particular events [29], p. 176, makes use of a primitive which he refuses to analyse. A particular walk will be a property of those times which are times of walking and in addition satisfy some other property, roughly being all times at which the very same event of walking occurs. One might consider an analysis by which a particular walk is the property of being a walk at t, but this would not allow us to say that the same walk could (in other worlds) occur at other times. If we want to say things like this, and I believe we do, then an analysis of events like KIM's (An event for KIM is a triple consisting of an individual, a property and a time[11])) is wrong in tying, as he appears to be doing, the time of the event to its essential nature.

In a semantics based on world-time pairs a particular walk would turn out to be a function from an individual a to a set of world time pairs (w,t) such that each t is an instance of a's walking in w and further that *they are all instances of the same walk*. The generic walk of course is the function which includes in its range for a all the (w,t) pairs which are instances of a's walking. The particular walk then is just a more specific function of the same kind as the generic walk. It is so also on MONTAGUE's account and we shall follow him in not giving a definition of particularity for walks.

We can also note that a walk in these semantics determines what was called a *basic individual* in [11], p. 94f., *viz* a function ρ such that for any world w, $\rho(w)$ is a set of space time points, thought of as the points occupied by ρ in w and described as the *manifestation* of ρ in w.[12] By extension $\rho((w,t))$ will be the spatial positions occupied by ρ in world w throughout the interval t.

4. Prepositional Phrases

In this section and the next I want to try to shew that the phrase *to the station* in

(1) *John's walk to the station*

has the same meaning that it has in

(2) *John walks to the station*

and I want to do this without reducing either one of these sentences to the other. In particular I want to treat prepositional phrases as one-place predicate modifiers in category $((0,1), (0,1))$ in a λ-categorial language with a semantics based on a domain D_1 of individuals, and a domain D_0 of sets of world-time pairs, where the first member is a possible world and the second a time interval. (Other context-dependence will be taken care of by BIGELOW quotation.)[13] One of the main tasks of [13] and [15] was to shew that a surprising amount of spatio-temporal material could be packed into a one-place predicate, for its meaning is a function from individuals to sets of world-time pairs; and when the time is an interval that means that we can make reference to the spatio-temporal path of the individual thought the interval in the world in question.

The semantics offered for certain adverbs and prepositions in [13] and [15] is crude. Many people have pointed out to me all sorts of inadequacies in it, and some, e.g. ARNIM VON STECHOW in [38], have proposed refinements. However it does give us something to work on and what I want to do is to shew how the semantics of these words, with all its crudity, can be taken over and applied to the semantics of event words.

We are now ready to discuss the formalization of (1) and (2). I will assume that (2) is represented in a λ-categorial language as

(3) $((\lambda, x, (John, (walks, (to, x)))), (the, station))$

where *John* is in category 1, *walks* in category $(0,1)$, *to* in category $(((0,1), (0,1)), 1)$ and *the station* in category $(0,(0,1))$. I shall say something in the next section about each of these expressions. All that is necessary here is to observe that when x is a variable in category 1 then the formation rules for λ-categorial languages described in section 10 will ensure that (3) is an expression in the category 0 of sentence.

(to,x) is therefore in category $((0,1), (0,1))$. We want to see how this applies to (1). In (1) *walk* is a common noun and therefore also in category $(0,1)$, so at least the syntactic category is right for the modification and

(4) $(walk, (to,x))$

will also be in category $(0,1)$. However we must now be very careful because of the problem noted in [13], section 7, the *walk* in (4) is represented by the predicate 'x is a walk', while the verb is 'x walks', and the problem is that the x which is the walk is clearly not the same as the x which walks. Now the semantics of *x walks to the station* requires that the x which is doing the walking be at the station at the end of the interval. If this phrase is unequivocal in the event expression *walk to the station* then it must mean that the walk, at the end of the interval is at the station. In other words, to maintain the analysis of prepositions offered in [15], we have to maintain that in all such nominalizations the spatio-temporal location of the event over the interval is the same as the spatio-temporal location of the actor. But, as remarked above, this is precisely the assumption that is being made by the limitations under which we are presently working.

This fact will also enable us to do something about the possessive morpheme *s* which appears when *walk* becomes *John's walk*. This morpheme was discussed briefly in [11], p. 206f., though hardly with a great deal of insight. In particular there was no hint of what kind of formal analysis could be given of the notation of an action performed by someone.

The first point to notice about the possessive morpheme is the difficulty of tying it down to anything definite. It has often been observed that *John's painting* can mean either the painting that John painted or the painting that John owns or the painting in which John is portrayed [37], p. 130. The moral of this is that it seems pointless at the moment to try to give any kind of precise semantics for *s*. And of course we are going to turn this fact to our advantage in saying what *s* means in the limited cases we are dealing with; as before in the hope that this may set us on the road to a more wide-ranging analysis. What we recall is that for the purposes of the adverbials we are now concerned with, the spatio-temporal position of John's walk at any interval may be identified with the spatio-temporal position of John throughout that interval.

5. Formal Semantics for Event Words

We shall now go through in detail the formalization of two sentences to show how the semantics works. The first is

(1) John's walk to the station occurs.[14)]

This has the λ-deep structure

(2) $(((John, s), (\lambda,x, ((\lambda,y, ((walk, (to, y)), x)),$

$(the, station)))), occurs)$

In this sentence we treat *John* in category 1 and *walk*, *station* and *occur* in category $(0,1)$, $(the\ station)$ is a nominal in category $(0,(0,1))$, while *s* is in category $((0,(0,1)), 1)$ and also makes a nominal, out of *John*. (2) is in category 0. By treating *John* as in category 1 we can achieve a slight economy (even though it is probably a nominal).[15] The semantics of *occurs* resembles that of *occ* in [12], p. 471, except that we shall try to give an analysis of the occurrence of an event in a world and a time interval. We shall make things explicit by giving semantics for (the noun) *walk* and the verb *occurs*.

What is the semantics for the noun *walk*? In particular how does its semantics link with the verb *walk*? In the manner of [13] the case of the verb would go like this,

$V(walk_V)$ is the function ω in $D_{(0,1)}$ such that a is in the domain of ω

iff a is a physical object, and for any such a and any $(w,t) \in W$,

$(w,t) \in \omega(a)$ iff t in w is an interval at which a walks.

(This last being intuitively understood.)

$walk_N$, the common noun, is related to $walk_V$, although as we shall see a precise connection cannot be stated. As MONTAGUE observes [29], p. 176, it is perhaps not possible for our language to express precisely just what any particular walk is. We shall therefore state $V(walk_N)$ in a such way that $V(walk_V)$ constrains its value but does not determine it.

We have supposed that a walk a is a thing (in D_1) which has a manifestation at every world time pair (w,t). We shall denote this manifestation by $a((w,t))$.

$V(walk_N)$ is a function ω in $D_{(0,1)}$ such that $a \in D_1$ is in the domain of ω iff for every $(w,t) \in W$, $a((w,t))$ is a section of the manifestation of an individual in the domain of $V(walk_V)$ and, for any $(w,t) \in W$ and a in the domain of ω, $(w,t) \in \omega(a)$ iff there is some b such that $a((w,t)) = b((w,t))$ and b walks at t in w.

We can see now that there is a semantic connection between $walk_N$ and $walk_V$ though we have not chosen to indicate this in the syntax. No doubt, many verbs have nouns which correspond to them in this way but I believe the matter at the moment is best treated lexically. It is better to treat it lexically because although $V(walk_N)$ is constrained by $V(walk_V)$, it does not seem to be determined by it. In particular there is no requirement that the entity a which is a walk by John in (w,t) be a walk by John in any other world. It may be that our notion of a particular walk does entail that being a walk is an essential property of it and if so then of course $V(walk_N)$ will reflect this. But nothing said so far demands either that this is so or that it is not.

If the connection between $walk_N$ and $walk_V$ is lexical and if, in general, the identity criteria for the noun are not predictable from the semantics of the verb then it would look as if the nominalizations discussed in section 3 and in [11], pp. 205-208, in which a complex predicate appears to be nominalized will always involve generic events and never particular ones. I believe that this is so, but it needs further evidence.

$V(occurs)$ is the function ω in $D_{(0,1)}$ such that a is in the domain of ω iff a is an event, and for any such a and any $(w,t) \in W$: $(w,t) \in \omega(a)$ iff $a((w,t)) \neq \emptyset$ (or, if we don't actually *identify* a in a world w with a set of space-time points, if the region occupied by a at (w,t) is not empty.)

$V(to)$ is as in section 4 of [13], viz:

$V(to)$ is the function ζ of category $(((0,1), (0,1)), 1)$

such that where $a \in D_1$, and $\omega \in D_{(0,1)}$, and $(\omega,t) \in W$ and $b \in D_1$:

$(\omega,t) \in ((\zeta(a))(\omega))(b)$ iff $(\omega,t) \in \omega(b)$ and t has a last moment m and there is a spatial point which is part of both the region occupied by a at m and the region occupied by b at m.

The idea of course is that something is proceeding to something else over a given interval if the position reached at the end of the interval overlaps with where that other thing is at the end of the interval. (But note the remarks made about V(*from*) in [15], section 2.)

The nominal phrase (*the*, *station*) makes use of BIGELOW quotation and in some appropriate manner refers to the particular station involved. V(*John*) of course is John and our last symbol is the possessive morpheme s. In view of what we said at the end of the last section we can give it the semantics:

V(s) is the function ζ in $D_{(((0,(0,1)), (0,1)), 1)}$ such that a in D_1 is in the domain of ζ only if a is a physical object and ω_1 and ω_2 are functions in $D_{(0,1)}$ whose domains are events or objects and for any such a, ω_1 and ω_2 and any $(\omega,t) \in W$

$(\omega,t) \in ((\zeta(a))(\omega_1))(\omega_2)$ iff

(i)　　there is exactly one b such that $(\omega,t) \in \omega_1(b)$ and b's spatio-temporal location in ω over t coincides with a's, and

(ii)　　for this b, $(\omega,t) \in \omega_2(b)$

For this semantics to work it is necessary to assume that for any particular time interval in any world there is exactly one walk by John with respect to that interval.

We are at last in a position to work out the semantics of (2).

(3) $(((John, s), (\lambda,x,((\lambda,y,((walk_N,(to,y)), x)),$
$\qquad (the, station)))), occurs)$

Let us work through this bit by bit.

(4) $V_\nu(((walk, (to,y)), x))$
$\quad = (V_\nu((to,y)) \ V(walk))(\nu(x))$
$\quad = ((V(to)(\nu(y)) \ V(walk))(\nu(x))$

Let V(*to*) be ζ, V(*walk*) be ω, $\nu(x)$ be a and $\nu(y)$ be b. Then

$(\omega,t) \in V_\nu(((walk, (to,y)), x))$ iff
$(\omega,t) \in ((\zeta(b))(\omega))(a)$

iff $(\omega,t) \in \omega(a)$ and t has a last moment m and there is a spatial point which is part of both the region occupied by a at m and the region occupied by b at m.

And of course $(\omega,t) \in \omega(a)$ iff there is some c such that c walks at (ω,t) and $a((\omega,t)) = c((\omega,t))$.

What it means is that a is a walk to b at (w,t) iff at the last moment of t, a's position overlaps with b's and there is a c whose manifestation at (w,t) is identical with a's and c walks at (w,t).

Put less formally, a is a walk to b at (w,t) iff there is some c whose walk a is and the final position of the walk a overlaps with the position of b.

We then abstract and put on the nominal *the station* and abstract again to get a phrase which means that a is a walk to the station:

(5) $((\lambda,y,((walk, (to,y)), x)), (the\ station))$

By a further abstraction we get the property of being a walk to the station:

(6) $(\lambda,x,((\lambda,y,((walk_N, (to,y)), x)), (the\ station))$

Let us suppose that the semantic value of this one-place predicate expression is ω_1 (i.e. ω_1 is the property of being a walk to the station.) And let us suppose that ω_2 is the property of occurring, as just discussed. Assuming that $V(John) =$ John we know by $V(s)$ that

(4) $(w,t) \in (V((John,\ s)(\omega_1))(\omega_2)$

iff (i) there is exactly one a such that $(w,t) \in \omega_1(b)$ and a's spatio-temporal location in w over t coincides with John's, and (ii) for this a, $(w,t) \in \omega_2(a)$.

We now recall that ω_1 is the property of being a walk to the station and ω_2 is the property of occurring.

So (4) holds iff a is a walk to the station at t in w, and a is identical with John at (w,t) and a occurs at (w,t).

Is the (2) of this section equivalent to the (2) of section 4? The question is almost straightforward but not quite, and the reasons, I think, are interesting. Suppose first that John walks to the station at (w,t) It would initially seem that there will certainly be an a such that $a((w,t)) =$ John $((w,t))$. There is indeed such a set theoretical entity; what is less clear is whether it should count as the kind of entity in the domain of $V(walk_N)$ *viz* an event. We know that John's walk at (w,t) is required to be unique, and what this requirement amounts to is that there be at most one entity which satisfies $V(walk_N)$ at (w,t) and coincides with John at (w,t). This implies a restriction of some kind on the domain of $V(walk_N)$ but does not say exactly what kind of restriction.

This is why the situation is only nearly straightforward. But I think we need not be troubled because it seems plausible to suppose that if John does walk at (w,t) then there is at least one entity in the domain of $V(walk_N)$ which coincides with John at that index.

What about the implication in the other direction? Suppose that John's walk occurs at (w,t) and is a walk to the station. Certainly then someone walks to the station at (w,t), further it is someone whose (w,t) manifestation is identical with John's (w,t) manifestation. To shew that it is John of course we need to assume that if John's manifestation at (w,t) is identical with someone who is walking to the station at (w,t) then John is walking to the station at (w,t). This assumption is entailed by the stronger assumption that no two distinct persons can occupy the same place at the same time. The stronger assumption has some plausibility but can cause problems as some recent discussions ([32] and [28]) of the logical possibility of a person dividing indicate. However the strong assumption is not needed. All we need to assume is that if two people have an identical manifestation then the first walks iff the second walks.

Again I think these formal results point to some of the problems that any useful theory of events and individuals must satisfy. It is perhaps worth remarking that the problems are parallel in both directions but in one direction the problem concerns the nature of events and in the other direction it concerns the nature of objects. But assuming suitable contraints in both directions we see that the two sentences are equivalent.

6. Event Nominalizations and Scope

We have seen that under suitable constraints the (2) of section 4 and the (2) of section 5 turn out to be equivalent. The fact that constraints are needed is actually important for its shews that these sentences are by no means semantically indifferent variants. It will be the first task of this section to see how $walk_V$ and $walk_N$ differ; in particular we shall look at the differences which arise because *John's walk* is a phrase of the kind called in [11], p. 130, a nominal. These are phrases in category $(0,(0,1))$ and because of that they can be involved in scope distinctions of the kind considered in [11], pp. 147-150. I wand to consider the sentence

(1) John's walk will amuse Arabella.

I want for the moment to pretend that the *will* here denotes a simple future tense and is a sentential operator in category $(0,0)$ with the semantics:

$V(will)$ is the function ω in $D_{(0,0)}$ such that for any $a \in D_0$, and any $(w,t) \in W$: $(w,t) \in \omega(a)$ iff $(w,t') \in a$ for some t' all of whose members are later than all of t s.

I am aware that tense is a much more complicated matter than this makes out[16] but the extra complexity does not matter here. I shall also assume that *amuse* is a two-place predicate whose meaning relates an event and a person where it need not be the case that the event is still occurring at the time it is doing the amusing.

I claim that (1) displays a scope ambiguity and that it can be represented by either of the following two λ-formulae:

(2) $(will,(((John,s),\ walk_N),\ (\lambda,x,(amuse,x\ Arabella))))$

and

(3) $(((John,s),\ walk_N),\ (\lambda,x,(will,\ (amuse,x\ Arabella))))$

(2) means that at some future interval the walk that John takes at that interval will amuse Arabella at that interval. (3) means that the thing which is John's walk at the present interval will amuse Arabella at some future interval.

Facts like these do not shew any important ontological difference between events and propositions. Of course I want to insist that there is an ontological difference between events and propositions, but I want to claim that the ambiguity in (1) is merely the result of picking something out by means of a nominal. It seems to me in fact that the same kind of scope difference can arise with *that* clauses in a sentence like

(4) That John runs will amuse Arabella

although it must be admitted that the requirement of tense in the subordinate clause makes the matter problematic.

It has been noted that definite descriptions in event nominalizations are referentially transparent. I shall now shew how this comes about when events are referred to by nominals.

In [12], p. 468, following DAVIDSON, it was noted that although the death of Scott is the same event as the death of the author of Waverley, yet the proposition that Scott died might not have been the proposition that the author of Waverley died, since Scott might not have written Waverley. I shall here go through the sentence

(5) Scott's death is the author of Waverley's death.

The semantics for *death* is analogous to that for $walk_N$, and in this case there is a phonetic variation between the noun and the verb. We shall treat *The author of Waverley* as a single unit with the semantic value ζ where:

$(w,t) \in \zeta(w)$ iff there is one and only one person a who writes Waverley in w and a completes Waverley before the end of t in w, and $(w,t) \in w(a)$.

(The temporal condition reflects the view that the author of Waverley only becomes the author of Waverley when the novel is completed.)

The *is* is as in [11], p. 182, the *is* of identity and has the semantics:

$V(is)$ is the function w in $D_{(0,1,1)}$ such that for any appropriate[17] a and b in D_1 and $(w,t) \in W$, $(w,t) \in w(a,b)$ iff $a = b$.

Scott will be presumed to be in category 1 and to denote Scott. We can now formulate the two nominals

(6) $((Scott, s), death)$

and

(7) $(\lambda, x_{(0,1)}, (the\ author\ of\ Waverley, (\lambda, x_1, (((x_1 s),$
$death), x_{(0,1)}))))$

These expressions are not semantically equivalent but in any world (and time) in which Scott is the author of Waverley we can see that the following sentence will be true.

(8) $(((Scott,s)death),(\lambda,x_1,((\lambda,y_1,(is,x_1,y_1)),$
$(\lambda,x_{(0,1)},$ (the author of Waverley, $(\lambda,x_1,(((x_1,s),$
$death),x_{(0,1)}))))))))$

(6) is a nominal true at (w,t) of any property ω if $(w,t) \in \omega(a)$ where a is the unique entity which is a death at (,) and is spatio-temporally identical with Scott's manifestation at (w,t).

(7) is true at (w,t) of any property ω such that $(w,t) \in \omega(a)$ when a is the unique entity which is a death at (w,t) and is identical with the manifestation of the author of Waverley at (w,t). But we are assuming that in (w,t) Scott is the author of Waverley so clearly they have the same spatio-temporal manifestation.

And since the semantics of   requires an unique death which spatio-temporally coincides with the individual in question at (w,t), then we have the identity which is expressed by (8).

It is easy to see that the proposition that Scott dies, i.e. the set of worlds in which Scott dies, is not the same as the proposition that the author of Waverley dies because there are worlds in which Scott is not the author of Waverley. Though even here one might be able to use the fact that *the author of* Waverley is a nominal to make a sentence which would mean something like

(9) Concerning the author of Waverley the proposition that he died is the same as the proposition that Scott died.

I do not think there is much call for sentences like (9) in which the wide scope of the nominal is involved, but they can certainly occur in the λ-categorial base language. This again means that there is no ontological importance to the scope phenomena.

There is another problem about event identity which this analysis will clear up. BEARDSLEY [3], p. 265, has argued that

(10) The fire burnt

and

(11) The fire burnt yellowishly

denote the same event. Using examples closer to [15] we can see that

(12) Scott's death

and

(13) Scott's death in the garden

will denote the same event provided Scott died in the garden, and will not denote any event at all if Scott did not die in the garden. To see how the argument would go it is sufficient to see why in example (2) of section 5, John's walk at (w,t) is the same event as John's walk to the station at (,). In the next section we shall look at some rather more controversial cases of event identity.

7. The Spatial Modification of Causative Verbs

The semantics of adverbials in [13] and [15] made the meaning of a one place predicate a function from individuals to sets of (w,t) pairs where w is a possible world and t a time interval. Spatial reference was obtained via the position of the argument of the predicate throughout the interval t in world w.

But there are some cases of transitive verbs in which it is the object of the verb whose spatial position is relevant. Consider

(1) John sent a parcel across the park.

In this sentence the path which is across the park is not the path traced out by John but rather the path traced out by the parcel. John is the agent which initiates a process of sending in which the thing most directly involved is the parcel. In

(2) John opened the door five centimetres.

it is not John but the door which moves five centimetres; and here there seems to be a more basic sense of *open* in

(3) The door opened five centimetres.

I shall not deal with (1) by case grammar though it may be that the kind of moves which suggest themselves can be regarded as steps towards a truth-conditional formalization of case grammar.

Although in (1) the preposition applies to the parcel it seems clear that it means pretty much the same as it does in applying to John in

(4) John walks across the park.

So that even if the analysis of prepositions in [15] needs refinement it is not any extra refinement that is involved here. Indeed *send a parcel* seems capable of pretty well the whole range of modification considered in [15].

(5) John sent a parcel five miles across a park and through a tunnel and around a tree to behind a bush.

sent is a transitive verb and will therefore be represented in a λ-categorial language by a two-place predicate in category $(0,0,1)$. This means that $(send, x,y)$ will be in category 0, and this in turn means that abstracting on the y we can make the one-place predicate.

(6) $(\lambda,y,(send,\ x,\ y))$

My suggestion then is that in case like (1) the prepositional phrase modifies (6). This means that we don't have to suppose that its meaning is any different here from that in the verbs of motion case. So (1) would become

(7) $((\lambda,z,(a\ parcel,\ ((\lambda,y,\ (John,\ sends\ y)),\ (across,\ z)))),$
$\quad (a,\ park))$

sends has the following semantics:

V(*send*) is the function ω in $D_{(0,1,1)}$ such that a and b are in the domain of ω if they are physical objects and for any (w,t) $\in$ W: $(w,t) \in \omega(a,b)$ iff a sends b somewhere over the interval t in world w, where t is the whole interval of b's journey.

It has been the policy of [13] and [15] not to attempt an account of what it is to do something like send something somewhere, but in view of the later discussion about the time of a sending, something more needs to be said. For one of the problems about a sending is that it seems very reasonable to say that John sent a parcel to Konstanz on Monday even though it never arrived until Tuesday. If we are to apply the semantics of *to Konstanz* which follow from V(*to*) or the semantics for *across a park* given in section 1 of [15], then (7) could only be true of an interval in which the parcel actually went across the park. This means that the sense of *send* involved in the formalism is the sense in which a sending is true only of the whole interval of the journey. (Though of course a sub-interval of a sending may still be a sending.)

How then are we to capture the idea that the sending is over as soon as John has done his bit?

One suggestion which is often made involves lexical decomposition. A common example is the decomposition of *kill* into *cause to die*, or if we are purists, *cause to become not alive*. (I have not seen any advocates of further decomposition of *alive* though presumably even this could be argued for.) Many authors, both linguists and philosophers, have pointed out that A can cause B's death without killing him. (And A can certainly cause a parcel to be sent across a park without sending it himself.) At least one, [21], has argued that the notion of cause is such that we cannot speak of an event as being *the* (unique) cause of anything without a lot of context built in. All seem to be agreed that the connection in *kill* is more direct than in the phrase *cause to die*.

I want to make use of a decomposition which is like the *cause to die*-variety but which is not, I hope, open to the same objections. Part of the reason why it escapes the objections is that I am not concerned with expressing *send* (or *kill*) in terms of what might be considered as semantically more primitive notions. Indeed I have often spoken out against the view that there is much to be gained from componential semantics. (Most recently in [15], section 1.) The reason for the decomposition is solely so that a temporal modifier can apply only to the causing or initiating of the sending. I will label the required morpheme *cause* but I will trust its semantics to show how it differs from the word *cause*. Cause is in category $((0,1),(0,1))$. We can then formalize (1) as

(8) $(John, (cause, (\lambda,x, ((\lambda,z, ((a, parcel), ((\lambda,y, (sends,x,y))$

$(across, z)))), (a, park))))$

The idea is that 'cause to send' is to be true of that initial bit of the interval which involves the agent of the sending. It is basically the idea that at a certain point there is nothing further which needs doing [36], pp. 115, 121.

V(cause) is the function $\zeta \in D_{((0,1),(0,1))}$ such that (w,t) $\in (\zeta(\omega))(a)$ iff there is an event e such that $e(w,t)$ coincides with $a(w,t)$, and an interval t' of which t is an initial segment, and $(w,t') \in \omega(a)$, and in the nearest world w' to w in which $(w',t') \notin \omega(a)$, $e((w',t')) = \emptyset$.

What this is intended to mean is that there is an event e which is an action of a's in an initial segment (w,t) of (w,t') (remember the semantics of s) and e is sufficient (other things being equal) to ensure that a satisfies ω at (w,t'). In the present case then it is true that a causes b to be sent to c at (w,t) iff there is an event e which is an action of a's at (w,t) and which is sufficient to ensure that a sends a parcel across a park (in the original sense in which that was only true of the longer interval of the parcel's going across the park) at (w,t') where t' is a longer interval of which t is an initial segment.

The notion of cause involved is intended to be reminiscent of DAVID LEWIS' [27]. His notion is defined for propositions (understood as those which record the occurrence of events) in such a way that p is said to be a cause of q iff q is true and if it had not been true then p would not have been true. This latter is explicated by saying that in the nearest world in which q is not true then p would not have been true. The version adopted here then is that the parcel was sent and e was an initial part of its being sent (the part connected with the sender) and if the parcel had not been sent then that event would not have occurred. In other words that event was sufficient for the sending.[18]

I am not absolutely confident that this formulation will turn out to be exactly right, but two observations are in order. First that an analysis of causation is beyond the scope of this paper, and second that the account here given does insist on the intimate connection between the causing and the sending, in that the causing is required to be an initial segment of the sending.

The whole sentence (8), unlike (7), will be true at any (w,t) which is a causing of the parcel to be sent across the park. It ought to be clear that the time of the causing need not include the whole interval during which the parcel travels across the park and therefore that if the whole sentence (8) is within the scope of a temporal modifier like *on Tuesday* the resulting sentence can be true even if the parcel did not get across the park until Wednesday.

There is another possible refinement. Suppose that John sends a letter to Konstanz but it never arrives. Can this be so? I am not absolutely sure but I am inclined to think that it can. If so then we would have to amend the semantics of 'cause' somewhat in the manner of DOWTY's analysis of the progressive in [17] so that it claims merely that there is some, reasonable of expectation, possible future caused by John's action in which there does occur a sending to Konstanz.

This raises the possibility of an interpretation with a non-specific reading. E.G. we might have

(9) John sent a parcel to a friend.

If it were required that the parcel get to its destination then of course there would have to be some particular friend to whom the parcel had been sent. However under the intensional interpretation of 'cause' it might be possible that John set in the train the sending of a parcel to different friends in different equally reasonable possible futures. I am not entirely confident about this sense of 'cause' but I think that the possibility is worth scrutiny.

8. The Time of a Killing

The title of this section is that of a paper by JUDITH JARVIS THOMSON [19)
in which questions are raised about the temporal properties of events.

In the example we discussed in the last section the modifiers of *send* are
spatial while the modifiers of 'cause' are temporal. Does this suggest that
there is a split between modifiers in sentences of this kind? First, even if
it is true of *send*, it does not seem to be true of *kill*. THOMSON's problem
was precisely that she did not know whether x' kills y' is to be true of the
whole interval, beginning with x's finger moving on the trigger and ending
with y's death. If the analysis given above of *send* were applied to *kill* then
we should expect at least the possibility of an ambiguity. It seems to me
that there may be an ambiguity. THOMSON asks us to imagine that a group of
students have set a bomb in the library but that it has not yet blown up.
The case is a bit loaded because we have to suppose that (a) the action which
causes the blowing up is sufficient to cause the explosion but (b) we know
this, although the building has not yet blown up. Part of the trouble is that
a situation in which (b) obtains is one in which it seems that steps might
yet be taken to prevent the explosion. I don't know exactly what difference
this makes but it seems the sort of fact which cannot really be ignored.

THOMSON's example involves someone walking past the library and telling
a friend about the student's activities. In that case it seems clear that it
would make sense to make the relevant interval the long one which does not
end until the explosion; but in other cases it seems possible that it only
applies to the action. One could imagine the students returning to the party
leader and being asked "Well, have you blown it up yet?" and their answering
(truthfully) "Yes".

There is a point worth noting in the blowing up example. For we can say

(1) The library blew up.

This is like FILLMORE's example with *open* [18, 27]. The semantically basic
predicate would be x *opens* y, but, as in the *send* case it would be interpreted
as true at an interval which was the whole opening of the door, not just x's
causing of it. (In the case of an action of opening a door the difference between the two is much slighter than in sending a parcel. Usually the door does
not go on opening for significantly long after the causing.) The thing about
open is that the agent argument can be suppressed. (Maybe because a door can
open without anybody opening it.)

But to get back to *send*; is it really true that the spatial modifiers all
modify the *send* and the temporal ones the Cause? Part of the explanation is
semantic, when a parcel is sent to Konstanz it is the parcel which makes the
journey, not the sender. It is therefore much easier and more natural that
the kind of modification represented by *to Konstanz* should apply to it rather
than to the sender. But other locatives seem to go with the sender.

(2) In Albuquerque, John sent a parcel to Konstanz

The real test case of course would be an adverbial which can apply to
either morpheme and which produces an ambiguity, or better where two contradictory morphemes combine consistently because each applies to a different
morpheme.

Examples are hard to come by but there are some which seem to me sufficiently good to suggest we are on the right lines:

(3) He sent the letter to Konstanz in the train.

I think that this can mean either that he was in the train and while in the train he sent the letter to Konstanz (there was a postbox, say, on the train) or that it was the letter that went in the train to Konstanz. The problem with this kind of example is that it is possible to argue that a different sense of *in* is involved. I don't believe that it is but it is very hard to prove that. I think that one can also get:

(4) He sent the letter to Konstanz in the train in the train.

It's easy to see why (4) is unnatural, but all that is necessary is to see that it is possible. Part of the problem is that the Cause does not really involve the idea of much movement.

If (3) and (4) are acceptable then it suggests that spatial modification can operate on the Cause. Is it possible that temporal modifiers should operate on *send*? Again the examples I have are less clear than I would like. I think one can say

(5) He sent the parcel to Konstanz by Tuesday.

meaning either that the parcel arrived by Tuesday, or merely that he had completed the sending by Tuesday. Thus

(6) He had sent the parcel to Konstanz by Tuesday
    but it didn't arrive until Wednesday.

But I'm not sure that one can have

(7) He had sent the parcel to Konstanz by Wednesday by Tuesday.

Perhaps (8) is better:

(8) At two o'clock that day he poisoned the inhabitants
    six months later.

A sentence like (8) is a little peculiar but it seems to me that the oddness is more because of the juxtaposition. (9) and (10) sound all right singly and I think they can have the required interpretation in the right context:

(9) At two o'clock that day he poisoned the inhabitants.

(10) He poisoned the inhabitants six months later.[20]

There is one final comment I would like to make about THOMSON's paper. Although the solution I have offered does seem to me to take care of most of what she says it is perhaps worth looking at a suggestion which she puts forward, though seems not entirely willing to adopt. She says that temporal expressions which refer to events might be intensional and therefore might not allow the inter-substitutability of expressions which refer to the same event. This may be all right as far as it goes but it hardly solves the problem. If this solution is right then we should expect the issue to involve the scope of nominals; (on the assumption that referential opacity is at bottom a matter of scope.) but the difficulty here is that THOMSON's problem can be stated, and is stated, in terms of the adverbial modification of sentences, and sentences do not have scope. What I think would have to be done would be to say that the temporal modifier is not strictly a property of the event which is the shooting or the killing but a property of a pair of events, (x,y) where x is the shooting and y is the being shot; and this pair would be opposed to the pair (x,z) of the killing (= the shooting) x and the being killed z. In general referential opacity arises when we have something which masquerades as a property of a single thing but which is really a property of something else, e.g. of a concept which happens to pick out the thing. In this case (x,y) and (x,z) are different pairs so (x,y) can occur at one time interval and (x,z) at another.

An analysis of this kind has been given in a very pretty unpublished paper by I.J.A. BARWELL called 'by-ways'. BARWELL is interested in defending DAVIDSON's analysis of events according to which when a person does A by doing B the two actions are identical. What her analysis comes to is in fact that x is an action of doing A by doing B if (x,y) is the doing of A and (x,z) the doing of B and x causes y and y causes z. Because it need not be the case that z causes y the by relation is not symmetrical. BARWELL does not formalize her solution and so, as in THOMSON's case it is not possible to compare it with the one given in this paper. But what is significant about both solutions, if my account is a fair one, is that they seem to work by splitting the meaning of the verb up into two parts and claim identity only in the case of the first part. It would be nice to think that a formalization of their ideas would be only trivially different from the one given here.[21]

9. Intervals and Recursiveness

In section 3 we discussed the problems which arise when we have negative event expressions. The solution was to treat the negative as applying inside the scope of a nominalizer. Assuming that the basic sense of not is as a sentential modifier and that other uses, e.g. in predicates, can be accounted for by abstraction we must give a semantics for not in interval semantics.

The simplest semantics is (where $V(not)$ is $\omega_{\sim}$): $(w,t) \in \omega_{\sim}(a)$

iff $(w,t) \notin a$ where $a \in D_0$.

This is the semantics for not which I think that I prefer, but it is worth a few comments. Suppose e.g. that t is a minimal interval of walking in some world w, this means that any subinterval t' of t will not be an interval of walking in w. This means that it will be an interval of not walking. We might, for instance, have the sentence

(1) John does not walk.

as true while at the same time

(2) John is walking.

is also true (because of the analysis of the progressive; vide [17]).

Part of the problem is pragmatic, when a sentence is uttered the t is often taken to be the present, but how big an interval the present is is very much a matter of context. If a sentence like (1) is uttered within an interval of walking it is quite likely that it would be held to be false because that most pragmatically appropriate interval to evaluate the sentence at is the whole interval of walking.

Of course it may be that there are operators which, so to speak, act like quantifiers which bind the intervals, and that negation is never applied until the interval place is closed up. It may indeed prove that it is best to have the argument place explicitly displayed.[22] All this however is outside the scope of this paper.

The semantics given for *not* is a very classical semantics. It may be that some other non-standard semantics is more suitable. The richness of intervals for exploring the semantics of "logical words" was explored in [14] and whatever one might think of the detailed solutions offered there at least it was shewn what a variety of alternatives there are. In fact the semantics there offered for *every* can help us solve an apparent difficulty in our semantics for words like $walk_N$. It was observed in section 5 that for any person in any world at any particular interval there had to be at most one thing which could count as a walk. But consider a sentence like

(3) Every walk John took yesterday amused Arabella.

The problem about (3) arises because the word *walk* has to occur inside the past tense operator and the sentence should therefore be understood as claiming that there was an interval yesterday such that everything which was a walk of John's at that interval amused Arabella. It would be embarrassing if there could be only one such walk. The problem is not solely a problem about events, and in [14] was discussed in conjunction with the sentence

(4) John polishes every boot.

The idea is that a sentence of the form 'every α is β' is to be understood as true at an interval if when α is true at a subinterval of t so is β. This is a little rough but should give an indication. It should be clear that some such solution will also work for (3).

10. λ-Categorial Languages

The aim of this appendix is essentially to summarise the basic semantic framework of the paper. The framework is fully set out in [11], though this paper will follow [13] and [15] in assuming that sentences are assigned sets of world-time pairs. That will take care of all the context-dependence considered here without the need for the complicated context-theory set out in chapter 8 of [11].

The set syn of syntactic categories is the intersection of all sets S such that

(i) $0 \in S$ and $1 \in S$

(ii)   If $\tau \in S$, $\sigma_1 \in S$, ..., $\sigma_n \in S$
      then $(\tau, \sigma_1, ..., \sigma_n) \in S$.

0 is the syntactic category sentence and 1 the category name. These are the two basic categories. $(\tau, \sigma_1, \ldots, \sigma_n)$ is the category of a functor which makes an expression of category τ out of expressions of categories $\sigma_1, \ldots, \sigma_n$ respectively.

A λ-categorial language Z is a triple (F, X, E) in which F, X and E are all functions from Syn. The values of F_σ for each $\sigma \in$ Syn are finite sets (and all but finitely many of them are empty). If $\alpha \in F_\sigma$ then α is called a symbol of category σ. X_σ for each σ, is a denumerably infinite set of variables of category σ. E_σ is the set of simple or complex expressions of category σ and there must be no overlap between E_σ and E_τ for $\sigma \neq \tau$. There is one improper symbol λ to denote abstraction and the formation rules which determine the members of each E_σ may be stated as follows:

(1) $F_\sigma \subseteq E_\sigma$

(2) If $\delta \in E_{(\tau, \sigma_1, \ldots, \sigma_n)}$ and $\alpha_1, \ldots, \alpha_n$ are in

$E_{\sigma_1}, \ldots, E_{\sigma_n}$ respectively then $(\delta, \alpha_1, \ldots, \alpha_n) \in E_\tau$

(3) If $\alpha \in E_\tau$ and $x \in X_\sigma$ then $(\lambda, x, \alpha) \in E_{(\tau, \sigma)}$

In certain cases (λ, x, α) can be read 'is an x such that α', though this only makes literal sense when α is in E_0. (λ, x, α) is called an abstract. In a formula with variables of more than one category I frequently write x_σ. In general I omit the subscript only when all the variables are in category 1. The commonest abstracts are those formed from a variable in category 1 and an expression in category 0 to form a one-place predicate in category $(0,1)$. Any x in α is bound in (λ, x, α). An expression with every variable bound is called a closed expression.

An interpretation for a λ-categorial language is obtained by first specifying a domain of values for expressions of each category. D_0 is the domain of propositions,[23) the values of sentences. Where W is the set of all pairs (w, t) in which w is a possible world and t a time-interval then $D_0 = PW$. D_1 is the domain of things and contains everything that we want to talk about. In fact $D_\sigma \subseteq D_1$, for all $\sigma \in$ Syn. (But see the caveats in [11], p. 99f.).

$D_{(\tau, \sigma_1, \ldots, \sigma_n)}$ is a set of partial function (some perhaps total) from $D_{\sigma_1} \times \ldots \times D_{\sigma_n}$ into D_τ. The requirement that $D_\sigma \subseteq D_1$ makes partial functions imperative and has the consequence that some

expressions of the language may turn out to be without a value.

Given the system D of domains an interpretation V can be defined on the members of each F_σ so that where $\alpha \in F_\sigma$ then $V(\alpha) \in D_\sigma$. Such a V induces an unique value for all closed expressions of α. Expressions which are not closed only receive a value with respect to an assignment ν which is a function such that for any $x \in X_\sigma$, $\nu(x) \in D_\sigma$. Where $a \in D_\sigma$ $(\nu, a/x)$ is the function exactly like ν for all variables except that $(\nu, a/x)(x) = a$. We can now define an assignment V_ν to all expressions of α as follows

(1) If $\alpha \in F_\sigma$ then $V_\nu(\alpha) = V(\alpha)$

(2) If $\alpha \in X_\sigma$ then $V_\nu(\alpha) = \nu(\alpha)$

(3) If $\delta \in E_{(\tau, \sigma_1, \ldots, \sigma_n)}$ and $\alpha_1 \in E_{\sigma_1}, \ldots, \alpha_n \in E_{\sigma_n}$
then $V_\nu((\delta, \alpha_1, \ldots, \alpha_n)) = V_\nu(\delta)(V_\nu(\alpha_1), \ldots, V_\nu(\alpha_n))$

(4) If $\alpha \in E_\tau$ and $x \in X_\sigma$ then $V_\nu((\lambda, x, \alpha))$ is the function ω in $D_{(\tau, \sigma)}$.

(It is undefined if that function is not in $D_{(\tau, \sigma)}$) such that

for every $a \in D_\sigma$, a is in the domain of ω if $V_{(\nu, a/x)}(\alpha)$

is defined and in that case $\omega(a) = V_{(\nu, a/x)}(\alpha)$.

It should be easy to see how closed expressions do not depend on ν. In such a case we can simply write $V(\alpha)$. (For a proof vide [11], p. 87.)

An expression α in category 0 is said to be true at a pair (w, t) with respect to an interpretation V iff $(w, t) \in V(\alpha)$.

Notes

1. The most elaborate formal treatment along these lines is in BARTSCH [1]. On p. 172 BARTSCH, in discussing PARSONS' predicate-modifier view of adverbs in [30], seems to think of it as complementary to her own analysis. If this is right it would be nice. What I am doing in this paper would then be regarded as an investigation of the nature of events as far as spatio-temporal modification is concerned.

2. The early transformationalist position of LEES [25] was of course in favour of such a derivation. Interesting as this question is however we can I think agree with the comment of BARTSCH [1], p. 167, that the semantic primacy (or of course otherwise, though this is not BARTSCH's concern) of events, process and the like is independent of the question of their morphological derivation.

3. One of the best criticism of Davidson is probably still CLARK's [10], though I think that CLARK's own analysis needs refinement. FODOR also in [19] has some useful things to say.

4. E.g. CHAFE [9] and BARTSCH [1] among the linguists. Among the philosophers the distinction was elaborated by VENDLER [37] and by KENNY [22] who got it from Aristotle. Neither KENNY nor TAYLOR [34] who gave formal expression to the distinction seems to have thought of these words as denoting things in different ontological categories.

5. This distinction was discussed in [11], pp. 205-208, using the terminology *verbal* and *nominal* gerund.

6. There is of course a meaning of this sentence in which the quickly modifies *cause*. That meaning is clearly not involved here.

7. Given ω as a function from times to sets of worlds we can define the associated set a of world-time pairs as $(\omega,t) \in a$ iff $\omega \in \omega(t)$ and given a we can say that $\omega \in \omega(t)$ iff $(\omega,t) \in a$. (The only time these would not be equivalent would be if not all times were in the domain of ω.)

8. Chapter 5 of VENDLER's [37] would seem to support not calling MONTAGUE's generic events.

9. I am treating common nouns as in category (0,1). GUPTA [20] wants to build in their identity criteria in a more explicit way. He may be right, though BENNETT [4], (see footnote 28), does not seem to think so, but the questions he raises don't concern events any more than other entities.

10. [23], p. 210 and [24], p. 42. (Vide also examples (13) - (16) in [13].) KIM's claim about Xanthippe has been disputed by BEARDSLEY [3], p. 269, but BEARDSLEY seems plainly wrong. Indeed it is so intuitively obvious to me that one cannot become a widow in prison without being in prison that I find myself at a loss when someone doubts it.

11. [24], p. 42. KIM says that he finds "much to recommend in an account of events according to which an event is a structure consisting of a concrete object, a property exemplified by it, and the time at which it is exemplified."

12. BRAND [8] seems to be arguing that any two events which have the same spatio-temporal location in each world should be identified. I am sympathetic to the identification even though this paper does not depend on it.

13. Essentially BIGELOW quotation relies on the idea that aspects of the context in which a sentence is uttered can be added as symbols to the very sentence itself to make its meaning more specific. The view is presented in BIGELOW's [5] and [6] and applies to the analysis of prepositions in [15].

14. Sentences like (1) are a little unhappy without an adverbial of time or place. It is more natural to have something like 'John's walk to the station occurred yesterday.' This fact does not affect the points made in the text.

15. *Vide* e.g. [11], pp. 132f and 177f and BOER [7] for some remarks about possible treatments of proper names in λ-categorial languages.

16. E.g. recent work by BÄUERLE [2] and BENNETT [4] makes it highly likely that different kinds of temporal adverbials work in quite different ways.

17. An example of an inappropriate member of D_1 would be $V(is)$ itself. We would like the domain of arguments of $V(is)$ to be as big as it consistently can.

18. Quite a bit of work has been done in [39] and elsewhere by DOUG WALTON on the possibility of decomposing action sentences into expressions which involve a 'bringing about' operator. WALTON is usually more concerned with what an agent is able to do, and shews in [40] how crucial time is to this in a discussion of [26]. In section 3 of [41] WALTON considers expressions in which 'x brings it about that p' is logically equivalent to p. What the present paper shews is that, even if this equivalence holds, the possibili-

ties of adverbial modification of the complex expression are greater than the possibilities of modifying the simple expression.

19. [36]. THALBERG [35], p. 781, has divided event theorists into 'unifiers' and 'multipliers' according to their inclination or otherwise to identify events which are picked out by different descriptions. The position of this paper is a sort of half-way house. BEARDSLEY [3] comes close to it though he seems to be slightly more of a multifier than I am.

20. Examples like these raise a tricky methodological question. It has from time to time been noted that in matters of the kind discussed in this paper the crucial examples tend to involve rather subtle and almost esoteric nuances and shades of meaning. This is often put as if it were a criticism but I don't think it really need be. I see these examples as analogous to the experiments used to decide the difference between two rival physical theories. These theories are supposed to .be at work throughout the whole of time and space, but the experiment needed to decide between them may well consist in cooking up a very unusual and almost bizarre situation in which the particular consequences we have in mind can be tested. The fact that the test situation is unusual is no mark against its value. The case is so in language also. To test whether an operator has a certain scope eg. we may well have to look at some very peculiar sentences. Yet if we can get reasonably clear judgements, as we sometimes can, their peculiarity is no mark whatever against their use in the testing of this or that hypothesis.

21. An interesting class of verbs which shews somewhat analogous behaviour to those discussed in this section is verbs of perception. BARTSCH [1], p. 124, gives the example 'Hans sees the evening star in the west' where of course on its most natural interpretation it is the evening star and not Hans who is in the west. BARTSCH, loc cit, also cites some other interesting cases such as 'Hans is playing on the table'. She is of course arguing for a spatial location for the process independent of the actor. Maybe this is the sort of case which does require a spatial index.

22. This is advocated by PARTEE [31] and supported, I think, by BENNETT [4] and BÄUERLE [2]. BARTSCH [1], p. 187 and pp. 317-322, has something to say about the relative scope of negation and other adverbials.

23. There is some terminological variation here. STALNAKER [33] has argued that it is better to take a proposition is merely a set of worlds. On p. 386 he claims that it is propositions in this sense which are the objects of illocutionary acts and propositional attitudes. If we adopt STALNAKER's line then the meanings of sentences (the members of D_0) are not propositions but things which determine propositions with respect to a fixed time-interval. Perhaps the word 'open proposition' used in [11], p. 115, is an appropriate one.

References

1. R. Bartsch: The Grammar of Adverbials. Amsterdam (North Holland Publishing Co., 1976)

2. R. Bäuerle: Tense logics and natural language. Synthese 40 (1979), 225-230

3. M.C. Beardsley: Action and events: The Problem of Individuation. In: American Philosophical Quarterly, Vol. 12 (1975) pp. 263-276

4. M. Bennett: A Guide to the Logic of Tense and Aspect in English. (mimeograph)

5. J.C. Bigelow: Contexts and Quotation I. In: Linguistische Berichte, Vol. 38 (1975) pp. 1-21

6. J.C. Bigelow: Contexts and Quotation II. Ibid., Vol. 39 (1975) pp. 1-21

7. S.E. Boër: Proper Names and Formal Semiotic. Synthese (Forthcoming)

8. M. Brand: Identity conditions for events. In: American Philosophical Quarterly, Vol. 14 (1977) pp. 329-337

9. W.L. Chafe: Meaning and the Structure of Language. Chicago (University of Chicago Press, 1970)

10. R.L. Clark: Concerning the Logic of Predicate modifiers. In: Noûs, Vol. 4 (1970) pp. 311-335

11. M.J. Cresswell: Logics and Languages. London (Methuen, 1973)

12. M.J. Cresswell: Adverbs and Events. Synthese, Vol. 28 (1974) pp. 455-481

13. M.J. Cresswell: Adverbs of Space and Time. Formal Semantics and Pragmatics for Natural Languages, ed. by F. Guenthner and S.J. Schmidt, Dordrecht (Reidel, Forthcoming)

14. M.J. Cresswell: Interval Semantics and Logical Words. On the Logical Analysis of Tense and Aspect, ed. by Ch. Rohrer, Tübingen (TBL-Verlag Narr, 1977) pp. 7-29

15. M.J. Cresswell: Prepositions and Points of View. In: Linguistics and Philosophy, Vol. 2 (1977) (Forthcoming)

16. D. Davidson: The Logical form of Action sentences. The Logic of Decision and Action, ed. by N. Rescher, Pittsburgh (University of Pittsburgh Press, 1967) pp. 81-95

17. D.R. Dowty: Toward a Semantic Analysis of Verb Aspects and the English 'Imperfective' Progressive. In: Linguistics and Philosophy, Vol. 1 (1977) pp. 45-77

18. C.J. Fillmore: The Case for Case. Universals in Linguistic Theory, ed. by E. Bach and R.T. Harms, New York, (Hold, Rinehard and Winston, 1968) pp. 1-88

19. J.A. Fodor: Troubles About Actions. Semantics of Natural Languages, ed. by D. Davidson and G.H. Harman, Dordrecht (Reidel, 1972) pp. 48-69

20. A.K. Gupta: The Logic of Common Nouns. An Investigation in Quantified Modal Logic (Ph.D. dissertation, University of Pittsburgh)

21. C.D. Johnson: Davidson on Primitive Actions that Cause Deaths. In: Analysis, Vol. 32 (1972) pp. 36-41

22. A.J.P. Kenny: Action, Emotion and Will. London (Routledge and Kegan Paul, 1963)

23. J. Kim: Events and Their Descriptions: Some Considerations. Essays in Honor of Carl G. Hempel, ed. by N. Rescher, Dordrecht (Reidel, 1970) pp. 198-215

24. J. Kim: Noncausal Connections. In: Noûs, Vol. 8 (1974) pp. 41-52

25. R.B. Lees: The Grammar of English Nominalizations. The Hague (Mouton & Co., 1960)

26. K. Lehrer and R. Taylor: Time,Truth and Modalities. In: Mind, Vol. 74 (1965) pp. 390-398

27. D.K. Lewis: Causation. In: The Journal of Philosophy, Vol. 70 (1973) pp. 556-567

28. D.K. Lewis: Survival and Identity. The Identities of Persons, ed. by A.O. Rorty, Berkeley (University of California Press, 1976) pp. 17-40

29. R.M. Montague: Formal Philosophy, ed. by R.H. Thomason, New Haven (Yale University Press, 1974)

30. T. Parsons: Some Problems Concerning the Logic of Grammatical Modifiers. Semantics of Natural Language, ed. by D. Davidson and G.H. Harman, Dordrecht (Reidel, 1972) pp. 127-141

31. B.H. Partee: Some Structural Analogies Between Tenses and Pronouns in English. In: The Journal of Philosophy, Vol. 70 (1973) pp. 601-609

32. J. Perry: Can the Self Devide? In: The Journal of Philosophy, Vol. 69 (1972) pp. 463-488

33. R.C. Stalnaker: Pragmatics. Semantics of Natural Language, ed. by D. Davidson and G.H. Harman, Dordrecht (Reidel, 1972) pp. 380-397

34. B. Taylor: Tense and Continuity. In: Linguistics and Philosophy, Vol. 1 (1977) pp. 199-220

35. I. Thalberg: Singling out Actions, their Properties and Components. In: The Journal of Philosophy, Vol. 68 (1971) pp. 781-787

36. J.J. Thomson: The Time of a Killing. In: The Journal of Philosophy, Vol. 68 (1971) pp. 115-132

37. Z. Vendler: Linguistics in Philosophy. Ithica, N.Y. (Cornell University Press, 1967)

38. A. von Stechow: Direktionale Präpositionen und Kontexttheorie. Wortstellung und Bedeutung; ed. by Maria-Elisabeth Conte, Anna Giacalone Ramat and Paolo Ramat, Tübingen (Niemeyer, 1978), pp. 157-166

39. D.N. Walton: Logical Form and Agency. In: <u>Philosophical Studies</u>, Vol. 29 (1976) pp. 75-89

40. D.N. Walton: Time and Modality in the 'Can' of Opportunity. <u>Action Theory</u>, ed. by M. Brand and D.N. Walton, Dordrecht (Reidel, 1976) pp. 271-287

41. D.N. Walton: Pure Tensed Action Propositions. (Forthcoming)

Conditional Necessity and Possibility

Angelika Kratzer

Max-Planck-Gesellschaft, Projekt Psycholinguistik, Berg en Dalseweg 79
Nijmegen, The Netherlands

Introduction: Conditionals Are Important but Troublesome

Conditionals are important and have always been considered to be so. In the
times of the Greek poet KALLIMACHOS, even the crows worried about them:

"Lo and behold how the crows on the roof-tops tell us by croaking which
conditionals are true and also how we shall get reborn."

This means that, to know which conditionals are true, was considered to
be just as important as to know what happens after our death. It was the conditionals which divided DIODOROS KRONOS and his pupil PHILO. Later, CHRYSIPPOS
joined the quarrel and they all died without reconcilement.

I do not want to say anything about why conditionals seem to be so important. But I do want to say a few words about why I think they caused such a
lot of trouble.

Chapter one: If-Clauses Have no Meaning Apart from the Quantifier They Restrict

In "Adverbs of Quantification"[1], DAVID LEWIS presents the following list of
sentences:

(1) Always
     Sometimes   } a man who owns a donkey,
     Usually   beats it now and then.
     Often

     Never   } a man who owns a donkey,
     Seldom   does beat it now and then.

In a more logic-like notation, we could rewrite these sentences in the following way:

(2) Always
     Sometimes   } if x is a man, if y is a donkey, and if x owns
     Usually   y, x beats y now and then.
     Often

     Never   } if x is a man, if y is a donkey, and if x owns
     Seldom   y, does x beat y now and then.

In these sentences, DAVID LEWIS considers the adverbs "always", "sometimes" .... etc. to be quantifiers over cases, cases being construed as the "tuples of their participants". These participants are values of the variables that occur free in the open sentence modified by the adverb. A time-coordinate may also be needed. The cases quantified over are those cases which satisfy the three if-clauses.

We have a construction consisting of three parts: the adverb of quantification, the if-clauses and the modified sentence. That is schematically for one if-clause:

(3) Always
     Sometimes
       .
       .   } , if α , β
       .

A sentence like (3) is true if and only if β is true in all, some, most ... admissible cases. A case is admissible if it satisfies the if-clause.

The important question is now, whether it is possible to get the same effect by first combining α and β into one conditional sentence and then taking this conditional sentence to be the sentence modified by the adverb. Following this proposal, we would have:

(4) Always
     Sometimes
       .
       .   } ,(if α , β)
       .

As DAVID LEWIS shows, there is no way to interpret the conditional sentence "if α, β " in a way that makes (4) equivalent to (3) for all adverbs he considers. For "always" we get the proper equivalence by interpreting it as the truth-functional material implication "$\alpha \supset \beta$ ". If the adverb is "sometimes" or "never", the corresponding interpretation would have to be the conjunction " $\alpha \wedge \beta$". In the remaining cases, there is no natural interpretation.

Here, DAVID LEWIS concludes, that the "if" in his restrictive if-clauses "should not be regarded as a sentential connective. It has no meaning apart from the adverb it restricts."

This remains true for if-clauses which restrict other kinds of quantifiers: "probably"[2], "necessarily", "must", "would", "possibly", "can" or "might". We might consider them as quantifiers over possible worlds.

As soon as we conceive of if-clauses in general as devices for restricting quantification, two more sources of trouble arise: If-clauses do not always have an explicit quantifier when we come across them. There might be misunderstandings about which quantifier should be filled in.

And furthermore:

Quantifiers depend for their interpretation on what GEORGE BOOLE called a "universe of discourse".[3] This is the domain over which the quantification takes place. It is this universe of discourse which makes the interpretation of quantifiers context-dependent: If we talk about people we may perhaps talk about just those people which are swimming in the Danube right now. And talking about times, our domain may be eternity, our lifetime or the actual moment. During one and the same conversation, the universe of discourse need not stay once and for ever the same. So there might arise misunderstandings about the domain of a quantifier which gets restricted.

We can imagine by now, why conditionals have always been so difficult to handle:

Their if-clauses have not been considered as devices for restricting different kinds of quantifiers with variable domains.

One lesson to draw from all this is the following:

In this paper, I will not be able to give a general account of conditionals. If if-clauses have no meaning apart from the quantifier they restrict, I will have to restrict myself to some of these quantifiers.

I chose the modals "necessarily", "must", "would", "possibly", "can" and "might" not only because I have done some work on modals already[4], but also because I believe that the concepts of conditional necessity and possibility are a key to the understanding of many conditionals which actually occur[5].

In the chapters to come, I will adopt the following strategy: First, some basic notions concerning possible-worlds-semantics and its application to the semantics of modals will be introduced. Then, a pair of counterfactuals will serve as a guideline for the development of the concepts of conditional necessity and possibility.

Other theories of counterfactuals will turn out to be special cases. In a further chapter, I will discuss some rules of use for indicative and subjunctive conditional sentences. Finally, it will be shown that certain characteristic differences between these two kinds of conditional sentences come out quite naturally by combining their rules of use with my account of conditional necessity.

Chapter two: Propositions, Modality and Conversational Backgrounds

When a sentence like

(1) I am here

is uttered in a situation, it usually expresses a proposition. When Arnim uttered it on the first of August 1978 at five o'clock in the afternoon, he thereby expressed the proposition

that Arnim is in his office at the University of Constance on the first of August 1978 at five o'clock in the afternoon.

Let us call this proposition "p".

By accident, Max uttered (1) at the same time as Arnim did. But he did not express the same proposition p with his utterance. Two different utterances of the very same sentence may express different propositions. The proposition expressed by Max uttering (1) was:

that Max is in his bed in his house in Wellington (New Zealand) on the second of August 1978 at four o'clock in the morning.

Let us call this proposition q. p and q could also be expressed by different sentences uttered in different situations, for example by:

(2) You are there

or

(3) He was here

So, one and the same proposition can be expressed by the utterance of different sentences in different situations. p and q are actually true. But we could conceive of states of affairs or <u>possible worlds</u> where p or q or both are false:

Arnim could have been on the top of the Matterhorn on the first of August 1978 at five o'clock in the afternoon and Max could have been in his bed in his house in Waikanae on the second of August at four o'clock in the morning.

Each proposition divides the set of possible worlds into two disjoint subsets: the set of worlds where it is true and the set of worlds where it is false.

p and q do so in a different way: there are worlds where p is true and q is false and vice versa.

In possible-worlds-semantics, a proposition is construed as the set of possible worlds where it is true. Starting with the set W of all possible worlds, the following definitions are commonly given:

<u>Propositions</u>:
A proposition is a subset of W.

<u>Truth of a proposition</u>:
A proposition p is true in a world $w \epsilon$ W if and only if $w \epsilon p$. Otherwise, p is false in w.

<u>Logical consequence</u>:
A proposition p follows from a set of propositions A if and only if p is true in all worlds where all propositions of A are true.

<u>Consistency</u>:
A set of propositions A is consistent if and only if there is a world $w \epsilon$ W such that all propositions of A are true in w. Otherwise, A is inconsistent.

<u>Logical compatibility</u>:
A proposition p is compatible with a set of propositions A if and only if $A \cup \{p\}$ is consistent.

W is the <u>logically true proposition</u>, $\emptyset$ is the <u>logically false proposition</u> and all other propositions are <u>contingent propositions</u>.

Consider now the two following sentences:

(4) In view of what we know, Marion du Fresne must have been eaten by the
     Ngā-Puhi tribe.

(5) In view of what we know, Marion du Fresne might have been eaten by the
     Ngā-Puhi tribe.

When I uttered sentence (4) a moment ago, I thereby expressed a proposition
which I want to call "r".

And when I uttered sentence (5) right after (4), I thereby expressed a proposition which I want to call "s".

r is true in a world w, if and only if it follows from what we know in w
that Marion du Fresne has been eaten by the Ngā-Puhi tribe. s is true in a
world w, if and only if it is compatible with what we know in w that Marion
du Fresne has been eaten by the Ngā-Puhi tribe.

r and s are both contingent propositions. They are true or false in a world
depending on what is known in this world.

I could have expressed the same propositions by uttering the two shorter
sentences (6) and (7):

(6) Marion du Fresne must have been eaten by the Ngā-Puhi tribe.

(7) Marion du Fresne might have been eaten by the Ngā-Puhi tribe.

If I had chosen to utter the sentences (6) and (7) instead of the sentences
(4) and (5) respectively, the context of utterance would have had to provide
whatever my utterance of the phrase "in view of what we know" contributed to
the fact that the propositions r and s and not some other propositions were
expressed by my utterances of (4) and (5).

I have argued elsewhere[6] that this contribution of the phrase "in view of
what we know" is a conversational background. A conversational background is
the kind of thing I refer to when I utter such a phrase.

What we know is different from one world to another. And what we know in
a world, is a set of propositions. So, in possible-worlds-semantics, a conversational background will get construed as a function which assigns a set
of propositions to every possible world. For our example, it would be that
function, which assigns to every world w the set of propositions which we
know in w.

This is an epistemic conversational background. Given, that only true propositions can be known, epistemic conversational backgrounds are special cases
of objective conversational backgrounds: An objective conversational background
is one which assigns to every possible world a set of facts of a certain kind.
A deontic conversational background may be one which assigns to every world
w the set of propositions which are commanded in w. There may also be mixed
conversational backgrounds which contain for example epistemic and deontic ingredients. And there are a great many more possibilities which I am not going
to discuss here.

All modals depend for their interpretation on a conversational background
which will be provided by the context of use in most cases. This interpreta-

tion is based on a logical relation between a proposition and a set of propositions.

Different modals may be based on different such relations. For "must", "would"[7] or "necessarily", this relation is logical consequence, whereas for "can", "might" or "possibly" it is logical compatibility.

A general account of (relative) necessity and compatibility would then look as follows:

Necessity:

Suppose that a sentence of the form:

(8) $\left.\begin{array}{l} \text{must} \\ \text{would} \\ \text{necessarily} \end{array}\right\}$, α

is uttered in a situation, where the proposition p is expressed by the utterance of the whole sentence, the proposition q is expressed by the utterance of α, and where H is the conversational background.

Then, p is true in exactly those worlds $w \in W$, where q follows from $H(w)$[8].

Possibility:

Suppose that a sentence of the form:

(9) $\left.\begin{array}{l} \text{can} \\ \text{might} \\ \text{possibly} \end{array}\right\}$, α

is uttered in a situation, where the proposition p is expressed by the utterance of the whole sentence, the proposition q is expressed by the utterance of α, and where H is the conversational background. Then p is true in exactly those worlds $w \in W$, where q is compatible with $H(w)$.

When a modal is modified or "restricted" by an if-clause, it is to be expected that this modification somehow affects the conversational background of the logical relation on which the modal is based. This question will be attacked in the next chapter from a new starting-point.

Chapter three: Conditional Necessity and Possibility

Imagine the two following situations:

First situation:
In the conference-room of the finest philosophy department in the Southern Hemisphere, there are exactly three men, George, Max and Chris.
They all prefer hokey-pokey-cookies to anything else in the world.

Second situation:
In the conference-room of the finest philosophy department in the Southern Hemisphere, there are exactly three men, George, Max and Chris. George and

Max prefer hokey-pokey-cookies to anything else in the world. Chris does not care about hokey-pokey-cookies at all.

Consider now sentence (1) and sentence (2):

(1) If all but one of the men in the room disappeared, there would still be one man in the room who prefers hokey-pokey-cookies to anything else in the world.

(2) If all but one of the men in the room disappeared, there might still be one man in the room who prefers hokey-pokey-cookies to anything else in the world.

I take it, that, in the first situation, I say something which is true in this situation, when I utter sentence (1) or sentence (2)[9]. But in the second situation, I say something which is false in this situation, when I utter sentence (1). What I say, when I utter sentence (2) would still be true in this situation.

I shall try now to describe what is going on here. Naturally, I will make use of all kinds of simplifications.

I suppose that, when I utter one of the two sentences in one of the two situations, roughly the same conversational background is established in all four cases. Let us call this conversational background "H". H is an objective conversational background: it reflects in a certain way the conditions which are relevant in a situation where I utter sentence (1) or sentence (2). For each possible world, H yields the answers to the two following questions:

Question one:
Which men are in the room?

Question two:
Which men in the room prefer hokey-pokey-cookies to anything else in the world and which ones don't?

H may be identified with what is expressed by these questions. H does not yield the answers to any of the following questions, which are completely irrelevant in a situation where I utter sentence (1) or sentence (2):

How many chairs are there in the room?
Who is not in the room?
Who was the most cruel emperor of Rome?
Are there turtles hibernating in Sicily?
etc.

If w_1 is a world where the first situation described above holds, $H(w_1)$ will be the set which contains nothing but the following propositions:

g_1: that George is a man in the room
m_1: that Max is a man in the room
ch_1: that Chris is a man in the room
g_2: that George prefers hokey-pokey-cookies to anything else in the world
m_2: that Max prefers hokey-pokey-cookies to anything else in the world
ch_2: that Chris prefers hokey-pokey-cookies to anything else in the world

Let us now return to the two sentences (1) and (2). I assume that sentence (1) expresses the same proposition p_1 whether it is uttered in the first or in the second situation. And that, likewise, sentence (2) expresses the same proposition p_2 in both cases. p_1 and p_2 are conditionals with identical antecedents and consequents. I shall change the antecedent in such a way that it expresses the result of the men's disappearing rather than the disappearing itself. That will do no harm but be more convenient. So we have:

the <u>antecedent</u> q: that there is only one man in the room
the <u>consequent</u> r: that there is still one man in the room
                               who prefers hokey-pokey-cookies to anything else in the world

So far, I have introduced an example which I shall use for the presentation of suitable notions of conditional necessity and possibility.

We have two situations, two sentences and certain intuitions about the truth of the corresponding propositions in the corresponding situation, given a certain conversational background.

Our aim is to find out for the two sentences the truth-conditions which fit best with our intuitions and lend themselves to further generalisations.

If we followed RODERICK CHISHOLM[10] or NELSON GOODMAN[11] we would now have to add the antecedent q to $H(w_1)$ and see whether the consequent r follows from the set $H(w_1) \cup \{q\}$. If this is so, p_1 would be considered to be true in w_1. The same holds for the world w_2. As for sentence (2), we would have to add the antecedent q to $H(w_1)$ as well, but this time, we would have to see whether r is compatible with $H(w_1) \cup \{q\}$. If this is so, p_2 would be considered to be true in w_1. Again, the same holds for the world w_2.

In our case, this does not lead to a satisfying result, as the addition of the antecedent q to $H(w_1)$ or $H(w_2)$ results in an inconsistent set of propositions. That George, Max and Chris are all three in the room is not compatible with the supposition that there is only one man in the room.

Given an inconsistent set of propositions, we find ourselves in the unpleasant situation, that any proposition follows from such a set and no proposition is compatible with it.

NICHOLAS RESCHER considered inconsistencies in a different framework and with different assumptions.[12]

If we accommodated his proposals to what we are doing here, we would try out the following procedure:

Take the set $H(w_2)$ as an example:

$$H(w_2) = \left\{ \begin{matrix} g_1 \,, \ m_1, \ ch_1 \\ g_2, \ \ m_2, \ -ch_2 \end{matrix} \right\}$$

If we add q to $H(w_2)$, we get the inconsistent set $H(w_2) \cup \{q\}$:

$$H(w_2) \cup \{q\} = \left\{ \begin{matrix} g_1, \ m_1, \ ch_1, \\ g_2, \ m_2, \ -ch_2 \end{matrix} \quad q \right\}$$

We consider now all the <u>maximal consistent subsets</u> of $H(w_2) \cup \{q\}$ which contain q.

In general, a subset C of a set of propositions A is a <u>maximal consistent subset</u> of A if and only if the following conditions hold:

(1) C is not the empty set
(2) C is consistent
(3) For any propositions $p \in A$:
     if $p \notin C$ then $C \cup \{p\}$ is inconsistent.

There are exactly three maximal consistent subsets of $H(w_2) \cup \{q\}$, which contain q:

$C_1 = \{q, g_1, g_2, m_2, -ch_2\}$
$C_2 = \{q, m_1, g_2, m_2, -ch_2\}$
$C_3 = \{q, ch_1, g_2, m_2, -ch_2\}$

Each set represents one way of making the antecedent q compatible with as many propositions of $H(w_2)$ as possible. In each case, two of the men have to leave the room and one may stay. For this, there are exactly three possibilities. In the first two cases, there is still one man left in the room, who prefers hokey-pokey-cookies to anything else in the world. In the third case, this is no longer true.

For NICHOLAS RESCHER, the proposition p_1 would be true in w_1 if and only if the consequent r follows from the <u>preferred</u> one of the three sets C_1, C_2 and C_3. I have chosen the example in a way which makes RESCHER's proposal very implausible. Which way of making the antecedent true should we prefer? Shall we ask George, Max or Chris to stay in the room?

I think we have to take into account <u>all three possibilities</u>. If the consequent r follows from all three sets, p_1 should be true in w_2. In fact, r does not follow from C_3. So p_1 should be false in w_2. And this fits exactly with the intuitions we had.

We shall examine now, what happens if sentence (1) is uttered in the first situation, that is, we consider the set

$$H(w_1) = \begin{Bmatrix} g_1, m_1, ch_1, \\ g_2, m_2, ch_2 \end{Bmatrix}$$

If we add q to this set, we get the inconsistent set $H(w_1) \cup \{q\}$:

$$H(w_1) \cup \{q\} = \begin{Bmatrix} g_1, m_1, ch_1, \\ g_2, m_2, ch_2, \end{Bmatrix} q$$

Again, there are exactly three maximal consistent subsets of $H(w_1) \cup \{q\}$ which contain q:

$C_1 = \{q, g_1, g_2, m_2, ch_2\}$
$C_2 = \{q, m_1, g_2, m_2, ch_2\}$
$C_3 = \{q, ch_1, g_2, m_2, ch_2\}$

The consequent r follows from each of these sets. p_1 should therefore be true in w_1, according to the criterium proposed above. Concerning sentence (1) and p_1^1, our intuitions have been matched by this criterium. But we still lack a corresponding criterium for sentence (2) and p_2.

If we stick very close to our example, we might want to require that p_2 is true in w_1 if and only if r follows from one maximal consistent subset of $H(w_1) \cup \{q\}$ which contains q. And that p_2 is true in w_2 if and only if r follows from one maximal consistent subset of $H(w_2) \cup \{q\}$ which contains q.

This would give us the right result, as in both cases, there is at least one maximal consistent subset from which r follows.

I think, however, that this condition is too strong for other cases. p_2 should be true in a world, if and only if, supposing that there is only one man in the room, it does not follow that there is no man in the room, who prefers hokey-pokey-cookies to anything else in the world.

Following these lines, p_2 would be true in a world w, if and only if there is a maximal consistent subset of $H(w) \cup \{q\}$ which contains q and with which r is compatible.

May be, this looks quite convincing. But there is a general draw-back in the use of maximal consistent subsets: As soon as we consider sets of propositions which have a more respectable size, we cannot always be sure that all their consistent subsets can be extended to a maximal consistent subset.[13]

The following proposals are designed to avoid these difficulties, while saving the advantages of the earlier attempts.[14]

Final criterium for the truth of p_1:

For some world w ∈ W, let $\mathscr{S}$ be the set of all consistent subsets of $H(w) \cup \{q\}$ which contain q. Then, p_1 is true in w if and only if for every set in $\mathscr{S}$, there is a superset in $\mathscr{S}$, from which r follows.

Final criterium for the truth of p_2:

For some world w ∈ W, let $\mathscr{S}$ be the set of all consistent subsets of $H(w) \cup \{q\}$ which contain q. Then, p_2 is true in w if and only if there is a set in $\mathscr{S}$ such that r is compatible with all its supersets in $\mathscr{S}$.

The reader may check for himself, that these criteria coincide with the proposals they are meant to replace for the case where every consistent subset of $H(w) \cup \{q\}$ which contains q can be extended to a maximal consistent subset of $H(w) \cup \{q\}$. But they do not presuppose the existence of such sets.

There is another point which is easy to prove:
Suppose that for some world w ∈ W, $H(w) \cup \{q\}$ is consistent. Let $\mathscr{S}$ be the set of all subsets of $H(w) \cup \{q\}$ which contain q. Every set in $\mathscr{S}$ is consistent, as they are all subsets of a consistent set. It could be proved now that r follows from $H(w) \cup \{q\}$ if and only if for every set in $\mathscr{S}$ there is a superset in $\mathscr{S}$ from which r follows. And r is compatible with $H(w) \cup \{q\}$ if and only if there is a set in $\mathscr{S}$ such that r is compatible with all its supersets in $\mathscr{S}$.

This means that our criteria coincide with CHISHOLM's and GOODMAN's proposals for the case where the addition of the antecedent q to H(w) does not yield an inconsistent set.

I misused the three philosophers George, Max and Chris in order to construct a rather contrived example for the use of conditionals. I hope nevertheless that the example exhibits enough properties which could lead to interesting generalisations. The generalisations I aimed at are the truth-conditions for those conditional sentences whose interpretation is based on the concepts of conditional necessity or possibility.

In detail, these truth-conditions would be the following:

Conditional necessity:

Imagine that a sentence of the form

(3) $\left.\begin{array}{l} \text{necessarily} \\ \text{must} \\ \text{would} \end{array}\right\}$, if α, β

is uttered in a situation, where:
H is the conversational background, p is the proposition expressed by the whole sentence, q is the proposition expressed by α , and r is the proposition expressed by β .

Suppose that for some $w \in W$, $\mathcal{S}$ is the set of all consistent subsets of H(w) $\cup$ {q} which contain q. Then, p is true in w if and only if there is for every set in $\mathcal{S}$ a superset in $\mathcal{S}$ from which r follows.

Conditional possibility:

Imagine, that this time, a sentence of the form

(4) $\left.\begin{array}{l} \text{possibly} \\ \text{can} \\ \text{might} \end{array}\right\}$, if α, β

is uttered in a situation, where:
H is the conversational background, p is the proposition expressed by the whole sentence, q is the proposition expressed by α and r is the proposition expressed by β .

Suppose that for some $w \in W$, $\mathcal{S}$ is the set of all consistent subsets of H(w) $\cup$ {q} which contain q. Then, p is true in w if and only if there is a set in $\mathcal{S}$ such that r is compatible with all its supersets in $\mathcal{S}$.

It is time to draw this chapter to a conclusion: I proposed a concept of conditional necessity and possibility which displays certain proposals of CHISHOLM, GOODMAN and RESCHER as special cases.

The example I used for motivation, was chosen in a way that would make it apparent that my concept is not too general after all: It seems plausible to suppose that - at least sometimes - we have to reason from an inconsistent set of propositions in order to tell whether a conditional is true or false in a given situation. Doing this, we cannot always be sure that there is just one preferred way of dealing with this inconsistency.

What has been neglected so far, was the idea that there might be nevertheless preferences and weights guiding the choice of ways to make the best out of an inconsistent set.

I prefer to consider these preferences and weights to be themselves components of the conversational background. Conversational backgrounds could then - for example - appear in the form of "systems of spheres"[15].

It will be the main topic of the next chapter how systems of spheres can be used for the interpretation of what DAVID LEWIS calls "counterfactuals" and how this treatment, too, turns out to be a special case of my account of conditional necessity.

Chapter four: Similarity and Systems of Spheres

Consider the following sentence:

(1) If Goethe had survived the year 1832, he would nevertheless be dead by now.

I think, that what I just said is true in our actual world. Goethe was born in 1749, now we are in 1978, and people do not get as old as that. In examining whether what I said by uttering (1) is true or not in our world, I took into account when Goethe was actually born and how old people actually get. In letting Goethe survive the year 1832, I still tried to leave our world as intact as this supposition permits.

For ROBERT STALNAKER[16], the proposition I expressed by my utterance would be true in a world w if and only if Goethe is dead by now in that world, which - of all worlds where he survives the year 1832 - is the one which is closest or most similar to w.

Against this, it has been argued that there may be several worlds of this kind which are all equally close to w.

DAVID LEWIS went even further with his objections: he stressed that it may very well be that there are worlds where Goethe survives the year 1832 which get closer and closer to w without there being any closest world at all.

This seems to be very plausible in our case, if we accept the kind of sophisticated argumentation which is common in philosophy: A world where Goethe dies in 1833 is closer to our actual world than a world where he dies in 1835. A world where he dies on the first of January 1833 is closer to our world than a world where he dies on the fifth of September of the same year. A world where he dies at one o'clock in the morning of the first of January 1833 is closer to our world than a world where he dies at five o'clock in the afternoon of the same day ... And we could go on. For DAVID LEWIS, the proposition which I expressed by my utterance of (1) is (non-vacuously) true in a world w if and only if there is a world where Goethe survives the year 1832 and is dead by now, which is closer (or more similar) to w, than any world where Goethe survives the year 1832 and is not dead by now.

Technically, DAVID LEWIS captures the idea of similarity between possible worlds by means of a <u>system of spheres</u> $, which assigns to every possible world w a set of sets of possible worlds $_w . For every world w, the elements of $_w are <u>nested</u> around w.

The following picture shows the case, where $_w contains just the four sets { w }, S_1, S_2, and S_3:

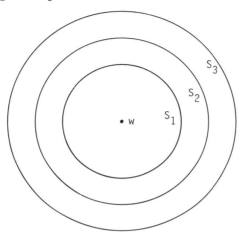

{ w }, S_1, S_2 and S_3 are <u>spheres</u> around w.
{ w } is a subset of S_1, $\overline{S_1\ \text{is a}}$ subset of S_2 and S_2 is a subset of S_3.

Any world within a sphere is closer (or more similar) to w than any world outside it.

The precise definition of a system of spheres runs as follows:[17]

<u>Systems of spheres</u>:
Let $ be an assignment to each possible world w of a set $_w of sets of possible worlds. Then $ is called a <u>(centered) system of spheres</u>, and the members of each $_w are called <u>spheres around w</u>, if and only if, for each world w, the following conditions hold:

(C) $_w is <u>centered</u> on w; that is, the set {w} is a sphere around w.
(1) $_w is <u>nested</u>; that is, whenever S and T belong to $_w either S is a subset of T or vice versa.
(2) $ is <u>closed under unions</u>; that is, whenever $\mathcal{S}$ is a subset of $_w, then $\overline{\cup\mathcal{S}}$ is a sphere around w.
(3) $_w is <u>closed under (non-empty) intersections</u>; that is, whenever $\mathcal{S}$ is a non-empty subset of $_w, then $\cap\mathcal{S}$ is a sphere around w.

Systems of spheres are created for carrying information about the overall similarity of worlds. They form the base for DAVID LEWIS' more formal account of the truth-conditions for counterfactuals:[18] Slightly adapted to our present way of speaking, these truth-conditions look as follows:

DAVID LEWIS' truth-conditions for counterfactuals:

Suppose, a sentence of the form

(2) Would, if α , β

is uttered in a situation, where p is the proposition expressed by the utterance of the whole sentence, q is expressed by the utterance of α and r by the
utterance of β . Then p is true in a world w ∈ W <u>with respect to a system of
spheres</u> $, if and only if <u>one</u> of the following conditions hold:

(i) q is false in all worlds of all spheres of $ ₓ. In this case, p is <u>vacuous-
     ly</u> true.
(ii) <u>There</u> is a sphere S of $ ₓ, such that S contains at least one world where
     q is true and r is true in all worlds of S where q is true.

Again, a picture will illustrate the case where p is non-vacuously true:

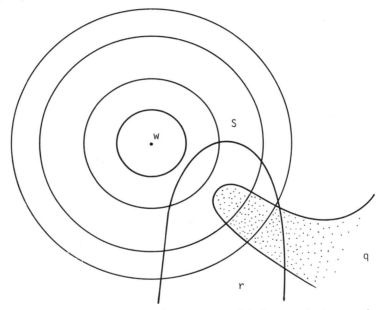

S is a sphere which contains at least one world where q is true and r is true
in all those worlds.

A system of spheres is a function which assigns sets of sets of possible
worlds to every possible world. A set of possible worlds is, however, a proposition. That means that a system of spheres is just a very special kind of
conversational background.

I want to show now that DAVID LEWIS' truth-conditions for counterfactuals
coincide (for the non-vacuous case) with my account of conditional necessity
if we restrict ourselves to conversational backgrounds which are systems of
spheres.

I do not worry very much about the vacuous case. Here, our intuitions are poor enough and if they were clear we could easily find a technical solution. Consider again an arbitrary utterance of the sentence

(2) Would , if α , β

where the proposition q is expressed by the utterance of α and the proposition r by the utterance of β.
Let $ be a system of spheres such that for any world w $\in$ W, there is at least one sphere in $_w$ which contains at least one world where q is true.
What I claim is, that the following two statements are equivalent for any world w $\in$ W.

First statement:
There is a sphere S in $_w$ such that S contains at least one world where q is true and r is true in all worlds of S where q is true.

Second statement:
For every subset of $_w$ with which q is compatible, there is a superset $\mathcal{P}$ such that
(i) $\mathcal{P}$ is a subset of $_w$
(ii) q is compatible with $\mathcal{P}$
(iii) r follows from $\mathcal{P}\cup\{q\}$.[19]

My claim will be proved in both directions:

Direction $\Rightarrow$:
If the first statement holds, then the second will:
We suppose that there is a sphere S in $_w$ such that S contains at least one world where q is true and r is true in all those worlds.
That is:

(a) $(\exists w \in W)$ $(w \in S \wedge w \in q)$

(b) r follows from $\{S, q\}$

Let $\mathcal{P}$ be any subset of $_w$, with which q is compatible. That is:

(c) $(\exists w \in W)$ $(w \in \cap\mathcal{P} \wedge w \in q)$

We have to show now, that there is a superset of $\mathcal{P}$ for which the three conditions (i) to (iii) mentioned above hold.
Consider, for this, simply the set:

$\mathcal{P} \cup \{S\}$

This set is a superset of $\mathcal{P}$, a subset of $_w$ and r follows from $\mathcal{P} \cup \{S\} \cup \{q\}$, as r follows already from $\{S,q\}$ according to (b).

What we have to prove is, that q is compatible with $\mathcal{P} \cup \{S\}$, that is that:

(d) $(\exists w \in W)$ $(w \in \cap\mathcal{P} \wedge w \in S \wedge w \in q)$

In the case where $\mathcal{P}$ is the empty set, there is nothing to prove. Then (d) holds because of (a) alone. If $\mathcal{P}$ is not the empty set, then $\cap\mathcal{P}$ is a sphere of $ according to the definition of a system of spheres. The same definition prescribes that $_w$ be nested, that is that either:

$$\cap \mathcal{S} \quad \subseteq \quad S$$

or:

$$S \quad \subseteq \quad \cap \mathcal{S}$$

Let us consider the <u>first case</u>, namely that

$$\cap \mathcal{S} \quad \subseteq \quad S$$

From this, it follows that:

$$\cap \mathcal{S} \quad \cap \quad q \subseteq \quad S$$

that is:

(e) $((\forall w_{\varepsilon W}) \; (w \varepsilon \cap \mathcal{S} \wedge w \varepsilon q) \supset w \varepsilon S)$

Because of (c), there is a $w \varepsilon W$, such that $w \varepsilon \cap \mathcal{S}$ and $w \varepsilon q$. Therefore, (d) holds in the first case.

Consider now the <u>second case</u>, namely that

$$S \quad \subseteq \quad \cap \mathcal{S}$$

from this, it follows

$$S \cap q \quad \subseteq \quad \cap \mathcal{S}$$

that is:

(f) $(\forall w_{\varepsilon W}) \; (w \varepsilon S \wedge w \varepsilon q) \supset w \varepsilon \cap \mathcal{S}$)

Because of (a), there is a $w \varepsilon W$ such that $w \varepsilon S$ and $w \varepsilon q$. Therefore, (d) holds also in this case.

This concludes the proof of direction $\Rightarrow$.

Direction $\Leftarrow$:
If the second statement holds, the first will.

We suppose that for every subset of $\$_w$, there is a superset $\mathcal{S}$ such that

(i) $\mathcal{S}$ is a subset of $\$_w$
(ii) q is a compatible with $\mathcal{S}$
(iii) r follows from $\mathcal{S} \cup \{q\}$

The supposition we made about $\$$, allows us to infer that $\$_w$ contains a sphere in which there is at least one world in which q is true. Let S be such a sphere. Then there is a subset of $\$_w$, with which q is compatible. Such a set could be $\{S\}$.   According to the supposition above, there must be a superset $\mathcal{S}$ of $\{S\}$ such that $\mathcal{S}$ fulfills the conditions (i) to (iii). In addition, $\mathcal{S}$ is not the empty set, as it is a superset of $\{S\}$, which is not the empty set either. That $\mathcal{S}$ fulfills condition (i) means that $\mathcal{S}$ is a subset of $\$_w$. That $\mathcal{S}$ fulfills condition (ii) means that there is a world in $\cap \mathcal{S}$ where q is true.

That $\mathcal{S}$ fulfills condition (iii) means that r is true in all worlds of $\cap \mathcal{S}$ where q is true.

As $\mathcal{S}$ is not the empty set, $\cap \mathcal{S}$ is a sphere of $\$_w$, according to the definition of a system of spheres. Therefore, there is a sphere in $\$_w$ such that it contains at least one world in which q is true and r is true in all its worlds where q is true.

This concludes direction $\Leftarrow$ and the whole proof.

In a so to speak "technocratic" argument, I have shown that David Lewis' truth-conditions for counterfactuals are a special case of my account of conditional necessity if we neglect the vacuous case.

The question is now, whether there are any good reasons to assume that conversational backgrounds are as special things as systems of spheres.

Consider again my utterance of sentence (1):

(1) If Goethe had survived the year 1832, he would nevertheless be dead by now.

It may be that what I expressed by this utterance is roughly that:

In view of what gets as close as possible to what is actually the case, Goethe would be dead by now, even if he had survived the year 1832.

Here, a system of spheres $\$$ could perhaps be thought to be the right reconstruction of what is expressed by the phrase "What gets as close as possible to what is actually the case".

If w is the actual world, then $\{w\}$, the center of $\$_w$, gets closest to what is actually the case in w. The more "deeply" a proposition is nested in $\$_w$, the more precise a description of the facts in w it represents.

I leave it to further investigations whether counterfactuals depend on conversational backgrounds which are in general as special as systems of spheres.

My analysis, at least, does not require this.

Systems of spheres are not meant to deal with indicative conditional sentences. My analysis aims to include this kind of sentences as well, as long as conditional necessity or possibility is involved.

Chapter five: Indicative and Subjunctive Conditional Sentences:
            Their Rules of Use

The following story is reported about ancient Rome:
When Caligula left the arena one day, suddenly the doors shut behind him and he was attacked by his own body-guard.

The crowd in the arena heard him screaming but they could only guess what had happened.

May be Caligula was dead, may be he was still alive.

In these moments of tension and uncertainty, Marcus, Tullius, Sejanus and Naso, four men in the arena, did the following utterances:

Marcus:
(1) If Caligula is dead now, I will necessarily get promoted.

Tullius:
(2) If Caligula is still alive, I will necessarily get promoted.

Sejanus:
(3) If Caligula were dead now, I would get promoted.

Naso:
(4) If Caligula were still alive, I would get promoted.

Some minutes later, the doors of the arena open and in comes Caligula, greeting the crowd.

Let us imagine now a rather absurd situation:

While Marcus, Tullius, Sejanus and Naso watch Caligula stepping in, they all repeat the very same sentence they had uttered before.

What would happen?

If Marcus repeated his sentence, that would sound very inappropriate. Perhaps we would think that he lost his mind, having to bury all hopes for promotion.

If Tullius repeated his sentence, that would not sound much better. May be we should silently replace the word "if" by "since" and let him pass.

There would be nothing peculiar about Sejanus uttering sentence (3). But if Naso repeated his sentence, we would be somehow puzzled again.

Given the new situation, the utterance of the three sentences (1), (2) and (4) would not be appropriate any more, while the utterance of sentence (3) still would.

Let us try to find out the reasons.

Before the appearance of Caligula, that he was dead or still alive, were both compatible with what was then commonly known.

But after the appearance of Caligula, that he was dead, was not compatible any more with what was then commonly known.

These observations (which seem to hold for all kinds of conditional sentences) may motivate the following rules of use for conditional sentences of the kind in which we are interested here:

Rules of use for indicative conditional sentences:

Consider an arbitrary utterance of an indicative conditional sentence of the form:

(5) must
$\left.\begin{array}{l} \text{must} \\ \\ \text{necessarily} \end{array}\right\}$, if α , β

where q is the proposition expressed by the utterance of α and w the world where the utterance takes place.

Such an utterance will only be appropriate if q and its negation are both compatible with what is common knowledge in w.[20]

This rule "rules out" the use of the sentence (1) and (2) after but not before the appearance of Caligula.

Similar restrictions are mentioned by other authors as well. In "Indicative Conditionals"[21], ROBERT STALNAKER states the following rule:

"It is appropriate to make an indicative conditional statement or supposition only in a context which is compatible with the antecedent".

Pushed by different considerations, JOHN BIGELOW[22] formulates a rule which is meant to hold for conditionals in general:

"We may stipulate that the sphere of resonance must always be chosen to be at least large enough to include some worlds in which the antecedent is false."

As implied by JOHN BIGELOW, this rule has to be assumed for subjunctive conditional sentences as well. The following rule takes up this idea:

Rule of use for subjunctive conditional sentences:

Consider an arbitrary utterance of a subjunctive conditional sentence of the form:

(6) would, if α , β

where q is the proposition expressed by α and w the world where the utterance is performed.

This utterance will only be appropriate if the negation of q is compatible with what is common knowledge in w.

This rule excludes the use of sentence (4) after but not before the appearance of Caligula; it does, however, not prohibit the use of sentence (3) in either situation.

There is a frequent use of subjunctive conditional sentences, which we might call their counterfactual use.

Here, the stronger requirement is made, that the antecedent should be incompatible with what is common knowledge in the world of the utterance.

Put into a rule, we have the following:

Rule of use for counterfactuals:

Suppose that a subjunctive conditional sentence of the form

(6) would, if α, β

is uttered in a situation where q is the proposition expressed by α and w
the world where the utterance is performed.

This use of a subjunctive conditional sentence is a counterfactual use if
and only if q is incompatible with what is common knowledge in w.

Whether a conditional sentence is <u>appropriately</u> used, depends on what is
<u>common knowledge</u> in the world of the utterance.

But whether the proposition expressed by the utterance of a conditional
where a modal is modified, is <u>true</u> in the world of the utterance depends on
the conversational background, which is responsible for the interpretation
of the modal.

There might be a connection between what is common knowledge in a world
where such a conditional sentence is uttered and the set of propositions
which the corresponding conversational background assigns to this world. But
these two sets need not be identical:

1.
There are uses of modalised conditional sentences where the truth of the
corresponding proposition in the world of the utterance depends on facts
which are not commonly known.

2.
There are appropriate uses of modalised indicative conditional sentences
where the antecedent is not compatible with the set of propositions which
the conversational background assigns to the world of the utterance.

An illustration of 1.:[23]

Consider again Tullius' utterance in the arena:

(2) If Caligula is still alive, I will necessarily get promoted.

Suppose that Caligula has just signed a paper which provides that Tullius
has to take care of the imperial geese instead of being promoted. Even if nobody but Caligula knows about the existence of this document, the proposition
expressed by Tullius is very likely to be false in such a situation.

An illustration of 2.:[24]

Suppose that the law in Rome provides

that nobody murders Caligula
and
that Caligula will be made a god, if he gets murdered

Imagine that, before the appearance of Caligula in the arena, Marcus says to
his neighbour:

(7) If Caligula has been murdered, he must be made a god.

As we have seen, this use of an indicative conditional sentence is appropriate, as it is compatible with what is commonly known in this situation, that Caligula has been murdered.

Given that the conversational background for the use of this "must" is formed by what the law provides, the set of propositions, which this conversational background assigns to the world of the utterance, is not compatible with the supposition that Caligula has been murdered.

I said that there might be a connection between what is common knowledge in a world, where a modalised conditional sentence is uttered, and the set of propositions, which the corresponding conversational background assigns to this world.

Such a connection is not to be expected in the case of a purely deontic background, but it is very likely in the case of an objective one. Here, relevant parts of the common knowledge may be components of the conversational background.

This seems to lead to a tendency, that with an objective conversational background, the antecedent of a modalised indicative conditional sentence which is appropriately used, is also compatible with the set of propositions which the conversational background assigns to the world of the utterance. And that likewise, the antecedent of a subjunctive conditional sentence which is counterfactually used, is not compatible with the analogous set.

I do not think that one could easily provide irrefutable arguments, that this is more than a tendency. But I think that, nevertheless, this tendency is plausible enough to support my guess, that the behaviour of modalised conditional sentences in certain inferences follows naturally from their rules of use in combination with my account of conditional necessity. This does not exclude that the influence of the rules of use is not as direct as one might be tempted to suppose.

The next chapters will examine some typical properties of modalised conditional sentences with respect to the three inference patterns "strengthening the antecedent", "transitivity" and "contraposition".

Chapter six: Valid Inferences

First of all, let us see what these threee inference patterns look like:

Strengthening the antecedent:

If Arcimboldo invented the merry-go-round, it must be that the merry-go-round was invented in Prague.

Therefore:

If Arcimboldo invented the merry-go-round and the emperor Rudolph liked merry-go-rounds, it must be that the merry-go-round was invented in Prague.

Transitivity:

If Arcimboldo invented the merry-go-round, it must be that the merry-go-round was invented in Prague.

If the merry-go-round was invented in Prague, it must be that the first merry-go-round was seen in the Hradschin.

Therefore:

If Arcimboldo invented the merry-go-round, it must be that the first merry-go-round was seen in the Hradschin.

Contraposition:

If Arcimboldo invented the merry-go-round, it must be that Vermeer painted a merry-go-round.

Therefore:

If Vermeer did not paint a merry-go-round, it must be that Arcimboldo did not invent the merry-go-round.

If a modalised indicative conditional sentence is used appropriately in a world w with an objective conversational background H, its rule of use induces a tendency that the corresponding antecedent is compatible with H(w). That is, in this case, no inconsistency arises.

I have mentioned in chapter three, that my account of conditional necessity reduces to logical consequence as soon as we deal with consistent sets of propositions. And for logical consequence, the three inference patterns hold.

Let A be any set of propositions and q, r and s any propositions. What we have now is:

Conditional necessity and logical consequence:

Suppose that q is compatible with A, and $\mathcal{S}$ is the set of all subsets of $A \cup \{q\}$ which contain q.

Then the following holds:

r follows from $A \cup \{q\}$ if and only if every set in $\mathcal{S}$ has a superset in $\mathcal{S}$ from which r follows.

Strengthening the antecedent:

If r follows from $A \cup \{q\}$,
then r follows also from $A \cup \{q \cap s\}$

Transitivity:

If r follows from $A \cup \{q\}$,
and s follows from $A \cup \{r\}$,
then s follows also from $A \cup \{q\}$

Contraposition:

If r follows from A ∪ { q},
then -q follows from A ∪ {-r}.

We can conclude that the rules of use for indicative conditional sentences and my account of conditional necessity predict that there is a tendency,
that the three inference patterns hold for modalised indicative conditionals
as long as the conversational background is objective and does not change
during the inference.

It may be objected, that the requirement that the conversational background should not change during the inference is probably too strong. Consider again the merry-go-round-inferences. They are all valid.

But it is quite likely that the conversational background does change during the inferences: The conversational background does not get established
independently of the modalised sentence itself. So the suppositions that the
emperor Rudolph liked merry-go-rounds, that the merry-go-round was invented
in Prague or that Vermeer did not paint a merry-go-round may very well contribute new kinds of premises to the ongoing inference. Our concept of conditional necessity can cope with this case: We need not stipulate that the
conversational background does not change at all during one and the same inference. We only have to insist that it does not change beyond the limits set
by logical consequence.

Imaginable cases out of a whole scale of possibilities could be the following: (Let A be any set of propositions and q, r and s any propositions).

Strengthening the antecedent:

Let B be any superset of A.
Then we have:
If r follows from A ∪ {q},
then r follows also from B ∪ {q∩s}

Transitivity:

Let B be any set of propositions.
What we have then is:
If r follows from A ∪ {q}
and s follows from B ∪ {r},
then s follows also from A ∪ B ∪ {q}.

Contraposition:

Let B be any set such that r follows from B ∪ {q}.
We may then state the following:
If r follows from A ∪ {q},
then -q follows from B ∪ {-r}

What we can now conclude, is, that the rules of use for indicative conditional sentences and my account of conditional necessity predict that there
is a tendency, that the three inference patterns hold for modalised indicative
conditional sentences as long as the conversational background is objective
and does not change during the inference beyond the limits set by logical
consequence.

The next chapter will examine some cases where the three inference patterns fail.

Chapter seven: Fallacies[25]

The three inference patterns may fail with indicative and with subjunctive modalised conditional sentences. Popular candidates for these fallacies are counterfactuals with objective backgrounds and those uses of modalised indicative conditional sentences, where the background is not an objective one. In both cases, there is the danger, that the antecedent of the conditional is not compatible with the set of propositions which the conversational background assigns to the world of the utterance. In the second case, the rules of use do nothing to prevent this inconsistency, in the first case, they even favour it.

Here are some examples for the failure of "strengthening the antecedent", "transitivity" and "contraposition":

Deontic fallacies:

Strengthening the antecedent:

If I bring you a cherry-cake, you must say: "Thank-you, that's really nice of you."

Therefore:

If I bring you a cherry-cake and throw it into your face, you must say: "Thank-you, that's really nice of you."

Transitivity:

If Caligula tries to kill Tiberius, Claudius must kill Caligula. If Claudius kills Caligula, Claudius must be decapitated.

Therefore:

If Caligula tries to kill Tiberius, Claudius must be decapitated.

Contraposition:

Even if Caligula tries to kill his wife, it must be that Claudius does not kill him.

Therefore:

If Claudius kills Caligula, it must be that Caligula does not try to kill his wife.

Counterfactual fallacies:
Strengthening the antecedent:

If I had kept my old job, I would have stayed poor.

Therefore:

If I had kept my old job and inherited one million guilders, I would have stayed poor.

Transitivity:

If I were in New Zealand now, I would sleep.
If I would sleep now, I would get fired.

Therefore:

If I were in New Zealand now, I would get fired.

I have to mention, that I am sitting in my office in Nijmegen at the moment. It is four o'clock in the afternoon and I am supposed to work. At the antipodes, however, it is night now and there would be nothing wrong, if I just slept. By the way, I think it would be highly appreciated by the organisation I work for, if I spent some time in New Zealand.

Contraposition:

If Goethe had survived the year 1832, he would nevertheless be dead by now.

Therefore:

If Goethe were not dead by now, he would not have survived the year 1832.

In both cases, I have no difficulties with the failure of contraposition: It simply fails. Contrapositions are likely to fail or sound funny for all kinds of reasons: The rules of use may be violated, the conversational background may change radically, the temporal order may get reversed.[26]

But with the other two inference patterns it's different: I sometimes think that they are excellent examples of fallacies. And at other times, I think that thinking this is itself a fallacy. I want to examine these two feelings carefully. I will start with the latter, restricting myself to counterfactual fallacies.For other kinds of fallacies, analogous observations can be made.

If it is really true that I would have stayed poor if I had kept my old job, should that not include the case where I inherit a fortune while keeping my job?

I did not think of this possibility when I uttered that sentence, but it still is a possibility. Dialogues like the following one are not uncommon in daily Tife:

Violetta: If I had kept my old job, I would have stayed poor.

Mrs. B.: Not necessarily. You might have inherited one million guilders.

Here, Mrs. B.'s reply is an objection to what Violetta said and not just a further supposition.

Most counterfactuals are vulnerable by this kind of objection. My example for the failure of transitivity could be destroyed in the very same way:

Angelika: If I slept now, I would get fired.

Veronika: Not if you were in New Zealand. Over there, it is night right now
and you could sleep without harm.

It seems to follow from such a <u>sceptical</u> strategy for handling counterfactuals, that, once a counterfactual supposition is made, anything is possible as long as it is compatible with this supposition. This would mean
that, given such a supposition, nothing but what follows from it, is necessary.

Working with this strategy, <u>strict implication</u> would be the right interpretation for <u>counterfactuals</u>.

We can capture this intuition by combining conditional necessity with a
conversational background H which assigns the set $\{w\}$ to every world w.

Let q be the antecedent, and r be the consequent of a conditional which
is expressed by the utterance of a sentence of the form "would, if α, β" in
a world w.

Suppose that H is the conversational background for this utterance and
that q is false in w (This follows from the fact that we consider a counterfactual use of the sentence above).

As q is false in w, the set of all consistent subsets of $H(w) \cup \{q\}$ which
contain q is simply $\{\{q\}\}$. This means, that there is for every set in $\{\{q\}\}$
a superset in $\{\{q\}\}$ from which r follows, if and only if r follows from $\{q\}$.

This should fit the sceptic's taste: He relies on everything which is
actually the case. Once the slightest change is assumed, you cannot be sure
what happens to the rest: it may develop freely within the limits of logical
possibility.

For strict implication, the two inference patterns hold.

So, working with the sceptical strategy, we may very well get the feeling
that, thinking that there are counterfactual fallacies, is itself a fallacy.

The sceptical strategy has certain advantages: If you follow it, you have
a free-pass for excursions into the realm of fancy.

Children, very often, seem to push this possibility to the extreme without
making a clear distinction between what is possible and what is necessary
under a counterfactual supposition.

The following dialogue took place between an adult and a three year old
child. It is reported by Kuczaj and Daly. [27]

Adult:	Child:
What would you think would happen, if you saw a crocodile?	
	I'd bite a crocodile.
You'd bite him?	
	Yeah. When I would turn into a tiger.

Adult:	Child:
When you turned into a tiger, you'd bite him?	
	Yeah.

In other examples reported by the same authors, the adult tries -with or without success- to make the child stay a bit closer to the facts. The following dialogue took place between an adult and an almost four year old child. [28]

Adult:	Child:
What would have happened if they couldn't have found any water?	
	They gotted a hose.
Oh. What would have happened if the hose had broken?	
	Then they would have a short hose.
Do you think they would have had trouble putting the fire out with a short hose?	
	Yeah. They would have to say "come here, fire. Come here, fire."
Why would they say that?	
	Because the hose, because a broked hose wouldn't reach the fire.
Oh. Do you think the fire would listen?	
	No. Fires aren't alive, silly.

In this dialogue, the child starts off with a strategy which we might call "keep-close-to-the-relevant-facts" -strategy. He switches then into fancy. Here, it is challenged by the adult, who tries to put him back on his original track.

I think that I follow this keep-close-to-the-relevant -facts-strategy, whenever I have the feeling that inferences like the ones mentioned above are really good examples of counterfactual fallacies. In what follows, I shall present a cautious reconstruction of what happens during the first inference, whenever I keep to this strategy. Naturally, this reconstruction is a bit simplified.

When I utter the sentence

(1) If I had kept my old job, I would have stayed poor.

a conversational background H is established whose main components could (approximately) be represented by the following questions:

?(q) : Did I keep my old job?
?(e) : How much could I earn in this job?
?(o) : Did I have any other kind of income up to now?
?(p) : Who is poor?

For w, the world of my utterance, the answers are the following:

(-q): that I did not keep my old job.
(e) : that I could not earn more than 800 guilders a month in this job.
(o) : that I did not have any other kind of income up to now.
(p) : that anyone who has less than a thousand guilders a month is poor.

We have now:

H(w) = {-q,e,o,p}

Let q be the proposition that I kept my old job and r the proposition that I stayed poor. q is the antecedent and r the consequent of the conditional I express by my utterance of (1). Adding q to H(w), we get the inconsistent set.

H(w) ∪ {q} = {q -q,e,o,p}

The set $\mathcal{S}_1$ of all consistent subsets of this set which contain q, would be:

$$\mathcal{S}_1 = \left\{ \begin{array}{c} \{q\}, \{q,e\}, \{q,o\}, \{q,p\}, \\ \{q,e,o\}, \{q,o,p\}, \{q,e,p\}, \\ \{q,e,o,p\} \end{array} \right\}$$

In $\mathcal{S}_1$, there is for every set a superset from which r follows: r follows from {q,e,o,p} and this set is a superset for every set in $\mathcal{S}_1$.

What I say by the utterance of (1) should therefore be true in w according to the criterium of conditional necessity.

I assume now that the conversational background does not change when I utter (2) shortly after (1):

(2) If I had kept my old job and inherited one million guilders, I would have stayed poor.

(2) too, is counterfactually used. Consider now the set $\mathcal{S}_2$ of all consist-ent subsets of H(w) ∪ {q ∩ s}, which contain q ∩ s, that is the proposition, that I kept my old job and inherited one million guilders:

$$\mathcal{S}_2 = \left\{ \begin{array}{c} \{q \cap s\}, \{q \cap s,e\}, \\ \{q \cap s,p\}, \{q \cap s,e,p\} \end{array} \right\}$$

Here, besides -q,o has been discarded, as the supposition that I inherited one million guilders is not compatible with the actual fact, that I had no other kind of income up to now (besides the kind of income one gets from a job).

There is no set in $\mathcal{S}_2$ from which r follows.

The proposition which I express by the utterance of (2) should therefore be false according to the criterium of conditional necessity.

And consequently, the whole inference should fail.

An important result of the above speculations is, that -for uses of modalised conditional sentences, where the antecedent is incompatible with the set of propositions which the conversational background assigns to the world under consideration, the inference pattern "strengthening the antecedent" may fail, even if we assume that the conversational background does not change during the inference.

I have presented two different strategies for counterfactual reasoning: the sceptical and the keep-close-to-the-facts-strategy. The examples above suggest that these two strategies may be used to challenge each other: If I keep close to the relevant facts, I may be challenged by a remark that, under a counterfactual supposition, anything is possible. If I take the sceptical strategy for a long-distance-flight from reality, I may be challenged by a remark that I should keep closer to the facts.

The changing feelings which I had towards the first two counterfactual inferences above, may perhaps be the result of a conflict between these two strategies.

For the first strategy, these inferences are sound, but for the second one, they are fallacious. Conversational backgrounds are slippery, fugitive and hard to grasp. If modalised conditionals depend on them, they will be themselves slippery, fugitive and hard to grasp. And so they are.

What is not slippery, fugitive and hard to grasp, is how modalised conditional depend on conversational backgrounds, once we have got them to grasp.

To show this was the aim of this paper.*

Notes

* A good deal of research for this paper was done while I was still a member of the Sonderforschungsbereich 99 "Linguistik" in Konstanz.
I am grateful for discussions with John Bigelow, Max Cresswell, Urs Egli, David Lewis and Arnim von Stechow.

1 Lewis (1975)

2 See Lewis (1976)

3 Boole (1854)

4 Kratzer (1977) and (1978)

5 See v. Kutschera (1974) for a similar view

6 Kratzer (1978)

7 I take "would" to be some kind of marked form. Phrases like "he would possibly ..." also occur.

8   I neglect here the case where H(w) is inconsistent. For a more adequate treatment, see Kratzer (1977) and (1978)

9   This does not exclude that it would be rather inappropriate to utter sentence (2) in the first situation.

10 Chisholm (1946)

11 Goodman (1947) and (1955)

12 Rescher (1964) and (1973)

13 I do not want to require the compactness of the set of propositions which a conversational background assigns to a world.

14 I was told by Hans Kamp, that Frank Veltman gave a talk in Amsterdam where he made similar proposals. See also his contribution in "Amsterdam Papers in Formal Grammar", volume, 1.

15 See Lewis (1973)

16 Stalnaker (1968)

17 Lewis (1973), pp. 13,14

18 For a discussion of this term, see the next chapter.

19 This formulation is equivalent to the one presented under the heading of conditional necessity.

20 For a discussion of the notion of common knowledge, see Lewis (1969) or Schiffer (1972)

21 Stalnaker (?)

22 Bigelow (1976)

23 I owe this kind of example to Max Cresswell.

24 This is a variation of the Samaritan-Paradox of deontic logic. See for example Hansson (1969)

25 For a discussion of these fallacies, see Hansson (1969), van Fraassen (1972) or Lewis (1973)

26 See Settekorn (1974)

27 Kuczaj and Daly (1978)

28 Kuczaj and Daly (1978)

References

Bigelow, J.C. (1976): If-then meets the Possible Worlds. In: Philosophia, vol. 2.

Boole, G. (1854): An investigation of the Laws of Thought. Reprint. New York (Dover Publications).

Chisholm, R. (1946): The Contrary-to-fact Conditional. In: Mind, 55.

Hansson, B. (1969): An Analysis of some Deontic Logics. In: Noûs 3.

van Fraassen, B. (1972): The Logic of Conditional Obligation. In: Journal of Philosophical Logic, 1.

Goodman, N. (1947): The Problem of Counterfactual Conditionals. In: Journal of Philosophy, 44.

Goodman, N. (1955): Fact, Fiction, Forcast. Deutsche Übertragung Frankfurt (Suhrkamp) 1975.

Kratzer, A. (1977): What "must" and "can" must and can mean. In: Linguistics and Philosophy, 1.

Kratzer, A. (1978): Semantik der Re'de. Kontexttheorie, Modalwörter, Konditional-sätze, Königsstein (Scriptor).

Kuczaj, S.A. (1978): The Ontogenesis of Hypothetical Reference. 10th Stanford Child Language Research Forum.

v. Kutschera, F. (1974): Indicative Conditionals. In: Theoretical Linguistics 1.

Lewis, D.K. (1969): Convention. Cambridge, Mass.

Lewis, D.K. (1973): Counterfactuals. Oxford.

Lewis, D.K. (1975): Adverbs of Quantification. In: Keenan, E. (ed.): Formal Semantics of Natural Language. Cambridge.

Lewis, D.K. (1976): Probabilities of Conditionals and Conditional Probabili-ties. In: Philosophical Review, 85.

Rescher, N. (1964): Hypothetical Reasoning. Amsterdam.

Rescher, N. (1973): The Coherence Theory of Truth. Oxford.

Schiffer, S. (1972): Meaning. Oxford.

Settekorn, W. (1974): Semantische Strukturen der Konditionalsätze. Kronberg (Scriptor).

Stalnaker, R. (1968): A Theory of Conditionals. In: Rescher, N. (ed): Studies in Logical Theory. Oxford.

Stalnaker, R. (?): Indicative Conditionals. Manuscript.

Veltman, F. (1976): Prejudices, Presuppositions and the Theory of Conditionals. In: Amsterdam Papers in Formal Grammar, 1.

A Semantic Analysis of German 'Erst'

Ekkehard König

Technische Universität Hannover, Englische Sprachwissenschaft,
Im Moore 21, D-3000 Hannover 1, Fed. Rep. of Germany

0. In this paper I would like to report on some aspects of comparative work on certain particles in German and related elements in English. The particles belong to the class of so-called 'degree particles' (Gradpartikel[1]) and include a large number of elements in German, viz. auch, ausgerechnet, erst, gleich, gerade, jedenfalls, noch, nur, schon, sogar, zumindest etc. In English the corresponding class is very small and comprises also/too/... either, even, only and perhaps one or two further elements. English counterparts of the German particles listed above also include the comparative construction as Ad as MP (=measure phrase) (e.g. as early$_2$ as ten, as many as five, etc.) and a few other constructions.

Syntactically, the particles listed above combine with any constituent (possibly more than one) of a sentence and an appropriate open sentence, i.e. an open sentence with a free variable of the same category as the element with which the particle is in construction. Following KARTTUNEN's terminology (cf. F. and L. KARTTUNEN, 1977:121) we call the open sentence the 'scope' and the other element the 'focus' of the particle. Degree particles are very much like quantifiers in their syntactic and semantic behavior. However, instead of relating a constituent of a sentence to the remaining open sentence most degree particles may also directly combine with a sentence, i.e. they may be used as sentence operators or conjunctions. Most elements also have a use as 'modal particle'. Using CRESSWELL's framework (CRESSWELL, 1973), in which all sentences of a natural language would have a representation in a formal base language called λ-categorial language, degree particles would combine with an element of various syntactic categories and an abstract. Thus, a sentence like (1) would roughly have the following representation in the base language:

(1) Paul likes even Mary.

(2) $\langle\langle \lambda, x_1 \langle$ Paul, likes, $x_1\rangle\rangle$ even, Mary$\rangle$

It is perhaps an unfortunate consequence of adopting this framework that degree particles would belong to many syntactic categories depending on the focus constituent (cf. KÖNIG, 1977). This drawback can be avoided if one follows KARTTUNEN's proposal to introduce particles syncategorematically. KARTTUNEN introduces

the elements under discussion by a quantification rule. This rule
applies to sentences containing an unbound pronoun and replaces
that pronoun with an element of the appropriate category adding
a particle to the front of it (cf. F. and L. KARTTUNEN, 1977:121).

As far as the semantic interpretation is concerned degree
particles pick out other values for the abstract than the one
denoted by the focus constituent and either imply or deny that
these other values satisfy the open sentence. Some but not all
particles require a strict ordering between the values under consideration. Most degree particles do not make any contribution
to the truth conditions of the sentence in which they occur. Thus,
the aspects of meaning just mentioned are generally not part of
what is asserted in a sentence but rather conventional implicatures. Like conversational implicatures and presuppositions,
conventional implicatures are conditions on the smooth functioning of communicative acts. A characterization of conventional
implicatures cannot only be found in GRICE (]975) but also in
a number of articles by KARTTUNEN and PETERS (1975, 1976).

Elements which are here considered as belonging to the class
of degree particles in English, viz. _only_, _even_ and _too_ have been
analysed in a large number of articles in recent years. Many of
these analyses show that it is very tempting to put too much
into the content, presuppositions or implicatures of these elements. The apparent properties of a particle are often due to
specific contexts one has in mind or at least to the interaction
of the conventional implicatures and certain contexts. An example
of this is the claim made in FRASER (1971), ANDERSON (1972) and
F. and L. KARTTUNEN (1977) that a sentence like _Even Bill likes_
Mary implicates (or presupposes) that other people like Mary
besides Bill. This is certainly a reasonable inference in most
situations. However, it is easy to think up$_3$examples and situations where this implication does not hold. Many more examples
of unjustifiably overloading the semantic description of _even_
or _only_ can be found in SHANON (1978), who tries to account for
the 'ungrammaticality' of sentences like _He is short; he is even_
of average height as well as the 'ungrammaticality' of (3) in a
temporal as opposed to a concessive sense:

(3) He died even after he prayed.

As a further example of the tendency to overspecify the meaning
of degree particles one could cite the claim made in HORN (1969:
101 f.) that the focus constituent of _only_ - provided it is not
a noun phrase - denotes something of low scalar value in contrast
to other values under consideration. FINNIS gives a great variety
of examples which refute this claim.

1. In what follows I shall try to give a semantic analysis of
German **erst**. In contrast to many other degree particles _erst_
cannot be used as a sentential operator. The use of _erst_ as degree
particle presents some notorious problems to the **analyst**. There
seem to be at least two different meanings or uses so that frequently two or more homophonous lexical elements are postulated
(cf. BLUMENTHAL, 1974). The first use that comes to mind is the
temporal use of _erst_ in examples like the following:

(4) Die Gäste gingen erst um Mitternacht.
    'The guests did not leave until midnight.

In this use erst is associated with an implicature of relative
lateness of the event considered. This implicature is also apparent in certain selectional restrictions of erst:

(5) erst später; erst allmählich; erst nach langer Zeit; *erst
    bald; *erst nach kurzer Zeit; erst vor kurzer Zeit; schon
    bald; schon nach kurzer Zeit, etc.

The two unacceptable combinations involve incompatible evaluations
of a point in time or interval. Note that schon is acceptable
in precisely the collocations where erst is not and vice versa.
One of the English counterparts of this use of erst (viz. not...
until) is only used in a temporal sense. Another possible translation of erst in (4), viz. as late as..., makes the implicature
just mentioned explicit.

    The following two examples show that erst does not only com-
bine with time expressions as focus constituent:

(6) a. Erst drei Biere machen dich fahruntüchtig.
       'It takes three pints to make you unfit to drive.'

    b. Erst ein Oberstudienrat wäre ihr als Schwiegersohn angenehm.
       'Only an O. would be acceptable to her as a son-in-law.'

The connection between (6) and (4) is fairly obvious. Erst marks
a relatively advanced point on a scale of values, where all values
preceding the one given do not satisfy the open sentence in the
formal representation of (4) or (6). It is much more difficult
to relate another use of erst to the one in (4):

(7) (Ich weiß wie er über dieses Problem denkt.) Ich habe erst
    gestern mit ihm gesprochen.
    'I talked to him only yesterday.'

Here the qualification of gestern by erst amounts to the appositive comment 'which is not long ago'. The interval denoted by
gestern is evaluated as relatively near to the point of speech.
The connection between (4) and (7) is obvious as soon as one
realizes that these two uses represent two complementary ways
of looking at and evaluating a point in time or interval. Seen
from an anterior point the interval given is evaluated as relatively late and this brings it near to a posterior point, the
moment of speech. These two complementary points of view always
seem to exist whenever erst (as well as noch and schon) has a
time phrase as focus and this time phrase specifies an interval
with reference to a posterior point or interval (cf. KÖNIG, 1979).
It is the context which makes one point of view more plausible
than the other. In English only is normally used for cases like
(7). In order to make future reference easier we will mark erst
as used in (4) to (7) with the subscript '1' ($erst_1$). The use
most difficult to link up with the one in (4) occurs in sentences like (8):

(8) a. Paul kennt erst drei Personen hier.
      'Paul only knows three people here so far.'

    b. Es ist erst 10 Uhr.
      'It's only ten o'clock.'

The evaluations introduced by erst in (8)a. and b. are the exact
opposite of what we found in (4) and (6). Erst in (8)b. amounts
to the comment that it is relatively early and the number in (8)a.
is evaluated as relatively small. In (8) only is the appropriate
English translation of erst. Only, however, can also translate
nur. English, just like French, does not have a lexical distinction parallel to nur - erst. In (8)b. erst is the only possibility,
nur is not acceptable in this context. In cases like (8)a., where
both are possible with a clear difference in meaning, additions [5]
like so far or yet have to be used in English to translate erst:

(9) I've only glanced at your article yet, so I can't pass comment.
    'Ich habe Ihren Artikel erst flüchtig durchgesehen...'

Erst as used in (9) will from now on be referred to as $erst_2$.

2. The preceding discussion has shown that the main problem in
the semantic analysis of erst is to account for the relationship
between erst in (4) and in (9)[6]. How is it possible that contrary
evaluative implicatures are associated with the same lexical item
or with two lexical elements of the same form? As was indicated
in (6) an adequate semantic analysis also has to account for a
few particles closely related to erst, viz. nur, schon, noch.
The distinction between erst and nur has no parallel in English.
In German many syntactic and semantic contexts permit both erst
and nur, with a clear difference in meaning. Another particle
we will have to consider is schon. Schon can always replace erst.
The difference between these two concerns the nature of the evaluation. Erst and schon imply contrary evaluations. If we replace
erst by schon in (4) the time of the guest's departure would be
evaluated as relatively early, a substitution of schon for erst
in (8)b. would change the implicature to 'it is relatively late'.
So our problem of examining the relationship between two uses of
erst with apparently contrary implicatures now also applies to
two uses of schon. Moreover, the contrast between erst and schon
has an exact parallel in the contrast between nur and auch:

(10) a. Es ist schon 11 Uhr, nicht erst 10 Uhr.

     b. Paul kommt auch mit, nicht nur Hans.

Thus, nur and schon are closely related to erst and can be considered field neighbours of erst. A complete analysis would therefore
have to characterize the place erst occupies in the field by describing similarities and differences between its members.

3. After characterizing the class of which erst is a member, the
various uses of this element and its field neighbours we can now
turn to the semantic analysis. We will first give an informal
characterization of the various aspects of meaning associated
with erst and then go on to a tentative formalization of our
intuitions.

As was pointed out above a description of the meaning of degree
particles must make reference to the focus constituent, the open
sentence or abstract and to the particle itself. What basically
happens in sentences with these particles is that other values,
comparable to the one denoted by the focus constituent, are considered and the question of their satisfying the open sentence is
raised. The proposition expressed by the sentence in which one
of these values replaces the focus constituent functions as pragmatic backdrop, as condition of use of the particle. The first
specific point to note about erst is that a strict order must
obtain between the value assigned to the focus constituent and the
other values under consideration. Thus the focus constituent of
erst is very often a time expression or numerical expression.
However, an order may also be obtained by mapping various entities
onto time intervals or points in time. Thus the following sentence
implies that everything served before the fruit was not to the
speaker's taste:

(11) Erst das Obst schmeckte mir gut.
     'I didn't like anything before the fruit.'

As was mentioned above erst contributes an implicature to the
meaning of a sentence that some event occurs relatively late,
that some quantity is relatively small, etc. Schon always reverses
the evaluation. It is a well-known fact at least since SAPIR that
gradable adjectives used predicatively are implicitly comparative.
So it might be a good idea to look for a comparative explication
of our intuitions concerning the implicature of erst. We shall
do so by saying that erst and schon involve expectations - in a
very broad sense of the word - which are in conflict with reality,
either ahead of reality or lagging behind. The expectations can
be those of the speaker, only then can an utterance like (4) be
initiating. But they may also concern the interlocutor. In the
latter case the speaker is contradicting the hearer in using a
sentence like (4). Let us look in more detail at our example (4),
where erst has a time expression as focus. Let us use two lines
to represent (a) the expectation of either speaker or hearer,
symbolized as 'e' and (b) reality (r). If φ stands for Die Gäste
gingen, we can illustrate the meaning of erst in (4) by the following diagram:

(12)

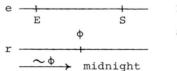

E = expectation point associated
    with erst
S = expectation point associated
    with schon

A sentence like (4) implicates that φ is expected for an interval
anterior to the interval specified in the sentence. Let us call
this interval the 'expectation point'. Schon reverses the order
between expectation point and interval given in the sentence. Erst
does not only imply the existence of such an expectation, this
particle also implies that this expectation is incompatible with

the assertion of the sentence. In fact, erst does not only exclude the expectation from being true in a situation where the
assertion is true but also contextually relevant values ordered
exactly like the expectation point with respect to the value given
in the sentence. Note the difference between nur and erst in the
following minimal pair:

(13) Ich fahre erst am Donnerstag nach Hannover.
     'I won't go to Hanover until Thursday.'

     b. Ich fahre nur am Donnerstag nach Hannover.
        'I only go to H. on Thursday.'

The first sentence excludes that the speaker goes to H, before
Thursday whereas (13)b. can also exclude days after Thursday. Thus,
erst does not only impose an order on the values under consideration, it also differs from nur in considering only values 'on
one side' of the value specified in the sentence. Erst introduces
a certain directionality. In uttering a sentence with erst one
goes from excluded values to included values for the variable in
the λ-categorial representation of the sentence. Erst marks a
boundary between excluded and included values. In sentences like
(13) nur can be paraphrased by sonst nicht/nie whereas vorher
nicht would be an appropriate paraphrase for erst.

(14) a. Ich fahre am Donnerstag nach H., vorher (fahre ich) nicht.

     b. Ich fahre am Donnerstag nach H., sonst (fahre ich) nie/nicht.

The function of sonst is very similar to that of degree particles:
Sonst selects certain alternatives to some value determined by
the co-text or context and restricts the predication of the sentence in which it occurs to these alternatives (cf. WUNDERLICH,
1978). Sentences like (4) or (13) give the impression that the
values excluded always have a low rank on the scale under consideration. This, however, is not the case. True, the flow of time
is normally conceived as irreversible and one needs a time machine
to go from excluded higher to included lower values:

(15) Erst im 15. Jahrhundert kannst du Ritter in Rüstungen sehen.
     'Only in the 15th century can you see knights in full armour.'

Whenever scales other than temporal ones are involved going from
high to low values and vice versa is no problem:

(16) a. Erst ein Regierungsinspektor wäre ihr als Schwiegersohn
        recht.
        'Only a R. would be acceptable to her as a son-in-law.'

     b. Erst ein Regierungsinspektor wurde von der Kulturrevo-
        lution verschont.
        'Only a R. was not affected by the Cultural Revolution.'

Given these two possibilities of selecting values on a scale how
can one tell where the expectation point and the area of excluded
values are located? The answer, I think, is that only the context
will tell you. (16)a. is a sentence about a woman who places high
demands on the professional rank of her future son-in-law. There-

fore values lower than the one given are excluded. (16)b., on the other hand, excludes higher values on the scale in a context where it is known that persons of high rank are particularly affected by a cultural revolution. Whenever events are placed in time, apparently only one way of viewing the matter is possible, unless a time machine is available. We will return to this point below.

4. So far we have only been dealing with $erst_1$. Let us now turn to the apparently more complicated uses of the particle in sentences like (8) or (9). The use of erst exemplified by (7) can be regarded as establishing a link between (4) and (8). In (7) the point of view is reversed and complementary to the one adopted in (4). The connection is even clearer if we look at the two following examples: Let us assume that (17)a. is uttered at 12 o'clock:

(17) a. Hans arbeitet erst seit 9 Uhr.
'H. has only been working since 9 o'clock.'

   b. Hans arbeitet erst (seit) drei Stunden.
'H. has only been working for three hours so far.'

Uttered at 12 o'clock the two sentences amount to the same thing. Whereas erst in (17)a. evaluates the beginning point of an event, the particle in (17)b. evaluates the time span of that event's duration, which is after all a consequence of the location of the beginning point. The expected value in (17)b. is larger than the value given in the sentence. The excluded values are the hours H. hasn't been working. Thus, we can say that the point of view adopted in (17)b. is opposite to that of (17)a. The situation can be illustrated by the following diagram:

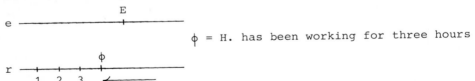

In all the examples considered previously the value specified in the sentence marks the beginning of an event, or the beginning of a range of values for some state of affairs. In (17)b. as well as in (8) and (9) there is an accomplished portion, a state which is the result of a process leading up to it. In spite of these differences it seems possible to give a unified semantic analysis for $erst_1$ and $erst_2$. The obvious differences between the two uses seem to be due to the meaning of the rest of the sentence and the context. Note that we can observe some very clear parallels in the interpretation of $erst_1$ and $erst_2$ and in the relations they contract with their field neighbours. First, the relationship to schon is exactly the same in the two uses: schon reverses the evaluation given by erst. Secondly, parallel to (15) and (16) processes evaluated by erst, provided they are reversible, can be considered from both 'angles'. A sentence like the following could be uttered both in a situation where one is heating up water and in a situation where one is cooling down the water of a hot-spring:

(18) Das Wasser ist erst lauwarm.
'The water is only lukewarm so far.'

To mention one more point, the complementarity in the placing of the expectation point of $\underline{\text{erst}}_1$ and $\underline{\text{erst}}_2$ also shows up in a complementarity of the selectional restrictions. The first and the last of the following examples are unacceptable because the rest of the sentence excludes the existence of the expectation point implied by erst:

(19) a. *Erst der Anfang des Rennens bereitete ihm Mühe.

b. Das ist erst der Anfang des Rennens.

c. Erst der Schluß des Rennens bereitete ihm Mühe.

d. *Das ist erst der Schluß des Rennens.

5. Let us now try to give a more precise characterization of the contribution of $\underline{\text{erst}}_1$ and $\underline{\text{erst}}_2$ to the truth conditions of a sentence. The framework in which we will give this characterization will be that of CRESSWELL (1973). This means that we have to translate our German sentences into a formal base language of the kind called λ-categorial language and we assume as given an interpretation which provides a domain of semantic values for the expressions of each syntactic category and a procedure for determining the semantic value of all complex expressions on the basis of an assignment of values to the symbols of the language. Since we are only concerned with the interpretation of degree particles we will simplify matters a great deal. Thus we will not adopt CRESSWELL's complicated treatment of context dependence and regard contexts as indices consisting of a time and a possible world index. We will also simplify matters by looking only at the syntax and semantics of degree particles and by leaving the rest of the sentence unanalysed. Let us first look at an example with $\underline{\text{erst}}_1$:

(20) Paul schwimmt erst abends.
'Paul does not go swimming until the evening.'

A sentence like (20) would have roughly the following representation in the base language, if ϕ abbreviates $\underline{\text{Paul schwimmt}}$:

(21) $\langle\langle \lambda, \ x_{\langle 0,0\rangle} \ \langle x_{\langle 0,0\rangle} \ \langle\phi\rangle\rangle\rangle \ \underline{\text{erst}}, \ a\rangle \quad (=\alpha)$

Truth conditions for (21) can now be defined as follows:

(22) $V_{w,t}(\alpha) = 1$

iff: a. $V_{w,t}(\langle\langle\phi\rangle \ \underline{a}\rangle) = 1$

b. there is some expression $\underline{b}$ such that $V(\underline{b}) \in D_{\langle 0,0\rangle}$ and $V(\underline{b}) < V(\underline{a})$ and $(\exists x)(x \text{ expects } ((\phi)\underline{b})\overline{)}$

c. $V_{w,t}(\langle\langle\phi\rangle\underline{b}\rangle\wedge\langle\langle\phi\rangle \ \underline{a}\rangle) = 0$ for all $\underline{b}$ such that $V(\underline{b}) < V(\underline{a})$

These truth conditions summarize all the facts about $\underline{\text{erst}}_1$ discussed so far: (a) As is the case with most, if not all, degree particles, sentences with $\underline{\text{erst}}_1$ have an entailment which can be described by the corresponding sentences without erst. (b) In

contrast to nur, erst imposes a strict order on the alternative
values under consideration. (c) Erst excludes these alternative
values as incompatible with the entailment mentioned in (a).
(d) The alternative values include an expectation point or expected value. Condition b. is meant to characterize the conventional
implicature associated with erst, a condition of use the violation
of which results in inappropriateness of the utterance but not
falsity of the sentence uttered. For schon in the position of
erst in (21) the order between V($\underline{b}$) and V($\underline{a}$) would have to be
reversed and the value '1'(true) would have to replace the value
'0'(false) in c. Let us now turn to an example with erst$_2$.

(23) Peter hat erst sechs Äpfel gegessen.
    'Peter has eaten only six apples so far'.

If we neglect the specific lexical content, (23) can be analysed
as a sentence of the following general form (P stands for predicate, i.e. the rest of the open sentence):

(24) $\langle\langle\lambda,\ x_{\langle\tau\rangle}\langle x,\ \underline{P}\rangle\rangle$ erst, $\underline{n}\rangle$ $(=\alpha)$

Truth conditions can now be defined analogously to (22):

(25) $V_{w,t}(\alpha) = 1$
    iff: a. $V_{w,t}(\langle\underline{n},\ \underline{P}\rangle) = 1$
        b. there is some expression $\underline{m}$ such that $V(\underline{m}) \in D_{\langle\tau\rangle}$ and
          $V(\underline{n}) \langle V(\underline{m})$ and $(\exists x)(x$ expects $(\underline{m},\ \underline{P})$
        c. $V_{w,t}(\langle\underline{m},\ \underline{P}\rangle\wedge\langle\underline{n},\ \underline{P}\rangle) = 0$ for all $\underline{m}$ such that
                    $V(\underline{n}) \langle V(\underline{m})$

Here, too, schon differs from erst in exactly the same way in
which it differed from erst in (21). Condition b. is again meant
to characterize a conventional implicature.

    The similarities between (22) and (25) are obvious. It is only
the focus of erst that differs and also - and this is the crucial
point - the order between the expectation point (as well as area
of values excluded) and the value specified in the sentence. How
do we know then where to place the expectation point associated
with erst with respect to the value given? If we want to avoid
postulating two lexical elements erst$_1$ and erst$_2$ the complemen--
tarity in the implicatures and truth conditions of the two uses
of erst must be accounted for by some independent principle.
Only then can the claim be substantiated that a common meaning
underlies all the uses of erst discussed in this paper. Let us
now investigate how the area of values excluded can be specified
independently of any reference to a specific meaning or use of
erst. There are no problems in those cases referred to as erst$_2$
so far, with the exception of (8)b. In (23), for instance, values
lower than six cannot be excluded because the sentence is perfectly consistent with such a situation. (23) in fact entails all
sentences where a number r $(1 \langle r \langle 6)$ replaces sechs. So the values
excluded by erst can only be values larger than the one given.
Again there are no problems with sentences such as (16) where
erst$_{(1)}$ combines with a non-temporal expression as focus constituent.

In our discussion of (16)a. and b. it was pointed out how the
context determines the expectation point and with it the area
of excluded values.

Things are more complicated whenever we have a temporal expression as focus constituent as in the following two examples
(as well as in (8)b., (4), (14) and (20)):

(26) Er unterschrieb den Vertrag erst um 12 Uhr. ($erst_1$)
     'He didn't sign the contract until 12 o'clock.'

(27) Es ist erst 12 Uhr. ($erst_2$)
     'It's only 12 o'clock.'

In (26) a time coordinate is assigned to an event whereas in (27)
a name (out of the set available for times of the day) is given
to the 'now', or more generally, to some point of reference of
the speaker. Before we try to find out whether the principles
relevant for (23) and (16) can also be applied to these cases
we may note another feature common to all uses of erst. It has
not been mentioned so far that sentences like (23) imply that
there is a possible future course of events such that a value
larger than the one given satisfies the open sentence. This is
the only difference between nur and erst in sentences like (23)
where a number functions as focus constituent of the degree particle. On the basis of this implication we can now make the following generalization: in all uses of erst the expectation conventionally implicated by the particle is ahead of reality. Because
of this, in all cases where a time coordinate is assigned to an
event, there will be an implicature that the event occurred later
than expected. This also holds mutatis mutandis for those uses
of $erst_1$ where a scale other than a temporal one is involved. If,
on the other hand, a name is assigned to the 'now' of the speaker
as in (27) an expectation which is ahead of reality looks at numbers further advanced on the dial and therefore we get the implicature 'it is earlier than expected'.

This common feature of all uses of erst, however, seems more
a consequence than a reason of principles determining the area
of excluded values. We must therefore ultimately look for a principle similar to the one invoked for (23) to account for the fact
that in all uses of $erst_1$ with a time phrase as focus the area
of excluded values precedes the time given in the sentence. Even
if it cannot be argued that the proposition expressed by (26) is
consistent with situations described by sentences where some t
(12<t) replaces '12', we can still say that there are results or
consequences for points in time later than 12 which are consistent
with (26):

(28) Um 13 Uhr war der Vertrag unterzeichnet.
     'By one o'clock the treaty was signed.'

Some principle of this sort seems to be ultimately at work in all
uses of erst. The fundamental difference between $erst_1$-contexts
and $erst_2$-contexts is that in the former case the beginning of
some state, process etc. is considered whereas in the latter case
an accomplished portion of a process etc. is under consideration.

An account of the complementarity in the meaning of both erst and schon must ultimately be related to this difference.

6. Our analysis has been considerably simplified in one aspect so far: the point or value to which erst and schon relate the value of the focus constituent has been referred to as the 'expectation point' so far. However, the expectations of either speaker or hearer are only one way of contextually specifying and determining such a point for either erst or schon. This is clearly shown by examples such as the following where neither speaker nor hearer expect Paul to be older than he is:

(29) Paul kann seine Rente noch nicht beantragen. Er ist erst 61.
    'Paul cannot apply for his pension yet. He is only 61.'

The point or value to which the value of the focus constituent is related is the age where one gets one's old age pension, say the age of 62. Analogous examples could be constructed for schon. This shows that we have only been considering special, if frequent, uses of erst so far. Obviously, there are many ways of contextual determination for a 'point of comparison' for erst or schon. It may even be the case that several points are specified by one speaker in the same situation. Let us assume that the following sentence is uttered in a situation where the election of the chairman of the Young Socialists (Jungsozialisten) is at issue and that the maximum age for membership in this organisation is 35:

(30) Wir können Paul wählen, denn er ist erst 34. Aber wir sollten
    ihn nicht wählen, da er schon 34 ist.
    'We could elect Paul, because he is only 34. But we should
    not elect him because he is 34 already.'

In (30) the point of comparison for the first part is determined by the legal possibilities: membership and therefore chairmanship is possible up to the age of 35. The relevant point in the second sentence, however, is determined by what the speaker thinks should be the case: no one should be elected who is near the age limit.

Thus, we have to give up our term 'expectation point'(as well as our formal explication of this intuition) and replace it by 'point of comparison','relevance point' or 'threshold point'. All that is required by erst or schon is that such a 'threshold point' be specified by the context to which the value of the focus constituent can be related. Expectations of either speaker or hearer are only one way of specifying this point.

To sum up, like other degree particles erst and schon raise the question of alternative values (to the one denoted by the focus constituent) for the open sentence. Erst excludes the alternative values under consideration as inconsistent or incompatible with part of the assertion. These values are always ahead of reality. Schon, on the other hand, includes the alternative values brought into play as consistent with part of the assertion. Here these values lag behind reality. It is only natural that it is the particle with an expectation ahead of reality which has negative implications, i.e. excludes alternative values.

Notes

1 This term is used in ALTMANN (1976) and has gained a certain currency since then.

2 In Europe this comparative construction only occurs in English and in the Scandinavian languages Danish, Swedish and Norwegian. This suggests that the origin of this construction in English is due to Scandinavian influence (cf. KÖNIG, 1979).

3 A situation which excludes this implication would be the following: a mother of two encourages one of her sons to eat porridge in the following way: "Come on, eat it. It is not bad. Even your brother had some (and he is very particular)". Given the fact that neither father nor mother ever eats porridge there would be no other value which satisfies the open sentence 'x had some porridge'. It is, however, relevant that the sentence is used as an encouragement or request, which means that another value for the variable of the open sentence is under consideration. Thus, the relevant implicature seems to be a 'weaker' version of the one postulated by FRASER, ANDERSON, etc.

4 If <u>only</u> occurs initially in the sentence the two complementary viewpoints are associated with different word order:

(i) Only two months ago you could get good coffee beans at 9o p a pound. (= not long ago)

(ii) Only two days later did the authorities admit that anything was wrong. (= relatively late)

5 It is interesting to note in this connection that $erst_2$ has a near-paraphrase which is exactly parallel to <u>only...yet</u>:

(i) Noch habe ich Ihren Aufsatz nur flüchtig durchgesehen.

The exact relationship between <u>erst</u> and <u>noch...nur</u>, which incidentally cannot occur in juxtaposition, is an interesting problem which cannot be pursued further in this article.

6 cf. KARTTUNEN (1974:296 n.§) and BLUMENTHAL (1974).

7 I have no solution to the problem of formally explicating the distinction between truth conditions and conventional implicatures.

8 This is as good a point as any to mention that $erst_2$ cannot be paraphrased by $erst_1$ <u>jetzt</u>:

(i) Peter hat erst jetzt seinen Aufsatz fertig.
    'Peter has only now finished his essay.'

(ii) Peter hat erst seinen Aufsatz fertig.
    'Peter has only finished his essay so far.'

These two sentences are clearly not synonymous.

9 Thus the following condition must be added to (25):
$V_{w',t'}(\langle \underline{m}',\underline{P}\rangle) = 1$, for some t' (t<t'), w' = w up to and including t, and some $\underline{m}'$ $V(\underline{n}) < V(\underline{m}'))$

References

Altmann, H. (1976). Die Gradpartikel des Deutschen. Untersuchungen zu ihrer Syntax, Semantik und Pragmatik. Tübingen:Niemeyer.

Anderson, S. (1972). "How to get even". Language 48. 893-9o6.

Blumenthal, P. (1974). "Eine kontrastive Präsuppositionsanalyse: nur/erst-seulement". Linguistik und Didaktik 17. 5o-58.

Cresswell, M. (1973). Logics and Languages. London: Methuen.

Finnis, N. (1978). "The Meaning of only". Unpublished Ms. Department of Linguistics, Cambridge.

Fraser, B. (1971). "An Analysis of even in English." In Fillmore, Ch.F. and Langendoen, D.T. (eds.) Studies in Linguistic Semantics. New York: Holt, Rinehart and Winston. 151-18o.

Grice, H.P.(1975), "Logic and Conversation." In P. Cole and J. Morgan (eds.), Syntax and Semantics. Speech Acts. New York: Academic Press.

Horn, L. (1969). "A Presuppositional Analysis of only and even." In CLS 5: Papers from the Fifth Regional Meeting. Chicago Linguistic Society. Chicago, Ill. 98-1o7.

Karttunen, L. (1974). "Until." In CLS 1o: Papers from the Tenth Regional Meeting. Chicago Linguistic Society. Chicago, Ill. 284-297.

Karttunen, L. and Peters, S. (1975). "Conventional Implicature in Montague Grammar." In BLS 1: Proceedings of the First Annual Meeting of the Berkeley Linguistic Society. Berkeley, Ca. 123-1

Karttunen, L. and Peters, S. (1976). "What Indirect Questions Conventionally Implicate." In CLS 12: Papers from the Twelfth Regional Meeting. Chicago Linguistic Society. Chicago, Ill.

Karttunen, Frances and Lauri (1977). "Even Questions". In Kegl, Nash and Zaenen (eds.), Proceedings of the Seventh Annual Meeting of the Northeastern Linguistic Society. Cambridge, Mass. 115-34.

König, E. (1977). "Zur Syntax und Semantik von Gradpartikeln." In K. Sprengel, W.-D. Bald and H.W. Viethen (eds.), Semantik und Pragmatik. Akten des 11. Linguistischen Kolloquiums.Tübingen: Niemeyer.

König, E. (1979). "Direkte und indirekte Bewertung von Zeitintervallen durch Satzadverbien und Gradpartikeln im Deutschen und Englischen." In H. Weydt (ed.), Die Partikeln der deutschen Sprache. Berlin: De Gruyter.

Shanon, B. (1978) "Even, only and almost hardly." Studies in Language 2. 35-7o.

Wunderlich, D. (1978). "Analyse einiger Funktionen von sonst - ein Beitrag zur Kontextabhängigkeit von Bedeutungen." Unpublished Ms., Düsseldorf.

Meaning and Context-Dependence

Dieter Wunderlich

Universität Düsseldorf, Inst.-Gr. III, Moorestr. 5
D-4000 Düsseldorf 1, Fed. Rep. of Germany

1. What BLOOMFIELD's Story Left Out

(A) Suppose that Jack and Jill are walking down a lane. Jill is hungry. She sees an apple in a tree.

(B) She says: "Look, there is an apple. I'm so hungry. Could you fetch the apple for me?"

(C) Jack vaults the fence, climbs the tree, takes the apple, brings it to Jill, and places it in her hand. Jill eats the apple.

As you have remarked, I gave to the well-known story of BLOOM-FIELD's another middle part (B). The original part was:

(B') She makes a noise with her larynx, tongue, and lips.
  (BLOOMFIELD 1935[2], 22)

The full story describes a speech event (B), and two series of practical events; one (A) precedes the speech event, the other one (C) follows it. According to BLOOMFIELD, the meaning of a linguistic form is the situation in which the speaker utters it and the response which it calls forth in the hearer (BLOOM-FIELD 1935[2], 139). BLOOMFIELD, however, in his original story only described a meaning of (B) - call it meaning$_B$ - without taking account of the linguistic form. What I did was to recons-truct from the given meaning$_B$ one possible linguistic form. This is a process of <u>verbalization</u>. Obviously, many other linguistic forms could have been reconstructed to fulfil our purpose, i. e. to match the practical events in (A) and (C). These linguistic forms could belong also to any other language, say German, or Japanese, or Yoruba.

BLOOMFIELD described the speech event (B') in terms of physio-logical activities of the speaker, whereas I described it in (B) by using quotation marks. This means that the speakeress, Jill, <u>uttered</u> the quoted sentences of English, by means of activities of her voice apparatus - probably also accompanying it by a gazing, or gesture. I take the position that the relevant linguistic form is a <u>sentence</u>, or a chain of sentences, but the way in which it comes to play a role within practical events is the <u>utterance</u>.

We can easily see now that meaning$_B$ is an <u>utterance-meaning</u>.

Let's say, the practical events described in (A) define a <u>situation</u>
consisting of two persons engaged in a certain cooperative
activity at a certain place, having at their disposal certain
mental attitudes and strategies. Jill's utterance <u>transforms</u> this
situation in a new one, and in <u>response</u> to this Jack behaves in
a certain way. Jack must have learned from Jill's utterance what
she wanted him to do. Jill's utterance is characterized by two
sorts of features, firstly it matches some properties of the
given situation, and secondly it anticipates some properties of
the responsive behavior. Only if we construe the force of the
utterance in this way, we are able to understand that the meaning
of the utterance may involve both series of practical events,
those that precede the speech event, and those that follow it.

2. Utterance-Meaning and Sentence-Meaning

Let's have a look now at Jill's utterance itself. The first part
of it, "look", directs Jack's attention to a certain place, or
a certain state of affairs (it is this part of the utterance,
we think, which might have been accompanied by a gazing, or
gesture).

The next two parts, "there is an apple" and "I'm so hungry",
both state a property of the given situation. These two properties
may stand in a goal-accomplishment-relation. We all know that,
given there is an apple and this apple could be brought into
our possession and we would eat it, then this might satisfy our
desire which springs from our property of being hungry. This
factual knowledge is activated if we hear someone stating these
two properties in a sequel. These parts of the utterance may
thus transform the given situation in terms of the mental states
of the participants. It might well be the case that a hearer
would presently react in the same way as Jack did.

The last part of the utterance, "could you fetch the apple for
me", asks for the performance of an action designed to bridge
the local distance between the object and the subject of desire.
Whereas the two preceding parts of the utterance were concerned
with properties of the given situation, this one deals with a
future responding behavior of the addressee.

It is a well-known practice of linguists to split an utterance-
meaning into two related parts: what is said, or its <u>propositional
content</u>, and its <u>illocutionary force</u>. What Jill said in the
described situation is the following:
(a) that Jack looks (to a certain place identified by a pointing
    gesture of Jill's);
(b) that an apple is at this place;
(c) that Jill is hungry;
(d) whether Jack could fetch this apple for Jill (or: that Jack
    fetches this apple for Jill).

The respective illocutionary forces are:
(a) to induce Jack to look at that place (i. e. to cause it that
    Jack makes the proposition Pa true);

(b) to inform Jack that the important thing about that place
is its property of being occupied by an apple (i. e. to
display to Jack the truth of Pb);
(c) to inform Jack that Jill is hungry (i. e. to assert the
truth of Pc) - and, possibly, to induce Jack to think of
the relationship between an apple and the property of being
hungry;
(d) to induce Jack to fetch the apple for Jill (i. e. to cause
it that Jack makes the positive proposition Pd true).

There is no doubt that the utterance-meaning of (B) could be
subjected to further exploration. We did enough, however, to
show the intrinsic relationship between the practical events
and the utterance-meaning: some of the properties of the given
situation make some of the things which are said true, and
some of the properties of the transformed situation or the
responding behavior make some other things which are said true.
It is, i. a., the task of the different illocutionary forces to
relate the things which are said with the given or transformed
situation, or, in other words, the hearer learns from the
illocutionary force how he is expected to further develop the
situation.

Another practice of linguists is to relate the utterance-meaning
not only with the situation but also with the linguistic form.
Jill uttered a chain of sentences in English. We presume that
these very sentences have something to do with the utterance-
meaning just outlined. The reconstruction of the sentences
quoted in (B) was, of course, based on this presumption. Though
I could have come to another chain of sentences, I could not
have chosen any arbitrary chain of sentences.

Each sentence could, however, be uttered in a quite different
situation. Each sentence can thus be ascribed a certain sentence-
meaning as a function from possible situations onto an utterance-
meaning. In correspondence with the above mentioned decomposition
of an utterance-meaning, we can say that each sentence-meaning
includes both a propositional and an illocutionary force
potential. The sentence-meaning is constituted by the meaning
of the individual words of the sentence, by virtue of the morphological and syntactical constructions in which the words are
used.

But words may be ambiguous - as may constructions. E. g., "fence"
can denote a barrier made of wooden or metal stakes, or a
person who receives stolen goods, or the activity of fighting
with foils or swords, whereas "vault" can denote an arched roof,
or a cellar, or the activity of jumping in a single movement,
with the hand resting on something. In the sentence "Jack vaults
the fence", however, "vault" is determined to denote an activity of Jack, and "fence" is determined to denote an object of
this activity, which - at least in the situation of the story -
can rarely be a person. Thus the sentence turns out (at least
in our story) to be non-ambiguous. In a way we might say that
the rest of a sentence provides a context which can disambiguate
an ambiguous word.

It seems to be a good strategy, however, not to stress the possible ambiguity of words. On the contrary, one should, as far as possible, conceive of the meaning of a word as unique, if possibly rather abstract. If used in a sentence, the individual word becomes then more specific, on basis of rather the same syntactical and semantical processes which are responsible for disambiguation. Again, we might consider the rest of the sentence as a context for that word. For instance, in the combination "you fetch the apple" "fetch" denotes a specific activity, which is different from 'fetch' in "these books won't fetch much" or "she fetched a deep sigh". These 'fetch' have, however, something in common, even if we may find it difficult to identify it. (Perhaps: 'to bring something into the reach of a person'.)

Turkish "almak" can mean 'take', or 'buy', or 'get'. Again, we will be well advised if we take something like the transition of an object into the disposal of a person to be the meaning of this Turkish word, and avoid to consider this word as threefold ambiguous. In most of its uses, however, "almak" becomes more specific such that it is readily translatable by one of its English equivalents. The same is true of many other words in every language of the world.

Going back to BLOOMFIELD's story in its extended version, we are quite sure that the sentences quoted there have a specific describable sentence-meaning. So far we have looked from the situation described in (A) and (C) at the utterances. Now, let us look from these sentences at the possible use we can make of them. From this point of view we speak, more generally, of a <u>possible context</u> of a sentence. Such a context may be a verbal context, i. e. a preceding utterance or inscription, or it may be a nonverbal situation in which the sentence is uttered. Almost every sentence is <u>context-dependent</u>, in the very simple sense at least that it bears a certain propositional and a certain illocutionary force potential, which are specified only in case of its utterance. But there are also some more specific features of context-dependence.

The sentences Jill uttered display some indexicality. "There", "I", and "you" are words which pick up some features of the situation, a place, the speaker, and the addressee resp. If we want to describe the sentence-meaning, we have to employ context-variables ranging over an appropriate set of objects. We might try to decontextualize the sentence by quoting the respective values of the situation, for instance:

(B'') Jill was saying something like: 'You, Jack, look right now at that place where I, Jill, now am looking and pointing at, and you, Jack, will see at that place an apple. ... I, Jill, want you, Jack, to fetch this apple for me, Jill, right now.'

Without doubt, we can find more and more elaborated sentences supplemented with various situational features thus making explicit the hidden connections. However, we don't seem to be able to ever fully decontextualize the sentences.

The newly introduced indexical word "now" could be replaced by the respective time of the utterance, but then we have to refer back to the whole utterance. The speech event itself introduces the origo for the time evaluation. Whenever we have indexical expressions in a sentence, these can be replaced by the appropriate values provided by the situation. But the fact that these values are related to the speech event itself cannot be eliminated, unless we have for each of these values appropriate proper names at hand.

Another remaining property is the anaphoric relationship between different parts of the sentences, expressed by "that" or "this". This simply serves to secure the identity of the referents. It finds its counterpart in the use of one and the same variable in a logical formula with bound variables.

3. Indexicality and Anaphora

Let me say some more words about the indexical (or deictic) and the anaphoric relationships.

The anaphoric relationship presupposes the preceding introduction of an object, and this very same object is used a second (or third etc.) time. This is not simply a relationship between linguistic forms or word-meanings, rather it calls for a contextual analysis. A preceding utterance of an anaphoric sentence changes the context in introducing some new object into the relevant world of consideration.

Jill sees an apple in a tree: this describes a perceptive process of Jill's as part of the situation. Jill says: "Look, there is an apple": by the quoted utterance, Jill introduces an apple into Jack's range of attention. We cannot be certain that Jack will identify an apple, much less that he will focus the same apple as Jill - this depends on the accuracy of the concomitant gesture and on further circumstances. Nevertheless, the utterance suffices at least to build up in the hearer a model of the world Jill is considering.

And then Jill says: "Fetch the apple for me.": the definite article in the quoted utterance marks the identity with a presupposed apple, and if any apples were previously introduced, the identity relation holds with the one which was introduced most recently. Again, Jack can understand the purpose of Jill's utterance if he identifies it with the apple in his model of the world Jill is considering; he can, however, only comply with Jill's request if he is at least able to identify some apple in the external world.

Now, Jill makes a pointing gesture with her forefinger and says: "There is an apple." The gesture is a particular pointer, it introduces a vector origo: in its deictic field are all the places along the vector, i. e. within one spatial direction. The quoted existential sentence might be interpreted as: move in that direction up to the point where you see an apple. There is, however, a certain opposition between, e. g., "here", "there", and "over there". These words relate the denoted place in an increasing distance to the vector origo. Thus, "there" informs the hearer that he should look in a medium distance.

To establish a deictic relationship, always an <u>origo-introducing pointer</u> is needed. Compare the following utterances:

(1) The speaker points with his finger on a map and says: "<u>Hier</u> ist das Gasthaus. <u>Dort</u> gibt es guten Fisch." ('Here is the inn. They have a good fish there')

(2) The soccer-reporter comments in a broadcasting transmission: "Kempes, der sich <u>hier</u> zuhause fühlt, auch wenn er von Valencia kommt. Aber <u>hier</u> im Rosaria-Zentralstadion, allerdings im alten, <u>dort</u> wuchs er auf, <u>dort</u> ist er groß geworden, <u>hierher</u> ist er zurückgekehrt und <u>hier</u> wird er stark gefeiert." ('Kempes who feels here at home, though he comes from Valencia. But here in the Rosaria central stadion, of course in the old one, there he grew up, there he became great, to here he returned and here he is celebrated')

(3) From a novel: "Sie gelangten schließlich in einen großen Saal. <u>Hier</u> kamen immer mehr Leute <u>herein</u>." ('Finally they got into a large hall. More and more people came in'.)

(4) Alternative to 3: "Sie gelangten schließlich in einen großen Saal. <u>Dort</u> kamen immer mehr Leute <u>hinein</u>." ('Finally they got into a large hall. More and more people went in'.)

In all these examples, "hier" ('here') is deictically, and "dort" ('there') is anaphorically used. (It is, however, possible to use German "dort" also deictically.) "Dort" takes up the inn in (1), the old central stadion in (2), the large hall in (4) resp. "Hier" always denotes a locality (of a variable seize depending on the further context) which includes the respective local origo. But how does the hearer know which is the origo? There seem to be three different procedures of origo-introduction:

(a) A concomitant gesture of the speaker serves as the pointer. This is the case in example (1) - as before in Jill's utterance -: "hier" denotes a piece of paper including the part the tip of the finger is directed at. Since we know, however, that a piece of paper will never be an inn we interpret that this piece of paper represents the inn.

(b) The speech event itself serves as the pointer. Any speech event determines at least a time, a place, and a speaker. This is the case in example (2): "hier" denotes a locality which includes the position of the speaker.

(c) A certain movement described in the preceding utterances
serves as the pointer. This is the case in example (3).
Beyond the origo or perspective determined by his utterance,
any speaker can shift to a new perspective within the world
he considers. The speaker can take the view as if he himself
were one of the persons or things that are moving around.
During their wandering some persons got into a large hall;
there their movement was temporarily terminated thus pointing
at a new locality; "hier" in example (3) denotes a locality
part of which is the place where these persons are. This
internal perspective forces the use of "hereinkommen" (Engl.
'come in') as opposed to "hineinkommen" (Engl. 'go in') in
example (4). "Herein" is directed to the origo, whereas
"hinein" is directed from the origo away. The speaker of (4)
keeps the origo determined by the speech event, which is
external to the described events, thus he relates to the
large hall anaphorically by "dort". The speaker of (3)
shifts the origo. We see this, however, only from the use of
"hier". Whether or not a movement described in an utterance
serves as a pointer, can only be recognized from the
following use made of this movement.

It is evident that one could say much more about the deictic and
the anaphoric relationships. Beyond these, there are surely a
lot more types of context-dependence to observe. In the following
I want to consider another point.

4. What a Sentence Tells Us About Its Context

Every sentence defines a number of restrictions which a context
has to meet in order to be a possible context of that sentence.
On every isolated sentence we can perform a certain process of
contextualization, we can, in other words, make predictions about
possible uses of this sentence. We can construe the possible contexts and the use which has to be made of them in terms of three
interrelated types of conditions:

(a) a use-condition,
(b) a condition of context-selection, and
(c) a truth-condition.

The use-condition singles out the class of contexts for a proper
use of this sentence. In any other context an utterance of the
sentence cannot receive a straightforward interpretation. In
cases of discrepancy it is, however, possible to reinterpret
either the context or the sentence. Under the assumption that the
speaker intends to make a senseful contribution to the current
discourse, we have certain pragmatic strategies at hand to solve
the seeming inappropriateness in one of these two ways.

Since the sentence-meaning only supplies a potential for the
utterance, it cannot by itself determine the utterance-meaning,
exhaustively. For completion, the utterance-meaning has to
rely on the context. This is, e. g., obvious for the propositional

content in the deictic or the anaphoric case, where we have to select appropriate values for the context-variables used in the description. The sentence tells us the type of the entities to be selected, and sometimes also some strategy for their selection. Other cases of propositional incompleteness are all kinds of ellipsis and of hidden parameters, for instance in the use of scaled adjectives. Illocutionary incompleteness is particularly often found with declarative sentences, where the 'point' or purpose of the utterance has to be established from the context.

Not surprisingly the use-condition and the condition of context-selection often go hand in hand. One feature of a proper or possible context is that it supplies the necessary entities. Analytically, these two conditions should, however, be distingui-shed; and generally they don't coincide.

Finally, each sentence tells us some minimal property of the world under consideration (or rather of every one of the set of worlds which are compatible with what is considered) in order that the proposition expressed by the sentence and, possibly, completed by the context be true. Thus the sentence can guide us whether we have to take the world under consideration as in-cluding the context of utterance or as only indirectly re-lating to the context of utterance.

The truth-condition is connected with some satisfaction-conditions of the illocutionary point or purpose. For instance, an assertion is satisfied if and only if the speaker can hold the claim that the expressed proposition is true, and an order is satisfied if and only if the addressee behaves in such a way that the ex-pressed proposition becomes true. Since the sentence expresses some illocutionary potential as well, it also determines - via the truth-condition and, again, under the assumption that the speaker wants to make a substantial condition - how the utterance is to be understood; in other words, it determines partly the change of the context brought about by the utterance.

For the sake of illustration, let us consider these sentences:

(5) Draußen regnet es. ('It is raining outside'.)

(6) Drüben regnet es. ('It is raining over there'.)

(7) Düsseldorf liegt rheinabwärts. (lit. 'Düsseldorf is the river downstream situated', i. e. 'Düsseldorf is further down the Rhine'.)

(8) The blanket is too long.

(9) The blanket is too short.

(10) This wall must be painted till tomorrow.

Sentences (5) and (6), though seemingly very similar, require quite a different context. A property of each proper context of utterance of (5) is that the speaker is inside a sheltered place (this does not mean that the sentence couldn't be uttered seriously elsewhere, but this would require special contextual modification), whereas (6) requires that the speaker faces a kind of local barrier. This condition enables the selection of the proper context value: in each proper utterance of (5) something is said about the local part of the context which is outside of the speaker's place and within a certain distance of that place; in (6) something is said about the local part which is beyond the barrier, again within a certain (visible?) distance from the speaker. And finally, in order for the proposition to be true in the given world it is necessary that in the local part just delimited there is an atmospheric process as a result of which the earth is wettened.

It is a property of sentences (5) and (6) that their utterances have the force of an assertion, which can serve, however, - given the appropriate situation - a number of different functions such as explanation, prediction, or warning.

The process of contextualization can only expound the sentence-meaning, whereas the utterance-meaning can be and usually is much more specific. We may distinguish then between a rough and a fine context. A _rough_ or, let's say, a _neutral context_ is defined by the sentence itself. It is confined to supplying the requisite values; thus it gives the so-called literal meaning of the utterance. A _fine context_, however, can have a much wider range consisting in a full-fledged situation. It may contain all kinds of mental states of the participants: their beliefs, expectations, and preferences, their conception of social relationships, social purposes, mutual obligations and institutional roles, their perception of preceding actions, utterances and the environment. Such a fine context allows the identification of non-literal utterance-meaning and of all kinds of suggestions.

The theoretical treatment of fine contexts requires other methods than rough contexts. In my view, the borderline between pragmatics and semantics can sensefully be drawn according to the methods for the treatment of these different kinds of contexts. As we have seen we can predict from a sentence a proper context of its utterance. Therefore it doesn't make much sense to make such a distinction just between the notions of utterance versus sentence, as it is often done.

Sentence (7) can only be uttered at places along the river Rhine. The expressed proposition is, then, true if and only if

(a) Düsseldorf is located at the river Rhine (which is indeed the case), and

(b) the place of utterance is located between the Rhine spring and Düsseldorf,

whereas it is false if and only if (a) as above and

(b') the place of utterance is located between Düsseldorf and the Rhine mouth.

Obviously, (a) is a presupposition of the proposition expressed by (7).

Though (7) has a very restricted use-condition, there seems to be nothing of a context selection. This is because of the elliptic nature of (7): "rheinabwärts" is a relative adverb which calls for a second relatum, e. g.

(11) Düsseldorf liegt von Mainz aus rheinabwärts.

Sentence (11) can be uttered at all places. In case this second relatum is omitted we have to select the place of utterance, i. e. (7) means the same as

(12) Düsseldorf liegt von hier aus rheinabwärts. ('Düsseldorf is from here the river Rhine downstream situated'.)

It can easily be proved that the substitution of "Mainz" by "hier" changes the truth-condition of (11) into that of (7). We also see that in condition (b) above the proper context selection has already been made.

With sentences (8) and (9) we observe another type of context-dependence. Any proper context of (8) as well as of (9) where a certain blanket has been introduced, must provide us with a certain required range. If we have a plus-adjective (which is used for the respective dimension) - as in (8) -, it is said that the seize of the object (or, more generally, its value on the respective dimension) is above the maximum of the required range. If we have a minus-adjective, the antonymous item in the dimension - as in (9) -, it is said that the size of the object is below the minimum of the required range. What is it now that constitutes a required range? The object must have a certain use function, i. e. a user employs it in some circumstances for some purpose. If we want to be more explicit we could select elements of this use function to specify the required range, e. g.

(13) The blanket is too short for me.
(14) The blanket is too short for this bed.
(15) The blanket is too short to cover the wine-shelf.

Still another type of context-dependence is shown by sentence (10) It has been pointed out by Angelika KRATZER (e. g., 1978, 12) that the proposition expressed by (10) is true in a world under consideration w if and only if (roughly)

(a) there exists exactly one set of background assumptions ('Redehintergrund') H in the situation of utterance, and
(b) the set of propositions which H attaches to w entails logically that this wall is painted till tomorrow. (Evidently, this latter proposition is again context-dependent.)

Thus, the context of utterance must supply a substantial set of background assumptions which justifies the use of "must". Yet we have no clear strategy of selection from the context. All we can do is to pursue a detailed investigation of the exact circumstances of the utterance situation.

If (10) is uttered with respect to all what one knows about the progress of the painting work, it is used epistemically and with the force of a prediction. If by contrast (10) is uttered with respect to whatever the authorities demand, then it is used deontically and possibly with the force of an order.

5. Concluding Remarks

In sections 1 and 2, I constructed a chain of sentences the utterance of which could match a given nonverbal situation and its sequel. I considered the propositional content and the illocutionary force of an utterance and their relationship to both the sentence-meaning and the situation of utterance.

Some thoughts about the contextual analysis of the anaphora and the contextual introduction of an origo as the source of indexicality were outlined in section 3.

In section 4, I considered what a sentence by itself can tell us about the nature of its contexts. I tried to defend the view that there are at least three kinds of conditions for the identification of a proper utterance-meaning connected with a sentence. Firstly, we have to delimit the set of proper or possible contexts; secondly, we have to select certain entities from the context in order to complete the expressed proposition; and thirdly, we have to state certain properties of the context in crder for the expressed proposition to be true.

Suppose there is yet another variant of the BLOOMFIELDian story where Jill said

(16) Jack, get the apple, otherwise I'll kill you.

Now consider the anaphora "otherwise". Its functions are manifold. It demands for a preceding context with some expression of necessity ; it selects the proposition that results by stripping off the necessity operator; and it states - together with the sentence in which it occurs - some happening in all the courses of affairs alternative to those where the selected proposition is true.

I am grateful to Florian Coulmas for his generous advice.

References

L. Bloomfield (1935[2]), Language.

A. Kratzer (1978),   Semantik der Rede.

D. Wunderlich (1979), Analyse einiger Funktionen von "sonst" - ein Beitrag zur Klärung von Kontextabhängigkeit. In: I. Rosengren (ed.) Lunder Germanistische Forschungen.

Scorekeeping in a Language Game

David Lewis

Princeton University, Department of Philosophy, 1879 Hall,
Princeton, NJ 08540

Example 1: Presupposition[1]

At any stage in a well-run conversation, a certain amount is presupposed.
The parties to the conversation take it for granted; or at least they purport to, whether sincerely or just "for the sake of the argument". Presuppositions can be created or destroyed in the course of a conversation.
This change is rule-governed, at least up to a point. The presuppositions
at time t' depend, in a way about which at least some general principles
can be laid down, on the presuppositions at an earlier time t and on the
course of the conversation (and nearby events) between t and t'.

Some things that might be said require suitable presuppositions. They
are acceptable if the required presuppositions are present; not otherwise.
"The king of France is bald" requires the presupposition that France has
one king, and one only; "Even George Lakoff could win" requires the presupposition that George is not a leading candidate; and so on.

We need not ask just what sort of unacceptability results when a required
presupposition is lacking. Some say falsehood, some say lack of truth value,
some just say that it's the kind of unacceptability that results when a required presupposition is lacking, and some say it might vary from case to
case.

Be that as it may, it's not as easy as you might think to say something
that will be unacceptable for lack of required presuppositions. Say something that requires a missing presupposition, and straightway that presupposition springs into existence, making what you said acceptable after all.
(Or at least, that is what happens if your conversational partners tacitly
acquiesce -- if no one says "But France has three kings!" or "Whadda ya mean,
'even George'?"). That is why it is peculiar to say, out of the blue, "All
Fred's children are asleep, and Fred has children". The first part requires
and thereby creates a presupposition that Fred has children; so the second
part adds nothing to what is already presupposed when it is said; so the second part has no conversational point. It would not have been peculiar to
say instead "Fred has children, and all Fred's children are asleep."

I said that presupposition evolves in a more or less rule-governed way
during a conversation. Now we can formulate one important governing rule:
call it the rule of accommodation for presupposition.

If at time t something is said that requires presupposition P to be acceptable, and if P is not presupposed just before t, then -- ceteris paribus and within certain limits -- presupposition P comes into existence
at t.

This rule has not yet been very well stated, nor is it the only rule governing the kinematics of presupposition. But let us bear it in mind nevertheless, and move on to other things.

Example 2: Permissibility[2]

For some reason -- coercion, deference, common purpose -- two people are both willing that one of them should be under the control of the other. (At least within certain limits, in a certain sphere of action, so long as certain conditions prevail.) Call one the _slave_, the other the _master_. The control is exercised verbally, as follows.

At any stage in the enslavement, there is a boundary between some courses of action for the slave that are permissible, and others that are not. The range of permissible conduct may expand or contract. The master shifts the boundary by saying things to the slave. Since the slave does his best to see to it that his course of action is a permissible one, the master can control the slave by controlling what is permissible.

Here is how the master shifts the boundary. From time to time he says to the slave that such-and-such courses of action are impermissible. Any such statement depends for its truth value on the boundary between what is permissible and what isn't. But if the master says that something is impermissible, and if that would be false if the boundary remained stationary, then straightway the boundary moves inward. The permissible range contracts so that what the master says is true after all. Thereby the master makes courses of action impermissible that used to be permissible. But from time to time also the master relents, and says to the slave that such-and-such courses of action are permissible. Or perhaps he says that some of such-and-such courses of action are permissible, but doesn't say just which ones. Then the boundary moves outward. The permissible range expands, if need be (and if possible), so that what the master says is true. Thereby the master makes courses of action permissible that used to be impermissible.

The truth of the master's statements about permissibility -- one aspect of their acceptability -- depends on the location of the boundary. The boundary shifts in a rule-governed way. The rule is as follows; call it the rule of accommodation for permissibility.

If at time t something is said about permissibility by the master to the slave that requires for its truth the permissibility or impermissibility of certain courses of action, and if just before t the boundary is such as to make the master's statement false, then -- _ceteris paribus_ and within certain limits -- the boundary shifts at t so as to make the master's statement true.

Again, this is not a very satisfactory formulation. For one thing, the limits and qualifications are left unspecified. But more important, the rule as stated does not say exactly how the boundary is to shift.

What if the master says that some of such-and such courses of actions are permissible, when none of them were permissible before he spoke. By the rule, some of them must straightway become permissible. Some -- but which ones? The ones that were closest to permissibility beforehand, perhaps. Well and good, but now we have a new problem. At every stage there is not only a boundary between the permissible and the impermissible, but also a relation of comparative near-permissibility between the courses of action on the impermissible side. Not only do we need rules governing the shifting boundary, but also we need rules to govern the changing relation of comparative near-permissibility. Not only must we say how this relation evolves when the master says something about absolute permissibility, but also we must say how it evolves when he says something -- as he might -- about comparative near-permissibility. He might say, for instance, that the most nearly permissible courses of action in a class A are those in a subclass A'; or that some courses of action in class B are more nearly permissible than any in class C. Again the rule is a rule of accommodation. The relation of comparative near-permissibility changes, if need be, so that what the master says to the slave is true. But again, to say that is not enough. It does not suffice to determine just what the change is.

* * *

Those were Examples 1 and 2. Examples of what? I'll say shortly; but first, a digression.

Scorekeeping in a Baseball Game

At any stage in a well-run baseball game, there is a septuple of numbers $\langle r_v, r_h, h, i, s, b, o \rangle$ which I shall call the <u>score</u> of that game at that stage. We recite the score as follows: the visiting team has r_v runs, the home team has r_h runs, it is the hth half (h being 1 or 2) of the ith inning; there are s strikes, b balls, and o outs. (In another terminology, the score is only the initial pair $\langle r_v, r_h \rangle$, but I need a word for the entire septuple.) A possible codification of the rules of baseball would consist of rules of four different sorts.

(1) <u>Specifications of the kinematics of score</u>. Initially, the score is $\langle 0, 0, 1, 1, 0, 0, 0 \rangle$. Thereafter, if at time t the score is $\underset{\sim}{s}$, and if between time t and time t' the players behave in manner m, then at time t' the score is $\underset{\sim}{s}'$, where $\underset{\sim}{s}'$ is determined in a certain way by $\underset{\sim}{s}$ and m.

(2) <u>Specifications of correct play</u>. If at time t the score is $\underset{\sim}{s}$, and if between time t and time t' the players behave in manner m, then the players have behaved incorrectly. (Correctness depends on score: what is correct play after two strikes differs from what is correct play after three.) What is not incorrect play according to these rules is correct.

(3) <u>Directive requiring correct play</u>. All players are to behave, throughout the game, in such a way that play is correct.

(4) <u>Directives concerning score</u>. Players are to strive to make the score evolve in certain directions. Members of the visiting team try to make r_v large and r_h small, members of the home team try to do the opposite.

(We could dispense with roles of sorts (2) and (3) by adding an eighth component to the score which, at any stage of the game, measures the amount of incorrect play up to that stage. Specifications of correct play are then included among the specifications of the kinematics of score, and the directive requiring correct play becomes one of the directives concerning score.)

Rules of sorts (1) and (2) are sometimes called <u>constitutive rules</u>. They are said to be akin to definitions, though they do <u>not have the form</u> of definitions. Rules of sorts (3) and (4) are called <u>regulative rules</u>. They are akin to the straightforward directives "No smoking!" or "Keep left!"

We could explain this more fully, as follows. Specifications of sorts (1) and (2) are not themselves definitions of "score" and "correct play". But they are consequences of reasonable definitions. Further, there is a systematic way to construct the definitions, given the specifications. Suppose we wish to define the <u>score function</u>: the function from game-stages to septuples of numbers that gives the score at every stage. The specifications of the kinematics of score, taken together, tell us that the score function evolves in such-and-such way. We may then simply define the score function as that function which evolves in such-and-such way. If the kinematics of score are well specified, then there is one function, and one only, that evolves in the proper way; and if so, then the score function evolves in the proper way if and only if the suggested definition of it is correct. Once we have defined the score function, we have thereby defined the score and all its components at any stage. There are two outs at a certain stage of a game, for instance, if and only if the score function assigns to that game-stage a septuple whose seventh component is the number 2.

Turn next to the specifications of correct play. Taken together, they tell us that correct play occurs at a game-stage if and only if the players' behavior at that stage bears such-and-such relation to score at that stage. This has the form of an explicit definition of correct play in terms of current score and current behavior. If current score has already been defined in terms of the history of the players' behavior up to now, in the way just suggested, then we have defined correct play in terms of current and previous behavior.

Once score and correct play are defined in terms of the players' behavior, then we may eliminate the defined terms in the directive requiring correct play and the directives concerning score. Thanks to the definitions constructed from the constitutive rules, the regulative rules become simply directives to strive to see to it that one's present behavior bears a certain rather complicated relation to the history of the players' behavior in previous stages of the game. A player might attempt to conform to such a directive for various reasons: contractual obligation, perhaps, or a conventional understanding with his fellow players based on their common interest in enjoying a proper game.

The rules of baseball could in principle be formulated as straightforward directives concerning behavior, without the aid of definable terms for score and its components. Or they could be formulated as explicit definitions of the score function, the components of score, and correct play, followed by directives in which the newly defined terms appear. It is easy to see why neither of these methods of formulation has found favor. The first method would pack the entire rulebook into each directive; the second would pack the entire rulebook into a single preliminary explicit definition. Understandably averse to very long sentences, we do better to proceed in our more devious way.

There is an alternative analysis -- the baseball equivalent of operationalism or legal realism. Instead of appealing to constitutive rules, we might instead claim that the score is, by definition, whatever some scoreboard says it is. Which scoreboard? Various answers are defensible: maybe the visible scoreboard with its arrays of light bulbs, maybe the invisible scoreboard in the head umpire's head, maybe the many scoreboards in many heads to the extent that they agree. No matter. On any such view, the specifications of the kinematics of score have a changed status. No longer are they constitutive rules akin to definitions. Rather, they are empirical generalizations, subject to exceptions, about the ways in which the players' behavior tends to cause changes on the authoritative scoreboard. Under this analysis, it is impossible that this scoreboard fails to give the score. What is possible is that the score is in an abnormal and undesired relation to its causes, for which someone may perhaps be blamed.

I do not care to say which analysis is right for baseball as it is actually played. Perhaps the question has no determinate answer, or perhaps it has different answers for formal and informal baseball. I only wish to distinguish the two alternatives, noting that both are live options.

* * *

This ends the digression. Now I want to propose some general theses about language -- theses that were exemplified by Examples 1 and 2, and that will be exemplified also by several other examples.

Conversational Score

With any stage in a well-run conversation, or other process of linguistic interaction, there are associated many things analogous to the components of a baseball score. I shall therefore speak of them collectively as the score of that conversation at that stage. The points of analogy are as follows.

(1) Like the components of a baseball score, the components of a conversational score at a given stage are abstract entities. They may not be numbers but they are other set-theoretic constructs: sets of presupposed propositions, boundaries between permissible and impermissible courses of action, or the like.

(2) What play is correct depends on the score. Sentences depend for their truth value, or for their acceptability in other respects, on the components of conversational score at the stage of conversation when they are uttered. Not only aspects of acceptability of an uttered sentence may depend on score. So may other semantic properties that play a role in determining aspects of acceptability. For instance, the constituents of an uttered sentence -- subsentences, names, predicates, etc. -- may depend on the score for their intension or extension.

(3) Score evolves in a more-or-less rule-governed way. There are rules that specify the kinematics of score:

If at time t the conversational score is s, and if between time t and time t' the course of conversation is c, then at time t' the score is s', where s' is determined in a certain way by s and c.

Or at least:

... then at time t' the score is some member of the class S of possible scores, where S is determined in a certain way by s and c.

(4) The conversationalists may conform to directives, or may simply desire, that they strive to steer certain components of the conversational score in certain directions. Their efforts may be cooperative, as when all partici- pants in a discussion try to increase the amount that all of them willingly presuppose. Or there may be conflict, as when each of two debaters tries to get his opponent to grant him -- to join with him in presupposing -- parts of his case, and to give away parts of the contrary case.

(5) To the extent that conversational score is determined, given the history of the conversation and the rules that specify its kinematics, these rules can be regarded as constitutive rules akin to definitions. Again, constitu- tive rules could be traded in for explicit definitions: the conversational score function could be defined as that function from conversation-stages to n-tuples of suitable entities that evolves in the specified way.

Alternatively, conversational score might be operationally defined in terms of mental scoreboards -- some suitable attitudes -- of the parties to the con- versation. The rules specifying the kinematics of conversational score then become empirical generalizations, subject to exceptions, about the causal de- pendence of what the scoreboards register on the history of the conversation.

In the case of baseball score, either approach to the definition of score and the status of the rules seems satisfactory. In the case of conversational score, on the other hand, both approaches seem to meet with difficulties. If, as seems likely, the rules specifying the kinematics of conversational score are seriously incomplete, then often there may be many candidates for the score function, different but all evolving in the specified way. But also it seems difficult to say, without risk of circularity, what are the mental representations that comprise the conversationalists' scoreboards.

It may be best to adopt a third approach -- a middle way, drawing on both the alternatives previously considered. Conversational score is, by defini- tion, whatever the mental scoreboards say it is; but we refrain from trying to say just what the conversationalists' mental scoreboards are. We assume that some or other mental representations are present that play the role of a scoreboard, in the following sense: what they register depends on the his- tory of the conversation in the way that score should according to the rules. The rules specifying the kinematics of score thereby specify the role of a scoreboard; the scoreboard is whatever best fills this role; and the score is whatever this scoreboard registers. The rules specifying the kinematics of score are to some extent constitutive, but on this third approach they enter only in a roundabout way into the definition of the score. It is no harm if they underdetermine the evolution of score, and it is possible that score sometimes evolves in a way that violates the rules.

Rules of Accommodation

There is one big difference between baseball score and conversational score. Suppose the batter walks to first base after only three balls. His behavior would be correct play if there were four balls rather than three. That's just too bad -- his behavior does not at all make it the case that there are four balls and his behavior _is_ correct. Baseball has no rule of accommodation to the effect that if a fourth ball is required to make correct the play that occurs, then that very fact suffices to change the score so that straightway there are four balls.

Language games are different. As I hope my examples will show, conversational score does tend to evolve in such a way as is required in order to make whatever occurs count as correct play. Granted, that is not invariable but only a tendency. Granted also, conversational score changes for other reasons as well. (As when something conspicuous happens at the scene of a conversation, and straightway it is presupposed that it happened.) Still, I suggest that many components of conversational score obey rules of accommodation, and that these rules figure prominently among the rules governing the kinematics of conversational score.

Recall our examples. Example 1: presupposition evolves according to a rule of accommodation specifying that any presuppositions that are required by what is said straightway come into existence, provided that nobody objects. Example 2: permissibility evolves according to a rule of accommodation specifying that the boundaries of the permissible range of conduct shift to make true whatever is said about them, provided that what is said is said by the master to the slave, and provided that there does exist some shift that would make what he says true. Here is a general scheme for rules of accommodation for conversational score.

If at time t something is said that requires component s_n of conversational score to have a value in the range r if what is said is to be true, or otherwise acceptable; and if s_n does not have a value in the range r just before t; and if such-and-such further conditions hold; then at t the score-component s_n takes some value in the range r.

Once we have this scheme in mind, I think we will find many instances of it. In the rest of this paper I shall consider some further examples. I shall have little that is new to say about the individual examples. My interest is in the common pattern that they exhibit.

Example 3: Definite Descriptions[3]

It is not true that a definite description "the F" denotes x if and only if x is the one and only F in existence. Neither is it true that "the F" denotes x if and only if x is the one and only F in some contextually determined domain of discourse. For consider this sentence: "The pig is grunting, but the pig with floppy ears is not grunting." (LEWIS) And this: "The dog got in a fight with another dog." (McCAWLEY) They could be true. But for them to be true, "the pig" or "the dog" must denote one of two pigs or dogs, both of which belong to the domain of discourse.

The proper treatment of descriptions must be more like this: "the F" denotes x if and only if x is the most salient F in the domain of discourse, according to some contextually determined salience ranking. The first of our two sentences means that the most salient pig is grunting but the most salient pig with floppy ears is not. The second means that the most salient dog got in a fight with some less salient dog.

(I shall pass over some complications. Never mind what happens if two F's are tied for maximum salience, or if no F is at all salient. More important, I shall ignore the possibility that something might be highly salient in one of its guises, but less salient in another. Possibly we really need to appeal to a salience ranking not of individuals but rather of individuals-in-guises -- that is, of individual concepts.)

There are various ways for something to gain salience. Some have to do with the course of conversation, others do not. Imagine yourself with me as I write these words. In the room is a cat, Bruce, who has been making himself very salient by dashing madly about. He is the only cat in the room, or in sight, or in earshot. I start to speak to you:

The cat is in the carton. The cat will never meet our other cat, because our other cat lives in New Zealand. Our New Zealand cat lives with the Cresswells. And there he'll stay, because Miriam would be sad if the cat went away.

At first, "the cat" denotes Bruce, he being the most salient cat for reasons having nothing to do with the course of conversation. If I want to talk about Albert, our New Zealand cat, I have to say "our other cat" or "our New Zealand cat". But as I talk more and more about Albert, and not any more about Bruce, I raise Albert's salience by conversational means. Finally, in the last sentence of my monologue, I am in a position to say "the cat" and thereby denote not Bruce but rather the newly-most-salient cat Albert.

The ranking of comparative salience, I take it, is another component of conversational score. Denotation of definite descriptions is score-dependent. Hence so is the truth of sentences containing such descriptions, which is one aspect of the acceptability of those sentences. Other aspects of acceptability in turn are score-dependent: non-triviality, for one, and possibility of warranted assertion, for another.

One rule, among others, that governs the kinematics of salience is a rule of accommodation. Suppose my monologue has left Albert more salient than Bruce; but the next thing I say is "The cat is going to pounce on you!" If Albert remains most salient and "the cat" denotes the most salient cat, then what I say is patently false: Albert cannot pounce all the way from New Zealand to Princeton. What I have said requires for its acceptability that "the cat" denote Bruce, and hence that Bruce be once again more salient than Albert. If next I say "The cat prefers moist food", that is true if Bruce prefers moist food, even if Albert doesn't.

The same thing would have happened if instead I had said "The cat is out of the carton" or "The cat has gone upstairs". Again what I say is unacceptable unless the salience ranking shifts so that Bruce rises above Albert, and hence so that "the cat" again denotes Bruce. The difference is in the type of unacceptability that would ensue without the shift. It is trivially true, hence not worth saying, that Albert is out of the carton. ("The carton" denotes the same carton as before; nothing has been done to raise the salience of any carton in New Zealand.) It may be true or it may be false that Albert has gone upstairs in the Cresswells' house in New Zealand. But I have no way of knowing, so I have no business saying that he has.

We can formulate a rule of accommodation for comparative salience more or less as follows. It is best to speak simply of unacceptability, since it may well be that the three sorts of unacceptability I have mentioned are not the only sorts that can give rise to a shift in salience.

If at time t something is said that requires, if it is to be acceptable, that x be more salient than y; and if, just before t, x is no more salient than y; then -- ceteris paribus and within certain limits -- at t, x becomes more salient than y.

Although a rule of accommodation, such as this one, states that shifts of score take place when they are needed to preserve acceptability, we may note that the preservation is imperfect. It is not good conversational practice to rely too heavily on rules of accommodation. The monologue just considered illustrates this. Because "the cat" denotes first Bruce, then Albert, then Bruce again, what I say is to some extent confusing and hard to follow. But even if my monologue is not perfectly acceptable, its flaws are much less serious than the flaws that are averted by shifts of salience in accordance with our rule of accommodation. Confusing shifts of salience and reference are not as bad as falsity, trivial truth, or unwarranted assertion.

(It is worth mentioning another way to shift comparative salience by conversational means. I may say "A cat is on the lawn" under circumstances in which it is apparent to all parties to the conversation that there is some one particular cat that is responsible for the truth of what I say, and for my saying it. Perhaps I am looking out the window, and you rightly presume that I said what I did because I saw a cat; and further (since I spoke in the singular) that I saw only one. What I said was an existential quantification; hence, strictly speaking, it involves no reference to any particular cat. Nevertheless it raises the salience of the cat that made me say it. Hence this newly-most-salient cat may be denoted by brief definite descriptions, or by pronouns, in subsequent dialogue: "No, it's on the sidewalk." "Has Bruce noticed the cat?" As illustrated, this may happen even if the speaker contradicts my initial existential statement. Thus although indefinite descriptions -- that is, idioms of existential quantification -- are not themselves referring expressions, they may raise the salience of particular individuals in such a way as to pave the way for referring expressions that follow.)

Example 4: Coming and Going[4]

Coming is movement toward a point of reference. Going is movement away from it. Sometimes the point of reference is fixed by the location of speaker and hearer, at the time of conversation or the time under discussion. But sometimes not. In third-person narrative, whether fact or fiction, the chosen point of reference may have nothing to do with the speaker's or the hearer's location.

One way to fix the point of reference at the beginning of a narrative, or to shift it later, is by means of a sentence that describes the direction of some movement both with respect to the point of reference and in some other way. "The beggars are coming to town" requires for its acceptability, and perhaps even for its truth, that the point of reference be in town. Else the beggars' townward movement is not properly called "coming". This sentence can be used to fix or to shift the point of reference. When it is said, straightway the point of reference is in town where it is required to be. Thereafter, unless something is done to shift it elsewhere, coming is movement toward town and going is movement away. If later we are told that when the soldiers came the beggars went, we know who ended up in town and who did not.

Thus the point of reference in narrative is a component of conversational score, governed by a rule of accommodation. Note that the rule must provide for two sorts of changes. The point of reference may simply go from one place to another, as is required by the following text:

When the beggars came to town, the rich folk went to the shore. But soon the beggars came after them, so they went home.

But also the point of reference is usually not fully determinate in its location. It may become more or less determinate, as is required by the following:

After the beggars came to town, they held a meeting. All of them came to the square. Afterwards they went to another part of town.

The first sentence puts the point of reference in town, but not in any determinate part of town. The second sentence increases its determinacy by putting it in the square. The initial fixing of the point of reference is likewise an increase in determinacy -- the point of reference starts out completely indeterminate and becomes at least somewhat more definitely located.

Example 5: Vagueness[5]

If Fred is a borderline case of baldness, the sentence "Fred is bald" may have no determinate truth value. Whether it is true depends on where you draw the line. Relative to some perfectly reasonable ways of drawing a precise boundary between bald and not-bald, the sentence is true. Relative to other delineations, no less reasonable, it is false. Nothing in our use of language makes one of these delineations right and all the others wrong. We cannot pick a delineation once and for all (not if we are interested in ordinary language), but must consider the entire range of reasonable delineations.

If a sentence is true over the entire range, true no matter how we draw the line, surely we are entitled to treat it simply as true. But also we treat a sentence more or less as if it is simply true, if it is true over a large enough part of the range of delineations of its vagueness. (For short: if it is true enough.) If a sentence is true enough (according to our beliefs) we are willing to assert it, assent to it without qualification, file it away among our stocks of beliefs, and so forth. Mostly we do not get into any trouble this way. (But sometimes we do, as witness the paradoxes that arise because truth-preserving reasoning does not always preserve the property of being true enough.)

When is a sentence true enough? Which are the "large enough" parts of the range of delineations of its vagueness? This is itself a vague matter. More important for our present purposes, it is something that depends on context. What is true enough on one occasion is not true enough on another. The standards of precision in force are different from one conversation to another, and may change in the course of a single conversation. AUSTIN's "France is hexagonal" is a good example of a sentence that is true enough for many contexts, but not true enough for many others. Under low standards of precision it is acceptable. Raise the standards and it loses its acceptability.

Taking standards of precision as a component of conversational score, we once more find a rule of accommodation at work. One way to change the standards is to say something that would be unacceptable if the standards remained unchanged. If you say "Italy is boot-shaped" and get away with it, low standards are required and the standards fall if need be; thereafter "France is hexagonal" is true enough. But if you deny that Italy is boot-shaped, pointing out the differences, what you have said requires high standards under which "France is hexagonal" is far from true enough.

I take it that the rule of accommodation can go both ways. But for some reason raising of standards goes more smoothly than lowering. If the standards have been high, and something is said that is true enough only under lowered standards, and nobody objects, then indeed the standards are shifted down. But what is said, although true enough under the lowered standards, may still seem imperfectly acceptable. Raising of standards, on the other hand, manages to seem commendable even when we know that it interferes with our conversational purpose. Because of this asymmetry, a player of language games who is so inclined may get away with it if he tries to raise the standards of precision as high as possible -- so high, perhaps, that no material object whatever is hexagonal.

UNGER has argued that hardly anything is flat. Take something you claim is flat; he will find something else and get you to agree that it is even flatter. You think the pavement is flat -- but how can you deny that your desk is flatter? But "flat" is an absolute term: it is inconsistent to say that something is flatter than something that is flat. Having agreed that your desk is flatter than the pavement, you must concede that the pavement is not flat after all. Perhaps you now claim that your desk is flat; but doubtless UNGER can think of something that you will agree is even flatter than your desk. And so it goes.

Some might dispute UNGER's premise that "flat" is an absolute term; but on that score it seems to me that UNGER is right. What he says is inconsistent does indeed sound that way. I take this to mean that on no delineation of the correlative vagueness of "flatter" and "flat" is it true that something is flatter than something that is flat.

The right response to UNGER, I suggest, is that he is changing the score on you. When he says that the desk is flatter than the pavement, what he says is acceptable only under raised standards of precision. Under the original standards the bumps on the pavement were too small to be relevant either to the question whether the pavement is flat or to the question whether the pavement is flatter than the desk. Since what he says requires raised standards, the standards accommodatingly rise. Then it is no longer true enough that the pavement is flat. That does not alter the fact that it was true enough in its original context. "The desk is flatter than the pavement" said under raised standards does not contradict "The pavement is flat" said under unraised standards, any more than "It is morning" said in the morning contradicts "It is afternoon" said in the afternoon. Nor has UNGER shown in any way that the new context is more legitimate than the old one. He can indeed create an unusual context in which hardly anything can be called "flat", but he has not thereby cast any discredit on the more usual contexts in which lower standards of precision are in force.

In parallel fashion UNGER observes, I think correctly, that "certain" is an absolute term; from this he argues that hardly ever is anyone certain of anything. A parallel response is in order. Indeed the rule of accommodation permits UNGER to create a context in which all that he says is true, but that does not show that there is anything whatever wrong with the claims to certainty that we make in more ordinary contexts. It is no fault in a context that we can move out of it.

Example 6: Relative Modality[6]

The "can" and "must" of ordinary language do not often express absolute ("logical" or "metaphysical") possibility. Usually they express various relative modalities. Not all the possibilities there are enter into consideration. If we ignore those possibilities that violate laws of nature, we get the physical modalities; if we ignore those that are known not to obtain, we get the epistemic modalities; if we ignore those that ought not to obtain -- doubtless including actuality -- we get the deontic modalities; and so on. That suggests that "can" and "must" are ambiguous. But on that hypothesis, as KRATZER has convincingly argued, the alleged senses are altogether too numerous. We do better to think of our modal verbs as unambiguous but relative. Sometimes the relativity is made explicit. Modifying phrases like "in view of what is known" or "in view of what custom requires" may be present to indicate just which possibilities should be ignored.

But sometimes no such phrase is present. Then context must be our guide. The boundary between the relevant possibilities and the ignored ones (formally, the accessibility relation) is a component of conversational score, which enters into the truth conditions of sentences with "can" or "must" or other modal verbs. It may change in the course of conversation. A modifying phrase "in view of such-and-such" does not only affect the sentence in which it appears, but also remains in force until further notice to govern the interpretation of modal verbs in subsequent sentences.

This boundary may also shift in accordance with a rule of accommodation. Suppose I am talking with some elected official about the ways he might deal with an embarrassment. So far, we have been ignoring those possibilities that would be political suicide for him. He says: "You see, I must either destroy the evidence or else claim that I did it to stop Communism. What else can I do?" I rudely reply: "There is one other possibility -- you can put the public interest first for once!" That would be patently false if the boundary between relevant and ignored possibilities remained stationary. But it is not false in its context, for hitherto ignored possibilities come into consideration and make it true. And the boundary, once shifted outward, stays shifted. If he protests "I can't do that", he is mistaken.

Take another example. The commonsensical epistemologist says: "I know the cat is in the carton -- there he is before my eyes -- I just can't be wrong about that!" The sceptic replies: "You might be the victim of a deceiving demon." Thereby he brings into consideration possibilities hitherto ignored, else what he says would be false. The boundary shifts outward so that what he says is true. Once the boundary is shifted, the commonsensical epistemologist must concede defeat. And yet he was not in any way wrong when he laid claim to infallible knowledge. What he said was true with respect to the score as it then was.

We get the impression that the sceptic, or the rude critic of the elected official, has the last word. Again this is because the rule of accommodation is not fully reversible. For some reason, I know not what, the boundary readily shifts outward if what is said requires it, but does not so readily shift inward if what is said requires that. Because of this asymmetry, we may think that what is true with respect to the outward-shifted boundary must be somehow more true than what is true with respect to the original boundary. I see no reason to respect this impression. Let us hope, by all means, that the advance toward truth is irreversible. That is no reason to think that just any change that resists reversal is an advance toward truth.

184

Example 7: Performatives[7]

Suppose we are unpersuaded by AUSTIN's contention that explicit performatives have no truth value. Suppose also that we wish to respect the seeming parallelism of form between a performative like "I hereby name this ship the Generalissimo Stalin" and such non-performative statements as "Fred thereby named that ship the President Nixon". Then we shall find it natural to treat the performative, like the non-performative, as a sentence with truth conditions. It is true, on a given occasion of its utterance, if and only if the speaker brings it about, by means of that very utterance, that the indicated ship begins to bear the name "Generalissimo Stalin". If the circumstances are felicitous, then the speaker does indeed bring it about, by means of his utterance, that the ship begins to bear the name. The performative sentence is therefore true on any occasion of its felicitous utterance. In LEMMON's phrase, it is a sentence verifiable by its (felicitous) use.

When the ship gets its name and the performative is verified by its use, what happens may be described as a change in conversational score governed by a rule of accommodation. The relevant component of score is the relation that pairs ships with their names. The rule of accommodation is roughly as follows.

If at time t something is said that requires for its truth that ship s bear name n; and if s does not bear n just before t; and if the form and circumstances of what is said satisfy certain conditions of felicity; then s begins at t to bear n.

Our performative sentence does indeed require for its truth that the indicated ship bear the name "Generalissimo Stalin" at the time of utterance. Therefore, when the sentence is felicitously uttered, straightway the ship bears the name.

The sentence has other necessary conditions of truth: the ship must not have borne the name beforehand, the speaker must bring it about that the ship begins to bear the name, and he must bring it about by uttering the sentence. On any felicitous occasion of utterance, these further conditions take care of themselves. Our rule of accommodation is enough to explain why the sentence is verified by its felicitous use, despite the fact that the rule deals only with part of what it takes to make the sentence true.

A similar treatment could be given of many other performatives. In some cases the proposal may seem surprising. "With this ring I thee wed" is verified by its felicitous use, since the marriage relation is a component of conversational score governed by a rule of accommodation. Is marriage then a linguistic phenomenon? Of course not, but that was not implied. The lesson of performatives, on any theory, is that use of language blends into other social practices. We should not assume that a change of conversational score has its impact only within, or by way of, the realm of language. Indeed, we have already seen another counterexample: the case of permissibility, considered as Example 2.

Example 8: Planning

Suppose that you and I are making a plan -- let us say, a plan to steal some plutonium from a reprocessing plant and make a bomb of it. As we talk, our plan evolves. Mostly it grows more and more complete. Sometimes, however, parts that had been definite are revised, or at least opened for reconsideration.

Much as some things said in ordinary conversation require suitable presuppositions, so some things we say in the course of our planning require, for their acceptability, that the plan contain suitable provisions. If I say "Then you drive the getaway car up to the side gate", that is acceptable only if the plan includes provision for a getaway car. That might or might not have been part of the plan already. If not, it may become part of the plan just because it is required by what I said. (As usual the process is defeasible. You can keep the getaway car out of the plan, for the time being at least, by saying "Wouldn't we do better with mopeds?") The plan is a component of conversational score. The rules governing its evolution parallel the rules governing the kinematics of presupposition, and they include a rule of accommodation.

So good is the parallel between plan and presupposition that we might well ask if our plan simply _is_ part of what we presuppose. Call it that if you like, but there is a distinction to be made. We might take for granted, or purport to take for granted, that our plan will be carried out. Then we would both plan and presuppose that we are going to steal the plutonium. But we might not. We might be making our plan not in order to carry it out, but rather in order to show that the plant needs better security. Then plan and presupposition might well conflict. We plan to steal the plutonium, all the while presupposing that we will not. And indeed our planning may be interspersed with commentary that requires presuppositions contradicting the plan. "Then I'll shoot the guard (I'm glad I won't really do that) while you smash the floodlights." Unless we distinguish plan from presupposition (or distinguish two levels of presupposition) we must think of presuppositions as constantly disappearing and reappearing throughout such a conversation.

The distinction between plan and presupposition is not the distinction between what we purport to take for granted and what we really do. While planning that we will steal the plutonium and presupposing that we will not, we might take for granted neither that we will nor that we won't. Each of us might secretly hope to recruit the other to the terrorist cause and carry out the plan after all.

One and the same sentence may require, and if need be create, both provisions of the plan and presuppositions. "Then you drive the getaway car up to the side gate" requires both a getaway car and a side gate. The car is planned for. The gate is more likely presupposed.[8]

Notes

1 This treatment of presupposition is taken from STALNAKER [20], [21].

2 This treatment of permissibility is discussed more fully in LEWIS [17].

3   Definite descriptions governed by salience are discussed in LEWIS [15] and McCAWLEY [18]; a similar treatment of demonstratives is found in ISARD [10]. PINKAL [19] notes a further complication: if some highly salient things are borderline cases of F-hood, degree of F-hood and salience may trade off. In-

definite descriptions that pave the way for referring expressions are discussed in CHASTAIN [5] and KRIPKE [12].

4 See FILLMORE [6], [7].

5 See the treatment of vagueness in LEWIS [16]. For arguments that hardly anything is flat or certain, see UNGER [22]. For another example of accommodating shifts in resolution of vagueness, see the discussion of back-tracking counterfactuals in LEWIS [14].

6 See KRATZER [11]. The accessibility semantics considered here is equivalent to a slightly restricted form of Kratzer's semantics for relative modality. Knowledge and irrelevant possibilities of error are discussed in GOLDMAN [8].

7 See AUSTIN [2] for the original discussion of performatives. For treatment along the lines here preferred, see LEMMON [13], HEDENIUS [9], and ÅQVIST [1]. ISARD [10] suggests as I do that performative utterances are akin to other utterances that "change the context".

8 I am doubly grateful to STALNAKER: first for his treatment of presupposition here summarized as Example 1 which I have taken as the prototype for parallel treatments of other topics; and second, for valuable comments on a previous version of this paper. I am also much indebted to ISARD, who discusses many of the phenomena that I consider here in [10]. Proposals along somewhat the same lines as mine are to be found in BALLMER [3], [4]. An early version of this paper was presented to the Vacation School in Logic at Victoria University of Wellington in August 1976; I thank the New Zealand-United States Educational Foundation for research support on that occasion. The paper also was presented at a workshop on pragmatics and conditionals at the University of Western Ontario in May 1978.

References

1. L. Åqvist: Performatives and Verifiability by the Use of Language (Filosofiska Studier, Uppsala, 1972)

2. J.L. Austin: Philosophical Papers (Oxford University Press, Oxford, 1971) 220-39

3. T. Ballmer: in Linguistische Pragmatik, ed. by D. Wunderlich (Athenäum-Verlag, 1972)

4. T. Ballmer: Logical Grammar: with Special Considerations of Topics in Context Change (North-Holland, 1978)

5. C. Chastain: Minnesota Studies in the Philosophy of Science 7, 194-269 (1975)

6. C. Fillmore: in Linguistik 1971, ed. by K. Hyldgaard-Jensen (Athenäum-Verlag, 1972)

7. C. Fillmore: in Pragmatik/Pragmatics II, ed. by S.J. Schmidt (Wilhelm Fink Verlag, 1976)

8. A. Goldman: Journal of Philosophy 73, 771-91 (1976)

9. I. Hedenius: Theoria 29, 1-22 (1963)

10. S. Isard: in Formal Semantics of Natural Language, ed. by E.L. Keenan (Cambridge University Press, Cambridge, 1974) 287-96

11. A. Kratzer: Linguistics and Philosophy 1, 337-55 (1977)

12. S. Kripke: Midwest Studies in Philosophy 2, 255-76 (1977)

13. E.J. Lemmon: Analysis 22, 86-89 (1962)

14. D. Lewis: Noûs 13 (1979)

15. D. Lewis: Counterfactuals (Blackwell, Oxford, 1973) 111-7

16. D. Lewis: Synthese 22, 18-67 (1970)

17. D. Lewis: in Essays to Honour Hintikka, ed. by R. Hilpinen, I. Niiniluoto, M.B. Provence, E. Saarinen (Reidel, Dordrecht)

18. J. McCawley: Syntax and Semantics 11 (1979)

19. M. Pinkal: in Semantics from Different Points of View, ed. by R. Bäuerle, U. Egli, A. von Stechow (Springer-Verlag, Berlin, 1979)

20. R. Stalnaker: Journal of Philosophical Logic 2, 447-57 (1973)

21. R. Stalnaker: in Semantics and Philosophy, ed. by M.K. Munitz, P.K. Unger (New York University Press, New York, 1974) 197-213

22. P.K. Unger, Ignorance (Oxford University Press, Oxford, 1975) 65-8

On Pragmatic Demarcation of Language

Asa Kasher

Bar-Ilan University, Ramat-Gan, Israel

A happy utterance may invoke a variety of rules, of different forms and on distinct grounds. Thus -- we are told by William of Sherwood -- "the science of discourse...has three parts: grammar, which teaches one how to speak correctly; rhetoric, which teaches one how to speak elegantly; and logic, which teaches one how to speak truly."[1] To be sure, there is more to happiness of utterances than correct phrasing, elegant wording and truth of the matter. Under some circumstances, a happy utterance of "I see strangers in the gallery" will play its standard role within the rule-governed activity of assertion, and under special circumstances it will count as part of a formal proposal to exclude the public from an ongoing parliamentary session.[2] The institution of assertion and the parliamentary Order are clearly beyond the explanatory power of grammar, rhetoric and logic.

Some of the rules which a happy utterance of a single sentence may invoke are of a purely linguistic nature, whereas other rules thus invoked would not count as such. The demarcation of language is the cleavage of all these rules into classes of linguistic rules and non-linguistic rules. This is, indeed, a generalized form of the semantic problem of distinguishing between analytic truth and synthetic truth.

Our present aim is to demonstrate that *if* an adequate demarcation of language is possible in Pragmatics, *then* it is possible also in Semantics. More accurately, if an adequate distinction between linguistic institutions and non-linguistic institutions is possible, then so is an adequate distinction between analytic truths and synthetic truths.

Assumption One: Standard uses of language are made within institutions, i.e. systems of non-natural rules that govern activities, by assigning roles and instituting facts.

Scholium. The theoretical goal of Pragmatics is here taken to be specification and explanation of the *constitutive* rules of the human competence to use linguistic means for effecting certain, standard purposes.[3] Any pragmatic demarcation of language will therefore be sought in the realm of uses of language.

Uses of language are numerous and possible uses of it are perhaps innumerable, but at the moment many of them are readily left out of our consideration. Thus excluded are, for example, some surrealist "secret alphabets" -- visual puns such as two daggers linked by a stream of a blood in a torso, interpreted as "F".[4] Since fluency in surrealist secret alphabets is not a prerequisite of mastery of any natural language, any pragmatic demarcation of language should leave such a use of linguistic means outside the confines of language.

The central family of uses of language here under consideration consists of institutional uses, such as asserting, promising and acquitting. Putting a sentence to such a use is subjecting the activity of producing it in a certain context of utterance to some system of non-natural rules. Institutions comprise such rules which regulate human activities. They specify the standard point of the governed activity and the linguistic means which may be employed for effecting it, as well as who is in a position to employ these means under the circumstances and what are the standard products of their use under such conditions.[5]

Since language is independent of any judicial procedure, the institutional rules which regulate acquittings are not linguistic rules. Linguistic knowledge does not suffice for a specification of the legal conditions of setting free an accused person by pronouncing a sentence which counts as a verdict of not guilty. On the other hand, it seems that all natural languages include an institution of assertion among their institutions, which means that all the rules which define and regulate the activity of asserting are part of language. In contrast to these clear examples, the institution of promising does not seem to be as central as the institution of asserting or as non-linguistic as the institution of acquitting. Its case, so it seems, is going to be decided by the theory.

Assumption Two: If an adequate demarcation of language is possible in Pragmatics, then it induces a distinction between linguistic institutions and non-linguistic institutions.

Scholium. This assumption rests on our previously mentioned conception of Pragmatics and on Assumption One.

For the sake of simplicity we use in the sequel the term 'linguistic institution' as if a distinction between linguistic and non-linguistic institutions has been adequately introduced.

Assumption Three: From the rules of every linguistic institution *Inst* of language L it follows, for any sentence p (of language L) and any context of utterance C, either that (utterance of) sentence p is appropriate to context C according to the rules of institution *INST*, or that (utterance of) p is inappropriate to context C according to these rules.

Scholium. The rules of any institution which governs a human activity specify, *inter alia*, the institutional purposes of the rule-governed actions as well as the institutional possible means of effecting these purposes. Where an institution essentially employs linguistic means -- sentences of a language, utterances and contexts of utterance -- the rules of the institution should determine under which circumstances, which sentences of the language may be used for attaining a given institutional purpose, by one of them being uttered, in order for the speech act thus performed to count as a happy performance within the institution. Thus, for example, within the institution of Question (in English) every normal utterance of "Go!" is inappropriate for any ordinary circumstances.

The rules which define an institution establish also its roles. For playing a role in a certain institutional activity, a person is required to fulfil several conditions. For instance, a promisor has to believe that his promised action is thought by the promisee to be in the promisee's favour. Clearly, violations of such role-conditions render (utterances of) certain sentences

inappropriate for certain contexts of utterance, from the involved institutional point of view.[6]

Notice that when utterance of a sentence is inappropriate for some context
of utterance, according to the rules of a given institution, the inappropriateness verdict is always accompanied by its reasons. The only justification for
marking (an utterance of) a sentence inappropriate for a context of utterance,
within a certain institution, is that pairing the two would violate certain
rules. Since each of these violated rules takes a definite part in defining
the institution through its constituents -- purposes and means, roles and
products -- the inappropriateness verdict is explicitly rooted in some features
of the paired sentence and context being discordant to conditions imposed by
the definition of one or more of these constituents.

Definition I. A sentence p (of language L) is _extreme_, with respect to an
institution _Ins_ (of language L) if, and only if, for every context of utterance
C it follows from the rules of institution _Ins_ that (utterance of) sentence
p is inappropriate to context C, according to the rules of institution _Inst_.

Definition 2. A sentence p (of language L) is _linguistically extreme,_
with respect to an institution _Inst_ (of language L) if, and only if,
institution _Inst_ is linguistic and sentence p is extreme with respect to it.

Scholium. The adequacy of these definitions rests indeed on our previous
assumptions.

Since reasons for inappropriateness may vary with context of utterance,
linguistically extreme sentences may be divided into disjoint classes according
to the extent of variation of reasons each of them involves. Of particular
interest are those linguistically extreme sentences which involve a minimal
extent of variation.[7] Thus,

Definition 3. A sentence p (of language L) is _extreme/linguistically extreme_
for reasons of role, with respect to an institution/a linguistic institution
Inst (of language) if, and only if, for every context of utterance C it
follows from the rules of institution _Inst_ that (utterance of) sentence p
is inappropriate to context C, according to the rules of institution _Inst_,
because utterance of sentence p at context C would violate one or more of
the rules which specify the institutional roles within institution _Inst_.

If it is assumed that nobody ever holds true very simple contradictions[8]
and it is granted that a person has the speaker's role within the presumably
linguistic institution of asserting only when he or she believes what is being
asserted to be true, then simple sentences of the conspicuous form _Alpha and_
not Alpha are extreme for reasons of role, with respect to the institution of
asserting.

Similarly, if it is assumed that according to the common knowledge nobody
ever fails to hold true very simple tautologies[8] and it is granted that the
speaker's role within that institution is played only by one who believes
that what is being asserted is not self evidently true[9], then simple sentences
of the form, say, _If Alpha and Beta, then Alpha_, are extreme for reasons of
role, with respect to the presumably linguistic institution of asserting.

Whether these cases of extremity are also cases of linguistic extremity,
with respect to assertion depends just on whether the institution of asserting
is linguistic or not.

Assumption Four: If there are linguistic institutions at all then assertion is a linguistic institution.

Scholium. In defence of this assumption we suggest the following line of argument:

First, institutional uses of language are made only by those who entertain thoughts.[10] This is fairly clear, given that such institutional uses involve intentions, desires, preferences, reasons and other mental elements.

Secondly, "having a thought requires that there be a background of beliefs"[11]. Consequently, any institutional use of language requires a system of entertained beliefs.

Thirdly, beliefs are results of acts of judgment, which are "interiorizations"[12] of external acts of assertion. Hence, fourthly:

The institution of assertion is prior to all other institutions of language use. Since the assertoric use of language is prior to all other uses of langauge, it is also prior, in the same sense, to all other uses of language which are completely governed by the rules of the language itself, if there are any. Therefore, if there are linguistic institutions, then the institution of assertion is one of them. QED.

It follows that if there are linguistic institutions, then extremity of sentences with respect to assertion is linguistic extremity. (We call this observation 'conclusion 1.')

Under the same conditions it also follows that extremity, with respect to assertion, of simple sentences having conspicuous tautological or contradictory forms is linguistic extremity. (This observation we call 'conclusion 2.')

Moving from pragmatic grounds to semantics we make the following assumptions:

Assumption Five: For a definition (or a theory) of "Analyticity" to be adequate, the following adequacy conditions have to be satisfied:

(1)   It explicates the intuitive notions of 'linguistically established truth' and 'linguistically established falsity';

(2)   The defined (or induced) set of analytic sentences is finitely representable, in a strict sense;[13]

(3)   It is not circular.

Assumption Six: The notion of 'logical closure' is well-defined within some linguistically adequate logical theories.[14]

We proceed now to propose the following programmatic definition of Analyticity:

Definition 4. (I) A sentence (of a language) is analytically true if, and only if, it belongs to the logical closure of the class of sentences (of that language) which are true and are extreme, for reasons of role, with respect to the institution of assertion.[15]

(II) A sentence (of a language) is analytically false if, and only if, its denial is analytically true.

Scholium. If we show that from our assumptions it follows that the proposed definition of analyticity may be reasonably taken to be adequate, in the sense of our Assumption Five, then we may regard our case as stated, because pragmatic demarcation of langauge is thus shown to lead to semantic demarcation of it.

Under our assumptions, the first adequacy condition of analyticity definitions seems to obtain. Sentences which are according to our definition 4 analytically true are also linguistically established truths because they are either linguistically extreme truths and thus linguistically established truths, or truths which belong to the closure of the class of linguistically extreme truths and thus also linguistically established truths, because logical closure does not take us beyond the borders of language.

A similar argument shows that all linguistically established truths are linguistically extreme truths, for reasons of role, with respect to assertion.

The second adequacy condition of analyticity definitions also seems to be satisfied. Institutions are finite systems of rules; the class of sentences of a natural language is reasonably assumed to be finitely representable; and the number of different kinds of context of utterance which are involved in considerations of institutional appropriateness is finite.[16] From these assumptions it follows that the class of linguistically extreme sentences (of a language), with respect to assertion, is finitely representable. Similarly, the class of sentences (of a language) which are linguistically extreme for reasons of role with respect to assertion is also finitely representable.

Since the definition of linguistic extremity for reasons of role with respect to assertion is free of allusions to analyticity, the third required adequacy condition also obtains.

Thus,

Conclusion 3: If an adequate distinction between linguistic and non-linguisti institutions is possible, then so is an adequate distinction between analytic truths and synthetic truths. QED

Our conclusion is conditional, and we do not have at our theoretical disposal a pragmatical demarcation of language which would render the antecedent of our conclusion true. However, at the moment we do not see a reason to give up pursuit of an adequate distinction between linguistic and non-linguistic institutions, unless, indeed, one has been convinced by Quine's arguments that no adequate definition of analyticity is possible. In the latter case, our paper should be read as an outlined demonstration of the impossibility of drawing an adequate distinction between linguistic and non-linguistic institutions, that is between linguistic and non-linguistic institutional uses of linguistic means.[17]

Notes

* This is a slightly revised version of a paper entitled differently and read to the Konstanz colloquium on Semantics. A different version of the paper is forthcoming in *Theoretical Linguistics*.

Thanks are expressed to the DFG for partial support through a grant to the Ruhr Universität, Bochum, and to the Israel Academy of Sciences and Humanities for partial support through a grant to Tel-Aviv University.

I am grateful to Leo Apostel, Dirk Batens, David Lewis, Ruth Manor, Herman Parret, Barbara Partee, Dov Samet, Helmut Schnelle, Gershon Weiler and Dieter Wunderlich for comments on earlier presentations of the present paper.

1 William of Sherwood (1966:21).

2 This holds, I am told, in the British Parliament.

3 For our view of Pragmatics and elucidations of some central notions, see Kasher (1977a) and (1977b).

4 See Anthony Earnshow, Seven Secret Alphabets, second edition, Cape 1977. Also in the T.L.S. 3913 (11 March 1977), p. 257.

5 For details see Kasher (1977b).

6 Searle, in his (1969), discusses such violations, but since he does not use a theory of institutions or any similar general framework his lists of rules carry an air of arbitrariness.

7 Notice that a sentence may be inappropriate for a context because of more than one rule which is violated by the pairing.

8 Excluded here are contexts of language acquisition, of lexical misunderstanding, etc.

9 This hinges on the purposefulness of linguistic activity.

10 See Davidson (1975). "Thought" is used in a broad sense.

11 See Davidson (1975:9).

12 See Dummett (1973:e.g. p. 362).

13 Since some of the definitions of "Analyticity" may primarily apply to non-linguistic entities, such as propositions, the definition of the corresponding class of sentences is induced in some cases, rather than simply given.

14 The logical closure of a class of formulas is the class of formulas which logically follow from the former. For our purposes, a definition of this logical relation should be shaped to fit the linguistic framework.

15 Instead of ascribing analytic truth directly to sentences, one might have defined "analytically true" in terms of sentences and propositions they stand for.

194

16 Every institutional rule determines a contextual requirement and contextual variation beyond these requirements are of no importance here.

17 Quine's arguments are weaker, but that is the lesson they are commonly taken to carry. See Quine (1961).

References

Davidson, D. (1975), Thought and Talk, in: S. Guttenplan (ed.), *Mind and Language*, Clarendon Press, Oxford, pp. 7-23.

Dummett, M. (1973), *Frege, Philosophy of Language*, Duckworth, London.

Kasher, A. (1977a), Foundations of Philosophical Pragmatics, in: R.E. Butts and J. Hintikka (eds.), *Basic Problems in Methodology and Linguistics*, Reidel, Dordrech-Boston, pp. 225-242.

Kasher, A. (1977b), What is a Theory of Use? *Journal of Pragmatics* I, pp. 105-120.

Quine, W.V.O. (1961) *From a Logical Point of View*, second edition, Harvard University Press, Cambridge.

Searle, J.R. (1969) *Speech Acts*, Cambridge University Press, Cambridge.

William of Sherwood (1966), *Introduction to Logic*, translated with an introduction and notes by Norman Kretzmann, University of Minnesota Press, Minneapolis.

Constructive Pragmatics and Semantics

Friedrich Kambartel

Universität Konstanz, Philosophische Fakultät,
Postfach 5560, D-7750 Konstanz, Fed. Rep. of Germany

Constructive pragmatics and semantics, many of you will not
know what that is. Serious knowledge of this activity means
getting involved in it in the way of a practical insight. As
far as I can see this insight would amount to a change of life
for many linguists. So obviously, as normal for a morally serious discourse, we cannot settle the matter this afternoon,
and the SFB 99 can be hopeful that the semantics-festival will
go on with only a rather short pragmatic interruption.

In a radically pragmatic understanding, language structures
are throughout reconstructed not as **objects** but as part of a
rational practice. And indeed such a pragmatic reconstruction
cannot reach back to those conceptions of language and logic,
that at present are dominant in formal logic and linguistics.
These are mostly based on the so called '**semantic** point of
view' which, in its modern form, goes back to A.TARSKI. Here
one has to take the word 'semantic' not just in the general
Greek sense indicating only, that the meaning of language expressions is treated. Rather, the word 'semantic' refers to a
quite peculiar theory of meaning. This theory assumes that
language consists of special (structured) objects, which become meaningful by their being related to certain other objects so to speak "in the world". Among these other objects
we have to imagine such abstract objects as functions, especially truth functions. These meaning relations are introduced and analysed by using another language (or level of
language) which is usually called (the) 'metalanguage'. In the
metalanguage, so we are informed, we can speak about the object language, i.e. that language which is the 'object' of our
considerations.

As an illustration let us consider the following example. In
logic books written from a semantic point of view, one can
find truth-conditional definitions of the universal quanti-
fier of the following kind: '$\wedge_x \underline{a}(\underline{x})$' is by definition true if
and only if for all 'admitted' substitutions $\underline{x}|\underline{n}$ the resul-
ting $\underline{a}(\underline{n})$ is true. - More sophisticated versions using the
possible worlds concept go roughly like this: A possible world
$\underline{w}$ belongs to the meaning of a universal sentence '$\wedge_x \underline{a}(\underline{x})$' if
and only if for all substitutions $\underline{x}|\underline{n}$: $\underline{w}$ is an element of the
meaning of $\underline{a}(\underline{n})$.

Strictly speaking, from the semantic viewpoint we characterize by such definitions abstract objects like sets or functions and coordinate them as meanings with certain other objects, called language expressions or symbols. - Quite obviously this type of explaining universal quantification involves
serious deficiencies: Besides the unjustified ontological framework it already uses expressions like 'for all x'. Therefore it
is not helpful for learning or understanding universal quantification, contrary to what we would expect from logic books. This
deficiency is not avoided, as most logicians since TARSKI think,
by just taking '$\wedge_x$' as a symbol of the object language and 'for
all x' as an expression of English, taken as a metalanguage to
the language of formal logic. For if we want to understand the
use of universal quantifiers, it would be a petitio principii
to use just metalanguage translations of (or equivalents to)
those terms of the object language that we want to introduce.
Also it would be a (more indirect) petitio principii, if such
a translation or equivalent is used to build up the metalanguage level. Nevertheless methodical circles of this kind are characteristic for the semantic point of view. Not taking them
seriously means to give up the goal of understanding what we do
when we use language, especially when we use logical expressions and symbols.

So a semantical analysis of the TARSKI-type does not provide
us with a rational understanding of meaning, neither of the lexical nor of the categorical component of meaning. Semantics
in this sense may give us a very general description of language structures, a description though, which works only on the
presupposition, that we have already acquired all the relevant
lexical and categorical competence. Hence this sort of semantics has nothing to do with the intensional part of language
analysis - if we still want to use the words "Sinn" and "intension" in the FREGE-CARNAP-tradition.

Another point is worth mentioning. Treating language and the
realm of meanings as a set of objects linked by functional relations often has dangerous consequences for the attempt to
install rational practice. For it takes us away from the obvious fact, that language is a human activity which can be reasonable or irrational, understandable or confused in a pragmatic sense. As one can experience in science and in the humanities, the semantic point of view supports descriptive attitudes to one's own ordinary and theoretical language as well as
the refusal to understand and justify these languages step by
step.

But couldn't we take the pragmatic approach of AUSTIN, SEARLE
and others as an alternative? - Linguistic pragmatism, in its
general formulations, surely points to a trivial truth, namely that language is a system of acts, not objects. Nevertheless in its concrete performance the "pragmatic" approach is
only pseudopragmatic. Very often pragmatic linguists just take
the traditional semantical or logico-grammatical categories
and "invent" speech acts on the verbal level, as in the case
of "propositional acts" derived from the stipulated abstract

objects called propositions. Thus pragmatics here depends on non-pragmatic distinctions and an objectifying surface-understanding of language. Therefore this kind of pragmatics still gives us no knowledge of how we can learn speech acts without having at our disposal a semantic conception of language. It gives us no knowledge e.g. of how we can learn a propositional act a without just defining it as "expressing the proposition a". Let me therefore propose a radicalisation of the pragmatic approach, which (re)constructs language as a rational system of acts without semantic rests at its basis and which I like to call constructive pragmatics.

Speech acts are first of all acts. Let us therefore as a next step try to agree about the concept of an act.

I hope you are all intentionalists, i.e. you do not rank acts among natural events as behaviorists do. Then we perhaps do not differ in characterizing acts as events, which do not just occur to the agent, but are brought about by him. As WITTGENSTEIN has put it: "I should not say of the movement of my arm, for example: it comes when it comes, etc. ... And this is the region in which we say significantly that a thing doesn't simply happen to us, but that we do it. 'I don't need to wait for my arm to go up - I can raise it.'" (Philosophical Investigations I, 612, editor's English translation).

You all know this distinction, I hope, 'exemplarisch' (by examples) or by Lebenswelt-experience. Nevertheless it will be good to add some more precise details about what we all know: To perform an act (a definite act!) means to exert an ability which we have acquired, as a rule by learning with a teacher or just by trying again and again ourselves. Therefore, if you can act in a certain way, you should be able to produce more than one single occurrence. Rather it will be necessary to have at your disposal a certain type of occurrence, at least under suitable circumstances, if you want to be independent from chance and nature. This leads us to the distinction between act schemes and concrete acts as actualisations of a certain act scheme.[1]

On the basis of this distinction there is no difficulty to understand the intentionality of acts: The relevant situation is that someone presupposes some occurrence to be a (concrete) act. Asking for the intention then is equivalent to the question, what the agent is doing there, and that is asking for the act scheme which he is actualizing.

There may be several intentions to one 'act occurence': Someone operates a switch, thereby turns on the light and thereby gives some information (signals something).

In every day English (and similarly in German) the word "intention" can be used for aims too. Our definition of intention means that we distinguish between e.g. the act of running which someone is actualizing, and the psychosomatic condition he wants to preserve or attain by regular running, which I propose to call the aim of his performance.

There are acts which we do (actualize) by doing (actualizing) other acts, like putting on the light by operating a switch or, as we shall see, speech acts. I propose to call an act **mediated** by other acts if and only if this act, by its definition, can be actualized by actualizations of one or several of these other acts. We may speak of **mediated acts** (absolutely) if and only if an act can be performed in a mediated way only.

Let us now come directly to those mediated acts which constitute language and other human institutions. I prefer to call them **symbolic acts**. Symbolic acts serve the purpose to agree upon the situation, in which we are, and to cooperate (pragmatically) by having influence on other people's actions. They, in a sense, make rational life possible. We construct (constitute) symbolic acts by giving a special (symbolic) use to other acts. This is done by **agreements** which restrict (explicitly or tacitly) the actualization of these acts to certain situations or lay down for them certain consequences in the course of our actions. Think e.g. of a certain phonetic act "come" (or rather $k \wedge m$) which by agreement has to be understood as a certain demand. A person who has uttered a demand - by the sort of agreements which are characteristic for demands - must be prepared to see his demand fulfilled by the addressee (no sanctions however implied, because **demands** are not necessarily **commands**).

The performance of symbolic acts is built on the possibility of **following rules**. However we should not confuse symbolic action with just following a rule, e.g. prescribing that an act **a** is allowed to be done only in certain situations or has to be done in certain other situations. A rule $R(\underline{a})$ just concerns a regular way of doing or forbearing **a**. That is: we have a different rule, if we regulate a different **a'** in the same way R. Drinking tea every morning is different from drinking coffee in the morning. Whereas in the case of a symbolic act the **a** underlying the regulation R does not really matter; it is **methodically** arbitrary, though there may be historical and mnemotechnical reasons for a selection. Any **a'**, on which we can make the same agreement $(\underline{R})$ as on **a**, in principle will be good for the same symbolic intention, though in fact naturally we do not and cannot make all possible agreements. Thus actualizing the symbolic act belonging to the rule or rule system $\underline{R}$ means to perform **one of the** acts, which by agreement are given the same symbolic use. This makes clear the particular way in which agreements and mere conventions are combined in symbolic acts. (Sometimes somewhat absurd examples make things clearer: we might indeed drink coffee or tea to indicate that it is morning time. Obviously drinking beer will do as well, but has side effects, which we should not want at the beginning of a philosophical day.)

As generally in the case of mediated acts in the performance of a symbolic act we follow at least two intentions, the **direct** one of the mediating act and the **indirect** one of the symbolic act. We shall say that the direct intention 'carries' the symbolic one. **Phonetic** acts that are mediating symbolic acts may be called **speech acts** (in the narrow sense). In the same way we may understand <u>writing acts,</u> the carrying intentions then consisting in the production of figures (spatial forms). Speech acts and writing acts then form the <u>speech acts in the broad (usual) sense</u> of the term. - Now we have laid the foundation for a pragmatic reconstruction of 'intensional meaning': I propose to define as <u>intensions</u> the symbolic intentions of speech acts in the broad sense.

The defining agreement <u>constitutes</u> a symbolic act <u>s</u>. Naturally we might in addition to actualizing <u>s</u> also just follow rules, which would then best be called <u>regulative</u> rules.

A symbolic act <u>s</u> has <u>informative</u> meaning with reference to the conditions which by agreement make the performance of <u>s</u> a correct one, and <u>performative</u> meaning because of the constitutive pragmatic consequences. Obviously mixed cases are possible.

But does not this approach lead us into serious methodical problems? Are we not forced to go back to descriptions (or articulations) of the agreements constituting certain symbolic acts? Since these descriptions make use of language already, we seem to get into an infinite regress or into the same circle which we criticised with respect to the semantic point of view: For it seems as if we have to use a descriptive meta-language to learn the acts of a pragmatically understood object language.

A closer look on elementary speech situations will, I hope, convince us, that in a pragmatic understanding of language there is no such circle. As you know by your own practice, in such situations we can learn an elementary symbolic act <u>s</u> by exemplification and we can <u>pragmatically</u> control our understanding of the agreement which is intended. That is, we just get acquainted with examples and counter-examples of a correct actualization of <u>s</u> in an appropriate pragmatic context. And in order to control and correct our understanding we can, in elementary situations, always return to what we <u>do</u>, especially what we do in non-symbolic action. (Take for an example the demand "come!", which I mentioned beforehand.) Therefore in the elementary case, in order to acquire a symbolic act, we, in principle at least, need no descriptions using other symbolic acts.

In natural language it is sometimes not clear what kind of elementary symbolic acts are performed, if we do not have an exact knowledge of the situation. E.g. uttering "bricks" may carry symbolic intentions like:
1. Bricks are over there.
2. Get me some bricks!
3. Bricks are over there, get me some!

Let me now from elementary symbolic acts go over to elementary statements. Elementary statements can be built up in two steps. For the first step let me take a proposal made by H. SCHNEIDER:

Obviously elementary symbolic acts can be rather ambiguous
in most, especially complex, situations. E.g. we may not know
whether a warning 'hot' concerns the soup or the pan. In such
cases, if we want to make clear what we have in mind, it is
often helpful just to connect the corresponding symbolic act
Q with a further symbolic act P. So in our example we could
say 'soup hot' or 'pan hot'. Naturally a suitable P must be
already at our disposal, i.e. there must be a well known use
of P in the considered language community. Let us in the
speech situation call P a specification of Q, and let us
write specifications in the form P-Q. In natural English or
German we may use quite a variety of grammatical structures,
e.g. the statement form 'P is Q' (with emphasis on P) or adverbial constructions (like 'hot soup').

Remaining disambiguities might be dissolved by using additional deictic or indexical expressions like "this", "that",
"here", "there", and, naturally, the personal pronouns. But
all this clearly does not lead us to "invariant" statements
about the situation (as opposed to "variant" statements in
the sense of utterances having situation-relatively changing
symbolic intentions), statements e.g. like "Peter is small".

Now I propose to reconstruct elementary statements as follows:
Let P, Q be informative elementary symbolic acts. Then in
many relevant cases we may agree upon rules of the following
type:

$$P \Rightarrow P\text{-}Q$$
(read: if P is correct, then Q (specified by P)
is correct or misleadingly: P-situations are
Q-situations)

Examples are:

Peter ⇒ tall   (Peter is tall)
horse ⇒ animal   (horses are animals)

Further elementary statements are the negative counterparts

$$P \nRightarrow P\text{-}Q$$
(read: if P is correct, then Q (specified by P)
is incorrect or misleadingly: P-situations are
not Q-situations)

What is the use of invariant statements "P is Q" in our
life? - Well, whereever an elementary statement "P is Q" is
correct ("valid"), then in a P-situation (that is: a situation, where P can be correctly performed) you have the possibilities to act which are characteristic for a P-Q-situa-
tion. This means that e.g. in the case of a correctly done
elementary statement "Peter is small" we take it that in
situations, where "Peter" is correct (objectively spoken:
where Peter is involved), we may rely on the situation allowing a correct performance of "small" (in connection with
"Peter"). Normally this holds only for a certain range of

Peter-situations, which is different e.g. for the usual sense of "Peter is small" and "Peter is lecturing". By elementary statements we thus take the first step towards agreements treating situations "generally", "in an abstract way". This enables us to go, via language, beyond the present, concrete situation.

Elementary statements may by agreement carry a further symbolic intention and thereby be transformed into the basic form of assertions (elementary assertions). The need for elementary assertions arises in situations, where action depends already on correctly performed elementary statements and where the participants do not agree on the correctness of such a performance. In this case one can either give up common orientation by using elementary statements, or try to overcome private opinions by a new level of transsubjectivity, namely by argumentation. What does argumentation mean (in this case)? - Well, quite simply all attempts to settle differences on the basis of previously or newly established agreements. Thus e.g. we may go back to other elementary statements, which are not at issue, or reproduce (resp. once more realize) the original learning situation for the words involved. In the first case e.g. if we have already agreed upon P is Q and Q is R, this might stop further discussion on P is R. Often it will be helpful (or even necessary) to remember the aims and activities which originally gave rise to the terms of a disputed elementary statement. This may be sufficient to show, what activities we can enter into for the purpose of justifying an elementary statement by arguments. Someone who now not only just states something, but asserts what he is stating, must be prepared to establish by argumentation a transsubjective agreement that his statement has been made correctly. In this way statements characteristically come to carry a further "assertive" symbolic intention, and then are called assertions.

Assertions are, in our everyday and scientific life, one of the language institutions, whereby we can rely on others in our orientation. Therefore they make possible division of labor in building up a knowledge of our situation. Trivially the reliability of assertions is undermined, if people make assertions without having the corresponding justifications at hand. Often this is done with bad intentions, as e.g. in the case of propaganda. Less harmful seems (but only seems) a practice, which is widely spread in universities, namely substituting mere assumptions for statements. Making assumptions may be a good thing when there is no knowledge in sight. Saying moreover, that your assumptions are formulated in a so-called theoretical language, in most cases dispenses people even from the necessity of introducing step by step the terms they use. Thus the orientation these theories provide us with is often something like fog with elaborated formal syntax.

We shall now consider logically complex assertions and show that, once have elementary assertions, it is helpful to proceed to more complex activities related to the logical words of our language.

In planning common practice e.g., it is in many cases advisable to make action depend on more than one justified orientation. Thus it may be that one has to do two things, justify _a_ and justify _b_, to make someone else do _h_. Whoever thinks himself capable of fulfilling both these justification-tasks, claims that he can do a complex justification-work, as we may well say. This claim is raised in English in the form of a complex statement, the conjunction 'a and b', in logical symbols: 'a∧b'. But is not there still a petitio principii in this reconstruction of logical conjunction? Did we not use the word 'and', when we put the relevant complex justification task as follows: 'to do two things, justify _a and_ justify _b_? - Indeed we did. But here (in this formulation) the word 'and' is not a logical connective (junctor), but a word, which we use to form expressions for complex acts, e.g. in the case of commands. And what it means to perform an act by doing several (in our case two) other acts we can learn in practice by corresponding examples. This practical ('empragmatic') learning does not imply that we need to speak about this learning situation and use, in doing this, logical conjunction. Thus there is no circle of definition.

In a similar way we come to logical adjunction 'a or (vel) b', in symbols: 'a∨b'. Adjunction serves e.g. the purpose of planning action which is dependent of several possibilities (alternatives). Again first we have to establish a pragmatic basis for logic, namely learn a sort of pragmatic complexity, which we may express as doing one of two things (acts). Knowing this we know in particular what it means to fulfil one of the (two) justification-tasks related to assertions _a_, _b_. And this new justification-claim we may again attach to a new complex statement 'a or b' ('a∨b').

The purpose e.g. of dividing up justifications in parts, leads us to logical subjunction 'b, if _a_' ('a→b'). In this case the constitutive claim is: let me have a justification of _a_, then I shall be able to construct one for _b_. This should, for invariance reasons, include the case, that I have an independent justification of _b_.

As to the negator 'not' ('¬'): whoever puts forward a negation¬ _a_ (not _a_), claims to have a procedure, by which we can be sure, that attempts to justify _a_ will fail. In short: the proponent of a negation ¬ _a_ must be able to refute _a_. Obviously negations provide us with an important kind of knowledge, because with them we can e.g. give up trying to justify the negated _a_ or reflecting on courses of action presupposing the validity of _a_. - Again negation makes use of a pragmatic distinction, namely between succeeding and failing to do something (to act in a certain way).

Now we are already able to settle e.g. the question of tertium non datur: Is _a_ ∨ ¬_a_ valid independently of the content of _a_, i.e. valid by taking into account nothing else but the meaning of the logical words ∨ ,¬? Obviously not, because there are _a_'s for which we have neither justifications nor refutations at hand.

The <u>contradiction principle</u> on the other hand holds, i.e.
— (a∧¬a) is logically valid. This is so, because nobody can
do both, justify an assertion <u>a</u>, and at the same time show us,
that an attempt to justify <u>a</u> must fail.

Logical quantifiers may be treated similarly: Asserting 'for
all <u>x</u>: <u>a(x)</u>', in symbols: '∧_x <u>a(x)</u>' (<u>universal quantification</u>)
means having a <u>procedure</u> at hand to justify <u>a(n)</u> for an arbi-
trary substitution <u>x/n</u>. To know a procedure does not necessarily imply descriptions using universal quantifiers: to know how
to get nails into a concrete-wall does not imply understanding
<u>sentences</u> like 'all nails are in the wall' or 'for all nails I
know how to get them into the wall'.

Who asserts 'there is an <u>x</u>, such that: <u>a(x)</u>', in symbols:
'∨_x <u>a(x)</u>' (<u>existential quantification</u>) claims to have a substitution <u>x/n</u> at hand, so that he can give a justification for
the corresponding <u>a(n)</u>. Existential quantification in this sense is 'effective': you have to know <u>how to 'construct'</u> the substitution which is necessary to defend the existential assertion.

Obviously no logical platonism or axiomatic formalism is
necessary to understand the meaning of the logical words and
symbols and to judge on logical validity. You just have to reconstruct their rational pragmatic place in our life, i.e., you
have to understand them as part of rational action, namely in
this case argumentation.[2]

Let us look back on the systematic way, especially the method,
which we have followed. We may call our considerations and proposals critical reconstructions of an activity, which we all
know in use, namely language. Reconstructions being <u>construc-
tions</u>, let me first dwell upon this point. 'Construction' in my
use is a term of the <u>theory of action</u>. In a (pragmatic) <u>con-
struction</u> we build up, step by step, systematically connected
actions. Pragmatic constructions are <u>justified</u>, in so far as
they lay the basis for a rational life. To intend justified
constructions implies that, besides the question of how we can
acuire step by step certain acts, we have to consider the connection between our acts and our aims: That is to say we have
to judge the consequences of performing those acts, i.e. evaluate the resulting situations. In this sense justified <u>prag-
matic</u> constructions include <u>teleological</u> considerations.

In most cases of pragmatic constructions, we do not enter
for the first time into the corresponding actions. Rather we
are already involved in them in a confused and sometimes seriously distorted way. Thus in some sense we always know what
we do, and in some sense we do not know; i.e. we know how to
do certain things without having a clear awareness either of
the pragmatical construction of this ability, or of its teleo-
logical place in our life. This leads us to misunderstand our
activities and sometimes thereby to become subject to a misuse
of our life without our realizing it. Therefore in those situations it is advisable to work out clear pragmatic and teleo-

logical constructions for the actions we are involved in, in
short: to <u>reconstruct</u> what we do. I think that this is an
endeavour for <u>enlightenment</u>; and obviously the actual use of
<u>language</u> often is confused enough by itself and moreover by
logicians and linguistics to need this enlightenment.

Notes

1) This terminology ("Handlungsschema", "Aktualisierung eines
   Handlungsschemas") has been introduced by W. KAMLAH: Cf.
   KAMLAH/LORENZEN (1967), II, § 2. G.H. VON WRIGHT (1963) uses
   a similar distinction between "generic acts" and "individual
   acts".

2) Obviously the proposed reconstructions of complex assertions
   are related to the <u>dialogical logic</u> of P. LORENZEN and K. LO-
   RENZ (now documented in the collection P. LORENZEN/K.LORENZ
   (1978); cf. also LORENZEN (1969), LORENZ (1973)). The dialogical approach too claims to characterize, by schematic rules,
   the logical aspect of concrete argumentation as exemplified
   e.g. by PLATO's dialogues. And yet the short history of dialogical logic shows that it has not led to a full overcoming
   of the distortions caused by the mathematization of logic.

   Already the first version in LORENZEN (1960) stylizes argumentation as following formal rules in a dialogical 'game',
   analogous to the moves in chess. LORENZ in (1961), (1968) then
   has worked out this gametheoretical reconstruction of formal
   obligations in argumentation and of logical validity. He gave
   precise and schematically applicable formulations not only
   for the steps dependent on the <u>logical particles (particle
   rules</u>), but also for the <u>general frame</u> which has to be observed by making whatever particle-related moves (<u>frame ru-
   les</u>). For all these rules, especially for frame rules, we
   can arise the question of justification, namely whether they
   are an adequate reconstruction of logical complexity in
   concrete argumentation. And here the adequacy control can
   lead to a reasonable regulation only if we already <u>under-
   stand the rational place of logically complex argumentation
   in our life</u>. (This perspective has been worked out to some
   degree in C.F. GETHMANN (1978 a), (1978 b) and KAMBARTEL
   (1978). Already LORENZ in (1967) took some steps in this
   direction.)

   The above proposals for an argumentative use of the logical
   words are meant to be such an understanding. Classically
   spoken, they play the role of a semantics in relation to
   the 'monological' or 'dialogical' formal systems.

References

GETHMANN, C.F. (1978 a): Die Ausdifferenzierung der Logik aus
der vorwissenschaftlichen Begründungs- und Rechtfertigungs-
praxis, in: Zeitschrift für allgemeine Wissenschaftstheorie 9,
forthcoming.

GETHMANN, C.F. (1978 b): Protologik - Untersuchungen zur formalen Pragmatik von Begründungsdiskursen, Habilitationsschrift Universität Konstanz.

KAMBARTEL, F. (1977): Symbolic Acts - Remarks on the Foundations of a Pragmatic Theory of Language, in G. RYLE (ed.): Contemporary Aspects of Philosophy, Oxford, 70-85.

KAMBARTEL, F. (1978): Überlegungen zum pragmatischen und zum argumentativen Fundament der Logik, i K. LORENZ (ed.): Konstruktionen versus Positionen, Berlin.

KAMLAH, W./LORENZEN, P. (1975, [2]1973): Logische Propädeutik - Vorschule des vernünftigen Redens, Mannheim.

LORENZ, K. (1961): Arithmetik und Logik als Spiele, Dissertation Universität Kiel, partly repr. in LORENZEN/LORENZ (1978), 17-95.

LORENZ, K. (1967): Die Ethik der Logik, in: H.C. GADAMER (ed.), Das Problem der Sprache, München, pp. 81-86.

LORENZ, K. (1968): Dialogspiele als semantische Grundlage von Logikkalkülen, in: Archiv für mathematische Logik und Grundlagenforschung 11, 32-55, 73-100, repr. in LORENZEN/LORENZ (1978), 96-162.

LORENZ, K. (1970): Elemente der Sprachkritik, Frankfurt.

LORENZ, K. (1973): Rules versus Theorems - A new Approach for Meditation between Intuitionistic and Two-Valued Logic, in: Journal of Philosophic Logic 2, 352-369.

LORENZ, K. (1976): Sprachtheorie als Teil einer Handlungstheorie. Ein Beitrag zur Einführung linguistischer Grundbegriffe, in: D. WUNDERLICH (ed.), Wissenschaftstheorie der Linguistik, Kronberg, pp. 250-266.

LORENZEN, P. (1960): Logik and Agon in: Atti del XII Congresso Internazionale di Filosofia (Venezia, 12-18 Settembre 1958) vol. 4, Firenze, 187-194, repr. in LORENZEN/LORENZ (1978), 1-8.

LORENZEN, P. (1969): Normative Logic and Ethics, Mannheim/Zürich.

LORENZEN, P./LORENZ, K. (1978): Dialogische Logik, Darmstadt, Wissenschaftliche Buchgesellschaft.

LORENZEN, P./SCHWEMMER, O. (1973, [2]1975): Konstruktive Logik, Ethik und Wissenschaftstheorie, Mannheim; pages refer to the second edition 1975.

SCHNEIDER, H.J. (1975): Pragmatik als Basis von Semantik und Syntax, Frankfurt.

VON WRIGHT, G.H. (1963): Norm and Action, London.

Explanation and Understanding in the Theory of Language

Hans Schneider

Universität Konstanz, Philosophische Fakultät,

Postfach 5560, D-7750 Konstanz, Fed. Rep. of Germany

I will be dealing here with a meta-scientific question, namely, what type of theory should a theory of language be? The words that I have used in the title of my paper, 'explanation' and 'understanding' express two main possibilities and at the same time they indicate a contention that I hope you will share. It is the following: When we, as philosophers or linguists, work on a theory of language, it is not enough to subscribe to the simple syllogism 'all interesting subjects should be treated scientifically; language is an interesting subject; therefore language should be treated scientifically'. We have to go further and ask: What is the specific interest we take in language? What is it that we want to know? Information of what type will we accept as answers to our questions?

Due to the division of labor in the modern university, these might well be taken as 'philosophical' questions, there is nothing wrong with such a classification. But a mistake is made, I think, when they are treated as 'merely' philosophical in the sense that linguists feel they can ignore them.

I will start my considerations with a very brief discussion of the concepts of explanation and understanding as they have very clearly and to my mind convincingly been worked out by G.H. VON WRIGHT[1] To explain an event e_2 means to bring it under a general law that connects it with another event e_1 by stating the following: Whenever e_1 will occur, e_2 will of necessity occur also. Laws of such a type allow us to predict, to explain, to produce, or to supress events of the type e_2 by noting, producing or supressing an event of the type e_1. So far this is a description of the deductive-nomological type of explanation according to the classical HEMPEL-OPPENHEIM scheme.

Now VON WRIGHT has argued that the concept of a law that this account makes use of can be distinguished from that of an accidental regularity only with recourse to the concept of an action. More specifically: To say that two types of events e_1 and e_2 are lawfully connected with one another, or, in other words, that the occurrence of e_1 necessarily results in the occurrence of e_2, means to say that by producing e_1 we can produce e_2. Note that this ability to produce the one by the other is not a consequence of the law, but is the defining condition of there being a law in the first place[2] According to this analysis, to look for explanations means to look for possibilities of isolating systems of events in such a way that an event of the type e_2 can be produced by producing another event of the type e_1. For example: An electic current can be produced by rotating a magnet in a magnetic field. Physics and chemistry are prominent examples of this type of system-building.

I now turn to the second concept, that of understanding. Adherents to the HEMPEL-OPPENHEIM scheme have always tried to defend the view that there is no difference between the explanation of natural events and the understanding of human action. Both would bring a particular event under a general law. And as long as the concept of lawlikeness was unclear, it was hard to oppose this view, because regularities we find in the field of human action as well as in the field of natural events. So it would have been easy, e.g. for a linguist, to describe his particular endeavour by saying that he is looking for the regularities of his subject-matter, language, like anybody else in scientific investigations. But the more detailed analysis that VON WRIGHT has given of the concept of explanation has changed the situation. We can now see that there are two types of investigation: An understanding of human action as it is sought in history and (partly) the social sciences is of another character, quite different from the explanation of natural events[3]. Roughly, to understand an action a means to be able to give a so-called 'practical syllogism' that consists in a statement of the agent's motives and opinions and concludes from them that he would get ready to do the action a. The philosophically central point here is that it can be shown that motives and beliefs are no causes, so that the practical syllogism differs strongly from an explanation in the sense discussed above. Furthermore, quite obviously practical syllogisms are not detected by experimentally searching for systems of events that can be manipulated and thus be brought under laws. For example: When we understand a person's action of having published an obituary in a daily paper, we do not do so on the basis of experiments in the course of which we learned how to make people do the considered action. Rather, to understand an action means, among other things, to understand how it serves the agent's motives and goals.

This short review of the two concepts shows that it makes an important difference in the construction of a theory whether it is considered as a means for explanations of the type prominent in the natural sciences, or as a means for understanding human action, as in the social sciences. We can now address ourselves to the question what the proper place would be for a theory of language. Should it be of the explanatory or of the understanding type? But before I discuss this question, I will briefly look at what seems to be a third type of scientific investigation, namely that of a formal science as exemplified by arithmetic. Is there a subject matter that is _explained_ by arithmetic itself, before it is applied? Quite obviously not. But there is nothing outside arithmetic that is _understood_ with its help, either. Rather to do arithmetic is itself a human activity that can be understood; and to learn arithmetic (or mathematics, generally) means, in the first place, to learn this activity.

It may be useful to remember that there has been some controversy about just what it means to <u>understand</u> mathematics. Is it enough to operate with symbols according to given rules, like a high school student who knows how to use his table of logarithms? Or should mathematics be seen like a language the elements of which have to be understood as meaningful, and, correspondingly, the formulas as true sentences? QUINE and GOODMAN, in an early paper, express this difference clearly, when they say about a purely formal approach to mathematics: "We can thus handle much of classical logic and mathematics without in any further sense understanding or granting the truth of the formulas we are dealing with."[4]

I will return to this problem later and will now take up the central question of this paper: Where, in relation to the background I have sketched, does the theory of language belong? Is it to be construed as an explaining theory that enables us to explain events with recourse to laws of nature? Is it a theory that makes us understand systems of actions? Or has language itself to be seen as a system of formal operations, so that a theory of language has to be a formal science of the mathematical type? Or, last not least, is it possible that we have a mixture of these cases; e.g., is language an understandable activity, certain aspects of which can be described mathematically? I will discuss these possibilities now one after another.

Firstly, is the theory of language a natural science, explaining events of language use by bringing them under general laws? I think no linguist or philosopher of language holds this view in its simple form; CHROMSKY's critique of SKINNER's 'Verbal Behavior' was too convincing for that.[5] There is a more sophisticated form of it, however, which I will discuss at a later point. So I proceed to the second question: Is it or should it be the goal of the theory of language to help us understand a system of actions? This question, I think, deserves a more careful investigation.

A number of arguments that have been developed by philosophers of language point to a positive answer. Since they are quite well known, it will be sufficient to shortly mention them. Considerations about the concept of meaning have led WITTGENSTEIN to give up the picture-theory of semantics and replace it by his use-theory. This led to the consequence that language as a whole was seen by him as a system of social activities governed by constitutive rules. 'Constitutive' here means that the actions of language use are no secondary phenomena, like the use one can make of a stone or a piece of wood. Rather, they constitute language so that to understand language <u>means</u> to understand these actions.

Secondly, CH.S. PEIRCE has discovered the speech act;[6] AUSTIN has repeated this discovery, and J. SEARLE has clarified the

concept further. It directs our attention to language uses
which cannot possibly be understood as picturing or representing something, and so it points into the same direction as
WITTGENSTEIN's work.

Finally, PEIRCE's Pragmaticism and the investigations of
words like indexicals have, among other influences, led to
the recognition of the field of linguistic pragmatics. All
these well known lines of thought point into one and the same
direction, namely, that the theory of language should be of
the understanding type. Its goal should be to make us understand in an explicit and reflected way our intuitive capacity
to make use of the complicated system of verbal actions that
we call a language. What then does it mean to __understand__ that
capacity?

Here is the point where the general considerations about explanation and understanding have to be applied, and different
options lead to quite different approaches. One takes the word
'capacity' in a mechanistic or naturalistic sense and thinks
of it as a device that is comparable to a machine or to a biological organ. This is the realm of explanation, of natural
science, of laws of nature. Another option takes the word 'capacity' as to refer to conscious, intentional action, to the
realm of motives and choices. This is the domain of understanding; it implies the necessity to talk about a person's
purposes and about the benefits of verbal activities. Here the
goal is not to have a theory about a biological device, but to
understand a system of meaningful actions as if it had been
consciously developed. I am arguing here for the second alternative, the understanding side, and to make that clear it will
be helpful to confront it now with the more sophisticated form
of its opposite, namely, the theory of CHOMSKY.

It is remarkable and to my mind unfortunate, that CHOMSKY,
despite his SKINNER-review, sticks to the side of explanation.
Let me elaborate. I fully agree with him where he criticizes
behaviorist empiricism. I am grateful, when he stresses the
point that a formalism producing correct sentences (and being
in this sense descriptively adequate) is not enough, because
it does not really explain anything, or, as I would prefer to
say, it brings no full understanding. Furthermore, I see it as
one of CHOMSKY's great merits to constantly point to the problem of the goals and the explanatory power of a linguistic
theory. But I do not think that we have to "study the acquisition of a cognitive structure such as language more or less
as we study some complex bodily organ"[7] and that we should,
in principle "be able to account for it in terms of human biology"[8]. Here he opts for the side of explanation in the sense
described above, and that means: for laws of nature, for cau-
sality, and, I am sorry to say, for the study of behavior. I
think the real alternative to behaviorism is not the kind of
theory that he envisages and that could be called 'Cartesian
biology', but a theory of human action. Consequently, the value of a descriptively adequate grammar should not be measured by the degree in which it fits into a biological theory

of cognitive development but by the contribution it can or
cannot make for an understanding of the activity of using a
language; an understanding in the strong sense I have used
throughout this paper.

But what kind of contribution can we expect? Is this kind
of formal approach to language of any value at all when we
pursue the goal of understanding an activity? With this question we are taking up a point that has been left open above,
namely the question whether the theory of language should be
construed as a formal science like mathematics. I take it for
granted, that no one holds that language is nothing but a system of formal operations, so our question can only be: to
what extent can and should certain aspects of it be treated in
a 'formal' way?

I cannot treat this question here in any satisfactory manner,
but in order to approach one aspect that is relevant for this
discussion, I will ask: What would it mean to say that language structure is of such a kind as to <u>necessitate</u> a formal treatment? Such a position, I think would have to hold that the
rules that constitute language have no relation to the motives and beliefs of the speakers. Whereas it is reasonable to
ask someone why he gave a certain command, one might argue
that it does not make sense to ask him, why he used the syntactical form he did. The use of the form is not governed,
one might say, by the speaker's motives, except by his desire
to be understood, to speak the language correctly.

If this were the whole truth, what it means to speak a language correctly would have to be specified in a first step,
by some kind of calculus; and only after that a consideration
of the motives of language-users would be possible. From the
calculus we would expect descriptive adequacy but in no way
we could meaningfully set ourselves the goal to understand it.
We would take it as a purely formal device in the sense that
QUINE and GOODMAN hesitated to accept as an appropriate understanding even of mathematics. We were forced to say that language as a <u>system</u> of actions cannot be understood. The rules
that produce correct concatenations would be taken to be objects of natural science, and of scientific <u>explanation</u>. The
only possible object of our <u>understanding</u> would be a social
act, i.e. an utterance in a certain context. And not its structure, but only its place in relation to other actions could we
understand. If this were a true and complete picture of the
situation, our desire to look for more than descriptive adequacy would indeed have no other place to turn to than cognitive biology. From there we could expect explanations, but
no theory that allows us to understand.

Fortunately, the picture just sketched is not the whole
truth. Although language has a formal aspect, (something that
nobody doubts and to which I will address myself later), it is
at the same time possible to see language as a system of action with an internal structure that can, in significant parts
at least, be understood. For example, one can understand that,

when the action of making an assertion has been acquired by
a person, it is a meaningful expansion of this capacity when
he goes on to learn how to ask questions. It is another meaningful expansion to proceed to logically complex assertions.
So in the structure of language there is something to understand, something that a pure description is unable to cover.
This aspect of language structure becomes more visible, when
the dimension of time, the diachronic aspect is brought in. Language
has been developed by man, and every new member of the species
has to acquire it. I do not deny that there are biological characteristics in the human cognitive apparatus without which we
would be unable to learn language. But at the same time the
process of language acquisition is one in the course of which
meaningful actions are acquired, and the differentiation and
enrichment to the full system is one that proceeds in meaningful steps and for that reason can be understood.[9]

So in spite of the fact that language structure, when taken
as a readymade whole, has a lot of features that cannot be
understood as directly intentional, the coming into existence
of this structure can be understood as the result of the building up of a system of meaningful actions. So it should be possible to work out a reconstruction of a language as a system
of actions in such a way that, as a result, we are indeed understanding what we are doing when we are using language. And
this has been our goal, when we opted for a theory of language not of the explaining, but of the understanding type.

For the rest of my paper I will leave the methodological
and philosophical level and discuss a problem we encounter at
a very early stage of the reconstruction, namely the step from
one-word-utterances to the capacity to make structured two-
word-utterances of the subject-predicate type. After that, I
will discuss an instance where syntax becomes, in a certain
sense, autonomous. To understand this possibility is of great
importance, I think, to understand the structural aspect of
language the degree in which a formal treatment is meaningful, and the precise meaning of the concept of a 'system of
actions'.[10]

The task now is the following: Can we describe a way in
which the use of a complex utterence of the form 'x is P' is
acquired which satisfies the following conditions: (1) The use
of the complex utterance-type rests on the capacity of using a
simpler one. (2) The step (or steps) from the simple to the
complex can be understood as an enrichment of the possibilities to act that is (a) pragmatically meaningful (i.e. it
makes sense in a subject's system of nonverbal and verbal com-
petences to act) and can (b) be imagined to be acquired step
by step in a non-circular way. (3) The description does not
speak of mental acts of such a kind that is systematically dependent on a semantic terminology. E.g. it will be excluded
as a petitio principii to speak of a mental act of referring
to objects (or actions, or whatever). On the contrary, the
specific characteristics of referring (as contrasted, e.g. to
predicating) are to be explained.

Now I take it that it is reasonably clear how simple one-word utterances of a certain type can be acquired along the lines described already by WITTGENSTEIN with his famous example of the building site." The example is made up in such a way that the pragmatic meaningfulness is clear from the beginning: The acquisition of language takes place in a situation in which people engage in actions; language in some obvious way 'helps' in this engagement. So I take it that a number of one-word sentences of the type 'slab', 'red', 'hot' are among the repertoire of the speakers. How can we now think of a step towards a complex sentence with a subject-predicate structure, that satisfies the conditions given above?

Considering that we are looking for a pragmatically meaningful expansion, we look for a situation in which the one-word competence comes to the boundaries of its helpfulness and in which an additional action of uttering a second word may turn out to be pragmatically meaningful. So I imagine that the word 'hot' has been introduced and has been used in a number of ways, e.g. as a warning when hot meals are brought to the table. Now the boundaries of its helpfulness are reached in a situation that has (from the point of view of the established practice) to be considered as non-standard; e.g. when not the meal but the plates are hot. So even if the word 'hot' has been used in other (non-eating) contexts, a misunderstanding may be anticipated (or experienced) by the speaker, and, in order to avoid it, he or she may invent (as a new step that transcends the conventions established so far) the possibility of uttering the two words 'plate hot'. Of course this utterance might not be understood; there is no rule yet according to which it was spoken. On the other hand we all know from travelling in countries with languages we do not speak, how a single word can be the key to a situation which is just one step away from being understood pragmatically: the one word enables us to act correctly. So the invention of the complex act might be helpful and become a first instance of a new convention.

With this example in mind, I now return to the conditions given above and ask if they are satisfied. For the first condition the answer is positive. We have postulated that both parts of the complex utterance ('plate' and 'hot') are known as separately performable linguistic acts. The second condition asks for pragmatic meaningfulness, which is satisfied quite obviously; the complex act helps to avoid a dangerous action (burning one's fingers) in a better way than a simple one could. And such a combination of two known acts can be imagined to be learned, it seems to me, in one step. The third condition is satisfied insofar as the description did not make use of a vocabulary for 'linguistic' mental acts, such as 'to refer to'. We imagined a situation in which a combination of two words of the same kind is used to cope with a particular type of ambiguity. It was not necessary to speak of mental acts as conditions that define or make possible certain speech acts.

So if an extension of the competence to perform linguistic acts is possible along the lines just sketched, how far does this take us towards an understanding of the subject-predicate structure of sentences? One point to be observed is that so far there occurred in the reconstruction only words of one single category ('predicators'). We have not introduced proper names, and we did not differentiate kinds of words according to semantic functions. Instead, we have introduced a step that gives a new pragmatic function to a word of the old (and only) category of predicators. In the complex utterance 'plate hot' the word 'plate' takes over a <u>new</u> role, a fact that is clearly seen when we compare its role in the complex utterance with the one it has in a one-word sentence. An utterance of 'hot' makes sense or is meaningful in so far as it changes the possibilities to act on the side of the hearer; mentalistically spoken: when the speaker informs the hearer of something he does not know. In the structured utterance 'plate hot' this is indeed the function of the word 'hot'; but the added element 'plate' does not so function: both partners have equal access to the linguistic act of uttering 'plate'; again in mentalistic terminology: both know there are plates in front of them. The new function of the word 'plate' (the 'subject') is to resolve an ambiguity that the utterance of 'hot' alone (the 'predicate') would have. Other acts like that of pointing could be introduced to fulfill the same function.

So if this functional difference, the difference in the use of words in the type of situation described, is understood, then we can on this basis differentiate between the roles of words in sentences; we have a necessary (though not sufficient) condition to speak of subjects and predicates and of the subject-predicate structure of sentences.

Instead of elaborating, why the given condition is not sufficient, I will now go on to a further expansion of the sketched mini-language. So far we have words of only one category but two syntactic functions. These functions directly mirror pragmatic functions, as was explained: For a word to be the predicate of a sentence means that with it the speaker performs the specific act of predicating. So the syntactic function is directly related to the pragmatic aspect of language and therefore can be understood.

This situation changes, when in a next step yes-no-questions are introduced as tentative assertions. Again: a new use is made of an old capacity; a tentative assertion of the kind to be considered here is no assertion, but a question, and it is easy to think of a convention (like raising one's voice or using a question mark) that expresses this new character of the action in a way that can be perceived by the hearer. So by making use of the already known action of stating, the new action of asking a question is developed; from stating 'plate hot' we proceed to asking 'plate hot?'. [Following SEARLE[12] one could use the symbolism '? (P_1, P_2)'.] On the level of <u>actions</u> we have a new action that makes use of an old one, without in any literal sense incorporating it as its part. Someone who asks is not doing two things, asserting and doing something

additional. Asking questions is a new possibility. At the same
time, this new possibility can be <u>understood</u>: it is a meaningful expansion of the capacity of stating; we understand in
what sense the one presupposes the other and the second makes
use of the first.

On the level of <u>symbols</u> (when we think of written language)
we have an enlarged structure that makes use of a smaller one
by adding another element (the question mark). The rest of the
chain of symbols remains the same. So on the level of symbols
what has been done can be described as: The old concatenation
(P_1, P_2) has been written, and a question mark has been added.
So the result is a disparity between the two levels: We have a
new action, in which the old elements take over new functions,
and in which it does not make sense to say the new action 'contains' the old one. But on the level of symbols we <u>can</u> say:
the new expression contains the old one, and therefore we can
describe the structure of the expression by speaking of its
subject and predicate. But when we do so and use the old terminology for talking about the functions of the constituents,
i.e. when we say of the second expression of the question that
it is the predicate-expression, then in this classification
the word 'predicate' has changed its meaning. Someone who asks
a question does not assert the truth of a predicator of an object; on the contrary: only when he is uncertain of the truth
will he ask the question. So (contrary to what SEARLE tries
to prove)[13] he is not predicating. Consequently, to say of a
word that it is the predicate of a sentence in the new sense,
no longer means to talk about its function in the activity of
speaking, but about a place that a symbol holds in a concatenation of symbols.

So here we have a case in which syntax becomes in a certain
sense autonomous (and by that deserves the title 'syntax'),
because it does not directly mirror an aspect of a speech act
that can be understood. This autonomous character of syntax
has been mentioned above as a possible motive for doubting
the possibility of constructing a theory of language as one of
the understanding type. But now we can see that we are able to
understand how the act of stating makes possible the act of
asking, and that it is a useful and simple convention to perform the new action, on the level of inscriptions, by doing no
more then adding to the old one another sign. So the process
that led to this kind of autonomy of syntax can itself be understood quite well. In this sense even an autonomous syntactic
structure can be understood if it is reconstructed in the way
just demonstrated.

So the type of reconstruction sketched helps us to understand both: the character of language as a system of meaningful actions, and the 'formal' side of this system, an aspect
that at first seemed to be in opposition to the first. And we
have some clarification now of the concept of a structured
'system of actions'. The relation between the actions that
constitute the system has (in the discussed example) turned out
to be that of one action making possible another, or, conver-

sely, the second making a meaningful use of the first. This
type of relation between actions is certainly an important
aspect of the system-character of language and is surely something that has to be understood, if it is to be grasped at all.
It is outside the reach of formal descriptions and explanations
of the kind employed by the natural sciences.

Notes

1) G.H. VON WRIGHT, Explanation and Understanding, London 1971

2) For a more detailed discussion of this concept of causali-
ty cf. H.J. SCHNEIDER, Die Asymmetrie der Kausalrelation,
Überlegungen zur interventionistischen Theorie G.H. VON
WRIGHTs. In: J. MITTELSTRAß, M. RIEDEL (eds.), Vernünftiges
Denken. Studien zur praktischen Philosophie und Wissenschafts-
theorie. Berlin, New York 1978, pp. 217-234.

3) The hermeneutic tradition has claimed this all along, of course, but VON WRIGHT's new arguments seem to be much more convincing for thinkers in the Analytic tradition.

4) N. GOODMAN, W.V.O. QUINE, Steps toward a Constructive Nomi-
nalism, JSL Vol. 12, 1947, pp. 105-122, quote: p. 122.

5) N. CHOMSKY, Review of Skinner's 'Verbal Behavior'. Language
35, 1959, pp. 26-58.

6) CH.S. PEIRCE, Collected Papers vols. I-VI, ed. CH. HARTS-
HORNE and P. WEISS, Cambridge (Mass.) 1931-35. 5.546 ff.

7) N. CHOMSKY, Reflections on Language, Glasgow 1976, p. 10.

8) ibid. p. 34.

9) Cf. M. MILLER, Zur Logik der frühkindlichen Sprachentwick-
lung, Stuttgart 1976.

10) Cf. F. KAMBARTEL, H.J. SCHNEIDER, Constructing a Pragmatic
Base for Semantics. To appear in a publication of the 'Institut International de Philosophie', Paris. The concept of
a pragmatic foundation for a theory of language is developed in detail in: H.J. SCHNEIDER, Pragmatik als Basis von
Semantik und Syntax, Frankfurt 1975.

11) L. WITTGENSTEIN, Philosophical Investigations, ed. G. ANS-
COMBE and R. RHEES, Oxford 1955, § 2.

12) J.R. SEARLE, Speech Acts. An Essay in the Philosophy of
Language. Cambridge 1970, p. 32.

13) SEARLE, pp. 121 ff. For a more detailed criticism of SEAR-
LE's concept of predication cf. H.J. SCHNEIDER, Ist die
Prädikation eine Sprechhandlung? To appear in: K. LORENZ
(ed.), Konstruktionen versus Positionen. Beiträge zur wis-
senschaftstheoretischen Diskussion. Berlin.

A New Approach to Formal Syntax

Klaus-Jürgen Engelberg
Universität Konstanz, Sonderforschungsbereich 99, 'Linguistik',
Postfach 5560, D-7750 Konstanz, Fed. Rep. of Germany

This paper presents a new formalism for the syntactic description of natural languages.

1. Introduction

It is quite common practice in linguistics to use constituent-structure trees for the syntactic description of languages. This article is going to show how to set up an algebraic system that deals with trees in a way quite analogous to the usual algebraic treatment of (natural) numbers. The formalism presented later on - the theory of recursive tree functions (or rather tree relations) - establishes a direct formal parallelism between primitive-recursive mappings of natural numbers and mappings of trees. Empirical evidence gathered so far suggests that in fact it is feasible to treat the transformations usually discussed in Generative Grammar within this framework.

Due to its close relationship to long established mathematical methods, this approach permits one to gain more easily general insights in the formal nature of the apparatus than seems possible for the formalism of traditional Transformational Grammar. Such a recursive tree relation grammar is equally suitable for synthesis as for analysis.

But the theory certainly draws its main importance from the fact that it allows the setting up of a very plausible hypothesis on the recursive nature of generative grammars of natural languages in general. This is done by restricting heavily the algebraic type of definition equations permitted in this system.

Unfortunately, owing to the very limited space available in this study, it is only possible to give a rather brief and sketchy account of the theory.

2. Recursive Tree Functions

Before considering mappings on trees we have to define the latter in an appropriate way. The following inductive description of trees corresponds to the ordinary description of terms in a formal system.

A Trees

Whereas the set of natural numbers can be obtained by using one single one-place successor function with O being the least element (Peono Axioms!), we define (simplifying) the free tree monoid B_Σ on a ranked alphabet Σ as follows:

We assume each symbol of the alphabet to be associated with a natural number (its rank) that gives the number of descendents (or branchings) of a node labeled with that symbol.

a) The terminals (elements having rank 0) are the least elements of the free tree monoid.

b) If $y_1 \ldots y_k \in B_\Sigma$ and if A_j^k (Nonterminal) has rank k, then the A_j^k-successor-tree to $y_1 \ldots y_k$ also belongs to the free tree monoid that is

$$\underset{y_1 \quad y_k}{\overset{A^K}{\diagup | \diagdown}} \in B_\Sigma$$

This abstract definition makes the notion 'tree' independent of a special representation (labelled brackets or two dimensional graphs etc.).

These successor operations will function as the most elementary functions available in the theory.

It is important to note that the algebraic fundation of the formalism precludes arbitrary many branchings of a node; so coordinate structures have to be defined in the recursive fashion known from context-free grammars. Besides, context-free grammars can serve to specify a subset of a free tree-monoid.

In order to make trees comparable with each other it is useful to introduce a norm on trees (analogous to the length of a word in word monoids).

Definition: The norm $\| y \|$ of a tree y is the maximal number of paths from the root node ot one of the terminal nodes.

Example: If   NP   then $\| y \| = 2$

$$y = \underset{\text{Jimmy} \quad \overset{N}{\underset{\text{Carter}}{|}}}{\overset{NP}{\diagup \diagdown}}$$

B   Tree mappings

Primitive recursive functions in general are defined inductively by specifying a set of trivial initial functions and then giving some operations for obtaining additional functions from those already defined.

Almost all functions 'practically' needed in arithmetic have turned out to be primitive recursive.

Consider the following example of a typical recursive tree function φ_1 on an appropriately chosen tree-monoid for the usual Pseudo-English

218

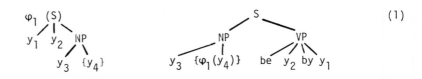

(1)

(In fact there are two definitions: one with the tree-variable y_4 on both sides, the other without any y_4.)

At the left-hand side of this definition equation we see a structural description, on the right-hand side we have a tree-expression consisting mainly of the resulting 'new' structure.

We are now going to apply φ_1 to a carefully chosen argument tree (called b_1):

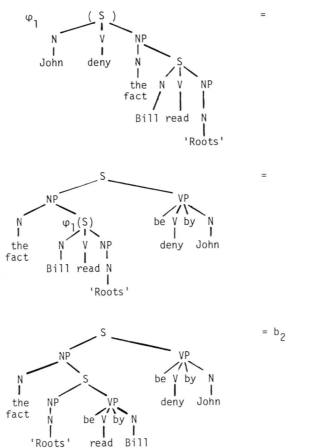

$= b_2$

This 'passivization'-transformation elucidates some basic facts about this formalism:

1) Recursive tree functions map trees into trees by iterative processes of local structure-building transformations ('cycling through' the tree).

2) The computation stops after a finite number of steps.

3) Recursive tree functions are partial functions defined only for trees meeting some structural analysis. (In general there are several disjunct structural descriptions for a function.) This 'partiality' provides for the 'filtereffect' of a recursive grammar.

This example function φ_1 was of a very simple top-down type. By a slightly more complicated definition it is possible e.g. to have functions that extract constituents from arbitrary deep embeddings of a tree structure (as needed for 'WH-Fronting').

Still more complicated would be 'Pronominalization'. There we would need a 'double recursive' function: one function scans the whole tree for all possible antecedents, the other function having the antecedent as parameter inserts a pronoun in all appropriate places in the tree. This 'double recursion' mechanism is the usual treatment for 'unbounded rules' in this formalism.

Investigations done so far into the theory suggest that in fact it is possible to write a recursive tree function for any of the transformations usually discussed in Generative Grammar, though more single rules and more explicitness may be needed that is perceivable in most of the current descriptions of Transformational Grammar.

A *recursive tree-grammar* would be the composite of several such basic functions. By this provision a strict order for the syntactic operations would be determined.

But at last we have to remedy the biggest inadequacy of the theory presented so far: Functions deliver for an input tree only one tree-structure as the result. This seems highly inadequate with regard to optional rules. But it is relatively easy to devise an algebraic mechanism that allows the computation of several alternative tree functions in parallel.

So what we are really doing in this theory is computing tree relations where individual trees (arbitrarily many in general) stand in the relation of combination. For describing optional transformations one would use the identity function as one alternative.

3. Elementary Invertible Functions

It is certainly one of the most important and interesting goals of linguistic theory to give a precise characterization of the notion *possible grammar of a natural language*. Many people will feel that the attempts undertaken so far in that respect within the formal framework of Transformational Grammar have not yet produced satisfactory results.

The approach to that problem in the formalism of recursive tree relations will be to have a close look at the inverse functions. Our claim is that precisely the condition of analyzability is appropriate to single out the rather restricted class of tree mappings needed in Generative Grammar.

First we shall give an intuitive account of the basic ideas. Reconsider example (1). The inverse function (or analysis-function) $\overline{\varphi}_1$ to the function φ_1 is.

$$\overline{\varphi}_1 \; (\; S \;) \qquad\qquad = \qquad\qquad S \qquad\qquad\qquad (2)$$

Apparently $\overline{\varphi}(b_2) = b_1$. Note that $\overline{\varphi}$ has the same simple top-down type as the original function φ.

Now the question arises whether this 'reversing' of a definition equation is always possible. Algebraists, of course, will know that it is not. We give two types of primitive recursive definitions that we are going to exclude from linguistic considerations.

Consider the example

$$\varphi_2 \; (\; S \;) \qquad\qquad = \qquad\qquad S \qquad\qquad\qquad (3)$$

Finding the inverse function in such a simple way as in example (1) now seems impossible since the variable y_2 appears twice in two different terms on the right-hand side of the definition. Now we see that constructing the definition of the inverse tree function has got something to do with what is generally called 'solving' a equation for the independent variable. As anyone who has some knowledge of elementary algebra will know it is always possible to isolate an independent variable in a definition equation by successively applying the inverse functors on both sides of the equality sign, provided this variable appears only once in the compound defining term.

But now we have to turn to the linguistic significance of recursive definitions with multiple occurrences of variables. The fact is that these definitions lead to a strange reiteration of the same lexical material in the resulting trees (e.g. φ_2 could map 'John thinks and Bill drinks' into 'John thinks and Bill drinks and Bill drinks'). This recursive repetition of an arbitrary number of words (though possibly in different syntactic constructions) is usually an uninteresting or undesired effect in natural languages. So we are going to call the universal 'constraint' that excludes definitions of the aforementioned type the 'condition for the absence of redundancy'.

It is surely one of the great mysteries of this theory that two things that have got nothing to do with each other at first glance - i.e. the possibility of effectively 'reversing' definitions and the absence of (some sort of) redundancy in the generated tree language - have the same formal status in the theory.

But we have to keep away from yet another type of definition. Consider the 'degenerated' definition

$$\varphi_3 \left(\begin{array}{c} A \\ \diagup \diagdown \\ a \quad y_1 \end{array}\right) = \varphi_3 (y_1) \qquad (4)$$

If we were to 'reverse' that definition we wouldn't have any structural description at all for the inverse function! As can be seen very easily functions like φ_3 are capable of deleting an arbitrary amount of information irrecoverably e.g. φ_3 could map a structure of any depth (or length of the terminal string) into one single terminal symbol (by adding $\varphi_3(a) = a$). We shall call the formal condition that makes 'degenerated' definitions like φ_3 impossible the 'condition of monotony'. Monotony of a function means that with an increase in the size of the argument the size of the function value will also increase, e.g. if we consider a transformation for the prepositioning of adjectives (that maps 'man who is bald and who is old' into 'old bald man') we recognize that the more relative clauses the input structure has the more adjectives appear in the resultant structure. (Though the latter is smaller than the former) The condition of monotony has its linguistic significance in that it ensures that with a quantitative increase in the amount of information contained in the input tree, the information contained in the output tree will also increase. Thus it seems a necessary condition for meaning-preserving transformations. Furthermore it can be mathematically shown that this condition guarantees the existence of the inverse function.

It is perhaps helpful to remember that, in contrast, the rules of inference of propositional calculus are not information monotonous. Logical deduction generally leads to an irrecoverable loss of information. But it is not this type of deduction that is being considered in Generative Grammar.

4. Formal System

Now the idea of analyzability in this theory will be stretched as far as possible, i.e. we are going to define a recursive definition system that is completely symmetrical in synthesis and analysis functions. For any tree function definable in the system the inverse function will also belong to the system.

We give a rather loose formal definition of the system of elementary invertible tree functions (EI) on a free tree-monoid.

A. Initial Functions: Generalized partial successor functions

  f ∈ EI if

$$f(n_k(y_1,\ldots,y_r)) = m_k(y_1,\ldots,y_r) \quad k = 1\ldots k_{max}$$

where n_k and m_k are functions that have been composed from elementary tree-successor-functions (cf. 2 A b).

Inverse function

$$\overline{f}(m_k(y_1,\ldots,y_r)) = n_k(y_1,\ldots,y_r) \quad k = 1\ldots k_{max}$$

B. Scheme of (simple) composition

If g, $h \in EI$, then $f \in EI$ if

$$f(y,x) = g(h(y,x),x)$$

In general there may be no parameter x or there may be several.

This scheme allows one to define a function f where the output of one function h serves as the input to another function g.

Inverse function

$$\overline{f}(y,x) = \overline{h}(\overline{g}(y,x),x)$$

C. Scheme of recursion

If $n_i,m_i,h_j,g_j \in EI$, then so is f if (end of recursion)

$$f(n_i(t_1,\ldots,t_p,x),x) = m_i(t_1,\ldots,t_p,x) \quad i = 1\ldots i_{max}$$

The $t_1\ldots t_p$ are terminals.

(Recursion)

$$f(h_j(y_1,\ldots,y_s,x),x) = g_j(f(y_1,x),\ldots,f(y_s,x),y_1\ldots,y_s,x) \quad j = 1\ldots j_{max}$$

Once again there may be no parameter x or there may be several.

f can be regarded as the iterated function of the 'generating' function g_j.

The definitions of φ_1 and $\overline{\varphi}_1$ comply with the last scheme.

Constraints for the scheme of recursion -

Condition of Monotony

$$\| h_j(y_1,\ldots,y_s,x) \| > \| y_i \| \text{ and}$$
$$\| g_j(y_1,\ldots,y_s,x) \| > \| y_i \| \text{ for any argument } y_i \ (i = 1 \ldots s)$$
$$\text{and each function } h_j \ g_j \ (j = 1 \ldots j_{max})$$

A similar condition has to apply to the terminal strings (omitted here).

It can be mathematically proved that this condition leads to a similar (albeit more general) form of monotony of the tree functions as known from number theory functions.

Note that this condition excludes a definition like φ_3 since there the 'generating' function g_1 would be the identity function.

Condition for the absence of redundancy. This condition is hard to capture in a 'contextfree' definition scheme. It may be described roughly as follows:

A variable y may never appear both in the 'bound' form f(y) (Argument 1...s) and the 'free' form y (Argument s+1...2s) within the term g_j.

This condition excludes definitions like that for φ_2.

D. Constraint on the recursion number

Empirical data seem to suggest that it is possible for linguistic purposes to restrict the function definitions possible up to now even further.

We claim: All tree transformations (as used in Generative Grammar) can be obtained by using at the most two successive recursions.

That means that the generating functions g_j themselves may be defined from some other g_j', but the latter in turn have to be defined in terms of elementary functions.

The recursion number may be used to classify functions into a hierarchy of recursive complexity.

It should have become apparent that the class of elementary invertible tree functions will contain only a very restricted subset of all computable functions. Furthermore this definition system EI can be shown (by adding some more technical details) to be effectively symmetrical in function and inverse function, or - as algebraists like to say - to be closed under the operation of function-reversing.

5. Conclusions

This paper shows how it is possible in syntax to use formal means quite naturally comparable to method developed in mathematics a long time ago. So recursive tree relations turn out to be a rather promising tool for the syntactic description of natural languages.

The approach taken here of singling out the relevant tree mappings from the linguistic point of view is fundamentally based on the idea of combining the concept of recursive functions with considerations as to the algebraic type of permitted definition equations. Thus the formulation of a definition system is possible that is completely symmetrical in regard to both synthesis and analysis. This approach may be considered tantamount to reconstructing a speaker's/hearer's linguistic competence in a way in which speech-production and speech-understanding processes have the same recursive complexity. We believe that this symmetry principle is a well motivated one that makes linguistics distinct from other sciences and that necessitates adequate formal treatment.

But as nice as the whole theory may look from the mathematical viewpoint its ultimate justification has to rest with empirical data. Investigations done so far into the theory to indicate that in fact it is capable in principle of dealing with the vast amount of data accumulated in the field of Generative Grammar and that it covers in formal terms not much more than these linguistic data. The theory leads (among other things) to the mathematically somewhat curious consequence that transformations normally used in linguistics may induce (at most) a linear, exponential or logarithmic dependence (of the lengths) of the output strings on the input strings; but there may be no transformations showing a power-serial relationship (i.e.

of the type $\lambda x \cdot x^2$, $\lambda x \cdot x^3$ etc.) of these values. This is a prediction that can at least in principle be tested against empirical data (in as far as anything at all is empirical in linguistics).

The symmetry principle has led to the discovery of two very plausible universal principles underlying transformations in Generative Grammar: Transformations have to be (information-) monotonous and free of (recursive) redundancies. It is important to note that these principles can be defined in purely formal terms and hence are independent of any particular natural language. But these principles seem to hold whether the formalism is applied in the field of Standard Theory, Generative Semantics, Montague Grammar or translations between natural languages.

From a different angle we might argue that this theory allows one to delineate (more) precisely the borderline between syntax proper and other areas of investigation. It wouldn't be possible to formulate a full inference algorithm for first order predicate logic (that could be implemented on a Turing machine) as an elementary invertible function (or relation) - an undertaking we would rather attribute to the realm of semantics.

Although the theory presented so far primarily purports to serve as a descriptive tool it seems nevertheless attractive to look shortly at the (seemingly) far reaching implications it has in a broader sense. First the so-called Universal Base Hypothesis: given the very limited expressive power of the elementary invertible tree functions it seems reasonable to assume that one single universal base tree monoid for all languages cannot possess an arbitrary simplicity.

Another problem the theory is capable of making a contribution to might be the theory of the learnability of languages. Here the conclusion to be drawn seems to be that for a child to learn the syntactic component of a language (paraphrases etc.) might not be so terribly difficult since generative grammars turn out to have a relatively simple recursive nature - if we think in terms of relationships between tree structures.

A final remark has to be made: Although this theory seems to deliver many answers long thought for in Linguistics, much work still remains to be done along the lines outlined here.

References

1. W.S. Brainerd and L.H. Landweber: Theory of Computation (New York, 1974)

2. K.-J. Engelberg: Funktion und Transformation (Neue Aspekte der formalen Syntaxtheorie), Arbeitspapiere Nr. 24 & 28 des SFB 99 (Konstanz, 1978)

3. F.W. Henke: Primitive rekursive Transformationen, GMD-Bericht Nr. 92 (Bonn, 1974)

4. H. Hermes: Enumerability, Decidability, Computability (Berlin, 1965)

5. R. Peter: Recursive Functions (New York, 1967)

6. W.C. Rounds: <u>Mappings and Grammars on Trees</u>, Mathematical System Theory 4, (1970), 257-287

7. R. Wall: <u>Introduction to Mathematical Linguistics</u> (Prentice Hall, 1972)

8. B.S. Baker: <u>Tree Transducers and Tree Languages</u>, Information and Control 37 (1978), 241-266

Visiting German Relatives

Arnim von Stechow

Universität Konstanz, Sonderforschungsbereich 99, 'Linguistik',
Postfach 5560, D-7750 Kostanz, Fed. Rep. of Germany

1. The Problems

To my knowledge, there exists no formal treatment of the syntax and semantics
of German relatives. In this article I shall try to fill this gap partially
by offering a description of some important aspects of German relative clauses.
This will be done within a Montague framework. It will be obvious that the
proposal presented here is influenced in many respects by articles of Rodman
and Bach & Cooper.

Most of the problems arising with relatives are syntactic problems. The
semantics of relatives seems to be pretty clear: relatives seem to express
properties. Yet this does not mean that the interpretation of rules which
combine relatives with terms is an easy matter.

I shall now give a brief survey of the problems to be solved:

a) The restrictive-appositive distinction

The following seems to be the case. Relatives modifying quantifying phrases
or general terms have a restrictive effect while relatives modifying individual or definite terms behave like predicates.[1] Relatives of the first kind
are called *attributive* or *restrictive* relative clauses. Relatives of the
second kind are called *appositive* or *explicative* relative clauses.

(1) Lidia, die eine Römerin ist, liebte den Duce. (Apposition)

    Lidia, who a   Roman   is , loved   the Duce.

(2) Niemand, der Adolf kennt, mag ihn. (Restriction)

    No one   who Adolf knows   likes him.

(3) Er legte die Kränze, die der Wind umgeworfen hatte, wieder an ihre Stelle.

    He put   the garlands which the wind overthrown had again   at their place.

    (Apposition or restriction)

The relative clause in (3) is an apposition, if it modifies the definite
term "die Kränze". It is a restriction, if it modifies the general term
"Kränze".

b) Relatives and negation

If we are given a sentence of the form Subject + Relative + Predicate we may infer that the subject has the property expressed by the relative and the property expressed by the predicate, if the relative is in apposition. If the relative is an attribute, such an inference is not valid. Thus

(1) implies (4), but (2) does not entail (5).

(4) Lidia ist eine Römerin, und sie liebte den Duce.

    Lidia is a   Roman   and she loved the Duce.

(5) Niemand kennt Adolf, und niemand mag ihn.

    No one knows Adolf and no one likes him.

Usually, (4) is even considered as being equivalent to (1). From this assumption, some people conclude that there is a problem about negation. The negation of (1) is (6), and the negation of (4) is equivalent to (7). But (6) and (7) certainly do not mean the same. (6) rather means something like (8).

(6) Lidia, die eine Römerin ist, liebte den Duce nicht.

    Lidia who a   Roman   is   loved the Duce not.

(7) Lidia ist keine Römerin oder sie liebte den Duce nicht.

    Lidia is no   Roman or she loved the Duce not.

(8) Lidia ist eine Römerin und sie liebte den Duce nicht.

    Lidia is a   Roman   and she loved the Duce not.

This problem arises only if you make the assumption that the negation particle in (6) is a sentence modifier. I shall treat it as an adverb which negates the predicate. This will avoid the problem.

I admit that there is another problem connected with (1). Given the conjunctive analysis for relatives in apposition, (1) will be synonymous with the following sentence.

(9) Lidia, die den Duce liebte, ist eine Römerin.
    Lidia who the Duce loved is a   Roman.

Yet, we feel that the *main information* which (1) gives us about Lidia is that she loved the Duce, whereas the relative gives us the *background information* that she is a Roman. (9) is, of course, the other way round. I cannot capture this difference in my semantical analysis. I put it into the pragmatic waste-basket.

c) The problem of quantifier restriction

The nominal in sentence (2) should have the following syntactic analysis

(9) [*Niemand*]   [*der Adolf kennt*]

    (no one)NP   (who Adolf knows)RC

    [[*niemand*] [*der Adolf kennt*]   ]   (Relativization rule)
         NP   RC NP

I am using the label RC for relative clauses. The problem is now to interpret the rule which combines the NP *niemand* (no one) with the RC *der Adolf kennt* (who Adolf knows). In Montague Grammar, NPs are second order properties. *Niemand* denotes the second order property which is true of a property ϕ *iff* there is no person a such that ϕ is true of a. Let us denote this property by

(10) $\lambda\phi$ [$\sim$($\exists$a) (Person (a) & ϕ (a))]

Furthermore, let ψ be the property of knowing Adolf. The relativized NP [*niemand*] [*der Adolf kennt*] should then denote the second order property
    NP   RC

(11) $\lambda\phi$ [$\sim$($\exists$a) (Person (a) & ψ (a) & ϕ (a))]

The interpretation of the relativization rule should then be an operation which makes (11) out of (10) and ψ. And, of course, this operation must also account for the cases where the NP is an existential, a universal quantifier and so on. It seems to be a very hard thing to define such an operation. I cannot prove that this is not possible, but as far as I know, no one has ever succeeded in doing so. Try to solve this problem and you will see that it is difficult.

There is a straightforward way to solve this problem. One has to assume the presence of a deictic pronominal element within indefinite pronouns. Such an assumption is both supported by historical considerations[2] and by sentences in which the deictic pronoun of the quantifier phrase occurs at the surface:

(12) Ich antwortete ihm, ich sei ein Gelehrter, ein Theologe, Grammatiker,
    I   answered   him I be   a   scholar   a theologist grammarian

Dichter und Schönschreiber. "*Alles dieses* wird hier zu Lande nicht
poet   and calligrapher   "*All   this*   is   here in the country not

gesucht" antwortete der Schneider.
searched" answered   the tailor.   (Story of the second calender)

It is clear from the context that the value of the pronoun *dieses* may be any of the properties mentioned in the preceding sentence, i.e. *dieses* may refer to 'being a scholar', to 'being a theologist', to 'being a grammarian' and so on. So the nominal *alles dieses* is, in a certain sense, an anaphoric phrase. The same is true of a pure quantifying phrase like *nichts* (nothing).

(13) Ich habe vieles versucht. *Nichts* hat geklappt.
    I   have much   tried.   *Nothing* has worked.

Nichts clearly means here 'nothing of what I have tried'. This motivates the assumption that the NP *nichts* should have the structure [[*neg*] [*pro$_i$*]], where the pronoun *pro$_i$* refers to a property   Det
      CNNP
given by the context.

We can then reanalyze the nominal *niemand der Adolf kennt* (no one who knows Adolf) in the following way.

(14) 1. $[[neg] [pro_i]]$ 2. $[der\ Adolf\ kennt]$
      Det   CN NP   RC

3. $[[[neg] [pro_i]] [der\ Adolf\ kennt]]$ (Relativization)
    Det   CN NP   RC NP

Bach & Cooper have provided a semantics for a relativization rule of this kind.[3] It is straightforward, indeed. Suppose, $V_\nu([[neg][pro_i]])$ is the value of our NP with respect to the variable assignment ν. This is the following property:

(15) $\lambda\phi\ [\sim(\exists a)\ (Person(a)\ \&\ \nu\ ([pro_i]_{CN})\ \&\ \phi\ (a))]$

Suppose furthermore that the content of the RC *der Adolf kennt* is the property ψ. Then the content of the relativized NP (14.3) is simply

(16) $V_{(\nu,\psi/[pro_i]_{CN})}\ ([[neg][pro_i]]_{NP}\ )$

In other words, the relativization rule modifies the variable assignment. It replaces the value of the pronoun under the assignment ν by the value of the relative clause. Thus (16) is

$\lambda\phi\ [\sim(\exists a)\ (Person(a)\ \&\ \psi\ \&\ \phi\ (a)]$.

And this is what we are after.

Notice that the relativization rule sketched here cannot be iterated because the free variable in the nominal is bound after the application of the rule. Yet, in English it is to have more than one restrictive RC.

(17) Nothing I have ever known which is personally delightful is decent.
     (Wilde, somewhat adapted)[4]

In such cases of double restriction ('relative stacking') it is always possible to conjoin the two relatives by an 'and'.
Therefore I would analyze (17) as follows:

(18)
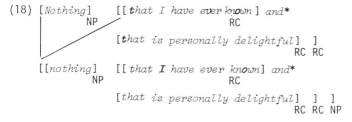

Given an appropriate conjunction rule, such an analysis does not require an iteration of the relativization rule. Wilde's original sentence is this:

(19) The only artists I have ever known who are personally delightful are
     bad artists.

It has three analyses. One where the first RC modifies the CN and the second the whole NP, one where the conjunction of the two RCs modifies the CN (this is the most natural reading) and one where the conjoined RCs modify the NP. None of these analyses requires an iteration of the rule sketched above. But, if you want to allow for an iteration of the rule, this can easily be achieved.[5]

d) The problem of movement control

I shall call the phrase containing the relative pronoun of the RC *the relative phrase of the RC*. As in English, the relative phrase may be an NP, a PP or an adverb (AdV).

(20) Er reichte ihr die zwei Goldstücke, [*die*] sie ⎯⎯ aber beleidigt
                                        NP
     He reached her the two gold coins   which she however offended

zurückwies. (Goethe)
refused.

(21) Wir langten abends in einem freundlichen Dörfchen an, [wo] wir die
                                              AdV
     We arrived at night in a   friendly   village at   where we the

Nacht ⎯⎯ verbrachten.
night spent.

(22) Das Betragen ist ein Spiegel, [*in welchem*] jeder   sein Bild zeigt.
                                    PP   (Goethe)
     The behavior is a   mirror   in which   everyone his picture shows.

I have indicated the place occupied by the relative phrase before the movement transformation by a 'trace'. In classical German, prepositional adverbs occur as relative phrases, too.

(23) Tief in den Fels ist eine Grotte gesprengt, [*wohin*]   des Himmels
                                                AdV
     Deep into the rock is a   grotto blast   whereto   the heaven's

Strahl nicht   leuchtet. (Goethe)
ray   not   shines.

It is then very plausible that the rule of relative formation does the following. It moves a pronominal phrase to the beginning of a sentence. Furthermore, the pronoun of the pronominal phrase is substituted by a relative pronoun.

$$[\alpha[..pro_i..]\beta]_{[+pro]S} \;\Rightarrow\; [\;[..rel\text{-}pro_i..]_{[+rel]}\;\alpha\;\beta\;]_{RC}$$

The semantical effect of this rule is just property abstraction, i.e. if S has the 'logical form' $\phi(x_i)$, then RC has the logical form $\lambda x_i\,\phi(x_i)$.

Thus movement is, in this case, just a syntactic device for expressing variable binding. Ideas of this kind have been expressed in 'trace theory' at many places.[6] The problem of movement control is now this. We cannot just front *any* NP, PP or AdV occurring in the RC. Consider the following examples.

(24) Die Frau, [mit der] Klaus-Jürgen   -   zu schlafen hofft
              PP
     The woman with whom Klaus-Jürgen   to sleep   hopes

(25)* die Frau, [mit der]   Klaus-Jürgen   hofft   daß er - schläft
               PP   hopes   that he   sleeps

These sentences show that we can move a pronominal phrase out of an infinitival complement, but not out of a sentential complement. Hence we must control movement in an appropriate way. Movement control is, of course, one of the central themes of transformational grammar. There exists an enormous amount of literature and I am not able to touch even the most important questions. It will be seen from my proposal how I shall control some cases of movement. Very tricky cases will be left out of consideration.

e) Some remarks concerning the syntax of relatives

The examples discussed so far suggest that German relatives behave exactly like their English counterparts. There are, however, differences.

The most important difference is that German relatives are not complementizer sentences, i.e. sentences of the structure COMP + S. This is so because all the English relatives which seem to have this structure have no grammatical German counterparts.

(26) a) The man *that* shot Liberty Valance.

     b)*Der Mann *daß* Liberty Valance erschoß.

(27) a) The woman I shot.

     b)*Die Frau ich erschoß.

One could say that relative clauses are just sentences of a special kind. Yet in the system I shall propose, sentences always express propositions whereas relative clauses express properties. Thus semantically, relatives behave more like adjectives or predicates. They also share some syntactic features with adjectives: both adjectives and relatives agree in number and gender with the term they modify (adjectives agree, in addition, in case and inflectional type). And, indeed, Thomason regards relatives as adjectives.[7] There are, however, differences between adjectives and relatives. Relatives can be extraposed to the right according to a movement rule for 'heavy constituents', which we must assume for German. Adjectives cannot be extraposed. Look at our example (23) again:

(23) Tief in den Fels ist eine Grotte ___ gesprengt,[wohin des Himmels

     Strahl nicht leuchtet].
              RC

These considerations motivate the assumption that relatives belong to a syntactic category of their own.

There is another difference between German and English relatives: they have a different word order. This, however, is a consequence of the general rules for German word order. Let me briefly illustrate this point. In German, we have three kinds of sentences, according to the position of the finite verbs:

(28) a) *Ist* Ede da?　　　　　　　(Initial position of the finite verb)
　　　Is　Ede there?

　　b) Ede *ist* da　　　　　　　　(Second position of the finite verb)
　　　Ede *is*　there

　　c) Ede da *ist*　　　　　　　　(Final position of the finite verb)
　　　Ede there *is*

In general, subordinate clauses belong to the c-type, i.e. the finite verb occurs at the end. Relatives are special subordinate clauses. If we apply the rule of relative movement sketched in the proceeding section to (28 c), we get the following relative clause:

　　d) *rel-da*　　Ede ── ist
　　　⎵⎵⎵⎵
　　　= *wo*
　　　where　　Ede　　is

Let me finish this section with a historical remark. In Old High German, there was no distinction between relative and demonstrative pronouns. Whether a clause was an RC or not was only clear from its syntax, which seemed to have the same movement rule as today. Consider the following sentence.

(29a) Fon　théro burgilûn　Bethleem,　*thâr* Davîd was,　quimit　Christ.
　　　From the　　castle　　Bethleem　*there* David was,　comes　Christ.
　　　　　　　　　　　　　　　　　　　　　(=where)

(Old High German)

But during the Middle High German period demonstrative relative pronouns were gradually replaced by interrogative pronouns. Yet, in poetry, the use of demonstratives instead of interrogative pronouns survives until recent times:

(30) Dies　ist　der　Tag,　*da* Tauris　seiner　Göttin　für　wunderbare
　　　This　is　the　day,　*there* Tauris his　　Goddess for　wonderful

　　neue Siege dankt. (Goethe)
　　new victories thanks.

And the most important relative pronoun, namely *der, die, das* (= the), is a demonstrative even today.

In Old High German, even pronouns of the first and second person could be used as relative pronouns.

(29b) Thaz　bin　ih,　giloubi　mir,　[*ih* hiar sprihu　mit　thir].
　　　　　　　　　　　　　　　　　　　　　　　　　　　　　　RC
　　　that　am　I　　trust　　me　　*I* here speak　with thee.
　　　　　　　　　　　　　　　[= who I]

(Old High German)

In modern German, we have to express the RC in (29b) either as (29c) or (29d):

(29c) *der* hier mit dir spricht
who here with thou speaks

(29d) *der ich* hier mit dir spreche
who I here with thou speak

The relative phrase in (29d) *der ich* still contains the pronoun of the first person, *ich*. This raises an interesting semantic problem. I have said that RCs express properties which are extracted from open sentences by property abstraction. But how can this be in the case of (29d)? (29d) is derived from

(31) Ich hier mit dir spreche
I here with thee speak

But this sentence contains no 'free variable'. Every term denotes. Well, my solution will be that, in this case, property abstraction applies vacuously. (29d) will express the property which is true of an a if I speak here with you. This will yield the right result.

f) Generalized relatives

(32) Wer hier eingeht, des' Nam' und Sein ist ausgelöscht,
Whoever here enters those's name and being is erased

er ist verweht. (Traven)
he is blown away.

(33) *Wo* du wirst geh'n und stehen, da nimm' mich mit. (Hymn)
Wherever thou willst go and stay, there take me with.

(34) Mach' *was* du willst!
Do *whatever* you want!

Generalized relatives are nominals. They seem to behave like 'attributive' definite terms. As in English, we can express the idea of 'generalization' by supplementing the relative pronoun by a quantificational particle: "wer *auch immer*" (= whoever), "wo *auch immer*" (= wherever) and so on. I shall try to treat generalized relatives by a rule which transforms RCs into NPs and gives them the appropriate reading.

2. The Syntactic-Semantic Framework

Before spelling out the formal syntax and semantics of relatives in German, I shall briefly expose the most important syntactic and semantic notions.

a) Syntactic notions

The language generated by our grammar will consist of labelled trees. Each label is composed of a *category* and possibly some *syntactic features*.

I shall use a self-explanatory notation, which is very similar to conventions found in transformational grammar.
The categories of the grammar are defined recursively as follows:

2.1 a) N and S are *basic categories*.
b) If A, $B_1, \ldots, B_n$ are categories, then $(A/B_1 \ldots B_n)$ is a *derived category*.
The set of all categories is *Cat*.

I shall usually omit the parentheses, i.e. $A/B_1 \ldots B_n = (A/B_1 \ldots B_n)$.
N are the 'names', S the 'sentences'. Furthermore, I shall use the following abbreviations:

CN: = S/N   'the common nouns'
NP: = S/CN   'the nominals'
RC: = S/A   'the A-type relative clauses'
<A>

$$V_{<A_1, \ldots, A_n>} := VP_{<A_1, \ldots, A_n>} = S/A_1 \ldots A_n$$

These are the n-place verbs which require complements of categories $A_1, \ldots, A_n$. $<A_1, \ldots, A_n>$ may be considered as a 'complement frame'.

Det: = NP/CN   'the articles'
AdV: = PP = VP/VP
<A>   <A> <A><A>

I shall reserve the letters

A, B, C, A_i, B_i, C_i, ...

in order to refer to categories. Complex categories will have the form

$[A, \delta_1, \ldots, \delta_n]$,

where δ_i is a syntactic feature. The notation '$-\delta_i$' means that the feature δ_i is not present.

I shall use the letters

X, Y, Z, X_i, Y_i, Z_i, ... in order to denote *trees*.

α, β, γ, α_i, β_i, γ_i ...

will serve for the representation of *trees*, *sequences of trees*, or *terminal strings*. The trees representing grammatical expressions are built up by means of syntactic rules.

2.2 A *syntactic rule r* has the following form:

$$\alpha_1, \ldots, \alpha_n \Rightarrow [\beta_1]_A$$
$$\vdots$$
$$[\beta_m]_A$$

$\alpha_1, \ldots, \alpha_n$ are the input structures (premisses) of r and $[\beta_i]_A$ is the ith output of r. $[\beta_i]_A$ is obtained from $\alpha_1, \ldots, \alpha_n$ by means of a *syntactic operation* $f_{i,r}$, i.e. $[\beta_i]_A = f_{i,r}(\alpha_1, \ldots, \alpha_n)$. Each function $f_{i,r}$ must be computable.

It is permitted that a rule have no premiss at all. Such a rule is called a *lexical rule*. The rules having premisses are the *syntactic rules proper*. A syntactic rule may be considered as a 'generalized transformation rule' in the sense of classical transformational grammar. [8] But in the system proposed here, there is no 'core grammar'.

b) Semantic notions

We will now discuss the general semantic framework. We shall make use of the method of *double indexing*. The general idea is this: A sentence like

(35) I am hungry.

will express a proposition only with respect to an appropriate context of utterance. In one context, it might express the proposition that Angelika is hungry and, at another occasion, it might express the proposition that Ede is hungry. The *meaning* of (35) may be regarded as the function that assigns to each context of utterance the proposition which is expressed by (35) with respect to that context. Let us call what is expressed by an expression with respect to a context a *content*. So we have to distinguish between *meanings* and *contents*. Generally, a meaning is a function from contexts to contents.[9]

2.3 For the purposes of this paper[10] we shall identify a *context* k with a sequence $<w,t,p,S,H,v>$, where w is a *possible world*, t is a *time*, p is a *place*, S is a person (the *speaker* at k), H is a person (the *addressee* or *hearer* at k) and v is a *variable assignment*. The components of k will be denoted as w_k, t_k, p_k, S_k, H_k and v_k, respectively.

The primitives of the theory are the *possible worlds* (or rather: *world histories*) W, the set of *possible individuals* U and the set of *times* T. I shall assume that T is a set of *time intervals* ordered in an appropriate way. Furthermore, there is a set P of *places*. We may assume that P and T (and even W) are subsets of U. But it is more perspicuous to distinguish these sets. Variable assignments are defined in the usual way. An explicit definition is given in the next paragraph.

We shall now make precise the notion of 'content'. Then it will be easy to say what the exact meaning of the term 'meaning' is. To each category A corresponds a set D_A of *appropriate contents*. Intuitively, contents are what can be expressed by expressions with respect to a particular context of use.

2.4 The *system of appropriate contents* $(D_A)_{A \in Cat}$, which is based on U, W, T, P, is defined as follows:

a) $D_N = U \cup T \cup P$

b) $D_S = \mathbb{P}(W \times T \times P)$[11]

The clauses (a) and (b) concern the basic categories. If C is a derived category of the form $(A/B_1,...,B_n)$ then

c) $D_C = D_A^{D_{B_1} \times ... \times D_{B_n}}$[12]

It is a consequence of this definition that the following equations hold:

$$D_{CN} = D_S^{D_N} \qquad\qquad D_{NP} = D_S^{D_{CN}} \qquad\qquad D_{RC} = D_{S/A}^{<A>}$$

$$D_V^{<A_1,\ldots,A_n>} = D_{VP}^{<A_1,\ldots,A_n>} = D_{S/A_1,\ldots,A_n}$$

$$D_{AdV}^{<A>} = D_{PP}^{<A>} = D_{VP}^{<A>} {}^{D_{VP}^{<A>}}$$

$$D_{Det} = D_{NP/CN}$$

If ϕ is an element of D_A, then we shall say that ϕ is a *content of category* A. D^+ is the set of all contents, i.e. $D^+ = \underset{A \in Cat}{U} D_A$.

The contents of category S will be called *propositions*. We say that *a proposition* p *is true (false) in   world* w *at time* t *and place* p iff $<w,t,p>$ is (is not) in p. A similar terminology applies to properties. If ω is a property in $D_{S/A_1 \ldots A_n}$, and $a_1 \ldots a_n$ are entities in $A_1, \ldots A_n$, respectively, then ω is *true (false) of* $a_1, \ldots a_n$ in w at t and p iff the proposition $\omega(a_1, \ldots, a_n)$ is true (false) in w at t and p.

Notice that properties may be quite complicated entities. In our grammar, we shall work with even fourth-order properties.

Now it is easy to say what is a meaning of category A.

<u>2.5</u> If A is a category and K is the set of all contexts, then the set

$$M_A: = D_A^K \text{ is called the } set\ of\ meanings\ of\ category\ A.$$

The set of all meanings is called M^+, i.e. $M^+ = \underset{A \in Cat}{U} M_A$.

A similar notion of meaning is found at many places in the literature. Vide, for instance, [33], [18], [22], [11], [19], [20] and, of course, Montague's UG.

Now, we are in a position to say what is an appropriate interpretation of the syntactic rules.

<u>2.6</u> Suppose we are given a system $A = <U,W,T,P,K>$ and a set of syntactic rules R. The members of the sequence A are nonempty sets. In particular, U is a set of individuals, W a set of worlds, T a set of times, P a set of places and K a set of contexts. An *interpretation of* R which is based on A is a function F which meets the following requirement:

If r is any syntactic rule of the form

$$[\alpha_1]_{A_1} ,\ldots, [\alpha_n]_{A_n} \Rightarrow \begin{array}{l} f_{1,r} \, ([\alpha_1]_{A_1} ,\ldots,[\alpha_n]_{A_n}) \\ \vdots \\ f_{m,r} \, ([\alpha_1]_{A_1} ,\ldots,[\alpha_n]_{A_n}) \end{array}$$

where the output trees are of category B[13], then

F_r is a meaning in $M_{B/A_1 \ldots A_n}$.

Montague called the interpretation of a rule r its *semantic operation*. In PTQ, the role of semantic operations is played by assigning to each syntactic rule an operation forming a new expression of intensional logic out of expressions already given.

We are now in a position to interpret the trees generated by our grammar. We must be a little bit careful because one and the same tree may be generated in more than one way. Therefore, we shall interpret *tree analyses*. These are pairs consisting of a tree together with the syntactic rule which has built up the tree. This will guarantee uniqueness.[14]

<u>2.7</u> Suppose, we are given a system /A as in 2.6, a set of rules R, and an interpretation F of R which is based on /A.

Then, the *interpretation* $V^{/A,R,F}$ *of the tree analyses* is the unique function V from the tree analyses into M^+ which satisfies the following condition:

If $<X,r>$ is a tree analysis and k is a context and X is obtained from the input tree analyses $<Y_1,r_1>,\ldots,$ $<Y_n,r_n>$ by means of the rule r, then

$$V(X,r)(k) = F_r \, (k) \, (V(Y_1,r_1) \, (k), \ldots, V \, (Y_n,r_n) \, (k)).$$

This is a very general definition. Usually, one requires of an interpretation that the variables, the deictic words like 'now', 'today', the logical words like 'and', 'every' and so on, be interpreted in the right way. One could easily formulate such restrictions. But I am not interested in a class of logically possible interpretations, for I have in mind just one, namely the actual interpretation of the rules of German. A part of this will be given - tentatively of course - in the next section.

3. A Fragment of German

In this section I will describe a fragment of German. The core will be the relatives, of course. Nevertheless, since language is a system of rules, I have to state some other rules as well. Let us begin with the personal pronouns.

a) Pronouns

<u>L1</u>. Syntax:

[*ich* cas(a)]
$$ \text{N } 1.\textit{Pers Sing } \text{cas(a)}$$

a = *Nom*, *Dat*, *Acc*, *Gen*;

Semantics: $F_{L1}(k) = S_k$, for any k.

Remember that S_k is the speaker at the context k (vide 2.3). cas(a) is a case variable, and the condition of the syntactic part of (L1) says that it may be specified by the nominative, the dative, the accusative or the genitive morpheme. Hence (L1) permits us to generate four different output trees from no input. These will be 'realized' on the surface as 'ich', 'mir', 'mich' and 'meiner', respectively.

This notation is still somewhat tedious. Therefore I shall henceforth fuse the syntactic and the semantic parts of the lexical rules in a self-explanatory way. This is seen from the next entry.

<u>L2</u>. $F_{[\textit{du } \text{cas(a)}]}(k) = H_k$
$$ [\text{N } 2.\textit{Pers Sing } \text{cas(a)}]$$

Thus, the pronoun of the second person singular always denotes the addressee. Pronouns of the third person will have indices. pro_0, pro_1,... will refer to entities in D^+. $pro\text{-}t_0$, $pro\text{-}t_1$,... refer to times only and $pro\text{-}l_0$, $pro\text{-}l_1$,..., $pro\text{-}l_{17}$,... will denote locations (i.e. places).

The interpretation of the third person pronouns requires to make precise the notion of variable assignment.

Let *Pro* be the set of all the labelled proforms, i.e. any element in *Pro* has the form $[pro_i]_A$, $[pro\text{-}t_i]_A$ or $[pro\text{-}l_i]_A$.

3.1 A *variable assignment* is a function from PRO into D^+ which meets the following conditions:

   a) $\nu(\;pro_i\;\beta]_N) \in D_N$
   b) $\nu(\;pro\text{-}t_i]_N) \in T$
1 c) $\nu(\;pro\text{-}l_i]_N) \in P$
   d) $\nu(\;pro_i]_{A/B_1...B_n}) \in D_{A/B_1...B_n}$

<u>L3</u>. $F_{[pro_i\;\alpha]}(k) = \nu_k([pro_i]_N)$
$$ \text{N }\alpha$$

α = *3.Pers* + *Sing* + cas(a) + gen(b)

If $\alpha = pro_i$ + *3.Pers* + *Sing* + *Nom* + *Mas*, then $[pro_i\;\alpha]_{N\alpha}$ will be realized as *er* or *der* (=he, the) and so on. There are pronouns of other categories as well. Consider, for instance, the following sentences.

(36) Kreusel is a sycophant. Knauth slaps him. *That's* nice.

Here, *that* refers to what is expressed by the preceding sentence. Hence *that* refers to a proposition. Such a possibility is captured by the following rule.

L4. $F_{[pro_i \, \alpha]_{\overline{S}}}$ (k) $= \nu_k \, ([pro_i]_{\overline{S}})$, where $= 3.Pers \; Sing \; cas(a) \; Neut$
$\qquad\qquad \overset{[\alpha]}{}$

$\overline{S} = S, + comp$ is the category of sentential complements.
A pronoun may also denote properties. Consider the following sentence.

(37) *What* Knauth does is nice.

Here, *what* denotes a property, say 'Slapping Kreusel'. This motivates the next rule.

L5. $F_{[pro_i + \alpha]_{\overline{VP}}}$ (k) $= \nu_k \, ([pro_i]_{\overline{VP}})$, where α is as in (L4).
$\qquad\qquad\quad \overset{}{[\alpha]}$

$\overline{VP} = [VP, - fin]$ is the category of infinitival complements.

Certain proforms are not realized at the surface at all. They will be used for the representation of context dependent words only. This is the background of the following rule.

L6. $F_{[pro_i]_A}$ (k) $= \nu_k \, ([pro_i]_A)$, for any A $\in$ Cat.

Deictic local and temporal adverbs like *here*, *da* (here, there) and *jetzt*, *da*, *als* (now, there, when) can be treated by the same techniques. The following two complex rules account for these words.

L7. Let ω^+ be any property in D_{VP}, let ζ be any A-content and $\alpha = hier, jetzt$.
Then $<w,t,p> \in F_{[\alpha]_{AdV}^{<A>}}$ (k) $(\omega^+) \, (\zeta): \Leftrightarrow <w,t*,p*> \in \omega^+ \, (\zeta)$, where

$\quad t* = t \; \& \; p* = p_k$, if $\alpha = hier$,
$\quad t* = t_k \; \& \; p* = p$, if $\alpha = jetzt$.

Thus *hier* shifts the evaluation place into the utterance place and *jetzt* shifts the evaluation time into the time of utterance.

L8. Suppose, ω^+ is any property in D_{VP} and ζ is any content in D_A,
$\alpha = pro\text{-}t_i, \; pro\text{-}l_i$. Then $<w,t,p> \in F_{[\alpha]_{AdV}^{<A>}}$ (k) $(\omega^+) \, (\zeta): \Leftrightarrow$

$\quad <w,t*,p*> \in \omega^+ \, (\zeta)$, where

$\quad t* = \nu([pro\text{-}t_i]_N) \; \& \; p* = p$, if $\alpha = pro\text{-}t_i$,
$\quad t* = t \; \& \; p* = \nu([pro\text{-}l_i]_N)$, if $\alpha = pro\text{-}l_i$.

240

$[pro\text{-}l_i]_{AdV}$ is realized as *da* or *wo*. $[pro\text{-}t_i]_{AdV}$ is realized as *da* or *als*.
　　　　<A>　　　　　　　　　　　　　　　　　　　　　<A>
Clearly, these words are demonstratives. They shift the time and place of evaluation into the time and place of utterance respectively.

b) Verb phrases and nominals

Let me start this section by writing down the derivation of a very simple sentence. More complex examples will be treated later.

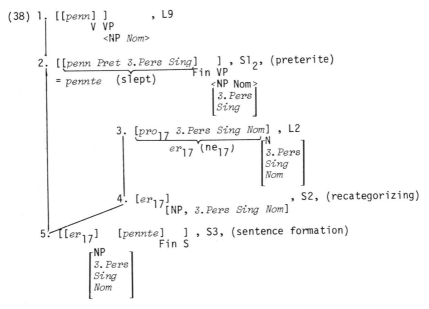

The tree derived at step (38.5) will be realized as the sentence

(39) Er_{17} pennte.[15]

He_{17} slept.

From this generation tree, the strategy followed is already visible. The sentence generated at step (38.5) has more internal structure than just the NP er_{17} and the finite verb *pennte*. But I have saved only as much structural information as I need for movement transformations. In most cases, at each step, only the immediate constituents of a tree are represented. The internal structure of the constituents is of no concern for our purpose. If it is needed, it can be recovered from the derivational history.

Let me now state the tense rules. I cannot motivate them here. But I refer to [20] and [4].

$\underline{(S1}_i)_{i = 1,2,3}$ *Basic tenses*

Syntax:

$[\alpha[\beta]\ ]$, β is the only V without suffix
  V VP
    [-*fin*]

---

1. $[\alpha[\beta+\gamma\ Pres]\ ]$
     $V_\gamma\ VP_\gamma$

2. $[\alpha[\beta+\gamma\ Pret]\ ]$
     $V_\gamma\ VP_\gamma$

3. $[\alpha[\beta+Inf]\ [werd+\gamma]\ ]$ γ = per(a) num(b)
    V $V_\gamma\ VP_\gamma$

Semantics:

Let X be $[\alpha[\beta]\ ]$, and let ζ be any member of D_{NP}.
     V [VP - *fin*]
Then $<w,t,p> \in F_{S1_i}$ $(k)(V(X,r)(k))(\zeta)$ *iff*

a) $(\exists t^*)(t^*$ is a subinterval of t)

   & $\begin{cases} t^* \text{ is not before } t_k \\ t^* \text{ is before } t_k \\ t^* \text{ is after } t_k \end{cases}$), and

b) $<w,t^*_*,p> \in V(X,r)(k)(\zeta)$, where t^*_* is the maximal subinterval of t which is

  $\begin{cases} \text{not before } t_k \\ \text{before } t_k \\ \text{after } t_k \end{cases}$

The verbs which are not specified with respect to number and person are subclassified as $-fin$. The other verbs are $+fin$. Instead of [V + fin], we shall write *Fin*.

The above rule is a schema for three rules. The distinction of cases in the semantic parts refers, of course, to the different rules.

The motivation of the semantics of this rule would require a whole paper.[16] Roughly speaking, the present tense gives us that part of the evaluation time which is not before the utterance time t_k, the preterite yields the part before t_k and the future the part after t_k. Thus, if we evaluated sentence (38.5) today at 11.00 A.M., it would express the proposition that he[17] sleeps today during the whole time before 11.00 A.M..

The following rule recategorizes Ns as NPs.

<u>S2</u>. *Recategorizing Ns as NPs*

$[\alpha]_N \Rightarrow [\alpha]_{NP}$, δ = per(a) num(b) gen(c) cas(d)
$[_\delta^N]$ $[_\delta^{NP}]$
$F_{S2}(k)(V([\alpha]_N,r)(k))(\omega)$ is true in w at t and p: $\Leftrightarrow \omega$ is true of $V([\alpha]_N)(k)$ in w at t and p, where ω is any property in D_{CN}.

And this is the sentence rule.

$\underline{\underline{S3}}_A$. *Sentence formation*

$$
\left.
\begin{array}{l}
[\alpha] \qquad\qquad , [\beta] \\
\ [VP<A_\gamma>,\delta_1] \qquad [A,\gamma,\delta 2] \\
A_\gamma = [NP\ cas(a)],\ \overline{S},\ \overline{VP} \\
\delta_1 = \delta_2 = per(b)\ num(e)\ \text{if } A = NF \\
\delta_1 = 3.Pers\ Sing\ \&\ \delta_2 = \emptyset, \\
\quad \text{if } A = \overline{S},\ \overline{VP}
\end{array}
\right]
\quad \Rightarrow \quad
\begin{array}{l}
[[\beta'] \quad \alpha] \\
\ [A_\gamma]\quad S
\end{array}
$$

$$
\text{where } \beta' = \begin{cases} \beta,\ \text{if } A \neq \overline{VP} \\ \beta_1[\beta_2+Inf],\ \text{if } A = \overline{VP} \text{ and } \beta = \beta_1[\beta_2] \\ \qquad\quad V \end{cases}
$$

$$
F_{S5}^A(k)(V([\alpha],r_1)(k),\ V([\beta],r_2)(k)) = V([\alpha],r_1)(k)(V([\beta],r_2)(k)).
$$
$$
\phantom{F_{S5}^A(k)(}VP\quad\ A\qquad\qquad\qquad VP\qquad\quad A
$$

As we would expect, the semantics is just functional application of the property expressed by the verb phrase to the value of the subject.

In order to evaluate sentence (38), we still need a meaning rule for the verb.

$\underline{\underline{L9}}$. Let ω_{sleep} be that property in $D_{S/N}$ which is true of an $u \in U$ in w at t and p *iff* u is asleep in w at t.

Let ω_{sleep}^+ be the corresponding property in $D_{S/NP}$, i.e. $<w,t,p> \in \omega_{sleep}^+ (\zeta)$ $\leftrightarrow \zeta(\omega_{sleep})$ is true in w at t and p, for any $\zeta \in D_{NP}$. Then

$$
F_{[[penn]\ ]} = \omega_{sleep}^+.
$$
$$
\phantom{F_{[}}V\ VP
$$
$$
\phantom{F_{[}}<NP\ Nom>
$$

Let us evaluate $V((38.5),\ S3_{NP})(k)$. This is the proposition which is true in w at t and p *iff*

a) $V((38.2),\ S1_2)(k)(V((38.4),\ S2)(k))$ is true in w at t and p. (By $S3_{NP}$)

Now, suppose that $V((38.4),\ S2)(k)$ is ζ_{Ede}, where ζ_{Ede} is that second-order property which is true of a first-order property ω in w at t and p iff $<w,t,p> \in \omega(Ede)$. By L2 and S2, this will be the case iff$v([pro_{17}])(k)$ $= Ede$. Then (a) is the case iff
$$
\phantom{= Ede. Then (a) is the case iffv([pro_{}}N
$$

b) $(\exists t*)(t*$ is a subinterval of t and t* is before t_k) and $<w,t*,p> \in V((38.1),\ L9)(k)(\zeta_{Ede})$, where t* is the maximal part of t which is before t_k. (By $S1_2$) And, by L9, this holds good, *iff*

c) $(\exists t*)(t*$ is a subinterval of t and t* is before t_k) and $<w,t*,p> \in \omega_{sleep}(Ede)$, where t* is the maximal part in t which is before t_k. Now, $<w,t*,p> \in \omega_{sleep}(Ede) \leftrightarrow Ede$ is asleep in w at t* and p. (By L9)

Thus, with respect to the context k, (38) roughly expresses the proposition that Ede is asleep in the past of t_k. This is what we were after.

The following two rules account for the fact that infinitival or sentential complements may occur as subjects or objects.

<u>S4</u>. *Formation of sentential complements*

$$[\alpha] \quad\Rightarrow\quad [da\beta\ \alpha]$$
$$[S,-comp] \qquad\qquad [S,+comp]$$

$$F_{S4}(k)(V([\alpha]\underset{S}{S3})(k)) = V([\alpha],S3)(k)$$

Thus, the interpretation of S4 is the identity mapping. In German, some verbs take infinitival complements having the preposition *zu* (=to), others take infinitives without *zu*. This is accounted for by the next rule.

<u>S5</u>. *Prepositional infinitives*

$$[\alpha[\beta]\ ] \Rightarrow [[\alpha][zu\quad \beta]\ ]$$
$$\begin{array}{cc} V\ VP & V\ VP \\ \begin{bmatrix} -fin \\ -zu \end{bmatrix} & \begin{bmatrix} -fin \\ +zu \end{bmatrix} \end{array}$$

The interpretation is identity. The rule for complex verb phrases is now easily stated.

<u>S6</u>.   *Verb phrases*
$$A_1 \ldots A_n$$

Syntax:

$$[\alpha]_{VP} \qquad\qquad , [\beta]$$
$$\langle A_1\delta_1,\ldots,A_n\delta_n\rangle \qquad [A_n\delta_n]$$

$$n > 1 \text{ and } A_n = NP\delta_n, \overline{S}, \overline{VP}$$

$$[\beta\alpha] \qquad\qquad\qquad , \text{ where}$$
$$VP$$
$$\langle A_1\delta_1,\ldots,A_{n-1}\delta_{n-1}\rangle$$

$$\gamma = \begin{cases} \begin{array}{l}[\beta] \\ [A_n\delta_n]\end{array} & , \text{ if } A_n = NP, \overline{S} \\[2ex] \beta_1[\beta_2 + Inf]_V, & \text{ if } A_n = \overline{VP} \text{ and } \beta = \beta_1[\beta_2]_V \end{cases}$$

Semantics:

$$\langle w,t,p\rangle \in F_{S6}^{A_1\cdots A_n}(k)(V([\alpha]_{VP}, r_1)(k), V([\beta]_{A_n}, r_2)(k))(\zeta_1,\ldots,\zeta_{n-1}): \Leftrightarrow$$

$$\langle w,t,p\rangle \in V([\alpha]_{VP}, r_1)(k)(V([\beta]_{A_n}, \mathring{r}_2)(k), \zeta_1,\ldots,\zeta_{n-1})$$

for any $\zeta_1,\ldots,\zeta_{n-1} \in D_{A_1} \times \ldots \times D_{A_{n-1}}$.

Thus, this rule makes an (n-1)-place verb out of an n-place verb. And the semantics transforms an n-place property into an (n-1)-place property.

Consider an example.

(39) daß Ede   zu   pennen   glauben   wird
    that Ede   to   sleep   believe   will

The derivation of this $\overline{S}$ will involve all our syntactic rules proper.

(40) 1. [[*penn*]]   , L9
           V VP
              <[+*Nom*]>

    2. [[*zu penn*]]   , S5
             V [VP,<[+*Nom*]>, +*zu*]

         3. [[*glaub*]]   , Lexicon
                V VP
                  <[+*Nom*]>, [$\overline{VP}$,+*zu*]>

    4. [[*zu penn* + *Inf*] [*glaub*]]   , S6
       $\underbrace{\qquad\qquad}$ V   V VP
       =*pennen*   <[+*Nom*]>

    5. [[*zu pennen*] [*glaub* + *Inf*] [*wird*]]   , S1$_3$
          V $\underbrace{\qquad\qquad}$ V   V VP
             = *glauben*   <[+*Nom*]>

         6. [*Ede*]   , Lexicon
           [N,*3.Pers Sing Nom*]

         7. [*Ede*]   , S2
           [NP,*3.Pers Sing Nom*]

   6. [[*Ede*] [*zu pennen*] [*glauben*] [*wird*]] , S3
      [NP]   V   V   Fin S

   7. [*daß*[*Ede*] [*zu pennen*] [*glauben*] [*wird*]   ] , S4
       NP   V   V   Fin $\overline{S}$

In order to evaluate this tree analysis, I have to introduce an interpretation of the two-place VP *glaub* (to believe), of course. Since this is somewhat tedious, I shall not do it here.[17]

Notice that (40) is not an awfully good German sentence. A nicer variant would be (41) where the $\overline{VP}$ *zu pennen* is moved over the finite verb.

(41) daß Ede - glauben wird ⌊zu pennen⌋
                           $\overline{VP}$

I shall assume an appropriate extraposition rule for 'heavy constituents'.[18] Our rule will even generate ungrammatical strings like

(42)* Ede [daß er pennt] glauben wird.
        $\overline{S}$

Here, the extraposition of the $\overline{S}$ is obligatory. Such cases must be excluded either by a filter[19] or by a stricter formulation of (S6).

c) Formation of relative clauses

The formation of the rule that forms relative clauses is a rather complicated matter. I shall first give a somewhat informal description which I will make precise in the sequel.

$\underline{\underline{S7}}_A$ *Formation of RCs*

Syntax:

$$[\alpha_1 [\beta]_A \alpha_2 \underset{[\delta]}{[\gamma]} \quad]_{\text{Fin S}}$$

$A = \text{NP}, \overline{S}, \overline{VP}, \text{PP}, \text{AdV}; \quad \beta$ is a pronominal phrase

$$[[\beta']_A \alpha_1' \; \alpha_2' \underset{[\delta]}{[\gamma]} \quad]_{\substack{\text{Fin RC} \\ < B > \\ [\delta]}} \quad , \text{ where the following conditions obtain.}$$

1. Let $pro_i \; \alpha \; (pro\text{-}t_i \quad pro\text{-}l_i)$ be the pronoun of β. Then β' is obtained

from β by substituting $pro_i \; (pro\text{-}t_i, pro\text{-}l_i)$ by $rel\text{-}pro \; (rel\text{-}pro\text{-}t, rel\text{-}pro\text{-}l)$.

2. $\alpha_1' \; \alpha_2'$ are obtained from α_1, α_2 by deleting the index 'i' of any pronoun occurring in α_1 or α_2.

Semantics:

Let $pro_i \; \alpha \; (pro\text{-}l_i, pro\text{-}t_i)$ be the pronoun of β, and let a be any element of D_B.

$<w,t,p> \in F_7^A(k)(V([\alpha_1 [\beta]_A \; \alpha_2 \; [\gamma]_{\text{Fin}}]_S, r)(k))(a) : \Leftrightarrow$

$<w,t,p> \in V([\alpha_1 [\beta]_A \; \alpha_2 \; [\gamma]_{\text{Fin}}]_S, r)(k^*)$, where k^* is like k with the only

difference that v_k is replaced by $(v_k, a/x_i)$, with $x_i = pro_i \; \alpha, \; pro\text{-}l_i, \; pro\text{-}t_i$.

The semantics of this rule sounds somewhat puzzling, but it is just property abstraction. The syntax is much more problematic. This is so because clause 1, which describes the transformation of demonstrative pronouns into the corresponding relative pronoun, is by no means clear. Firstly, we have to say what is meant by '*the* pronoun of the phrase β'. Secondly, a pronoun may occur at different locations. But we want to replace a particular *occurrence* of a pronoun by a relative pronoun. We can express condition 1 only by means of a recursive definition over the syntactic rules which generate NPs, $\overline{S}$s, $\overline{VP}$s, PPs and AdVs. These rules are not yet complete. We shall introduce them in this section and shall make condition 1 precise afterwards.

Let us illustrate before how rule (S7) is meant by means of some examples. A trivial case of relative formation is the following one:

(43) 1. $[[\underbrace{pro_{17} \; 3.\,Pers \; Sing \; Nom}_{= \; er_{17}}]_{NP} \; [pennte]_{\text{Fin S}} \quad]$, (38,5)

2. [[*rel 3.Pers Sing Nom*] [*pennte*]] , (S7$_{NP}$)
   $\underbrace{\qquad\qquad\qquad\qquad}_{NP}$ Fin   RC
   = *der, welcher* (who)   slept   \<N\>

A more complicated derivation is the following one:

(44) 1. [[*zu pennen*] [*glaub*]] , (40,4)
      to sleep ^{V} believe^V VP
                    \<NP\>

   2. [*pro-l$_{19}$*]   , L8
      $\underbrace{\qquad\quad}$ AdV
      = *da$_{19}$* \<VP\>

   3. [[*da$_{19}$*]   [*zu pennen*] [*glaub*]]   , S8, (Adverb rule)
           AdV   V   V VP
           \<VP\>   \<NP\>

   4. [[*da$_{19}$*]   [*zu pennen*] [*glaub-t*]]   , Sl$_1$, (present)
           AdV   V   Fin VP

   5. [*Ede*]   , (40,7)
        NP

   6. [[*Ede*] [*da$_{19}$*]   [*zu pennen*] [*glaubt*]] , S3
        NP   AdV   V   Fin S

   7. [[*rel-da*]   [*Ede*] [*zu pennen*] [*glaubt*]]   , S7
      $\overline{= wo}$ AdV   NP   V   Fin RC
      (where)   Ede   to sleep   believes \<N\>

Given an appropriate meaning rule for '*glaub*', (44,7) expresses the property which is true of a place p iff Ede believes that he is asleep at p. Notice that most relative clauses express properties of individuals. Yet, there are also RCs and RCs.
                              \<$\overline{S}$\>   \<$\overline{VP}$\>

(45) Suzanne will heiraten, *was* Klaus-Jürgen mißbilligt.
     Suzanne wants to marry   what Klaus-Jürgen disapproves of.

In this case, the *was* probably modifies the whole preceding sentence. Hence the RC has the subcategory \<$\overline{S}$\>. But consider the next example.

(46) Suzanne möchte heiraten, *was* sie besser bleiben lassen sollte.
     Suzanne wants to marry   what she better remain let   should.

In this case, the RC modifies only the infinitival *heiraten*, hence it is an RC. The relative in (46) is derived in the following way:
\<$\overline{VP}$\>

                          S7
(47) [[*was*] [*sie*] [*besser*]   -   [*bleiben*] [*lassen*] [*sollte*]]
      NP   NP   AdV   V   V   Fin RC
                                                     \<$\overline{VP}$\>

At this place, it is convenient to introduce some new syntactic rules. Let us begin with prepositional phrases.

<u>S8</u>. *PP-formation*

$[\alpha]_P \qquad , \qquad [\beta]_{NP} \qquad \Rightarrow \qquad [\alpha\beta]_{PP}$
$\quad$ <cas(a)> $\qquad$ [cas(a)]

$F_8(k)(V([\alpha]_P, r_1)(k), V([\beta]_{NP}, r_2)(k)) = V([\alpha]_P, r_1)(k)(V([\beta]_{NP}, r_2)(k)).$

$\underset{\text{<cas(a)>}}{P}$ is defined as $\underset{\text{<A>}}{PP}/[NP\ cas(a)]$.

The subcategory cas(a) is needed, because, in German, prepositions govern different cases. For instance, *in* governs the dative or accusative, whereas *während* (while) governs the genitive.

<u>S9</u>. *Modification of verbs*

$[\alpha\beta]_{VP}$, where α is a sequence of NPs, possibly empty.
$\begin{bmatrix} <A> \\ -fin \end{bmatrix}$ The first member of β is no NP.

$[\gamma]_B$, $\quad B = AdV, PP$
$\quad$ <A>

$[\alpha[\gamma]_B\ \ \beta]_{VP}$
$\quad$ <A> $\begin{bmatrix} <A> \\ -fin \end{bmatrix}$

The semantics of this rule is functional application of the value of $[\alpha]_\beta$ to the value of $[\alpha\beta]_{VP}$.

These rules enable us to generate sentences like the following two.

(48) Ede in Rom pennte.
$\quad$ Ede in Rome slept.

(49) in der Ede pennte
$\quad$ in which Ede slept

Let us derive the second sentence. It is more complicated than the first one.

(50) 1. [[*penn*]] , L9
$\qquad\qquad$ V VP
$\qquad\qquad$ <[*Nom*]>

$\qquad$ 2. [*pro*$_{19}$ *3.Pers Sing Fem*] , L2
$\qquad\qquad\qquad\qquad\qquad\qquad\qquad$ N
$\qquad\qquad$ = *der*$_{19}$ $\qquad\qquad$ [*Dat*]

$\qquad$ 3. [*der*$_{19}$] , S2
$\qquad\qquad\qquad$ [NP]
$\qquad\qquad\qquad\quad$ *Dat*

$\qquad\qquad\qquad$ 4. [*in*], P , L10
$\qquad\qquad\qquad\qquad\qquad$ <*Dat*>

$$5. \ [in \ der_{19} \ \text{PP}, \ S8$$

$$6. \ [[in \ der_{19}]_{\text{PP}} \ [penn] \ ]_{\substack{\text{V} \ \text{VP}}}, \ S9$$
$$<[Nom]>$$

It is a thorny problem to write a meaning rule for the preposition *in*. We meet the same kind of difficulty here that we have discussed in connection with quantifier restrictions by relatives. It would be easy to write a meaning rule for *in* under the assumption that *in* be of the category PP/N. Then the rule would be something like this:

$$<w,t,p> \in F_{[in]} \ (k)(a)(\omega\text{+})(\zeta) : \iff <w,t,p\text{*}> \in \omega\text{+}(\zeta),$$

where p* is 'the interior of a'.

But it is hard to have an NP-content at the place of a. Consider a sentence like

"Ede works in every town."

It should express the following proposition:

$(\forall x)(x$ is a town $\Rightarrow$ Ede works at x'), where x' is the interior of x. Here, the 'in' modifies a bound variable. How is this possible?
It would be easy to treat the sentence by means of the rule sketched above and a quantifying-in device:

$$((\text{Every town}), \ (\lambda, x_N \ (\text{Ede works in } x_N))).$$

That's the way Cresswell proceeds in [12]. A more complete grammar will need quantifying-in anyhow. But I don't like the idea of being forced to apply such an artificial procedure in the derivation of (50). So, I assume that a meaning rule for *in* can be written, even under the assumption that *in* is a PP/NP, although I have no idea how this can be done. Let us call this fictitious meaning rule <u>L10</u>.

The next three rules generate NPs.

<u>S10</u>. *Prepositional NPs*

$$[\alpha]_P \ , \qquad [\beta]_{NP} \qquad \Rightarrow \qquad [\alpha\beta]_{NP}$$
$$<cas(a)> \qquad [cas(a)] \qquad\qquad [cas(\alpha)]$$

The semantics is identity.

This rule is necessary in view of verbs having 'prepositional objects'.

(51) Ede denkt oft *an* Piroschka.
      Ede thinks often *of* Piroschka.

Here, the verb phrase *denkt an Piroschka* is generated as follows:

(52) 1. $[[denkt] \ ]_{\substack{\text{V} \ \text{VP}}}$, Lexicon
$$<NP \ Nom, \ NP \ an>$$

2. [*an Piroschka*]   , S10
　　　　　NP
　　　　　[*an*]

3. [[*an Piroschka*] [*denk*]] , S6
　　　　NP　　　　V VP
　　of Piroschka　thinks<NP *Nom*>

Thus, *denken* (think) is just a special two-place verb governing the pre-position *an*. In this case, the preposition has no literal meaning. It is rather something like a case. This is reflected by the notation.

S11. *NPs having articles*

$[\alpha]_{Det}$, $[\beta]_A$ ⇒ $[\alpha\beta]_{NP}$
$[\delta]$ 　 $[\delta]$ 　　$[\delta, 3.Pers]$

A = CN, CN (= CN/N)
　　　　<N>

CN is the category of relative terms, like *Vater* (father).
<N>
In case β is a non-relative CN, the semantics of S11 is simply functional application of the α-content to the β-content. If β is a relative term, the situation is more difficult.

(53)　Der　Vater　spricht.
　　　The　father speaks.

In (53), the nominal refers to the father of one or several salient persons. Since I have not introduced 'salient objects' into the context theory, I will not treat cases like (53). Let us now give the meaning rule for the definite article.

L11. *The descriptive sense of the definite article*

$$<w,t,p> \in F_{[def\ cas(a)\ gen(b)\ Sing]}(k)(\omega_1)(\omega_2): \Leftrightarrow$$

$$(\exists u)(\forall v)[[<w,t,p> \in \omega_1(v) \Leftrightarrow u = v] \& <w,t,p> \in \omega_2(u)]$$

This is Russell's definite description. The next rule captures the demonstrative use of the definite article.

L12. *Demonstrative articles*

$$<w,t,p> \in F_{[pro_i\ cas(a)\ gen(b)\ Sing]}(k)(\omega_1)(\omega_2): \Leftrightarrow$$

$$<w,t,p> \in \omega_1(v_k([pro_i]_N)) \& <w,t,p> \in \omega_2(v_k([pro_i]_N))$$

Instances of (L11) will be realized as *der*, *die*, *das* (the), instances of (L12) will appear at the surface as *der*, *die*, *das* or *dieser*, *diese*, *dieses* (this).

So Donnellan's 'attributive-referential' distinction is not captured via quantifying-in (as, for instance, in [11]) but via double-indexing (as in [18], [20], [19]).

Thus, the sentence

(54) Der Präsident ist ein Ehrenmann.
      The president is an honest man.

will express the proposition that Karl Carstens is president and that he is an honest man, if the article *der* is a *pro*. referring to Karl Carstens. And it expresses the proposition that the president, whoever this is, is an honest man, if *der* is derived from *def*.

The following rule transforms genitive NPs into determiners.

S12. *Genitive NPs become Det s*

$[\alpha]_{NP}$ $\Rightarrow$ $[\alpha]_{Det}$
  Geni

The semantics of this rule has to account for at least four different cases. Consider the following NPs:

(55) Edes Bruder
      Ede's brother

(56) Edes Wohnung
      Ede's flat

These two nominals are both definite terms, whose article may either have an attributive or a demonstrative sense. Furthermore, *Bruder* (brother) is a relative CN, *Wohnung* (flat) is not. Hence we must distinguish at least four cases, originating from the combination of the following features:

$\left\{ \begin{array}{l} \text{descriptive} \\ \text{demonstrative} \end{array} \right\}$ $\left\{ \begin{array}{l} \text{relative} \\ \text{non-relative} \end{array} \right\}$

I shall treat only two cases. In order to understand the interpretation of (S12), it is necessary to have the following two lexical entries:

L13. $<w,t,p> \in F_{[Wohnung\ \alpha]_{CN}}$ (k)(u): $\Leftrightarrow$ u is a flat in w at t and p.
                        $[\alpha]$
      α = num(a) cas(b) *Fem*.

L14. $<w,t,p> \in F_{[Bruder\ \alpha]}$ (k)(u)(v): $\Leftrightarrow$ v is a brother of u in w at t.
      α = num(a) cas(b) *Mas*

I will now give the interpretation of S12. I consider only two readings. It should be obvious how the other readings can be treated.

S12. a) *Semantics in the descriptive-relative case*

$<w,t,p> \in F_{12}^{1}$ (k)$(V([\alpha]_{NP},r)(k))(\omega_1)(\omega_2)$: $\Leftrightarrow$ $(\exists u)(\forall v)[[<w,t,p> \in V([\alpha]_{NP},r)$

(k)$(\lambda^*a(\omega_1(a,v)])$ $\Leftrightarrow$ v = u] & $<w,t,p> \in \omega_2(u)]$ for any $\omega_1 \in D_{CN/N}$ and $\omega_2 \in$

D_{CN}.

b) *Semantics in the descriptive-non-relative case*

$$<w,t,p> \in F^2_{12}(k)(V([\alpha]_{NP},r)(k))(\omega_1)(\omega_2): \Leftrightarrow (\exists u)(\forall v)([[<w,t,p> \in \omega_1(v) \ \&$$

$$<w,t,p> \in V([\alpha]_{NP},r)(k)(\omega_{owns\ v})] \Leftrightarrow v = u] \ \& \ <w,t,p> \in \omega_2(u)), \text{ where } \omega_1, \omega_2$$

$$\in D_{CN} \text{ and } <w,t,p> \in \omega_{owns\ v}(u): \Leftrightarrow u \text{ owns } v \text{ in } w \text{ at } t \text{ and } p.$$

Thus a nominal like (56) is true of a property ω, if there is exactly one flat owned by Ede and if *this* flat has the property ω. The derivation of (56) is the following:

(57) 1. $[Edes]_{NP}$, Lexicon
$\quad\quad [Geni]$

2. $[Edes]_{NP}$, S2
$\quad\quad [Geni]$

3. $[Edes]_{Det}$, S12   4. $[Wohnung]_{CN}$, L13

5. $[Edes\ Wohnung]_{NP}$, S11
$\quad\quad$ Ede's flat

Notice that, according to (S12), a term like

(58) Keines   Präsidenten   Wohnung
     no   president's   flat

will denote the apartment which is owned by no president. The more natural reading for (58) is, of course, 'No apartment which is owned by some president'. I do not get this reading, and it would be worthwhile to inquire into the reasons why I don't get this reading. But I cannot go into this here.

The rules generating NPs, $\overline{S}$s, $\overline{VP}$s, PPs and AdVs are now complete. Therefore, we are able to define condition 1 of (S7) in a precise way. This is done by means of the syntactic relations R_1 and R_2, whose intuitive meanings are the following ones:

$\alpha R_1 \beta: \Leftrightarrow \beta$ is a pronominal phrase and α is the main pronoun of β.

$\alpha R_2 \beta: \Leftrightarrow \alpha$ is the location of the pronominal phrase β.

3.1 The syntactic relation R_1

1. Let α be *ich Nom*, *du Nom*, $pro_i\text{-}t$, $pro_i\text{-}l$ or $pro_i\beta$. Then $\alpha R_1[\alpha]_A$, where $A = N$, NP, $\overline{S}$, $\overline{VP}$.

2. Suppose $[\beta\gamma]_{PP}$ is obtained from $[\beta]_P$ and $[\gamma]_{NP}$ by rule (S8). Suppose further that $\alpha R_1 [\gamma]_{NP}$. Then $\alpha R_1 [\beta\gamma]_{PP}$.

3. Suppose $[\beta\gamma]_{NP}$ is obtained from $[\beta]_P$ and $[\gamma]_{NP}$ via rule (S10). Suppose further that $\alpha R_1 [\gamma]_{NP}$. Then $\alpha R_1 [\beta\gamma]_{NP}$.

4. Suppose $[\beta]_{Det}$ is derived from $[\beta]_{NP}$ by (S12) and $\alpha \; R_1 \; [\beta]_{NP}$ holds good. Then $\alpha \; R_1 \; [\beta]_{Det}$.

If we did not forget any relevant rule, then the relation R_1 is defined for all the cases we have in mind. Notice that recursive definitions of the same spirit as here are found in Montague's UG (cf. the definitions of 'main verb' and 'main verb location', UG p. 238-239).

3.2 The syntactic relation R_2

1. Let $[\alpha]_A$ be as in 3.1 (1). Then $[*]_A \; R_2 \; [\alpha]_A$.

2. If $[*]_{NP} \; R_2 \; [\alpha]_{NP}$ and $[\beta\alpha]_P$ is obtained from $[\beta]_P$ and $[\alpha]_{NP}$ by means of (S8), then $[\beta*]_{PP} \; R_2 \; [\beta\alpha]_{PP}$.

3. If $[*]_{NP} \; R_2 \; [\alpha]_{NP}$ and $[\beta\alpha]_{NP}$ is obtained from $[\beta]_P$ and $[\alpha]_{NP}$ by means of (S10), then $[\beta*]_{NP} \; R_2 \; [\beta\alpha]_{NP}$.

4. If $[\alpha]_{Det}$ is obtained from $[\alpha]_{NP}$ by (S12) and $[*]_{NP} \; R_2 \; [\alpha]_{NP}$, then $[*]_{Det} \; R_2 \; [\alpha]_{Det}$.

Let us consider two examples. Look at (50,5), $[in \; der_{19}]_{PP}$. It is easily checked that

$$pro_{19} \; 3.Pers \; Sing \; Fem \; R_1 \; [in \; der_{19}]_{PP}.$$

Hence we have recovered the main pronoun of the pronominal PP. And, of course, the following is true:

$$[in \; *]_{PP} \; R_2 \; [in \; der_{19}]_{PP}.$$

$\underline{\underline{S7}}_A$. *restated*

$[\alpha_1[\beta]_A \quad \alpha_2[\gamma]_{Fin}]_S$, A = NP, $\overline{S}$, $\overline{VP}$, PP, AdV.
$\quad [\delta]$
There is an α such that $\alpha \; R_1 \; [\beta]_A$.

$[[\beta']_A \quad \alpha_1' \; \alpha_2' \; [\gamma]_{Fin}]_{RC}$
$\quad [\delta] \qquad\qquad\qquad \begin{bmatrix} <B> \\ \delta \end{bmatrix}$

1. Let α be the expression such that $\alpha \; R_1 \; [\beta]_A$. Let $\beta*$ be the tree such that $[\beta*] \; R_2 \; [\beta]_A$. Then β' is obtained from $\beta*$ by substituting $*$ by rel-α', where α' is α without the index.

2. α_1' and α_2' are obtained from α_1 and α_2 by deleting the index of α in any pronoun occurring in α_1 or α_2.

We are now able to generate most of the relatives discussed so far. Consider an example again:

(58) 1. $[[du\ Nom]_{NP}\ [im\ Himmel]_{PP}\ [bist]_{Fin}]_S$, (S3)
        thou   in heaven   art

   2. $[[\underline{rel-du\ Nom}]_{NP}\ [im\ Himmel]_{PP}\ [bist]_{Fin}\ ]_{RC}$, (S7)
      $= der\ du$ (who) in heaven   art   <N>

The only relatives we can't get yet are the generalized relatives. The
following rule accounts for some of them.

S13. Generalized relatives

$[\alpha]_{RC \atop \langle N \rangle}$ $\Rightarrow$ $[\alpha']_{NP}$, where α' comes from α by substituting *rel* by *gen*.
$[\delta]$ $[\delta]$

$F_{13}(k)(V([\alpha]_{RC},r)(k))(\omega)$ is true in w at t and p *iff* $(\exists u)(\forall v)[[<w,t,p> \in$
$V([\alpha]_{RC},r)(k)(v) \Leftrightarrow u = v]$ & $<w,t,p> \in \omega(u)]$, where $u,v \in D_N$.
Look at an example again:

(59) 1. $[[\underline{rel-der}]_{NP\ Nom}\ [hier]_{AdV}\ [ein]_{Aff}\ [geht]_{Fin}\ ]_{RC}$, (S7)
        who   here   enters   <N>

   2. $[[\underline{gen-der}]_{NP\ Nom}\ [hier]_{AdV}\ [ein]_{Aff}\ [geht]_{Fin}\ ]_{NP}$, (S13)
      $= wer,$ here   enters   *[Nom]*
      wer auch immer
      (who ever)

According to (S13). (59,2) is a description denoting the person entering
this place, whoever this may be. (S13) certainly needs some refinement. We cannot
yet treat cases like the following ones:

(60) Wo du bist, da bin auch ich.
       Where you are, there am also I.

(61) Wenn du gehst, dann gehe ich auch.
       When you go   then go   I   too.

Yet, the general line I would like to take should be clear from (S13).

d) Modification by relatives

I will now state the rule which combines RCs with terms. This rule is complicated. In order to ensure a better understanding, I shall therefore give
some examples first.

(62) A case of restriction

  1. $[Mann]_{CN}$ 2. $[der\ Liberty\ Valance\ erschoß]_{RC}$, S7

  3. $[Mann$ $[der\ Liberty\ Valance\ erschoß]_{RC}\ ]_{CN}$, S14

    4. [der]_{Det} , L11

5. [der Mann   [der Liberty Valance erschoß]_{RC}]_{NP} , S11
   the man   who L. V.   shot

(63) A relative in apposition to a demonstrative NP

1. [der_{17} Mann]_{NP} , S11

    2. [der L.V. erschoß]_{RC} , S7

3. -[der_{17} Mann   [der L.V. erschoß]_{RC}]_{NP} , S14
   the   man   who L.V. shot .

(64) Apposition to names

1. [Rom]   , S 2
   [$^{NP}_{Dat}$]

    2. [[wo] [Ede] [zu pennen] [glaubt]] , (44.7)
        AdV   NP   V   Fin RC
                                       <N>

3. [Rom [[wo] [Ede] [zu pennen] [glaubt]]] , S14
        AdV   NP   V   Fin RC [$^{NP}_{Dat}$]

    4. [in] , L10
        P
        <Dat>

5. [in Rom [wo Ede zu pennen glaubt]] , S8
                          RC PP

    6. [[leb]]   , Lexicon
              VP
            <[Nom]>

7. [[in Rom [wo Ede zu pennen glaubt]] [leb]] , S9
                          RC PP   V NP
                                       <[Nom]>

8. [[in Rom [wo Ede zu pennen glaubt]] [leb-t]] , S1_1
                          RC PP   Fin VP
                                          <[Nom]>

    9. [Lidia] , Lexicon
           NP
           [Nom]

10. [[Lidia] [in Rom [wo Ede zu pennen glaubt]] [lebt]] , S3
     NP   RC PP   S
    Lidia   in Rome where Ede to sleep believes   lives

(65) Quantifier restriction

1. [*neg pro*   *3.Pers Sing Nom Mas*] , L15
                                  NP
    = *niemand* (= no one)

      2. [*der Ede kennt*] , S7
                   RC

3. [*niemand* [*der Ede kennt*]] , S14
                           RC NP
   no one   who Ede knows

(66) Apposition to sentences

1. [*Suzanne will heiraten*]
                     S
    S.   wants to marry

      2. [*was Klaus-Jürgen mißbilligt*] , S7
                             RC
        what K.-J. disapproves   <S>

3. [*Suzanne will heiraten* [*was K.-J. mißbilligt*]] , S14
                                        RC S
   S.   wants to marry what K.-J. disapproves

(67) Apposition to infinitivals

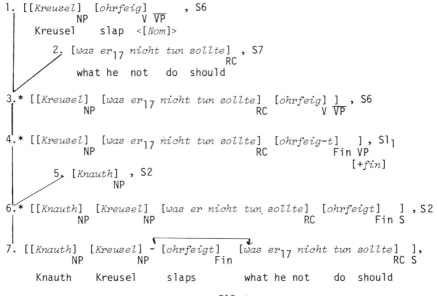

1. [[*Kreusel*] [*ohrfeig*]   , S6
         NP   V $\overline{VP}$
    Kreusel   slap <[*Nom*]>

      2. [*was er₁₇ nicht tun sollte*] , S7
                               RC
        what he not do should

3.* [[*Kreusel*] [*was er₁₇ nicht tun sollte*] [*ohrfeig*]] , S6
        NP   RC   V $\overline{VP}$

4.* [[*Kreusel*] [*was er₁₇ nicht tun sollte*] [*ohrfeig-t*]] , S1₁
        NP   RC   Fin VP
                                        [+*fin*]

      5. [*Knauth*] , S2
             NP

6.* [[*Knauth*] [*Kreusel*] [*was er nicht tun sollte*] [*ohrfeigt*]] , S2
        NP   NP   RC   Fin S

7. [[*Knauth*] [*Kreusel*] – [*ohrfeigt*] [*was er₁₇ nicht tun sollte*]],
        NP   NP   Fin   RC S
    Knauth   Kreusel   slaps   what he not   do should

                             S19, 'Extraposition of heavy
                                constituents'.

These examples show that a relative can modify a CN, a demonstrative NP, a name, an indefinite pronoun an S or a $\overline{VP}$. Hence we have to distinguish these cases, when we formulate the rule of relativization. This is a little bit tedious, of course.

$\underline{S14}_A$. *Modification by relatives*

Syntax:

$$[\alpha] , \quad [\beta] \quad \Rightarrow \quad [\gamma] \quad , \text{ where the following conditions hold:}$$
$$\quad A \quad \quad RC \quad \quad \quad \quad A$$
$$\quad \quad \quad <B>$$

1. $\gamma = \alpha \underset{RC}{[\beta]}$ and A = CN, S, $\overline{S}$ or NP. In the last case, α is either a name,

   a demonstrative phrase, or an indefinite pronoun; <u>or</u>

   $\gamma = \underset{RC}{[\beta]} \, \alpha$ and A = $\overline{VP}$.

2. α is not modified by an RC, i.e. $\alpha \neq \alpha_1 \underset{RC}{[\beta]}$ and $\alpha \neq \underset{RC}{[\beta]} \, \alpha_1$.

3. The relative pronoun of β agrees in number, gender and type with α.

Condition 1 could be made more precise by means of an inductive definition like 3.1 or 3.2, given in the last section. Condition 3 means the following. If A is subcategorized by num(a) gen(b), then the '*rel-pro* in β is followed by num(a) and gen(b), too, or it is an AdV. If A = S, $\overline{VP}$, then the relative pronoun is a *neutrum singularis*. Agreement in type means, that B is S, VP, if A = S, VP. Otherwise, B = N.

$\underline{S14}_A$. *Modification by relatives*

Semantics:

1. Let A be CN.

   $<w,t,p> \in F^1_{14}(k)(V(\underset{CN}{[\alpha]},r_1)(k),V(\underset{RC}{[\beta]},r_2)(k))(u): \leftrightarrow$

   $<w,t,p> \in V(\underset{CN}{[\alpha]},r_1)(k)(u)$ & $<w,t,p> \in V(\underset{RC}{[\beta]},r_2)(k)(u)$ for any $u \in U$.

2. A = NP and α is a name or a demonstrative term.

   $<w,t,p> \in F^2_{14}(k)(V(\underset{NP}{[\alpha]},r_1)(k),V(\underset{RC}{[\beta]},r_2)(k))(\omega): \leftrightarrow$

   $<w,t,p> \in V(\underset{NP}{[\alpha]},r_1)(k)(\omega) \cap V(\underset{NP}{[\alpha]},r_1)(k)(V(\underset{RC}{[\beta]},r_2)(k))$.

3. Suppose A = NP and α is an indefinite pronoun which has the form α_1

   $pro_i \, \alpha_2$. Then

   $<w,t,p> \in F^3_{14}(k)(V(\underset{NP}{[\alpha]},r_1)(k),V(\underset{RC}{[\beta]},r_2)(k))(\omega): \leftrightarrow$

   $<w,t,p> \in V(\underset{NP}{[\alpha]},r_1)(k*),$

   where k* is like k with the only exception that ν_k is replaced by

   $(\nu_k, V(\underset{RC}{[\beta]},r_2)(k) \, (\underset{CN}{[pro_i]}))$.

4. Suppose $A = S, \overline{S}$. Then

$<w,t,p> \in F_{14}^4(k)(V([\alpha]_A,r_1)(k),V([\beta]_{RC},r_2)(k)):\Leftrightarrow$

$<w,t,p> \in V([\alpha]_A,r_1)(k)$ & $<w,t,p> \in V([\beta]_{RC},r_2)(k)(V([\alpha]_A,r_1)(k))$.

5. Suppose $A = \overline{VP}$. Then

$<w,t,p> \in F_{14}^5(k)(V([\alpha]_{VP},r_1)(k),V([\beta]_{RC},r_2)(k))(\zeta):\Leftrightarrow$

$<w,t,p> \in V([\alpha]_{VP},r_1)(k)(\zeta)$ & $<w,t,p> \in V([\beta]_{RC},r_2)(k)(V([\alpha]_{VP},r_1)(k))$.

This rule accounts for all the examples we have discussed so far. Let us consider two examples.

L15. $F_{[neg\ pro_i\ 3.Pers\ Sing\ cas(a)\ gen(b)]}(k)(\omega)$

  is true in w at t and p: $\Leftrightarrow$

  $\sim(\exists u)[u$ is a person in w at t and $\nu([pro_i]_{CN})$ is true of u in w at t

  and p & $<w,t,p> \in \omega(u)]$.

Consider now (65.3). Suppose that $V([der\ Ede\ kennt]_{RC}, S7)$ (k) is the property of knowing Ede. Then F_{14}^3 makes sure that $V([niemand\ [der\ Ede\ kennt]_{RC}]_{NP}$, S14,) is true of a property ω iff $\sim(\exists u)[u$ is a person & u knows Ede & $\omega(u)]$. This is what we want.

Or consider (66.3), i.e. the sentence

$[Suzanne\ will\ heiraten\ [was\ Klaus\text{-}J\ddot{u}rgen\ mi\beta billigt]_{RC\ S}]_{<\overline{S}>}$
Suzanne wants marry   what K.-J. disapproves

Suppose $[Suzanne\ will\ heiraten]_S$ denotes the proposition that Suzanne wants to marry. Suppose further that $[was\ Klaus\text{-}J\ddot{u}rgen\ mi\beta billigt]_{RC\ <\overline{S}>}$ denotes the property which is true of a proposition p iff Klaus-Jürgen disapproves of p. Then, according to F_{14}^4, (66.3) denotes the proposition that Suzanne wants to marry and that Klaus-Jürgen disapproves that she wants to marry.

Next, consider (62). Suppose $[der\ Liberty\ Valance\ erscho\beta]_{RC}$ denotes the property which is true of a u if u shot Liberty Valance. Then. F_{14}^2 makes sure that $[Mann\ [der\ Liberty\ Valance\ erscho\beta]_{RC}]_{CN}$ is true of u if u is a man and u shot Liberty Valance.

Last, look at (63). Suppose, $V([der_{17}\ Mann]_{NP})$, S11, (k) is true of ω iff Tom Doniphon is a man and Tom Doniphon has ω. Then, by F_{14}^2, $V([der_{17}\ Mann$

[*der L.V. erschoß*]]   S14) (k) is true of ω iff Tom Doniphon is a man
               RC NP'
and he has ω and he shot Liberty Valance.

I think these examples show that the rule of relativization works quite nicely.

e) The last rules

I want to finish this article by stating some additional rules, which will enable the reader to also derive sentences that do not have the word-order of subordinate clauses. The most important rule in this respect is the movement rule which fronts the finite verb.

S15. *Fronting of the finite verb*

[[α]β]   ], A = [VP<B>], [S,-*comp*, -*top*]
   Fin A

[[β] α]
   Fin A

The semantics is identity.

S16. *Topicalization* (Drach's rule)

[[α] $β_1$[γ] $β_2$]
   Fin   A   [S-*top*]

A = NP cas(a), where a ≠ *Nom* or
A = $\overline{S}$, $\overline{VP}$, PP, AdV

[[γ] [α] $β_1β_2$]
   A   Fin   [S+*top*]

The semantics is identity. Consider an example

(68) 1. [[*im Bahnhof*]   pennte]   ]   , Sl_2
         | PP   Fin VP
         | <[*Nom*]>
         |
      2. [[*pennte*]   [*im Bahnhof*]] ,   S15 (fronting of *Fin* in *VP*)
         | Fin   PP VP
         | <[*Nom*]>
         |
         3. [*Ede*]   , S2
              [NP]
              [*Nom*]
         |
      4. [[*Ede*] [*pennte*]   [*im Bahnhof*]] , S3
           NP   Fin   PP S
           Ede   slept   in the station

(69) 1. [[*Ede*] [*im Bahnhof*] [*pennte*]] , S3
    NP   PP   Fin S

  2. [[*pennte*] [*Ede*] [*im Bahnhof*]] , S15 (fronting of *Fin* in *S*).
     Fin   NP   PP S

  3. [[*im Bahnhof*] [*pennte*]   [*Ede*]] , S16 (topicalization)
      PP   Fin   NP S
    in the station slept   Ede

Notice that there is a certain asymmetry between (68) and (69). In (68), the finite verb is moved within the VP. In (69), it is moved within the sentence. One could restrict *Fin*-movement to sentences and liberalize the topicalization rule (S16) in such a way that nominative NPs could also be topicalized. That is the way Thiersch proceeds.[20] This would permit a 'unified' analysis of (68) and (69), according to the following idea: first (S15) applies and then (S16), i.e., (68) would be derived just like (69):

(68a) *Thiersch's analysis of (68)*

  1. [[*pennte*]   [*Ede*] [*im Bahnhof*]] , (69.2)
     Fin   NP   PP S

  2. [[*Ede*] [*pennte*]   [*im Bahnhof*]] , S16 liberalized
     NP   Fin   PP S
    Ede   slept   in the station

I don't like this solution for two reasons. The first is a purely emotional one: I feel that the subject of (68) does not get moved. Its position is the normal unmarked place. The second reason is this: I want to generate coordinate predicates having different tenses directly, and without any rule like equi-NP-deletion. Consider a case like the following:

(70) Ede   pennte   gestern   im   Bahnhof
     Ede   slept   yesterday in   the station

     und   wird   morgen   auf   der   Polizeiwache   pennen.
     and   will   tomorrow at   the   police station sleep

The structure of the predicate should be something like the following:

(71) 1. [*pennte gestern im Bahnhof*]   , S15
                                 VP

    2. [*wird morgen auf der Polizeiwache pennen*]   , S15
                                               VP

  3. [[*pennte gestern im Bahnhof*] *und*
                             VP
    slept yesterday in the station and

    [*wird morgen auf der Polizeiwache pennen*]] , S17$_{VP}$ (VP-Conjunction)
                                         VP VP
    will tomorrow at the police station sleep

Evidently, in Thiersch's approach, the predicate of (70) can't have this structure. The following rule generates conjunctions.

$\underline{\underline{S17}}_A$. *Conjunction*

$$[\alpha_1]_{[A\delta]} \quad ,\ldots, \quad [\alpha_n]_{[A\delta]} \quad , \quad A = S,\ \overline{S},\ VP,\ \overline{VP},\ RC$$
$$\phantom{[\alpha_1]_{[A\delta]} \quad ,\ldots, \quad [\alpha_n]_{[A\delta]} \quad ,} <B>\ <B>\ <B>$$

$$[[\alpha_1]_{[A\delta]} \quad (und)\ [\alpha_2]_{[A\delta]} \ \ldots\ \{und\}\ [\alpha_n]_{[A\delta]} \ ]_{[A\delta]}$$

The first n-2 *und*'s are optional, and the last *und* is almost obligatory. The semantics is conjunction, i.e.

$$F_{17}^{S}(k)(V([\alpha_1]_A,r_1)(k),\ldots,V([\alpha_n]_A,r_1)(k)) =$$
$$V([\alpha_1]_A,r_1)(k)\ \cap\ \ldots\ \cap\ V([\alpha_n]_A,r_1)(k),\ \text{if}\ A = S,\ \overline{S}$$

and

$$F_{17}^{VP}(k)(V([\alpha_1]_A,r_1(k),\ldots,V([\alpha_n]_A,r_1)(k))(\omega) =$$
$$V([\alpha_1]_A,r_1)(k)(\omega)\ \cap\ \ldots\ \cap\ V([\alpha_n]_A,r_1)(k)(\omega),\ \text{if}\ A = VP,\ \overline{VP},\ RC.$$
$$\phantom{V([\alpha_1]_A,r_1)(k)(\omega)\ \cap\ \ldots\ \cap\ V([\alpha_n]_A,r_1)(k)(\omega),\ \text{if}\ A = } <B>\ <B>\ <B>$$

It is possible, of course, to conjoin expressions belonging to other categories as well. But here I will not be concerned with this.

$\underline{\underline{S18}}$. *VP-negation*

$$[\alpha\beta]_{VP}\ \begin{bmatrix} <A> \\ -fin \\ -neg \end{bmatrix} \quad , \text{ where } \alpha \text{ is a sequence of NPs, possibly empty.}$$

The first member of β is no NP.

$$[\alpha\ nicht\ \beta]_{VP}\ \begin{bmatrix} <A> \\ -fin \\ +neg \end{bmatrix}$$

$F_{18}(k)(V([\alpha\beta]_{VP},r_1)(k))(\zeta)$ is true in w at t and p iff

$V([\alpha\beta]_{VP},r_1)(k)(\zeta)$ is false in w at t and p.

We can now generate sentence (6):

(72) 1. [*Lidia, die eine Römerin ist*] , S14
　　　　　Lidia who a　　Roman　is NP

　　　　　2. [[*den Duce*] [*lieb*]] , S6
　　　　　　　　　　　NP　　　V VP
$$\begin{bmatrix} -fin \\ -neg \end{bmatrix}$$

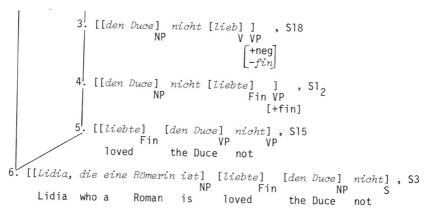

3'. [[*den Duce*] *nicht* [*lieb*]] , S18
     NP   V VP
$$\begin{bmatrix} +neg \\ -fin \end{bmatrix}$$

4'. [[*den Duce*] *nicht* [*liebte*]] , Sl$_2$
     NP   Fin VP
                [+fin]

5'. [[*liebte*] [*den Duce*] *nicht*] , S15
     Fin   VP   VP
    loved   the Duce not

6. [[*Lidia, die eine Römerin ist*] [*liebte*] [*den Duce*] *nicht*] , S3
                 NP   Fin   NP   S
   Lidia who a Roman is loved the Duce not

Given an appropriate meaning rule for [*lieb*]$_V$(=love), (72.6) expresses the proposition that Lidia is a Roman and Lidia did not love the Duce.

The last rule is a very rough sketch of the movement rule which extraposes 'heavy constituents'.

<u>S19</u>. *Extraposition of heavy constituents*

The premiss of the rule is either of form (1) or of form (2),where B = [VP<C>] or S.

1. $[\alpha_1 [\beta]\ \alpha_2\ [\alpha_3]\ ]$, where A = $\overline{VP}$, $\overline{S}$, PP, RC
      A   V B
2. $[\alpha_1 [\beta_1 [\beta]\ \ \ ]\ \alpha_2\ [\alpha_3]\ ]$, where A$_1$ = NP, PP
          RC A$_1$ V R

The conclusion has the form (1) or (2), respectively:

1. $[\alpha_1 \alpha_2 [\alpha_3]\ [\beta]\ ]$
           V A B
2. $[\alpha_1 [\beta_1 \beta_2]\ \alpha_1\ [\alpha_3]\ [\beta]\ ]$
          A$_1$ V RC B
The semantics is identity.

An example where the first clause of this rule did apply was (67.7). Clause (2) is needed for a derivation of the following kind:

(73) 1. [[*Klaus-Jürgen*] [*möchte*] [*die Frau*
          NP   Fin
    Klaus-Jürgen wants   the woman
   [*die er liebt*]] [*heiraten*]] , S3
          RC NP   V S
   whom he loves   marry

2. [[*K.-J.*] [*möchte*] [*die Frau*] [*heiraten*] [*die er liebt*]] (S19,
     NP   Fin   NP   V   RC case 2)

From these examples, it should be clear how I treat movement. There are, of course, more complicated cases than the ones treated here. It would be an intriguing task to integrate the recent work of M.I.T. linguists into a Montague framework. It is one of the purposes of this paper to give further evidence that Montague Grammar and Transformational Grammar are not incompatible at all.[21]

Let me finish this article with a remark concerning the problem of 'double-binding'. If you do not carefully control movement, then you are able to iterate the rule of relative-formation. In Thomason's fragment[22] you can derive a sentence like the following one:

(74) The fish which John has dated a woman who loves swims.

This sentence is supposed to express the following proposition:

(75) The fish such that John has dated a woman who loves that fish swims.

The essential step in the derivation of (74) is 'double-relativization':

(76) $wh\text{-}him_{17}$ [John has dated a woman [who loves $\quad-\quad$]]
$$\text{S} \quad \text{S}$$

You may say that a movement such as that in (76) violates some island constraint. Or you may formulate the rule of relative formation in a rather strict way. I have done the latter. It is easily checked that 'double-binding' is not possible in my grammar.

Notes

1 Cf. [32].

2 All indefinite pronouns seem to originate from a combination of quantificational particles and deictic words. For instance, *niemand* (no one) comes from *nio* + *man* (= never man). This fact gives some support to David Lewis' analysis of quantifiers in [21].

3 Cf. [3]. Bach & Cooper use a different notation.

4 Cf. [14 , p. 37ff.]

5 Although I like Bach & Cooper's NP-S-analysis, I don't like the way they treat the iteration. They introduce a new free variable into the relative clause. This seems to be unmotivated. I would simply restrict the assignment ν in (16). It should be $(\nu, \psi \cap \nu([pro_i]_{CN}) / [pro_i]_{CN}$, where "$\cap$" denotes property conjunction. This would make iteration possible.

6 Vide, for instance, [8].
  Cf. also [32].

7 Cf. [37].

8 Cf. [1].

9 This is, more or less, Kaplan's terminology. Cf. [18].

10 A more sophisticated context-theory is found in [20].

11 $\mathbb{P}(M)$ is the power set of the set M.

12 M^N is the set of all functions from N into M.

13 In 2.2, we stipulated that the outputs of a rule were all of the same category.

14 Cf. EFL, section 7, where this technique is explained in detail.

15 Unfortunately, German orthography always suppresses the index '17'.

16 Vide [5].

17 Notice that having infinitivals as complements of 'believe' fits nicely with what D. Lewis says about this verb in a recent paper called 'Attitudes de Dicto and de Se'.

18 Cf., for instance, [36], where this point is discussed in more detail.

19 Cf. [8].

20 Cf. [36].

21 Cf. also [10].

22 Cf. [37]. Thomason is aware of this problem, of course.

References:

1. BACH, E.: 'Montague Grammar and Classical Transformational Grammar'. Conference on Montague Grammar, Philosophy and Linguistics. State University of New York, Albany, April 23-24, 1977

2. BACH, E.: 'The order of elements in a transformational grammar of German'. Language 38, pp. 263-269, 1962

3. BACH, E. and Cooper, R.: 'The NP-S -Analysis of Relatives and Compositional Semantics'. Linguistics and Philosophy 2, 1978

4. BÄUERLE, R.: 'Tempus, Temporaladverb und temporale Fraġe'. Diss., Konstanz 1977

5. BÄUERLE, R. and von STECHOW, A.: 'Finite and non-finite temporal constructions in German'. To appear in the proceedings of the Stuttgart Conference Tense and Quantifiers, April 1979

6. BIERWISCH, M.: Grammatik des deutschen Verbs. Studia Grammatica II, 8. Aufl. 1973

7. BLATZ, F.: Neuhochdeutsche Grammatik Vol. 2, Lang'sche Verlagsbuchhandlung, Karlsruhe 1896

8. CHOMSKY, N.: 'On Binding'.
   Manuscript 1978

9. COOPER, R.: 'Toward a semantic account of constraints on movement rules'.
   Manuscript, Chicago 1977

10. COOPER, R. and PARSONS, T.: 'Montague Grammar, Generative Semantics
    and Interpretive Semantics'.
    in: [28], pp. 311-362

11. CRESSWELL, M.J.: Logics and Languages. London 1973 (Methuen)

12. CRESSWELL, M.J.: 'Prepositions and point of view' (1977).
    To appear in Linguistics and Philosophy.

13. DONNELLAN, K.S.: 'Proper names and identifying descriptions'.
    Synthese 21.

14. DRUBIG, H.B.: Untersuchungen zur Syntax und Semantik der Relativsätze
    im Englischen. Diss. Stuttgart 1970

15. EMONDS, J.: A Transformational Approach to English Syntax.
    Academic Press 1976

16. EVANS, G.: 'Pronouns, Quantifiers, and Relative Clauses'.
    Canadian Journal of Philosophy, Vol. VII, no. 3., Sept. 1977

17. GRANDY, R.E.: 'Anadic Logic and English'.
    Synthese 1975
    (The paper originally presented at the conference was much in the spirit
    of this article.)

18. KAPLAN, D.: Demonstratives. An Essay on the Semantics, Logics, Meta-
    physics and Epistemology of Demonstratives and other Indexicals.
    Manuscript (UCLA), March 1977

19. KLEIN, E.: On Sentences which report beliefs, desires ans other mental
    attitudes.
    Diss. Cambridge 1978

20. KRATZER, A.: Semantik der Rede. Kontexttheorie - Modelwörter - Kondi-
    tionalsätze.
    Königstein/TS. 1978 (Scriptor)

21. LEWIS, D.K.: 'Adverbs of Quantification'.
    In: Keenan, E. (ed.): Formal Semantics of Natural Language.
    Cambridge 1975 (University Press)

22. LEWIS, D.K.: Index, Context and Content.
    Manuscript, Princeton 1977

23. McCLOSKEY, J.: Questions and Relative Clauses in Modern Irish.
    Diss. Austin (Texas) 1977

24. MONTAGUE, R.: Formal Philosophy.
    ed. by R.H. Thomason, Yale Univ. Press 1974

25. MONTAGUE, R.: 'The proper Treatment of Quantification in Ordinary English', (= PTQ). In [24], pp. 247-270

26. MONTAGUE, R.: 'English as a Formal Language', (= EFL). In: [24], pp. 188-221

27. MONTAGUE, R.: 'Universal Grammar', (= UG). In: [24], pp. 222-246

28. PARTEE, B.H. (ed.) Montague Grammar. Academic Press 1976

29. PARTEE, B.H.: 'Some Transformational Extensions of Montague Grammar'. In: [28], pp. 51-76

30. PARTEE, B.H.: 'Montague Grammar and the Well-Formedness Constraint'. L.A.U.T., No. 45, 1977

31. REINHART, T.: The Syntactic Domain of Anaphora. M.I.T.-Diss. 1976

32. RODMAN, R.: 'Scope Phenomena, Movement Transformations - and Relative Clauses'. In: [28], pp. 165-176

33. STALNAKER, R.: Assertion. Manuscript 1975

34. von STECHOW, A.: 'Deutsche Wortstellung und Montague Grammatik'. In: Working papers of the SFB 99 'Linguistics', 1978 to be published in: Koerner & Meisel (ed.): Generative Grammar and Word-Order

35. von STECHOW, A.: 'Presupposition and Context', to appear in: Drubig/Günthner/Mönnich (eds.): Philosophical Logic

36. THIERSCH, C.L.: Topics in German Syntax. M.I.T.-Diss. 1978

37. THOMASON, R.H.: 'Some Extensions of Montague Grammar'. In: [28].

The Stoic Concept of Anaphora

Urs Egli

Universität Konstanz, Sonderforschungsbereich 99, 'Linguistik',
Postfach 5560, D-7750 Konstanz, Fed. Rep. of Germany

Two theories of the Stoics will be reconstructed systematically and compared
with modern concepts. First, the historical antecedents from the Stoa onwards
of MONTAGUE's semantics for noun phrases will be discussed. I will give
translations and interpretations of texts by the Stoics LOCKE, LEIBNIZ,
the logicians of PORT-ROYAL, FREGE and MONTAGUE. This discussion will con-
firm and expand LEWIS' presentation, in his "General Semantics", of the
relation between historically given theories and modern systems.

   Several difficulties with FREGE's and MONTAGUE's approach to noun phrase
semantics will then arise. One of these concerns the semantic treatment of
sentences like

> "If anyone is in Athens, it is not the case that he is
> in Rhodos." (CHRYSIPPUS)

Most current theories treat this sentence as if its form were:

> "For every x: if x is in Athens, it is not the case that x is
> in Rhodos."

   But the Stoics gave another account of these natural language phenomena,
in that they interpreted these constructions directly without recourse to
paraphrase. In order to show how this can be done I will present the Stoic's
and ancient grammarians' theories of anaphora. At first sight these might
seem rather obscure. But by trying to make sense of them, we are able to
construct a NP+anaphora logic which turns out to be a viable alternative
to the more usual Bound-variable+quantifier logic. While being justifiable
from the logical point of view, it nevertheless directly treats some natural
language phenomena which before had to be paraphrased in order to be amenable
to a semantic treatment.

I.

SEXTUS, who in this is influenced somehow by the Stoics, says at Adversus
Mathematicos 7.246:

> "Of men some are Greeks, some are barbarians, but the generic man is
> neither Greek - because otherwise every specific man would be Greek -
> nor barbarian for the same reason."

The generic man, according to SEXTUS, does not possess a property if and only if not every man has that property. Put positively, the generic man has a property if and only if every man possesses it. But according to this criterion, there are properties that the generic man has not and whose negation he has not either. This is incompatible with the principle of bivalence, but can be avoided if we do not maintain that the generic man is an individual, but rather that he is a set of properties, viz. those every man has. This seems to be the effect of the Stoic definition of generic entities at DIOGENES LAERTIOS 7.60:

"A generic entity is a collection of several concepts which cannot be taken away (from the collection), e.g. the generic animal. This extends to the individual animals."
Let me briefly comment upon this passage. We first have the individual animal and the concepts of them (*ennoêma*). With the concepts of individuals we associate concepts of properties possessed by the individuals. A maximal specific generic entity (*eidikôtaton*) which corresponds to a given individual concept is the collection of property concepts associated with this individual concept. If we take away from the specific general entities corresponding to individual men every concept that is not common to all of them we get the generic man who consists of the concepts of properties every man possesses.

LOCKE in his Essay 4.7.9 speaks of the general idea of a triangle which is *neither* rectangular nor equilateral, but all the same *both* rectangular and equilateral. The first part of the characterization is clear: The generic triangle is an analogue to the generic man familiar to us by now.But either the generic triangle consists of those properties every triangle has - it then is not rectangular - or it consists of the properties some or other triangle has - then it is rectangular. Both alternatives make sense, but they have to be distinguished. So we are led to accept both the universal generic man, who consists of the properties every man has, and the particular generic man, who consists of the properties that some or other man has. LEIBNIZ writes:
ed. GERHARDT 2, 131:

"Je supplie V.A. de demander à M. ARNAULD comme d'elle même, s'il croit veritablement qu'il y a un si grand mal de dire que chaque chose (soit espece, soit individu ou personne) a une certaine notion parfaite, qui comprend tout ce qu'on en peut enoncer veritablement, selon la quelle notion Dieu (qui conçoit tout en perfection) conçoit la dite chose."
ibid. 43:

"Après cela je croy tous les doutes doivent desparoistre, car disant que la notion individuelle d'Adam enferme tout ce qui lui arrivera à jamais, je ne veux dire autre chose, si non ce que tous les philosophes entendent en disant praedicatum inesse subjecto verae propositionis."

Here the universal generic man is distinguished from the property or species man. It is called the perfect notion of man. Further, the perfect notion of an individual is introduced, i.e. the collection of properties this individual possesses. Third, a truth condition for subject-predicate sentences is given. A sentence consisting of subject and predicate is true iff the property expressed by the predicate is in the collection of properties expressed by the subject. This is offered by LEIBNIZ as an explication of the traditional Aristotelian dictum: the predicate is contained in the subject of a true proposition. Thus, the generic man must be considered to constitute the semantic counterpart of the noun phrase "every man" rather than of the common noun "man".

The construction of the perfect notion of an individual is closely related with LEIBNIZ' thesis of the identity of indiscernibles. According to it two individuals are identical iff the properties of the first are just the properties of the second. We can use this fact in two ways:

1) as a definition of the concept of identity between individuals

2) as the statement of a one-to-one correspondence between the set of properties an individual has and the individual itself.

LEIBNIZ' perfect notion of Adam exemplifies the second use of the principle of the identity of indiscernibles.

The subdivision of the concept of idea in the logique du PORT-ROYAL is closely connected with this line of thought. Somewhat simplified it is as follows:

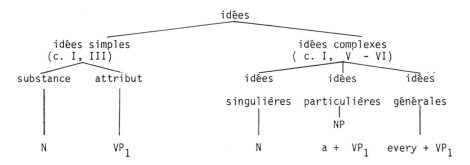

The syntactic categories indicated give an idea of the ways in which we can use the categories of ideas as semantic counterparts of linguistic categories. By the way, the concept of substance is sometimes identified with the singular idea, the concept of attribute with the universal idea. Both identifications are justified by a one-to-one correspondence between the respective entities.

The next step was made by GOTTLOB FREGE who pointed out that the noun phrase "four" has a second order concept as its semantical value which is possessed by first order concepts. He paraphrased the article "kein" (no) by "nichts" (nothing) or "0":

(1) Venus has no moon

(2) Nothing is a moon of Venus

In a similar way "vier" (four) used as an article is paraphrased by an autonomous use of this word as a noun phrase:

(3) The carriage of the emperor is drawn by four horses

(4) Four are the horses that draw the carriage of the emperor

Nothing and Four are then regarded as concepts of the second level predicated of concepts of the first level like horses that draw the carriage of the emperor. (Grundlagen der Arithmetik p. 59ff.)

In "Begriff und Gegenstand 197ff. "alle" (all) is regarded as a two place second order predicate which holds between "man" and "is mortal", though GEACH in Reference and Generality 1968, p. 58 has pointed out that LEIBNIZ' solution would have been compatible with FREGE's approach too. In a way, this solution is contained in FREGE's Begriffsschrift.

A reduction of a good many noun phrases to "all" considered as a second order concept, "if-then" considered as meaning material implication and "not" is given in FREGE's Begriffsschrift. According to this theory the syntactical positions of quantifiers and proper names are totally different. The sentences "everybody is glad" and "John is glad" are given structures of the following kind:

(5) every x: x is glad

(6) John is glad

FREGE was aware himself that this treatment of quantifiers was a radical novelty:

Begriffsschrift 4:

Bei dem ersten Entwurfe einer Formelsprache ließ ich mich durch das Beispiel der Sprache verleiten, die Urtheile aus Subject und Prädicat zusammenzusetzen. Ich überzeugte mich aber bald, daß dies meinem besondern Zwecke hinderlich war und nur zu unnützen Weitläufigkeiten führte.

Begriffsschrift p. VII:

Insbesondere glaube ich, daß die Ersetzung der Begriffe *Subject* und *Praedicat* durch *Argument* und *Function* sich auf die Dauer bewähren wird. Man erkennt leicht, wie die Auffassung eines Inhalts als Function eines Argumentes begriffsbildend wirkt. Es möchte ferner der Nachweis des Zusammenhanges zwischen den Bedeutungen der Wörter: *wenn, und, nicht, oder, es giebt, einige, alle* u.s.w. Beachtung verdienen.

One of the side effects of these novelties was that for the first time FREGE could give a reasonable representation of quantifiers in object position. In a sentence like

(7) Peter sees a house

there is no part which corresponds to an attribute which could be thought to be included in the particular generic house, i.e. in the set of properties possessed by at least one house. FREGE, in effect, pointed out that implicitly there is such an attribute present: Take

(8) a sees b

We can forge an attribute

(9) to be seen by a

or more explicitly

(10) the attribute which an individual x possesses if a sees x

(11) Lx (a sees x)

Now this attribute must be in the particular generic house, if the sentence

(12) a sees a house

is to be true.
FREGE then introduced the further novelty of writing

(13) Vx fx $\quad(\overset{x}{\frown}\,fx)$

as shorthand for

(14) V Lx fx

MONTAGUE's theory of noun phrases (MONTAGUE 1975, 241: definition
$H_0 - H_4$) is a combination of FREGE's ideas and those of FREGE's predecessors,
esp. those of LEIBNIZ. He in effect constructed a language containing the
category of noun phrases, but he showed how to translate these constructions
into a FREGE-type language. His languages are intensional, but this is an
inessential feature, as I showed in EGLI 1974 that there is an extensional
version of noun phrase semantics which has just the expressive power of
quantification theory. I also constructed a deductive system of noun phrase
logic and introduced some novelties like the treatment of NP-conjunction.

By now we have reached a point where we can fully appreciate LEWIS' remarks
in LEWIS 1972, 202f.

II.

Now, there are some problems with the MONTAGUE-FREGE approach to quantification considered as a model for the use of natural language noun phrases and
articles.

1) In FREGE's scheme, noun phrases are torn to pieces. A noun phrase like
"every man" does not survive translation into standard quantificational
language.

(15) every man is mortal

is rendered as

(16) for *every* x: *if* x is a *man*, then x is mortal

From the standpoint of naturalness, this seems to be a severe defect of
FREGE's scheme. MONTAGUE avoided it by interpreting noun phrases as having

characters as semantical counterparts. Characters are entities like the generic man, i.e. bundles of properties. One problem remains: is every set of properties a character? If we answer this question positively, we are forced to make sense of the bundle consisting of the properties an individual has if and only if p.
Which noun phrase corresponds to:

(17) Lf p ?

If, however, we answer the question negatively: how are we to draw the line between those sets that are characters and those that are not?

2) In FREGE's scheme the noun phrases do not appear at the places where they appear in natural language. Thus, a sentence like

(15) every man is mortal

is rendered as (16). In MONTAGUE's scheme the sentence is translated into a form of the following type:

(18) (every man) Lx (x is mortal)

The noun phrase is "exported" from the original place it appears in the natural language sentence. It leaves a bound variable at the original place which is bound by an occurrence of the same variable occurring after L ("x such that"). In a way, the equivalence of structures like (15) and (18) is offered by MONTAGUE as an explanation of the meaning of (15).

3) Even the official notation of MONTAGUE does not leave every occurrence of a noun phrase unchanged, if applied properly. In a way that is barely understood theoretically the noun phrase changes its quality if exported in contexts like

(19) if anyone (jemand = someone) is in Athens, he is not in Rhodos

These are called CHRYSIPPUS sentences. The standard formalization of sentence (19) has a universal quantifier instead of the particular one occurring at the surface.

(20) for every x: if x is in Athens, x is not in Rhodos

In the original sentence (19) an analogue of variable binding occurs. It is difficult to interpret. We traditionally say that the pronoun "he" is related anaphorically with "anyone" in the antecedent. But "he" does not stand in the scope of "anyone", as ordinary quantification theory would have it.

4) A similar phenomenon is the so-called BACH-PETERS sentences which only have paraphrases in standard quantification theory very far away from their natural language form:

(21) a schoolboy who deserves it wins a prize he deserves

(22) for some x: (x is a schoolboy and for some y: (y is a prize and x deserves y and x desires y and x wins y))

5) A final difficulty is constituted by those German sentences in which scope is indicated not by surface word order, but rather by suprasegmental means.

(23) eíne Sprache sprechen alle/ a language is spoken by everyone

(24) eine Sprache sprechen álle/ everyone speaks a language

paraphrased respectively as

(25) für ein x (x ist eine Sprache und für alle y (y spricht x))

(26) für alle y: für ein x: (x ist eine Sprache und y spricht x)

In the rest of this paper I will mainly be concerned with the third and fourth problems, viz. sentences like (19) and (21). I am working with Stoic type Greek, but in order to make the presentation easier to follow I shall translate the relevant Greek sentences into English. The main difference between the Greek structures considered and the English translations lies in the fact that English makes a some-any distinction which is absent from Greek (and German and French as that).

III.

I now shall proceed in the manner suggested by the historical sketch of NP-semantics. I shall sketch a tentative solution of the problems in the dark ages of logic and shall then try to make sense of this solution. The main concept involved is Anaphora. This word seems to have been used for the first time by the Stoics in a sense which basically is the traditional one. They invented this concept within the framework of their semantics of the article and the deictic noun phrase. The problem was to give an inter- pretation of four kinds of atomar sentences:

(27) with definite subject 1)   he is a linguist

(28) with quasi-definite subject 2)   John is a linguist

(29) with quasi-indefinite subject 3)   a man is a linguist
(Greek without "a")

(30) with indefinite subject 4)   someone is a linguist
(Greek someone = anyone)

The truth conditions of sentences of Type 2) - 4) stipulate that the sentence is true iff the logical product of the class of individuals related with the subject and the class related with the predicate is not null. "Someone" is associated with the universal class, the proper name "John" with the unit class consisting of John.

It proved to be more difficult for the Stoics to give sentence (27) a truth condition. They took the deictic use as their point of departure: We are pointing at a person in uttering the sentence. The sentence is then true according to this pointing (*Deixis)* iff the person pointed at is a linguist, i.e. an element of the class related semantically with the predicate. If, however, we consider sentences like

(31) If John is a linguist, then he is no philosopher

we are no longer entirely free to point at whatever we like if we are to explain the word "he". We need a new theory. "He" is used anaphorically, the Stoics said, it is understood with reference (*anaphora*) to "John". If we understand it to be explained deictically, the deixis must perforce be something different, a kind of mental pointing to John (*deixis tou nou*). Every definite subject thus can be used both deictically and anaphorically, the Stoics said. The definite subject is standing for the quasidefinite subject "John", for it could be substituted for it *salva veritate*. This fact lies at the origin of calling definite words of this type pronouns (standing for a noun). However, in the case of a definite subject being related anaphorically with an indefinite subject, substitution no longer preserves the truth value. Consider a sentence like

(32) If anybody (=somebody, *tis*) is a linguist, it is not the case, that he is a philosopher

Substituting "anybody" for "he" we get:

(33) If anybody is a linguist, it is not the case that anybody is a philosopher

which is not equivalent to sentence (32). This is called the paradox of general (indefinite and quasi-indefinite) terms by CHRYSIPPUS though of course the Stoics were well aware that this sentence is to be understood in a universal sense. They even called CHRYSIPPUS sentences universal (*katholika*). But they never succeeded to really give an exact theory of anaphora. By the way, the ordinary interpretation of Stoic sentence theory as an exact counterpart of modern formation rules of propositional logic is valid only for sentences having no anaphory relationships, as CLAUDE IMBERT seems to have noted first.

IV.

I shall now discuss an artificial language A whose syntactic rules are given in the context free grammar of Appendix 1) and for which precise transformation rules can be given (see Appendix 2). The language is expressively equivalent to quantification theory, but syntactically much closer to natural language by admitting

1) pronouns instead of variables

2) anaphora relationships instead of variable binding

3) scope relationships instead of automatically indicated scope

Some examples of sentences of this language can be found in Appendix 3).

Reflexives and relative clauses are not interpreted as cases of anaphoric relationship. They rather get an explanation involving predicate functors in the sense of QUINE. The reflexive pronoun is a predicate functor which identifies the first and last places of a predicate. Relativization is explained with the help of a predicate functor which fronts the argument being relativized.

(34) rasiert x x = (sich rasiert) x

(35) sieht a x   = (perm sieht) x a = (a perm sieht) x

(36) den a sieht = (rel a perm sieht) = Lx (a perm sieht) x

In languages like German the case of the relative pronoun indicates the argument place which is relativized and which in language A is the place of the fronting functor.

I am strictly separating two different problems lumped together by SMABY: I only give an explanation of possible anaphora relationships without trying to treat the problem of the most probable anaphora relationships associated with a sentence when uttered in a certain context. I think that problems of the second kind can be solved better if we already have a theory of possible anaphora.

Our notation was anticipated by BOURBAKI's official notation of set theoretic formulas though in practice he uses bound variables. Anaphora relationships are noted by writing a "+" beneath every item related anaphorically in the same row. In the general case we thus have several rows to work with. The problem of noting scope of indefinite pronouns and articles is separated from the problem left unsolved to decide whether an indefinite pronoun is to be taken in a specific sense (ein bestimmter) or in the unspecific sense (ein gewisser). We always presuppose the unspecific use of the indefinite article. The syntax of our language is similar to that of SMABY.

What is certainly unexpected in the present approach is the contention that rules very similar in nature to the interpretation rules of interpretive semantics (cp. COOPER-PARSONS) arise already in logic. It was known that there exist systems of logic with the same expressive power as quantification theory which do not contain bound variables. QUINE's predicate functor logic is an example. Language A is one more such system. It is specifically designed to solve the problem of CHRYSIPPUS sentences, and Stoic type anaphora theory in general.

V.

I now want to give the motivation behind the rule dealing with CHRYSIPPUS sentences. I am proceeding in five steps.

Step 1. I first note that the standard formalization of

(44) somebody + predicate

is

(45) for some x: x + predicate

Step 2. This formalization is not applicable to every occurrence of a construction like (44). In a sentence of the type

(46) if (anybody (= somebody) + predicate), then sentence

this translation is correct only if, in the consequent, there are no items related anaphorically with "somebody" in the antecedent. An example where this condition is not met is:

(47) if anybody (somebody) is in Athens, he is not in Rhodos

A general rule for somebody/anybody in this context would have to export the existential quantifier changing it to a universal one.

Step 3. But is such a procedure valuable in the case in which no anaphora relationships hold? E.g.

(49) if anybody is in Rhodos, I also go there

Yes, for there is the logical theorem

(50) (for every x: if fx then p) iff (if for some x: fx then p)

Step 4. If there is to be a general rule of exportation of the quantifier at all we have to start from such a theorem and then to interpret the cases with anaphora relationships correspondingly.
Let us test another case:

Step 5. There is the theorem:

(51) (for some x: (fx and p)) iff ((for some x: fx) and p)

therefore

(52) somebody did that, and he left instantly

should mean

(53) for some x: (x did that, and x left instantly)

And this really is the case.

Thus, we have arrived at the following criterion for the interpretation of nonexported quantifiers:

(54) If
('connective + quantifier + fx + p' iff
'quantifier' x connective fx p')
is a law of quantification theory, then
'connective quantifier f p' is to be interpreted as
'quantifier' connective e f p' in language A.

We now have to treat two exceptions.

1) There are cases where anaphoric relationships are very unusual.

(55) if everybody does that, he will be punished.

Our criterion would assign a meaning to this sentence even if "he" is related anaphorically with "everybody".

(56) for some x: if x does that, then x will be punished.

But this fact does no harm, as sentence (55) is unacceptable syntactically. The syntactical constraints can be formulated independently by something very much like surface structure constraints.

2) There is no rule of quantification theory covering "if and only if". We thus have to interpret this as "if ..., then ..., and conversely".

(57) if, and only if anybody did that, he will be punished

(58) if anybody did this, he will be punished,
and conversely if anybody will be punished, he did this.

The criterion now is applicable.

3) English has two quantifiers in place of one in German and French:

(59) jemand - quelcun - tis - somebody/anybody

I am tentatively offering the following explanation:
"anybody" in English is standing for "jemand" if by application of the rules of our system this "jemand" (=S) can be traced back to a "everybody" (=P).

VI.

To conclude, I wish to make the following points:

1. The Stoic concept of anaphora can be made precise. The problems connected with it can be treated adequately in logic.

2. Our treatment is similar to modern treatments in linguistics, e.g. those of HINTIKKA and COOPER.

3. Special emphasis has been laid on CHRYSIPPUS sentences. The treatment contains a solution both for CHRYSIPPUS and BACH-PETERS sentences.

4. In addition to anaphoric pronouns, anaphoric articles are treated.

5. Use is made of predicate functors in the sense of QUINE in order to treat reflexives and relativization.

6. The resulting system has just the expressive capacity of quantification theory though it does not use bound variables, but rather anaphoric pronouns. The system is a variant of quantification theory very much like QUINES predicate functor logic. The rules given are translational. Whether they could be replaced by a kind of semantical rules is an open problem.

Appendix 1: Syntactic rules of the language A

S 1	Text → S (text)	Texts
S 2	S → Kon_2 SS	molecular sentences
S 3	S → Kon_1 S	negative sentences
S 4	S → NP VP (!)	subject-predicate sentences
S 5	S → NP S	left dislocation formation
S 6	VP_n → NP VP_{n+1}	noun phrase insertion
S 7	VP_n → sich VP_{n+1}	reflexive insertion
S 8	VP_n → perm VP_n	fronting of relativized argument
S 9	Rel S → rel VP_1/ such that S	relative phrase formation
S 10	VP_1 → (VP_1) Rel S	relative phrase insertion
S 11	VP_n → Kon_1 VP_n	predicate negation
S 12	NP → Art VP_1	article + appellative as noun phrase
S 13	NP → N	nouns as noun phrase
S 14	NP → Kon_2 NP NP	noun phrase composition
S 15	NP → Kon_1 NP	
S 16	NP → P, S, O, e every, some, no, he	
S 17	Art → P, S, O, d every, some, no, the	
S 18	Kon_1 → N not	constants
S 19	Kon_2 → B, C, K, A p, if q; if p,q, both p and q, p or q	
S 20	VP_2 → is	

Appendix 2: Transformation rules

R 1. $(- Q\ VP_1 -)$ /   Q (Konn (e VP_1) (- e -)
         +   +   +   +

      if Q = O, S, d,   then Konn = K

      if Q = P   ,   then Konn = C

Restriction: The left construction must be an atomar sentence without ! at the end. No quantifier with scope priority over that mentioned in the rule occurs in the atomar sentence.

R 2. $(S\ VP_1^!\ VP_1!)$ / $C(S\ (S\ VP_1)\ is\ (e\ VP_1^!))$
          +   +   +
                                                              +

R 3.   d (   )   /   (   )
         e

Restriction: The construction within the parentheses has to be a sentence.

R 4.   (e such that (-))   /   (-)
                        +   (+)   (+)
              +   +

Restriction: The construction (-) is a sentence. Every item anaphorically related with "such that" is put in the same anaphora class as the e mentioned.

R 5.   (- Q -)   /   (Q (- e -))
              +   +   +

Restriction: The quantifier is occurring autonomously. No quantifier with scope priority over that mentioned in the rule occurs in the sentence (-- Q --).

R 6. $N(Q...)$ / $Q'(N...)$
          +   +

$(Q...)$ is an VP_n or an S.

If Q = P then Q' in S and vice versa. If Q = 0 then Q' = SN

R 7.   (- NN -)   /   (- -)

R 8. a) C Q(-) ( )   Q' C (-) ( )
          +   +

        C (- Q -) ( )   Q' C (- e -) ( )
             +   +   +

        B ( ) Q (-)   Q' B (   ) (-)
              +   +

        B ( ) (- Q -)   Q' B (   ) (- e -)
                  +   +   +

    b) K   ' K
       A   Q(-) ( )   Q (A (-) ( )
       B   +   + B

       K   K
       A   (- Q -) ( )   Q (A (- e -) ( ))
       B   +   + B   +

```
K                              K
A   ( ) Q( - )                 Q(A ( ) ( - ))
C        +                     + C

K                              K
A   ( ) (- Q - )               Q(A ( ) ( - e - ))
C          +                   + C            +
```

Restriction: The rule is to be applied only if there is no quantifier in the whole construction which is prior to that mentioned.

R 9. a) $(e\ VP_1\ rel\ VP_1')$ / $K(e\ VP_1)\ (e\ VP_1')$
            +   +   +

b) $(e\ VP_1\ such\ that\ (-))$ / $K(e\ VP_1)\ (-)$
                            +   (+)
         +   +   (+)

R 10.   n times

$(e\ e\ ...\ e\ \ \ perm\ VP_n)$ / $(e\ e\ e\ ...\ VP_n)$
   +   +
      +   +
         +   +

R 11.   n times

$(e\ \ .\ .\ .\ e\ N\ VP_n)$ / $N(e\ ...\ e\ VP_n)$

R 12.   in times

$(e\ \ .\ .\ .\ e\ such\ VP_{n+1})$ / $(e\ .\ .\ .\ e\ e\ \ VP_{n+1})$
   +   +   +

R 13. $Q(\ .\ .\ .\ e\ .\ .\ .\ e\ ...\ )$ / $Qx(\ ...\ x\ ...\ x\ ...)$
           +   +   +

Restriction: No one of the rules 1-12 is applicable to the construction; there are no anaphora relationships of the Q mentioned outside the construction. Every e anaphorically related with the Q is replaced by x. There is no capture of variables; i.e. "x" is not free for e at every place it is replaced by x.

Appendix 3: Some examples of sentences

(1)   every man is mortal

```
P       man     mortal
|        |        |
Art     VP_1     VP_1
  \_NP_/
      \___S___/
```

(a)   P man mortal
       +

(b)   P C e man e mortal
R 1   + +   +

(c)   Px Cx man x mortal
R 13

(2)   if anyone is in Athens, then he is not in Rhodos

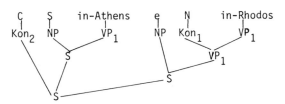

(a)   C S in-Athens e N in-Rhodos
         +   +

(b)   P C e in-Athens e N in-Rhodos
R 8   + +   +

(c)   P C e in-Athens N e in-Rhodos
R 11 + +   +

(d)   P x C x in-Athens N x in-Rhodos
R 13

(3)   The schoolboy who deserves it wins a prize he desires

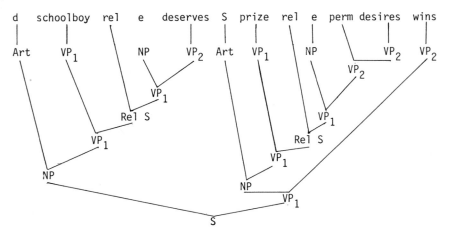

(a) d schoolboy rel e deserves S prize rel e perm desires wins
     +   +
                         +   +

(b) dK(e schoolboy rel e deserves)(e(S prize rel e perm desires wins))
R 1 + +   +   +
                            +   +

(c) K(e schoolboy rel e deserves)(e(S prize e perm desires)wins)
R 3   +   +   +
                       +   +

(d) K(e schoolboy rel e deserves)SK(e prize rel e perm desires)(e e wins)
R 1   +   +   +
                       +   + +   +

(e) SK(e schoolboy rel e deserves)K(e prize rel e perm desires)(e e wins)
R 8   +   +   +
     +   +   +   +

(f) SKK(e schoolboy)(e e deserves)KK(e prize)(e e perm desires)(e e wins)
R 9   +   +   +   +
     +   +   +   +   +

(g) SKK(e schoolboy)(e e deserves)KK(e prize)(e e desires)(e e wins)
R 10   +   +   +   +
     +   +   +   +   +

(h) SxKK y schoolboy yx deserves KKx prize yx desires yx wins
R 13

(4)   not any cat is a reptile

   (a)   N S cat reptile
                +

   (b)   N S K e cat e reptile
   R 1   +   +   +

   (c)   P N K e cat e reptile
   R 6   +   +   +

   (d)   P x N K x cat x reptile
   R 13

(5)   anyone who is rather stupid is incompetent

   (a)   S rel stupid incompetent !

   (b)   C S S rel stupid is e incompetent
   R 2   +   +
                   +

   (c)   P C e S rel stupid is e incompetent
   R 8   +   +
             +   +

(d)   P C S K e rel stupid e e is e incompetent
R 1   + +   +   +
      +   +

(e)   P P S K e rel stupid e e is e incompetent
R 8   + +   +   +
      +   +

(f)   P P C K e stupid e e is e incompetent
         + +   +   +
R 9 a) +   +

(g)   P y P x C K x stupid y x is x incompetent
R 13

   This is logically equivalent to

   P x C x stupid x incompetent

   if "is" is taken to be identity

References

1. R.H. Cooper: Montague's Semantic Theory and Transformational Syntax.
(Ann Arbor, Xerox Univ.Microfilms, 1975)

2. R.H. Cooper/T. Parsons: Montague Grammar, Generative Semantics and Interpretive Semantics. in Montague Grammar , ed. by B. Partee (New York etc.,
Academic Press, 1976)

3. U. Egli: Semantische Repräsentation der Frage. in Dialectica 27, 363-370
(1973)

4. U. Egli: Ansätze zur Integration der Semantik in die Grammatik. in
Forschungen Linguistik und Kommunikationswissenschaft 3 (Scriptor, Kronberg
1974)

5. J. Hintikka: Logic, Language-Games and Information. (Clarendon Press,
1973)

6. J. Hintikka: Quantifiers vs. Quantification Theory. in Linguistic
Inquiry 5, 153-177 (1974)

7. J. Hintikka: Quantifiers in Logic and Quantifiers in Natural Language.
in Philosophy of Logic, ed. by St. Körner (Basil Blackwell, Oxford, 1976)

8. J. Hintikka: Quantifiers in Natural Languages: some Logical Problems II.
in Linguistics and Philosophy 1, 153-172, (1977)

9. J. Hintikka/L. Carlson: Pronouns of Laziness in Game-Theoretical Semantics.
in Theoretical Linguistics 4, 1-29, (1977)

10. J. Hintikka/E. Saarinen: Semantical Games and the Bach-Peters Paradox.
in Theoretical Linguistics 2, 1-19 (1975)

11. C. Imbert: Sur la Méthode en Histoire de la Logique. in ISILC Logic Conference, ed. by G.H. Müller, A. Oberschelp, K. Potthoff. Proceedings of the International Summer Institute and Logic Colloquium, Kiel 1974. (Springer, Berlin/Heidelberg/New York, 1975) 363-383

12. D. Lewis: General Semantics. in Semantics of Natural Language, ed. by D. Davidson, G. Harman (Reidel, Dordrecht, 1972) Synthese Library

13. B. Mates: Leibniz on Possible Worlds. in Logic, Methodology, and Philosophy of Science III, ed. by B. van Rootselaar, J.F. Staal (North-Holland, Amsterdam, 1968)

14. R. Montague: Formal Philosophy. Selected Papers of Richard Montague, edited and with an Introduction by R.H. Thomason. (Yale University Press, New Haven /London, 1974)

15. R.T. Schmidt/K.-H. Hülser/U. Egli: Die Grammatik der Stoiker. Deutsch von K. Hülser. Bibliographie von U. Egli. (SFB 99 Linguistik, Konstanz, 1978) Especially p. 60-63

16. R. Smaby: Ambiguity of Pronouns. (Mimeo University of Pennsylvania.)

17. R. Smaby: Ambiguous Coreference with Quantifiers. (Mimeo Univ.of Pennsylvania)

Expression and Content in Stoic Linguistic Theory

Karlheinz Hülser

Universität Konstanz, Sonderforschungsbereich 99, 'Linguistik',
Postfach 5560, D-7750 Konstanz, Fed. Rep. of Germany

During the last decades interest in the dialectics of the Stoics has grown
remarkably. It contains a lot of linguistic and logical points which are of
historical originality and are considered to anticipate many modern ideas.
Thus the interpretation of the Stoic linguistic theory has made important
progress. Nevertheless the overall structure of Stoic dialectics is still an
unsolved problem since neither the concept nor the classification of dialectics is quite clear. The Stoics characterized their discipline by some definitions which are very different from one another, and they subdivided it in
a way which has not yet been sufficiently accounted for. The two parts of dialectics were entitled *peri sēmainontōn* and *peri sēmainomenōn*, i.e. in verbal
translation: 'On the signifying' and 'On the signified' respectively. Other
translations of a more or less interpretive character are: 'On expression /
On content', 'On language / On discourse', 'On utterance / On utterance as
meaningful'. All these translations are considered in the specialist literature.[1] Their diversity points to the problem of interpretation. In the title
of this paper I used the rather imprecise translation 'expression' and 'content' in order to indicate this problem. In what follows I will try to clarify
the Stoic concept of dialectics, to determine the fundamental aim of the dialectics, and to develop the classification of this discipline. But first the
problems encountered in this field should be delineated.

I

The Stoics divided philosophy into three parts: logic, physics, and ethics.
Diogenes Laertius writes in 7,39 that Zeno of Citium, the founder of the Stoa,
was the first to make this division. But in 7,2 he reports that Zeno was a
hearer of Xenocrates; and from Sextus Empiricus, Adv. Math. 8,16, we know that
the tripartition of philosophy was first formulated by Xenocrates, and that
the Peripatetics and the Stoics took it over. Thus there was a commonly accepted reorganisation of philosophy. But some people had reservations. On the
strength of a erroneous interpretation of Aristotle's they recognized logic
not as a part of philosophy but only as an instrument (*organon*) of it.[2] Probably this was the reason why the Stoics gave special arguments for the tripartition of philosophy, and why they especially defended the partial character of logic.[3] However, from the proofs as well as from other indications it
follows that the logical part of philosophy was to deal with all questions of
language, of argumentation, and of cognition. This is in accordance with the
broad significance of the word *logos*, although, as the Stoics employed it,
physics and ethics, too, are concerned with the Logos.[4]

Logic was subdivided into the theory of cognition, dialectics, and rhetoric. On this point the Stoics had some discussions. As Diogenes Laertius reports, some of them did not want to separate the theory of cognition and dialectics, but wanted to incorporate the first discipline into the second one (7,43f.), while the other view was that the theory of cognition had to precede dialectics (7,49). The latter account is followed in the fragment of Diocles (7,49ff.), and it fits in conveniently with all the other sources.[5] It is also in better correspondence with the content of the Stoic theory of cognition which centers around the concept of cataleptic presentation; thus it could so far be grouped with physics more than with dialectics. Finally the separation of the theory of cognition and of dialectics is in full accordance with the definitions of dialectics which will be considered later, in that these definitions seem to presuppose the concept of truth as clarified previously and not as a problematic concept. Hence it is adequate to subdivide Stoic logic not only into dialectics und rhetoric but into the theory of cognition, dialectics, and rhetoric, as was already done by H. v. Arnim in his collection of the fragments.[6] At what time this subdivision arose in the Stoa cannot be determined with certainty. From Zeno we do not have any sources explicitly dealing with the question; but on account of his theory of cognition, and of his statements on dialectics (and rhetoric) the tripartition is unavoidable (cf. SVF I 47-51. 52ff. 75), provided he considered the theory of cognition to be a genuine part of logic at all. Cleanthes subdivided each part of philosophy into two; therefore he enumerated six parts of philosophy. Logic then fell into dialectics and rhetoric (D.L. 7,41). Obviously he preferred the bipartition; but whether or not this is of any importance in the present context is not quite sure, since the same reservation could be made as in Zeno's case, or alternatively since nothing is said about a further subdivision of dialectics. With respect to Chrysippus we may establish that he incorporated the theory of cognition into logic, since his new ideas in these fields are closely interrelated.[7] The tripartition then results. A further question is how to interpret the subdivision of logic when it is seen from the standpoint of the reorganisation of the philosophical disciplines. I omit this question here; when we consider the constitution of dialectics it will come up again.

In the sources we find different definitions of dialectics. One of them is a definition by division. On account of it dialectics is composed of two parts, one of which deals with the *sēmainonta*, the other with the *sēmainomena*, i.e. with the signifying and with the signified respectively. This subclassificatory definition was coined by Chrysippus (D.L. 7,62). Occasionally later Stoics changed the titles of the two parts into '*peri phōnēs* / On voice' and into '*peri lektōn* / On what is or can be said' or '*peri pragmatōn* / On subject-matters' respectively (cf. D.L. 7,43. 62f.; Sextus Empir., Adv. Math. 8, 12). But in substance they took the definition over, so that even Diocles, who himself was not a Stoic, followed the classification of Chrysippus in his systematic survey of Stoic dialectics (cf. D.L. 7,55-82). In his exposition he (or Diogenes Laertius respectively) informed us at the same time of the themes which were discussed in the two parts of dialectics (s.a. D.L. 7,43f.). The list of themes completes the organisation of Stoic dialectics. The overall structure of the discipline is shown by the scheme on the next page.

Additionally we should notice that the Stoics did not merely distinguish the three parts of philosophy; but they stressed their interrelatedness as well (D.L. 7,40; Sextus Empir., Adv. Math. 7,17-19). Correspondingly they considered dialectics under ethical aspects, too (cf. D.L. 7,46-48). And in accordance with their physical ideas they said that things which are discussed in the first part of dialectics are corporeal, while the subject-matters of

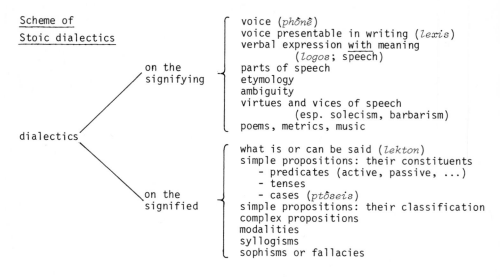

Scheme of
Stoic dialectics

dialectics

on the signifying
- voice (*phônê*)
- voice presentable in writing (*lexis*)
- verbal expression with meaning (*logos*; speech)
- parts of speech
- etymology
- ambiguity
- virtues and vices of speech (esp. solecism, barbarism)
- poems, metrics, music

on the signified
- what is or can be said (*lekton*)
- simple propositions: their constituents
  - predicates (active, passive, ...)
  - tenses
  - cases (*ptôseis*)
- simple propositions: their classification
- complex propositions
- modalities
- syllogisms
- sophisms or fallacies

the second part were incorporeals (Sextus Empir., Adv. Math. 8,11f.; cf. D.L. 7,55). This information completes the overall view. This treatment makes a very systematic impression on the reader.

The subclassification of philosophy, of logic, and especially of dialectics is seemingly an outstanding product of the famous Stoic interest in the formation of a philosophical system. On account of this, and as language is evidently the subject-matter of dialectics, it is normally assumed that the Stoics considered language from two points of view, that these two approaches homogeneously define the first and second part of dialectics respectively, and that they determine all the single points. Sometimes this assumption is only presupposed, or it is explicitly made without further explanation.[8] Other authors specify the two approaches in one way or another. But what they say is not sufficient in order to justify the assumption. Thus the overall structure of Stoic linguistic theory is as yet unknown. And the time has come to raise the question as to whether the standard assumption can be justified at all, or whether the apparently systematic character of Stoic dialectics has quite another origin. The first possibility is highly unconvincing, and the second very probable, as we shall see in the next section.

II

The problem of how to make the division of the Stoic linguistic theory intelligible was already seen by Rudolf Schmidt, who was the first to give a comprehensive representation of Stoic grammar. But what he offered as a solution is by no means a systematically developed answer and at best some sort of explanation of the question.[9] His failure brings out two points which are also valid for other approaches, namely 1. that it is very difficult to justify the adequacy of the terminology used in order to reconstruct the division of Stoic dialectics, and 2. that it is not easy to avoid contradictions between the reconstruction and the extensive lists of dialectical themes.

Nowadays the classification of dialectics evokes other intuitions than in R. Schmidt's time. But they do not stand up to examination either. The titles of the two parts of dialectics might remind us of F. de Saussure's distinction between the signifying and the signified, or of the distinction between syntax and semantics. But these distinctions are not helpful in understanding the Stoic linguistic theory; we have to give them up soon. For in the Stoic theory we neither find the psychologism nor the important distinction between 'langue' and 'parole' of de Saussure; furthermore the Saussurean concept of sign is incompatible with the Stoic thesis that all words are ambiguous.[10] Since this doctrine is developed in the first part of dialectics this part contains some semantical components. On the other hand we find relevant syntactical features in the propositional theory of the second part.[11] Hence the Stoic classification does not coincide with the distinction between syntax and semantics either. To assume this would be even more inadequate if we were to connect our distinction with the semiotic concept of Ch.W. Morris, because then we would have to ask also for a pragmatical part of dialectics, and to state that it is not so much absent as fused into the second part.[12] Thus the first two approaches cannot lead to a sufficient account of the division of dialectics.

A third intuition might be the distinction of grammar and formal logic, probably supported by the two catalogues of subjects which are enumerated by Diogenes Laertius in 7,43f.[13] But closer examination of these lists and even more of the more elaborated ones which we got from Diocles' text above, shows that what the second part of dialectics deals with, is significantly more than what we would assign to formal logic; but we would assign to it some subjects of the first part, e.g. divisions and amphiboly. On the other hand from the first part at least the poetical questions are surely not recognized as a piece of grammar, while in the second part there are found some important grammatical subjects. Hence Stoic grammar exceeds the first part and, vice versa, is divided by the Stoic classification of dialectics. This is spoken from a material point of view and leads to the question whether or not what we formally call 'grammar' in a broad sense was known to the Stoics at all. Recently M. Frede put this formal question, and needed a lot of pages to give a positive answer; he argued that there are some subjects in the first part which fulfill our formal criteria for grammar.[14] Thus from a formal point of view the Stoics were familiar with grammar. But it was not yet developed, and formed only a few elements of the first part of dialectics. Therefore our concepts of grammar and formal logic are not suitable for an interpretation of the Stoic division of dialectics even when their application is guided more by formal criteria than by material ones.

In becoming more cautious we might remember the variety of modern theories of meaning, and examine whether by their application we reach at least a partial understanding of the Stoic ideas. Since the second part of dialectics according to its title is a semantic one, and since the first part contains semantical components, too, but is of quite another character, we may expect that different theories of meaning are applicable to them. Indeed, we could argue that the second part of dialectics fits Wittgenstein's 'meaning-as-use'-theory while the semantical aspects of the first part correspond to a semantics of a Tarskian type. I omit the arguments for this thesis, since it creates new difficulties. Not only would our result be a partial one with respect to the first part but also we have to realize the precarious systematic relation between the semantics of a Tarskian and that of a Wittgensteinian type, and we have to ask how the Stoics handled this relationship. In the sources we find no sufficient answer to this question, so that our progress in interpreting the classification of dialectics is at best a superficial one.

After such disappointment we must state: The division of Stoic dialectics reminds us of some familiar distinctions. But none of them leads us to a sufficient account of the Stoic division. Thus one will seek for other points of departure. For instance the concept of dialectics might be appropriate for delineating the division of dialectics. Besides the definition by division cited above some other definitions of dialectics have been handed down to us:

1. Augustine reports that the Stoics called dialectics *sollertia disputandi* (SVF II 106). Evidently this expression is intended as a Latin translation of *dialektikê technê* which means 'the art or skill of discussing'; Augustine's translation prefers the sense of 'skill' in contrast to that of 'art' or 'science'.

2. Rather often we read the following definition: Dialectics is the science of discussing correctly (or well), while rhetoric is considered to be the science of speaking well (see SVF II 131. 288-294, III 267). Diogenes Laertius says in greater detail: 'the science of discussing correctly subjects by question and answer' versus 'the science of speaking well on matters set forth by plain narrative (7,42). He adds a further definition which he offers as a consequence of the foregoing one:

3. 'Hence', he says, dialectics is 'also' defined 'in this manner': science of the true, of the false, and of that which is neither true nor false (ibid.). This definition is also reported by Sextus Empiricus (Adv. Math 11,187); and Diogenes mentions it in another place again where he attributes it especially to Poseidonius (7,62).

4. Alexander of Aphrodisias used the formula 'science of speaking well' which normally defined rhetorics, in order to characterize dialectics; and he adds that speaking well consists in speaking the true and the suitable (SVF II 124).

5. Zeno of Citium compared 'the arts of the dialecticians' to the just measures when they are applied to rubbish instead of useful things; and he recommended dialectics as it is capable of solving the sophisms or fallacies (SVF I 49f.).

Thus the Stoics defined their dialectics in rather multifarious manners. Although Diogenes and Alexander indicate certain material connections between the definitions they do not explicate them. To do this is an important claim when we are interested in a homogeneous concept of dialectics, and when we want to see whether the definition by division given by Chrysippus can be explained against the background of the other definitions. In studying these things one has also, of course, to compare the numerous single themes of dialectics. In particular the subjects of the first part should be kept in mind since they seem to be very unspecific to justify their subsumption under the heading of any definition of dialectics. Furthermore what the Stoics say about the 'virtues and vices of speech' contains even rhetorical elements;[15] these then are not completely excluded from dialectics despite the classification of Stoic logic. Finally the poetical subjects fit very badly with the definitions of dialectics; when seen in the light of Aristotle's work their place in 'logic' ought to be as autonomous as that of rhetoric. Without doubt, the definitions are in some sense starting points to make dialectics intelligible. But evidently they also involve substantial problems which need a sufficient answer.

In addition to the aforesaid difficulties there are at least two further delicate tasks, the solution of which is essential for an overall understanding of Stoic dialectics. The two parts of the discipline were distinguished sharply; this is particularly evident from the fact that their subjects were characterized as corporeal and as incorporeal respectively. In accordance with this sharp distinguishing line the Stoics developed different terminologies in the two fields; and at the same time they were able to introduce a certain isomorphism between them. For instance the *logos* and its parts, the 'parts of speech', e.g. *onoma* (proper name) and *rhēma* (verb), are classed in the first half of dialectics since they are signs, although signifying ones. What they signify, namely the *lekta* (especially a *axiōma* or proposition, a *ptōsis* or case, and a *katēgorēma* or predicate respectively), is classed in the second part and must be well distinguished from the things which we meet in our world (*tygchanonta*); these are corporeal again, and by signifying meanings the linguistic signs refer to them (Sextus Empir., Adv. Math. 8,11f.). Now, the sharp distinction of the signs and their meanings involves a problem. The *logos* is distinguished from the *lexis*, which is also dealt with in the first part, in that having meaning is essential to it (D.L. 7,57). Hence to examine the *logos* is just to examine its meaning, i.e. the *lekton*; but to examine this, while it is distinguished from the object or fact the *logos* refers to, is the same as to examine the *logos*. From this point of view the strong separation of the linguistic signs and the meanings is questionable.[16] Why did the Stoics nevertheless adhere to it? This must be solved by a reconstruction of dialectics and its division.

Furthermore, for what reason did the Stoics use the terms 'corporeal' and 'incorporeal' in the field of dialectics? These terms originate from physics. Evidently language can be made a subject of research in the philosophy of nature. But in this case it belongs to the field of physics instead of that of logic and dialectics. Such a shift was not intended by the Stoics. We must assume, therefore, that the physical terminology has a certain function in the linguistic theory. This assumption cannot be dismissed by remarking that the Stoics insisted on a systematic interrelation between the three parts of philosophy. But it can be strengthened by an additional observation, namely that the physical terminology was apparently used only in the field of dialectics and not in that of rhetoric as well. Finally, it could be questioned what the evidence is on account of which, for instance, the parts of speech are established to be corporeals, i.e. to be acting and acted upon, and on account of which it is generally denied that the meanings of linguistic signs could fulfil the criterion of corporality (see e.g. SVF I 90. 98. 146, II 140. 363); don't the linguistic signs have some effect just because of their meaning? This question also leads to the aforesaid assumption. Always in Stoic dialectics there seems to be a linguistic difficulty which the Stoics were unable to solve by linguistic means. Whether this is true, and what in that case the difficulty consists in, is clearly a very important question in the context of a reconstruction of dialectics and its division.

The list of problems of interpretation could be lengthened. But it is already extensive enough to show that the usual assumption about the overall structure of Stoic dialectics is misleading or even false. For even if we succeeded in discovering a homogeneous point of view for each part of dialectics, and if the points of view ascertained are appropriate to answer the last two of the forementioned questions, there are, nevertheless, at least two conditions the fulfilment of which seems on the one hand to be impossible while on the other hand it is demanded by the assumption: a) It is very doubtful that the point of view belonging to the first part of dialectics is also analytically productive. In the sense of the assumption it is not enough to point out a criterion which is met by all topics of the first part; the point of view indicated must also determine positively the various topics; it must lead to the phonetical themes as well as to the poetical ones. If it does not do so, the assumption is invalidated. But even if it does, the assumption is not yet

justified, since the two points of view, so far accepted, have to fulfil a
further condition. b) The assumption is directed towards a homogeneous concept
of dialectics; it entails the idea that there exists a homogenous (though
probably debatable) linguistic concept. Hence the two points of view which
determine the first and second part of dialectics respectively, have to proceed from such a concept of language, or must lead back to it. If they do not
do so, the assumption is again weakened. Now, in view of the difficulties
which centre around the definitions of dialectics, it is doubtful whether precisely the same points of view which fulfil all the foregoing conditions are
capable of meeting the additional condition, namely of leading us back to a
homogeneous concept of language and of dialectics. It is extremely improbable
that they could do so. Thus, we ought reckon with systematic dislocations in
the overall structure of Stoic dialectics. However, the starting point of the
interpretation must be independent of the standard assumption concerning the
concept of dialectics and its classification.

III

Like the subclassification of philosophy the subclassification of logic was
taken over by the Stoics from Xenocrates; he was probably the first to divide
logic into rhetoric and dialectics (Sextus Empir., Adv. Math. 2,6f.). Nevertheless the Stoic concept of dialectics ought to be considered on its own. For
on the one hand, we do not know any details of the dialectics of Xenocrates
and are, therefore, unable to specify the influence on the Stoics. On the
other hand, we are quite sure that the Stoic ideas were also influenced by the
so-called Dialectical school, the existence of which was recently made evident
by D. Sedley.[17] The most prominent members of this school were Diodorus Cronus
and Philo. Zeno 'studied dialectics under Diodorus', and had many discussions
with Philo (D.L. 7,25. 16). And all the topics which we are sure that Diodorus
spoke about[18], also appear in Stoic dialectics. Thus, at least two very different influences on the Stoic concept of dialectics are manifest. This concept, then, cannot be identified either with the dialectical ideas of Diodorus or with those of Xenocrates. This conclusion is of some importance with
regard to the use of the term 'dialectic': It is by no means trivial to use
this term in order to name a science, as was done by the Stoics (and Xenocrates). For in earlier times the term had significantly different meanings; and
yet when it was used to name a science (e.g. Plato, Soph. 253 b-e), this use
was only a subordinate one. As the predominant and only one it was a new
phenomenon in the history of Greek thought. When we combine this observation
with the foregoing consideration of the relative independence of the Stoic
concept of dialectics, we are entitled to assume that the Stoic dialectics
was not only a science but also a new one, and that it was named by changing
the sense of an old word. Accordingly two problems arise: 1. We have to consider the basic meaning of the term 'dialectic' and the history of its special meanings in order to find out how it became possible or even indispensable to change the meaning of the term such that it denoted a science which
was concerned with linguistic theory. 2. The more important problem is related to the question of what the unity of Stoic dialectics consists in: If it
is true that Stoic dialectics was a new science, then in the light of all the
well known details of this discipline we have to ask for what reasons the new
science was constituted by the Stoics. Is there, for instance, a fundamental
problem in the history of Greek thought which demanded a new answer and thus
also a new discipline? - In this section of the paper I shall comment on the
first question.

The first place where we meet the word 'dialectic' in Greek literature is the dialogues of Plato. From the beginning he gives a special meaning to the word. But on different occasions as well as in different ways he, nevertheless, gives us to understand that beside his own specific use of the word there is a more general or basic one.[19] We are reminded that the Greek expression *hē dialektikē* is elliptic; completed it has the form *hē dialektikē techne*, a point which was also obvious at later times, and could also be easily illustrated by passages from other authors. According to its completed version, in the first instance 'dialectic' has no other meaning than 'the skill (or art) of conversing (or discussing)'. The applicability of either part of the expression as well as of the expression as a whole is a very wide one. Correspondingly the meaning is as general as it is basic. In comparison it is only a rather small restriction to substitute 'conversing (or discussing)', and to interpret 'dialectic' to mean 'the skill (or art) of questioning and answering'. In ancient philosophical circles this formula served as an equivalent to the first one, and was seemingly considered to be a mere analytical explanation. For it was cited in all philosophical schools and did not influence their special uses of the term 'dialectic'. The need to differentiate the meaning of the term and its applicability respectively arises only if the terms 'conversation' or 'discussion', and 'question and answer' are used in a more specific way than that suggested by their basic meaning. Whatever these specifications are, there is a corresponding specific sense of *techne*, be it the meaning of 'mere skill' or that of 'art' or that of 'method' or that of 'knowledge' or ... or even that of a particular personal ability. Such then is the direction in which the ancient philosophers developed their special concepts of dialectic from the basic meaning of the term.

But in order to reconstruct the Stoic concept one must also consider another approach. After the dialectical concept of Plato, after that of Aristotle, after the so-called Dialectical school, and after the dialectics of Xenocrates, the Stoic concept was (at least) the fifth one. Although these five more precise uses or meanings of the term 'dialectic' are very different there is a certain historical continuity between them. Plato idealized the art of discussing according to the example of Socrates, and declared it to be the only genuine philosophical method, the path to the being. Thus the members of his school exercised this method, and instituted training-discussions.[20] But since these discussions were not seriously philosophical in character they undermined Plato's dialectical concept, and were considered by him to be dubious in character (cf. Pol. 537e - 539d). Aristotle realized this and took them as the historical model for his own concept of that of what dialectic 'really' was to be.[21] But at the same time the historical basis of his new concept disappeared as in the case of Plato. For Aristotle complains about the fact that the members of the Academy were no longer able to ask clear questions which needed no further clarification and could be answered by a simple 'Yes' or 'No' (Soph. El. 17. 175 b 10-14). The more specific 'skill or art of discussion' became unusual to such a high degree that it became possible to consider it to be a personal ability of certain people, and to use 'dialectic' to name a certain philosophical school the members of which 'put their arguments into the form of question and answer' (D.L. 2,106). Thus in spite of their great differences the first three special senses of 'dialectic' are interrelated not only indirectly by the very general basic sense of the word but also directly in that under certain historical conditions the later ones were stimulated by the earlier ones. Hence we have also to ask whether the use of the term 'dialectic' in order to name a discipline dealing with language was called forth by something similar. As noted above, this use was not a totally new one. But what stimulated its becoming the predominant and only one?

It is not yet possible to give a satisfactory answer to the latter question. For we do not know enough about the historical model (if there is one) Xenocrates had in mind when applying the term 'dialectic' predominantly to a science. And with regard to the Stoics we ought to be aware that there was no historical change or event which could stimulate their use of the term and serve as a model for it. Otherwise it would not have been of any interest to relate dialectics explicitly to the basic meaning of *hê dialektikê technê* by speaking of the *sollertia disputandi*, as Augustine says, i.e. by pointing out the character of a skill in contrast to that of an art or science. In order to give at least a preliminary answer to the questions concerning the Stoic use of the term 'dialectic', we can do only two things for the moment. 1. We can point out that if one was interested in establishing a new science of language, as the Stoics evidently were, it was adequate to call this science 'dialectics' inasmuch as each earlier philosophical sense of the term 'dialectic' involved a certain relation to linguistic theory (though in each case a different one).[22] And 2. we can check more precisely the relationship between the Stoic use of the term 'dialectic' and the term's basic meaning. We shall see how small the analytical force of those definitions of dialectics is which refer to discussions in the form of question and answer; these definitions have very little to do with the actual scope of Stoic dialectics.

The division of philosophy was made on the basis of different subject-matter. The Stoics followed the same principle in the subdivision of both ethics and physics (cf. D.L. 7, 84. 132), and it was appropriate to follow it also by subdividing logic. Accordingly dialectics as well as rhetoric is constituted by a certain subject-matter. Therefore and since we do not yet know what the subject-matter of dialectics actually is, we could examine how far it is possible to reconstruct this discipline by considering it to be the complement of rhetoric. In starting from logic and its subject-matter it is practically unavoidable to first distinguish between rhetoric and something else. For in hellenistic Greece the range of rhetoric was perfectly clear for a long time, and its social relevance was very great so that it would have been pointless to undermine the independence of this discipline. Thus rhetoric had to appear at the first level of the subclassification of logic, and it was suitably defined in a traditional manner. What rhetoric is distinguished from, the 'something else', so far only turns out to be what is left over. What is its specific subject-matter, what is its definition, and what is its name?

The name obviously is 'dialectics'. For its adequacy we can only recall the above considerations, as the 'rest' of logic had to deal with many linguistic topics, among them with many themes of Diodorus Cronus, i.e. of the 'Dialectical' school. - As regards the definition, an old formula was then used in that discussions in the form of question and answer were referred to. This formula now even included poetics since this field did not belong to rhetoric but to the 'rest' of logic. Hence the definition was so far materially inadequate, and necessarily anachronistic when considered to involve a suitable positive description of dialectics. But as a delimitation from rhetoric it served very well. In fact, most of the sources which quote this Stoic definition of dialectics quote it together with the definition of rhetoric, and do not cite the formula alone as was previously usual. This is not a mere accident, as is plainly shown by Sextus Empiricus, Adv. Math. 2,6ff. Nevertheless, in order to balance the one-sided use of the classical explanation of the term 'dialectic' a little bit, it was easy to recall the basic meaning of *hê dialektikê technê* by calling, as Augustine tells us, dialectics *sollertia disputandi*, i.e. by pointing out the character of a skill instead of an art or a science. By this it is perhaps indicated that what dialectics deals with, is a natural thing inasmuch as to discuss is a specific human ability (cf. Sextus Empir., Adv. Math. 8,275f.). - Finally the present approach leads to a vague hint at the subject-matter of dialectics: The subject-matter of rhetoric, for instance the speaking of an orator could be considered typical of a use of language for practical purposes. Thus, on the contrary, what dialectics is dealing with is probably typical of a use of language which is unburdened by the compulsions of everyday life. This idea indicates at the propositions to be the predominant subject-matter of dialectics, and consequently it throws some light upon the fact that the definition of dialectics which refers to discussions in the form of question and answer, was explicated by other definitions which refer to the true and to the false.

Such then is the utmost we can attain in reconstructing dialectics merely as the complement to rhetoric. The result is completely unimportant in that it does not bring out the scope of dialectics. But it includes the full range of that definition of dialectics which refers to discussions in the form of question and answer. Hence it shows us (1) that this definition served merely to differentiate dialectics from rhetoric, and does not positively describe the discipline; it is not really interrelated with the basic meaning of 'dialectic', and completely open to interpretation by any other definition of dialectics. (2) In order to determine the real subject-matter of dialectics and ascertain its scope, it is unavoidable to take up the other main question: For what reason did the Stoics constitute their new science of language, which was then called 'dialectics'? To answer this question a point of departure is needed which is totally different from that of the present considerations.

IV

As is well known Greek philosophy was strongly influenced by Parmenides as well as by Heraclitus. Their doctrines in ontology and in the philosophy of nature had important linguistic consequences. And later philosophers were not least engaged in solving the problems connected with these consequences. Parmenides' doctrine of the One-True-Being which does not permit any multiplicity or any Not-Being beyond itself, destroyed the relationship of language to reality, and even language itself. For its consequence was that the multiplicity of linguistic signs, the differences in meaning, and grammatical structures did not have any relevance with respect to reality. At best all expressions whatever their difference may be, refer to one and the same object. But even this is impossible as Plato realized (Soph. 244 b-d) since language ultimately had to coincide with the One-True-Being. On the other hand Heraclitus taught that all things are in permanent flux. As a consequence of this the stability as well as the intersubjective commitment of the meanings of both words and sentences is absolutely unjustified with respect to reality. Thus, this doctrine also destroyed the relationship between language and reality. That there is a difference between language and reality was naturally known; it could at any time be additionally supported by indicating the multiplicity of languages. But that this difference amounted to a mutual exclusion of language and of reality was a new thesis, and evidently not at all acceptable. Certainly, a mere refutation of the Parmenidean and Heraclitean views would not have been adequate, even if it was supported by such tricky arguments as those of the sophist Gorgias.[23] But the question was to establish another ontology and / or philosophy of nature, one which is in correspondence with the relationship which language was required to have to reality. Hence, and as this claim relates especially to statements or propositions, the semantic structure of the proposition widely became the guiding principle of the heuristic approach to ontology and to the philosophy of nature; and these disciplines may be characterized in an important sense as justifications of the proposition, or as analyses of the conditions of propositions. This was the semantic-ontological program which both Parmenides and Heraclitus assigned to Greek philosophy. Of course, the fallacies also demanded an answer in this context, since they were produced be it to defend Parmenides or be it from other motives, and as they were at times employed to undermine the relation of language to reality.[24] But compared with the original semantic-ontological question the sophisms clearly constituted a rather superficial problem, and were not basic since they use precisely the relation of language to reality in order to confuse it.

The basic semantic-ontological problem dominated the doctrines of Antisthenes [25] as well as Plato's doctrine of ideas[26]. It also determined Aristotle's theory of substance in that this theory was developed as an ontological reflection on the form of elementary propositions; intended as a metaphysical justification of this form it explained how it is possible that, what a logical subject refers to, without losing its identity is also something else, namely all that which can be predicated of it in correspondence with the categories or without contradiction respectively.[27] In comparison with earlier efforts this theory led to enormous progress since it was the first one to account for the functional asymmetry between subject and predicate. But nevertheless, its solution of the basic problem was insufficient. For 1. the theory of substance justified far too small a section of language; it gives no satisfactory account even of elementary relational propositions and of the complex propositions of propositional logic. 2. Semantically like all the earlier theories it follows the model of proper names; the functional asymmetry of subject and predicate is translated into an ontological asymmetry of the corresponding objects of reference, but the relationship between word and object is the same in either case, so that for Aristotle what we call 'state of affairs' or 'fact' merely appears as an organism of dissimilar things.[28]

In addition to this we should note that as concerns the claim contained in the questions posed by Parmenides and Heraclitus, it goes further than the propositions: Non-assertoric forms of speech also have a subjectively interpolated function and a commitment which includes a certain relation to reality. Thus they also need justification. On the other hand, they show even more impressively than the sophisms that language is capable of much more than of expressing reality. Therefore a semantic-ontological justification of language is not a sufficient claim. To answer Parmenides' and Heraclitus' questions fully there is needed something other than a semantics which is delimited by the postulate of translatability into ontology. Aristotle hinted at this demand by saying that all speech has a meaning such that each non-assertoric sentence was also considered to be a *logos*; but then he banished these sentences into the field of 'rhetoric or poetics', and was no longer interested in them in his studies into the logic of language (De interpr. 4. 16 b 33 - 17 a 7). The Stoics were much more conscious of the problem. Under the heading of the *lekta* in the second part of their dialectics beyond propositions they distinguished eight forms of non-assertoric sentences, and in each case they gave a definition of the attached meaning.[29] Furthermore at least the imperative was inquired by them in more detail, and with some success.[30] Accordingly we may assume that they were sceptical about the ontologisation of semantics which had been conventional up to that time, and that they intended to form another kind of semantic justification of language. Whether this assumption is correct, which other paths the Stoics pursued, and how far they succeeded in doing so, all this must, of course, become evident not so much in the field of the non-assertoric sentences, but rather in the discussion of the propositions.

If we relate Zeno's description of dialectics, namely that it has to solve the sophisms or fallacies (SVF I 50), to our present problem, then the founder of the Stoa avoided this field in the first instance, and switched over to the related surface-problem. Even this could be interpreted as a reservation with regard to the semantic-ontological justifications of language. However, the solution of sophisms demanded a lot of linguistic research on the linking of words and on consequential relations; hence Zeno included them in the tasks of dialectics (SVF I 51, also 49). Thus his description of dialectics stimulated many of the individual topics of the discipline. But though this research might be very extensive, so far it only serves a defensive purpose, namely to solve fallacies, and this aim of dialectics is not sufficient in order to grasp the later overall structure of the discipline. For merely for the solution of fallacies it is not necessary to divide dialectics into two strongly distinguished parts, to develop the theory of the *lekta*, and to introduce terms of the philosophy of nature in order to interpret language; nor can one see how the defensive aim of solving fallacies could lead to questions for poetics and for precise definitions of the meanings of non-assertoric sentences.[31] Therefore and as it was not possible at all to answer the basic problem of the justification of language convincingly by only discussing the fallacies, we have to return to this problem again. Now, the sources do not indicate any Stoic considerations dealing with the adequacy or inadequacy of the semantic-ontological standard-form of the problem of justification of language; they were seemingly unable to refute this form explicitly. But if at the same time it is true that they wanted to escape it, we may assume that they did not accept it by giving a half-hearted answer; in other words: they tried to 'avoid' it by establishing a new kind of ontology and of semantics as well.

With regard to the semantic-ontological level, especially to the relationship of propositions to reality, two thoughts of Zeno are of considerable interest: 1. Zeno had also attended the discussions of the Megarian Stilpo (D.L. 2,114. 120; cf. 7,24), who 'demolished the ideas, and said that who asserts the existence of Man means no individual, for he did not assert the existence of this man or of that one' (D.L. 2,119). Thus Stilpo taught the metaphysical primacy of the individual above the universal. The Stoics from Zeno on took this thesis over.[32] They considered 'This is P' to be the basic form of assertoric sentences, and analysed all propositions in such a way that their subjects refer not to ideas or substances but always to one or several of the individual objects which we encounter in our world. 2. Probably stimulated by the same Stilponean discussions Zeno reinterpreted the ideas of Plato and considered them no longer as metaphysical entities, but as *ennoêmata hôsanei tina*, i.e. as psychological quasi-somethings (SVF I 65; cf. 92). - Additionally we may assume that Zeno did not accept Aristotle's theory of substance. For this theory involved a certain concept of possibility (cf. Aristotle, Metaph. IX) which was at least debatable, and was strongly attacked by Zeno's teacher in dialectics, namely by Diodorus Cronus, in that he formed an alternative concept.[33]

With regard to the question of the semantic justification of language the first thesis does not necessarily imply that the meaning of nominators is identical with individual objects. But it does imply that this meaning is guaranteed in some manner by individual objects. And this is clearly an ontological answer to the question of justification. But it is not yet a sufficient answer because the meaning of propositions is constituted not only by the meaning of the nominators but by that of predicates also. Now, the meaning of a predicate cannot be correlated immediately to the reality encountered like that of the nominators. For in this case the undesirable Aristotelean theory of substance and accidence or something similar is unavoidable; propositions would be again justified only in that they are capable of representing reality; and the research would not lead to aspects which could serve as starting points for extending the studies into non-assertoric sentences. Thus the predicates have to relate to the world in a manner quite different to that of the nominators (especially to that of the singular terms). The meaning of predicates must be guaranteed in a different way. Thus it requires another ontological status. This was probably the reason why Zeno considered the ideas of Plato (i.e. in Plato's perspective: the meanings of words and especially that of predicates) as psychological quasi-somethings.

By this he reaches a position which is most remarkable from a modern analytical point of view. The nominators and the predicators signify not only different things but do this in different manners; their functions in the constitution of the sentence-meaning are complementory, and the meaning of propositions may be compared to our states of affairs. That Zeno's successors took this intention over, may be drawn from the fact that in the second part of dialectics the sentence - meanings are demonstrated in the first place and are called 'complete' *lekta* while the parts of speech have 'incomplete' meanings (D.L. 7.63). Thus, Zeno's ideas in the field of linguistic theory were, on the one hand, most interesting. But on the other hand, they were also formulated most imperfectly, namely in a quasi-nominalistic manner: Zeno accepted the semantic-ontological question in the field of the nominators, and avoided it in the field of the predicates by establishing a psychological concept of meaning. This answer was very unsatisfactory since the psychological character of the meanings of predicates was not appropriate to guarantee the obligatory force of argumentative speech. On the very contrary it must be interpreted as an indicator of mere subjectivity. Thus, the pressure of the semantic question for an ontological justification of language must again increase and direct itself especially against the meaning of predicates and consequently against that of sentences as wholes. If one wanted to continue with the basic linguistic ideas, and to resist the question without being able to show its inadequacy, then it was necessary to find answers of systematic originality.

Cleanthes took the next step in introducing the term *lekton* in order to designate the meaning of the predicate (SVF I 488). Subsequently Chrysippus applied the new term generally to the meaning of the proposition (cf. SVF II 166ff.). He could do that easily as well as adequately both due to the principal problem of justification and to the meaning of the term itself which is: 'what is or can be said'. By these steps two things were achieved: 1. The new term adequately characterized the meanings (*sêmainomena*) as the matters expressed (*pragmata*) which in speaking are said and understood by the members of a linguistic community and which are not understood by people who do not speak the same language (cf. Sextus Empir., Adv. Math. 8,11f.). In this way the meanings are extracted from the non-obligatory sphere of mere subjectivity without being identified with so-called objective reality. Thus the property of language is characterized in a genuine manner. 2. The unsettled question of the semantic-ontological justification of language is directed at the *lekta* now and compels the assumption of a special ontological sphere for them. The meanings or *lekta* must be distinguishable in this new sphere and therefore be considered somethings (*tina*) again. Zeno's psychological quasi - somethings were transformed into somethings of a special, although unspecified ontological sphere. These special somethings which the foreigner is unable to identify, can now be separated from that which the foreigner nevertheless hears, namely from speech and linguistic signs inasmuch as they do not constitute the obligatory force of argumentation; moreover it is possible now to oppose the signs and the meanings to each other, and to develop, then, an isomorphism between them.

Clearly, even at this stage the question of the justification of language is still unsettled because the ontological sphere of the *lekta* is not yet described and guaranteed in a positive way. Any hints as to how to do this, could not be provided by further reflection of a genuine linguistic character, since even the starting point of the Stoic reflections, i.e. the practice of understandable speech, does not permit one to recognize why predicates should have a thinglike meaning at all. Therefore one needed means of a heterogeneous kind in order to characterize the special ontological sphere of the *lekta* positively. Thus categories of the philosophy of nature were utilized and the meanings were described as incorporeal while all that the foreigner is able to understand besides the linguistic content, was considered corporeal: it has some effect upon him. That the physical interpretation of language resulted from a theoretical calamity is also shown by the difficulties the Stoics encountered in trying to make it plausible that the meanings of predicates are incorporeal; their exemplifications sounded sophisticated.[34] Nevertheless through the introduction of physical components the main problem of justification of both the independence and the objectivity of language in regard to reality was solved inasmuch as the semantic-ontological questions had no further point of contact. Thus, we have now to examine what the outcome of all this is in regard to both the concept and the classification of dialectics.

V

We have considered the problem of the justification of language which was a fundamental one in Greek philosophy. After having sketched its development with the Stoics we return to the definitions and to the classification of dialectics. Especially since ontological or physical solutions of the problem of the justification of language are insufficient in principle, the Stoics adequately tried to handle the question as one which genuinely belongs to the philosophy of language. Accordingly it was part of the subject-matter of their logic, and especially of dialectics. More precisely we have to assume that the problem of the justification was the basic problem of Stoic dialectics; in the Stoic version it constituted just that new science in the history of Greek thought which was then called 'dialectics'.

As yet this assumption is supported by the following points: 1. Zeno's general statements about dialectics and his linguistic comments fit in excellently with the problem of the justification of language. They indicate a new solution to the problem which was, nevertheless, not yet satisfactory inasmuch as the handling of the traditional ontological aspects of the problem could not yet convince. Hence Zeno's successors developed and reformulated his new ideas in such a way that they could count as a sufficient answer to the problem of the justification of language. 2. Precisely on the line of this development of the Stoic answer to the ancient question of the justification of language there was introduced the division of dialectics which became usual from Chrysippus on. At the beginning of the development the classification was not yet possible. For, if having differentiated relations to reality and, therefore, being appropriate for argumentation and for the acquisition of knowledge, is an essential property of language, and if the question of justification refers precisely to this property, then it makes no sense to separate in the elaboration of dialectics the linguistic sign from its meaning (though a mere distinction is always possible). That it, nevertheless, must be introduced results from the fact that it was factually impossible to settle the question of justification by other means than by ontological ones although these are necessarily inadequate for the realisation of the relative semantic independence of language in regard to reality. Thus, in order to realize it nevertheless, the Stoics assumed a special ontological sphere which had to contain all those aspects of language which fell under the question of justification. This sphere then must be distinguished from those linguistic phenomena which did not need either a justification or a special ontological sphere. Accordingly Chrysippus divided dialectics into two parts, the second of which dealt with the elements of the special ontological sphere. Though this division was necessary, it is at the same time obvious that it was a problematic one. 3. Our reconstruction of the dividing line between the two parts of dialectics corresponds with the criterion reported by Sextus Empiricus, Adv. Math. 8,11f., that the meanings are that which in speaking is said and understood by the members of a linguistic community and which is not understood by people who do not know that language. The meanings were the subject-matter of the problem of justification, and when adequately characterized in such a pragmatic way, they showed not only the relation of language to reality but also the relative semantic independence of language in regard to reality. They are, therefore, precisely the elements of the special ontological sphere which was required by the Stoics. 4. In answering the question of justification the Stoics had to attribute to the meanings a thinglike character. The meanings, therefore, could appear as homogeneous subject-matter which was constituitive for the second part of dialectics. This part, then, was a uniform subdiscipline, and it was not necessary to introduce further subdivisions similar to those which were to be expected in view of e.g. the Organon of Aristotle, but could now be considered to be unimportant. 5. Our reconstruction shows how physical terminology entered into the dialectics, and how it was superimposed the separation of the linguistic sign and its meaning. Indeed, it served to solve a linguistic problem which one was not able to solve by genuine linguistic means.

These points are important enough to make it evident that Stoic dialectics is basically concerned with the ancient problem of the justification of language and with the new ideas of the Stoics in this field. And vice versa, they show that the reconstruction given in the foregoing section of this paper, solves some main problems of the interpretation of the overall structure of Stoic dialectics. Additionally it solves the problems which centre around the definitions of dialectics:

As the linguistic problem of justification predominantly related to the propositions, many definitions insistently indicated the true and the false. Of course, as a consequence of the division of dialectics, these definitions, then, pointed much rather to (the greater part of) the second part of dialectics than to the whole field of the discipline. The Stoics sometimes corrected this one-sidedness by adding to the definitions that dialectics also deals with that which is neither true nor false. This privative description has two ranges. In the first instance it applies to the meanings of non-assertoric sentences which are without exception declared to be neither true nor false (D.L. 7,66-68). On the other hand, the privative description has also a good sense when it is applied to the linguistic signs which are separated from their meanings. Hence the additional element covers all those fields in the second and first part of dialectics respectively which do not belong to the scope of the original definition, and it does so in full accordance with our account of Stoic dialectics. According to Diogenes Laertius 7,42 there is a relationship of consequence between our present definition that dialectics deals with the true, with the false, and with what is neither true nor false, and that definition of dialectics which refers to discussions in the form of question and answer. In order to elucidate this relation it is now enough to remember the respective comments towards the end of section III of this paper. The latter definition is predominantly a negative one; in order to determine its positive sense, one has to interpret it on the basis of a heterogeneous approach. This approach, then, is indicated be the first definition, and is delineated by our reconstruction of Stoic dialectics.

Having succeeded so far in accounting for the overall structure of Stoic dialectics, we have to consider our result with respect to the first part of dialectics. According to the present approach the first part of dialectics is a mere complement to the second part; it deals with the linguistic signs, i.e. with those aspects of language which are separated from their meanings and, therefore, fall outside the question of the semantic justification of language. The identity-criterion of the first part appears as a negatve or a minimal one, which does not yet indicate what research in this field is really interested in. When seen systematically the Stoic linguistic research did not start at the linguistic signs and end at their meanings but vice versa: Coming from the meanings the Stoics had only then to think over the aim of their studies in the field of the linguistic signs. In order to determine the positive scope of the first part of dialectics a point of view was required which must unavoidably be as additional as heterogeneous, and introduce a further systematic dislocation into the overall structure of dialectics.

Thus on the one hand, our present result requires completion, and is not yet a satisfactory account of the first part of dialectics. But on the other hand, it is, nevertheless, quite adequate. This is shown by the following points: 1. By pointing out the forementioned minimal identity-criterion of the first part of dialectics our result involves an explanation as to why poetics belongs to that part though in view of the definitions of dialectics one does not expect it there. And by postulating an additional point of view the result fits in conveniently with the fact that not so much Zeno and Chrysippus but later Stoics (for instance Diogenes of Babylon) introduced systematically developed definitions and rules into the field of the linguistic signs. 2. The first part of dialectics contains semantic components, and these presuppose the second part of dialectics. For instance the Stoic definitions of the parts of speech are semantic in character, and must be interpreted in the light of their meanings which are explicated in the second part of dialectics (cf. D.L. 7,58). And the semantic thesis that all words are ambiguous, presupposes an opposition between words and meanings, and considers the words in the light of their meanings. 3. Our result is compatible with what M. Frede recently found out about the history and the inner organisation of the first part of dialectics.

Frede is interested in the question whether it is adequate or only anachronistic to consider the first part of Stoic dialectics not only to be the historical point of departure but also to represent on its own the first form of that discipline which was later called grammar; and he arrives at a positive answer.[35] Frede's main point of view is the reorganisation of the philosophical disciplines during the hellenistic period, especially of the different linguistic disciplines. Aristotle had reiterated some topics at different points in his 'linguistic' studies. For instance his ideas on diction in general (*lexis*) appear in both his rhetoric (Rhet. III 1. 1404 a 28-39) and his poetics (Poet. 19. 1456 b 8-18). Thus, it was appropriate to extract such general topics from the different disciplines, and to incorporate them into a new linguistic discipline which was the most general one inasmuch as it preceded all the other linguistic disciplines. This new discipline constitutes an important part of the first part of Stoic dialectics. By this we can recognize a certain unity of the different topics of the first part. Additionally we get a positive interpretation of the title 'On the linguistic sign'. And finally, the sharp distinction between the two parts of dialectics can now be supported even from the standpoint of the first part, in that this part contains all the topics which are preliminaries to the special linguistic disciplines and must then also be distinguished from the themes of the second part of dialectics. But precisely at this point we can also see that Frede's principles concerning the formation of the first part of dialectics are subordinated to our own approach. For if Frede's point of view were to be basic with regard to the overall structure of dialectics as a total, then the new discipline which deals with the most general linguistic topics, ought to have the same affinity to all the special linguistic disciplines. But in the system of Stoic dialectics the affinities are in fact very different. The affinity of the themes 'On diction' to poetics, i.e. to another field of the first part of dialectics, is much closer than the affinity to the second part of dialectics; and this affinity is again much closer than with respect to rhetoric which is not even included in dialectics. This asymmetry shows that the formation-principle pointed out by Frede only determines the first part but not the overall structure of dialectics; and we may conclude, therefore, the adequacy of our own insufficient account of the first part of dialectics.

On the other hand, there remain some open questions. For, what does it mean with regard to our approach to the overall structure of Stoic dialectics when this structure is broken up by the transformation of the first part of dialectics into an independent discipline of grammar? Furthermore, in what way and how far is our approach capable of accounting for the fact that some Stoics wanted to integrate the theory of cognition with dialectics? And finally, the development of the Stoic answer to the question of the justification of language which has been sketched ought to be interrelated with other points of Stoic thought. For instance, there is also a development from Zeno to Chrysippus in the theory of cognition and in the concept of truth. An essential relationship between the two developments is to be expected. But it must be demonstrated!

Notes

1 See e.g. J. Pinborg, Classical Antiquity: Greece. In: Th.A. Sebeok (Ed.), Current Trends in Linguistics. Vol. 13,1. The Hague - Paris 1975, p.79; A.C. Lloyd, Grammar and Metaphysics in the Stoa. In: A.A. Long (Ed.), Problems in Stoicism. London 1971, p. 58ff.

2 On this point see I. Düring, Aristoteles. Heidelberg 1966, p. 53.

3 Cf. SVF II 49. (SVF = Stoicorum Veterum Fragmenta, collegit I. v. Arnim. Vol. I - III. Stuttgart 1903-1905. Reprint 1964.)

4 Cf. D.L. 7,83. On the *logos* in the Stoa see e.g. Ch.H. Kahn, Stoic Logic and Stoic LOGOS. Archiv für Geschichte der Philosophie 51, 1969, p. 158-172.

5 Cf. above all Sextus Empiricus, Adv. Math. VII and VIII: He separated his discussion of the theory of cognition, and of the dialectical questions.

6 On this question see e.g. G.B. Kerferd, The Problem of Synkatathesis and Katalepsis. In: Les Stoiciens et leur logique. Actes du colloque de Chantilly 18-22 septembre 1976. Paris 1978, p. 251f.

7 See for instance Chrysippus' introduction of the common noun as the fifth part of speech (D.L. 7,57) on the one hand, and his criticism of the traditional doctrine of the *entypôsis* (Sextus Empir., Adv. Math. 7,227ff. 370ff.) on the other hand. For the second point cf. K. v. Fritz, Zur antisthenischen Erkenntnistheorie und Logik. Hermes 62, 1927, p. 473ff.

8 Cf. J. Pinborg, loc. cit. p. 79f.

9 Cf. R.T. Schmidt, Stoicorum grammatica. Halle 1839. Reprint Amsterdam 1967, p. 15ff. 49ff. For a detailed critique of Schmidt's ideas in this field see my introduction to the German translation of Schmidt's book: R. T. Schmidt, Die Grammatik der Stoiker. Einleitung, Übersetzung und Bearbeitung von K. Hülser. Mit einer Bibliographie zur stoischen Sprachwissenschaft von U. Egli. Braunschweig 1979, p. 17ff. (forthcoming).

10 C. Imbert, Théorie de la représentation et doctrine logique. In: Les Stoiciens et leur logique p. 235f.

11 See U. Egli, Stoic Syntax and Semantics. In: Les Stoiciens et leur logique p. 135-154.

12 Cf. for instance the determinations of the different complete *lekta* in D.L. 7,65-68, and the form 'This is (or does) P' which is basic for all statements: Sextus Empir., Adv. Math. 8,96ff.

13 Cf. A.C. Lloyd, loc. cit. p. 60.

14 M. Frede, Principles of Stoic Grammar, In: J.M. Rist (Ed.), The Stoics. Berkeley - Los Angeles - London 1978, p. 27-75.

15 See e.g. M. Frede, loc. cit. p. 37ff.

16 Cf. A.C. Lloyd, loc. cit. p. 60. - The problem indicated throws some light on the fact that in some sources tne terminology of the two fields is not sharply distinguished or is even confused; see the collection of G. Nuchelmans, Theories of the Proposition. Amsterdam - London 1973, p. 72-74.

17 D. Sedley, Diodorus Cronus and Hellenistic Philosophy. Proceedings of the Cambridge Philological Society 203, 1977, p. 74ff.

18 Cf. D. Sedley, loc. cit. p. 84-104.

19 See e.g. Men. 75 cd ('more dialectic'); Pol. 537e - 539d (the very important empirical fact of a degenerate dialectic); Theaet. 167d - 168c (the
rules of the question/answer-discussion are capable of being used in an
eristic manner as well as for serious philosophical claims). - Since Plato himself hints at a basic meaning of 'dialectic' and since at times
'dialectic' was used to name a philosophical school, it is inadequate
(and in fact unfruitful) to say that 'dialectic' was originally used only
to characterize the form of discussion especially cultivated by Socrates,
and to develop the different meanings of 'dialectic' in Plato, in Aristotle, and in the Stoics on the lines of different interpretations of the
kind of discussion cultivated by Socrates. This approach was chosen, for
instance, by C.A. Viano, La dialettica stoica. Rivista di Filosofia 49,
1958, p. 179-227.

20 Very well descripted by E. Kapp, Syllogistik. RE Vol. IV A,1, p. 1056.

21 See his Topica, especially the books I and VIII.

22 In the Cases of Plato and Aristotle this could be developed systematically on the basis of their respective concepts of dialectic; but in the present context it is enough to point at some passages: Plato, Crat. 390 c-e;
Soph. 253 b-e; Aristotle, Top. esp. VII; Metaph. A 6. 987 b 29-33. In the
case of Xenocrates the relationship between his dialectics and linguistic
theory follows from his subclassification of philosophy. In the case of
the Dialectical school we have no programmatic evidence but only indirect
testimony: From the fact that Zeno studied dialectics under Diodorus Cronus (D.L. 7,25) we may conclude that Diodorus was a famous teacher in especially those topics which were considered by the Stoics to fall under the
heading of dialectics; from this, then, it follows that Diodorus was dealing with linguistic theory, and that the Dialectical school was familiar
with this field.

23 Cf. H.-J. Newiger, Untersuchungen zu Gorgias' Schrift Über das Nichtsei-
ende. Berlin - New York 1973.

24 See e.g. D. Sedley, loc. cit. p. 89ff.

25 Cf. K. v. Fritz, loc. cit. p. 455ff.

26 This is well to see from the dialogues of Plato, and was explicitly displayed by Aristotle: Metaph. A 6. 987 a 29ff.

27 Aristotle himself indicated that the theory of substance was an ontological interpretation of the form of (elementary) propositions: e.g. Metaph.
H 6. 1045 a 7-29. - That this starting point also leads to an interpretation which is both careful in detail and critical in systematic respects,
may be seen from E. Tugendhat, *TI KATA TINOS*. Freiburg 1958. The influence
of linguistic points of view on Aristotle's philosophy of nature was first
investigated by W. Wieland, Die aristotelische Physik. Göttingen 1962.

28 The relevance of the semantic model of proper names up to Aristotle was
recently stressed by A. Graeser, On Language, Thought, and Reality in Ancient Greek Philosophy. Dialectica 31, 1977, p. 359-388.

29 D.L. 7,66-70; Sextus Empir., Adv. Math. 8,70-74; Ammonius, In Aristot. de
interpr. 2,26 - 3,6 Busse; Simplicius, In Aristot. categg. 406,20-28 Kalb-
fleisch.

30 On this point see P. Pachet, L'impératif stoicien. In: Les Stoiciens et leur logique, p. 361-374.

31 This way of reasoning as well as the following argumentation entails that Chrysippus did not radically change the thoughts of his Stoic predecessors but in reforming the Stoa continued to ask certain main systematic questions raised by the founder of the school.

32 For more details see J.M. Rist, Zeno and the Origins of Stoic Logic. In: Les Stoiciens et leur logique, p. 393ff.

33 See K. Döring, Die Megariker. Kommentierte Sammlung der Testimonien. Amsterdam 1972, fragments 130ff. For further comments cf. ibid. p. 132ff., and D. Sedley, loc. cit. p. 96ff.

34 On this point G. Nuchelmans, loc. cit. p. 45-47.

35 See above note 14. Cf. also K. Barwick, Remmius Palaemon und die römische ars grammatica. Leipzig 1922. Reprint Hildesheim - New York 1972, p. 215-223.

Réparer – Reparieren. A Contrastive Study

Christoph Schwarze

Universität Konstanz, Sonderforschungsbereich 99, 'Linguistik', Postfach 5560, D-7750 Konstanz, Fed. Rep. of Germany

Introduction

In my communication I am going to give a contrastive account of the meanings of German and French verbs[1] belonging to the lexical field of repairing, such as the items corresponding to <u>repair</u>, <u>mend</u>, <u>patch</u>, <u>restore</u>, <u>renovate</u>, <u>heal</u>, <u>cure</u>, <u>stop</u> etc.

1. Overall semantic properties

In the first part of this paper, I will make some remarks on the features shared by all items belonging to that lexical field and on the parameters according to which they differ from each other.

The fundamental meaning of these verbs may be stated as follows:

1.1 There is an action, and as for all actions, there is an agent, which may be specified or not:

> *The car has been repaired by the mechanic*
> *Repairing this car will be expensive*

Consequently, all verbs of repairing will have an agent in their case frame.

1.2 The action is always one which includes accomplishment, that is for a sentence like:

> *John repaired his car*

it holds that if this sentence is true, then it is also true[2] that the action has reached a result (which we will specify below); correspondingly, in a sentence like:

> *I will repair your car*

I promise that I will be successful in my action, and in

> *He is repairing his car*

when this sentence is true, then it is also true that the result will be obtained if the action is not interrupted.

Those verbs which have this component of meaning we call
resultative verbs; resultative verbs can of course be used in
sentences the meaning of which is not resultative; e.g. when
they are accompanied by operator verbs like try: in a sentence
like:

He is trying to repair his car

the action the sentence refers to may be materially the same,
but the meaning of the sentence does not include that the
action will be successful.

All verbs of repairing will have the feature predicate
'resultative' in their complete analytical indices.

1.3 There always is an object of the action. It is presupposed that this object is in a state of defectiveness, that
is a negatively valued state in respect of integrity or sound-
ness. There are two possibilities: the object may be damaged
or destroyed. The meaning of verbs may differ according to
this distinction; cf.

The car has been repaired (damage)
The temple has been rebuilt (destruction)

If the defectiveness is damage, then the object of the
action of repairing is an affected object. If it is destruction, then the situation is more complicated: the object
which has been destroyed does not exist any longer at the time
of the 'repairing action'; another object is brought into being by this action. We might say consequently that the object
of the action, in the case of destruction the original object,
is an effected object. But this does not account for the fact
that in words like restore, reconstruct, rebuild etc. the prefix re- relates the identity of the object which is brought
about by the action to the identity of the object which had
been there before and which was destroyed: in a very natural
sense a city which has been completely destroyed by an earth-
quake and which is reconstructed remains identical to itself.

Probably this identity must rest upon some real (material
or social) continuity, e.g. the place, and what is more important, the name of the old and the new city. How can we
solve this problem? All we have to do is to determine the
meaning of 'destroyed' in such a way that it does not exclude
existence. We will say that if a destroyed entity is the object of an action of repairing, then its existence must have
been virtualized, but it is not completely annihilated. This
permits us to treat the destroyed and reconstituted object of
an action of repairing as an affected object. The change from
virtual to real existence then is implied for all verbs for
which the defectiveness is specified as destruction.

Each verb of repairing will thus have in its case frame an
obligatory 'affected object' case.

The success of the action I spoke about above consists,
roughly speaking, of eliminating the defectiveness of the

affected object. This may mean to reestablish the state in
which the object was before being damaged or destroyed, as it
is the case for a verb like restaurer. But it may also mean
simply that the result state corresponds just in one relevant
point to the original state. This point may be the functioning
of the affected object as in

> *John repaired the cable*

(where the cable may have some insulating tape on it that it
had not in its original state); it may be the integrity and
clearness of the surface as in

> *La façade a été ravalée*

(where the colour of the new coat of painting may be quite
different from that of the old one) etc.

Thus an action of repairing presupposes three states of
the affected object:

a. an original state of integrity
b. a subsequent state of defectiveness
c. a resultative state of eliminated defectiveness

This makes it possible for us to mark off the verbs of repairing from other verbs the meaning of which is closely related, and which may also be used for referring to actions of
repairing, but which are not verbs of repairing as to their
lexical meaning. Verbs of this sort are e.g.:

> amender, améliorer,

verbs that is which do imply a change from worse to better
(corresponding to the transition from b. to c.), but which do
not presuppose an original state of integrity (a.). Another
type of verb which we do not include in the lexical field of
repairing is represented by, e.g.:

> remplacer, redresser

These verbs are often interpretated in terms of repairing,
but they do not determine this interpretation by their
meaning: we just know that substituting parts or straightening
things is a frequently employed method of repairing, that is
why we interpret sentences like the following as describing
actions of repairing:

> *Jean a fait remplacer les freins de sa voiture*
> *Jean a fait redresser l'antenne de son téléviseur*

But these verbs are far from always describing actions of
repairing; cf.:

> *Jean a remplacé sa 2 CV par une 504*
> *Jean a redressé les roues de sa voiture*

We will have to return to these "method"-verbs when treating translational relations between French and German verbs.

Returning now to the affected object of the action of repairing, there is another parameter according to which verb
meanings may differ: there may be various restrictions on the
nature of the affected object itself. There may be very general criteria, as e.g. the abstract-concrete and the animate-
inanimate distinctions, cf., in German, the difference between
reparieren, to be used only for concrete inanimate objects,
and wiederherstellen, to be used without restrictions on the
affected object.

There may be, on the other hand, very special distinctions
as to the nature of the affected object; thus in French we
have the verb dépanner, to be used only in reference to engines and vehicles.

Restrictions on the affected object will be expressed as
feature predicates in the analysis indices of the verbs.

1.4. If the presupposed state of defectiveness is that of
damage, the kind of damage may be specified, as in e.g.

John will repair the leak

We account for this by saying that speakers treat a damage
as an ideal object. One might think of categorizing these objects equally as affected objects of the actions, since they
appear as direct objects (accusatives in German) just like the
"objects-which-are-damaged", and they may even be coordinated
with each other:

John repaired the car and the leak in the swimming pool

But this analysis would lead us into difficulties: the
affected object of an action of repairing has been defined as
an object which runs through the three states of original integrity, of defectiveness and of eliminated defectiveness;
this definition would make no sense if we included the damage
in the category of affected objects. Consequently we introduce a new deep case notion: whenever the presupposed state of
defectiveness of the affected object is one of damage (as opposed to destruction), then there is an abstract individual,
involved in the action of repairing, which we call "damage";
this individual may be specified or not; for certain verbs,
it cannot be specified in the same nuclear sentence, see below. Notice that there are certain lexical items which have
being a damage as part of their meaning, as e.g. the word
damage itself, or wound, fissure, leak, French déchirure,
fêlure, cassure etc., but there are many other words which do
not have being a damage as part of their meaning, such as
hole, dampness, stiffness etc., but which may still refer to
ideal objects involved as damage in an action of repairing.

The meanings of verbs may differ according to the kind of
damage specified for the affected object: so stop may be used

only if the damage is a <u>hole</u> or <u>leak</u>, <u>heal</u>, if it is a wound or illness etc.

Accordingly, most verbs of repairing either have the feature predicate 'destroyed', the argument of which is identical with the argument of the 'affected object' case predicate, or the verb has, as an alternative, the case predicate 'damage', which has an ideal entity as its argument. In the latter case, the damage may of course be specified, and the specification of the damage may be a feature predicate of the verb. There are a few verbs however, the meaning of which does not specify whether the defectiveness is damage or destruction.

1.5 Further there may be a <u>method</u> of the action, that is other actions, by means of which the action of repairing is accomplished. The method too is a parameter for distinguishing the meaning of verbs, so German <u>flicken</u> and <u>stopfen</u> refer to two different methods of mending holes in tissue or cloth.

The method may involve an object used as an <u>instrument</u>, this may be referred to by a prepositional phrase, as in:

She mended the hole with a needle

We account for this fact by using the well-known notion of instrumental case, and we say that in any action of repairing there may be an individual involved as instrument.

The method may also involve a material or substance; this may be referred to exactly in the same way as the instrument, and we treat it accordingly, that is, as an optional deep case.

How shall we treat <u>by</u>-clauses (or what corresponds to them) indicating the method? I will give a very rough idea of this by the following example: Consider the sentence:

John repaired the car by replacing the clutch

We would say that there are two actions, the first one is John's repairing the car, and the other one is his changing the clutch, and we would add the statement that the second action is the method employed in accomplishing the first one.

Thus each verb of repairing optionally has an 'instrument' and a 'material' in its case frame; it may have a 'method' among its features.

1.6 The action may be accomplished for the benefit of someone, who is then involved as a beneficiary, as in:

He will repair anything for you

1.7 Finally the meaning of a verb of repairing may convey information on how the speaker evaluates the action. So we have in French <u>raccommoder</u> vs. <u>rafistoler</u>; the latter characterizing the action as being accomplished in a superficial way, whereas the former is neutral in that respect.

Thus a verb of repairing may have something like 'done in a superficial way' among its feature predicates, the argument of this predicate being the variable of the action itself.

1.0.1 Let me resume:

All verbs of repairing are resultative verbs of action. Their case frame contains the following <u>obligatory cases</u>:

> agent (AG)
> affected object (AO)
> damage (DA)(excluded for those verbs the feature predi-
> cates of which specify the defectiveness as 'destruc-
> tion'; obligatory for all others)

and the following <u>optional cases</u>:

> instrument (IN)
> material (MA)
> beneficiary (BE)

Further, all verbs referring to actions of repairing pre-suppose that the affected objects undergo a change from a state of integrity to a state of defectiveness and, from this state, to a state free from that defectiveness.

The meanings of verbs of repairing may differ in that they convey (or do not convey) information about the following points:

> - the nature of the affected object
> - the sort of defectiveness (damage vs. destruction)
> - in the case of damage: the nature of the damage
> - the method employed in accomplishing the action
>   (determinateness vs. indeterminateness of the method)
> - in case of determinateness of the method: the speci-
>   fied method employed
> - evaluation of the quality of the action

Before going on to analyze and compare the meanings of a set of German and French verbs belonging to the semantic field of repairing, we will briefly examine their syntactic properties.

2. Overall syntactic properties

We are now giving a survey of the main types of surface syntax properties of the verbs under discussion. Since for all these verbs it holds that in an active sentence the agent, if there is any, becomes the subject, we will not mention the subject. We can distinguish the following syntactic types:

2.1 German:

2.1.1 AO $\rightarrow$ accusative

> *Karl repariert den Zaun*

2.1.2 DA $\rightarrow$ accusative

Karl repariert das Loch

All verbs which admit of construction 2 also may have a realization of the "AO case" in the same surface sentence, as
part of the "damage-NP". Two possibilities must be distinguished:

2.1.3 DA $\rightarrow$ accusative, AO $\rightarrow$ prepositional phrase incorporated in the damage-NP, the preposition being a local one govern-
ing the dative.

Karl repariert das Loch im Zaun

2.1.4 DA $\rightarrow$ accusative, AO $\rightarrow$ genitive phrase incorporated in
the DA-NP:

Karl heilt Augusts Wunde

The choice between 3 and 4 does not arbitrarily depend on individual lexical items; it is governed by the features of AO:
if AO is an inanimate object (including a part of the living
body!), then 3 must be chosen; if it is an animate being, then
AO is realized according to 4.

In an autonomous syntax, constructions 3 and 4 would of
course be derived from relative clauses. This is not necessary
in a semantically based case grammar, but the consequences of
the treatment suggested here are still to be studied.

2.1.5 $AO_1 \rightarrow$ accusative, $AO_2 \rightarrow$ $\begin{cases} \text{coordinated accusative NP} \\ \underline{\text{mit}} + \text{NP} \end{cases}$

Karl versöhnt Fritz $\begin{cases} und \\ mit \end{cases}$ *August*

(There is of course a difference of perspective between both
variants, which we neglect here.)

2.1.6 AO $\rightarrow$ dative

Karl gibt Fritz Genugtuung

All verbs which admit of this construction also may have a
realization of the "damage case" within the same sentence. We
then have:

2.1.7 AO $\rightarrow$ dative, DA $\rightarrow$ $\underline{\text{für}}$ + NP

Karl gibt Fritz Genugtuung für die Beleidigung

2.1.8 IN $\rightarrow$ subject, AO $\rightarrow$ accusative

Diese Behandlung hat ihn wieder auf die Beine gebracht

This construction of course presupposes the agent to be unspecified.

2.1.9 There are cases in which indicating a construction in terms of constituency would not account for the linguistic reality, even if restricted in terms of semantic features: certain verbs have typical phraseological complements, such as *sanieren* in the expression *einen Entzündungsherd sanieren*. These cases should be included in the analysis of syntactic properties, whenever the lexical comparison is to have any practical application. We must limit ourselves here to merely mentioning the problem.

2.2 French:

French has very similar constructions for the verbs of the lexical field we are discussing; we express this similarity by using the same numbers for analogous constructions. There is however one systematic difference between French and German with respect to constructions 3 and 4 of the preceding list; cf. below.

2.2.1 AO $\rightarrow$ direct object

> *Jean répare la clôture*

2.2.2 DA $\rightarrow$ direct object

> *Jean répare le trou*

2.2.3 DA $\rightarrow$ direct object, AO $\rightarrow$ local preposition phrase incorporated in the DA-NP

> *Jean répare le trou dans la clôture*

It must be added however that this construction is near to ungrammatical: French either prefers construction 4 (which consequently is not restricted as it is in German) or it realizes the incorporation of the "damage-NP" by using a relative clause:

> *Jean a réparé le trou qui était dans la clôture*

This contrast with German is not directly related to the verbs we are treating here, but it is a consequence of the differences the noun phrase structure has in both languages.

2.2.4 DA $\rightarrow$ accusative, AO preposition phrase with de, incorporate in the "damage-NP"

> *Jean répare le trou de la clôture*

According to what has been said above, the German constructions 3 and 4 in French coincide in 4. There are however different implicational relations of the surface sentences belonging to type 4, which reflect the distinctions of German:

> *Le trou de la clôture*

implies

    a. *La clôture a un trou*
    b. *Il y a un trou dans la clôture*

implication b. being more "natural" than implication a. Quite differently from this, a phrase like

    La plaie de Jean

does not imply a surface sentence formally corresponding to b., the only possibility being a:

    a. ₊*Jean a une plaie*
    b. *Il y a une plaie dans Jean*

2.2.5 $AO_1 \rightarrow$ direct object, $AO_2 \rightarrow$ coordinated direct object $\underline{avec}$ + NP

    Jean remet Paul $\genfrac{}{}{0pt}{}{et}{avec}$ Pierre

2.2.6 $AO \rightarrow + \underline{à}$ + NP

    Jean donne satisfaction à Paul

2.2.7 $AO \rightarrow \underline{à}$ + NP, $DA \rightarrow \underline{de}$ + NP

    Jean donne satisfaction à Paul de cette offense

2.2.8 IN $\rightarrow$ subject, AO $\rightarrow$ direct object

    Ce remède va le remettre rapidement

2.3 Observations on the syntactic properties:

2.3.1 All verbs which have construction 2 also have constructions 1 and 3/4. These verbs form a clearly distinct group:

    guérir, raccommoder, rafistoler, rapetasser, recoudre, réparer, repriser

in French, and

    ausbessern, flicken, reparieren, stopfen

in German

2.3.2 There is another important group, that is the group of those verbs which do not admit the DA to be expressed as an object or prepositional phrase, as:

    dépanner, désintoxiquer, rapiécer, ravaler, ravander, rechaper, refaire, remettre à neuf, remettre en état, remettre en ordre, rénover, ressemeler, restaurer, rétablir, rétaper in French, and

> *auffrischen, entlausen, erneuern, ersetzen, instand-*
> *setzen, renovieren, restaurieren, versöhnen, wieder-*
> *aufbauen, wiederherstellen, wieder in Ordnung bringen*

in German.

In some cases, this property can be explained on semantic grounds: some of the verbs have the kind of damage they presuppose as part of their lexical meaning, so it would be pointless (and regarded as pleonastic) to refer to the damage in form of an object of that same verb; cf. e.g.

> **dépanner une panne*
> **désintoxiquer une intoxication*
> **Läuse entlausen*

Other verbs do not presuppose a damage done to, but destruction of the AO; so obviously the damage cannot be stated. This is the case for, e.g.

> *rétablir*
> *wiederaufbauen*
> *wiederherstellen*

There are other cases however, in which the lack of construction 2 cannot be explained semantically; we then have to do with purely surface restrictions. This is the case in e.g.:

> *remettre en état*
> *instandsetzen*

These surface restrictions possibly may differentiate from each other verbs which are synonymous with respect to their semantic features, but I did not find such a case in my material.

3. Polysemy

Many of the verbs analyzed have more than one reading. The basic semantic analysis we have made for the whole lexical field makes it possible for us to isolate the points at which various readings of one lexeme differ, exactly in the same way as we distinguish the meanings of the various lexemes from each other. Thus the French verb raccommoder has, in one reading, the following restrictions: the affected object is an inanimate object of everyday use, and the damage is 'being broken, torn, having a hole'. In another reading, the AO is 'two or more persons' and the damage is a 'state of hostility'.

How do we express relations of this kind? We distinguish two possibilities: If the relation between the two readings is a structural relation we also find in other polysemous lexemes, we formulate the underlying principle as a rule generating derived meaning, and we specify for each lexeme, taken in one determinate reading, the polysemy rules which apply to it. (In a formalized version of our account, these rules would be functions which apply predicates into predicates.)

In our lexical field we have the following polysemy rules:

1° For a meaning specifying the method employed, there is a derived meaning, where the method is not specified, but where there is a specification of the evaluation of the action of repairing qualifying it as superficial or provisional.

To give an example: German <u>flicken</u> in one reading specifies as method 'putting on a patch'. (cf. <u>eine Hose</u>, <u>einen Schlauch flicken</u>). According to rule 1, there is another reading, where no method is specified, but where the action is characterized as accomplished superficially, in a provisional way (cf. <u>eine Leiter</u>, <u>eine Maschine flicken</u>).

2° For a meaning specifying the damage as a physical phenomenon, there is a derived meaning recategorizing the damage as a moral or psychological phenomenon.

As an example, consider French <u>désintoxiquer</u> which in one reading specifies the damage as a poisoning or addiction (cf. <u>désintoxiquer un alcoolique</u>), and in another as some negative influence on beliefs and opinions (cf. <u>désintoxiquer les esprits</u>).

Moreover, the example shows that the recategorization of the damage may imply a recategorization of the affected object: For the basic reading the affected object is a human being, considered under a physical aspect; for the derived reading a non-physical aspect is referred to.

It does not seem necessary here to formulate an independent rule for the recategorization of the AO, since we can form one set of possible AOs from various subsets. So we can account for the "metaphorical" meaning of French <u>raviver</u> (cf. <u>raviver les couleurs d'une robe</u> vs. <u>raviver un vieux souvenir</u>) by uniting ideal and inanimate objects into the set of possible AOs. That is consequently what we will do in analogous cases.

But there are more complicated cases. The recategorization of the affected object may be accompanied by a change of register. Here it is not sufficient to postulate merely a composed set of possible affected objects: we have to distinguish two different readings, and we can relate both to each other by a polysemy rule which reads as follows:

3° For a meaning where the AO is specified, there is a derived meaning, where this is not the case. The use of the lexeme in this reading is restricted to the register of familiar conversation.

To give an example: French <u>ravaler</u> presupposes the AO to be a building or a wall (cf. <u>ravaler une façade</u>, <u>ravaler un</u>

palais). But _ravaler_ may be used metaphorically as in Elle a
ravalé son visage (for: elle a maquillé son visage). This use
belongs to the register of familiar conversation.

Here a remark has to be made: I have formulated the rule
in purely negative terms, that is, as an abolition of a restriction, instead of, positively, as a change from one category to another. This might prove to be inadequate, since not
just anything can be the AO of metaphorical _avaler_. Hence rule
3 would need reexamination.

Consider also the following example: French rebâtir (as well
as reconstruire and German wiederaufbauen) has one reading in
which the AO is a 'building, part of a building, or settlement'.
But there is also a metaphorical reading, where the AO is an
ideal object, generally considered as a positive value, as in
se rebâtir une existence. This second reading implies a change
of the method specification: the method is no longer 'building' in the concrete sense. Here one would intuitively say
that it is the change of the AO which is basic (as opposed to
the change of the method). This intuition is reflected by
practical experience: it is much easier to define the change
of the AO than to define the change of the method specification. We can therefore formulate another rule of AO-recatego-
rization:

4° For a meaning which specifies the AO as a physical
   object or an animate being, there is a derived meaning, where the AO is an ideal object.

There is a third polysemy rule concerning the AO:

5° For a meaning which specifies the AO as a physical
   object, there is a derived meaning where the AO is
   specified as a human being. In this case, either the
   evaluation 'accomplished in a superficial way' is
   added, or the use is restricted to the register of
   familiar conversation.

Examples are German flicken and French recoudre (cf. Die
Ärzte haben ihn wieder zusammengeflickt vs. les médecins l'ont
recousu).

Notice that in these examples, polysemy rule 1 applies conjointly. In those cases where two polysemy rules apply conjointly to derive one reading, we join the numbers representing the rules by the plus symbol (+). (For another example,
cf. replâtrer un mur vs. replâtrer un marriage, where polysemy
rules 1 and 4 apply conjointly.) - Where different rules can
be applied independently, so that each application yields a
different reading, I separate the rule numbers by a comma.

Within our lexical field, rules 4 and 5 are the most important; cf. the following table:

Distribution of the application of the polysemy rules:

| rule N° | applies to | | total |
	German lexemes	French lexemes	
1	1	2	3
2	1	2	3
3	-	2	2
4	2	6	8
5	1	5	6

(The higher frequencies for the French words seem to be due to the fact that French has more words in the lexical field we are discussing here, the ratio being of 44 to 19; for an explanation of this fact, see below, 4.2.)

But not all polysemies can be accounted for in terms of polysemy rules, at any rate if one does not want to formulate rules which apply to just one item. Where the readings of a verb cannot be accounted for by means of polysemy rules, the word is split up into more than one lexeme, spelled identically and differentiated by indices. (The alleged racommoder is one of these cases.)

4.   Interlingual equivalence and translational relatedness

4.1 Equivalence

Interlingual equivalence, as has been pointed out above, is postulated according to the standards and the depth of our analysis. It is understood as a semantic relation holding between lexemes, but does not claim that the same polysemy rules apply to these lexemes. Thus German flicken and French rapiécer are treated as equivalent, even though flicken has polysemically derived readings rapiécer has not. (Notice that our analysis does not ignore this difference: it is expressed by the polysemy rule number figuring (or not figuring) in the entry.)

This treatment of polysemy is a methodological approach which makes it possible to have a relatively high number of interlingual equivalence relations, that is, to state similarity of word meanings in a rather simple way without violating descriptive adequateness.

I should like to emphasize, in this context, that I never split a word meaning for the sole purpose of getting more equivalence relations: a word meaning should only be split when it is not possible to give a consistent analysis of the semantic, syntactic and pragmatic properties of the word itself while still preserving the unity of the lexeme. I espe-

cially never split up a word meaning because the word has several non-synonymous translational correspondences in another
language.

4.2 Translational relations without semantic equivalence

For a certain number of verbs, there is no equivalent transla-
tional· correspondence. In this case we indicate usual non-
equivalent translations. If an analysis of the translationally
correspondent verb has been made, this analysis shows what information the translator possibly needs to choose the right
word, or what part of information is lost in the translation.

However the reader will notice that we have not analysed
all the verbs given as translational correspondences. The main
reason for this is that the translationally correspondent verb
often are not verbs of repairing. Thus recoller une assiette
may quite normally be translated with einen Teller kleben, and
recoudre un bouton with einen Knopf annähen, translations which
literally correspond to coller and coudre. These translational
correspondences can be accounted for on two levels. Firstly, they
rest upon the fact that many actions, which are not actions of
repairing in themselves, can be methods of actions of repairing. Gluing, e.g., is not in itself an action of repairing,
but I can repair certain objects by gluing. As a consequence,
I can refer to an action of repairing by using the word indicating the method and leave it to the hearer to understand
that he is supposed to establish a reference to an action of
repairing. Secondly, and this is a point concerning the specific languages we are examining, French and German have different devices for forming verbs of repairing on the base of
"method" verbs. French uses a normal prefixation device: the
morpheme re- (r-, ré-) is prefixed to the method verb (rebâtir, reconstruire, recoller, recoudre etc.). German however
has no analogous device: in order to obtain the designation
of an action of repairing from a verb of method, it can use
the adverb wieder (wiederaufbauen, wieder annageln, wieder annähen, wieder kleben etc.) Accordingly, recoller is a genuine
verb of repairing, whereas wieder kleben is a phrase, and
strictly speaking, there is no corresponding verb for recoller
in German.

This is, by the way, the main reason for the disproportion
between the German and the French inventory of verbs of repairing: of the 19 German verbs, 4 are formed with wieder,
whereas of the 44 French verbs, 19 have a productive re- prefix, and there are still others which have a lexicalized re-.

To this morphological difference between French and German
must be added the fact that there is a difference of language
use: in German the use of wieder in reference to actions of
repairing is optional and often avoided, whereas in French the
re-derivation of the verb must be used if the action is an
action of repairing. This phenomenon, by the way, is not restricted to our lexical field; cf. the following translation
relations:

<u>Er hat den Hörer aufgelegt</u> - <u>il a raccroché</u>
<u>Man hat ihn aus der Seine gefischt</u> - <u>on l'a repêché</u>
<u>dans la Seine</u>
<u>Ich habe meine Geldbörse gefunden</u> - <u>j'ai retrouvé ma</u>
<u>bourse</u>
<u>Man hat den Ausbrecher gefaßt</u> - <u>on a rattrapé l'évadé</u>

In German the use of <u>wieder</u> is of course possible, but in
many cases one would only use it under special circumstances.
In the first sentence one would use it for instance to indicate that the person the sentence is about has replaced the
receiver immediately after taking it off; the French sentence
would be completely anomalous without the prefix <u>re-</u>; in the
second sentence, <u>wieder</u> would be used if reference to the previous state was explicitly to be made (in e.g. <u>Man hat ihn in</u>
<u>die Seine geworfen und dann wieder herausgefischt</u>); in the
French sentence, <u>re-</u> can be omitted, but the sentence then
would be about something which is normally in the river, for
instance a fish.

5. Conclusion

I have tried to show how the notional apparatus of a semantically based deep case grammar can be used for the comparative
analysis of the lexemes different languages have for a deter-
minated lexical field. I have not tried to bring my results
into canonical form, and accordingly, there is only a very
intuitive control of the consistency of my analysis. I am conscious too of the fact that my heuristics is open to improvement: I have not had the time for a careful empirical control
of the analysis I have made on the base of my knowledge of the
two languages, the consultation of dictionaries and the statements of a few informants I interviewed on points I was not
quite sure about. Finally, I have not analysed all the verbs
belonging to the lexical field.

What I claim to have shown however is this:

- One can realize an interlingual lexical comparison
  with the same methodological approach as a monolingual
  analysis.

- One can attain a relatively high number of interlingual semantic equivalences by a proper treatment of
  polysemy, without splitting up meaning on merely comparative grounds.

- One can reasonably organize meaning components by
  distinguishing between feature predicates, case predicates and predicates (restrictions) on the arguments
  of the case predicates.

Appendix: A French-German dictionary of verbs of 'repairing'

Abbreviations: s_1: "state of defectiveness previous to the repairing action. AO: "affected object of the repairing action".
- DA: "damage". - M: "Method". - E: "Evaluation of the action
of repairing". - PR: "Polysemy rules". - C: "Syntactic constructions". - =:"Semantically equivalent interlingual corres-
pondance". - ut: "Usual, but not equivalent translation".

How to read the entries: If an expression e is given after s_1,
AO, DA, M and E, this is to be read as "s_1, AO, DA, M, E is
specified by the lexeme meaning as having the property e". If
s_1, AO, DA, M and E are not mentioned in the entry, this means
that the lexeme meaning does not specify these meaning components. The specifications are often given in form of several
words, separated by commas or the word or. This is never to be
understood as a disjunction of contradictory terms, but as a
notation for simple predicates which do not exist in ordinary
English. - The numbers after PR and C indicate the polysemy
rules and the syntactic constructions, respectively, which
hold for the lexeme. - Those meaning components which all 'repairing' verbs have in common, are not mentioned in the dictionary.

FRENCH-GERMAN

dépanner s_1: damage, AO: engine, technical device, DA: break-
down, C: 1, PR: 5, ut: reparieren

désintoxiquer s_1: damage, AO: animate being, DA: intoxication,
poisoning, addiction, C: 1, PR: 2, ut: von einer Sucht heilen, wieder zu Kräften bringen, entschlacken

guérir s_1: damage, AO: animate being, part of body, DA: disease, illness, wound, PR 2, C: 1, 2, 4, = heilen

épouiller s_1: damage, AO: inanimate object, DA: having lice,
C: 1, = entlausen

raccommoder 1 s_1: damage, AO: inanimate object of every day
use, DA: being broken, torn, having a hole, C: 1, 2, 4,
ut: flicken, stopfen, ausbessern, reparieren, instandsetzen

raccommoder 2 s_1: damage, AO: two or more persons, DA: state
of hostility, C: 5, = (miteinander)versöhnen

radouber s_1: damage, AO: ship, fishing net, PR: 3, C: 1,
ut: reparieren, überholen

rafistoler s_1: damage, AO: inanimate object, DA: broken or
fallen into pieces or worn out, E: executed in a superficial way, C: 1, 2, 4, = flicken 2 (i.e. flicken after
application of PR 1)

ranimer 1 s_1 damage, AO: animate being, DA: loss of consciousness, C: 1, = wiederbeleben

ranimer 2 s_1: damage (!), AO: animate being, DA: death, PR: 4,
C: 1, = auferwecken

<u>rapetasser</u> s_1 damage, AO: inanimate object (espec. mattress), E: executed in a superficial way, C: 1, = <u>flicken 2</u>

<u>rapiécer</u> s_1: damage, AO: inanimate object, M: putting on patches, C: 1, 2, 4, = <u>flicken</u>

<u>ravaler</u> s_1 damage, AO: building, wall, DA: dirt, wear and tear, M: cleaning, whitewashing on the outside, PR: 3, C: 1, ut: <u>renovieren</u>

<u>ravauder</u> s_1: damage, AO: old clothes, cloth, net, DA: hole, wear and tear, M: by sewing, C: 1, ut: <u>flicken</u>, <u>ausbessern</u>, <u>stopfen</u>

<u>raviver</u> s_1 damage, AO: ideal or inanimate object, espec. color, DA: loss of freshness, fading, C: 1, = <u>auffrischen</u>, ut: <u>erneuern</u>, <u>neu beleben</u>

<u>réanimer</u> s_1 damage, AO: animate being, DA: coma, M: medical treatment, PR: 4, C: 1 ut: <u>wiederbeleben</u>

<u>rebâtir</u> s_1: destruction, AO: settlement, building, part of building, M: building an object presenting the conditions required for identity with AO, PR: 4, C: 1, = <u>wiederaufbauen</u>

<u>rechaper</u> s_1 damage, AO: tyre, DA: tyre casing worn out, M: vulcanizing a layer of rubber, C: 1, = <u>runderneuern</u>

<u>recoller</u> AO: inanimate object, DA: broken, torn, M: gluing, C: 1, = <u>wieder kleben</u>, ut: <u>kleben</u>

<u>réconcilier</u> s_1 damage, AO: two or more persons, DA: state of hostility, PR: 4, C: 5, = <u>versöhnen</u>

<u>reconstituer 1</u> AO: something having shape, structure or meaning, DA (if s_1 is a damage): alteration, mutilation, M: finding out original shape structure or meaning by inference, possibly constructing model of AO, C: 1, ut: <u>rekonstruieren</u>

<u>reconstituer 2</u> s_1: damage, AO: stock, DA: diminuition, consumption, PR: 5, C: 1, ut: <u>ergänzen</u>, <u>erneuern</u>

<u>reconstruire</u> s_1: destruction, AO: settlement, building, part of building, M: building an object presenting the conditions required for identity with AO, PR: 4, C: 1, = <u>wiederaufbauen</u>

<u>recoudre</u> s_1: damage, AO: inanimate object, part of body, DA: hole, disconnected part, wound, M: sewing, PR: 1+5, C: 1, 2, 4, ut: <u>nähen</u>, <u>annähen</u>, = <u>wieder annnähen</u>

<u>remettre à neuf</u> s_1: damage, AO: inanimate object, DA: decay, wear and tear, E: executed thoroughly, so that AO appears new, C: 1, ut: <u>renovieren</u>, <u>überholen</u>, <u>instandsetzen</u>

<u>remettre d'accord</u> s_1: damage, AO: two or more persons, DA: state of hostility, C: 5, = <u>versöhnen</u>

<u>remettre en état</u> s_1: damage, AO: inanimate object, C: 1, = <u>instandsetzen</u>

<u>remettre en ordre</u> s_1: damage, DA: being in a state of disorder, C: 1, = <u>wieder in Ordnung bringen</u>, ut: <u>in Ordnung bringen</u>

rénover s_1: damage, AO: district, building, room, furniture, DA: decay, wear and tear, M: conserving substance of AO, E: executed thoroughly, so that AO appears new, C: 1, = renovieren

renouveler 1 M: replacing AO or part of the substance of AO, C: 1, = erneuern 1

renouveler 2 AO: ideal object, DA: loss of strength or validity, C: 1, = erneuern 2

réparer 1 s_1: damage, AO: inanimate object, DA: concerning integrity of substance or functioning, C: 1, 2, 4, = reparieren

réparer 2 s_1 damage, AO: human being, DA: moral injury, offence or suffering, M: compensating for DA, C: 2, = wiedergutmachen

replâtrer s_1: damage, AO: inanimate object, M: plastering, PR: 1+4, C: 1, 2, 4, ut: vergipsen

repriser s_1: damage, AO: of cloth, DA: hole, M: interweaving yarn with needle across hole, C: 1, 2, 4, = stopfen

ressemeler s_1: damage, AO: shoes, DA: soles worn out, M: replace soles, C: 1, ut: besohlen

restaurer 1 s_1: damage, AO: inanimate object of esthetic value DA: wear and tear, decay, E: original state reproduced, C: 1, = restaurieren 1

restaurer 2 s_1: destruction, AO: ideal object, C: 1, = restaurieren 2, ut: wiederherstellen

restaurer 3 s_1 damage, AO: human being, DA: loss of strength, esec. caused by hunger, M: feed (well), C: 1,8, ut: ?

restituer s_1 damage, AO: text, monument, DA: alteration, mutilation, M: finding out original form by inference, C: 1, ut: wiederherstellen

rétablir 1 s_1: destruction, AO: ideal object, C: 1, ut: wiederherstellen

rétablir 2 s_1: damage, AO: text, DA: alternation, mutilation, M: finding out original wording by inference, C: 1, ut: wiederherstellen

retaper s_1: damage, AO: inanimate object in a generally bad state, E: executed in a superficial way, PR: 5, C: 1, ut: flicken, reparieren

stopper s_1: damage, AO: made of subtle texture, DA: hole, M: interweaving yarn with neddle across hole, C: 1, 2, ut: stopfen

GERMAN-FRENCH

auffrischen s_1: damage, AO: inanimate object, ideal object, espec. color, DA: loss of freshness, fading, C: 1, = raviver, ut: renouveler 2 ausbessern s$_1$: damage, AO: inanimate object (engines, machines excluded), DA: slight damage, C: 1, 2, 3, ut: réparer, refaire, ravauder, raccommoder, restaurer 1, repriser

entlausen s$_1$: damage, AO: animate being, inanimate object, DA: having lice, C: 1, = épouiller

erneuern 1 M: replacing AO or part of the substance of AO, C: 1, = renouveler 1

erneuern 2 AO: ideal object, DA: loss of strength or validity, C: 1, = renouveler 2

flicken s$_1$: damage, AO: inanimate object, DA: hole, M: putting on patch, PR: 1, 1+5, C: 1, 2, 3, = rapiécer

Genugtuung geben s$_1$: damage, AO: human being, DA: offence to AO's honor, C: 6, ut: donner satisfaction

heilen s$_1$: damage, AO: animate being, part of body, DA: disease, illness, wound, PR: 2, C: 1, 2, 4, = guérir

instandsetzen s$_1$: damage, AO: inanimate object, C: 1, = remettre en état

renovieren s$_1$: damage, AO: district, building, room, furniture, DA: decay, wear and tear, M: conserving substance of AO, E: executed thoroughly, so that AO appears new, C: 1, = rénover

reparieren s$_1$: damage, AO: inanimate object, DA: concerning functioning or integrity of substance, C: 1, 2, 3, ut: réparer

restaurieren 1 s$_1$: damage, AO: inanimate object of esthetic value, DA: wear and tear, decay, E: original state reproduced, C: 1, = restaurer 1

restaurieren 2 s$_1$: destruction, AO: ideal object, C: 1, = restaurer 2

stopfen s$_1$: damage, AO: of cloth, DA: hole, M: interweaving yarn with needle across hole, C: 1, 2, 3, = repriser

versöhnen s$_1$: damage, AO: two or more persons, DA: state of hostility, PR: 4, C: 5, = remettre d'accord, réconcilier

wiederaufbauen s$_1$ destruction, AO: settlement, building, part of building, M: building an object presenting the conditions required for identity with AO, PR: 4, C: 1, = rebâtir, reconstruire

wiederbeleben s$_1$: damage, AO: animate being, DA: loss of consciousness, C: 1, = ranimer 1

wiedergutmachen s$_1$ damage, AO: human being, DA: moral injury, offence or suffering, M: compensating for DA, C: 2, 3, = réparer 2

wiederherstellen s$_1$ destruction, C: 1, ut: rétablir, remettre en état

Notes

1 This paper is a result of a project supported by the Deut-
sche Forschungsgemeinschaft, on "comparative lexicology".
The project is described in Ch. Schwarze, Vergleichende
Lexikologie. Bericht über ein Forschungsprojekt, paper at
the Third International Colloquium on Contrastive Linguis-
tics and the Science of Translation, Trier and Saarbrücken,
September 1978. - The main sources of inspiration are Ch.
Fillmore's articles Verbs of judging, in: Ch. Fillmore/
C. Langendoen (eds.), Studies in Linguistic Semantics, New
York 1971, p. 273-290 and Types of lexical information, in:
F. Kiefer (ed.), Studies in Syntax and Semantics, Dordrecht
1969, p. 109-137; the lexicological analyses are to be integrated into a predicate calculus based comparative grammar as has been outlined in: Ch. Schwarze (ed.), Kasusgram-
matik und Sprachvergleich, Tübingen 1978; for the formal
treatment of the lexicon in a comparative grammar see Ch.
Schwarze, Le lexique dans une grammaire comparée du fran-
çais et de l'allemand, in: Ch. Rohrer (ed.), Actes du Colloque franco-allemand de linguistique théorique, Tübingen
1977, p. 231-240.

2 In using these expressions, I claim that lexical features
can be treated as predicates in a truth-functional semantics of sense relations. I do not want however to specify
whether the feature information is to be formalized as a
proper implication or as a (semantic) presupposition. - I
cannot enter into the details of the criticism which has
been developed recently of a feature semantics (cf. H.
Putnam, Meaning, Reference and Stereotypes, in: E. Guenthner and M. Guenthner-Reutter (eds.), Meaning and Translation. Philosophical and Linguistic Approaches, London 1978,
p. 61-81); I would just like to state that I do mean to
give analytical meaning components of the lexemes as they
are conventionally used. (I may of course fail in doing so
in those cases where my analysis has not been made thoroughly enough.) The main reason for maintaining this position is that treating lexical meanings as stereotypes would,
in a cross language analysis, easily make word meanings
which cannot be treated as equivalent in translation coincide. I furthermore suspect that the argumentations exemplified on words like 'gold' and 'cat' might seem less convincing when related to verb meanings like 'yield', 'put',
or 'ask'.

SALAT:
Machine Translation Via Semantic Representation

Christa Hauenschild, Edgar Huckert, and Robert Maier

Universität Heidelberg, Angewandte Sprachwissenschaft,
Landfriedstr. 12, D-6900 Heidelberg, Fed. Rep. of Germany

This paper is to show how some semantic problems are handled in
the machine translation system S A L A T (= System for Automatic
Language Analysis and Translation)[1]. Therefore it will be necessary to give a rather comprehensive introduction into the system.
Otherwise the topic could not be treated in a satisfactory way,
and it would be impossible for the reader to get a sufficiently
detailed and concrete idea of the involved problems and proposed
solutions.

1. Basic Principles of S A L A T

In the development of S A L A T the following principles have
been and are being respected:
- theoretical orientation of the project;
- independence of individual languages;
- strict separation of data from algorithms;
- translation via a logico-semantic interlingua representing
  meanings of translated sentences and knowledge about the
  situation and the world ("Situations- und Weltwissen").

1.1 Theoretical Orientation

The project of S A L A T aims at theoretical rather than at
practically applicable results, i.e. its main orientation is not
towards problems of large-scale application (e.g. optimizing of
programs, preparation and processing of comprehensive data sets),
but towards the investigation of the prerequisites for fully
automatic high-quality translation.

By this term coined by Y. BAR-HILLEL in the early sixties we
understand (as he did e.g. in (1) and (2)) machine translation
without pre- or post-editing respecting the usual standards of
human translation. We agree with Y. BAR-HILLEL that such a translation must be based on a full-fledged semantic analysis, i.e.
on the 'understanding', of the translated text by the computer,
which is possible only if "good general background knowledge"
(p. 331 in (1), "knowledge about the world" in our terms) as
well as supplementary information about the situation of utterance is available; for otherwise e.g. the resolution of many
ambiguities would be impossible. But we do not agree that therefore fully automatic high-quality translation is a priori in-
feasible nor that the only way is to confine oneself to machine-

aided translation or to utterly restricted domains, as was claimed by Y. BAR-HILLEL in (1) and (2).

Rather do we hold that it still makes sense to try and approximate high-quality machine translation by working out concepts for the necessary components of an appropriate translation system, including a data base (containing knowledge about the situation and the world) and an inference-making device (for a realistic data base would have to be very large, but nevertheless could not comprise all the information needed for any special translation problem), and by defining the corresponding algorithms in a way which allows them to be programmed and tested on gradually enlarged sets of examples. The main difficulty in designing such a system lies in the absence of an entirely satisfactory theory - not only of knowledge representation, but of the translation process as a whole - that would make it possible to formulate problems and solutions in a way precise and explicit enough for computational processing.

Thus such a project can be promising only if it is paralleled by the development of efficient theoretical approaches for its different parts and based on further results of linguistic, logical and artificial-intelligence research. Then it may contribute to a general theory of translation and serve as an appropriate tool for the verification of the adequacy of the different sub-theories, linguistic or other. So the theoretically oriented approach to machine translation makes sense, even if it turned out that fully automatic high-quality translation was in fact impossible (which would be very difficult to prove, as the underlying theories can surely always be improved), on account of the lots of useful insights gained on the way as to its precise limits and the linguistic or other reasons therefor.

1.2 Independence of Individual Languages and Separation of Data from Algorithms

In accordance with the theoretical orientation of S A L A T , the translation procedure is not dependent on special source or target languages: it is being tested on German, English, French, and Russian data, which is documented in (6) (esp. Vol.II), (12), (13), (14), (15), (17).

As identical formalisms and algorithms ought to be applicable for the translation between different language pairs, one of the main programming principles consists in a strict separation of data (e.g. lexica, rules) from algorithms (e.g. application of rules). This is convenient, too, for the division of labour between the linguist and the programmer. Moreover, the rule systems can be revised and completed without changing the programs (the reverse is only partially true; mostly, however, a revision of programs does not require substantial, but just formal changes of rules, if any), which is of great importance in the testing phase of a machine translation system.

1.3 Logico-Semantic Interlingua

The translation process goes via a logico-semantic interlingua
which serves as a general representation system for the meanings
of translated sentences as well as for those of sentences containing supplementary information about the situation and the
world, possibly not inferable from the translated text, but
needed for high-quality translation. As the interlingua representations of these latter sentences are to be stored in a data
base and operated on by special deduction systems, the interlingua must be flexible enough to represent natural-language
meanings in a way that facilitates the formulation of logico-
semantic deduction rules.

The interlingua of S A L A T is the core of the whole system, as it were, for it serves as a basis for the solution of
semantic translation problems. Its form is described in some
more detail in 2.1, while its functioning is explained and illustrated in several passages in chapters 3 to 5.

2. Formalisms Used in S A L A T

For the different levels of natural-language description and for
the connections between them the following formalisms have been
developed or adapted for S A L A T :
- ε-λ-context-free syntax for "deep structures" (= expressions
  of the interlingua);
- quasi-normal two-step context-free syntax in complex notation
  for "surface structures";
- transformational rules establishing relations between deep
  and surface structures or among deep structures.
The rôles of these formalisms in the different parts of S A L A T
are explained more fully in chapters 3 and 4.

It ought to be kept in view that, while the formalisms as such
seem to be satisfactory, this does not hold for the present versions of the respective rule systems, which are rather limited
in scope and precision, but can nevertheless serve as a basis for
realistic tests of the system. Moreover, the flexibility of the
formalisms facilitates the adaptation of analyses of natural-
language phenomena formalized differently. So the rule systems
can easily be revised and completed, in order to cover gradually
enlarged fragments of natural languages and of the translation
relations between them.

In the following paragraphs, the formalisms used in S A L A T
will not be described at full length, but rather illustrated with
the aid of hopefully illuminating examples.

2.1 ε-λ-Context-Free Syntax

The interlingua of S A L A T is an ε-λ-context-free language
designed by A. v. STECHOW (21) with reference to ideas by R.
MONTAGUE (23), P. SUPPES (22), M. J. CRESSWELL (7), and U. EGLI
(9), which was modified by us according to the special needs of

our project [19], [20]: a context-free syntax, the terminals of
which are "semantemes" mainly representing lexical meanings of
natural languages, is enlarged by rules introducing variables and
the abstractors ε and λ for classes and functions respectively
(in the present version only λ is used). The deep structures,
i.e. expressions of the interlingua, generated by this "deep
syntax" can be understood as representations of type-theoretic
expressions in the form of trees and therefore have nearly nothing in common with Chomskyan deep structures. They allow a
model-theoretic interpretation which is used in the heuristics
of the deduction rules, for the control of their correctness,
and for the formulation of meta-theoretical statements.

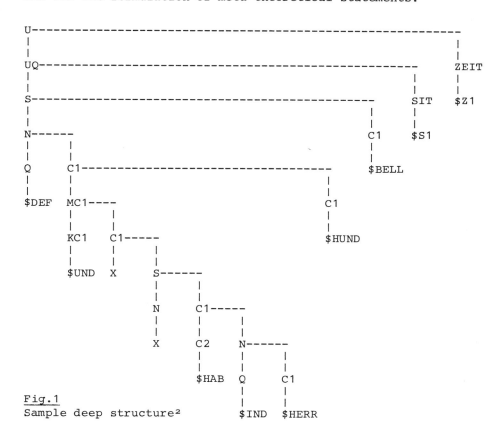

Fig.1
Sample deep structure[2]

The deep structure in Fig.1 represents the German sentence
"Der Hund, der einen Herrn hat, bellt.", which translates into
"The dog which has a master barks."[3]. The non-terminal node
labels, i.e. "deep categories", to be found in the example correspond approximately to the following constituents (mainly of
surface syntax):

```
U     - utterance
ZEIT  - time of utterance
UQ    - utterance without time specification
SIT   - situation of utterance
S     - sentence, clause
N     - noun phrase, proper name
Q     - quantifier, determiner
C1    - "one-place contentive" = noun, one-place verb
        or verb phrase, intersective adjective, ...
C2    - "two-place contentive" = two-place verb or verb
        phrase, ...
MC1   - modifier of one-place contentive
KC1   - connective for one-place contentives
```

The terminal labels of the deep structure are variables
("X"es, the indices of which are contained in a special list
omitted here) and semantemes (marked by "$") corresponding to
German lexemes with the exception of "$Z1" and "$S1", which are
arbitrary names of the time and the situation of utterance respectively. The other semantemes may be related to the following
English lexemes:

```
$DEF  - the
$UND  - and
$HAB  - have
$IND  - a
$HERR - master
$HUND - dog
$BELL - bark
```

The embedded "S" of Fig.1 shows the typical deep structure
of a relative clause. The rule introducing this "S" originally
contained "λ" (C1 → λ X_i S), which is left out here just for
technical reasons (binarity of the structure), but is of course
considered in the model-theoretic interpretation. Interpreting
the "sentential part" of the sample deep structure, i.e. without
the categories referring to the utterance and its specification,
would yield the following result:
$BELL ιx($HUNDx & $\exists y$($HERRy & $HAByx))

"$HAByx" is to be read as "x has y", which does not correspond
to the usual order of arguments in the predicate calculus. The
full sequence of the steps of interpretation is given in [14],
pp.14-15.

2.2   Two-Step Context-Free Syntax in Complex Notation

Surface structures of input or output sentences in S A L A T
are expressions of a context-free language defined by a quasi-
normal two-step context-free syntax in complex notation, where
"two-step" refers to the fact that it consists of a "word syntax"
(roughly: morphology) and a "sentence syntax" (for the details
of the formalism and the corresponding analysis procedure see
[4], more or less comprehensive rule systems written in this
formalism for fragments of different languages are contained in
Vol.II of [6] and in [15]).

The following figure shows the context-free surface structure
of the English sentence "The dog which has a master barks.",
i.e. of the sentence corresponding to the German expression
represented in the deep structure of Fig.1. This surface structure was the output of a sample translation with S A L A T
described in (14), pp.29-63.

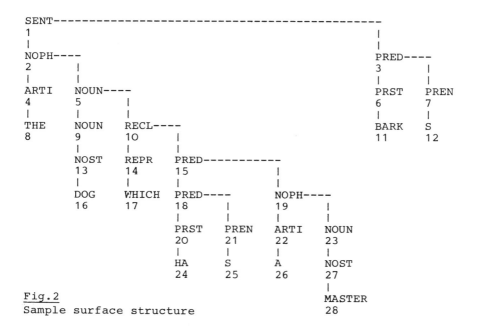

Fig.2
Sample surface structure

The meanings of the syntactic categories in Fig.2 should be
to some extent self-explanatory by virtue of the structure assigned and the abbreviations employed. The boundary between
word syntax and sentence syntax is defined by the "transition
categories" (here: "ARTI" - article, "NOUN" - noun, "REPR" -
relative pronoun, "PRED" - verb). The labels of the nodes dominated by them belong to the word syntax (here: "NOST" - noun
stem, "PRST" - verb stem, "PREN" - verb ending).

The digits under the node labels are the canonical node numbers, which could not be omitted here (as in Fig.1) because of
their function in the following list of "subcategories", which
is an integral part of the surface structure.

Figure 3 contains the "syntactic šubcategories", which are
related to their respective "main categories" (i.e. non-terminal
labels of the surface structure) by the canonical node numbers
of the latter, listed in the left column. Together they form
"complex categories"; so this is just a special notation for
complex node labels which keeps the tree structures within

sensible dimensions[4]. The "specifications" of the subcategories
(comparable to values assigned to variables) are given in parentheses behind the subcategory names.

node number	subcategories
2	NUM(1)
3	ERG(1) NUM(1) PER(3)
4	NUM(1)
5	NUM(1) ART(2)
6	ERG(1) PTY(2)
7	NUM(1) PER(3) PTY(2)
9	NUM(1) ART(2)
10	NUM(1) ART(2)
13	ART(2) NTY(1)
14	ART(2) CAS(1)
15	ERG(1) NUM(1) PER(3)
18	ERG(2) NUM(1) PER(3)
19	NUM(1)
20	ERG(2) PTY(1)
21	NUM(1) PER(3) PTY(1)
22	NUM(1)
23	NUM(1) ART(1)
27	ART(1) NTY(1)

Fig.3 Subcategory list

   Subcategories are the core of the complex notation of syntactic rules (cf. [4], pp.56-57); e.g. they are responsible
for number and person agreement of subjects and predicates, for
number (and gender) agreement within noun phrases etc. The range
of possible functions of subcategories (even for more 'semantic'
phenomena) is very wide; they are employed not only in the context-free syntax, but also in the transformational rules of
S A L A T (cf. 2.3).

   The names of the subcategories occurring in Fig.3 are partly
self-explanatory ("NUM", "PER", "CAS"); the rest shall not be
explained in detail here (it is done in [14], pp.49-50). Only
some remarks showing, hopefully, the flexibility of the subcategory device: "ERG" is responsible for verb valency, "PTY"
and "NTY" specify the inflectional types of the stems and the
corresponding endings of verbs ("PTY") and nouns ("NTY"). "ART"
indicates the types of nouns with respect to potential relative
clauses modifying them, namely whether they are to contain "who"
or "which" ("ART(1)", indicating the "who" type, and "ART(2)",
indicating the "which" type, are assigned to the nouns "master"
and "dog" respectively, cf. nodes 23 and 9). The corresponding
specifications characterize the relative pronouns (here: node
14 with complex label "REPR ART(2) CAS(1)", dominating "WHICH")
and are 'inherited' from them by the relative clauses (here:
node 10 with complex label "RECL NUM(1) ART(2)"), so that an
'agreement' of "ART" specification between the noun and the
relative clause can be stated in the corresponding syntactic
rule of noun modification[5].

2.3 Transformational Rules

Transformational rules are applied in S A L A T for the transduction of surface structures into deep structures (second part
of analysis) and vice versa (synthesis) as well as for deductions
and other transformations in disambiguation and transfer. Like
the S A L A T deep structures, they exhibit little similarity
to the Chomskyan concepts having the same name; they are just
mappings of (sequences of) trees on (sequences of) trees. They
are of a very flexible type conceived with reference to ideas
by U. EGLI (9). In particular, they allow the formulation of
supplementary conditions of application using decidable predicates with structures and parts of structures as their arguments.
These predicates must hold true for the "object trees", i.e. the
trees where the transformations are to operate, or else the respective rules will not be applicable (for a more comprehensive
description see (14) and (16)).

The following figure shows a very simple sample rule with
a decidable predicate occurring in it. The rule is given in tree
notation, which is easier to read than the S A L A T input
notation (cf. Fig.5), especially in the case of more complicated
structures. Moreover, the subcategories are combined with their
main categories to build up complex node labels.

```
$BELL    --->    ?PRED
                 ERG(1)
                 |
                 |
                 ?BARK
```

Condition:
DOMS(S(N*C1),1)   Fig.4   Sample rule 1 - tree notation

The sample rule is taken from the translation with S A L A T
described in (14), namely from the "lexicon of semantemes and
lexemes" (cf. chapter 3) of the English synthesis. It contains
a semanteme on its left-hand side and a "lexeme" and an "intermediate category" on its right-hand side. Lexemes (in the
S A L A T sense of the word) appear only in the course of synthesis as "intermediate" labels between the semantemes and the
terminal labels of surface structures. They belong to the intermediate categories (intermediate between deep and surface categories), which are all prefixed with "?", in order to distinguish
them from the surface categories, from which they are different
by virtue of their usually incomplete subcategory string.

The rule in Fig.4 will apply, if there is a terminal node
labelled "$BELL" to be found in the object tree and if the se-
quence of its predecessors (in the ascending direction) starts
with any number of "C1" nodes followed by one "S" node[6]. This
condition is coded in the two-place predicate "DOMS", the first
argument of which is an expression defining the properties to
be fulfilled by the sequence of predecessors (here: one "S"

dominating n times "C1") of the node referred to by the second
argument. The latter is the canonical number of the respective
node in the "rule tree" of the left-hand side of the transformational rule (here: "1" refers to the one and only node of
the left-hand side).

This supplementary condition, called "structural restriction",
could not be expressed easily in the left-hand rule tree on
account of the indefinite number of "C1" nodes that may occur
in the sequence of predecessors of "$BELL".

There are other decidable predicates defined in S A L A T
with different types of arguments. They can be combined to more
complex structural restrictions with the aid of the operators
of propositional logic (cf. [16], chapter 3.2.1); in particular,
they can be negated. E.g. "CONTA" is frequently used with negation, claiming that a special substructure is <u>not</u> <u>contained</u>
in a specified subpart of the object tree. It is not obvious,
how this condition might be expressed in the rule tree without
using a predicate (for an example of "CONTA" see the deduction
rules in 5.2).

If the rule in Fig.4 is applicable, the terminal node of the
left-hand side (i.e. the semanteme "$BELL") is substituted in
the object tree by the terminal structure of the right-hand side
(i.e. the lexeme "?BARK", dominated by "?PRED ERG(1)").

<$BELL>.
BED.:<DOMS(S(N*C1)1)>.
--->
<1.?PRED(?BARK)>.
1.ERG(1)

<u>Fig.5</u> Sample rule 1 - S A L A T notation

In the notation used for transformational rules in S A L A T ,
both sides of the rule, as well as the structural restriction,
are given in the form of bracketed expressions corresponding to
the rule trees in Fig.5 and to a bracketed Polish notation of
the structural restriction ("BED" is short for "Bedingung", i.e.
"condition"). Here, the subcategories are related to their respective main categories by reference numbers ("1.", "2." etc.),
which is very convenient in cases where different main categories
and/or different occurrences of one main category have the same
sequence of subcategories: they then get the same reference
number, and the respective subcategory string has to be written
down only once (cf. Fig.6).

In the next figure we give another example of a transformational rule to be applied in the English synthesis. This rule,
too, stems from the sample translation in [14]. It describes
the substitution of the deep category "N" by the intermediate
category "?NOPH" and the completion of the subcategory string
of "?NOUN".

Another facet of the flexibility of the transformational
formalism employed in S A L A T is shown here, namely the
use of variables of different types. Again, we have chosen a
very simple, but nevertheless realistic rule, in order not to
introduce too much complication that would only obscure the
principles to be illustrated (for more complex rules see 5.2
and the rule systems in [12], [13], [14], [17]).

```
N--------              --->    ?NOPH
|        |                     NUM(A)---
|        |                     |      |
?ARTI    ?NOUN                 |      |
NUM(A)   ART(B)                ?ARTI  ?NOUN
|        |                     NUM(A) NUM(A)
|        |                     |      ART(B)
ΔA       ⊓B                    |      |
                              ΔA      |
                                      ⊓B
```

```
<N(1.?ARTI(ΔA)2.?NOUN(⊓B))>.
--->
<1.?NOPH(1.?ARTI(ΔA)3.?NOUN(⊓B))>.
1.NUM(A)
2.ART(B)
3.NUM(A)ART(B)
```

<u>Fig. 6</u> Sample rule 2 - tree notation and S A L A T notation

The prefixed "A"s and "B"s occurring in Fig.6 as terminal
labels of the rule trees are variables ranging over substructures of the object tree to which the rule is applied. As identical values have to be assigned to different occurrences of
one variable on both sides of the rule (as well as, by the way,
in the structural restriction), the corresponding substructures
are left unchanged in the course of the transformation, but they
need not be specified, so that the rule can apply in different
environments.

The different prefixes of the substructure variables serve
for the distinction between different subtypes of them: "Δ"
variables, "⊓" variables, and "◊" variables correspond to exactly
one edge in the object tree, to a non-empty sequence of edges,
and to a (possibly empty) sequence of edges respectively. Such
a distinction is convenient for the sake of the efficiency of
the algorithm.

The "A"s and "B"s that appear in Fig.6 in "NUM(A)" and
"ART(B)" are variables ranging over subcategory specifications.
They are needed in the complex notation of transformational
rules: the sample rule comprises, as it were, 4 elementary rules
with constant specifications, for the occurring subcategories
can both be specified in two ways, namely "(1)" or "(2)" (cf.
the explanations to Fig.3), and all the combinations of speci-

fications are permitted. In the case of more complicated rules
with numerous subcategories and a great number of possible specifications, this leads to an important economy of rules and aug-
ments the transparency of the rule systems.

It is impossible to give a complete survey of the different
possibilities of using variables in the transformational rules
of S A L A T in the space available for this paper. There are
other devices, that were not at all mentioned here, e.g. the
description of several subparts of the object tree in one transformational rule or the generalization of the formalism to many-
place rules which operate on a sequence of object trees. The
latter is exemplified in the deduction rules in 5.2 (for further
details see (16)).

3. Major Parts of the Translation Process

The translation procedure of S A L A T comprises three main
programs, COSY (context-free syntax), TRANSFO (transformations),
and DEDUKT (deductions), with different versions for disambiguation and transfer), which are employed in the following major
parts of the translation process:

- two-step context-free analysis (COSY),
- transformational analysis (TRANSFO),
- disambiguation (TRANSFO and DEDUKT I),
- transfer (TRANSFO and DEDUKT II),
- transformational synthesis in two phases (TRANSFO).

3.1 Flow Chart of S A L A T

The flow chart in Fig.7 illustrates the interconnections of the
main subprocedures of S A L A T with their input and output
and with the data used in them.

The left column contains the input and output of the whole
translation procedure as well as the intermediate results produced in the course of a translation. The central column shows
the succession of the main parts without indication of their
internal modular structure. In the right column, there appear
the more or less permanent data used for several translations.
They include rule systems for the description of the source
language (SL), of the target language (TL), and of the relations
between them as well as deduction rules and supplementary information coded in the data base in the form of deep structures.

The data base is the only component of the right column that
will have to be partially changed in the course of one translation, for e. g. information contained in the input sentences
will have to be added to the data base, in order to allow inferences referring to the context. Ideally, some parts of the
data base and the rest of the data used are absolutely permanent, but in the testing phase of a translation system they will
have to be gradually revised and completed.

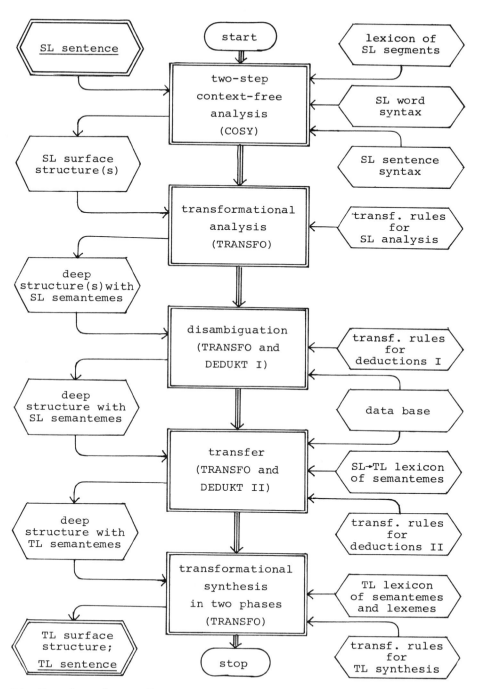

Fig.7 Flow chart of S A L A T

3.2 Analysis and Synthesis

In describing the different parts of the translation process
of S A L A T , we do not proceed chronologically, but rather
treat together analysis and synthesis. These have much in common,
being the more 'syntactic' components compared to the essentially
semantic steps of disambiguation and transfer, which are dealt
with in 3.3.

By "analysis" we understand the transduction of source-
language sentences into expressions of the interlingua, where
several deep structures correspond to one sentence, if it has
more than one reading. For reasons of efficiency the first part
of analysis is accomplished by the context-free parser COSY,
described in [5], which applies a two-step context-free syntax
as illustrated in 2.2. This does not imply a general limitation
of accepted languages to context-free ones, for the first part
of the analysis may be skipped for non-context-free phenomena
(if such exist[7]) or else the context-free syntax may accept some
non-grammatical sentences which are then eliminated by the fil-
tering power of the transformational part of the analysis.

The output of the context-free analysis is one or, in case
of syntactic or lexical ambiguity (not e.g. in case of ambiguity
of pronominal reference, which is dealt with in the transformational part of analysis), several surface structure(s) assigned
to the input sentence.

The second, transformational, part of the analysis transduces
surface structures into deep structures, thereby augmenting -
if necessary - the number of different structures for one input
sentence. The transformational rules of this step are applied
by the procedure TRANSFO, described in [16], which constitutes
an algorithm generating all the derivations rendered possible
on the basis of the input sets of object trees and of transformational rules.

TRANSFO does not, by itself, guarantee the termination of the
derivation process, for it accepts e.g. also cyclically operating rules which may be applied an infinite number of times.
This is avoided by the special form of the rule systems used in
S A L A T : they exhibit an intrinsic rule ordering that is based
on the utilization of mutually disjunct partial vocabularies for
node labels, related to different states of the translation
process. We think that an _extrinsic_ rule ordering is not necessary, for all the phenomena mentioned e.g. in [18] can surely
be treated without it, if some fixed ideas on the possible and
permissible forms of deep structures and transformational rules
are given up. For more details regarding the rule ordering in
S A L A T see [11], [14], and [16]; for a short discussion of
the decidability problem connected with the use of transformational rule systems cf. [11], chapter 3.

TRANSFO is applied in synthesis, too; for "synthesis" means
the transformation of deep structures into context-free surface
structures of the target language the terminal strings of which

are the wanted target-language sentences. It seems advantageous
to guarantee well-defined (e.g. by a context-free syntax) output
structures for theoretical and practical reasons (the Chomskyan
surface structures are not well-defined in the sense intended
here).

On account of its intrinsic rule ordering, the transformational synthesis is divided into two phases:
- a bottom-up phase where semantemes are substituted by target-
  language lexemes with the aid of a set of transformational
  rules called "lexicon of semantemes and lexemes", which simultaneously attaches incomplete morpho-syntactic information
  in the form of syntactic subcategories to the preterminal
  nodes (see sample rule 1 in 2.3); this information is then
  transferred to the higher nodes and partially completed by
  other rules (see sample rule 2 in 2.3);
- a top-down phase where complete morpho-syntactic information
  is attached to every node, so that finally the lexemes at
  the terminal nodes can be substituted by inflected word forms
  or by "segments" (i.e. by stems and endings forming together
  inflected word forms).
In any of the two phases, structural changes can be carried out
if necessary.

3.3   Disambiguation and Transfer

In S A L A T the synthesis cannot start directly with the deep
structures resulting from the analysis. This is mainly due to
the ambiguities occurring in the translation process. There are
at least two kinds of them, namely ambiguities of the source
language without reference to any target language and ambiguities
of the source language in relation to a special target language.
Let's call them "internal" and "translation" ambiguities respectively.

Internal ambiguities are e.g. such of quantifier scope, of
pronominal reference, of homonyms; translation ambiguities occur
e.g. if a lexeme which is not ambiguous from the point of view
of the source language requires different translations into the
target language in different contexts and/or situations of utterance. This holds for instance for the translation of English
"put" into German "stellen, legen, ...", depending on properties
of the involved objects. Internal ambiguities ought to be dealt
with independently of the target language, whereas translation
ambiguities should be resolved in a phase where the dependence
of the target language is explicit.

However, it seems impossible to define a clear-cut boundary
between the two kinds of ambiguities in practice. There are many
uncontroversial cases, but numerous debatable ones, too. Nevertheless, there are good reasons to draw a provisional line separating them. It would be contrary to any principle of economy
(and, probably, even impossible) to resolve all the potential
translation ambiguities independently of the target language in
question, at least in a machine translation system which, in
principle, operates on any source or target language. A great

amount of disambiguation work, not needed for the target language at hand, but only for some other one(s), would have to be carried out.

On the other hand, it does not seem satisfactory either to resolve all the ambiguities (including the internal ones) in a phase where the target language already comes in. In our system, this would imply that a meaning representation had to be assigned to input sentences where even ambiguity of homonyms and of pronominal reference were not resolved, which would be rather counter-intuitive. Moreover, as the resolution of ambiguities is one of the core problems (may-be even the one core problem) of machine translation, it is convenient to split up the task into different sub-tasks, in order to reduce its complexity.

Accordingly, the two kinds of ambiguities are resolved in S A L A T in two different steps of the translation process: "disambiguation" and "transfer" deal with the internal and translation ambiguities respectively. Both components operate on the level of deep structures, which corresponds to the essentially semantic character of the involved problems.

Internal ambiguities are reflected in the following way: as the analysis may result in several deep structures representing the different readings of the input sentence, a disambiguation procedure is needed to find the reading(s) favoured by the context and/or situation, taking into consideration general knowledge of the world, too. So these decisions are based on information stored in the data base or inferable from it by logical deductions. These are transformations like those used for analysis and synthesis, but they are controlled in a different way by the procedure DEDUKT.

Translation ambiguities are mirrored in S A L A T in non-correspondences between the semantemes of the deep structures resulting from analysis or disambiguation, which are oriented towards the source language, (short: "SL semantemes") and the lexemes of the target language. So, before the lexicon of semantemes and lexemes (i.e. the first step of synthesis) can be applied, the SL semantemes have to be substituted by TL semantemes. This is accomplished by a set of transformational rules called "lexicon of semantemes". These rules contain special conditions of application referring to information stored in or deducible from the data base, in order to make the right choice among the different potential translation equivalents (represented by different TL semantemes). The procedure deciding whether these conditions are met is again a version of DEDUKT which may in some respects differ from the version for disambiguation.

While the algorithms constituted by COSY and TRANSFO for analysis and synthesis are by now available in a form which is next to final (they are implemented and tested for data sets of different languages), this is not true for the algorithms of disambiguation and transfer, which are only partially completed. A first version of DEDUKT II (transfer deductions) is illustrated in 4.3 and 5.3.

4. Solving Semantic Problems in the Transfer Step

The semantic task of resolving translation ambiguities in the
transfer step of S A L A T is described in some more detail
in this chapter and exemplified in chapter 5. Since the realization and partially even the conception of transfer is not yet
finished, only a first rather incomplete version with quite a
few obvious shortcomings is implemented and tested by now (cf.
chapter 3.6.1 of (17)). Nevertheless, it may serve for an illustration of the main principles and methods conceived so far for
the treatment of some semantic problems in S A L A T . Moreover, by running rather simple examples one can gain useful
insights into the involved problems and possible solutions,
which is a fertile basis for further developments.

The components of the present transfer version in S A L A T
are the following:

- lexicon of semantemes, containing transformational "transfer
  rules";
- data base;
- deduction rules, controlled by DEDUKT II.

4.1 Lexicon of Semantemes

In S A L A T no analysis into "semantic primitives" (as e.g.
in (24), pp.123ff.), "atomic semantemes" or anything similar
is performed. Rather there is one semanteme of the interlingua
corresponding to each internally unambiguous lexeme vs. to each
reading of an internally ambiguous lexeme of every involved
language. It is possible, but will not occur very often, that
one and the same semanteme is assigned to (the readings of) different lexemes of one language or even of different languages,
namely if they are synonymous in a strict sense of the word[8].
Thus the sets of SL semantemes and of TL semantemes (corresponding to (readings of) SL and TL lexemes respectively) may overlap.

Usually, if the semanteme in question does not belong to the
intersection of these two sets, there will be different potential
translation equivalents (represented by different TL semantemes)
the choice among which is to be made with regard to the context
and/or situation, including general knowledge of the world. For
instance, in translating English "put" into German "stellen" or
"legen" (this does, of course, not exhaust the possibilities of
translating "put") in S A L A T , the semanteme "$PUT" has to
be substituted by one of the semantemes "$STELL" or "$LEG". Under
normal conditions, "$PUT" has to be transferred into "$STELL",
if the involved object usually rather stands than lies, and into
"$LEG", if it rather takes a lying position. Obviously this is
just a first approximation; realistic descriptions of semanteme
correspondences (representing lexeme relations) will have to
consider much more complex information and a great number of
different cases.

The substitution of SL semantemes by TL semantemes, including the choice among the latter, is performed in S A L A T by the lexicon of semantemes. It is constituted by transformational rules the left-hand sides of which apply each to a single SL semanteme (in a certain structural context), while their right-hand sides contain TL semantemes or structures with only TL semantemes as terminal labels. If there are n possibilities of translating an SL semanteme, this yields at least n rules with this semanteme occurring on their left-hand sides.

The different cases are distinguished in the structural re-strictions of the transfer rules with the aid of a special de-cidable predicate "DAB" (short for "data base"). "DAB" does not refer to structural properties of the object tree, as structural restrictions usually do (cf. 2.3), but claims that the informa-tion represented by its argument (e.g. the information about the preferred position of the object in the "put" example) is to be found in or deduced from the data base by a suitable deduction procedure. This means that the arguments of "DAB" have to be deep structures, for the data base contains information only in the form of such. Since, moreover, the transfer is accomplished by transformational rules like those for analysis and synthesis, no new formalism is necessary for their formulation.

The transfer rules for a certain combination of source and target language constitute the lexicon of semantemes for this language pair.

There exist not only 'lexical', but also 'structural' trans-lation ambiguities. In the present version, no special rules of 'structural transfer' are provided for, because structural chan-ges can easily be carried out in the course of synthesis. Such rules might as well be included into the lexicon of semantemes in a form which would not refer to single SL semantemes only, but to bigger substructures of the SL-oriented object trees.

4.2   Data Base

The data base of S A L A T must provide all the information needed for the decisions to be made in disambiguation and trans-fer. This does not mean, however, that all the necessary in-formation has to be explicitly contained (in the form of deep structures), which is in fact impossible, but it must be logical-ly deducible from what is explicitly stored in the data base.

The relevant information cannot be contained in the deep structures alone due to the fact that their meanings are de-termined by the rules of model-theoretic interpretation only relative to an interpretation function for the semantemes. Such a function, however, does not exist explicitly anywhere in the implemented system (which would not be possible), but the inter-lingua expressions in the data base determine the meanings of semantemes - and thus the meanings of deep structures - in a quasi-axiomatic way (e.g. in the form of meaning postulates). So the data base replaces, as it were, an interpretation function for semantemes.

As can be concluded from diverse remarks on the function of the data base in several preceding paragraphs, there are different kinds of information, exhibiting different degrees of generality, to be stored in the data base:
- contextual information (from the input sentences),
- information about the situation and time of utterance,
- general knowledge of the world,
- meaning postulates.

Since there is no clear-cut boundary to be defined between these types of information, it is convenient to express all of them in one and the same formalism, namely in the ε-λ-context-free syntax of the S A L A T interlingua. This is possible, because the meaning of any natural-language sentence as well as any statement on situations and times of utterance, on facts about the world, and on meaning relations in the involved languages can, in principle, be represented by interlingua expressions, i.e. deep structures:
- the meaning of a natural-language sentence is, of course, represented by the deep structure that is or would be assigned to it by analysis and disambiguation;
- statements on situations and times of utterance are expressed by deep structures containing their names;
- general facts about the world can be expressed in natural-language sentences, so they are represented accordingly;
- meaning relations are reflected in deep structures marked as valid at all times and in all situations (examples of such meaning postulates are given in 5.2).

As was already pointed out in 3.1, the data base contains (ideally) constant as well as changing parts. Meaning postulates and general knowledge of the world are constant; situational and contextual information change, usually even in the course of the translation of one text.

4.3 DEDUKT (II)

For each decidable predicate occurring in the structural restrictions of transformational rules in S A L A T , a decision procedure must be available within TRANSFO. For the predicate "DAB", used in transfer rules, this procedure is DEDUKT II: TRANSFO calls DEDUKT II for the decision whether the argument of "DAB" can be found in or deduced from the data base by logical deductions (in the following paragraphs we shall often simply speak of "DEDUKT" without reference to its different versions, for most of what is said is true of DEDUKT I, too).

The logical deduction rules in S A L A T are mappings of (sequences of) deep structures - namely of data-base expressions or intermediate results of deduction - on (sequences of) deep structures - namely on intermediate results or, finally, the arguments of "DAB". Thus these rules are just like those used in other transformational components of S A L A T with the following exception: in general, they apply to more than one input structure and yield a corresponding number of output structures. This generalization to many-place rules is provided in the formalism of transformational rules in S A L A T (cf. 2.3); so no new formalism for deduction rules is needed. Moreover, since DEDUKT applies transformational rules, several subprocedures of TRANSFO can be used for it, though there are substantial divergencies between the two procedures.

It is advantageous, too, that the logical deductions operate on deep structures. Since deep structures can be viewed as typetheoretic expressions in tree notation, the deduction rules of type theory can serve as an orienting basis for the formulation of the deduction rules of S A L A T . Besides, correctness proofs for the latter are available on account of the modeltheoretic interpretation of the deep structures.

As the set of all the logical consequences from the data base is not decidable, DEDUKT cannot offer a decision procedure for this set precisely. In artificial-intelligence research, theorem provers are often used in similar cases (see e.g. [8]). Theorem provers are complete deduction algorithms deducing every logical consequence from a given set of sentences. Nevertheless, they do not constitute a decision procedure, for, if a sentence is not deduced after a certain number of steps, it is impossible to decide whether it is deducible at all. Moreover, theorem provers operate in rather an undirected way, producing lots of irrelevant results. Because of time limitation, only an arbitrary subset of the possible consequences is generally drawn in practice, often excluding the most interesting ones and even rather easily decidable cases.

Therefore, DEDUKT should not be based on a theorem-prover concept. It is not necessary to make all the inferences, but rather to find the useful and relevant ones in a reasonable amount of time, although this means that sometimes only an ad-hoc decision, if any, is attainable. This does still not exclude the possibility of fully automatic high-quality translation, for more than once even human translators have to content themselves with ad-hoc solutions of translation problems, if a perfect solution cannot be found in the time and with the information available. Besides, human translators obviously do not use complete decision procedures.

So, what is needed for DEDUKT, is a deduction strategy oriented towards the relevant inferences. Such a strategy must lead to a step-by-step procedure where each step corresponds to the application of an appropriate set of deduction rules in a suitable order to a suitably chosen subset of the data-base expressions and where any step is carried out only if no solution has been found in the preceding one.

As no comprehensive and satisfying set of heuristic principles for such a strategy is known by now, only some simple heuristic advices have been respected in the implementation of the first version of the transfer step:
- split up the contextual information into simple pieces and use it by preference[9];
- apply deduction rules to data-base structures only if the

latter have semantemes in common with the sentence (more
precisely: the structure) to be proved;
- specify general statements with regard to the actual parameters, e.g. by applying universally valid sentences to the
actual situation of utterance.

Obviously, these principles can be improved in several ways
and extended in different directions. It will be useful, for
instance, to conceive special decision procedures for easily
decidable cases or to classify the data-base expressions according to their relative import (e.g. information coded as semantic features in other approaches may be particularly important).
Since no strategy will be optimal for every case, different
strategies ought to be employed regarding e.g. the form of the
structure to be proved.

5. Transfer Example

In this chapter we give an example from German-French translation which comprises the following elements:
- deep structure of the translated sentence,
- transfer rules,
- data-base structures,
- deduction rules,
- steps of deduction.

5.1 Sample Sentence and Transfer Rules

The sentence to be translated is "Das alpine Gebiet ist klein."
("The Alpine region is small."), the deep structure assigned to
it (with a somewhat simplified representation of "klein"[10]) is
given in Fig.8 (for the meaning of the deep categories see the
explanation to Fig.1).

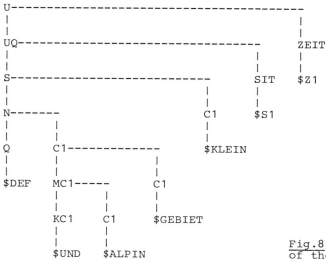

Fig.8 Deep structure
of the sample sentence

The translation of this sentence into French ought to yield:
"La région alpine est petite.". Ignoring other possible difficulties involved in this example, we focus our attention on the
translation of German "Gebiet" into French. Out of the different
potential translation equivalents we consider only "région" and
"domaine" (corresponding approximately to English "region" and
"domain").

The relevant rules of the German-French lexicon of semantemes
can be stated informally as follows:
1. Substitute the "Gebiet" semanteme by the "région" semanteme,
   if the "Gebiet" is a geographic one.
2. Substitute the "Gebiet" semanteme by the "domaine" semanteme,
   if the "Gebiet" is a scientific one.
This is, of course, only a first approximation of realistic transfer rules, which is indeed even desirable for the sake of the
transparency of the example.

In the linear S A L A T notation these rules read:

1. <U(UQ(◊C(◊F N(ⅡD C1(◊E($GEBIET)))◊Y)SIT(ΔB))ZEIT(ΔA))>.
   DAB.:<U(UQ(S(N(ⅡD C1($GEBIET))C1($GEOGR))SIT(ΔB))ZEIT(ΔA))>.
   --->
   <U(UQ(◊C(◊F N(ⅡD C1(◊E($RE1GION)))◊Y)SIT(ΔB))ZEIT(ΔA))>.

2. <U(UQ(◊C(◊F N(ⅡD C1(◊E($GEBIET)))◊Y)SIT(ΔB))ZEIT(ΔA))>.
   DAB.:<U(UQ(S(N(ⅡD C1($GEBIET))C1($WISSENSCH))SIT(ΔB))ZEIT(ΔA))>.
   --->
   <U(UQ(◊C(◊F N(ⅡD C1(◊E($DOMAINE)))◊Y)SIT(ΔB))ZEIT(ΔA))>.

As the linear notation is rather difficult to read, mainly
owing to the non-terminal variables "◊C" and "◊E", we give the
left-hand "structural description", which is the same for both
rules and is, moreover, identical to their right-hand sides
(with the exception of the semanteme), in tree notation.

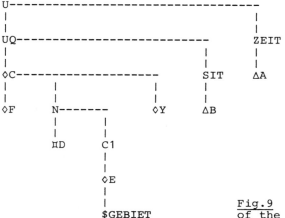

```
U------------------------------------
|                                    |
|                                    |
UQ------------------------------     ZEIT
|                            |        |
|                            |        |
◊C------------------         SIT     ΔA
|      |           |          |
|      |           |          |
◊F     N------     ◊Y         ΔB
       |     |
       |     |
       ⅡD    C1
             |
             |
             ◊E
             |
             |
          $GEBIET
```

Fig.9 Structural description
of the transfer rules

This structural description applies to any object tree with "$GEBIET" occurring somewhere under a node labelled "N", e.g. to the deep structure of the sample sentence (Fig.8), since the substructures assigned to the "◇" variables may be empty. Note that the different occurrences of the variable "ПD" (in the three components of both rules) stand for identical quantifiers. The semantemes appearing in the structural restrictions, "$GEOGR" and "$WISSENSCH", correspond to English "geographic" and "scientific" respectively.

The two occurrences of "$GEBIET" in each rule have to be referentially identical. In the present version of the rules this is only imperfectly guaranteed by the identity of situation and time of utterance (expressed by identical variables)[11].

5.2 Data Base and Deduction Rules

We assume the sample data base to contain the following meaning postulates, i.e. deep structures valid for the "universal situation" and the "universal time" (which is expressed by "$ALLS" and "$ALLZ"), given in linear notation:

1. <U(UQ(S(N(Q($ALL)C1($MISCHPULT))C1($ELEKTRON))
   SIT($ALLS))ZEIT($ALLZ))>.
   ("Every sound mixer is something electronic.")

2. <U(UQ(S(N(Q($ALL)C1($ELEKTRON))C1($TECHN))
   SIT($ALLS))ZEIT($ALLZ))>.
   ("Everything electronic is something technical.")

3. <U(UQ(S(N(Q($ALL)C1($TECHN))C1($WISSENSCH))
   SIT($ALLS))ZEIT($ALLZ))>.
   ("Everything technical is something scientific.")

4. <U(UQ(S(N(Q($ALL)C1($ALPIN))C1($GEOGR))
   SIT($ALLS))ZEIT($ALLZ))>.
   ("Everything Alpine is something geographic.")

Only the last of these meaning postulates is relevant for our example.

The present version of DEDUKT uses two kinds of deduction rules:
- "clause rules" that are applied to the deep structures assigned to translated sentences and that split them up into suitable pieces of information ("clauses");
- "inference rules" that are applied to data-base structures and to intermediate results of deduction.

The example was carried out with the following set of clause rules:

1. <S(◇G(N(Q(ΔA)C1(MC1(KC1($UND)C1(ПB))C1(ПC)))ΔD)))>.
   --->
   <S(N(Q(ΔA)C1(ПC))C1(ПB))>.
   (example: "The green apple is sweet." ---> "The apple is green.")

2.<S(N(Q(ΔA)C1(пB))C1(MC1(KC1($UND)C1(пC))C1(пD))))>.
  --->
  <S(N(Q(ΔA)C1(пB))C1(пC))>.
(example: "The apple is green and sweet." ---> "The apple is green.")

3.<S(N(Q(ΔA)C1(пB))C1(MC1(KC1($UND)C1(пC))C1(пD))))>.
  --->
  <S(N(Q(ΔA)C1(пB))C1(пD))>.
(example: "The apple is green and sweet." ---> "The apple is sweet.")

For the first clause rule to be valid it is, of course, necessary that the specifications of situation and time of utterance be the same for the antecedent and the consequent. This is, in fact, guaranteed: since the corresponding parts of the object tree do not appear in the rule structures, they remain unchanged in the course of the application.

The inference rules of the sample transfer read:

1.<U(UQ(S(N(Q($ALL)C1(пA))C1(пB))SIT(ΔF))ZEIT(ΔE)))>
  <U(UQ(S(N(Q(ΔD)C1(пC))C1(пA))SIT(ΔF))ZEIT(ΔE)))>
  <ZERO>.
  --->
  <U(UQ(S(N(Q($ALL)C1(пA))C1(пB))SIT(ΔF))ZEIT(ΔE)))>
  <U(UQ(S(N(Q(ΔD)C1(пC))C1(пA))SIT(ΔF))ZEIT(ΔE)))>
  <U(UQ(S(N(Q(ΔD)C1(пC))C1(пB))SIT(ΔF))ZEIT(ΔE)))>.
(informally: "If every A is a B at time E in situation F and if some C is an A at time E in situation F, then some C is a B at time E in situation F", where "some" may be replaced by other quantifiers except "no".)

2.<U(UQ(S(пY)SIT($ALLS))ZEIT($ALLZ)))>
  <U(UQ(S(пZ)SIT(ΔA))ZEIT(ΔB)))><ZERO>.
  BED.:<&(¬(CONTA(ΔA $ALLS)))¬(CONTA(ΔB $ALLZ))))>.
  --->
  <U(UQ(S(пY)SIT($ALLS))ZEIT($ALLZ)))>
  <U(UQ(S(пZ)SIT(ΔA))ZEIT(ΔB)))>
  <U(UQ(S(пY)SIT(ΔA))ZEIT(ΔB)))>.
(informally: "If a sentence Y is true at all times and in all situations, Y is also true for time B and situation A which are the utterance parameters of sentence Z.")

Both inference rules are three-place transformational rules with two structures (representing the antecedents) occurring identically on both sides and a third structure (which represents the result proper of the inference) replacing the empty structure "<ZERO>". The double occurrence of the first two structures is due to the fact that they must not be deleted in the course of rule application; for they are to remain in the data base. "<ZERO>" is needed on the left-hand sides, because the transformational formalism of S A L A T requires the rules to have the same number of structures on both sides.

The structural restriction of the second inference rule is to be read as follows: the substructure assigned to "ΔA" (in

applying the rule to an object tree) does not contain "$ALLS"
and the substructure assigned to "ΔB" does not contain "$ALLZ".
As in the present version of the deep syntax the categories
"SIT" and "ZEIT" cannot dominate more than one node each, this
is equivalent to: the node assigned to "ΔA" is not labelled
"$ALLS" and the node assigned to "ΔB" is not labelled "$ALLZ".
This condition is necessary, for if sentence Z were universally
valid, too, no new structure would be generated (the third structure being identical with the first).

The second antecedent structure of the second inference rule,
which might at a first glance seem superfluous, is necessary
for two reasons: firstly, without it no value could be assigned
to the variables occurring in the structural restriction, and
secondly, it would be useless to relate the universally valid
structure to a situation and a time that do not appear in any
other structure, for then no further deduction would be rendered
possible (compare the sample deductions in 5.3).

5.3 Steps of Deduction

Regarding the data of the example (sample sentence, transfer
rules, data base, and deduction rules), it is intuitively obvious, which deductions ought to be carried out for the choice
between the two potential transfer rules: since the referent
of "$GEBIET" has the property "$ALPIN" and since "$ALPIN" im-
plies "$GEOGR" according to the last data-base expression, the
"$GEBIET" is "$GEOGR", and hence it follows that "$RE1GION" is
the TL semanteme to be substituted for "$GEBIET".

Three steps of deduction are carried out by DEDUKT to attain
the desired result, two of them being preparatory, as it were.
First, the information contained in the object tree (Fig.8) has
to be split up into clauses by the clause rules. Only the first
of them is applicable. The result of its application (Fig.10)
is added to the data base.

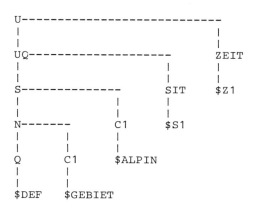

```
U---------------------------
|                          |
|                          |
UQ------------------       ZEIT
|                 |        |
|                 |        |
S-------------    SIT      $Z1
|         |   |        |
|         |   |        |
N-------  C1  $S1
|     |   |
|     |   |
Q     C1  $ALPIN
|     |
|     |
$DEF  $GEBIET
```

Fig.10 Result of the
first step of deduction

In the next step, DEDUKT applies the second inference rule
to the last data-base structure and to the result of the first
step. The result proper of the application (i.e. the third output structure, given in Fig.11) states that the universally
valid meaning postulate is true at time "$Z1" and in situation
"$S1" as well. As the rule operates on data-base structures
this result becomes a part of the data base, too.

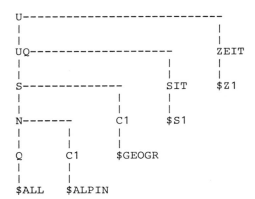

Fig.11 Result of the
second step of deduction

The second inference rule is not applied to any other data-
base structure, according to the principle (which is implemented
in DEDUKT) that data-base expressions are regarded only if they
have semantemes in common with the structure to be proved.

After these two preparatory steps the decisive deduction can
be carried out: the first inference rule is applied to the results of the first two steps, yielding the new deep structure
given in Fig.12.

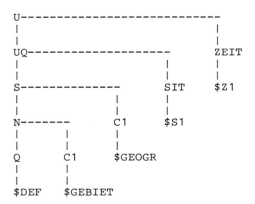

Fig.12 Result of the
third step of deduction

This is exactly the argument of "DAB" of the first transfer rule in tree notation, where the variables are, of course, replaced by their actual values stemming from the object tree (Fig.8). So the first transfer rule is applicable, and "$GEBIET" is replaced by "$RE1GION". Since the structural restrictions of the transfer rules for one SL semanteme are assumed to constitute mutually exclusive conditions of application, the first rule found to be applicable is the only one that will apply at all. So, in the case of our example, the second transfer rule need not be tested for applicability, in particular, its "DAB" argument need not be refuted by DEDUKT.

The preceding example has been tested with the present first transfer version of S A L A T (cf. chapter 3.6.1.2 of [17]). Needless to repeat that all its components are still in a more or less provisional form. Nevertheless, they will hopefully have contributed to the clarification of the principles respected and methods provided in S A L A T for the treatment of some semantic problems in machine translation.

Notes

1   S A L A T is being developed by the Project A2 "Automatische Übersetzung" ("Machine Translation") of the Sonderforschungsbereich 99 "Linguistik" at the Institut für Angewandte Sprachwissenschaft (Institute of Applied Linguistics) of the University of Heidelberg. The system is implemented on the IBM 370/168 of the computing center at the University of Heidelberg and is being tested on simple sample sentences. The project is headed by Prof. Dr. Klaus Brockhaus. It is sponsored by the Deutsche Forschungsgemeinschaft, as well as the whole Sonderforschungsbereich, most projects of which are located at the University of Konstanz.

2   For technical reasons it has been impossible to reproduce the original computer output of the examples, but they have been imitated as far as possible by typewriter. Some abbreviations have been introduced (in particular, the canonical node numbers of nearly every structure have been left out) and some special signs had to be replaced by others.

3   This is, of course, only one reading of the German sentence. By the way, an earlier version of the deep structure in Fig.1 occurred in a sample translation with S A L A T which is documented and described in some detail in [14]. That version of the interlingua did not explicitly represent time and situation of utterance in the deep structures assigned to translated sentences. Properly speaking, it is not sentences, but utterances (roughly: sentences in specific situations of utterance) that are translated. This is reflected in S A L A T in the following way: the utterance parameters (presently names of times and situations, more parameters might be needed) of the deep structures may be viewed as pointers to data-base expressions with the same names occurring in them. These expressions contain supplementary information about the utterance

specifications. The foregoing should be kept in mind if we speak of "translated sentences" in this paper.

4 Such a device is very convenient, as, for the purpose of control, the structures are printed out in tree form, and e.g. in the Russian context-free syntax of (10) there are maximally 16 subcategories belonging to one main category.

5 This is, of course, no complete description of relative modification in English. E.g. relative clauses containing neither relative pronouns nor "that" can modify any noun, so they would be specified as "ART(1,2)", which means that they can agree with "ART(1)" nouns as well as with "ART(2)" nouns.

6 This condition is motivated in the following way: it describes the typical position for a verb representation, which is necessary, because there are other positions typical for noun or adjective representations and in these cases the semanteme ought to be substituted by a noun lexeme ("barker") or by an adjective lexeme ("barking"). The decidable predicate of the sample rule holds true e.g. for the deep structure in Fig.1.

7 It is shown in (3) that the proofs usually adduced that natural languages are not context-free do not hold, for the property is proved only for subsets of the grammatical sentences (e.g. for "respectively" constructions), which, by itself, does not imply that the whole set of grammatical sentences has the property of being non-context-free.

8 For instance, the semantemes representing 'logical words' (some conjunctions, negations, quantifiers) belong to the set of 'international' semantemes. If the corresponding lexemes have non-logical readings, too, these have to be represented by other semantemes, which will often be specific to one language only.

9 This principle is motivated by the hypothesis that, in case of conflict, special information is to be preferred to more general information. In particular, information from the context seems to be able to override general knowledge or meaning postulates. The three principles mentioned here are respected in the transfer example (cf. 5.3).

10 "klein" ("small") is represented here as if it were an intersective adjective, but it is in fact a subsective one. This requires a more complicated representation, because a standard of comparison is needed (e.g. it is not the same to be "small" for an elephant or to be "small" for a mouse). The appropriate structure for subsective adjectives is given in (19), pp.6ff.

11 Indeed, this solution is not as bad as it might seem, since each sentence of a translated text gets a distinct specification of utterance time and situation (represented by distinct time and situation names, which may be related to each other

with the aid of suitable data-base expressions). However,
there might be cases where e.g. a definite description occurring twice in one sentence had different referents for
each occurrence. Thus a satisfactory solution of the problem
would require that at least different occurrences of noun
phrases be marked by differently specified utterance parameters.

References

1 Bar-Hillel, Yehoshua (1962): "Machine Translation: The End
   of an Illusion." Information Processing 62. Proceedings of
   the IFIP Congress 1962, ed. by Cicely Popplewell. Amsterdam:
   North-Holland Publ. Co. 1963, pp.331-332

2 Bar-Hillel, Yehoshua (1971): "Some Reflections on the Present
   Outlook for High-Quality Machine Translation." Feasibility
   Study on Fully Automatic High-Quality Translation. RADC-TR-
   71-295, Vol.I. December, 1971. Rome, N. Y.: Air Development
   Center, pp.72-76

3 Brandt Corstius, Hugo (1976): "The Proof that Natural Language
   is not Context-Free." Paper read at the International Colloquium of the Sonderforschungsbereich 100 "Elektronische
   Sprachforschung", 23.9.-25.9.1976 at Saarbrücken. Abstract
   in the Preprints. Saarbrücken: Universität des Saarlandes,
   pp.22-23

4 Brockhaus, Klaus (1975): "Ein Syntaxformalismus für Flexion
   und Wortbildung." Linguistische Berichte 40, pp.45-62.

5 Brockhaus, Klaus (1976): "Benutzungsanleitung für das Pro-
   grammsystem COSY. Version 2." Working paper B11 of SFB 99/A2.
   Brockhaus et al. 1976, Vol.I, pp.94-124

6 Brockhaus, Klaus / Hauenschild, Christa / Höfling, Jürgen /
   Huckert, Edgar / Maier, Robert (1976): Forschungsbericht
   1.11.1973-31.3.1976. Sonderforschungsbereich 99 "Linguistik"
   /Teilprojekt A2 "Automatische Übersetzung". Universität
   Heidelberg

7 Cresswell, Max J. (1973): Logics and Languages. London:
   Methuen

8 Dilger, Werner / Schneider, Martin (1976): Automatisierbare
   und automatisierte Beweisverfahren für die Logik 1. Stufe.
   Mit Anhängen von Heribert Ficht und Hubert Schleichert.
   Konstanz: Sonderforschungsbereich 99

9 Egli, Urs (1975): Ansätze zur Integration der Semantik in
   die Grammatik. Kronberg (Taunus): Scriptor

10 Hauenschild, Christa (1976): "Kontextfreie Satzsyntax für
   ein Fragment des Russischen." Working paper C7 of SFB 99/A2.
   Brockhaus et al. 1976, Vol.II, pp.70-240.

11 Hauenschild, Christa (1978): "S A L A T : System for Automatic Language Analysis and Translation." Paper read at the 7th International Conference on Computational Linguistics, Bergen (Norway) 14-18 August, 1978. To appear in the Proceedings

12 Hauenschild, Christa (in prep.): Pronominalisierung am Beispiel des Deutschen. Working paper C11 of SFB 99/A2. Heidelberg

13 Hauenschild, Christa (in prep.): Automatische semantische Analyse des Russischen: Artikelrekonstruktion. Diss. Heidelberg

14 Hauenschild, Christa / Huckert, Edgar / Maier, Robert (1978): " S A L A T : Entwurf eines automatischen Übersetzungssystems." Working paper CER1 of SFB 99/A2. Heidelberg. To appear in: Sprache und Datenverarbeitung

15 Huckert, Edgar (1976): Kontextfreie Wort- und Satzsyntax für einen Ausschnitt des Französischen. Working paper E12 of SFB 99/A2. Heidelberg

16 Huckert, Edgar (1978): TRANSFO. Ein System zur Erzeugung transformationeller Ableitungen. 2nd, rev. and enl. version of working paper E13 of SFB 99/A2. Heidelberg

17 Huckert, Edgar (in prep.): Automatische Synthese des Französischen aus einer logischen Basis. Diss. Saarbrücken

18 Koutsoudas, Andreas (ed.) (1976): The Application and Ordering of Grammatical Rules. The Hague-Paris: Mouton

19 Maier, Robert (1976): "Die ε-λ-kontextfreie Basis des Übersetzungssystems S A L A T ." Working paper R3/4 of SFB 99/A2. Brockhaus et al. 1976, Vol.I, pp.45-66

20 Maier, Robert (1978): Zur Syntax und Semantik der Basis von S A L A T - Stand Ende 1977. Working paper R13 of SFB 99/A2. Heidelberg

21 Stechow, Arnim von (1974): "ε-λ-kontextfreie Sprachen. Ein Beitrag zu einer natürlichen formalen Semantik." Linguistische Berichte 34, pp.1-33

22 Suppes, Petrick (1973): "Semantics of Context-Free Segments of Natural Language." Hintikka/Moravcsik/Suppes (eds.): Approaches to Natural Language. Proceedings of the 1970 Stanford Workshop on Grammar and Semantics. Dordrecht: Reidel, pp.370-394

23 Thomason, Richmond (ed.) (1974): Formal Philosophy: Selected Papers of Richard Montague. New Haven: Yale Univ. Press

24 Wilks, Yorick (1973): "An Artificial Intelligence Approach to Machine Translation." Schank/Colby (eds.): Computer Models of Thought and Language. San Francisco: Freeman, pp.114-151

Conceptual Impairment in Aphasia [1]

Rudolf Cohen, Stephanie Kelter, and Gerhild Woll

Universität Konstanz, Sonderforschungsbereich 99, 'Linguistik'
Postfach 5560, D-7750 Konstanz, Fed. Rep. of Germany

Abstract. Broca's and Wernicke's aphasics, brain-damaged patients without aphasia, and chronic schizophrenics were tested
in a non-verbal matching task where the subject had to indicate
which of two pictures was more closely linked to a clue picture.
Both aphasic groups performed worse than brain-damaged controls
when the identification of individual attributes or actions shared by clue and referent was required, but were unimpaired when
the two had a set of referential-situational associations in
common. Factor analyses including 8 additional verbal and non-
verbal reference tasks resulted for both groups in two factors,
one of which represents general Language Impairment. For the
Broca's aphasics this factor was closely related to general organic deficit as measured by the Trail Making Test; for the Wernicke's aphasics it was associated with tasks which might be considered illustrative of analytical competence in isolating and
comparing individual features of objects or concepts.

Introduction

In recent years considerable evidence has accumulated showing
that there are certain non-verbal tasks where impaired performance in brain-damaged patients seems related to the presence
of aphasic disorders. Non-verbal tasks where aphasics have been
found to perform worse than other brain-damaged patients include the matching of colours to black-and-white drawings of objects (1,2,3,4), recognition of typical sounds of objects (5,6,
7,8), object-sorting (9,10), identification of embedded figures
(11) and learning conditional responses to combinations of visual
shapes and backgrounds (12). Very little is known about the specific nature of aphasics' difficulties. Nor is it clear what constitutes the relationship between these difficulties and the patients' language impairment. There are several arguments (cf.,
1,4) which suggest that it is unlikely the aphasics' difficulties in non-verbal tasks are simply a consequence of verbal
impairments, for example, their impaired inner speech. The more
perceptual functions, on the other hand, seem to be unimpaired
in aphasics (cf.,3,4,6). Thus, one may conject that the deficit
occurs at some conceptual or possibly "preverbal" level. The aim
of the present study was to obtain some information that would
help to formulate a more precise hypothesis concerning the nature of such conceptual disorder. We focused on three questions:
(1) What are the specific properties of those tasks which were
repeatedly found to be especially difficult for aphasics? (2)

Are the crucial properties of these tasks interrelated or are
separate factors involved? (3) How might these factors be related to characteristic impairments in different forms of aphasia?
The theoretical and methodological approach of the study was
prompted by an unexpected finding from an earlier study (13).
Here, aphasics were found to be significantly poorer than other
brain-damaged patients in identifying which of two objects was
alluded to by a clue-object, when the link between referent and
clue was a shared attribute. However, they did perform as well
as the control groups when the referent and clue had a common
set of situational associations. Since the experimental paradigm
and the type of stimulus material were the same for all items the
discriminating property must be related to the difference between
the identification of shared attributes and that of shared situational associations. The aphasics seem to have difficulties in
matching by specific attributes alone. Such a view appears even
more plausible if one considers the tasks listed earlier: in all
these tasks individual attributes which are specific to the objects in question have to be identified. Moreover, even the discriminating power of the Token Test can be interpreted within
such a framework (cf.,14,15). Our supposition is, then, that a
distinctive feature of aphasic patients lies with their difficulty
in isolating analytically specific attributes of objects or concepts.
In order to improve the empirical basis of this hypothesis
the immediate goal of the present study was to determine whether the results from our earlier study could be replicated under more demanding methodology. First, a third scale was included with the link between the clue and the referent being a characteristic action. If aphasics' difficulties are confined to
more static attributes without immediate pragmatic value,
their performance should be unimpaired on this "Actions" scale.
Secondly, it was to be investigated whether this scale, which
discriminated aphasics and non-aphasics, correlated with the
other "classical" non-verbal tasks where aphasics are found
to fail. Thirdly, the relationship between the non-verbal and
the verbal impairment of the patients was to be investigated.
For this purpose three of the most commonly used verbal tests
were used.

Since the present study was intended to provide data concerning the characteristic impairment of aphasics, the control group
consisted of non-aphasic brain-damaged patients heterogeneous for
localization. A second control group comprising chronic thought-
disordered schizophrenics was included because language disorders may be difficult to discriminate from psychotic thought
disorders (cf.,16).

Method

Subjects
Subjects were 20 Wernicke's aphasics, 20 Broca's aphasics, 20
brain-damaged patients without aphasia, and 20 chronic schizophrenics. All patients were male, right-handed, and native German speakers. The four groups were comparable with respect to age
($47.2 \leq M \leq 48.2$; range 18-66; F (3,76)= 0.03) and a combined index
for level of education and occupation ($2.20 \leq M \leq 2.37$; F (3,76)=

0.17). In addition, the two aphasic groups and the brain-damaged control groups showed about equal levels of performance on
Form A of the Trail Making Test (17) which was used as a global
measure for severity of brain-damage ($1.99 \leq \underline{M}$ (log.sec.) ≤ 2.04;
$\underline{F}$ (2,57) = 0.26).

Aphasics were classified as Broca's or Wernicke's according
to the judgement of their therapists (18). Subjects in the brain-
damaged control group without aphasia were highly heterogeneous
as to the localization of their impairment. Patients with diffuse brain lesions were prevalent; subjects with only minor well-
circumscribed lesions were excluded. No patient in the control
group had a history of previous aphasic symptomatology in his
clinical record. There were no significant differences between
the three brain-damaged groups with respect to etiology ($Chi^2(6)$
=2.73, $\underline{p} > .10$), or duration of illness ($Chi^2(2)=0.61$, $\underline{p} > .10$).
The medians for duration of illness for the Broca's, Wernicke's
aphasics and the brain-damaged controls were 13.5, 12.0, and
18.5 months, respectively.

All schizophrenic patients had been diagnosed by the psychia-
tric staff of the respective hospital as chronic process schizophrenics with insidious onset and manifest thought disorders.
All had been hospitalized continuously for at least one year
prior to examination with no change in neuroleptical medication
within the last month. Patients who had an indication of neuro-
logical impairment in their clinical records were not considered, nor were patients showing predominantly paranoid symptomatology.

Material and Procedure

1. Picture-to-Picture Matching Task

This consisted of three sets of stimulus cards (17.5 cm x 23.5
cm). Each card showed three black-and-white drawings arranged
in the form of an inverted triangle. The two drawings on the
upper half of the card represented the "referent" and the "non-
referent", i.e., the two concepts between which the subject had
to choose. The picture located in the middle lower half of the
card was the "clue" by which the referent was to be identified.
For each item the referent and non-referent were similar in that
they had the same concept as one of their nearest possible super-
categories. The clue always belonged to another super-category.
The only connection between clue and referent was through one
specific aspect common to both, the "mediator". For example, one
stimulus card showed a swan and a turkey as referent and non-referent, and a snowman as clue; the mediator was "white". Another
item comprised pictures of a frog and a snail (as referent and
non-referent), and of a kangaroo (as clue); the mediator was
"jumping". Two pilot studies with normal Ss were run in order
to ensure that the items to be used in the present study met
the above criteria and to control for the pure associational
connections between the depicted objects (18). In the final version there were three sets of items:
"Attributes" scale: this consisted of 55 items where the mediator
was supposed to be a specific feature or property common to both
the referent and clue (e.g., 'rose' and 'tulip' as alternatives,

'hedgehog' as clue). Most normal subjects in the second pilot study who were asked to explain their choice between referent and non-referent used adjectives in naming the mediators of the items in this scale.

"Situations" scale: this consisted of 50 items. The aspect common to referent and clue was intended to be the typical context of the depicted objects, i.e., some common array of referential-situational associations (e.g., 'guitar' and 'violin' as alternatives, 'bullfight' as clue). The majority of subjects in the second pilot study used nouns to explain their choices.

"Actions" scale: this consisted of 50 items where the mediator was supposed to be an action (e.g., 'scavenger' and 'postman' as alternatives, 'washer-woman' as clue). Most subjects in the second pilot study used verbs to explain their choices.

From each of these sets only 28 items were retained for the final analyses. This was done in order to equate the three sets with respect to their distributions of difficulty and reliability in the control group of non-aphasic brain-damaged patients.

2. Non-Verbal Tasks

Sound-to-picture matching:
This task comprised 46 items similar to the auditory recognition task of FAGLIONI, SPINNLER, and VIGNOLO (6). The patients were required to match a meaningful sound (e.g., barking) presented by tape to one of four pictures which showed the natural source of the sound (for details see (8)).

Colour-to-picture matching:
This task consulted of 42 items similar to the colour-to-picture matching task of DE RENZI and SPINNLER (4). The patients had to indicate on a display of 24 colour strips the most appropriate colour for an object depicted in a black-and-white drawing (for details see (2)).

Picture-coordination "Parts":
Each of the 22 items of this task showed three pictures in a row, two of which were characteristic parts or accessories of a familiar object. The patients had to indicate these two pictures and to ignore the third picture showing a semantically closely related object (for details see (19)).

Picture-coordination "Situations":
This task also comprised 22 items with 3 pictures each. The two pictures which the patient had to indicate as belonging together showed things which are usually found in the situational context of a familiar object (for details see (19)).

3. Verbal Tasks

Token Test: This test originally constructed by DE RENZI and VIGNOLO (20) was administered in the version by ORGASS (21,22).

Peabody Picture Vocabulary Test: The German version (23) of the original test by DUNN (24) was used. For each of the 70 items the subject had to indicate which of the four pictures depicted an object denoted by a word spoken by the experimenter.

Picture-naming: The patients were asked to name each of 60 familiar objects depicted by black-and-white drawings.

There were four sessions per patient each lasting 60 to 90
minutes. The tests were assigned to the sessions in the same way
for all patients but the order of tests within a session was ran-
domized across subjects.
Instructions for all non-verbal tasks were illustrated by two
examples.

Results

In all cases where tasks from other studies were employed the differences in performance level between both aphasic groups and the
brain-damaged controls were as expected. As can be seen from Table 1, aphasics were significantly poorer than brain-damaged controls in the Token Test, the Peabody Picture Vocabulary Test, the
naming task, the sound-to-picture matching task, and the colour-
to-picture matching task (Mann Whitney $\underline{U}$ tests: $2.49 \leq z \leq 11.27$; p<
.05). In none of these tasks was there $\overline{a}$ significant $\overline{d}$ifference
between Broca's and Wernicke's aphasics ($0.03 \leq z \leq 1.45$; p > .10).
Schizophrenics also tended to make more errors than the brain-damaged controls, but the difference was significant only in the Token Test ($\underline{z}$ = 2.82; p < .01). The schizophrenics' performance in
this test was nevertheless significantly better than that of the
two aphasic groups; the same is true for the naming task ($3.33 \leq$
$z \leq 5.20$; $\underline{p}$ < .001). Of the two picture-coordination tasks only the
scale "Parts" discriminated between the aphasic groups and the
brain-damaged controls (z= 2.47; $\underline{p}$ < .05). In both scales, "Parts"
and "Situations", as well as in all other non-verbal tasks, the
differences between the two aphasic groups and the schizophrenics
were not significant (z ≥ 1.22).

Results for the picture-to-picture matching task are shown in
the lower part of Table 1. Both aphasic groups showed poorer performance than the brain-damaged controls in the "Attributes" sca-
le as well as in the "Actions" scale ($2.15 \leq z \leq 3.36$; $\underline{p}$ < .05). In
contrast, the differences between the groups are far from signi-
ficance in the "Situations" scale (z < 1.19). On the other hand,
schizophrenics made significantly more errors than the brain-damaged controls in all three scales ($2.05 \leq z \leq 2.64$; p < .05).

A within-groups comparison between the three scales revealed
that for both control groups of patients without aphasia the
three scales were of about equal difficulty (Friedman two-way
analysis of variance: $Chi^2(2) \leq 0.60$). However, for the two aphasic groups the scales differed significantly ($Chi^2(2) \geq 6.2$; p <
.05). For Broca's aphasics the "Attributes" scale as well as the
"Actions" scale were - according to the Wilcoxon test - significantly more difficult than the "Situations" scale; for Wernicke's
aphasics only the difference between the "Actions" scale and the
"Situations" scale reached the 5% level of significance.

Table 1. Medians of Error Scores in the 7 References Tasks and the Three Scales of the Picture-to-Picture Matching Task

T a s k s	Broca's Aphasics	Wernicke's Aphasics	Brain-Dama-ged without Aphasia	Chronic Schizo-phrenics	Kruskal-Wallis-Test $\underline{H}$ (3)
Token Test	29.5	19.5	0.2	1.4	53.9 * *
Peabody Picture Vocab. Test	10.0	5.5	0.3	1.4	25.2 * *
Picture Naming	33.5	25.0	0.3	1.1	41.1 * *
Sound-to-Picture Matching	9.5	8.5	5.0	7.5	9.0 *
Colour-to-Pictu-re Matching	5.6	4.9	3.7	4.0	8.4 *
Picture-Coord. "Parts"	4.0	4.2	1.8	3.0	8.7 *
Picture-Coord. "Situations"	2.5	2.5	1.5	2.3	3.8
Picture-to-Pictu-re Matching "Attributes"	5.0	2.7	1.4	4.6	11.7 * *
Picture-to-Pictu-re Matching "Situations"	1.7	2.1	1.9	3.7	4.2
Picture-to-Pictu-re Matching "Actions"	4.0	4.0	1.3	3.9	13.2 * *

* $\underline{p} < .05$ ** $\underline{p} < .01$

Spearman rank order correlations between all 10 tasks and the Trail Making Test used as a global measure for severity of brain-damage were determined separately for both the Broca's and the Wernicke's aphasics (cf., 18). Analogous analyses for the two control groups were not performed since the variances of error sco-res in these groups were too small to yield results for compari-son with the aphasics. The correlational matrices of the aphasic groups were then subjected to Principal Components Analyses with subsequent Varimax rotation. Only the two factor solutions will be considered here, since in both cases only the Eigenvalues of the first two factors exceeded unity to any extent (5.94 and 1.50 for the Broca's aphasics; 6.00 and 1.46 for the Wernicke's apha-sics). The rotated factor loadings are given in Table 2.

Table 2. Varimax Rotated Factor Loadings of the Error Scores from Verbal
and Non-Verbal Tasks

Tasks	Broca's Aphasics			Wernicke's Aphasics		
	I	II	h^2	I	II	h^2
Token Test	.92	.16	.87	.75	.37	.69
Peabody Picture Vocab. Test	.74	.31	.64	.90	.28	.88
Picture-Naming	.94	.21	.93	.87	.32	.86
Sound-to-Picture Matching	.62	.54	.67	.72	.30	.62
Colour-to-Picture Matching	.73	.30	.62	.17	.89	.82
Picture-Coord.: "Parts"	.14	.70	.51	.25	.67	.51
Picture-Coord.: "Situations"	.08	.82	.69	.16	.82	.70
Scale 1 ("Attributes")	.43	.60	.54	.87	.05	.75
Scale 2 ("Situations")	.33	.81	.77	.44	.64	.60
Scale 3 ("Actions")	.34	.63	.51	.74	.29	.63
Trail Making Test (Form A)	.80	.22	.70	.23	.57	.37
% Total Variance	39	29	68	39	29	68

For both groups the first factor is largely one of Language
Impairment with high loadings in the three verbal tasks (.75≤
a ≤.94). Independent of clinical diagnoses, the pattern of the
three measures is very similar for the Broca's and the Wernicke's aphasics, although the cluster of verbal impairment scores seems slightly tighter for the Wernicke's than for the Broca's aphasics (.84 ≤ r_s ≤ .93 for the Wernicke's aphasics; .60 ≤
r_s ≤ .85 for the Broca's aphasics). The relationship of this verbal cluster to the non-verbal tasks is less consistent across
the two groups of aphasics. For the Wernicke's aphasics the verbal cluster is closely intertwined with the matching of pictures according to "Attributes" and "Actions" (a = .87 and .74,
respectively). It seems much less related to the matching of
pictures according to "Situations" (a = .44), i.e., the task
where patients were found to be unimpaired. The only other task
that shows a substantial loading on this first factor for the
Wernicke's aphasics is the matching of sound-to-pictures (a =
.72). This task has also some loading on the Broca's first factor (a = .62). Otherwise, this first factor of Language Impairment in Broca's aphasics has some very distinct features. While
the three scales from the picture-to-picture matching task have
only medium and rather similar loadings (.33 ≤ a ≤ .43), this
factor correlates highly not only with colour-to-picture matching (a = .73) but also with the Trail Making Test (a = .80).
The rank correlations between the three verbal tests and this

measure of general deficit in visual-motor coordination and speed are systematically larger for the Broca's ($.51 \le r_s \le .79$) than for the Wernicke's aphasics ($.28 \le r_s \le .40$).

The second factor has high loadings ($.64 \le a \le .82$) in both groups for the two picture-coordination tasks and the picture-to-picture matching task Scale 2 ("Situations"). It seems to represent some General Knowledge about the World. For the Wernicke's aphasics the colour-to-picture matching task also has a high loading on this factor. In this group it covers about a third of the variance from the Trail Making Test. In contrast to the Wernicke's aphasics, the Broca's aphasics' second factor also covers a rather large proportion of the variance from Scale 1 ("Attributes") and Scale 3 ("Actions") of the picture-to-picture matching task, although about half of these scales' variances still remain unexplained by the first two factors ($h^2 = .54$ and $.51$).

Discussion

Our intention in this study was to follow up some of the numerous studies which show specific aphasic impairment in various non-verbal tasks. What do these non-verbal tasks have in common which differentiates aphasics from brain-damaged patients without aphasia? And how do such discriminative demands relate to the characteristic language impairment?

In close agreement with an earlier finding (13) the aphasics in the present study were found to be poorer in matching one of two pictures to a third picture according to a common specific attribute, but to be equal to the controls when the correct alternative was related to the third picture through a common set of situational-referential associations. Considering the discrepant results for the "Attributes" scale and the "Situations" scale one might suggest that the aphasics' difficulties result from an extremely pragmatic attitude where less attention is given to the more static or descriptive features of an object. Such a view would agree with the observation that at least some groups of aphasics rely more than normals on functional and global situational aspects when a set of stimuli has to be categorized (25,26). Similarly ZURIF, CARAMAZZA, MYERSON, and GALVIN (27) conclude in their study of word categorization that aphasics put undue weight on "perceived or imaged environmental situations " (p.185). However, this approach can hardly explain the fact that the aphasics also showed poorer performance on the "Actions" scale. This result supports our earlier conjecture: aphasics are equal to normals as long as they can base their judgement on a global comparison of the relative overlap of associative fields; they fail if the task requires the analytical isolation, identification, and conceptual comparison of highly specific individual aspects. For "Situations" items the isolation of individual features would not simply be irrelevant, it would be detrimental to task performance: in matching 'tulips' but not 'carnation' to 'windmill', one would be led astray if one were to think about specific features of Holland. Only when the sets of associations are treated globally can one expect correct solutions. Such an interpretation would accord with the hypothesis that left hemisphere damage has an effect primarily on the analytical and serial processing of information. Furthermore, it might also apply to tasks such as matching colours or sounds to objects, sorting a set of stimuli according to certain attributes, embedded figures, or conditional responses.

The above observations apply equally to Broca's and Wernicke's aphasics. In no task was there a significant difference between the two aphasic subgroups on mean performance level. This may result from the groups being matched according to overall severity of brain-damage (as estimated by the Trail Making Test). However, the main question which is posed by this result is whether due to the similarity in mean performance level the underlying deficits are basically the same. The results for the schizophrenics suggest that this conclusion may not be tenable: in all non-verbal tasks which differentiated aphasics from brain-damaged controls, schizophrenics were as equally impaired as the aphasics. This finding demonstrates that similar impairment in performance can be due to completely different functional deficits. It might be instructive to look more closely at which verbal and non-verbal impairments seem linked or are independent within the Broca's and the Wernicke's aphasics.

The three verbal tasks (Token Test, Peabody Picture Vocabulary Test, and picture naming) are closely intercorrelated for both groups of aphasics and determine most of the first factor's variance. This finding of a general factor of Language Impairment, evident for both expressive and receptive disorders, corresponds well to earlier analyses (14,28,29). For both groups the non-verbal sound-to-picture matching task also has considerable loadings on this factor: the correlations between this task and the Peabody Picture Vocabulary Test are equally high for Broca's and Wernicke's aphasics. This is at odds with LURIA's view (30), that the sensory aphasics' disturbance is due to impaired phonological discrimination. But it does corroborate the experimental evidence of BLUMSTEIN, BAKER, and GOODGLASS (31) indicating poorer phonemic discrimination in both anterior and posterior aphasics, and similarly that of TALLAL and NEWCOMBE (32) who found deficits in "responding correctly in rapidly changing acoustic stimuli whether verbal or non-verbal" (p.13) to be correlated with the Token Test. The second factor in both groups has high loadings on both the "Situations" scale and on the two picture-coordination tasks. It may be taken to represent a kind of General Knowledge about the World or the ease with which referential-situational associations come to mind about what might be encountered in a particular context. The aphasics were found to be unimpaired in these tasks. This sort of cognitive function seems largely unaffected by aphasia.

Besides these similarities these are also clear-cut discrepancies: for Broca's aphasics the first factor of Language Impairment also has a high loading on the Trail Making Test. Thus, it appears that Language Impairment and general organic deficit are more closely interrelated in this group of patients than in the Wernicke's aphasics. Also, their difficulty in matching pictures according to specific attributes or actions - although significantly correlated with the Token Test - seems to be rather independent of Language Impairment; both the "Attributes" scale and the "Actions" scale have higher loadings on Factor II than on Factor I.

In contrast, for the Wernicke's aphasics it is not the Trail Making Test which loads mostly on the factor of Language Impairment but rather the two scales which require, in our view, the analytical isolation and identification of characteristic aspects of a given object. Although the Wernicke's aphasics showed on average no greater impairment, their conceptual difficulties in analytical or "propositional" thinking appears more closely linked with Language Impairment than may be the case for Broca's aphasics. This might be seen, depending on one's taste for argument, as support for the view that Wernicke's is the primary aphasia.

Taken as a whole, our results suggest that both Broca's and Wernicke's aphasics are specificially impaired in the analytical ability to isolate and identify conceptually individual features of objects or concepts. This ability might be a primary requirement in the Token Test (cf.,15) and also in many of the non-verbal tasks shown to discriminate between aphasics and brain-damaged controls. The impairment of such analytical competence which may be crucial for propositional thinking seems to be more closely related to the language deficits of Wernicke's than of Broca's aphasia. Whether this impaired competence is a result of the disordered language capacity or whether the Language Impairment is a result of problems in propositional thinking cannot be decided on the basis of the available data. It might be equally plausible to assume that both faculties interact with one supporting the other; the disruption of one process decisively affecting the functioning of the other irrespective of any causal links.

Acknowledgements. This research was funded by a grant from the Deutsche Forschungsgemeinschaft. It was conducted at 18 clinics and rehabilitation centers of West Germany (cf., 18). We wish to express our sincere thanks to the neurologists, therapists and, last but not least, to the patients of these institutions for their support and cooperation. We are indebted to Ewald Neumann and Hans Strohner for their help in collecting and analysing the data, and to Brian Bell for his assistence with the English text.

Note

1 An extended version of this paper is to appear in Brain and Language (1980) under the title 'Analytical competence and language impairment in aphasia.'

References

1. A.Basso, P.Faglioni, H.Spinnler: Neuropsychologia, 14, 183 (1976)
2. R.Cohen, S. Kelter: Cortex, (in press)
3. E.De Renzi, P.Faglioni, G.Scotti, H.Spinnler: Brain, 95, 293 (1972)
4. E.De Renzi, H.Spinnler: Cortex, 3, 194 (1967)

5. D.G.Doehring, J.G.Dudley, L.Coderre: Fol. phoniat. 19, 414 (1967)

6. P.Faglioni, H.Spinnler, L.A.Vignolo: Cortex, 5, ·366 (1969)

7. H.Spinnler, L.A.Vignolo: Cortex, 2, 337 (1966)

8. H.Strohner, R.Cohen, S.Kelter, G.Woll: Cortex, 14, 391 (1978)

9. E.De Renzi, P.Faglioni, M.Savoiardo, L.A.Vignolo: Cortex, 2, 399 (1966)

10. S.Kelter, R.Cohen, D.Engel, G.List, H.Strohner: J. Psycholing. Res., 6, 279 (1977)

11. H.-L.Teuber, S.Weinstein: Arch. Neurol. Psychiat. 76, 369 (1956)

12. S.Weinstein, H.-L.Teuber, L.Ghent, J.Semmes: Am. Psychol. 10, 408 (1955)

13. S.Kelter, R.Cohen, D.Engel, G.List, H.Strohner: Cortex, 12, 383 (1976)

14. R.Cohen, S.Kelter, D.Engel, G.List, H.Strohner: Nervenarzt, 47, 357 (1976)

15. R.Cohen, S.Kelter, B.Schäfer: Z. Klin. Psychol. 6, 1 (1977)

16. G.Goldstein: Schiz. Bull. 4, 161 (1978)

17. R.M.Reitan: A Manual for the Administration and Scoring of the Trail Making Test.(Indiana University, Indianapolis 1959)

18. R.Cohen, S.Kelter, G.Woll: Forschungsbericht aus dem Sonderforschungsbereich 99 "Linguistik" No. 29, unpubl. Manuscr., University of Konstanz (1978)

19. G.Woll, R.Cohen, S.Kelter: Z. Klin. Psychol. (in press)

20. E.De Renzi, L.A.Vignolo: Brain, 85, 665 (1962)

21. B.Orgass: Diagnostica, 22, 70 (1976a)

22. B.Orgass: Diagnostica, 22, 141 (1976b)

23. C.Bondy, R.Cohen, D.Eggert, G.Lüer: Testbatterie für geistig behinderte Kinder, Weinheim: Beltz (1969)

24. L.C.Dunn: The Peabody Picture Vocabulary Test.Manual and Set of Plates. (Minneapolis 1959)

25. K.Goldstein, M.Scheerer: Psychol. Monogr. 53, whole No. 329 (1941)

26. E.Weigl: Z. Psychol. 103, 2 (1927)

27. E.B. Zurif, A.Caramazza, R. Myerson, J.Galvin: Brain and Language, 1, 167 (1974)

28. K.Gloning, G.Haub, R.Quatember: Neoropsychologia, 6, 141 (1968)

29. H.Schuell, J.J.Jenkins, J.B.Carroll:J. Speech Hear. Res. 5, 349 (1962)

30. A.R.Luria: Traumatic Aphasia (Mouton The Hague 1970)

31. S.E.Blumstein, E.Baker, H.Goodglass: Neuropsychologia, 15, 19 (1977)

32. P.Tallal, F.Newcombe: Brain and Language, 5, 13 (1978)

On the Representation of Classificatory and Propositional Lexical Relations in the Human Brain

Claus Heeschen

Physiolog. Institut der Freien Universität Berlin,
Arnimallee 22, D-1000 Berlin 33, Fed. Rep. of Germany

1. Introduction

The topic of this paper is very closely related to that of
R. COHEN and W. HUBER (s. their contributions in this volume).
I will also deal with the problem of lexical relations, specifically with the distinction between logical-classificatory
and propositional relations (for a definition see below), but
my starting point was a different one: I was not concerned so
much with aphasiological questions, but rather with questions
concerning the language abilities of the two cerebral hemispheres.

As is well known, in a normal population the overwhelming
majority of subjects has the language function represented in
the left or so-called dominant or major hemisphere. This is
the general rule - leaving aside the problem of some peculiarities of the cerebral organization of left-handers and, possibly, women (s. [1] for a comprehensive presentation of the
problems associated with cerebral dominance; for a comprehensive review of studies concerning sex differences s. [2]). Nevertheless, even in the clearly left-dominant subjects, the
right (or minor or subdominant) hemisphere has at least some
language abilities. Thus, intensive studies of split-brain-
patients have shown convincingly that the right hemisphere is
at least quite good in understanding language. Its ability to
comprehend individual single words in particular, is rather
well developed. According to ZAIDEL [3,4] the vocabulary which
the right hemisphere of a normal adult has at its disposal has
the extent of a 14 year old child, - which indeed is not small.
In contrast to these well developed lexical abilities, the
ability to understand larger constructions, such as whole sentences, seems to be extremely poorly developed. Thus, expressed
in linguistic terms, we can say that the right minor hemisphere
has no grammar, in particular no syntax, but quite a large lexicon. Nevertheless, maybe it is a little premature to speak of
a lexicon in this context. So far, that we know for certain is
that the right hemisphere is able to match a given word to a
presentation of a piece of reality and conversely. Thus, the
right hemisphere is able to associate the sound "lion" with a
four-legged, living, yellow and hairy object existing in some
regions of Africa, but - and this is a mere triviality - a
lexicon is not a mere list of sound-reality-associations, but
a structure, a list organized by a variety of internal rela-

tions between the single items of the list. Thus, the question remains whether the right minor hemisphere has indeed a lexicon in the full sense of the word or a mere list of sound-reality-associations; in other words: is the right hemisphere not only responsive to word-reality-relations, but also to word-word-relations?

In a series of experiments done at the university of Ulm, Department of Neurology, A. ROTHENBERGER, R. JÜRGENS and I were able to show, by means of the so-called dichotic listening, that the right hemisphere is as responsive to semantic relations as the left hemisphere (s. [5, 6]). For instance, it was easier for the right hemisphere to identify a pair of semantically related words, e.g. "Rekrut (recruit) - Offizier (officer)", than to identify a pair of semantically unrelated words, e.g. "Rekrut (recruit) - Apfelbaum (apple-tree)". In this respect, i.e. in the general responsiveness to semantic relatedness, there was no difference between the subdominant right and the dominant left hemisphere, - at least no quantitative difference. So we may ascribe a true lexicon, i.e. a list of words structured and organized by semantic relations between individual words, to the right hemisphere as well.

(N.B.: Throughout this paper I will speak of a lexicon in the right and a lexicon in the left hemisphere. I should like to stress that this is a mere metaphor used for convenience. The neuronal representation of what we may call - in functional terms - the lexical knowledge of a subject is probably much more complicated than these metaphors will suggest; the "lexicon" is probably something undivided in the human brain, extending over large areas and over both hemispheres. Accordingly, the metaphor "the left and the right hemispheric lexicon" is to be understood as the specific use of or access to the stored lexical knowledge by a specific hemisphere.) By the dichotic experiments just mentioned we were not able to answer the qualitative question with respect to the lexical structures in the two hemispheres, i.e. are the lexical structures in the right hemisphere the same as in the dominant left hemisphere or are the principles of semantic organization in the lexicon qualitatively different in the two hemispheres? To shed some light on this problem, F. REISCHIES and I devised an experiment using the technique of bilateral stimulation of the visual half fields (VHF). The experiment was carried out at the Physiological Institute of the Free University Berlin, Department of Neurophysiology (Director: Prof. Dr. O.-J. GRÜSSER). Although this was a team project, I alone am responsible for the report in this paper.

Before describing the experiment, it is perhaps expedient to give some explanatory remarks concerning the technique of bilateral stimulation of the VHF's. Experiments with this technique proceed as follows:

The subjects have to steadily focus on a given point, the so-called fixation point. Then, two visual stimuli are presented to the subject simultaneously in such a way that one stimulus appears in the left and the other in the right VHF. In

order to prevent involuntary eye movements during the exposure
of the stimuli, the exposure time must not exceed 150 ms. Under
these conditions, the anatomy of the visual pathways involves
the stimulus in the left VHF going primarily into the right
cerebral hemisphere and the stimulus in the right VHF into the
left one. Exchange of information between the two hemispheres
takes place via the corpus callosum, particularly its posterior
part, the splenium, However - and this is the crucial point - ,
such an exchange seems to occur <u>only after</u> the stimuli have
been at least partially processed by the hemisphere into which
they have primarily been projected. This has been demonstrated
- among others - by D. HINES [7] and there is also some evidence from neuroanatomical studies in monkeys which show that
there are no direct callosal connections between the two areas
17, at least not parafoveally. Thus, the subject's responses
to stimuli in the left VHF reflect what the right hemisphere
is doing and his responses to stimuli in the right VHF reflect
what the left hemisphere is doing. Admittedly, this is a very
simplified description of the true state of affairs, but I
think it is basically correct; anyway, it would not be very
meaningful in this context to go into the details of the methodological problems associated with the VHF-technique.
Now let us turn to our experiment.

2. Method

The subjects sat in front of a projection screen at a distance
of 2.5 meters. They were required to focus on a small bulb on
the screen, the bulb serving as the fixation point. By pres-
sing a button, the experimenter turned on the bulb, thereby
triggering the tachistoscopical projection of a slide on which
a pair of words was written in capital letters. This pair of
words was arranged in such a way that one word appeared on the
left side of the fixation point and the other on the right
side. Fig.1 gives a schematical outline of the experimental
situation and an example of a stimulus pair.

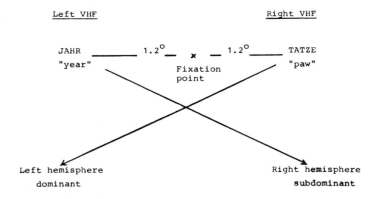

Fig.1 Example

The distance from the fixation point to the innermost letters
of the words was 1.2° visual angle, and to the outmost letters
2 - 3°, depending on the length of the respective words. Exposure time was 140 ms. Immediately after the appearance of such
a pair of words, the subjects simply had to tell what they had
read or what they believed to have read. There was a total of
60 pairs of words.

16 normal subjects (i.e. with no known disease of the central nervous system) were tested, 8 males and 8 females. All
subjects were clear right-handers and native speakers of German. The number of subjects having correctly identified a given word was taken as a measure for the recognizability of
that word. For example, the recognizability of "Tatze" was 1,
meaning that only one subject was able to identify "Tatze"
under the conditions just described.

Then, another group of 16 subjects (also 8 males and 8 females and all being normal right-handed native speakers of
German) was tested. The stimulus material and the method of
stimuli presentation was the same as before. This second group
of subjects, however, was assisted in identifying the words.
Before the projection of a pair of words, they were given an
additional word - orally by the experimenter - which was semantically related to one word of the following pair; e.g.,
before the projection of "Jahr" and "Tatze", the subjects were
given the word "Löwe (lion)" as an auxiliary stimulus. The
subjects were not told to which word of a pair the auxiliary
stimulus would be related. In 30 of the 60 pairs of words, the
auxiliary stimulus was related to the word in the left VHF,
and in the other 30 pairs of words the auxiliary stimulus was
related to the word in the right VHF. The number of subjects
having correctly identified a word, the recognition of which
was facilitated by an auxiliary stimulus, was taken once more
as a measure for the recognizability of that word.

Now we have 60 words for which we have two scores of recognizability. The score obtained under the condition with an
auxiliary stimulus will be called "facilitated recognizability" and the score obtained with no auxiliary stimulus will be
called "basic recognizability"; e.g. - as mentioned above -
the basic recognizability of "Tatze" was 1, the facilitated
recognizability - facilitated by the auxiliary stimulus word
"Löwe" - was 7, i.e. the item "Tatze" was identified with an
auxiliary stimulus by 6 more subjects than without such a stimulus.

The relations between the auxiliary stimulus words and the
words to be recognized were controlled for two variables: the
one variable being the linguistic type of relation and the
other being the associative strength. All stimulus words and
auxiliary stimulus words were taken from the Kent-Rosanoff-
lists of associations so that the associative strength between stimulus and auxiliary stimulus could be defined in quite
a straightforward manner as the number of subjects having the
stimulus word as their first association to the word functioning as auxiliary stimulus. In Tab.1 some examples are given.

<u>Table 1</u> Examples of stimuli

Auxiliary Stimulus	Stimulus	Associative Strength	Type of Relation
Löwe "lion"	Tatze "paw"	1	classificatory
Adler "eagle"	Geier "vulture"	9	classificatory
durstig "thirsty"	Bier "beer"	39	propositional
Baby	Wiege "cradle"	11	propositional

The associative strength between "Löwe" and "Tatze" is 1, i.e. from a total of 200 subjects, one subject had "Tatze" as his first association to "Löwe". An example of extremely high associative strength is "durstig (thirsty)" and "Bier (beer)". 39 subjects had "Bier" as their first association to the word "durstig".

As to the variable "Type of linguistic relation", we distinguished 2 levels: <u>logical-classificatory</u> and <u>propositional</u>. The logical-classificatory relations comprised part-of-relations, such as "Löwe" and "Tatze" and co-classificatory relations, such as "Adler (eagle)" and "Geier (vulture)". Relations which are termed propositional in this paper are mainly situational ones, i.e. the two words are tied together by the co-occurrence of their respective referents in a given situation, e.g. "Baby" and "Wiege (cradle)" or "durstig" and "Bier"; "durstig" is a quality characteristic of a situation in which "Bier" also functions as an important and characteristic accessory. Thus, the distinction between classificatory and propositional relations is exactly analogous to the distinction R. COHEN drew in his paper although his terminology is different.

In summary, the outcome of our experiment will be a set of data with the following structure: We have a total of 60 item words, 30 for each VHF. Each item is assigned a score for 5 variables:

<u>Variable 1:</u> The "facilitated recognizability" i.e. the number of subjects having identified the item after an auxiliary stimulus word has been given.

<u>Variable 2:</u> The "basic recognizability" i.e. the number of subjects having identified the item without an auxiliary stimulus.

<u>Variable 3</u>: The "linguistic type of relation" between auxiliary stimulus and the stimulus to be identified. This qualitative variable is coded arbitrarily as 1 and -1

<u>Variable 4:</u> The "associative strength" between auxiliary stimulus and the stimulus to be identified.

<u>Variable 5:</u> The interaction between variable 3 and 4. Because this latter variable had no relevant effect, I will not explain in greater detail what exactly is meant by the "interaction"; it is introduced here only for reasons of statistical completeness.

Table 2 exemplifies the data structure and gives an example for each VHF.

<u>Table 2</u> Data structure

Item	x_1 Facilitated recognizability	x_2 Basic recognizability	x_3 Associative strength	x_4 Type of relation	x_5 Type X Strength Interaction
.					
.					
Bier	11	8	39	1	11.92
.					
.					

Left VHF
n = 30

.					
.					
Tatze	7	1	1	-1	14.11
.					
.					

Right VHF
n = 30

3. Results

Let us first consider the difference between the two scores of recognizability.

On the average, a word is identified by 3.43 subjects if no auxiliary stimulus is given (=basic recognizability). If an auxiliary stimulus is given, the recognizability increases up to 5.23; the difference of 1.80 is significant as a correlated <u>t</u> test shows: t (59) = 6.43; p<.01. This holds after summing over the 2 VHF's. Fig.2 also shows the results separately for each VHF. As can easily be seen, the improvement from the basic recognizability to the facilitated recognizability is more or less the same in the two VHF's. The difference between the differences (2.07 and 1.54 equally .53) is insignificant as a 2 x 2 analysis of variance has shown.

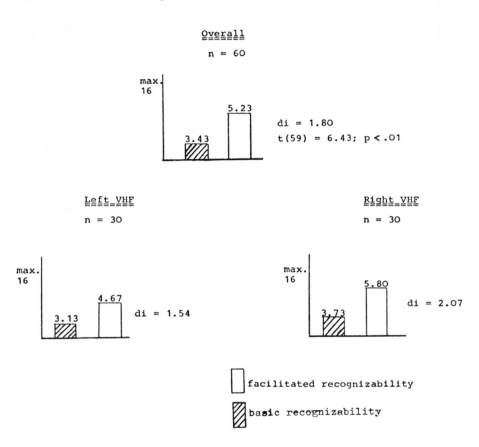

Fig.2 Mean values of recognizability

The data clearly indicate that a word can be more easily identified after a semantically related word has been presented. Now the crucial questions are:
- How far does this helping effect depend on the qualitative and quantitative aspects of the relation between the auxiliary word and the word to be identified?

- Are there any differences between the 2 VHF's with respect to these possible dependencies?

Before answering these questions, we have to construct an adequate numerical expression for the helping effect. The score "facilitated recognizability" as such is certainly not adequate in this respect, as can easily be verified by the following example: The word "Bier" was identified by quite a lot of subjects (11) after the presentation of the auxiliary word "durstig". "Bier", however, was also identified by a comparatively high number of subjects (8) without the auxiliary stimulus - probably because "Bier" is a high frequency word, because of its shortness etc.; i.e., only a certain portion of the score "facilitated recognizability" is a true expression of the helping effect of the auxiliary words. Statistically spoken, in order to evaluate the true helping effect, we have to "partial out" the variable "basic recognizability" from the variable "facilitated recognizability". What is left then from the original "facilitated recognizability" is indeed a true expression of the helping effect. I will call this residual variable the "gain in recognizability"; e.g. the gain in recognizability for the word "Bier" was 1.97, i.e. 1.97 more subjects have identified "Bier" after "durstig" has been given than would have been expected on the basis of the basic recognizability of "Bier". Table 3 shows the structure of this new reduced set of data.

We can now consider the variable "gain in recognizability" as the criterion variable and the variables "associative strength", "type of relation" and the interaction between these two variables as the predictor variables and can answer the above-men-

Table 3 Data after removing all variance due to "basic recognizability"

Item	x_1 Gain in recognizability	x_2 Associative Strength	x_3 Type of Relation	x_4 Interaction
Left VHF	·			
	·			
Bier	1.97	16.83	-1.44	16.51
	·			
	·			
Right VHF	·			
	·			
Tatze	2.97	-6.36	.65	12.74
	·			
	·			

tioned questions by means of multiple regression analysis. It should be mentioned that the stimulus material was chosen in such a way that the predictor variables are mutually independent, i.e. orthogonal.

Two multiple regression analyses applied separately to the data for the left and the right VHF yielded the following results:

Table 4   Results of multiple regression analysis

VHF	Variance of criterion "Gain in recognizability"	Variance explained	by Variable	Standard regression coefficient(beta)	
left	1.00	.18	Associative Strength	.42	$p<.05$
		.01	Type of Relation	.12	n.s.
		.04	Interaction	.21	n.s.
right	1.00	.01	Associative Strength	-.07	n.s.
		.22	Type of Relation	-.47	$p<.05$
		.04	Interaction	.19	n.s.

In the <u>left</u> VHF, 18% of the criterion variance is explained by the associative strength, which is a significant portion ($p < .05$), while the type of relation explains more or less nothing at all in the criterion (1%, which is insignificant). In the <u>right</u> VHF, the situation is reversed: a significant ($p < .05$) portion of 22% of the criterion variance is explained by the type of relation and more or less nothing (1%) is explained by the associative strength. More specifically, the greater the associative strength between auxiliary stimulus and the stimulus to be recognized, the greater the helping effect for words projected into the left VHF, while for words projected into the right VHF, the helping effect does not depend on the associative strength at all. Conversely, auxiliary stimuli standing in a classificatory relation to the stimuli to be identified help the identification more than auxiliary stimuli standing in a propositional relation, but this holds only for words projected into the right VHF, while for words projected into the left VHF, it does not matter at all whether the auxiliary stimuli stand in a classificatory or propositional relation. This last finding can be made clearer by another presentation of the data. For each VHF, there were 20 words with a propositional relation to the auxiliary stimulus and 10 words with a classificatory relation to the auxiliary stimulus. Table 5

shows the mean gain of recognizability for each group of words
in each VHF. A 2 x 2 analysis of variance appropriate for un-
equal group sizes shows a significant VHF x type interaction
$[F(1.56) = 5.92; p < .05]$, the decomposition of which into
simple effects shows that the gain in recognizability increases
from "propositional" to "classificatory" only for words in the
right VHF, while the effect of "Type" is absolutely insignificant for the left VHF.

Table 5 Mean gain in recognizability

Type

	classificatory	propositional
left	-.24 n=1o	.12 n=2o
right	1.53 n=1o	-.77 n=2o

VHF

Type x VHF -Interaction: $F(1,56) = 5.92; p < .o5$

Simple Effects:
Type for left VHF: $F(1,56) = .5o$
Type for right VHF: $F(1,56) = 8.90; p < .o1$

4. Discussion

As mentioned above, we can interpret the subjects' behaviour
to stimuli in a given VHF as a reflection of what the contra-
lateral cerebral hemisphere is doing. Thus, the fact that the
identification of words is equally facilitated by semantically
related auxiliary words in both VHF's indicates that both hemispheres are equally responsive to semantic relations. This
could already be demonstrated by our above-mentioned dichotic
experiments (s. also [8], a study on a split-brain-patient).
The new finding in our experiment is that this semantic responsiveness is qualitatively different in the two hemispheres.
The right hemisphere seems to be absolutely insensitive to the
type of relations between words: it does not make any difference whether the relation is of the classificatory or the pro-

positional type; this distinction has no meaning as far as
the lexical organization of the right hemisphere is concerned.
It is only the quantitative aspect of the association between
two words which has relevance for the right hemisphere. Thus,
we may conceive of the lexicon in the right hemisphere as a
list of words organized into associative fields on the basis
of the associative strength between the words. As far as the
precise qualitative nature of these associations is concerned,
the right-hemispheric lexicon seems to be organized only in
a vague and diffuse manner, if at all. On the other hand, the
left hemisphere is primarily sensitive to the qualitative nature of associations, i.e. to the logical linguistic type of
the associations: classificatory associations tie the words
more together than propositional relations, while the quantitative aspect of the relations (the associative strength) has
no relevance for the structure of the lexicon. Thus, we may
conceive of the left-hemispheric lexicon as a list of words
organized on the basis of a hierarchy of logical linguistic
relations with classificatory relations assuming the top position in that hierarchy. The left-hemispheric lexicon seems
to have a precise conceptual structure.

These findings fit excellently to the findings of R. COHEN.
If sensitivity to classificatory relations is a special domain
of the left hemisphere, it is quite natural that damage to
the left hemisphere (as occurs in aphasia) disturbs or even
makes impossible operations for which a classificatory analysis of the stimuli is a necessary prerequisite.

Our findings also fit some generalized theories concerning
the mode of operation of the two hemispheres. Nowadays it is
a generally assumed position among neuropsychologists that
the mode of operation of the left hemisphere can be characterized as sequential-<u>analytic</u> and of the right hemisphere as
more <u>wholistic</u> or "gestalthaft". From this it would follow
that the right subdominant hemisphere differs not only from
the left dominant hemisphere in that it has less linguistic
abilities, but also in that its linguistic abilities are
qualitatively different from those of the left hemisphere.
As a matter of fact, classification of words presupposes
their decomposition into individual meaning components or -
in other words - the analytical isolation of certain defining
meaning components, and this is a way of handling words typical for the analytical left hemisphere. On the other hand,
to group such words as "durstig" and "Bier" closely together
presupposes a wholistic handling of these words or at least
a "neglect" of their individual components and their mediat-
ion by a whole situational picture. Thus, the dependence
of the right hemisphere on the variable "associative strength"
and of the left hemisphere on the "type of linguistic relation"
is not by chance, but is rather a consequence of some basic
characteristics of the two hemispheres.

References

1. HECAEN, H. and ALBERT, M.L. Human Neuropsychology. Wiley, New York, 1978.

2. HARRIS, L.J. Sex differences in spatial ability. In Asymmetrical Function of the Brain, M. KINSBOURNE (Editor). Cambridge University Press, 1978.

3. ZAIDEL, E. Auditory vocabulary of the right hemisphere after brain bisection and hemidecortication. Cortex 12, 191-211, 1976.

4. ZAIDEL, E. Unilateral auditory language comprehension on the Token Test following cerebral commissurotomy and hemispherectomy. Neuropsychologia 15, 1-13, 1977.

5. HEESCHEN, C. and JÜRGENS, R. Pragmatic-semantic and syntactic factors influencing ear differences in dichotic listening. Cortex 13, 74-83, 1977.

6. HEESCHEN, C., ROTHENBERGER, A., JÜRGENS, R. Perception of semantic and syntactic paradigms in dichotic listening. Submitted for publication.

7. HINES, D. Independent functioning of the two cerebral hemispheres for recognizing bilaterally presented visual half-field stimuli. Cortex 11, 132-143, 1975.

8. SUGISHITA, M. Mental association in the minor hemisphere of a commissurotomy patient. Neuropsychologia 16, 229-232, 1978.

Events, Instants and Temporal Reference

Hans Kamp

Bedford College, University of London, Senate House,
London WC1E 7HU, England

I:

The truth of my claim: 'It is raining' depends on the time at which I made
it. It was true if and only if it was indeed raining (in my vicinity) at that
time. Similarly my assertion 'it has been raining', made at time t, is true
if there was a time t' preceding t such that it rained at t'.
But what is a time? In physics, where it has been standard practice to represent time as a structure isomorphic with the real numbers, we have become
accustomed to thinking of times as either durationless instants, or else
collections of such instants.
The concept of a durationless temporal instant is a quite sophisticated one,
the eventual response, after many centuries of experimentation, to Zeno's
puzzle. It contains at least two distinct mathematical ideas, both of which
are by no means obvious. In fact, they appear counterintuitive to many who
encounter them for the first time. The first of these concerns the possibility
of densely ordered structures, between any two elements of which there is a
third; the second the possibility that a collection of elements each of which
has zero size by itself, may nonetheless have a size bigger than 0. (Thus, in
particular, an interval may have finite duration even though each of the instants that constitute it has no duration whatever.)
These principles tend to strike non-mathematicians as particularly puzzling
when they are stated in the context of time; and one of the reasons for this
is no doubt that the instant-concept which would satisfy them is so very far
removed from the ideas that people ordinarily have of 'time' - however inar-
ticulate these ideas may be.

Is time really like the real numbers? Or is it rather like the rationals,
or like the integers, or has it some other structure? Before we can even make
an attempt at answering such a question, we must first determine what sort of
question it is. And the sort of question it is depends on what we take to be
the nature of time. If time is, as Kant suggested, a mental category, then
the question is about how, and to what extent, the structure of the mind determines the formal properties of this category. If we take - as, it seems,
Poincaré advocated - the structure of time to be a matter of theoretical convention, with no more justification, and no more need of justification, than
its utility to a highly successful complex of scientific theories, the question disappears. If we assume, with Leibniz, Einstein or Whitehead, that
time is no more than the totality of temporal relations between the events
and processes which constitute the history of our world, the question is
about the actual structural relations between these events and processes.
If we assume - as it appears Russell did at some stage - that statements about
time, like other statements which appear to be about the world outside us,
are in last analysis complex claims about actual and possible experiences,
then the question is about the structure of these experiences.

Only the last two of these different conceptions are relevant to what I wish to say below. These two views, however different in their general philosophical perspectives, are nevertheless quite similar in an important formal respect: Each takes as primary certain entities - be they mental experiences or physical events - which are generally - in fact it is reasonable to assume *always* - of finite duration. I shall refer to such entities henceforth as *events*. If we can talk about durationless instants at all, these must, on either of the two views, be constructs, built from elements which are themselves not without duration.

II:

There are various ways in which such a construction can proceed. The one which I shall present here goes back to Russell and Wiener.[1] This particular construction assumes that with the basic elements (be they mental or physical occurrences) are given two binary temporal relations, the relation of complete precedence, $\propto$, and that of temporal overlap, O. We assume that these relations satisfy the following postulates:

A1: $(\forall x \forall y) \ (x \propto y \rightarrow \neg \ y \propto x)$

A2: $(\forall x \forall y \forall z) \ (x \propto y \wedge y \propto z \rightarrow x \propto z)$

A3: $(\forall x) \ x \ O \ x$

A4: $(\forall x \ \forall y) \ (x \ Oy \rightarrow yOx)$

A5: $(\forall x \forall y) \ (x \propto y \rightarrow \neg \ xOy)$

A6: $(\forall x \forall y \forall z \forall t) \ (x \propto y \wedge yOz \wedge z \propto t \rightarrow x \propto t)$

A7: $(\forall x \forall y) \ (x \propto y \vee xOy \vee y \propto x)$[2]

Suppose that $\tau = \ <T,<>$ is such a strict linear ordering, that E is a set of non-empty intervals of τ; and that for e_1, $e_2 \in E$

$$e_1 < (\tau) \ e_2 \equiv_{df.} (\forall t_1 \in e_1) \ (\forall t_2 \in e_2) \ (t_1 < t_2); \text{and}$$

$$e_1 \ O(\tau) \ e_2 \equiv_{df.} (\exists t) \ (t \in e_1 \wedge t \in e_2).$$

Then the structure $<e, \propto (\tau), O(\tau)>$ satisfies each of A1 - A7. By verifying that this is so, the reader may discover the intuitive motivation behind these postulates. But in view of the use we wish to make of them such an argument would be circular if presented as a justification for adopting them. Indeed the only possible justification for A1 - A7 must derive directly from the intuitions regarding the events or experiences themselves and the temporal relations by which they are connected. Thus what justification can be given will depend largely on the metaphysical assumptions we make about the nature of time; and it is here that what we might refer to as the Russellian and the Whiteheadian approaches part company.[3]

I am not much attracted either by Russell's phenomenalism or by Whitehead's metaphysics; and so I shall not attempt to justify the postulates A1-A7 in the context of either of these two frameworks. I shall, in due course, come up with an interpretation of my own. But first let me describe how the instants may be constructed from events structured in accordance with A1-A7. The construction is to provide us with instants such that for each of the events there is a certain set of instants at each of which the event is 'going on'. This means that if i_1 is an instant at which e_1 goes on, i_2 is an instant at which e_2 goes on and $e_1 \propto e_2$ then i_1 must indeed be earlier than i_2. This indicates how we might define the earlier-later relation; but it does not show us how to construct the instants themselves.

When e_1 0 e_2, then, we would like to say, there ought to be some instant at which e_1 and e_2 go on simultaneously. Similarly, if e_1, e_2 and e_3 have a common overlap there ought to be an instant at which all three go on. Now, since 0 is a binary operator, the proposition that e_1, e_2 and e_3 have a common overlap cannot be expressed directly. However, we may convince ourselves that its content is given by the conjunction e_1 0 e_2 & e_1 0 e_3 & e_2 0 e_3. For, given that the events are, intuitively speaking, uninterrupted, how could the conjunction hold without there being common overlap?[4] Similarly, if x is a set of events such that for any two members e_1, e_2 of x e_1 0 e_2, then there ought to be an instant at which all events in x go on simultaneously.[5] Of course there might be several such instants. In fact there would have to be several such if there were events e_1 and e_2 such that $e_1 \propto e_2$ while both e_1 and e_2 overlap each of the events in x. For then there ought to be an instant at which all members of x U $\{e_1\}$ go on and an instant at which all members of x U $\{e_2\}$ go on, and of these the first must precede the second. This situation cannot arise, however, if x itself is *maximal*, i.e. if there is no event e which overlaps all the members of x and yet is not already in x. Even in this case we could assume without contradiction that there are distinct instants at which each of the members of x goes on; but the principle that any two which do *not* overlap do *not* share any instants does no longer force us to assume such multiplicity.
Indeed it is not difficult to show that if we identify instants with such maximal sets we get what we were looking for.

Formally:

Let ε = $<E, \propto , 0>$ be a structure which satisfies the postulates A_1-A_7.

Def.　a) An *instant of* ε is a maximal subset of E of pairwise overlapping events, i.e. i is an *instant of* ε iff i) i $\subseteq$ E; ii) for any e_1, $e_2 \in$ i　e_1 0 e_2; and iii) for any $e_1 \in$ E \ i there is an $e_2 \in$ i such that $\neg e_1$ 0 e_2.

　　b) Let I (ε) be the set of instants of ε.

　　c) For i_1, $i_2 \in$ I (ε), $i_1 < i_2$ iff there are $e_1 < i_1$ and $e_2 \in i_2$ such that $e_1 \propto e_2$.　•

Theorem:　Suppose ε = $<E, \propto, 0>$ safisfies A_1-A_7. Then $<I(\varepsilon), <_\varepsilon>$ is a strict linear ordering.

Proof:　We must show that ε safisfies the following conditions:

　　i)　　$i_1 < i_2 \rightarrow \neg i_2 < i_1$;

　　ii)　　$i_1 < i_2 \wedge i_2 < i_3 \rightarrow i_1 < i_3$;

　　iii)　$i_1 \neq i_2 \rightarrow i_1 < i_2 \vee i_2 < i_1$.

i) Suppose $i_1 < i_2$ so there are $e_1 \in i_1$ and $e_2 \in i_2$ such that $e_1 \propto e_2$. Suppose now that also $i_2 < i_1$. Then there would also be $e_3 \in i_1$ and $e_4 \in i_2$ such that $e_4 \propto e_3$. Since e_3 and e_1 belong to the same instant we have e_3 O e_1. So by A6 we infer from $e_4 \propto e_3$, e_3 O e_1, $e_1 \propto e_2$ that $e_4 \propto e_2$. But on the other hand e_4 and e_2 also belong to the same instant i_2. So e_4 O e_2. This contradicts A5.

ii) Suppose $i_1 < i_2$ and $i_2 < i_3$. So there is an $e_1 \in i_2$ and an $e_2 \in i_2$ such that $e_1 \propto e_2$. Also there is an $e_3 \in i_2$ and an $e_4 \in i_3$ such that $e_3 \propto e_4$. Finally since e_2, $e_3 \in i_2$, e_2 O e_3. So by A6 $e_1 \propto e_4$.

iii) Assume $i_1 \neq i_2$. So there is an e_1 such that either $e_1 \in i_1 - i_2$ or $e_1 \in i_2 - i_1$. Suppose $e_1 \in i_1 - i_2$. Then there is an $e_2 \in i_2$ such that e_1 O e_2. So by A7 either $e_1 \propto e_2$ or $e_2 \propto e_1$. If $e_1 \propto e_2$ then $i_1 < i_2$; in the other case $i_2 < i_1$. If $e_1 \in i_2 - i_1$ the argument proceeds similarly. q.e.d.

I shall refer to the structure $<I(\varepsilon), <_\varepsilon>$ also as '$\tau(\varepsilon)$'. Notice that if we assume that ε satisfies only A1-A6, then it is still possible to show that $<_\varepsilon$ satisfies i) and ii). But of course, it is then no longer possible to show that $<_\varepsilon$ is connected.

Given the way we have defined instants the relation which holds between an event e and an instant i when intuitively we would wish to say that e 'goes on' at i is simply the set theoretic relation of membership: 'e goes on at i' could be defined as 'e $\in$ i'. It is quite easy to show that for each e $\in$ E the set $\bar{e} = \{i \in I(\varepsilon): e \in i\}$ is a non-empty interval of $\tau(\varepsilon)$.

For suppose i_1, $i_2 \in e$ and $i_1 <_\varepsilon i <_\varepsilon i_2$. We must show that $i \in \bar{e}$, or, in other words, that $e \in i$. Suppose not. Then there is an $e_0 \in i$ such that $\neg e_0$ O e. So $e_0 \propto e$ or $e \propto e_0$. Suppose $e_1 \propto e$. There are $e_1 \in i_1$ and $e_2 \in i$ such that $e_1 \propto e_2$. Since e_0, $e_2 \in i$, e_2 O e_0. So by A6 $e_1 \propto e$. But e_1, $e \in i$, so e_1 O e: contradiction. The case where $e \propto e_0$ is treated analogously.

Of course, in general not every interval of $\tau(\varepsilon)$ will correspond in this way to an event of ε. Nor can we be certain that an interval that does not correspond to an event determines that event uniquely: there might be events which, although distinct, are yet perfectly simultaneous. Any two such events will stand, however, in exactly the same temporal relation to every other event of ε.

We have already seen how to define relations $\propto(\tau)$ and O (τ) for intervals of some strict linear ordering τ. It is also easily verified that if $e_1 \propto e_2$ then $\bar{e}_1 \propto (\tau(\varepsilon)) \bar{e}_2$, and if e_1 O e_2 then $\bar{e}_1$ O $(\tau(\varepsilon)) \bar{e}_2$. Thus the function e $\Rightarrow \bar{e}$ is a homomorphic embedding of ε into the structure $\varepsilon(\tau(\varepsilon)) = <E(\tau(\varepsilon))$, $<(\tau(\varepsilon))$, O $(\tau(\varepsilon)) >$, where $E(\tau(\varepsilon))$ is the set of all intervals of $\tau(\varepsilon)$. To the structure $\varepsilon(\tau(\varepsilon))$ we can apply the Russell-Wiener construction once again. This yields a linear ordering, to which I shall for notational simplicity, refer here as $\tau' = \langle T', <' \rangle$. In general τ' will not be an isomorphic copy of $\tau(\varepsilon)$. To see this suppose that ε consists of two denumerable sequences of events $\{e_1, e_2, e_3, \ldots\}$ and $\{f_1, f_2, f_3, \ldots\}$ and that $e_1 \propto e_2 \propto e_3 \propto \ldots$ $\ldots \propto f_3 \propto f_2 \propto f_1$. In this case each instant of ε will consist of precisely one event. Among the maximal sets of pairwise overlapping intervals of $\tau(\varepsilon)$ however there is in particular one which contains (among others) for each $j = 1,2,3,\ldots$ both the interval (e_1, f_j) and the interval (e_j, f_1). This set of intervals determines an instant of τ' which precedes all the f_j's and is preceded by all the e_j's. This instant does therefore not correspond to any instant of $\tau(\varepsilon)$.

In general the structure τ' will not be what we should like it to be. Thus in the example just discussed τ' would contain besides the points already in $\tau(\varepsilon)$, in addition *two* new instants i_1 and i_2 such that
$$\{\overline{e_1}\} < \{\overline{e_2}\} < \ldots < i_1 < i_2 < \ldots < \{\overline{f_2}\} < \{\overline{f_1}\}$$ where $\{\overline{e_i}\}$, $\{\overline{f_i}\}$ are the points of τ' corresponding to points $\{e_i\}$, $\{f_i\}$ of $\tau(\varepsilon)$. i_1 will be the maximal set containing all intervals of the form $\bigcup_{i>n}\{e_i\}$ where n is some natural number, while i_2 is the set which contains all intervals $\bigcup_{i>n}\{f_i\}$ for some n.

This is displeasing - it would have been much more satisfactory had τ' been the Dedekind closure of $\tau(\varepsilon)$, producing, in particular, in the example under consideration exactly one instant for the gap between the points $\{e_i\}$ and the points $\{f_i\}$. To obtain the Dedekind closure we must restrict the family of intervals of $\tau(\varepsilon)$ which enter into the construction of the instants of τ' to all closed intervals which are bounded by instants of $\tau(\varepsilon)$, i.e. all intervals of the form $[i_1, i_2]$ where $i_1, i_2 \in I(\varepsilon)$.

This alternative has its awkward side too, however, in as much as some structures ε contain events e such that the corresponding interval $\overline{e}$ of $\tau(\varepsilon)$ is not of the form $[i_1,i_2]$. This would be the case for instance if the event structure ε of our example contained besides the e_i and f_i and event g which overlaps all of the e_i but none of the f_i. The same would be true of an event h which overlaps all of the events f_i but none of the e_i. And as soon as we admit the intervals $\overline{g}$ and $\overline{h}$ together with all the closed intervals of $\tau(\varepsilon)$ in the construction of τ' we obtain again two instants i_1 and i_2, rather than one, to fill the gap of $\tau(\varepsilon)$. (i_1 would contain besides all intervals $[\{e_i,g\}, \{f_j,h\}]$ also $\overline{g}$ while i_2 would contain $\overline{h}$ as well as all these closed intervals).

It is thus not true in general that τ' is the Dedekind closure of $\tau(\varepsilon)$. It should be added however that in all cases the difference between τ' and the Dedekind closure of $\tau(\varepsilon)$ is slight. It can consist only there in that for certain gaps of $\tau(\varepsilon)$ τ' has a pair of instants where the Dedekind closure $\tau(\varepsilon)$ has got only one. I shall not investigate here the possibility of imposing additional conditions on ε which would warrant that τ' and the Dedekind closure of $\tau(\varepsilon)$ are indeed isomorphic.[6]

The event structure $\varepsilon(\tau')$ formed out of the intervals of τ' will be in general richer than $\varepsilon(\tau(\varepsilon))$. But after that we finally reach stability: $\tau(\varepsilon(\tau'))$ is isomorphic with τ'.

III:

In section I I asked, by way of an introduction to the discussion which followed, the question how one might determine the structural properties of time. Let us assume that time, presented as a linear ordering of points is derived from an underlying structure of events. Does this help us to answer that question?

The obvious strategy must now be i) to discover additional postulates for event structures which allow us to derive additional structural conditions on the derived ordering; ii) to find independent justification for these additional postulates. Russell made a valiant effort in this direction in his [12]. But his work seems to bear out the conclusion that this course is not as fruitful as one might have hoped. For the new postulates for ε tend to be just as plausible, or dubious, as the additional conditions on $\tau(\varepsilon)$ that can be derived with their help. To show that $\tau(\varepsilon)$ is dense, for instance, one has to adopt some such postulate as:

$$(\forall e_1)(\forall e_2) \ (e_1 \propto e_2 \rightarrow (\exists e_3)(\exists e_4) \ e_3 \propto e_2 \wedge e_1 \propto e_4 \wedge e_3 \ O \ e_4)).$$

It is evident that with this extra condition we can demonstrate the density of $<_\varepsilon$. But why should the postulate be accepted?

It is not for the sake of settling such problems however that I have discussed the Russell-Wiener construction. The two applications that I have in mind for it are in a quite different direction. The first of these applications is in fact quite distinct, I believe, from anything that the authors had contemplated themselves. And the second, though more commensurable, with their own intentions (as well as, for that matter, with those of Whitehead) is yet in important aspects different from what I expect either Russell or Whitehead would have accepted.

The first application is a purely linguistic one.
I have become increasingly convinced that there are certain linguistic phenomena for which we can only account via a systematic analysis of the ways in which discourse participants process the information with which the discourse provides them. Among these phenomena there are some which concern reference to time, and of such phenomena I shall give some examples later on. To illustrate what I have in mind let us consider a very simple situation, in which one person, S, does all the talking, and another, H, all the listening. We shall assume, moreover, that S utters a sequence $s_1,...,s_n$ of indicative sentences, as one would do when telling a story, or reporting on an event one has witnessed. As the discourse proceeds H will represent the information conveyed to him; and we shall suppose - another simplifying assumption - that he modifies his representation after each successive sentence that S utters. Thus H produces a series of representations $D_1,...,D_n$. Each next representation D_{i+1} results from incorporating the new information contained in S_{i+1} into the structure D_i which represents all the information obtained from $S_1,...,S_i$. Precisely how these D_i are structured will depend on many factors. Among these is the grammatical complexity of the sentences $s_1,...,s_n$. I shall later on illustrate, for some exceedingly simple language, how the operation which produces D_{i+1} out of D_i and s_{i+1} might actually be defined. For sentences drawn from fairly uncomplicated language fragment suffice it for now to point out that in many types of discourse much of the information communicated is about certain events; when this is so the discourse will often make clear how the different events are temporally related. Such information I propose to represent with the help of event structures of the kind discussed

in the preceding section. The elements of E will be labeled events (where the label tells us, what the event consists in); and the relations < and 0 will contain the information about the temporal order of the events.

In general, however, the information H receives will not specify the temporal order of the events completely.[7]
This means that we must abandon postulate A7. I shall discuss the consequences of this in the next section.
First, however, a preliminary sketch of the second application. As I already remarked, this application is more in accordance with the intentions of those who developed the theories of section II.

There is, I believe, a great deal of plausibility in the view that the nature of time is determined by the temporal connections of the events which constitute the history of our universe. I also believe that these temporal relations between events are objective - this is one of the important philosophical insights bequeathed by the theory of relativity. I do not believe, however, that a similar objectivity attaches to the concept of an event itself. What can count as an individual, separate, event depends on the means for singling it out; for recognizing it as the presence, in some limited area of space and time, of a certain condition, or alternatively, as the change within some area of space-time in regard of some conditon. But of conditions we can speak only where there is a conceptual scheme within which they can be expressed. And although conceptual schemes may well be partly determined by the nature of things, it would be unreasonable to assume that they are fully determined thereby. In particular, how rich the conceptual scheme is, (and therewith how rich the event structure it generates) depends not so much on intrinsic features of that in which the scheme is meant to create some order but rather on the needs and limitations of those who use it.

It would appear to be a consequence of the ways in which we learn and share concepts that many of them are vague. I do not have a conclusive argument that this is so. But, whether or not such an argument can be given, that many of the concepts we actually use are vague, is an undeniable fact. Let us consider for simplicity just unary concepts. The vagueness of such a unary concept manifests itself in the presence of entities which are of the type to which the concept applies, but are nevertheless such that the criteria associated with the concept do not determine whether the entity falls under the concept or not. In some cases where the discovery of an entity which is neither clearly inside nor clearly outside the extension of a concept c confronts us with the vagueness of c we experience this as a deficiency; in such cases we will often try to sharpen c in such a way that the given entity a, - as well as, hopefully, many others whose relation to the concept had thus far been undecided - now fall clearly on one or the other side of the boundary of c's extension; and our intention is that this modification of c be permanent. In other cases the encounter of such entities will not motivate us to do this, however. In fact it is arguable that some concepts, - such as e.g. *orange, clever, lonely, tiny, bald,* - are *essentially* vague; that in order to resolve the vagueness of these concepts we would have to alter them to a point where they would no longer fulfill their actual function: They would lose that flexibility which enables their users to adjust their extensions quite freely to the needs of the particular contexts in which they employ them. Although such concepts may be sharpened within particular contextual settings, the modification is meant to be provisional, and lapses when the context in question terminates. I have argued elsewhere[8] that vagueness is compatible with the laws of classical predicate logic, in as much as we can treat vague concepts as potentially sharp - although precisely *where* the boundary of the extension lies will be undetermined. In an earlier essay I may have given the impression that I believed that we must *always* take this attitude towards vague concepts. This would be an overstatement; and it is something which at that time I did not believe any more than I believe it now. It does seem to me to be correct, however, that we often treat vague concepts in this way. And that is all that is required for the following observation.

Suppose the sun is setting. First its colour is bright orange, then it turns into a bright red. At what time precisely does the sun cease to be orange, and become red? In as much as the borderline between orange and red is fuzzy this time can not be determined with arbitrary precision. But does this mean that there is an *extended period* p during which the sun is turning red, a period such that up to the beginning of p the sun is orange, during p the sun is in transition and from the end of p the sun is red? I don't think that that is what it means. For with regard to p the same sort of question arises again: where precisely does p begin and where precisely does it end? It is not so much that the time of change is *extended* - it is rather that it is *undetermined*. Indeed, in any potential semantic extension of the language in which the borderline between red and orange is fixed perfectly the change will be instantaneous.

Suppose now that while the sun is setting the sky right above the tree to my right, which was blue at first, turns green. Once more, the colour changes gradually; but when the different shades of blue end and the different shades of green begin is again an issue that it will be impossible to answer exactly. Consider now the event of the sun's turning red, and that of the sky's turning green together. How are they temporally related? That too may be undetermined. In fact it will be undetermined if i) it is semantically consistent to simultaneously fix the borderline between orange and red and that between blue and green in such a way that the first of these events occur according to this specification, before the second; and ii) it is also consistent to fix the borderline so that the first event occurs later than the second.

Thus if we admit both the sun's turning red and the sky's turning green as elements e_1, e_2 of the structure ε of all events, then once again given the way the world is *and* the present status of our concept we can assert neither $e_1 \propto e_2$ nor $e_1 \, 0 \, e_2$ nor $e_2 \propto e_1$. So once again A7 must be abandoned.

It is natural to ask whether we could not save A7 by excluding such events as the sun's becoming red from ε altogether. I do not think, however, that that would be reasonable. For then we would eliminate far too much. In the first case many, perhaps all, of those events would have to go which we identify as changes from a given condition into one of its opposites. What would remain? We often speak of an event where a certain condition pertains over a limited period of time; e.g. the nap I took two hours ago might be called an event. Such events, however, are always accompanied by a couple of changes, the beginning of the event - here the change from non-sleep to sleep -, and its end - here the change from sleep into non-sleep. And precisely the same considerations that led us to the conclusion that changes may be incomparable, leads therefore also to that conclusion in connection with events of the second type. How for example would one answer the following question: Did your nap completely precede mine, or was there a tiny overlap? Finally there are events that we might call *protracted changes*. Here we explicitly acknowledge that between the initial condition c_1 and the final condition c_2 there are intermediate stages during which conditions obtain that are incompatible with both c_1 and c_2. With regard to such protracted changes the same problem arises as with events of the second type: When for instance does the final condition c_2 obtain for the first time?

Thus, even if we shun the potentially instantaneous changes, we still have no guarantee that A7 is satisfied.

IV:

In each of the applications of the theory of events which I envisage the transformation of event structures into instant structures will play a central role. But, as we have just seen, we cannot, in the context of these applications, assume that the event structures satisfy A7. The instant structures into which the Russell-Wiener procedure translates them will therefore be in general only partially, but not linearly, ordered. This is unsatisfactory, for time is conceived as linear.[9]

There are various ways in which we can obtain a linear instant structure from the partial ordering that the Russell-Wiener construction gives us. In the first place, it is a familiar fact that each partial ordering $<T,<>$ can be extended to a linear ordering $<T,<'>$. This extension is of course not unique (except in the trivial case where $<T,<>$ is already linear itself, and $<T,<'>$ coincides with $<T,<>$). No one of these extensions deserves, any more than its alternatives, to be regarded as giving *the correct* structure of time. Rather we should consider only those properties definite features of temporal structure which all these extensions have in common.

Rather than first applying the Russell-Wiener method and then passing to extensions, we can also proceed in the reverse order: We first form an extension ε' of ε which satisfies A7, and then apply the Russell-Wiener transformation to ε'. Note in this connection that a model ε of A1 - A6 can always be extended to a model ε' of A1 - A7. For suppose $\tau' = <T,<'>$ is a linear extension of the result of applying the Russell-Wiener transformation to ε. Then τ' determines a model $\varepsilon' = <E, \propto', 0'>$ of A1 - A7 in the obvious way, vz. via the definitions: $e_1 \propto e_2$ iff $\overline{e}_1$ lies entirely before $\overline{e}_2$; and e_1 $0'$ e_2 iff $\overline{e}_1$ and $\overline{e}_2$ overlap in ε'. We have, moreover, that $\tau' = \tau(\varepsilon)$. Thus each linear extention of $\tau(\varepsilon)$ can be obtained from a corresponding extension ε' of ε.

In fact the second method is more general than the first: there may be linear orderings of the form $\tau(\varepsilon')$, where ε' is an extension of ε, which cannot be obtained as extensions of the instant structure $\tau(\varepsilon)$ into which the Russell-Wiener construction transforms ε. The reason for this is that the instants of ε' need not be the same as the instants of ε. Suppose for example that i_1 and i_2 are incomparable instants of ε, i.e. for no $e_1 \in i_1$ and $e_2 \in i_2$ do we have either $e_1 \propto e_2$ or $e_2 \propto e_1$. Then there will be at least one extension ε' of ε in which for any $e_1 \in i_1$ and $e_2 \in i_2$ e_1 0 e_2. Thus the two distinct instants i_1 and i_2 of ε collapse into a single instant i of ε'.[10]

It should be intuitively clear that all the instant structures which can be obtained via completion of ε to a structure satisfying A7 represent linear time structures compatible with, and thus potentially contained in, the partial event structure ε itself. The second method is thus preferable to the first. It is questionable, however, whether the partial information about temporal order that can be derived either from ongoing discourse or from the (limited) accuracy with which our concepts mark the boundaries of the events they determine, is best represented in the form of structures $<E\rho\propto,O>$. For we may on occasion will have information to the effect that e_1 is *not* completely before e_2: it may be that e_1 O e_2, that $e_2 \propto e_1$; and yet undetermined which of these disjuncts holds - certain being only that the third alternative is excluded. Similarly it may be definite that two events are not simultaneous, though not which prededed which. The best way to represent such information is to admit for each of the relations $\propto$ and O, a *negative* as well as a *positive* extension. The positive extension of, say, $\propto$ will contain, as before, those pairs $<e_1, e_2>$ such that e_1 definitely precedes e_2; while its negative extension is to contain the pairs such that e_1 definitely does not precede e_2.

Talk of positive and negative extensions will remind some readers of certain fairly recent proposals for the model theoretic treatment of vague predicates.[11] Indeed it would in principle be possible to use the framework developed in these proposals to treat the relations $\propto$ and O as vague relations. It seemed desirable to me, however, to stick in the present study with a conventional metalanguage in which to state and discuss the conditions that should be imposed on event structures. I shall therefore represent the positive and negative extensions as extensions of distinct predicates. This means that we shall henceforth consider event structures of the form $E\rho\propto^+\rho\propto^-,O^+,O^-$, where $\propto^+$ and $\propto^-$ represent the positive and negative extension, respectively, of the relation of complete precedence, and O^+ and O^- the positive and negative extension of the relation of overlap.

In order that a structure of this form can be regarded as a representation of the temporal relations between the events in its domain it must, as before, satisfy certain conditions. Among these are, in particular, the condition that $\propto^+$ and $\propto^-$, and the condition that O^+ and O^-, are mutually exclusive. But there are others, which derive from the constraints that are imposed on the vague relations $\propto$ and O in virtue of there being subrelations of relations which jointly satisfy A1 - A7. Which are these additional conditions?

If the structure $<E\rho\propto^+\rho\propto^-, O^+,O^->$ gives a complete specification of temporal relations, i.e. if $\propto^-$ is the complement of $\propto^+$ and O^- the complement of O^+, then these conditions can be immediately obtained from those we postulated in section I: we simply replace in A1 - A7 $\propto$ and O everywhere by $\propto^+$ and O^+. But, of course, this is precisely the situation in which we are not particularly interested right now. In the general case, where $\propto^-$ and O^- are included in, but not identical with the complements of $\propto^+$ and O^+, it is not so obvious what postulates the structure $<E\rho\propto^+\rho\propto^-,O^+,O^->$ must satisfy.

In fact this question is a special case of a much more general problem: Suppose that the analysis of a given number of concepts $c_1,...,c_n$ leads to the conclusion that in principle these concepts jointly satisfy the set of postulates T - i.e. that ideally any formal representation of the domain(s) in which these concepts are operative should take the shape of a structure $<U,R_1,...,R_n>$ which is a model of T. Suppose also that in practice the concepts tend to be less than fully defined, so that a more correct formalization of what is actually determined about the extensions of the concepts must rather be in the form of a structure $<U,R_1^+,R_1^-,...,R_n^+,R_n^->$, where R_i^+ and R_i^- represent the positive and negative extensions of c_i. This structure need not satisfy the postulates of T (or, more accurately, the results of replacing in them the occurrences of R_i by R_i^+); but it must be capable of extension to a structure that satisfies these postulates. It is natural to ask:

i) Is there a set of postulates T' such that $<U,R_1^+,R_1^-,\ldots,R_n^+,R_n^->$ satisfies T' iff it can be so extended?

ii) Is there a general method to derive what its postulates are from the original T?

The first of these questions does not always have a positive answer. It does have a positive answer however in a restricted class of cases which includes those in which we are specifically interested in the context of this paper. Moreover it is possible to give a quite simple characterization of T' in time of T. This characterization however is not as effective as one might wish, as it does not provide us with an effective method for determining from an explicitly given finite set of postulates T an explicit list of the postulates of T'.

To discuss these matters properly, it is indispensible to introduce a certain amount of terminology. Some of this will already be familiar from the theory of models.[12]

Def.1: Let $M = <U,R_1,\ldots,R_n>$ and $M' = <U',R_1',\ldots,R_n'>$ be relational structures of the same similarity type.

   i) We say that M is a *relational substructure* of M' if

     a) $U \subseteq U'$; and

     b) for $j = 1,\ldots,n, R_j \subseteq R_j'$.

   ii) M is a *strictly relational substructure* of M' iff M is a relational substructure of M' and moreover $U =. U'$.

   iii) For any first order theory T we shall understand by RS(T) the first order theory of the class of all relational substructures of models of T; and by SRS(T) the first order theory of the class of all strictly relational substructures of models of T.

Def.2: i) Let ϕ be a formula of first order logic which is in prenex disjunctive normal form. Then ϕ is called a *negative prenex formula* if each atomic subformula of ϕ which is not of the form $\sigma = \tau$ is preceded by a negation sign.

   ii) A formula is called *negative* if it is logically equivalent to a negative prenex formula, and *universal negative* iff it is equivalent to a negative prenex formula whose prenex consists of universal quantifiers only.

   iii) Let T be a first order theory. By Neg(T) we understand the set of all consequences of the negative theorems of T; and by Unneg(T) the set of all consequences of the universal negative theorems of T.

Proposition

   i) M is a relational substructure of M' iff M is a strictly relational substructure of some substructure of M'.

   ii) Unneg(T) $\subseteq$ RS(T).

   iii) Neg(t) $\subseteq$ SRS(T).

The proofs of these are trivial.

Theorem 2

Let T be any first order theory. Then

i) $\text{Unneg}(T) = \text{RS}(T)$;

ii) every model of $\text{Unneg}(T)$ is a relational substructure of a model of T;

iii) $\text{Neg}(T) = \text{SRS}(T)$;

iv) suppose T is a purely universal theory (i.e. the set of its theorems are derivable from some subset of purely universal theorems). Then every model of $\text{Neg}(T)$ is a strictly relational substructure of some model of T.

Note: Jonathan Stavi has recently pointed out to me that iii), which I had only verified for the special case where T is purely universal, holds for arbitrary first order theories. The proof for the general case parallels that of Lyndon's theorem that the positive sentences are precisely the sentences preserved under homomorphisms. I shall here present only the much simpler proof for the case where T is assumed to be an universal theory.

Proof: i). That $\text{Unneg}(T) \subseteq \text{RS}(T)$ follows from Prop. ii). To show that $\text{RS}(T) \subseteq \text{Unneg}(T)$ suppose $\phi \in \text{RS}(T) \setminus \text{Unneg}(T)$. Let M be a model of $\text{Unneg}(T) \cup \{\neg\phi\}$. Then M is not a relational submodel of a model of T. One easily verifies that this amounts to the statement that $D^+(M) \cup T$ is inconsistent, where $D^+(M)$, or the *positive diagram of* M, is the set of all formulae which have one of the following forms:

a) $P(\bar{u}_1,\ldots,\bar{u}_n)$, where P is an n-place predicate of the language of T, $\bar{u}_1,\ldots,\bar{u}_n$ are individual constants denoting the elements $u_1,\ldots,u_n$ of M and $\langle u_1,\ldots,u_n\rangle$ belongs to the extension of P in M;

b) $\bar{u}_1 = \bar{u}_2$ where $\bar{u}_1$ and $\bar{u}_2$ are names of the same element of M;

c) $\bar{u}_1 \neq \bar{u}_2$ where $\bar{u}_1$ and $\bar{u}_2$ name different elements of M.

Since $D^+(M) \cup T$ is inconsistent there are formulae $\alpha_1,\ldots,\alpha_k$ in $D^+(M)$ such that $T \vdash \neg(\alpha_1 \wedge \ldots \wedge \alpha_k)(\bar{u}_1,\ldots,\bar{u}_k)$, where $\bar{u}_1,\ldots,\bar{u}_k$ is an enumeration of all the constants which occur as arguments in any of the α_j. Since the $\bar{u}_i$ do not occur in T

(1) $T \vdash (\forall x_1,\ldots,x_k)(\neg\alpha_1 \vee \ldots \vee \neg\alpha_n)(x_1,\ldots,x_k)$

where the x_i are variables not occurring in $\alpha_1,\ldots,\alpha_k$, and $(\neg\alpha_1 \vee \ldots \vee \neg\alpha_n)(x_1,\ldots,x_k)$ is the result of replacing the $\bar{u}_i$ everywhere in $(\neg\alpha_1 \vee \ldots \vee \neg\alpha_n)$ by the x_i. The formula displayed in (1) is a universal negative sentence of T. So $\text{Unneg}(T) \vdash \neg(\alpha_1 \wedge \ldots \wedge \alpha_n)(\bar{u}_1,\ldots,\bar{u}_k)$. But this means that M is not a model of $\text{Unneg}(T)$, contrary to assumption. Therefore $\text{RS}(T) \subseteq \text{Unneg}(T)$.

ii) A similar argument shows that if $M \models \text{Unneg}(T)$ then M is a relational substructure of a model of T. For if not then $D^+(M) \cup T$ would be inconsistent and the argument proceeds as under i).

iii) As I announced in the Note I shall prove this part only for the special case where T is purely universal. Neg(T) $\subseteq$ SRS(T) holds in virtue of Prop.

iii). To prove the converse inclusion observe that if T is purely universal then

(2) M is strictly relational substructure of a model of T iff M is a strictly relational substructure of a substructure of a model of T (since T is preserved under taking substructures) iff M is a relational substructure of a model of T (in view of Prop. i)).

Suppose that $\phi \in$ SRS(T) $\setminus$ Neg(T). Then Neg(T) $\cup$ $\{\neg\phi\}$ has a model M which in virtue of (2) is not a relational substructure of a model of T. As under i) we infer that for some atomic $\alpha_1,\ldots,\alpha_n$ in $D^+(M)$ Neg(T) $\vdash$ $(\forall x_1 \ldots x_k)$ $(\neg\alpha_1 \vee \ldots \vee \neg\alpha_n)(x_1,\ldots,x_k)$.
So M is not a model of Neg(T), which once again contradicts our assumption.

iv) The argument is once more of the same form: Suppose M were a model of Neg(T) but not a strictly relational substructure of a model of T. Then M would in view of (2) not be a relational substructure of a model of T. So $D^+(M) \cup T$ is inconsistent, etc.

If T is not purely universal then it need not be the case that every model of SRS(T) is a strictly relational substructure of a model of T. For example let T_1 be the theory of strict linear orderings which satisfy the additional condition that each element which has a successor has an immediate successor:

$(\forall x)((\exists u)(x < u \rightarrow (\exists u)(x < u \wedge \neg(\exists y)(x < y \wedge y < u))$

Consider two structures: $M_1 = <U_1,R_1>$ and $M_2 = <U_2,R_2>$, defined as follows: Let $<U_1,S_1>$ be a linear ordering of order type $\omega^* + \omega^*$ and let $<U_3;S_3>$ be a linear ordering of order type $\omega^* + \omega + \omega^*$, and let $U_1 \cap U_3 = \emptyset$.
R_1 is to be the successor relation of the ordering $<U_1,S_1>$, $U_2 = U_1 \cup U_3$ and R_2 is to be the union of the two successor relations on $<U_1,S_1>$ and $<U_3,S_3>$ respectively. Then M_2 is a strictly relational substructure of a model of T_1. For we can completely order its universe as indicated in the following picture:

(Thus we mesh to two parts of type ω^* of U_1 with the corresponding parts of U_3.)

M_1 on the other hand cannot be extended to a model of T_1 without adding new elements to its domain. For the only way in which we can extend R_1 to a transitive relation is to make it into the relation S_1 and then the last point of the first ω^* part of U_1 will be without an immediate successor.

However, it is easy to show that M_1 and M_2 are elementarily equivalent (see Appendix). So, since $M_2 \models SRS(T_1)$ it follows that $M_1 \models SRS(T_1)$. So $SRS(T_1)$ has models which are not strictly relational substructures of any models of T_1.
A similar counterexample can be constructed for the theory of dense linear orderings.

As both these counterexamples involve theories which are only slightly more complicated than purely universal theories - each is axiomatizable by a set of postulates all but one of which are universal while the remaining axiom is either of prenex form $\forall\exists$ or of prenex form $\forall\exists\forall$ - one would suspect the failure of iv) for non-universal theories to be a quite general phenomenon. However, as I already adumbrated, this circumstance does not affect the applications with which we are concerned in this paper, as these only deal with the theory T_{ev} whose axioms are:

a) the axioms $A1^+ - A7^+$, obtained from $A1 - A7$ by replacing everywhere $\propto$ by $\propto^+$ and 0 by 0^+; and

b) the sentences

A8 $(\forall x,y)(x\propto^+ y \rightarrow \neg x <^- y)$ and

A9 $(\forall x,y)(x\ 0^+ y \rightarrow \neg x\ 0^- y)$

Even where T is universal there remains the question whether from a given axiomatization of T we can derive, in a more or less algorithmic manner, an explicit axiomatization for $Neg(T)$. It appears that the most satisfactory general solution to this problem is contained in the work of Barwise ([1]). But this is something I cannot go into here. That the problem is not trivial is indicated by the fact even where T is finitely axiomatizable this is in general not so for $Neg(t)$. An extremely simple example of such a theory T is the theory of strict partial orderings (i.e. the theory whose only axioms are $(\forall x,y)(x < y \rightarrow \neg y < x)$ and $(\forall x,y,z)(x < y \wedge y < z \rightarrow x < z)$. Another example is provided by T_{ev}. Axiomatizations of $Neg(T_2)$ and of $Neg(T_{ev})$ can be found in the Appendix.

The reader may wonder how relevant this general model theoretic discussion is to the particular problem in the theory of events which leads to it. When considering event structures of the form $< E,\propto,0 > I$ argued that the intuitively acceptable representations of event sets with partially defined temporal relations were the models of $A1 - A6$. Here the subtheory that characterizes the class of admissible relational substructures is just as finitely axiomatizable as the original theory itself. And, as it turns out, something similar can be definded in connection with the theory T_{ev}. For it appears plausible on intuitive grounds that the partial event structures $< E,\propto^+,\propto^-,0^+,0^- >$ which represent incomplete information about the temporal relations between the events in their domains must nevertheless satisfy each of the following postulates:

A10 $(\forall x,y)(x\propto^+ y \rightarrow y\propto^- x)$

A2$^+$ $(\forall x,y,z)(x\propto^+ y \wedge y\propto^+ z \rightarrow x\propto^+ z)$

A3$^+$ $(\forall x)(x\ 0^+ x)$

A4$^+$ $(\forall x,y)(x\ 0^+ y \rightarrow y\ 0^+ x)$

A7+ $(\forall x,y,z,u)(x<^+y \land y\ 0^+z \land z<^+u \rightarrow x<^+u)$

A11 $(\forall x,y,z,u)(x<^+y \land z<^-y \land z<^+u \rightarrow x<^+u)$

A12 $(\forall x_1,x_2,y_1,y_2,z_1,z_2)(x_1\propto^+y_1 \land y_1 0^- y_2 \land y_2\propto^+z_1 \land x_2\propto^+y_2 \land y_1\propto^+z_2 \rightarrow x_1\propto^+z_1$
$\lor\ x_2\propto^+z_2)$

It is easily checked that these formulae together with the principles

A8' $(\forall x,y)(x\propto^+y \rightarrow \neg x\propto^-y)$ and

A9' $(\forall x,y)(x\ 0^+y \rightarrow \neg x\ 0^-y)$

entail all axioms of $\mathrm{Neg}(T_{ev})$ as given in the Appendix.

Thus, while the theory of relational and strictly relational substructures may have some interest in its own right, and while it may yet be found to have other, more subtle, applications to conceptual analysis, some of the complications which we have encountered during the preceding discussion do not directly matter to what is primarily at stake here.

One further observation before I conclude this section. In section II and III I created the impression that only strictly relational substructures of models of T_{ev} are of importance for the intended applications. As regards the application to discourse representation this is essentially correct. But in connection with questions concerning the structure of time as determined by the ensemble of events which a given conceptual scheme is capable of isolating from the flow of nature this is not strictly right. I already argued for the possibility that the time at which a certain change, say, from orange to red, takes place, cannot be exactly pinpointed because of the inherent vagueness in the concept used to define the change. For exactly the same reason that the time can in general not be perfectly determined, however, we should also allow for the possibility that it may be undetermined whether a change actually took place at all.[13] For suppose a certain object a, which is unambiguously orange at first, changes colour in the direction of red; but before it has reached a shade which is unambiguously red it reverts back to the original, indubitable, orange. The question whether here we have a change from orange to red followed by a change from red to orange, or rather no change at all would depend on where the borderline between red and orange is drawn. If it is drawn near the central instances of orange then according to that semantic decision there will have been two changes. But if the line is drawn near the central cases of red then, according to that stipulation, a would never, in the period under consideration, have ceased to be orange at all and thus no such change would have taken place. Thus while the partial event structure ε which incorporates only such information as is already definite in virtue of the semantic conventions as they stand, will not contain changes from orange to red and back, some of the event structures representing the information conveyed by particular ways of eliminating the truth value gaps of the underlying concepts will contain such changes.

It is a further question how the presence of such additional events in some of the completions of the partial structure ε might affect the structure of time as it is (partially) determined by ε. This is as it stands not a very precise question; but one way, consistent with what I have said before about this issue, of making it precise is the following.
Let φ(ε) be the class of all completions of ε. Each such completion ε' determines a substructure $R(\varepsilon') = <E\ \propto^{+"}, \propto^{-"}, 0^{+"}, 0^{-"}>$ where the relations $\propto^{+"}$,

$\propto^{-}$",0^{+}",0^{-}" are the restrictions to E of the corresponding relations of ε'. (Thus, in the special case where the domain of ε' equals that of ε R(ε') = ε'.) Let $\phi'(\varepsilon)$ be the set of all these structures R(ε') for ε' in $\phi(\varepsilon)$. Furthermore let $\kappa(\varepsilon)$ be the class of all instant structures $\tau(\varepsilon')$ where $\varepsilon' \in \phi(\varepsilon)$ and let $\kappa'(\varepsilon)$ be the class of all instant structures $\tau'(\varepsilon)$ for $\varepsilon' \in \phi'(\varepsilon)$.

We may then ask if the set of structural properties shared by all members of $\kappa(\varepsilon)$ does or does not coincide with the set of all properties common to the members of $\kappa'(\varepsilon)$. This question is still not fully precise, for I haven't said what is to count as a 'structural property'. Here various options would seem reasonable. For instance, we could identify the structural properties with those properties which are first order definable in terms of <; or with the corresponding second order properties; or with those definable by formulae of monadic second order logic, etc.

To answer the question arising from the adoption of any of these options would involve us in conceptual as well, probably, as mathematical complications whose subtlety would exceed what I am able to handle at the moment. But I should at least make clear why I have raised the issue at all.

The description I gave of the case where the object a, plainly orange at first, changes its hue in the direction of red and then reverts to its original state, suggests that although it is indeterminate whether there have been changes e_1 from orange to red and e_2 from red to orange it is on the other hand definite that some other changes in colour took place at around that time. If those other changes are definable within the conceptual framework which provides the events of the partial structure ε they will already belong to ε itself. In view of this it is natural to ask whether the presence in a completion ε' of ε of the events e_1 and e_2, in addition to these other colour changes (which must belong to ε' since they already belong to ε) could have any impact on the structural feature of $\tau(\varepsilon')$. Suppose that this were not so; and moreover, that it were not so not only in the particular case considered but in all other cases where the completion of ε contains events that do not occur in ε. In that case we would have to conclude that although some of the completions of ε have larger domains than ε, nevertheless the structure of time as determined by ε must be assessed via a class of structures of which ε is a strictly relational substructure. The completions ε' of which ε is a relational but not a strictly relational substructure would only be immediately relevant, vz. as generators of the structures R(ε') which enter into the assessment directly and of which ε is a strictly relational substructure. I hope to have made it sufficiently clear however that much careful analysis will be necessary of these issues before mere speculation can be replaced by informed opinion.

I should like to add one last remark. As the preceding discussions should already have revealed implicitly one of the distinctive features of the concepts of time and temporal order which underlies the formal developments of this paper is the thesis that the structure of time depends on the conceptual framework that is employed in the determination of the events which, according to the present theory, form the basis of that structure. This seems to introduce into the notion of temporal structure an important subjective element. It is an interesting, but extremely difficult, question how much room the present conception nonetheless leaves for an objective component to the notion as well. Essentially this comes down to the question what conceptual schemes are possible: can we carve up the 'natural flow of things' in just any way we like - and thus extract from it any temporal structure you might wish -; or are the conceptual frames accessible to us restricted by an intrinsic order of nature, or by an intrinsic order in the interactions between nature and mind? On problems of this magnitude I would not dare to speculate. Suffice it to note their relevance for the philosophical implications of the view I have here advanced.

V:

All natural languages contain devices of temporal reference. To describe these devices formally we need to represent, in one way or another, the structure of time. In the course of the fairly short history of the model theory of temporal reference the representation has been without exception, I believe, 'atomistic': time was modelled as a linearly ordered structure of instants. This was true, in particular, of the first formal work in the area, Cocchiarella's model theoretic analysis of Prior's P,F-calculus (or, to be more explicit, of a formal language which combines the familiar apparatus of first order predicate logic - predication, quantification and boolean connection - with Prior's operators P ('it was the case that') and F ('it will be the case that')). Cocchiarella's models take the form of triples (τ, U, F), where τ is a linear order $(T, <)$, U is a non-empty set (of possible individuals) and F is a function which assigns to each non-logical constant γ of the language an appropriate extension at each instant t of T.[14] The truth definition then associates also with each complex expression α an appropriate extension at each t of T; and a sentence, in particular, is in this way assigned at each t a truthvalue. Systems of tense logic such as those developed by Prior are structurally quite simple. This can be an advantage where we are concerned to clarify, by way of formalization, certain conceptual questions whose true nature the complexities of the ordinary vernacular tend to conceal. But when our concern is rather the precise analysis of the temporal devices which natural languages actually employ, this simplicity can be, and in fact has been, very misleading. The semantic description of many of these devices appears to require a number of modifications of the framework Cocchiarella introduced.

One of these, which has received much attention in recent work on tense and aspect, relates to the temporal elements with respect to which such semantic notions as truth and satisfaction are (recursively) defined. For Cocchiarella these elements are simply instants; but in subsequent work it has been claimed that such semantic concepts must be analyzed as relations between expressions and intervals rather than relations between expressions and moments of time.[15]

The switch from instants to intervals has been motivated by various considerations. These considerations, which it would carry us too far to discuss individually with the care they deserve, fall, it seems to me, into two classes. Considerations of the first type concern the *recursive* part of the definition of truth, satisfaction (and, possibly, other semantic concepts). In the first place it has been argued that in order to arrive at a correct recursive characterization of the conditions under which assertoric utterances of certain complex sentences are true at the times at which they are made we must allow the recursion to pass through intermediate stages at which subexpressions of those sentences are evaluated with respect to intervals rather than to instants.
Consider for instance the sentence:

(1) Fritz always writes an article in less than a month.

Suppose we analyze (1) as the syntactic result of combining the subject 'Fritz' with the complex predicate

(2) (λx)(x always writes an article in less than a month)

To arrive at the right truth conditions for (1) we must associate with (2) the right function from individuals to sets of instants (those instants at which the individual in question satisfies the predicate). Suppose further that this function is to be obtained from (functions associated with) underlying expressions

(3) (λx)(x writes an article)
(4) always   , and
(5) in less than a month

The initial motivation for this requirement would be that (1) conveys that all occasions where Fritz writes an article are occasions of a certain kind, vz. occasions on which the writing takes less than a month. What function f_3 ought to be associated with (3) so that from it we can, given appropriate interpretations for (4) and (5), correctly determine the function f_2 that must be associated with (2)?

Suppose f_3 gives us for each individual a set of instants at which it is true that a is (in the process of) writing an article. To derive f_2 from such an f_3 we would presumably have to make use of a clause to the effect that an instant t belongs to f_2 (a) iff each continuous interval of instants all belonging to f_3(a) has a duration of less than a month.[16] But this would yield the correct result only if a always writes only one article at a time. If on the contrary a starts one article on, say, the 1-st of March and a second on the 15-th of March, finishes the first on the 21-st of that month and the second on the 7-th of April, then the proposed clause would imply that he did not satisfy (2). Thus it is wrong. Nor does there appear to be any other clause that determines f_2 correctly from such a function f_3. A function f_3 for (3) from which f_2 can be reconstructed would, it seems, have to relate with each individual a, a set of *intervals*, the set which contains for each of the articles written by a the duration of the writing of that article. It should be intuitively clear how from a function of this sort we could define f_2.

Suppose next that we take the function f_3 to be determined by the semantic entities associated with, respectively, the 2-place predicate

(6) $(\lambda x)(\lambda y)$(x writes y)

and with the quantifier phrase

(7) an article

It is natural to assume that this determination takes the form usually associated with the existential quantifier, vz. that f_3(a) is the union of f_6(a,b), where b ranges over all articles. In order that this operation should give the right value for f_3(a) it is necessary that f_6 also associate with each suitable pair (a,b), again, a set of intervals. Note however that even if we insist that f_6 be of this form it is nonetheless possible for that function to be fully determined by an underlying function f_6' which maps pairs (a,b) to sets of instants - f_6'(a,b) being the set of instants at which it is true that a is in the process of writing b. The difference between f_6 and f_3 lies therein that in the present case it might seem plausible that f_6(a,b) consists of precisely those intervals which are maximal uninterrupted stretches of instants belonging to $f_6'(a,b)$ - we saw that a similar assumption was unwarranted in connection with f_3.

It seems therefore that the function f_6 is reducible to a function which assigns instants; and thus the example suggests the following picture: at the basis of the recursion we have certain relations between individuals and instants; but at some point in the recursion we must switch from such relations to relations between individuals and intervals. Eventually however there is a return to notions involving instants, such as in particular that of the truth of a complete sentence at the instant it is used.

Of course the discussion of the example is very far from a conclusive argument that this is indeed the right picture. In the first place I have done nothing to show that (1) must be analyzed into components in precisely the way I proposed. To argue for this persuasively is possible only via careful semantic and syntactic considerations of all sentences of a substantial language fragment to which (1) belongs, and this would go not only beyond the scope of this paper but also beyond my present capacities.

As a matter of fact I do not really believe that the difficulties to which the discussion drew attention could really be circumvented via an alternative analysis of (1) into basic components. There was however another point in the discussion that is genuinely dubious, and which deserves more careful attention than I have given it so far. This is the point where I remarked - with appropriate diffidence - that 'it might seem plausible' that f_6 is determined by an underlying function f_6' which assigns sets of instants to pairs (a,b).

Is this really plausible? An interval which counts as the period during which a wrote a particular article b will as a rule not consist exclusively of instants at which a is actually writing, or even engaged in directly related activities such as reading up on the literature of the subject, looking up references in the library etc. Even the most devoted scholar will have to take out time for sleep and food unless his project - that of writing b - can be accomplished within less than, say, 24 hours.

What can be said about an instant which belongs to the period during which the article is written but at which the author actually was asleep? Earlier, when considering the reducibility of f_6 to f_6' I tried to dodge this issue by describing the relevant instants as instants at which the author is 'in the process of writing' the article. But how is one to tell that an instant at which he is actually asleep is also an instant at which he is in the process of writing? Only, surely, by evaluating the position of that instant within the stretch of time which contains also many instants when he is engaged in what we might coin 'writing his article in the strict sense', (i.e. writing, checking related papers and such like). This strongly suggests that in some cases the judgement whether the author is in the process of writing at a particular instant reduces to a conceptually prior judgement regarding whether he is writing *during* some interval to which the instant belongs.

From all I have said it would appear that this latter judgement depends in turn on judgements about the instants at which the author is writing in the strict sense. It is the distribution of these instants throughout the interval i which determines whether i counts as a period during which the author is in the process of writing. So could we not construct a semantic theory in which the truth conditions for (1) are spelled out along the lines sketched above, but in which f_6 is determined by an underlying function f_6'' that assigns to a pair (a,b) the set of instants at which a is writing b in the strict sense?

This is a difficult question to which I do not know the answer. It is difficult for two, related reasons. First it may be very hard to specify with any precision what it is for a to be writing in the strict sense. Which activities are to be taken as directly part of the actual writing? If looking up a reference in the library counts as such, should being on the way to the library in order to check a reference also count among these activities? And if that counts, what about having a nap so as to be able to carry on more efficiently with the writing afterwards?

Secondly, even if we assume that 'writing in the strict sense' could be defined with sufficient precision, which distributions within i of instants at which a is writing in this sense make i an interval during which a is writing b? If you stop to think for a moment about a *general* clause which would correctly define this class of intervals in terms of the corresponding distributions of instants, you will soon realize how very complicated such a clause would have to be. In fact it might well have to be so complex that we would not wish to incorporate it into a semantic theory whose purpose is to elucidate semantic relations - a purpose hampered by the surfeit of detail which the clause would introduce into the theory; in which case it would be better to treat f_6 , and similar functions that involve intervals rather than instants, as primitives.

But apart from these methodological considerations there may be an even more conclusive reason for treating f_6 as primitive: It is conceivable that f_6 is not uniformly reducible to notions involving instants in any way whatever. For even if it is true that the judgement that a was writing b during i is based on what went on at the various instants that constitute i the integration of information concerning the various instants which yields this judgement might occur at a level of mental processing which - unlike the semantic relations between grammatically complex expressions and their parts, to which formal methods of analysis have thus far been applied with some measure of success - defy description with the help of the discrete combinatorial techniques which have been the essence of all formal semantics to date.

It may seem that the example we have here considered - the relation 'a writes b' is a rather special one. Nevertheless the question to which it gave rise, vz. whether judgements about intervals are reducible to judgements about instants, is a perfectly general one, which can, and must be raised in connection with any predicate. Note however that what lends these questions their appearance of urgency is the particular temporal framework within which the theory of temporal reference has been operating: If we choose to represent time as an instant structure the choice between the use of instants and the use of intervals may look like the choice between greater theoretical simplicity on the one and greater empirical adequacy on the other hand. But from the perspective that we have developed in the preceding sections this dilemma simply disappears. For what, according to the advocates of the use of intervals in the better theory, and possibly the only theory that can do justice to the facts of natural discourse, now also appears as the theoretically simpler description, in that it evaluates expressions relative to what according to this new perspective are the basic constituents of time.

VI:

Let us briefly consider what such a semantic theory might be like. For the sake of simplicity we shall restrict our attention to languages L whose primitive expressions are singular terms and predicates and which combine formulae into larger ones with the help of certain logical operators, about which more below. As before I shall assume that time is given in the form of a partial event structure $\varepsilon = (E \propto^+ \propto^-, 0^+, 0^-)$. Furthermore we shall assume that an interpretation for L relative to ε takes the form of a function A which associates with each n-place predicate of L a function that assigns to any tuple $(a_1, \ldots, a_n)$ of appropriate arguments a subset of the event set E. Intuitively $A(Q)(a)$, where Q is a 1-place predicate and a an individual, is to consist of those events e during which a has Q.

Note that the absence of e from $A(Q)(a)$ should not be interpreted as conveying that throughout e a fails to have Q. For instance e may be the event of a's washing b; it temporally includes the event e' of a's rinsing b; thus e' will belong to $A('rinse')(a,b)$, while e will not. It is clear in this case that the condition 'a rinses b' does not fail throughout e. Thus the satisfaction relation relative to events is not bivalent; and the distinction between events during which an atomic sentence fails and events during which it partly fails and partly holds, which evidently is essential to the truth conditions of the negations of simple sentences, must somehow be made explicit by the interpretation. We shall do this by assuming that A assigns to Q and $a_1, \ldots, a_n$ not a single set $A(Q)(a_1, \ldots, a_n)$ but a pair of sets $A^+(Q)(a_1, \ldots a_n)$ and $A^-(Q)(a_1, \ldots, a_n)$ consisting, respectively, of the events during which $a_1, \ldots, a_n$ stand in the relation Q and the events during which $a_1, \ldots, a_n$ do not stand in that relation.

Suppose ε' is a model of T_{ev} which is a strictly relational extension of ε, and let t be an instant of $\tau(\varepsilon')$. Under what conditions would it be appropriate to say that a has Q at t? Our first guess might be that

(1) a has Q at t iff there is an $e \in E$ such that $e \in A^+(Q)(a)$ and $t \in e$.

However, our earlier discussion of the phrase 'a writes b' has already shown how problematic this clause is: If we allow for the possibility that e belongs to the set assigned by A to Q and (a,b) in virtue of e's being a 'period when a was writing b' then being an instant at which e occurs is not a sufficient condition for it being correct to say that at that instant a is writing b. (1) could therefore only be correct if we excluded from $A(Q)(a,b)$ all those events which contain parts during which strictly speaking a does not stand in the relation Q to b. But to do so would be to eliminate precisely that aspect of the new theory that renders it more promising than theories which build their semantic recursions on the basis of assignments that involve instants. It thus appears that (1) cannot be right. What we need instead is the following clause

(2) a has Q at t iff for each $e \in t$ there is an $e' \in E$ such that $e' \subseteq e$

and $e' \in A^+(Q)(a)$

(here ' $e' \subseteq e$ ' is short for: $(\forall e'')(e'' 0^+ e' \rightarrow e'' 0^+ e)$
this last formula is easily seen to be equivalent to
$(\forall t' \in T(\varepsilon'))(e' \in t' \rightarrow e \in t'))$

According to (2) a has Q at t iff no matter how short an event e occurring at t we consider there is an event e' temporally included in e during which a has Q. Thus (2) deals with the difficulty which we observed in connection with 'a writes b'; and I cannot see any other reason why it would be inadequate. Let us adopt it.

With the help of (2) we can convert the interpretation function A into a function A' which tells us for each n-place predicate Q, individuals $a_1,\ldots,a_n$ and instant t whether $a_1,\ldots,a_n$ satisfy Q at t. In this way we can pass from the pair (ε,A) to a structure $(\tau(\varepsilon'),A')$ which much resembles the models for tenselogic which were first introduced by Cocchiarella.

There is however an important difference which the existing similarities threaten to conceal. Cocchiarella's assignment functions are total: for the sentence $\neg Q(a)$ to be true at t in one of his models $M = (\tau,A)$ it is (necessary and) sufficient that t does not belong to the set of instants which the interpretation function A associates with Q and a. But it is far from obvious that we can deal with negation in the same simple fashion when we work with the models $(\tau(\varepsilon'),A')$ which are the products of our interpretations relative to event structures. We already noticed that the truth relation between statements and events is not bivalent: besides the possibilities: i) s is true during e, and ii) s is false during e, there is a third, vz. that s is true during some parts of e and false during others. By itself this does not necessarily produce failure of bivalence in the derived instant model. For nothing we have said so far excludes the possibility that for each s and each t there either is an event surrounding t during which s is true or else an event surrounding t during which s is false. There is however another reason why we should not expect, and indeed not *want*, bivalence even at the level of instants. In section IV I argued that among the events that are crucial to the determination of temporal structure there are in particular those which I termed changes. Suppose that e is an event of this kind, and that e is identified as an event of a's turning from not-Q into Q. Let us assume moreover that this change is ideally instantaneous, so that in $\tau(\varepsilon')$ there is an unique t(e) to which e belongs. Does a satisfy Q at t(e)? There are, it seems to me, in general no good grounds either for confirming this or for claiming that a does satisfy not-Q at t(e). t(e) is a time at which a is in transition in regard to Q, and this is a situation which is distinct both from that where a is in the state, or engaged in the activity, denoted by Q and from that where a is subject to the condition of not being in the state (or not being engaged in the activity).

Indeed we might find it tempting to represent this third kind of situation by a third 'truthvalue', distinct from 1, which the statement that a has Q should receive in a situation where a is in the state or engaged in the activity, and 0, which the statement would have in situations where a is subject to the opposite condition. If we decide to do this then we should introduce of course also a fourth value to represent those situations in which a is turning from Q into not-Q.

This would give rise to a type of four valued logic. But whether a viable logic emerges, will depend, as always, on the possibility of stating the values of complex expressions in terms of the values of their components. And, as usual, the possibility is severely limited. Indeed the languages for which this analysis seems at all workable are all very impoverished. An example would be the language L whose atomic formulae are of the form $Q(\alpha_1,\ldots,\alpha_n)$ where Q is an n-place predicate and $\alpha_1,\ldots,\alpha_n$ are singular terms; and in which complex formulae are formed only with the help of the connectives 'and', 'or' and 'not'. Moreover we must assume that any change from satisfaction of a predicate Q by individuals $a_1,\ldots,a_n$ to non-satisfaction of Q by these individuals - and similarly any change from non-satisfaction to satisfaction of Q - is ideally instantaneous; and finally - but this hardly seems a restriction - that a change from not-p to p, where p stands for a condition expressed by any atomic sentence of L, is flanked by an event during which not-p holds on the left and by another event during which p holds, on the right. Thus if p stands, say, for the condition expressed by the atomic sentence $Q(\alpha)$ and e is a change from not-p to p then e should satisfy in the structure (ε, A) the condition:

(3) $(\exists e_1)(e_1 \propto^+ e \,\&\, e_1 \in A^-(Q)(a) \,\&\, (\forall e')(e' \propto^+ e \rightarrow e_1 \propto^- e')) \,\&$

$(\exists e_2)(e \propto^+ e_2 \,\&\, e_2 \in A^+(Q)(a) \,\&\, (\forall e')(e \propto^+ e' \rightarrow e' \propto^- e_2)).$

Similarly a change from p to not-p should satisfy:

(4) $(\exists e_1)(e_1 \propto^+ e \,\&\, e_1 \in A^+(Q)(a) \,\&\, (\forall e')(e' \propto^+ e \rightarrow e_1 \propto^- e')) \,\&$

$(\exists e_2)(e \propto^+ e_2 \,\&\, e_2 \in A^-(Q)(a) \,\&\, (\forall e')(e \propto^+ e' \rightarrow e' \propto^- e_2))$

Under these conditions the truth values of complex sentences are, it seems, correctly determined by the following four-valued truthtable:

¬	
P	¬P
0	1
1	0
2	3
3	2

&

p\q	0	1	2	3
0	0	0	0	0
1	0	1	2	3
2	0	2	2	0
3	0	3	0	3

v

p\q	0	1	2	3
0	0	1	2	3
1	1	1	1	1
2	2	1	2	1
3	3	1	1	3

The joker hides in the table for 'and' and 'or'. His hiding places are the entries for (p = 2, q = 3) and (p = 3, q = 2). That the value of (p & q) must be 0 in these cases can be argued as follows. By assumption the event e at which p has, say, the value 2 and q the value 3 is instantaneous. So p is turning from false to true at the very instant when p turns from true to false. So the conjunction (p & q) which was false just before the change on account of p is also false just after the change on account of q. Consequently there is no change in truthvalue for (p & q) in the immediate vicinity of the instant of change. It would therefore seem reasonable to stipulate that (p & q) have that same value also at the instant of change itself. The same considerations lead us to postulate the value 1 for (p v q) in the case where p = 2 and q = 3 and that where p = 3 and q = 2.

The logical calculus which we obtain via these truthtables is perhaps mildly assuming. But the ideas behind it get us nowhere in general. In particular, as soon as we admit into the language L an operator, T say, which turns a sentence p into a sentence Tp which says that it is becoming the case that p, the plausibility of the truthtables vanishes. For clearly if e is a change from not-p to p then the value of Tp at t(e), if it is to be any one of the four values available to the present semantics, must be 1. This implies however that, since p itself has the value 2 with respect to e, (p & Tp) gets, according to the truthtable for 'and', the value 2. But this is strongly counterintuitive. The conjunction says that it both is the case that p and that it is becoming the case that p. This seems to be a contradiction and thus should receive the value 0.[17]

The four-valued system also loses its plausibility in the absence of the assumption that the changes are ideally instantaneous. For suppose the event e which constitutes a change from not-p to p and also a change from q to not-q corresponds to the interval (t_1, t_2) of $\tau(\varepsilon')$. Graphically we might represent this situation in some such way as the following:

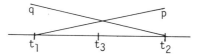

Here t_3 is some point interval to the interval (t_1, t_2). The diagram suggests, and I think rightly, that there is no good justification for giving (p & q) the value 0 at t_3, especially not if we give on the other hand (p v q) the value 1 at t_3. Nor would either of the values 2 and 3 be appropriate. For these indicate change; but neither (p & q) nor (p v q) does change in the vicinity of t_3, at least not in the sense in which we have understood change so far, i.e. as change either from definite truth to definite falsehood or as change from definite falsehood to definite truth.[18]

The upshot of all this is that in general we cannot hope for a complete specification of the values of complex sentences in terms of the values of their components even if we adopt the additional values 2 and 3. The best which it seems we have reason to expect is a partial truth definition. Let it be thought that this partial valuedness is a drawback of the present approach when compared with more familiar treatments of temporal reference I want to stress my belief that this is on the contrary a virtue.

It is a mistake to adopt a framework which makes it appear that there always ought to be an answer to the question: Is p true at time t?. If t is a time of change for p this question has in general no clear answer. Only in some particular cases specific considerations may persuade us that one of the two possible answers is more suitable than its opposite. Thus if p expresses the sentence 'object a is at rest relative to the object b' and t is a time where this sentence turns from true to false we may want to say that p is still true at t. The reason for this would be that, according to the received theory of motion, a has at times shortly after t a non-zero velocity relative to b while at times shortly before t the relative velocity will be zero. Moreover, the limit of the velocity at t', where t' approaches t from the right, is zero too. And, given the usual definition of instantaneous velocity this limit will in fact be equal to the velocity at t itself. Thus t shares with its temporal predecessors the property that a has zero velocity and differs in this respect from its near successors. This may, though it need not, sway us to count t as one of the instants of rest.

But even in cases such as this one the decision does not alter the status of t as an instant of change for p. Indeed, it is this feature of models for temporal reference based on event structures, i.e. that times of change are identified as such *directly*, and not as transition points between times of no change, which makes them very natural for the analysis of the logical properties of 'becoming'. In another paper[19] I shall analyze a number of formal languages which contain besides certain devices of temporal reference, such as tense operators, also the operator T ('it is becoming the case that') mentioned earlier in this section.

There are a number of different options between which one must choose when formulating the semantics for such languages. One of these I should at least mention here, as it is directly relevant to the discussion of section V. Suppose we are given a pair (ε, A) where ε is a partial event structure and A an interpretation relative to that structure. There are then three possible models with respect to which we could try and formulate the truth definition:

a) The model (ε, A) itself; or, alternatively, some model (ε', A) where ε' is some strictly relational extention of ε.

b) The model $(\tau(\varepsilon), A')$ where $\tau(\varepsilon')$ is the instant structure determined by some strictly relational extention ε' of ε and A' is obtained from A via (2).

c) The structure $(\iota(\tau(\varepsilon')), A'')$ where $\iota(\tau(\varepsilon'))$ is the interval structure determined by $\tau(\varepsilon')$ and A'' is determined by A.[20]

Which of these different models will provide the most suitable framework for the formulation of the truth definition of any particular language L will depend on the specific features of L. These questions too are better left to the later paper.

VII:[21]

In section III I briefly stated my intention to apply the theory of events to the analysis of discourse. In this last section I wish to say a little more about such applications. The reader will have to be content with a mere outline of the possibilities which arise in this connection and some discussion of certain methodological and conceptual implications. I hope to provide further details in the already mentioned [10].

We shall continue to limit our attention to the forms of discourse where A does all the talking (or writing) and B all the listening (or reading); where the discourse consists of a succession of indicative sentences $s_1, \ldots,$ s_n; and where B adjusts his representation of the information he has obtained after each successive sentence. Moreover I shall limit myself here to discourse that is exclusively in the past tense. Discourse that satisfies all these constraints one finds typically

i) in written and oral narrative prose;
ii) in reports about past events, such as those given, for instance, by eyewitnesses under interrogation.

Even in the presence of these severe restrictions one encounters phenomena whose significance can be properly understood only, I believe, within the framework that has been developed in the earlier sections of this paper. Central among these phenomena is the 'directive' function of certain devices that occur in natural language, of which I shall discuss a couple of examples.

The first of these is strictly speaking a combination of two contrasting devices, represented in French by, respectively, the Passé Simple and the Imparfait. Quite a bit has been written about the difference between these two tenses, but mostly by grammarians working in a non-formal framework, or at any rate in one very different from that of modeltheoretic semantics. It has been suggested: that the Passé Simple is used when one wants to emphasize the punctual character of the reported event, while the Imparfait stresses its durative aspect; that the Imparfait is used to provide the background to a certain event or sequence of events, whereas the succession of events which unfolds against this background is reported with the help of the Passé Simple; that the use of the Imparfait places the addressee as it were inside the locus of action, where the use of the Passé Simple would have kept him at what might be called an outside observation post.

Each of these contrasts contains an important element of truth; and no one can be captured, it would seem, within a theory of truth conditions: It does not seem possible to articulate those contrasts as differences in truthconditions between sentences in respectively the Passé Simple and the Imparfait. Exactly the same event can be correctly reported by the sentence

'Il y a deux ans la Compagnie acheta un navire de 100.000 tonnes.'

and by the sentence

'Il y a deux ans la Compagnie achetait un navire de 100.000 tonnes.'

Which tense is appropriate depends not on features of the event as such (e.g. the time that it took to conclude the deal) but rather on the role that is attributed to it, or the angle from which it is viewed in the context in which it is mentioned.[22]

The claim I wish to make is that what distinguishes Imparfait and Passé Simple does not so much lie in the contribution they make to the truth conditions of the sentences in which they occur, but rather in the different directives they convey to the addressee concerning how he is to represent to himself the contents of the sentences which these tenses mark.

As a first approximation we can say, reiterating one of the theses referred to above, that the Passé Simple indicates that the reported event is to be viewed as punctual, or temporally undivided. Let us assume that the discourse representations $D_1,...,D_n$ which B constructs in response to A's utterances of $s_1,...,s_n$ are partial interpretations of the form (ϵ,A) which we described in the previous section. Let (ϵ_k, A_k) be the structure B has constructed at the point where A has uttered $s_1,...,s_k$. Suppose s_{k+1} is a sentence in the Passé Simple, and moreover a particularly simple sentence of this sort, e.g.

'Jean ôta sa veste.'

If, as would normally be the case, this sentence gives new information, not yet conveyed by $s_1,...,s_k$, then B is to add to the event set E_k a new event e; the Passé Simple indicates that this event is to be treated as *punctual within* the representation of the discourse which B is in the process of building up. I shall interpret this formally as the condition that in ϵ_{k+1} e must satisfy the condition that it is not partitioned by other events:

$$(\forall e_1, e_2)(e_1 O^+ e \,\&\, e_2 O^+ e \rightarrow e_1 \propto^- e_2)$$

It is natural to ask whether this condition should be regarded as remaining in force in the course of the subsequent modification, which yield, in succession, $D_{k+2},...,D_n$. It seems that this is not always so. Consider for instance the following passage:

'Hamilcar continua seul à pied, sans escorte, car les réunions des Anciens étaient, dans les circonstances extraordinaires, toujours secrètes, et l'on s'y rendait mystérieusement.
D'abord il longea la face orientale de l'Acropole, passa ensuite par le Marché-aux-herbes, les galeries de Kinsido, le Faubourg-des-Parfumeurs. ... (Flaubert, Salammbô)

Here the first event is reported in the Passé Simple; and yet the passage continues to recount various stages of that event. There is a natural temptation to explain texts of this type by saying that a certain thematic 'break' occurs between the introduction of the event which is subsequently subdivided and the following sentences which effect the subdivision. Unfortunately it is not easy to formulate the concept of thematic 'break' in a way which protects such an explanation against circularity. I shall leave the problem of accounting for texts of this sort for a later occasion, and ignore this complication in the present section. Thus we shall make here the simplifying assumption that once a condition of the form (1) has been introduced into D_{k+1} it remains in force in all the subsequent $D_{k+2},\ldots,D_n$.[23]

Connected with the principle that the Passé Simple indicates punctuality appears to be the rule of narrative discourse that a succession of sentences in the Passé Simple is to be taken as reporting a similarly ordered sequence of successive events ('The Passé Simple pushes the action forward'). Indeed, although I do not think that there is any clear sense in which the principle can be said to *imply* the rule the following considerations may suggest how the former could have contributed to the development which established the latter.

Suppose e_1 and e_2 are events reported by two successive Passé Simple sentences s_1 and s_2. Let t_1 and t_2 be the time points these events determine. There are in principle three possibilities for their relative location:

  i) t_2 after t_1;
  ii) t_2 coincident with t_1; and
  iii) t_2 before t_1.

Why should possibilities ii) and iii) be ruled out? To begin with we should observe that neither is always precluded. The second possibility for instance represents a genuine interpretation of a two sentence sequence such as:

  'Pierre épousa Francine. Eduard épousa Chantale.'

The cases where a consecutive interpretation of the two events appears strongly preferred are typically those where their simultaneity implies that at least one of them must have lasted for some time. This arises in particular in contexts where the sentences s_1 and s_2 report actions by (or, more generally, events involving) one and the same individual. In some such cases it is down right impossible to be involved in both events at the same time (getting married and getting pregnant are arguably events of this sort, at least if we understand the former in the legal sense of the term); in which case coincidence of t_2 with t_1 is ruled out trivially. But more often it is rather that though the actions could be performed, or the events could happen, simultaneously, this is only possible if the individual involved in both 'meshes', so to speak, his involvements: he has to perform the second action, say, while engaged in, and perhaps briefly suspending, the first action. The interpretation of the two as simultaneous would then impose upon at least one of them a durative aspect which the use of the Passé Simple precludes.

The preference of i) over iii) has, I believe, a quite different origin. There is a natural preference for listing a collection of events in the temporal order in which they occurred rather than in some other order. This is so because only by following the actual order of the events in his account does the speaker enable his audience to 'live through' the events in their true succession. It is very plausible moreover that as soon as one way of recounting a series of events has some over all preferability over its potential competitors this one way becomes established as a convention. For clearly it is a practical advantage to be able to convey the actual order of events simply through the order of enunciation, rather than having to add explicit verbal information for this purpose. And, given that it is advantageous to have such a convention it should be expected that the one to establish itself is that which provides the most natural correlation between order of enunciation and order of occurrence.

It is important to notice in this connection that such a convention is only operative where the speaker can be assumed to know what the true order of events is - this is so in particular in fiction, where the order is, as much as any other aspect of the story, of the speaker's own making. In situations, on the other hand, where the speaker cannot be assumed to have complete knowledge as regards order, such as when a witness tries to recall the various events relevant to the case in connection with which he has been called, the convention does not hold: the witness may recall the events in the wrong order; and if he later on in his account he makes an explicit statement about the temporal order of two events which he introduced at some earlier point, he thereby invalidates his earlier statements no more if this order goes against that in which the events were introduced than it would if the two orders agreed.

While the Passé Simple is typically used to report the successive elements of the main course of action of a story, the Imparfait serves to present the setting in which the action is taking place.

Or course, as the story progresses the background may change as well. Therefore a sentence in the Imparfait, enunciated at a particular point in the narration will convey that the condition to which it refers obtains at the time to which the action has progresses at that point of the story. It may, but need not, obtain also at earlier or later parts of the course of events. Roughly therefore narrative prose is governed by the following principles.

1) The Passé Simple conveys punctuality of the event reported.
2) A succession of sentences in the Passé Simple conveys a similar temporal succession of the reported events.
3) A sentence in the Imparfait conveys that at the point to which the story has proceeded a certain condition obtains.

3) implies that a series of successive sentences in the Imparfait conveys that the corresponding conditions all obtain at the same time. If the discourse then continues with a sentence in the Passé Simple which introduces a new 'punctual' event these conditions may, but do not have to, hold also at this next time. There is one exception to this, vz. when the narrative starts with a number of sentences in the Imparfait which set the stage for the beginning of the action. Here it seems to be understood that the first event does fall in the time span where all the above mentioned conditions obtain. But the events introduced by Passé Simple sentences following this first one are again free of this constraint: at the times they represent the conditions mentioned at the start of the story need no longer be in force.

Evidently these rules cover only a relatively small part of a very special form of verbal communication. But they provide a simple framework within which it will be possible to discuss the few general points to which this section will be confined.

First I must say a little more about the sense in which the Passé Simple indicates 'punctuality'. I already suggested that this indication takes the form of a directive to the hearer and that formally this amounts to his adopting in the passage from D_k to D_{k+1} an instance of (1) involving the new event e which is introduced at that point. If e does satisfy (1) in ϵ_{k+1} then $\tau(\epsilon_{k+1})$ will contain a single instant at which e goes on; so that in precisely this sense e is indeed instantaneous in $\tau(\epsilon_{k+1})$. The same is true of the structures $\tau(\epsilon')$ where ϵ' is a strictly relational extension of ϵ_{k+1} satisfying A1 - A7, provided e also satisfies (1) in ϵ'. (Theorem 2 of section IV implies that a strictly relational extension satisfying this extra constraint will in fact always exist.)

The fact that e is instantaneous in $\tau(\epsilon')$ does of course not mean that e is instantaneous in any absolute sense. To be a little more precise let us assume that the discourse consisting of $s_1,...,s_n$ is non-fictional. In that case the question arises whether what was said was indeed true. Formally this should mean that in a model which represents the 'real world' as it develops through time the sequence of sentences is true at the time they were uttered. For the present discussion it is not so important how this real world model is precisely set up. Let us assume, to start, that it has the familiar form of a pair (τ,A) where τ is a strict linear ordering, e.g. an ordering isomorphic to that of the real numbers, and A is an interpretation function relative to τ of the primitive non-logical expressions of the language in question. I shall make the idealized, but harmless, assumption that the entire sequence $s_1,...,s_n$ is asserted at one single instant t_0.

Under these assumptions the question of truth is the question whether the sentences $s_1,...,s_n$ are all true in the model (τ,A) at the time t_0. Suppose that one of these sentences, s_k say, reports an event in the Passé Simple, e.g.

'Jean ferma la porte.'

If this sentence is true then there must be one or more instants of τ before t_0 at which the relevant event goes on, i.e. at which John and the door stand in the relevant relation (let us leave aside for now the question which relation this is). Now from a physical point of view events such as the closing of a door always take time. So, if (τ,A) describes the world from a physical standpoint it will contain an entire interval of points at which the relation holds. This is moreover something of which speakers are of course perfectly well aware, even when they treat the event as punctual: what emerges as an instant in the instant structure induced by the discourse representations D_i may nevertheless be a temporally extended event from another point of view; and that other point of view may moreover be the one that generally passes for the 'objective' point of view.[24]

In fact there ought to be, in those cases where A speaks truthfully, a natural correspondence between the discourse structures D_1 which B constructs in response to his words and the real world model (τ,A). In order to give an idea of the formal nature of this correspondence let us assume that the sentences $s_1,...,s_n$ are drawn from a very simple language L, all of whose sentences are of either one of two forms: $P_i q_j$ or $P_s q_j$. These sentences result from applying the operators P_i and P_s to underlying sentence symbols q_j. Intuitively the sentences $P_i q_j$ and $P_s q_j$ stand for certain simple French sentences in, respectively, the Passé Simple and the Imparfait such as

'Jean ferma la porte' and
'Francine se brossait les cheveux';

and the sentence symbols q_j which occur as parts of them can roughly be viewed as standing for the corresponding present tense sentences ('Jean ferme la porte', 'Francine se brosse les cheveux').[25]

The informal rules for the interpretation of narrative discourse now come to this: We distinguish two cases

a) s_1 is of the form $P_s q_j$; and

b) s_1 is of the form $P_i q_j$.

We first consider case a).

1) D_1 is to be the pair (ε_1, A_1), where E_1 is to contain two events, e_s - the event of utterance of the discourse $s_1, \ldots, s_n$ - and e_1, the event reported by s_1. ε_1 incorporates moreover the information that e_1 precedes e_s; and e_1 is put into $A^+(q_j)$.

2) Suppose D_k has already been constructed. s_{k+1} will be either of the form $P_s q_j$ or of the form $P_i q_j$. Suppose first that it is of the form $P_s q_j$. In this case we add a new event e to E_k and include the ε_{k+1} the information that it precedes e_s and is itself preceded by the event reported by the last Passé Simple sentence preceding s_{k+1}. Moreover e is put into $A^+(q_j)$. Suppose next that s_{k+1} is of the form $P_i q_j$. Then we also introduce a new event into E_k and into $A^+(q_j)$; but now we specify in that this event overlaps with the last event introduced by a Passé Simple sentence.

In case b) the construction is to proceed in almost the same way. The only difference concerns the beginning of the construction. Suppose that the first Passé Simple sentence of the discourse is s_{r+1}. Then each of the sentences $s_1, \ldots, s_r$ is to be taken as introducing an event which overlaps each of the others, and moreover does not lie entirely after e_s. The event introduced in response to s_{r+1} is also to overlap all of these first r events as well as to completely precede e_s. After that the construction follows the same rules as under a).

We assume that A spoke truthfully. But what precisely does this mean? It means, at the very last, that each of the sentences $s_1, \ldots, s_n$ is true in (τ, A) at t_0. However it might be argued that this is not by itself quite enough for A to have spoken the full truth; that in order for that to be so the times at which the underlying 'present tense sentences' q_j are true in (τ, A) must moreover be in the temporal order which the sequential order of the sentences $s_1, \ldots, s_n$ conveys.

I shall come back to this question soon. But for the moment let us assume that the order in which the mentioned events happened is indeed in accordance with that conveyed by the discourse.

To investigate the relation that obtains in this case between the discourse structures D_i and the real world model (τ, A) let us concentrate on the last structure D_n. As before I shall assume that D_n has the form (ε_n, A_n), where for each q_j $A_n^+(q_j)$ and $A_n^-(q_j)$ are disjoint subsets of E_n.[26] The function A on the other hand will be assumed to assign to certain combinations of a sentence q_j and a time $t \in T$ a truth value (1 or 0).

Let us first suppose that for each of the q_j that occur in any of the sentences $s_1, \ldots, s_n$ there is an unique interval i_j before t_0 consisting of all and only those points $t \in T$ such that $A(q_j, t) = 1$. Let $\iota = (I, \propto, 0)$ be the structure consisting of precisely these intervals, together with the one point interval $[t_0, t_0]$, where the relation $\prec$ and 0 are defined in the obvious way (see section II). It is easily verified that since $s_1, \ldots, s_n$ report the events in their true order, ι corresponds to a strictly relational extension of ε_n; i.e. there is such an extension $\varepsilon' = (E_n, \varpropto_n^{+\prime}, \varpropto_n^{-\prime}, O_n^{+\prime}, O_n^{-\prime})$ such that $(I, \varpropto, O)$ is isomorphic to $(E_n, \varpropto_n^{+\prime}, O_n^{+\prime})$. This isomorphism preserves moreover the semantic connection with the q_j: $e \in A^+(q_j)$ iff the corresponding interval i consists of all the points t at which q_j is true according to A.

Each instant of $\tau(\iota)$ will be a finite set of overlapping intervals. Let f be the function which maps each t that belongs to the union of all the intervals of I to that instant of $\tau(\iota)$ all members of which contain t. Then f is a homomorphism of a substructure of τ (that substructure which is determined by I) to the structure $\tau(\iota)$. f induces therefore a homomorphism g from that substructure of τ to a structure $\tau(\varepsilon')$ where ε' is some strictly relational extension of ε_n. It should be evident that this homomorphism also preserves truth, in the sense that if q_j is true at t according to A then there is an $e \in E_n$ such that $e \in g(t)$ and $e \in A^+(q_j)$, and conversely.

In general the sets of times at which the q_j are true according to A need not constitute single, uninterrupted intervals. There are at least two reasons why this need not be so. In the first place the actual past may contain several events of the type of q_j, only one of which the discourse in question reports. In the second place, as we observed in section IV, a certain period may qualify as the duration of a protracted event or process without it being strictly true that the conditions in terms of which the event or process is identified obtain at every single instant of that period.

Let us first assume that only the former of these two reasons is operative. In that case it remains possible to single out a set I of intervals of τ such that the structure $(I, \varpropto, O)$ determines a strictly relational extension of ε_n in the way described, and which is such that if the interval i of I corresponds to the event e of E_n then q_j is true, according to A, at each $t \in i$ iff $e \in A^+(q_j)$. But it will in general not be possible, as it was in the simpler case considered earlier, to *define* the members of I explicitly in terms of the information A provides about the q_j.

If the second reason is operative also then it need no longer be true that the interval of τ which, intuitively speaking, ought to correspond to the event e, introduced into ε_n in response to, say, the sentence $P_s q_j$, consists exclusively of instants at which q is true according to A. The correspondence between ι and ε_n will then no longer verify (2). An adequate description of the relation between D_n and the real world would in such cases seem to require that we represent the actual past also in the form of a model $M = (\varepsilon, A)$, where ε is a partial event structure. Each of D_n and M then induces its own instant structure and the second of these will be a 'refinement' of the first - as ε will contain so many more events than ε_n.

These extra complications do not alter the moral, however, that is implicit in our discussion of the simple case. - The moral is this. There is a perfectly legitimate sense in which we can, in a given context, treat, or look upon, certain events as punctual. Such an attitude does not imply any commitment to the belief that these events are indeed instantaneous absolutely. But it will determine (and manifest itself in) particular ways of talking about them, the interpretation of which leads to temporally ordered structures in which they do *play* the role of instants. There where discourse concerns real events, and reports them correctly, this structure can be regarded as containing, among other things, a possibly incomplete representation of part of the real world. This representation involves as a rule some sort of *contraction* of what are in physical terms protracted happenings to indivisible temporal units.

At two earlier points I already touched upon the question whether the difference between Passé Simple and Imparfait has anything to do with the contributions these respective tenses make to the truth conditions of the sentences in which they occur. I first expressed myself as if this were not so. However, subsequent discussions seemed to indicate that that was too rash a denial. More careful reflection upon the matter shows that what we should say here ultimately depend on the role we wish to attribute to the concept of truth.

What might appear to lend the denial some plausibility is the assumption - implicit in so much work within formal semantics - that truth conditions can be assigned to sentences in isolation. For, as already remarked, there is little, if anything in the respective truth conditions of two sentences which differ only in that the first has a Passé Simple where the second has an Imparfait to set them apart. The assumption that sentences determine their truth conditions individually, and that a bit of non-fictional assertoric language is true as a whole if and only if each of the sentences uttered as part of it is true separately arises naturally, but surreptitiously, from a conception of semantics that is too simple-mindedly compositional.

Yet the implausibility of that assumption flies in the face of anybody who stops to think about, for instance, the phenomenon of intersentence anaphora. As is has been realized for some time how close the parallels are between tenses and pronouns, and in particular how important anaphora is not only in connection with pronouns and demonstratives but also in connection with tenses,[27] it should be no surprise that the dubious assumption proves equally untenable within the present domain of enquiry - indeed the mechanisms of which I tried to give a description on pp. 410-1 might well be said to be themselves mechanisms of anaphora; for they allow us to infer the time of a reported event, or at any rate some information about the temporal position of that event, from preceding discourse.

Once we have accepted that it is only to the discourse as a whole that truth conditions can be assigned in a systematic way, we may find it natural to explicate the difference between Passé Simple and Imparfait at least partly in terms of their distinctive contributions to the truth conditions of the discourse. For as we saw the particular temporal order that the discourse conveys depends on where it uses the Passé Simple and where the Imparfait.

But is this order really part of the truth conditions of the discourse? After all the mechanisms that convey the order are operative only in certain types of discourse; and the question whether a particular discourse is of such a type may depend on such typically pragmatic factors as the speaker's knowledge about the order of the events which he recounts. There has been a strong tendency in the past to keep such pragmatic factors and their implications separate from typically 'semantic' notions such as truth conditions, a strategy which, as Grice was the first to point out, often has very striking advantages.

As a matter of fact the separation of pragmatic from semantic issues leads in some cases to considerable technical difficulties.[28] I do not know if such difficulties are to be feared within the context of the present phenomenon also. But let us assume for the sake of argument that they do not arise. The question whether the conveyed order of events is part of the truth conditions of the discourse is then, it seems to me, a question about the *status* of the mechanism for conveying it; and this status may differ from one case to the next. Thus we may become persuaded that with certain forms of language, in particular literary forms, the mechanism is associated in a strictly conventional manner, while in other cases the association is based on the consensus among the discourse participants that the necessary pragmatic preconditions for it obtain. In the former cases it would seem reasonable to regard the order as a matter of truth conditions; in the latter probably not.

Some of the issues to which I have tried to draw attention in this section also arise in connection with the second of the two examples which I promised to discuss. This is the English expression 'and next'. 'And next' has commanded a certain amount of attention within philosophy, primarily through the work of Von Wright, in whose theory of action and obligation it plays an important part. Von Wright analyzes 'and next' as a 2-place sentential operator, which combines sentences p and q into a compound sentence pNq which is stipulated to be true at a time t iff p is true at t and q is true at the next time after t. According to this stipulation N can be used non-trivially only in a context where time is discrete, i.e. where moments have immediate successors. Indeed it is only time of this type that Von Wright considers.

This strikes me as unsatisfactory - at least if things are left at just that. For most of us do not really believe that time is discrete. Yet we all use the expression 'and next' often, and apparently without effort or strain.

The explanation of this must, I think, once again be sought in the *directive* function that attaches to the expression: it instructs the addressee to treat the events e_1 and e_2 reported by the first and the second, respectively, of the two sentences which it combines as *consecutive*. By using 'and next' the speaker conveys to the hearer that within the context none of the events which from an 'objective' point of view do come between e_1 and e_2 are to be taken into account. It is precisely the element of stipulation that makes it often so difficult to fault a speaker on this score: if the event e_2 was indeed after e_1 how is one to make a convincing case that what the speaker said was wrong because other events, which he did not mention, intervened?

Nevertheless there are situations in which such an attack seems justified. Suppose you and I went to town this morning to do the shopping and have just returned to the cottage with the groceries. I say to may wife: 'First we went to the butcher and next we went to the bakery'. Whereupon you interrupt me, saying: 'No, that it is not quite right. After the butcher we went to the greengrocer's, and only then to the bakery'. Here it seems that if things were indeed as you say my account was in fact false. The reason is that the context *already* determines quite clearly which events are to count as significant. An enumeration which claims two of them to be consecutive while there is a third from this very same class which came in between therefore strikes us as being simply not true to the facts. But what appears in this case as part of the truth conditions will in others, where the class of significant events has not been fixed in advance, only be understood as a contribution to the definition of that class; as such it might have an effect on the truth conditions of subsequent sentences; but it cannot be itself attacked as being in breach of the truth.

Both examples we have discussed indicate how difficult it is to draw the fashionable distinction between 'semantic' and 'pragmatic' aspects of language. The difficulties we have encountered are twofold. In the first place it looks as if the effects of what is in each case essentially the same mechanism (the mechanism for conveying order of occurrence through order of enunciation) should sometimes be classified as pragmatic and sometimes as semantic. But to insist on such a classification is unhelpful. Not only is it likely to lead to quite arbitrary cuts in a continuous spectrum of types of discourse (stretching from those where, according to existing criteria for the distinction, the contributions are clearly pragmatic to those where the pragmatic element has become completely ossifed, and the contributions would count as semantic); also by attributing too much importance to the distinction we risk concealing from view the unifying principle that is in each case responsible for these contributions.

In the second place there is the status of the directive functions themselves. In as much as they are directives to the hearer they belong in the general theory of speaker-hearer interaction and thus might seem to qualify as pragmatic. At the same time however they have an important semantic aspect, as they serve the hearer in his effort to construct his representations of what is said; and what, if it isn't that, could be identified as his assigning a *meaning* to what he has been told?

Indeed it seems to me that the rules for the construction of discourse representations have at least as good a claim to being constitutive of meaning as the clauses which make up the definition of truth. Meaning after all attaches to fiction no less than to factual discourse. What distinguishes the two is that the latter, but not the former, can be (literally) true or false. But both induce the formation of structures that mirror their contents; and the rules that guide such formation are, we have seen, the same in either case.

APPENDIX I

Let $M_1 = (U_1, R_1)$ and $M_2 = (U_2, R_2)$ be as on p. 393.

By the *distance in M_1 from* the element u_1 of U_1 *to* the element u_2 of U_1 we understand: i) the unique positive integer n such that u_2 is the n-th successor of u_1, provided there is such an integer; ii) the unique number -n such that u_1 is the n-th successor of u_2, provided there is such an n; iii) ∞ if neither i) nor ii) applies. We write '$d(u_1, u_2)$, for this distance. In the same way we define the *distance in M_2 from* an element v_1 of U_2 *to* another element v_2 of U_2.

We shall refer to the elements of M_1 and M_2 which have no immediate successors as 'zero's' (of M_1 or M_2, respectively).

We say that a k-tuple $(u_1, \ldots, u_k)$ of elements of U_1 and a k-tuple $(v_1, \ldots, v_k)$ of elements of U_2 are *similar mod n* (in symbols: $(u_1, \ldots, u_k) \underset{n}{\sim} (v_1, \ldots, v_k)$) iff i) for each $i, j \leqslant k$ either $d(u_i, u_j) = d(v_i, v_j)$ or else both $|d(u_i, u_j)|$ and $|d(v_i, v_j)| > n$; and ii) for $i \leqslant k$ u_i and v_i either are at the same distance from a zero or each is from every zero at a distance whose absolute value is greater than n.

We associate with each formulae ϕ of the language of M_1 and M_2 a number $n(\phi)$ such that, assuming ϕ has k free variables, (1) if $(u_1,\ldots,u_k)$ $_{n(\phi)}^{\sim}$ $(v_1,\ldots, v_k)$ then $M_1 \vDash \phi[u_1,\ldots,u_k]$ iff $M_2 \vDash \phi[v_1,\ldots,v_k]$.

$n(\phi)$ is defined by induction on the complexity of ϕ:

i) if ϕ is atomic then $n(\phi) = 1$;

ii) if ϕ is $\neg\psi$ then $n(\phi) = n(\psi)$;

iii) if $\phi = \psi_1 \& \psi_2$ then $n(\phi) = \max(n(\psi_1),n(\psi_2))$;

iv) if $\phi = (\exists x_k)\psi(x_1,\ldots,x_{k-1},x_k)$, then $n(\phi) = 2.n(\psi) + 1$.

(1) is shown by induction on ϕ. The only interesting case is that where ϕ has the form $(\exists x_k)\psi(x_1,\ldots,x_{k-1},x_k)$.

Assume $(u_1,\ldots,u_{k-1})$ $_{n(\phi)}^{\sim}$ $(v_1,\ldots,v_{k-1})$.

Suppose $M_1 \vDash \phi[u_1,\ldots,u_{k-1}]$. Then there is a $u_k \in U_1$ so that $M_1 \vDash \psi[u_1,\ldots, u_{k-1},u_k]$. We distinguish the following cases:

i) $d(u_k,u_k) \leqslant n(\psi)$ for some $i < k$. In this case choose v_k at distance $d(u_i, u_k)$ from v_i. Note that this is possible even when $d(u_i,u_k) > 0$. For if v_i were less than $d(u_i,u_k)$ points from a zero of M_2 then u_i would have been that same number of points from a zero of M_1 and so the distance from u_i to u_k could not have been as much as $d(u_i,u_k)$. It is easy to see that $(u_1,\ldots, u_{k-1},u_k)$ $_{n(\psi)}^{\sim}$ $(v_1,\ldots,v_{k-1},v_k)$. Suppose e.g. that $|d(u_k,u_j)| \leqslant n(\psi)$ for some $j \neq i$. Then $|d(u_i,u_j)| \leqslant n(\phi)$. So $d(v_i,v_j) = d(u_i,u_j)$, and so, since also $d(v_i,v_k) = d(u_i,u_k)$, $d(v_k,v_j) = d(u_k,u_j)$. In the same way one argues that if $|d(v_k,v_j)| \leqslant n(\psi)$ for some $j \neq i$, then $d(v_k,v_j) = d(u_k,u_j)$, and also that if either u_k or v_k is at some distance from a zero which is less than or equal to $n(\psi)$ absolutely, then the other point is at the same distance from a zero too.

ii) For no $i < k$ $|d(u_i,u_k)| \leqslant n(\psi)$, but $|d(u_k,z)| \leqslant n(\psi)$ for some zero z of M_1. In that case we choose v_k to be a point of U_2 which has that same distance to some zero of M_2. Clearly $|d(v_i,v_k)| > n(\psi)$ for all $i < k$. For if for some i $d(v_i,v_k) \leqslant n(\psi)$ then v_i would be at a distance $\leqslant n(\phi)$ from a zero of M_2 and so u_i would have been at that distance from z. But then $d(u_i,u_k) = d(v_i,v_k)$ and so $|d(u_i,u_k)| \leqslant n(\psi)$, contrary to assumption. Thus we have again that $(u_1,\ldots,u_{k-1},u_k)$ $_{n(\psi)}^{\sim}$ $(v_1,\ldots,v_{k-1},v_k)$.

iii) For no $i < k$ $|d(u_i,u_k)| \leqslant n(\psi)$ and for no zero z $d(u_k,z) \leqslant n(\psi)$. In this case we choose a v_k which has distances $> n(\psi)$ to all v_i as well as to all zero's of M_2. Clearly $(u_1,\ldots,u_{k-1},u_k)_{n(\psi)}^{\sim}(v_1,\ldots,v_{k-1},v_k)$.

Since in each of the cases i), ii), iii) $(u_1,\ldots,u_{k-1},u_k) \; \widetilde{n(\psi)} \; (v_1,\ldots,v_{k-1},v_k)$ we may infer by the inductive hypothesis that $M_2 \models \psi [v_1,\ldots,v_k]$. So $M_2 \models (\exists x_k) \, \psi \, [v_1,\ldots,v_{k-1}]$.

It follows in particular that if ϕ is a sentence then $M_1 \models \phi$ iff $M_2 \models \phi$. So M_1 and M_2 are elementarily equivalent.

APPENDIX II

Let T_0 be the theory of strict partial orderings. (Thus T_0 is axiomatized by the two axioms $(\forall x,y,z)(x < y \;\&\; y < z \rightarrow x < z)$ and $(\forall x,y)(x < y \rightarrow \;\; y \not< x)$). Then $RS(T_0) = SRS(T_0) = Neg(T_0) = Unneg(T_0)$ is axiomatized by the set of all sentences ϕ_n of the form

$(\forall x_1,\ldots,x_n) \neg (x_1 < x_2 \;\&\; x_2 < x_3 \;\&\; \ldots \;\&\; x_{n-1} < x_n \;\&\; x_n < x_1)$,

where $x_1,\ldots,x_n$ are n distinct variables. (Intuitively such a sentence says that there is no cycle of n elements). It is easy to see that this set of axioms cannot be replaced by any finite set.

The axiomatization of $RS(T_{ev}) = SRS(T_{ev})$ is a little more complicated. Indeed, the statement of the axioms that I shall give here involves an element of recursion which did not enter into the axiomatization of $RS(T_0)$; and I do not know that this element could be eliminated from a perspicuous formulation of axioms for $RS(T_{ev})$.

The axioms will be the universal closures of disjunctions of negated 'basic' formulae (where these basic formulae are either atomic formulae or conjunctions of two atomic formulae). However, it will faciliate the subsequent description to take as axioms rather the equivalent forms in which the matrix of the sentence is the negation of a conjunction of basic formulae, and to identify any such axiom simply in terms of that conjunction.

Thus $x <^+ y \wedge y <^+ z \wedge z \; 0^+ \; x$ represents the axiom

$(\forall x,y,z) \quad (x <^+ y \wedge y <^+ z \wedge z \; 0^+ \; x).$

It is easily verified that all sentences represented, in the way just explained, by the following conjunctions are theorems of $RS(T_{ev})$:

(C1) $R_1(x_1,x_2) \wedge R_2(x_2,x_3) \wedge \ldots \wedge R_{n-1}(x_{n-1},x_n) \wedge R_n(x_n,x_1)$

where for $i = 1,\ldots,n$ each formula $R_i(x_i,x_{i+1})$ has one of the forms:

i) $x_i \;<^+\; x_{i+1}$

ii) $x_i \; 0^- \; x_{i+1} \wedge x_{i+1} <^- x_i$

iii) $x_{i+1} \; 0^- \; x_i \wedge x_{i+1} <^- x_i$

iv) $x_i \; 0^+ \; x_{i+1}$

v) x_{i+1} 0^+ x_i

vi) x_{i+1} $<^-$ x_i

and where in the cycle $\{1,2,\ldots,n,1\}$ any two formulae $R_i(x_i,x_{i+1})$, $R_j(x_j, x_{n+1})$ each of which has one of the forms iv), v), vi) are separated by a formula $R_k(x_k,x_{k+1})$ which has one of the forms i), ii), iii).

N.B. we shall henceforth refer to formulae on the forms i), ii) and iii) as *strong conjuncts* and to those of forms iv), v) and vi) as *weak conjuncts*.

We shall indeed adopt all formulae of the form (1) as axioms. But that is not enough. It cannot be enough since none of them contains any basic conjunct x_i 0^- x_{i+1}. (0^- cannot occur, but only in combination with $<^-$!)

There are however negative sentences which are valid in T_{ev} and in which 0^- occurs by itself e.g. $(\forall x,y)$ $(x\ 0^+\ y \rightarrow \neg x\ 0^-\ y)$. The difficulty with the relation 0^- is that $x\ 0^-\ y$ means intuitively that either $x <^+ y$ or $y <^+ x$, but which of these two is the case the formula does not specify. We cannot therefore have any 'cyclical' axioms of the by now familiar form, which contain a single occurrence of a conjunct $x\ 0^-\ y$. For example, although the sentence represented by $x <^+ y \wedge y <^+ z \wedge z <^+ x$ is valid, this is not the case for that represented by $x\ 0^-\ y \wedge y <^+ z \wedge z <^+ x$.

For $x\ 0^-\ y$ *might* be true because y lies before x, and not x before y.

Similarly the sentence represented by $x\ 0^-y \wedge x <^+ u \wedge u <^+ y$ is not valid. However the combined conjunction $x\ 0^-\ y \wedge y <^+ z \wedge z <^+ x \wedge x <^+ u \wedge u <^+ y$ does represent a valid sentence, which can be seen more clearly if we write that sentence in the form:

(2) $(\forall x,y,z,u)$ $[(x\ 0^-\ y \wedge y <^+ z \rightarrow \neg z <^+ x) \vee (x\ 0^-\ y \wedge x <^+ u \rightarrow \neg u <^+ y)]$

Since for any value u_1, u_2 for x, y we must have either $\bar{u}_1 <^+ \bar{u}_2$ or $\bar{u}_2 <^+ \bar{u}_1$, one of the conditionals in the matrix of (2) must be true, irrespective of what z and v are.

Generalizing we can observe the following:

(3) Suppose the conjunction (C3) $\phi_1 \wedge .. \wedge \phi_n$ and (C4) $\sigma_1 \wedge .. \wedge \sigma_m$ each represent a theorem of $RS(T_{ev})$; (and in particular that each of the $\phi_1,\ldots \phi_n$, $\sigma_1,\ldots,\sigma_m$ has one of the forms i) - vi) mentioned above). Suppose that v_1, v_2 are two variables so that there is a formula ϕ_i which has the form a) $v_1 <^+ v_2$ and a formula σ_j which has the form b) $v_2 <^+ v_1$.

Let (C5) be the conjunction of i) the result of replacing in (C3) all conjuncts ϕ_i which are occurrences of a) by $v_1\ 0^-\ v_2$; and ii) the result of replacing in (C4) all conjuncts which are occurrences of b) by $v_1\ 0^-\ v_2$.

Then (C5) represents again a theorem of $RS(T_{ev})$. Similarly we get the representation of a theorem by forming (C6) the conjunction of i) the result of replacing in (C3) all instances of a) by $v_2 \ 0^- \ v_1$, and ii) substituting $v_2 \ 0^- \ v_1$ for all instances of b) in (C4).

(3) offers a means of constructing new axioms out of pairs of sentences which have already been adopted as members of the axiom system.

It turns out that we only need to close the class of sentences represented by the conjunction of form (C1) under the construction step described under (3) to obtain a complete axiomatization for $RS(T_{ev})$.

Thus, summarizing, we put $A_5^0 =$ the set of all sentences represented by conjunctions of the form (C1); $A_5^{n+1} = A_5^n$ together with all sentences which can be obtained from pairs of sentences in A_5^n by applying the step described under (3). A_5 is then $\bigcup_n A_5^n$.

It should be noted that none of the theories $RS(T)$ we have considered is finitely axiomatizable even though the axiomatization of T was in all cases finite and in fact, one would feel, extremely simple.

That $RS(T_{par})$ is not finitely axiomatizable is seen very easily. For define for $n = 1,2,\ldots$ $\psi_n = \bigwedge_{i \leqslant n} \phi_i$. Then for $m > n \vdash \psi_m \to \psi_n$. On the other hand $\nvdash \psi_n \to \psi_m$. For let $M = (U,<)$ where $U = \{1,2,\ldots n+1\}$ and $< = \{(i,i+1): i \leqslant n\} \cup \{(n+1,1)\}$. Then $M \vDash \psi_n$ but $M \nvDash \phi_m$. So the ψ_n form a strictly increasing set of axioms for $RS(T_{par})$. This implies that the theory cannot be axiomatized finitely.

Similar, though somewhat more involved, arguments show that the other theories $RS(T)$ cannot be finitely axiomatized.

The proofs that the axiomatizations given here are indeed complete are not difficult but long and tedious. I therefore decided not to include them.

Notes

The research for this paper was done while the author was supported by the DFG-Projekt 'Die Beschreibung mit Hilfe der Zeitlogik von Zeitformen und Verbalformen im Französischen, Portugiesischen und Spanischen' at the University of Stuttgart.

1 Cf. [12], [15].

2 A2 is strictly speaking superfluous, as it can be deducted from A6 and A3.

3 I should point out in this connection that Whitehead himself used a different construction of instants out of processes from the one I shall discuss

here. However, the same fundamental issues that arise in connection with the present construction also arise in connection with his.
A discussion of many of the same concerns to which this paper tries to address itself, but which uses a construction more akin to that of White-head, is to be found in Van Benthem [3]. See also Whitehead [13].

4 It is easily seen that if e_1, e_2, e_3 are intervals of an ordering $<T,<>$ and 0 is defined as on p.3, then if $e_1 \; 0 \; e_2$, $e_2 \; 0 \; e_3$ and $e_1 \; 0 \; e_3$ there is always at $t \in T$ such that $t \in e_1 \cap e_2 \cap e_3$.

5 Actually there is a complication here when x is infinite. See also p. 383.

6 I should mention here an alternative method for constructing instants out of events which, it appears, was first studied by Walter (cf. [14] p.157ff). This method is based on the same idea that underlies Dedekind's construction of the real numbers from the rationals. Given an event-structure ε we can define a *cut of* ε to be a maximal pair (A,B) of the subsets of E such that for each $e_1 \in A$ and $e_2 \in B$ $e_1 \propto e_2$ - the pair is maximal in that for each event e not in A $\cup$ B there is an $e_1 \in A$ such that $e_1 \propto e$ and an $e_2 \in B$ such that $e \propto e_2$. It is easily shown that if we define instants as cuts and put $(A_1,B_1) < (A_2,B_2) \equiv$ df. $A_1 \subset A_2$, then we obtain again a linear ordering. This ordering moreover is already complete, so that τ' is in fact isomorphic with $\tau(\varepsilon)$ itself. It is easily verified that if (A,B) is a cut and e $\notin$ A $\cup$ B then there are $e_1 \in A$ and $e_2 \in B$ such that $e_1 \; 0 \; e$ and $e_2 \; 0 \; e$. This makes it reasonable to define the events that go on at (A,B) as precisely those events that belong neither to A nor to B. The problem with this approach is that if e is an instantaneous event - i.e. if there are no e_1, e_2 such that $e_1 \; 0 \; e$, $e_2 \; 0 \; e$ and $e_1 \propto e_2$ - then there will be no instant at all at which e_1 happens. It will become clear in section V why this makes the Walter approach ill-suited to the purpose of this paper.

7 This is particularly common in connection with eyewitness reports. The speaker tries to piece the events together as best he can. The various aspects of the case may come back to him more or less at random. Often he will be able to reconstruct the true temporal sequence of the occurrences he relates, and to communicate this additional information, only in the latter part of the discourse. Sometimes he won't arrive at a complete articulation of the temporal relations at all. In the former case some of the intermediate structures D_i, with $i < n$, will violate A7; in the latter case this will be true even of the final structure D_n.

8 See [9].

9 Relativity Theory has taught us that in one sense the relation of earlier and later is *not* connected: there may be two successive events e_1 and e_2 in one place neither of which is either earlier or later than a third event e_3 occurring at some distance from e_1 and e_2. But this circumstance arises only in connection with spacially distant events; and even in a case such as the one described connectivity fails only in the sense that e_1 nor e_2 is causally connected with e_3. If however an appropriate convention for measurement of time, vz. through synchronization of clocks at the respective place of the events, has been established in advance, the times of these events do become fully comparable, albeit in a way which is based on a partly arbitrary agreement.
It would be wrong therefore to regard the theory of relativity as having

proved the untenability of the traditional view that the order of time is a linear one.

10 Of course i may absorb additional instants of ε as well - i.e. we may find that $i_1 \cup i_2 \subsetneq i$. In general the class of instant structures of the form $\tau(\varepsilon')$ corresponds not to the class of linear extensions of $\tau(\varepsilon)$, but to the class of those structures $<T',<'>$ where the elements of T' are equivalence classes of elements of the structure $\tau(\varepsilon)$ under some equivalence relation which is also a congruence relation with respect to $<_\varepsilon$.

11 See, for instance, [7], [9].

12 See e.g. Chang & Keisler [5].

13 My attention was drawn to this possibility by David Lewis.

14 By 'appropriate' I mean here: a member of U if γ is an individual constant; a subset of U if γ is a 1-place predicate, etc.

15 As far as I know the first explicit proposal of this sort is Bennett and Partee [2]. Since the first (informal) circulation of that paper there have been many other similar proposals, but I have decided to refrain from attempting to give a representative list of these.

16 A general truthdefinition should of course contain, rather, a clause with two parameters of which the clause referred to in the text would result as a special instance if we were to substitute for these parameters the particular interpretations which the theory associates with, respectively, (4) and (5).

17 I had at first overlooked how soon the truthtables here presented become inadequate. Barbara Partee protected me from the embarrassment that would have resulted from my failure to observe this within the present, more generally accessible version of the paper.

18 One might be inclined to assign to (p & q) at t_3 some 'intermediate truth-value'; but not only would we thereby abandon the four-valued scheme that is under scrutiny; the introduction of such intermediate values leads in any case to notorious difficulties. See e.g. my 'Two Theories about Abjectives', in Edw.L.Keenan (ed.) *Formal Semantics of Natural Language*.

19 See my forthcoming contribution to the proceedings of the Conference on Quantifiers and Tense, Stuttgart, April 1979.

20 Precisely how A'' is to depend on A is not quite so simple a question. Clearly intervals of the form $\bar{e}$, where $e \in E$, will have to belong to $A''^{\pm}(Q)(a_1,\ldots,a_n)$ iff e belongs to $A^{\pm}(Q)(a_1,\ldots,a_n)$. But for intervals which are not of this form such questions are complicated by the problems which we encountered in our discussion of 'a writes b'. I must leave this question to the other, above mentioned paper.

21 The material presented in the present section owes much to the help and advice from members of the DFG project on tense and aspect in Stuttgart, in particular Franz Guenthner, Jaap Hoepelman and Christian Rohrer.

22 I do not want to go so far as to say that there are no events, processes or states which can be correctly reported with the help of only one of these tenses. For example it seems doubtful that one could ever be justi-

fied in the use of the Passé Simple in a sentence such as: 'Francois fut le fils du Directeur et Mme Delahaye'. Even of such a sentence however it is by no means evident that it is unacceptable because it is (necessarily) false. It is rather that certain events, processes or states cannot be viewed in a certain way or attributed a certain role, because the aspect that the viewpoint emphasizes or that is required for the fulfillment of the role, is entirely absent from them.

23 It follows from these remarks that strictly speaking a discourse representation D_i involves, besides a structure (ε_i, A_i) also a set C_i of conditions which stipulate the status of some of the members of E_i, and which are carried over to the next structure D_{i+1}. In most of what follows, however, I shall ignore this and speak of the D_i as if they consisted simply of the pairs (ε_i, A_i).

24 From what was said in earlier sections of this paper it follows that there is no such thing as *the objective* point of view in some absolute, uniquely determined sense.

25 It has been one of the basic assumptions of tense logics of the sort brief-ly alluded to in the opening paragraphs of section V that sentences in the simple past tense can be analyzed as resulting from applying a 'past tense operator' to an underlying sentence, often identified with the correspon-ding present tense version of the past tense sentence in question. This identification is notoriously problematic, especially in English. However, •whatever the precise relation may be between the past tense and the present tense sentence, it usually makes perfectly good sense to ask whether the conditions referred to in the sentence - whether it be in the past or in the present tense - obtain at a given time, e.g. if at a given time John and the door stand in the relation which obtains whenever John is closing the door. This is sufficient justification for the introduction of the sen-tence symbols q_j.

26 In discourse structures constructed in response to the special type of discourse we are considering now many, and possibly all, of these sets are either empty or singletons; moreover, as we have formulated the lan-guage L, the sets $A_n(q_j)$ will all remain empty. But in general these special conditions need not be satisfied.

27 See in particular B. Partee: Tenses and Pronouns. J. Phil. 1971

28 See e.g. my Semantics vs. Pragmatics. In Guenthner & Schmidt (eds.) *Formal Semantics and Pragmatics of Natural Languages*. Dordrecht 1979. Admittedly the issues there discussed are quite different from those which concern us here.

References

1. BARWISE, J.: Some Applications of Henkin quantifiers. Isr. J. of Math. Vol. 25, 1976.

2. BENNETT, M. & PARTEE, B.: Toward the logic of Tense and Aspect in English. Unpublished 1973. Published by the Indiana University Linguistics Club, 1978.

3. BENTHEM, J. Van: Points and Periods. To appear in the proceedings of the Conference on Quantifiers and Tenses, Stuttgart 1979.

4. BERGSON, H.: *Essay sur les Donnees immédiates de la Conscience.* Paris 1889.

5. CHANG, C.C., and KEISLER, H.J.: *Model Theory.* Amsterdam 1973.

6. COCCHIARELLA, N.: *Tense and Modal Logic. A Study in the Topology of temporal Reference.* Dissertation. UCLA 1966.

7. FINE, K.: Vagueness, Truth and Logic. Synthese, Vol. 30, 1975.

8. KAMP, H.: Semantics vs. Pragmatics. In: Guenthner, F., & Schmidt, S. (eds.), *Formal Semantics and Pragmatics of Natural Languages.* Dordrecht 1978.

9. KAMP, J.A.W.: Two Theories about Adjectives. In Keenan, Edw. (ed.), *Formal Semantics for Natural Language.* Cambridge 1975.

10. KAMP, H.: On the Logic of Becoming. To appear in the Proceedings of the Conference on Quantifiers and Tenses. Stuttgart 1979.

11. PRIOR, A.N.: *Past, Present and Future.* Oxford 1967.

12. RUSSELL, B.: On Order in Time. In: Russell, B. *Logic and Knowledge.* London 1956.

13. WHITEHEAD, A.N.: *Process and Reality.* Cambridge 1929.

14. WHITROW, J.: *The Natural Philosophy of Time.* London 1961.

15. WIENER, N.: A Contribution to the Theory of relative Position. In: Proc. of the Camb. Phil. Soc. Vol. 17, 1914.

16. WRIGHT, G.H. Von: 'And Next', Acta Phil. Fennica, Vol. 18, 1965.

1 Christoph Schwarze	15 Ede Zimmermann	30 Josef Bayer
2 Karlheinz Hülser	16 Klaus Mudersbach	31 Robert Maier
3 Wilfried Döpke	17 Barbara Hall-Partee	32 Walter Huber
4 Count Dracula	18 Wolfgang Sternefeld	33 Ede Huckert
5 Manfred Pinkal	19 David Lewis	34 Claus Heeschen
6 Christel Schwarze-Hanisch	20 Marie-Theres Schepping	35 Joachim Ballweg
7 Peter Hartmann	21 Thomas Ballmer	36 Renate Bartsch
8 Jaap Hoepelmann	22 Klaus-Jürgen Engelberg	37 Dieter Wunderlich
9 Irene Heim	23 Helmut Schnelle	38 Angelika Kratzer
10 Helmut Frosch	24 Ekkehard König	39 Max Cresswell
11 Hans Kamp	25 Ivar Tönisson	40 Arnim von Stechow
12 Rainer Bäuerle	26 Wolfgang Klein	41 Veronika Ullmer-Ehrich
13 Martin Rüttenauer	27 Suzanne Schlyter	42 Urs Egli
14 Hans Schneider	28 Christa Hauenschild	43 Roland Hausser
	29 Gerhild Woll	44 Günter Posch

Index of Contributors

G. Herdan

The Advanced Theory of Language as Choice and Chance

1966. 30 figures. XVI, 459 pages
(Kommunikation und Kybernetik in
Einzeldarstellungen, Band 4)
ISBN 3-540-03584-2

Contents: Introduction. – Language as
Chance I – Statistical Linguistics. –
Language as Choice I – Stylostatistics. –
Language as Chance II – Optimal Systems
of Language Structure. – Language as
Choice II – Linguistic Duality. – Statistics
for the Language Seminary. – Author
Index. Subject Index.

G. Hammarström

Linguistic Units and Items

1976. 17 figures. IX, 131 pages
(Communication and Cybernetics,
Volume 9)
ISBN 3-540-07241-1

Contents: Introduction. – Spoken
Language. – Written Language. – Written
Language in Relation to Spoken Lang-
uage. – Spoken Language in Relation to
Written Language. – The Tasks of
Linguistics. – Bibliography. – Author
Index. – Subject Index.

Springer-Verlag
Berlin
Heidelberg
New York

H. Hörmann

Psycholinguistics

An Introduction to Research and Theory
Translated from the German edition by H.H. Stern
1971. 69 figures. XII, 377 pages
ISBN 3-540-05159-7

„...provides a comprehensive introduction to the psychology of language by concentrating on the behaviourist conception...
the translation is written in a clear, concise and compact English...
The substance of this book, which has become a standard textbook in German as well as the brilliancy of its translation will certainly secure its position in the English speaking world as well." *IRAL (Deutschland)*

B. Malmberg

Structural Linguistics and Human Communication

An Introduction into the Mechanism of Language and the Methodology of Linguistics
Reprint of the 2nd revised edition 1967
1976. 88 figures. VIII, 213 pages
(Kommunikation und Kybernetik in Einzeldarstellungen, Band 2)
ISBN 3-540-03888-4

Contents: Introduction. – Signs and Symbols. The Linguistic Sign. – The Communication Process. – Preliminary Expression Analysis. Acoustic and Physiological Variables. Information. – Segmentation. Forms of Expression. Oppositions and Distinctions. – Paradigmatic Structures. – Redundancy and Relevancy. Levels of Abstraction. – The Distinctive Feature Concept. The Binary Choice. – Syntagmatic Structures. Distribution and Probability. – Content Analysis. – The Functions of Language. – Perception and Linguistic Interpretation. – Primitive Structures and Defective Language. – Linguistic Change. – Bibliographical Notes. – Author Index. – Subject Index.

Springer-Verlag
Berlin
Heidelberg
New York

"A general survey of modern structural linguistics by B. Malmberg...
The book is essentially intended for the advanced student, but others will also find it useful, since the author manages to deal lucidly and intelligibly with a difficult subject." *The Years Work in English Studies*